The Problem of Democracy

ALSO BY NANCY ISENBERG AND ANDREW BURSTEIN

Madison and Jefferson

Mortal Remains: Death in Early America (co-editors)

ALSO BY NANCY ISENBERG

White Trash: The 400-Year Untold History of Class in America

Fallen Founder: The Life of Aaron Burr

Sex and Citizenship in Antebellum America

ALSO BY ANDREW BURSTEIN

Democracy's Muse:
How Thomas Jefferson Became an FDR Liberal, a Reagan Republican, and a Tea Party Fanatic, All the While Being Dead

Lincoln Dreamt He Died:
The Midnight Visions of Remarkable Americans from Colonial Times to Freud

The Original Knickerbocker:
The Life of Washington Irving

Jefferson's Secrets:
Death and Desire at Monticello

The Passions of Andrew Jackson

Letters from the Head and Heart:
Writings of Thomas Jefferson

America's Jubilee: How in 1826 a Generation Remembered Fifty Years of Independence

Sentimental Democracy:
The Evolution of America's Romantic Self-Image

The Inner Jefferson:
Portrait of a Grieving Optimist

The Problem of Democracy

The Presidents Adams Confront the Cult of Personality

Nancy Isenberg

and

Andrew Burstein

VIKING

VIKING
An imprint of Penguin Random House LLC
penguinrandomhouse.com

Illustration credits
Title page: John Adams, sketch by Jacques Reich. National Portrait Gallery, Smithsonian Institution. John Quincy Adams, sketch by Jacques Reich. National Portrait Gallery, Smithsonian Institution. Page x: "A New DISPLAY of the UNITED STATES," 1799. Library of Congress. Page xxx: Letter, John Adams to John Quincy Adams, September 13, 1790. Collection of the Massachusetts Historical Society. Page 190: Letter, John Quincy Adams to John Adams, November 25, 1800. Collection of the Massachusetts Historical Society. Page 436: "Foot-Race," by political cartoonist David Claypoole Johnson. Library of Congress.

Library of Congress Cataloging-in-Publication Data

Names: Isenberg, Nancy, author. | Burstein, Andrew, author.
Title: The problem of democracy : the Presidents Adams confront the cult of personality / Nancy Isenberg and Andrew Burstein.
Description: New York, NY : Viking, [2019] | Includes bibliographical references and index. |
Identifiers: LCCN 2018039232 (print) | LCCN 2018054339 (ebook) | ISBN 9780525557517 (ebook) | ISBN 9780525557500 (hardcover)
Subjects: LCSH: Adams, John, 1735-1826—Political and social views. | Adams, John Quincy, 1767-1848—Political and social views. | Presidents—United States—Biography. | United States—Politics and government—1783-1865. | United States—Politics and government—Philosophy. | Democracy—United States—History.
Classification: LCC E322 (ebook) | LCC E322 .I74 2019 (print) | DDC 973.4/4092—dc23
LC record available at https://lccn.loc.gov/2018039232

Printed in the United States of America
1 3 5 7 9 10 8 6 4 2

Designed by Gretchen Achilles

Contents

There never was a Democracy yet
that did not commit suicide.

— JOHN ADAMS (1814)

In truth Human Nature itself is little more
than a composition of inconsistencies.

— JOHN QUINCY ADAMS (1814)

"A New DISPLAY of the UNITED STATES," 1799. The successor to a 1794 head-and-shoulders portrait of President George Washington surrounded by the seals of the states, this broadside features President John Adams as another uniter and protector at the center of the Union. The draping behind him is a staged presentation, symbolizing both grandeur and openness to light and truth; the whole reaffirms the chief executive's image as an embodiment of the nation. This is a rare example of an Adams being granted Washingtonian status.

EXORDIUM*

Mythic Democracy

They were the only two chief executives in the American republic's first half century to be turned out of office after a single term. There is no giant marble memorial to either of them in Washington, D.C.[1] Alive or dead, they do not embody the beau ideal of the democratic spirit. Who would claim that John and John Quincy Adams speak credibly, meaningfully, to the modern age? We would.

It is precisely because they are not obvious symbols of democracy that we find the two Adamses compelling subjects as we search for a better way to understand how the United States could have proceeded from its ecstatic opening pledge—the magnanimous "spirit of 1776"—to where it is today as a distressed political system. No historical investigator until now has committed to telling in any depth the story of the first father-and-son presidents. In these pages, we retie the broken threads of our nearly 250-year-old political inheritance. We see the Adamses' experiences and their unpopular (but not necessarily wrong) positions as an opportunity to present to the politically engaged of our own time an accurate picture of a political heritage too many Americans are loath to address. It includes, but is not limited to, the unfortunate tribalism of the two-party system.

* John Quincy Adams wrote in his *Lectures on Rhetoric and Oratory* (1810), "The exordium is defined by Cicero as 'a discourse to prepare the minds of the audience for the favorable reception of the remainder.' Hence you will observe it is not inherent in the subject; but a mere preliminary to conciliate the favor of the hearer. Though not always indispensable, it is often necessary; and when not improper should never be omitted" (lecture 17).

With a fixation on influence-buying, poll-shifting dollars, we live at a moment in history when confusion reigns as to the dependability of all high-sounding founding-era rhetoric. If you were to ask an average citizen what America stands for, he or she would most likely repeat something from grade school about freedom and democracy. The simplistic response is not to be mocked, but it does betray what's wrong: lack of definition. The framers of the Constitution did not erect a democracy. It was not their intent to do so. We must not assume that the United States is a democracy today either. That is why we have written this book. The presidents Adams are our vehicle in an effort to provide a germane, perhaps even urgent, interpretation of the nature of American politics. Persistent myths can no longer suffice.[2]

How, then, do we extend the discussion from what we *think* we know about the two Adamses to what we *should* know about them? John Adams, the second president, assumed a lead role in the looming Revolution, vocally defending the Declaration of Independence when it came before the Continental Congress. But that is not what we consider most memorable about him. John Quincy Adams, the sixth president, was the first president not to have been old enough to take part in the Revolution; he stood before the Supreme Court in 1841 and argued valorously in order to win freedom for the kidnapped Africans who had dispatched their captors on board the *Amistad*. But that is not what we consider most memorable about him. The best reasons we find for remembering the Adamses are those that concern their stubborn insights into human psychology. They understood the tricky relationship between human nature and political democracy, and how emotionally induced thought often undermined social and political justice.

To the extent that their critique has been dislodged from America's proud history, it is because it does not comport with the ecstatic, celebratory, self-congratulatory script that grew into the political faith we know as "American exceptionalism." If the emotive writer Thomas Jefferson planted the seeds of exceptionalism ("this whole chapter in the history of man is new," he pronounced), the presidents Adams cultivated a cautionary, less intoxicating political science favoring a balance of interests to counteract those urges that led a ruling few to undemocratic self-aggrandizement.[3]

The two shared a critical disposition in perceiving (much as we moderns claim we can perceive) the hollowness of celebrity. They saw how image supplanted truth and how the public mind was captured by a clever concept that hid a political agenda. They took note as popular personalities acquired power over citizens' minds. Thomas Jefferson and Andrew Jackson were perfect examples. But they were neither the first nor the last.

The presidents Adams knew that the powerful in government were elitists, no matter what they called themselves. There were those, like Jefferson, Jackson, and many of their fellow southerners, who skillfully employed a rhetoric that concealed their class interests, their impulse to protect those most like themselves; and there were those in the Adamses' New England who dismissed all social inferiors without apology. The two Adamses might have been snobs in their own way, but they hated all forms of deception and intimidation, subtle or direct, regardless of its origin. To the endless frustration of father and son, each spent the greater part of his political career facing the same charge: of holding an especially dangerous degree of elitist sympathy. Guilty or not, they took a perverse pride in refusing to court public opinion through dishonest means. They were, in short, pained politicians.

The presidents Adams were never very sanguine about the two-party system, and this may be the most distinguishing feature in their political profile. Others forecast a favorable outcome to party competition, convinced that voters could safely decide which of two candidates best represented the majority's interests. The Adamses balked at this vision. They decried the hypnotic sway of "party distinctions" and "party spirit" as the bane of political life.[4]

On the day of his own inauguration as president, betting against his father's prognosis for one brief shining moment, John Quincy Adams allowed that the two parties that dominated the early years of the Republic had both contributed "splendid talents" and "ardent patriotism" along with the more obvious "human infirmity and error." For these defects, he adjudged, a "liberal indulgence" was due. Inaugural addresses were, then as now, intended to inspire more than to describe a work agenda, and over the course of a long and ruffled career in deliberative bodies John Quincy would nevermore invoke party business without presenting it as a history of manifest intrigue. Political parties did not guarantee democracy to everyone; they merely protected the interests of their most influential members.

It is easy to relate to John Quincy's inauguration day remarks on the "collisions of sentiments and sympathies" that accompanied party rivalry. Father and son identified flaws built into the two-party system that would prove fatal to the Union in 1860, and that continue to harass political society even now. As conspicuously, they detested the provocative mania parties allowed for, when they roused an intense enthusiasm for select, heroically framed men without objectively assessing their merit first.

Few understand how much the Adamses worried about the emergence of one or another form of aristocracy in America, whether it was a moneyed oligarchy or a slave-owning planter contingent that spoke with a single voice. Any faction that held outlandish power over laws and lawmaking threatened good government. Their cure for malignant control was to be found in institutional solutions aimed at simultaneously mitigating personality-driven considerations and preserving a balance of power across social classes.

To synthesize, then, as much as this book centers on the Adamses' still fertile, endlessly rewarding world, it reassesses the roots of the fractured democracy of today. It tackles misperceptions, beginning with our common assumptions about democracy's historical inevitability as a function of ethical progress. It challenges the orthodox American faith in "government by the people." That hallowed phrase explains nothing. It ignores the real question: Who makes the wheels of power turn?

The world of John and John Quincy Adams encompassed the privacy of the hearth and the publicity of political councils. We encounter father and son on turbulent seas and inside crowded coaches ranging across continents. We see a lot of them in diplomatic garb as they faced the titled of Europe, unawed. In and out of legislative assemblies, they voiced what few politicians ever speak aloud: a conviction that "the people" are not always right, can be misled, and will arrive at conclusions with insufficient information.

In taking the temperature of heated times, the learned presidents Adams feared the effects of what was then called "popular enthusiasm." They personify an intellectual tradition too easily conflated with political conservatism and actually something apart. We describe it as a *dissent* from democracy. Theirs was, to be more precise, a nonpartisan rejection of the *impersonation* of democracy that the Jeffersonian-Jacksonian synthesis came to mean; theirs was an honest questioning of the sometimes slick democratic doctrine preserved in axioms that morphed into an enduring vision of a fair and impartial world predicated on American values. But we know implicitly, don't we, that our national ideal is just that, an ideal, and that democratic rhetoric masks undemocratic reality to the extent that powerful interests *everywhere* call the shots?

In their wide travels, the Adamses observed the abuses brought on by monarchy. But they also saw fundamental flaws in the quasi-religious adoration of the spirit of democracy. In 1800, from Berlin, John Quincy wrote of these paired problems to his then-president father. He saw across Europe evidence of "the ill consequences of power in hereditary succession," and he witnessed the concurrent failure of the French Revolution to produce good government. A decade after the fall of the Bastille, the rise of Napoleon Bonaparte proved to the younger Adams "the tendency of all the absurd and wicked theories of equality and fraternity, and representative democracy, to end in absolute and hereditary sway."[5]

It is remarkable, then, that John Q. Adams was the first to publicly proclaim—in his underappreciated inaugural address as president, twenty-five years later—that his country's system of government was "a confederated representative democracy." Nevertheless, he and his father both questioned whether there would ever be a way to guarantee that good judgment and moral excellence rose to the top in American politics. While humans remained subject to their passions, it was empirically true that the favored theory of Western democracy did not ensure positive outcomes. The Adamses sensed this and did not shy away from saying so.

This is dangerous territory; after all, no one wants to be told that the dynamic story of the rise of democracy is an exercise in mass self-delusion. But the fate of the presidents Adams provides a much-needed lesson in myth busting. We did something similar in our earlier collaboration *Madison and Jefferson* (2010), wherein we dispelled the long-held illusion that James Madison was Thomas Jefferson's dutiful political lieutenant. History largely ignored their coequal relationship, buried Madison's partisan identity, and portrayed his presidency in gloomy terms while greatly overstating his triumph at the Constitutional Convention.

The mismanagement of history around the Adamses is perhaps even greater. Father and son are seen as obstructionists, stuffed shirts, surly malcontents, who were resistant to the supposed good intentions embedded in Jeffersonian and Jacksonian democracy. Instead of viewing them as contrarians, we should know them as serious students of a road not taken, two who insisted that competence and rational judgment should supersede hollow celebrity and contrived popularity in a republic where votes ought always to register the choices of an informed citizenry.

This is where we turn next: to the Adamses' unqualified rejection of the "cult of personality" that diminished them in the national imagination.[6] When John and John Quincy Adams protested, in turn, the power of image over merit, and men over lawful institutions, they regarded personality as an illegitimate political force, a psychological tool designed to stimulate vulnerable citizens' desires. All humans craved notice, fame, renown; if they could not attain it themselves, they found an object to worship vicariously. In that sense, democracy was about representation, which required a certain theatricality or, as John Adams put it, "glitter." He bemoaned the fact that candidates had to promote themselves and "make the mob stare and gape."[7]

The phenomenon of political idol worship kept pace with the rise of parties, to the point of redefining the collective personality of Americans in the eyes of prominent European visitors such as Frances Trollope and Alexis de Tocqueville. Writing after the election of "the Hero" Andrew Jackson in 1828, these two, and others in their wake, made incisive remarks about a boisterous, impulsive, supremely self-confident race of people whose pride in democracy seemed unbounded. George Washington's personal aversion to the public's glorification of him had not taken root.[8]

In these pages, we adapt the term "cult of personality" to an all-embracing interest in the quasi-aristocratic bent that Americans refuse to see but that attaches not only to the historical Washington, Jefferson, and Jackson—monumental names—but also to families such as the Kennedys and Roosevelts. We have presidents Bush as well as presidents Adams because of the artificial weight accorded to names. Americans paradoxically prize the principle of equality and ogle admiringly at self-made billionaires and tabloid royalty. Force of personality has been at the heart of the American people's reflection on past actors, just as it plays a key role in quadrennial campaign hype. Force of personality does not apply to the presidents Adams, whose historical character stands in contrast to the democratic hero-worshipping compulsion.[9]

Disdaining the need to establish themselves as leaders of a political party, John and John Quincy Adams promoted themselves as worldly men who would make sound decisions. They were rejected at the polls for failing to galvanize the voting public. And yet their losses were narrow ones. Bright careers as patriots and public servants paved the way for their rise to the highest national office, while their stern moral values went largely unappreciated. America's evolving national self-image required a more freewheeling sense of what it meant to enjoy liberty than what they projected.[10]

This does not mean that "real democracy" ever supplanted an Adamsian version of government or national identity. It only means that others are seen to personify American democracy far better than they. Let us not lose this distinction. Our mythic democracy rejects the Adamses; it typecasts them as misfits, as poor representatives of a transformative idea that even now some lovers of country think of as divinely inspired. The Adamses are remembered as old-fashioned and curmudgeonly. Democracy is the opposite, a source of positive energy. As a revolutionary, John Adams helped to invent the myth. If he lost his way, his son never quite caught up to the pace of democratization either.

There could be only one national father: George Washington. His image was twisted and ultimately remolded into a supreme spirit, the self-contained One who embodied disinterested republicanism. Heaven sent and heaven returned, Washington was dead before the hate-spewing election of 1800 pitted the transactional opposites John Adams and Thomas Jefferson against each other. The success of Jefferson's party (Democratic-Republican or Republican), and later Andrew Jackson's (Democratic), allowed successful partisans to claim lineage to a desirable political style. If Jeffersonianism somehow registered the popular will, even though Jeffersonian officeholders were of the same class background as their supposedly elitist rivals, the so-called age of Jackson baked into America's apple-pie history the enchanting notion that popular democracy was an unstoppable force. Either you "got it" or you were a snob. We all know which category the Adamses were forced into by celebrants of the quintessential American idea.[11]

Good history must challenge popular assumptions when they are backed by uncertain evidence. It is in this way that we are able to learn that capital *D* "Democracy" did not magically "arise" (as many high school and college texts will assert) or lodge in the receptive hearts of eager voters, fulfilling the wise founders' collective vision. This mytho-pietistic narrative formula belongs to something called "consensus history." Adhering to its built-in limitations only guarantees repetition of the best possible America from one history book to the next, misleading generations of readers. Only one sharp thorn, slavery, stands out amid a rosy saga.

Consensus history does not particularly like the presidents Adams. They did not usher in a celebrated "age of" anything. They lost popular favor and, with it, a positive role in democracy's gloried trajectory. As writers, they shared a marvelous whimsicality that is overlooked. As humanists, they get overshadowed by Jefferson. As moral philosophers, they had a common lifelong fascination with the Roman statesman Marcus Tullius Cicero that reveals an assimilation of fine-tuned historical messages that should resonate but does not any longer.

There were many other thinkers, ancient and modern, who impressed the Adamses, but Cicero, in particular, was to them, and to many other knowledge seekers in post-Revolutionary America, a symbol of farsighted political courage. As a nineteenth-century translator of his political works said of Cicero, he considered himself "too great a man for party," and this was the two Adamses' idealized image of themselves as well. As the personification of Roman excellence, Cicero could (in the translator's words) waft "above all sects and schisms," draw from the good in competing party platforms, and, with a dastardly, well-honed wit, "lash their errors and corruptions with unsparing satire." That, as we shall see, was as Adamsian a political profile as it was Ciceronian. If the politician Cicero sided with the aristocrats of his day, it was only because the democrats he knew were "a very dangerous, precipitous, and violent body," too easily drawn to demagogues. They took unwise chances, "clamoured" recklessly for experimental acts, and did not as often act in the popular interest as their name might imply. As Cicero himself put it, the object of good government was to dispose of anxiety, not intensify it. The American idea of democracy had, built in, an intense contradiction: as a force for good, it offered freedom of expression, but it had a downside, too, in the dangerous fallout from high-spirited public performances that fueled hatreds.[12]

If educated Americans of the early nineteenth century embraced the familiar symbol of the rags-to-riches philosopher/inventor/diplomat Benjamin Franklin (John Adams's powerful nemesis), they were also taught to internalize Cicero's life well lived, a life cut short by political assassination. Their models of public speech and writing were not ours but are relatable in emotional suggestion to, say, Martin Luther King Jr.'s "I Have a Dream" speech—maxims and mottoes and imagery meant to prod individuals to virtue and achievement. Early Americans did not have the visual cues we do, however. Theirs was a typographical age, in which poetry (William Shakespeare, John Milton, Lord Byron, and lesser knowns then deemed great) served a large purpose in reimagining a distant past. Just as the poets found inspiration in antiquity, America's Revolutionary and post-Revolutionary writers borrowed the names and reputations of giants to enlarge the character of their men of consequence: Washington was popularly drawn as the manly and virtuous Roman Cincinnatus, the fiery orator Patrick Henry as the Greek Demosthenes. Today, when we enshrine the founders as unmatched and unimpeachable, we grant them the very status they assigned to classical models. All of these individuals symbolized sacrifice—the antithesis of political self-aggrandizement.

Image building was a constant in the politics of the early republic, just as it is today. No one felt as deeply as the two presidents Adams that image carried undue weight. So, does American history have some sort of problem with unimposing bald men? That sounds flip, of course, though the next one-term president after the Adamses, Martin Van Buren of New York, might concur. Tall presidents of the nation's formative years are the ones regarded as most striking: Washington, Jefferson, Jackson, and Lincoln all exceeded six feet in height, while the second and sixth presidents were among the shortest at five feet seven or thereabouts.

George Washington was as far from a backslapping politician as one can imagine. The soft-spoken Jefferson was imperturbable when he appeared in a public setting. The less than magnetic Jameses, Madison and Monroe, were not dramatic orators either. The dynamic, charismatic Alexander Hamilton and Aaron Burr, their names forever linked, were no taller than the Adamses. So, the presidents Adams actually fit right in. It is posterity that has, for its own purposes, accorded magnetic qualities to select members of the Revolutionary and post-Revolutionary generations.

By addressing the symptoms of political dysfunction, *The Problem of Democracy* reveals a good deal more than how father and son presidents constituted a damaged dynasty. One cannot fit something as amorphous as "democracy" into a rational category. It is not a given. The Adamses didn't suddenly wake up on the wrong side of democracy. Democracy was something that winners declared. They found it useful to them to exclude the presidents Adams from a mighty genealogy.

But the truth is that democracy is as mythic as it is real. When we revisit the "losers," if that's what the presidents Adams are, it is not to go against the grain but to harvest it.[13]

Now for the rules of the road. You may be entering the united worlds of the supremely well-educated "loser presidents" John (1735–1826) and John Quincy (1767–1848) Adams for the first time. An official chronology appears in the back of the book, but without entirely abandoning chronology, we focus on several dynamic themes and present an interdependent portrait of the presidents Adams as inhabitants of a world we only imagine we know.

To enter their domain, we engage the rich tradition of familiar letter writing and the still young culture of diary writing, which opens the door to everything else that matters: the truly remarkable emotional bond subsisting between father and son; their vast diplomatic activities across Europe over a period of several decades; the broad philosophical engagement that distinguishes them; the intermittent, often polemical writings that gained them notice; matching political styles that made it easy for their enemies to lump them together; and, finally, executive decisions that look surprisingly progressive in historical relief. As our commentary proceeds, the chronology gradually becomes fixed, but the story of the Adamses remains fluid.

Three full decades separated their births, and twenty-four years passed between the end of John's presidency and the start of John Quincy's. Yet their careers overlapped in significant ways. Each demonstrably influenced the other at key moments. We study cause and effect, consistencies and inconsistencies, coherence as well as disruptions. How father and son presidents differed in outlook or impulse is as interesting as marking out their shared beliefs or corresponding habits. This is, incidentally, where any author's subjectivity becomes most pronounced, which leads to one further explanatory admission: we refuse to accept the ordinary dictate that two generations—John's and John Quincy's, the founders and their immediate successors—are to be classified as distinct and separable eras. Tradition dictates that generations are to be studied as isolated units. We provisionally dissent. To isolate generations can sometimes be limiting, and we believe it is in this case.

What interests us is less what divides than what binds the two generations: a special reverence for all that stood behind the Declaration of Independence. The second and sixth presidents found themselves, at different intervals over the years, reinterpreting the Revolutionary moment. It was the touchstone around which a dynamic politics of memory operated, and they were, despite thirty-two years' difference in age, equally self-conscious actors in its unfolding history. This is why we want to listen in on their conversations. In charting the flights of memory they took, and by warily, sensitively manipulating the usual textbook chronology, we render time somewhat closer to what our co-subjects admitted to feeling.

There is more than one way to pass judgment on history. To stand to one side and wave the flag at a metaphysical parade of great presidents is the least original method of encountering its twists and turns. Pausing along the parade route to declare one or another transformational "age" is another conventional formula. Feeding our patriotic conditioning as it is catechized in primary and secondary school, even mature writers will fall back on the convenient story line of a "rise of democracy" from the "age of Jefferson" to the "age of Jackson."

It was, rather, an age of one-upmanship. The nation's formative years saw rival parties battle almost constantly. At one point, they appeared to reconcile. The interlude between the end of the War of 1812 and preparations for the 1824 election is conveniently styled an "Era of Good Feelings." The label has stuck, and yet throughout the period included in our study, American politics actually shed little of its volatility. For the two Adamses, the future of the United States remained ever worrisome and suspense filled.[14]

The "Era of Good Feelings" is a flawed taxonomic invention that leaves out the web of dissent that persisted from age to age, and it sidelines crucial personalities who were actively engaged in creating history. In this book, we recover a number of once-illustrious names that help us add vitality to the Adamses' story and contribute to a fuller understanding of American political culture. These include James Bayard, Francis Dana, Albert Gallatin, Elbridge Gerry, William Branch Giles, John Hancock, John Jay, Timothy Pickering, Benjamin Rush, John Trumbull, Martin Van Buren, William Vans Murray, and Mercy Otis Warren. We want readers to anticipate their appearance and pay attention to the roles played by these individuals as well as our main protagonists.

The first president Adams assumed office on March 4, 1797, when the federal government was still situated in the colonial-era capital of Philadelphia. Four years later, he lost his job to his own vice president, Thomas Jefferson, and exited under a cloud from the gloomy, marshy, newly named District of Columbia, or "Washington City." John and Abigail Adams were the first couple to occupy the President's House, which was only dubbed the White House in the heyday of their son. The second president Adams resided in that imposing palace, the executive mansion, from 1825 to 1829. He lost both the residence and the country to the upstart Andrew Jackson and spent the remainder of his years in the House of Representatives. His pattern of national service is one that no other president has ever cared to follow.

As the only single-term presidents in the nation's first five decades, the father and son Adamses are unique. They had everything going for them.

They were Harvard men with animated ideas about nation building. They had strong foreign policy chops, having each served long years in diplomatic posts: France, the Netherlands, and England for the father; the Netherlands, England, Russia, and Prussia for the son. Yet most historical treatments ignore everything else and emphasize ill temper, a disagreeable manner, to somehow justify their shared political failure as presidents.

The stirring to life of an American political style cannot be contained in symbolism or described in single adjectives. But as we have already begun to show, the changes wrought by the party system and the very language of partisanship add necessary context to the American story, inseparable from real or constructed personalities. Whether the matter at hand was of statewide or national concern, when they engaged in political talk the Adamses and their political contemporaries routinely judged "warm language" or a "cooling" of relations between men of principle in terms of the "state of parties."[15]

John and John Quincy Adams came of age before political parties as we know them existed. This fact matters greatly. There were certainly camps, schools of thought, but it was not until the decade of the 1790s that the self-consciously elitist "interest" known as Federalist and those who promised to accommodate nonelite participation in government, the self-styled Republicans, vied with each other heatedly. Until the next century, no one was comfortable identifying his "interest" as a formal party, because *party* was a divisive entity, destructive of public order. Federalists and Republicans both disowned the name "party." They accused their opposition of being the only group to practice the hideous "spirit of party."[16]

Others professed to renounce party spirit, but it was the two Adamses who, among the early presidents, best resisted the hardening of parties. They remained loyal to their common definition of nonpartisan statesmanship. They were, one might also argue, a party of two, adopting their own distinctive, if subdued, partisan identity. If they were outliers, it was owing to this quality of independence. They prescribed a politics that governed and didn't pander, a politics that operated against "turbulent and ungovernable" ambition, to use a pairing of adjectives to which newspapers and political pamphlets of their day often recurred. President Washington might have entered office as the unanimous choice, a preeminently nonjudgmental leader among those who lent their support to the Constitution, but party spirit became the nation's torment in the middle of his first term. As the majority marched in lockstep and joined the ranks of one of the two rival parties, John and John Quincy Adams refused to knuckle under to party pressure to conform. We should be struck that the outliers retained their stature under these circumstances.[17]

Each was elected president on the basis of a commitment to country, not because of subservience to anyone—not even George Washington. Yet they occupy a compromised position in the national story. It has been said over the years in faculty lounges and academic symposia, too glibly, that John Adams should have retired directly after the Revolution and not written treatises on government, if he wanted to be remembered heroically. As for John Quincy, few Americans give thought to his program as a one-term president, and these commenters tend to laud the sixth president mostly for his stand against slavery, which he came to only later, in his post-presidential career.

Along with a compulsion to locate heroes, Americans love nothing so much as a smooth, stable narrative. The truth is that the national story is rough and unstable. The country was busy doing things other than "building democracy."

For one, hardly anyone realizes anymore how much post-Revolutionary Americans cared about the nation's position relative to the Old World. The Adamses gave powerful opinions about European manners and prejudices and were profoundly nationalistic in appraising America's standing on the Continent. The early American republic did not exist in a vacuum. It was starved for news from abroad. Its cultural nexus was as much European as American inflected. At the same time, state and local matters often superseded a more general consciousness of national identity. Modern re-creations of the past tend to overlook the prominence of citizens at the local level who influenced national players and contributed meaningfully to critical debates. Admittedly, this is a lot to wade through. But it's worth the effort.

The Adamses force us to reevaluate "winner" and "loser" history. Must winners always have the last word? Must we assume that those who are vanquished at the polls were out of step with enlightened notions of progress? It would hardly seem so.

In the home library father and son shared, the European Enlightenment was not a utopian mission or a passing fancy. It was a template for useful knowledge and their common guide to a sophisticated tone of criticism. Before their presidencies, both saw up close, together and separately, at various intervals between 1780 and 1824, how sycophants and dronish functionaries behaved. Conscious of performing a different sort of duty, they did as earlier Enlightenment thinkers had done and translated historical experience into a species of political morality.

The past continued to speak to them. This is not to say John and John Quincy Adams were backward looking or swallowed whole the "genius" that came before. They were conceivers. No one ideology captured them in full. They constantly tested the waters, literally and figuratively. Taking into account the perils of an ocean transit at the time they lived, it is difficult to think of any president beyond these two who was able to boast greater preparation for high office based on an exposure to foreign capitals. They knew the physical world as well as any who was not a professional explorer. As they wandered through that world, they saw tremendous varieties of human settlement, high and low society. It all had an appreciable impact on them.

During their combined eight years in office, and due largely to their individual efforts, diplomatic resolution to crises prevailed instead of wars brought on by partisan excitement, newspaper headlines, and out-of-control war fever. The two Adamses were instrumental in readying the United States for expanded commercial engagement with the world. John Adams did not assent to his vitriolic fellow New Englanders or a militaristic Alexander Hamilton who pressed for war with France; his son, with an evenhandedness not expected of him, satisfied the slave states by adding Florida to the Union.

What did the multilingual Adamses do for their country? Without endorsing democracy in ways that posterity would celebrate, they added to national prestige and power. Nothing less. They were forceful in the national interest. Temperamental and occasionally indiscreet, they did not want the young, vulnerable United States beholden to either of the major powers of the age, England or France.

Our study is ambitious, because they were ambitious. In 1770, after the Boston Massacre, the attorney John Adams embraced controversy by defending the British soldiers charged with the five murders; he wore what might have been an unpopular stand as a badge of honor, making certain he would be noticed. In 1776, he championed the cause of independence in the Continental Congress, advocating liberty—and national dignity—obtained through law. Once again, he guaranteed that his voice was heard. In 1810, after several years in the U.S. Senate, John Quincy Adams authored a book on rhetoric and oratory, drawn from lectures he gave as a Harvard professor. Accentuating the faculty of invention, he became not only an expert in the rules of debate but also a lifelong student of the means of persuasion deployed from the pulpit, at the bar, and in popular assemblies. "Old Man Eloquent," they dubbed him in later years, when he baited adversaries with provocative speech.[18]

The pair witnessed crucial transformations. When John Adams became the nation's "first magistrate" (president) in 1797, the original states hugged the Atlantic coast; when John Quincy died in 1848, the Mexican War was nearing its end, and the entire continent lay in American hands. Between them, they forecast canals, road and railroad networks, and far-flung manufactories. They understood and approved this kind of national ambition. And once again, they embraced prescient ideas that belie the label of "conservative" that ordinarily attaches to them.

The Adamses judged harshly. They made political courage a core value, without any real attempt at consensus building. This might have been their most obvious flaw as political actors. Both lost the presidency to a southerner more popularly constructed and more creatively presented to the public. Seething as a result of their forced surrender of the presidency, both Adamses refused for years to speak to the men who wrested the presidential chair from them.

Imbued with similar substance, father and son had different things to prove. John Adams took long years to develop into a revolutionary, absorbed in the daily grind of a circuit-riding attorney when the real activists were meeting and planning. He made his bed, as it were, with his inspired cousin Samuel, remaining a junior partner until after the Boston Tea Party, when he finally seized his opportunity. John Quincy, witnessing that same Revolution unfold as a child, was at once a dutiful son and creatively distinct from his father. His directness in taking on dominant views exceeded that of his father.

The son came into his own as a barbed political writer during the tumult-filled Federalist decade of the 1790s, while his father grudgingly served in the unexciting role of vice president under George Washington. Appointed by Washington to a diplomatic post in Europe, JQA (as he often designated himself) determined to make his mark on the world on the basis of something other than nepotism. Though he worked hard to become his own man, the "curse" of a presidential father never completely dissipated.

By James Madison's presidency (1809–1817), JQA no longer had a Federalist character. He'd abandoned the party to which his father had nominally belonged. If he was, by now, an ally of Madison's, he was hardly a Jeffersonian. And so a strange transition took place: Madison, the more flexible of the two Virginians, had utterly detested John Adams in the 1780s and 1790s, when his political alter ego Jefferson unsuccessfully sought to temper that prejudice. After 1809, the past did not stop the senior Adams from becoming as unabashed a supporter of the fourth president as his son was in these years. Displaying his munificence, John Adams revived an old, and now dearer, friendship with the ideologically more rigid Jefferson, the man who had sent him into retirement.

The two Adamses' presidencies were similar only in superficial ways. John Adams was saddled with Washington's cabinet, composed of Hamilton men with little regard for their official boss. On the other hand, he engaged a generally supportive Congress. John Quincy Adams enjoyed excellent relations with his advisers, most conspicuously Henry Clay of Kentucky, a former rival who became his secretary of state. But the Congress he dealt with was largely directed by Jackson men, who made it abundantly clear that they would not permit the president to carry out a single one of his well-drawn policies.

As they approached their reelection campaigns, both of the presidents Adams held uncertain expectations. They did not mask their feelings of hurt or anger, but they were, at bottom, men of peace who were practiced in determining *when* and *where* to confront. They were not, by any measure, predictable, which makes them all the more fascinating as biographical co-subjects. To a moral economy we might describe as thrifty New England attributes writ large, they added a coherent tone of criticism we might call Adamsian, which usually involved finding a justifying authority in history—the art of politics and the art of living as prescribed by Cicero being one outstanding example of that. The presidents Adams profited from history without fetishizing past knowledge. And they sought to protect history from those they considered frauds and propagandists. If that makes them elitists, we don't think they would have rejected the label.

Their common prescription centered on two concepts: *independence* and *service to country*. Here we need to appreciate the power of language to feed both thought and emotion, to uncover both interiority and community. Independence of mind extended to national character; personal industry extended to patriotic service.

The Adamses did not periodize American history precisely as we would. But they did divide the Revolutionary era, in an emotional sense, from both its predecessor and its successor. "A nation was born in a day," John Quincy Adams proclaimed in an oration he delivered as James Monroe's secretary of state on July 4, 1821. Coming into his own as a senior politician, he could look back wistfully while stating that old "resentments" toward Britain were being properly "buried in oblivion." As the sixth president, he retained the memory of the first time he heard the Declaration of Independence read and the deep feelings it gave him as a nine-year-old in Boston, while his father labored in Philadelphia. On the day he died, July 4, 1826, John Adams delivered a final toast for the newspapers: "Independence forever." He had the unique experience to depart life while his eldest son was occupying the highest office in the land.

But it gets better. A year later, in the fall of 1827, the living president Adams woke one day to find that his first timepiece, acquired in France as a youth, had stopped ticking. It had been in his possession since he was a teen, pursuing his studies at the foot of a father just then in the process of negotiating American independence. As the sixth president noted the disablement of his old watch, his mind flashed to a day when his father had temporarily misplaced a relic dating to the same historic moment, the seal he had affixed to the 1783 Treaty of Paris. He'd felt it as the loss of a dear friend. A burst of emotion had seized John Adams then; it seized John Quincy now. Struggling with his memories, he wrote with heightened awareness in his regular diary, "Lean not on friendship or time."[19]

These words would have been a fit epitaph for either the father or the son.

New York Septr. 13. 1790

Dear John

I wrote you before to day: but I forgot to Say Several Things. — Have you ever attended a Town Meeting? You may there learn the ways of Men, and penetrate Several Characters which otherwise you would not know. There are Several Objects of Enquiry which I would point out to your consideration ~~and Enquiry~~ without making any noise or parade about them.

1. The State of Parties in Religion, Government Manners, Fashions.
2. The Leading Characters in Church and State.
3. The Machines, Arts and Channels by which Intelligence and Reports are circulated through the Town.
4. The Makers and Spreaders of Characters.
5. The State of the various Tradesmen and Mechanicks, their Views designs and Projects
6. The State, Hopes, Views, Plans, Passions, and Sentiments of the old Tories, and their Correspondencies abroad and at home in their own State and in other States.
7. The Dittos of the old Whigs of 1764 and 1774.
8. Ditto of the Neutrals.
9. Ditto of those who have Sprung up Since the Revolution.

Letter, John Adams to John Quincy Adams, September 13, 1790. While he was George Washington's vice president, the advice-giving father derived a comprehensive plan for his son, beginning with his attendance at Boston's democratically framed "Town Meeting." There, the struggling young attorney was to monitor the "State of Parties" in political society, the "Leading Characters in Church and State," and "old Tories," "old Whigs"—those who opposed and those who supported the innovative principles put forward at the Revolutionary moment.

PART I

PROGENITOR

In most father-son relationships, there comes a time—and it usually arrives unnoticed—when the elder finds himself yielding to the knowledge of the younger. The thirty years extending from John Quincy's birth through John Adams's accession to the presidency constitute the period when the "progenitor" ruled the roost, controlled the purse strings, and directed his son's choices. For about three decades, then, the "inheritor" tended to heed his father's advice, build a résumé, and wait his turn. He experienced a challenging apprenticeship as the son of a man who had risen to national prominence. Nothing had been given to the elder Adams beyond an education, nothing to assure him of success in life. If the expectations John Adams placed upon his son were great, it is no less true that the regular "approbation" John Quincy received from his father afforded him "exquisite" pleasure—those were the son's words, directed to his father, and a memorable testament to their extraordinary closeness.

ONE

EXEMPLARS

Fame, Fortune, Power say some, are the Ends intended by a Library.
The Service of God, Country, Clients, Fellow Men, say others.
Which of these lie nearest my Heart?
—DIARY OF JOHN ADAMS, *January 30, 1768*

John Adams, thirty-one, was absent for the birth of his eldest son. As a practicing attorney, he was riding the circuit and generating income, ever anxious about his public reputation. "It is a Life of Here and every where," he jotted in his diary, "a rambling, roving, vagrant, vagabond Life." On any given day, these "desultory" wanderings might find him in attendance at superior court, or sitting in the gallery of the colonial legislature, or browsing and buying at the shop of the bookseller John Mein, a Tory friend soon to become a client. His infant son was two months old when Adams's wife, née Abigail Smith, chastised her husband for his absences by repeating a line their two-year-old daughter, Nabby, sang as a lullaby to her new companion: "Come papa come home to Brother Johnny." Mr. Adams had heard such grumbling from his wife many times over, and it was never very subtle. Nor did it have to be. He was quick to acknowledge that his divided responsibilities made for a conflicted mind.[1]

John Adams was not exactly a homebody, nor was he known for the fidelity of his memory. Three and a half decades later, as the first president of the United States to lose office in a failed reelection bid, he began composing his autobiography, left blank the day of John Quincy's birth, and waited for his son to fill it in. His pen correctly marked the year as 1767, but then he gave the month as August instead of July. What does it say that he could forget his eldest son's birthday?[2]

In early adulthood, John Adams was self-conscious about his modest genealogy, all the while believing in his mind's potential for greatness.[3] From the mid-1750s, he regularly acknowledged to himself how much he longed to shine; his determination to become a lawyer reflected an undisguised desire to be heard and respected by the public. Angling for business in Boston's highly competitive legal marketplace, he consciously vied with older, more established attorneys. While still struggling to build his practice, he married and put down roots. By the year of John Quincy's birth, in the third year of the marriage, he finally felt he could afford to feed his passion for book collecting.

His partner in life equaled John Adams in enterprise and discernment. She had been denied Harvard-taught measures of useful knowledge, but she read widely and spoke with authority. Before the successive years of 1778 and 1779, when father and son traveled to Europe, trekked over treacherous terrain, and grew to be each other's closest confidant, they were alike Abigail's men. There was nothing in the least passive about this self-educated woman. During John Quincy's first decade, while his father ventured into politics, his mother acted as their intermediary.

The boy's middle name honored Abigail's maternal grandfather, Colonel John Quincy. Said Quincy had died in 1767, just days before his legatee was born. Ordinarily, that statement would stand on its own, but in this case the assignment of a middle name warrants a bit more study. The attribution of a middle name was not fashionable until the nineteenth century, at which point it became fairly routine. John Quincy was thus distinctive before he made himself distinguished. It also says, importantly, that Abigail's family lineage mattered, leaving her stamp between "John" and "Adams."[4]

When it came to his son's education, John Adams did not act unilaterally. "I am very thoughtfull and anxious about our Johnny," he wrote to his wife when their boy was six. In their world, this was a critical time in a male's education. "What School to send him to," John pondered, "what Measures to take with him. He must go on learning his Latin, to his Grandfather [Adams] or you, or somewhere. And he must write."[5]

John and Abigail's fifty-four-year-long marriage has been the focus of intense scrutiny and speculation. The consensus points to the Puritan inheritance in their shared commitment to a comprehensive education that emphasized steadiness, diligence, "habituation" to "industry"; a virtuous conception of manhood; and, no less material, the development of a "laudable" ambition.[6]

While even a rudimentary education was far from universal in Revolution-era America, well-educated people across the colonies did invest considerable energy in cultivating the intellect of their six-year-old sons. In an American child's upbringing, family honor was at stake, as was the fate of future property management and inheritance. By the same reasoning, written records were preserved in order to maintain a conscious connection between the present and earlier generations. The land a family held did not change hands without that history in mind.

BRAINTREE BEGINNINGS

John Smith (of Pocahontas fame) sailed along the Massachusetts coast in 1614 and appended to his subsequent *Generall Historie* a map imaginatively depicting the as yet unsettled town of Braintree/Quincy as the future "London" of New England. By 1625, a plantation existed on what would eventually become the Adamses' property, and in 1634 Braintree became a permanent settlement. In the seventeenth century, official documents from the place were often dated "Braintry, Newengland."[7]

Those whom John and John Quincy Adams called the "Pilgrim Fathers" were far less remote to the Adamses than the two early and outspoken American presidents are to us. Even before the Revolution, their sense of national beginnings reflected a keen awareness of the scope of their ancestors' hazardous undertakings. Until John Adams took up his post at the Continental Congress in Philadelphia in 1774, and until he took young Johnny with him to Europe in 1778, what mattered about the past, what filled historic memory, had all taken place nearby. Their village, quiet and drab, was eleven miles south of the center of Boston. Braintree formed the so-called northern precinct of the town of Quincy (also named after Abigail's maternal grandfather), into which it was incorporated in 1792. A finite number of surnames communed in New England cemeteries.[8]

In terms of its commercial position on the North American continent, the Adams property was well situated. The soil was of good quality. Yet we must recognize something else, too: until the Revolution, the entire

Massachusetts Bay Colony was regarded abroad as a deficient, dependent corner of Britain's sprawling empire. It is tempting to think otherwise, given Boston's central position in the political crisis that loomed, but eastern Massachusetts was less wealthy, per capita, than the middle Atlantic, Chesapeake, or Caribbean colonies. As traditional cottage industries such as spinning, weaving, cheese making, and shoe manufacture proceeded apace, a generally modest merchant class imported clothing, earthenware, china tea sets, and mahogany furniture. The region's agriculture could hardly keep up with population growth; as a result, the middle colonies were called upon to make up the difference. After the Revolution, the Commonwealth of Massachusetts offered subsidies to budding domestic enterprises, hoping to jump-start the postwar economy: paperhanging and stained-paper production were encouraged (a precursor of wallpaper, suspended like tapestries in area homes); sailcloth and other textile factories spoke to Boston's pride in manufacturing and helped reverse the easy tendency to look abroad for imported quality goods.[9]

The Braintree farm of John Adams's father (yet another John) grew wheat, corn, and oats. Theirs was an area of open pastureland fronting hills. On inheriting his property in 1761, John Adams planted. He studied husbandry along with the law. "My Thoughts are running continually from the orchard to the Pasture and from thence to the swamp," he wrote in his diary. He could be found at the plow, or "pruning Apple Trees, mending Fences, carting Dung. Sometimes in the Pasture, digging stones, clearing Bushes . . . digging stumps and Roots." Even with a top-notch education, he was something less than a "gentleman farmer." He worked the land, albeit with hired hands who shared in the labor.[10]

Close to the throbbing sea, the little town of Braintree gave even subsistence farmers the sense of connection. The sights and sounds they knew were not ours, of course. Nothing louder than church bells vibrated in the air. There was often a damp earth to contend with when they moved their produce to market. From season to season, tall masts and long wharves framed their vision; they built wooden houses with small-paned windows and traveled in unsteady carriages that plied the road to Plymouth. Beyond the thirty-acre farmers and merchants and artisans were men of letters whom the Adamses thought worth knowing. The descendants of Puritans boasted of their one institution of higher learning, Harvard College. Each annual commencement marked a major milestone in the life of greater Boston, celebrated much as official holidays were.

As a recent Harvard graduate and a barely tested attorney in 1759, John Adams found the town of Boston curiously peopled and cluttered with visual obstructions. Besides those he saw at the docks—shipwrights and fishermen, caulkers and carvers, sail and rope makers—tradesmen in Boston included cobblers and coopers, soap or sugar boilers, apothecaries, leather dressers, smiths, and masons. Quaintly, Adams recorded after one of his jaunts, "My Eyes are so diverted with Chimney Sweeps, Carriers of Wood, Merchants, Ladies, Priests, Carts, Horses, Oxen, Coaches, Market men and Women, Soldiers, Sailors, and my Ears with the Rattle Gabble of them all that I cant think long enough in the Street upon any one Thing to start and pursue a Thought."

By his own admission, he was awed by the well-established cadre of Boston attorneys, seniors to him in his chosen profession. A classic overachiever, he was discomfited in adopting as his necessary goal "to get a Character in Town." Making his way among more accomplished families, he used what connections he had to press forward—hobnobbing without appearing unctuous. But how to find his way into their society? "Shall I look out for a Cause to speak to, and exert all the Soul and all the Body I own," he posed to himself. "Shall I creep or fly?"[11]

His son grew up in a considerably different social environment. John Quincy would always know that his father was an established "Character" in the state. But that fact did not render the son's path smoother; he did all he could to make it in the legal profession on his own merit. The decade of his twenties was at least as hard for him as it had been for his father before him. He would experience the same struggle to be respected when he trod in his father's steps as a member of the diplomatic corps. The greatest difference in their respective careers was that the surname Adams held meaning by the time of John Quincy's entry into society. That said, poisonous feelings of self-doubt pursued both of the Adamses as young men.

Though an extremely hard worker, John Adams never became rich. Select Boston-area merchants did, but not he. In a post-presidential memoir, he recalled the advice he received from a distinguished attorney as he prepared for the bar. The first part was "Pursue the Law itself rather than the gain of it." The second part went, "I advize you not to marry early." Old John

Adams explains, "His Advice made so deep an Impression on my mind that I believe no Lawyer in America ever did so much Business as I did afterwards in the seventeen Years that I passed in the Practice at the Bar, for so little profit; and although my Propensity to marriage was ardent enough, I determined I would not indulge it, till I saw a clear prospect of Business and profit enough to support a family without Embarrassment." John Quincy received the same advice from his parents.[12]

John Adams lived modestly because he *had* to. In the middle of the Revolution, he questioned his ability to persist in politics, knowing that his former law colleagues were steadily pursuing a proper living while he labored, too much of the time, at a distance. During one home respite, he wrote to the family friend James Lovell, "When I see my Brothers at the Bar, here, so easily making Fortunes for themselves and their Families, and when I recollect that for four years I have abandoned myself and mine [to attend Congress], and when I see my own Children growing up, in something very like real Want, because I have taken no Care, it requires as much Philosophy as I am Master of, to determine to persevere in public Life." Indeed, while Adams *père* and *fils* alike were masters of the law, public service would prove to be their principal source of income.[13]

Money was scarce. Prior to the Revolution, Massachusetts Bay was a place where goods were used in payment at times when banknotes were not available. Small farmers were always extending credit to their neighbors. Currency shortages were a permanent feature of the provincial economy, leaving it to those most active to advocate for an expansion of banks to boost the colony's reputation within the family of nations. Men of commerce prodded each royal governor in turn to allow paper money to circulate. From mid-century, however, as John Adams came of age, Boston's shipbuilding industry saw a decline; the town's population slowly decreased, as the numbers of newly poor added up. A farming lawyer had to work overtime to provide for his family. And in the end, John Quincy, too, fared best by earning a government salary, a fact that caused some stir in the press as he was criticized for being what is today referred to as a career politician.[14]

From the moment he joined the Continental Congress in 1774, John Adams came to rely on his wife to manage their acreage, hire help, and keep their financial house in order. "You must take Care, my Dear, to get as much

Work out of our Tenants as possible," he wrote. Going down the list of his debtors, he appealed to her, "I can not loose such Sums as they owe me—and I will not." He was reluctant to take chances. He had little appetite for financial wheeling and dealing. Mrs. Adams took charge.[15]

After war erupted, management of their finances became more complicated. As the notes they held lost value, the Adamses came near to financial ruin. It was Abigail, with no formal training in such affairs, who found solutions by making wise investments. To combat the shortage of goods in the dark days of the Revolution, she took the initiative and arranged for her husband, while overseas, to ship cargoes home, which she sold through a male relative. This way, she would not be perceived as a woman who violated the dictates of prudence or challenged the public pose expected of a senior statesman's consort. From Europe, John hesitated once the British captured two early shipments. But Abigail persisted with her plan and through her efforts markedly improved their financial situation. More than just confident, she proved adept at finding business opportunities, while her husband confined his grand plans to the cause of the nation he was helping to build economically. She invested in depreciated public securities, reaping profits from state debts accrued during the war years. In this matter, she turned not to her husband for financial advice but to her uncle Cotton Tufts.[16]

"Had I followed my own Business with as much Attention and Industry as I have those of the Publick," John wrote to Tufts, a physician, in 1787, "I could have owned, the whole Town of Braintree at this hour, or the Value of it. . . . Now I must be content to be poor, and my Children too, unless they Should have more Wisdom." Without his wife's activities, he would have been in far worse shape than he was at the conclusion of his time abroad. And he knew it.[17]

Rural Obscene

Boston and Braintree were not the sole sources of John Adams's evolving sense of self. He took pride in his broader New England roots, proof of which lies in his early adoption of the pen names "John Winthrop" (whom he considered the progenitor of both the Massachusetts Bay Colony and

America itself) and "Novanglus," which translates from the Latin as "New England." When the aging French philosopher Abbé de Mably related his plan to write a history of the American Revolution, Adams prepared a long list of sources to consult, most of which emphasized the vitality of New Englanders. (The length of the list convinced Mably to abandon the project.) From Adams's perspective, republican traditions dug their deepest roots in his home region, where four institutions had seeded the ground for popular government: schools that advanced education, churches that sustained community morals, local militias that taught discipline, and most of all town meetings that gave citizens essential training in deliberation and debate.[18]

Yet this rosy picture tells only half the story. "Adams country" wasn't necessarily a haven for calm reasoning. Itinerant life as a lawyer put him in contact with all sorts of litigants: civil suits and criminal cases exposed him to the worst in human nature. There was *King v. Stewart* (1774), a civil action for damages over an assault and destruction of property. The cause was "Scurlogging" (either a curious local term or Adams's own invention), which described the crime of inciting a mob through scurrilous talk. Stewart, the perpetrator, was supposed to have instigated a riot upon the death of a horse. He had accused his wealthy neighbor, the aptly named King, of complicity in the death, but more conspicuously of his being a Tory whose haughty ways mimicked those of a despised British minister.

Adams represented the offended Mr. King. In his address to the jury, he accepted the fact that small towns and rural communities were subject to "vulgar" passions. Local knowledge was easily corrupted, and residents prone "to swallow down greedily all the Lyes and dirty Tales" and take delight in propagating them. The attorney Adams cursed the peevishness of small-minded folks and their peculiar resentments. "These private Mobs, I do and will detest," he wrote to his wife. The mob was not engaged to protect fundamental rights, but was, in his view, formed so as to cast blame on someone for unrelated private grievances.[19]

So, he had mixed sentiments about New England ways. Literacy rates were likely higher there than anywhere else in Anglo-America, but a common education had its limits. In 1755, before his career in the law began, John Adams was a schoolmaster in Worcester. Writing an ironic account of his students, he designated himself a "haughty Monarch," having to dispense "right and Justice" from the head of the classroom. And all for naught, because all the instruction he gave that mattered was that which he was obliged to convey with a "Birch" (that is, corporal punishment). "Scolding, then flattering, then Thwacking" were serially applied in order to retain the pupils' attention. The vaunted age of Enlightenment met its match at the local level, where conversation could devolve into incoherent quarreling. Whether the subject was radical deism, social leveling, or what Adams styled "rural obscene witt," the effect was the same: his people were an obstinate, rough-hewn, troublesome breed. He had little choice but to make peace with them all.[20]

In 1776, fellow members of the Continental Congress remarked upon New Englanders' backwardness. Which led John, in that notable year, to complain to Abigail that they were "Aukward and bashfull," "pert," lacking in "Art and Address," and modest in their "Knowledge of the world." They were not formed to be "heroes and statesmen." At least not yet. But it didn't matter. He confessed to a "local Attachment, that partial Fondness, that overweening Prejudice in favor of New England." Despite the obvious defects, feelings of place ran deep.[21]

John Adams's early use of the colorful moniker "Humphry Ploughjogger" was another, important example of his awareness of the human environment. He was probably inspired to adopt the graphic pseudonym after seeing a pamphlet on religious dissent, published in Boston, and signed "Richard Ploughjogger." Like the innovative "Richard," who opened his piece by apologizing for his "imperfection" as a mere "Man that follows the Plough," Adams's "Humphry Ploughjogger" embraced an unassuming pose. He was an unschooled yeoman taking a friend to task for social sycophancy. Adopting the vocabulary of a small farmer, Adams compared the politics conducted by "grate men" to the rude work of "breaking Heads, boxing Ears, ringing Noses and Kicking Breeches." His "Ploughjogger" advised the best of the Bay Colony's politicians that they were in need of a reality check: they should be putting aside their egos—no longer "fling[ing] dirt"; they should be standing apart from the howling crowd, talking sense, and "teeching mankind things they want to know." It was 1763.[22]

In 1782, the diplomat John Adams was still calling himself "Humphry Ploughjogger." This time, it related to his successful lobbying efforts at The Hague, suggesting that his provincial identity was not entirely shed, even after several years in the courts of Europe. Not long after, this

"Ploughjogger" fellow took on a life apart from the pen of John Adams, when the name appeared in debates over the ratification of the Constitution. In 1788, "Ploughjogger" was adopted by both Federalists and Anti-Federalists. The first saw the value of a rusticated pose in winning over the yeomanry to a grand cause; the second thought that rusticity in prose underscored their greater sympathy with the lower orders. The idea was that ordinary farmers were as capable of "guiding the machinery of the state" as they could "guide and govern the plough." As late as 1801, an anonymous writer who must have known "Humphry Ploughjogger" as Adams's pseudonym revived the name in a satire-laced attack on the newly elected president, Jefferson.[23]

John Quincy Adams would also invent pseudonyms once he took up the vocation of political essay writing. But his "Publicola," "Marcellus," and "Menander" were Roman and Greek. At no time in his long career would he ever pose as a rustic or rube. He enjoyed all the benefits of a gentleman's education, and his less entrenched provincialism would prove useful when he eventually broke with the Federalist Party in 1807, a party whose last stronghold was New England. His father had married Abigail Smith, of a neighboring town, whereas John Quincy would find his bride across the Atlantic in old England. So, there was that, too.

YANKEE ACCENT

We would love to know what these Adamses sounded like. To an extent, we do, even though contemporaries did not bring up problems in comprehension or mark curiosities in speech when northerners and southerners met. Linguistic scholarship indicates that "deep, geographically based, dialect differences marked early modern British speech," whereas "colonial English was significantly less differentiated" in North America. New England writers of the nineteenth century who peppered their stories with "old Yankee dialect" only did so as a means of depicting characters of the uneducated class. The poet James Russell Lowell marked the Yankee dialect as "racy with life and vigor and originality."[24]

The Adams diaries provide us hints of a speaking style. Starting out in Braintree, one variously "came into Boston" and "went into Boston." He "idled away" time, "pass'd an evening," "searched in vain," and "told of his misfortune"—the verbs are decisive. A satisfying event was "agreeable," a good day "agreeably spent." This constituted polite speech.

"I got my fire made," says John Adams, employing syntax that sounds colloquial, even unrefined, to modern ears. Yet he preferred the high-sounding Latinate over a stark, rusticated Saxon form, as when "enumerating" (rather than counting) the "excellencies" (worth) of a person. He frequently praised "intrepidity" and "magnanimity," was unable to "bear the least mortification," and recognized when a parent "inculcated" a "maxim" in attempting to influence his child's behavior.

Riding the circuit, the attorney John Adams was applauded by one gentleman after obtaining a successful verdict: "Sir, says he, I shall think myself forever obliged to you, for the Patriotick manner in which you conducted that Cause. You have obtained great honour." This language strikes us as highly affected, but for the recipient of a high compliment it was not. Affectation, for John Adams, was the preacher who spoke above his parishioners, with elaborate constructions that had no place in the pulpit, where the language spoken should always be "plain."[25]

John Quincy, when young, writes, "We were stopped a going out of the city," his colloquial "a going" adding a syllable to convey active movement and rhythm. Benjamin Bangs and his crew of New England whalers were "a bitterly scared" of an enemy sloop. (Appalachian American English of the modern era has preserved this particular colonial custom.) Bangs was a Cape Cod resident with a Braintree connection whose ancestry extended back nearly to the *Mayflower*. A bit older than John Adams, he kept a diary for twenty years. He used "nigh" for "near" when a neighbor taken with "Bloody flux" (a gastrointestinal disorder) "Lies now to appearance *nigh his End*." Bangs's son Isaac, a 1771 Harvard graduate, shared the Adamses' syntax, using the conditional tense in a way that strikes the modern ear as other than American: houses were "not so well constructed as I immagined we should have found them." Praising "a very civil Set of People with whom I lived very quietly" shows how established rules of civility demanded nonintrusiveness.

If eighteenth-century American English was less differentiated from colony to colony than British English was from shire to shire, a definable speech pattern did exist that eventually became known as a New England "drawl." Father and son might have pronounced "horse" as "hoss" and "pound" as "paund." Depending on where in New England you were, the verb form "heard" was variously pronounced "hard" or with a long *e* as in "heered"; "bombs" sounded more like "bums," "boil" as "bile." As the circuit-riding attorney John Adams described the fickleness of his world, he was "much pinched with a cold, raw, harsh, N.E. Wind." To be "pinched" under what we might describe as a "biting" wind may be an atypical word choice, but it's a thoroughly recognizable sensation. Note that he was conscious of the direction of the wind, which he described in his diary with not one but three adjectives.[26]

It was not until after the Revolution that a real concern for the composition of American English became the hobbyhorse of nationalists. It was, in fact, John Adams himself who first exhorted Congress in 1780 (from Amsterdam, and in the company of John Quincy) to establish an institution that would improve "eloquence and language" and work for greater uniformity across the states. For whatever reason, no action was taken on his proposal.[27]

From the Revolution forward, Americans liked to say that the English spoken in England was undergoing change, while American English retained the pure elements of an older, proper English. Trying to have it both ways, patriot-linguists claimed that American English was developing its own sound and structure: the Republic refused to be yoked to lifeless, aristocratic, metropolitan British English. The language of Shakespeare, while outmoded, would not have been described by these New Englanders as puzzlingly archaic. More important, John Adams, as "Ploughjogger," could imitate a farmer's voice while adoring the resplendent tones of the poet Milton.[28]

It was not the agricultural interest nor any academic persuasion that lit the sparks which fully ignited in the mid-1770s. It was Boston's merchant class. The powers granted to royal officials, and especially to customs authorities, caused the first stirrings of discontent among the people of Massachusetts in the early 1760s. The appointment of Thomas Hutchinson as a colonial administrator marked a turn for the worse; though a native of these parts, he gave primary allegiance to Great Britain. The rift between the Massachusetts Assembly and Governor Hutchinson widened as the 1760s bled into the 1770s; a petition for his removal, brought to the king's attention by the Bay Colony's agent in London, Benjamin Franklin, went nowhere.

Boston merchants led the resistance to decisions in Parliament that they deemed arbitrary and constraining. The Stamp Act crisis of 1765–1766 was the first so-called act of tyranny to produce massive cross-colonial defiance; the Harvard-trained physician Joseph Warren exclaimed, a bit prematurely, "The whole continent is inflamed to the highest degree." Opposition to parliamentary taxation resulted in a patriotic boycott of British products, which in turn prompted the stationing of troops in central Boston and the March 5, 1770, "Massacre" of five "inhabitants" of the town, who fell before a line of agitated soldiers near the customhouse. The attorney John Adams gained in honor and combativeness by representing the hated soldiers, ensuring that they received a fair trial. His visibility increased. Then came the Tea Act and the destruction of 342 chests of tea in Boston harbor at the end of 1773. As yet, no one was refusing to acknowledge George III as a rightful sovereign.

Massachusetts had been singled out for special treatment by the ministry in London. Boston was a flash point, and would remain so. As the crown removed responsibility from the colonial legislature and undertook to pay the salary of Governor Hutchinson, John Adams took up his pen at the behest of his political friends and asserted the colony's autonomy. He now stood at the forefront of the movement to declare rights and defend civil liberty.

Bursting Heart

His wife understood what drove him. While it was not always easy to accept his absences, she had a keen consciousness of the urgency of the times. She held on. They held on. John and Abigail Adams lived to celebrate more than half a century of marriage in an age when epidemics and early death were common. The same would be true of John Quincy Adams and his wife, Louisa Catherine (née Johnson). Both couples certainly beat the odds.

When she agreed to wed the twenty-nine-year-old lawyer in October 1764, nineteen-year-old Abigail Smith of the nearby town of Weymouth was arguably of superior social stock to her betrothed. Her father, a respected Congregationalist minister, officiated at the wedding. Nine months later, daughter Abigail (Nabby) was born to the couple; the next year, a second child was conceived, and on July 11, 1767, a date his father did not commit to heart, John Quincy entered the world. Like his father, JQA married when he was in his late twenties, and the bride, though not quite as young as Abigail, took her wedding vows at twenty-two. The younger generation began a family right away, too.

John Adams kept a cluttered law office in the house where his children were born, so Johnny (as he was known through his teens) probably experienced a childhood no grander than that his father had known—up to a point, anyway. The world enlarged for him quite suddenly when he was ten and accompanied his father to Europe. Crossing the Atlantic repeatedly during that decade and the next, the boy had a rare, and indeed an unconventional, education.

John Quincy was a prodigy, yes, but it was wholly owing to circumstances that he became one. He engaged with great "characters" wherever he went; he became a citizen of the world before his parents decided he had best return to New England and prepare himself to enter Harvard. This was all before he exited his teens. A first inkling of his promise is provided in his diplomat-father's diary record of 1779, during the then eleven-year-old's return voyage, after having spent a number of months in France. As his father watched, Johnny gave two high-ranking French officials English lessons. "The Chevalier de la Luzerne, and M. Marbois are in raptures with my Son," wrote the well-pleased father. "The Ambassador said he was astonished, at my Sons knowledge." In 1783, from Paris, John Adams wrote to his daughter, Nabby, of her sixteen-year-old brother, "He is grown to be a man, and the world says they should take him for my younger brother, if they did not know him to be my son." By then, the elder Adams was seeing quite a bit of himself in his son: "He is very studious and delights in nothing but books, which alarms me for his health; because, like me, he is naturally inclined to be fat." Despite these concerns, the proud father confided, "His knowledge and judgment are so far beyond his years, as to be admired by all who have conversed with him." He exemplified his parents' social aspirations.[29]

Was their compulsive sense of intellectual independence and avid book reading a congenital trait? The two Adamses conducted regular self-study, coldly assessing their natural faculties. Before the nation made them into historical subjects, John and John Quincy cast themselves as moral subjects whose declared common enemy was ignobility, cowardice, degradation. It is important to state this fact, because (as we shall see) the personal critique found its way into political commentaries. They expressed discomfort whenever they were called upon to placate a government colleague or navigate by verbal indirection. Relatedly, each appreciated the value of humor, picking up on irony in a multitude of circumstances (as we shall also see).

Abigail Adams's influence on the distinctive moral sense of her men is obvious. Her letters to husband and son are replete with willful exhortations. This attitude became almost her sole means of maintaining connections during John and John Quincy's shared years in Europe. She was obliged to become increasingly independent: five full years passed before her husband relented and gave his blessing for her to travel with Nabby to England, where they joined the Adams males in 1784.

As protective as she was of her men, Mrs. Adams was contemptuous of others' deceit and sycophancy. Much like her troublesome husband, she had a reputation for bluntness. Describing herself as the down-home New England antithesis of European courtier culture, she owned to an uncomplicated emotional cast, "taught to say the thing I mean, and to wear my Heart in my countenance." Father and son knew always to expect candor from her, and by all accounts they relished her combination of gentleness and toughness. There were definitely moments when her eldest son found her overbearing—depressingly so when she interfered with his selection of a wife—but his overall estimate of her was somewhere between respectful and reverent.[30]

For John Adams, so strongly associated in modern minds with the impetus toward revolution, an enlarged sense of political duty only unfolded in the year or so prior to the birth of John Quincy. The true political animal among the Adamses was his older, well-bred Boston cousin Samuel Adams. John was slow to commit himself to a cause that might lose him law clients. He wished to be known as competent but not controversial. Once he got his feet wet in politics, his patriotic commitment magnified. In addition to Cousin Samuel, he communed with such agreeable Sons of Liberty as the charismatic Dr. Joseph Warren. Warren and Samuel Adams attended the same church; he and John Adams entered into friendship after Warren inoculated the roaming attorney against smallpox.

The Warren-Adams friendship grew strong over the trying decade of their colony's confrontation with London.[31]

These were already, as Thomas Paine was to record, the times that tried men's souls. In mid-April 1775, Dr. Warren dispatched Paul Revere on his storied ride to Lexington and Concord, warning the local militia to be prepared for British regulars coming from Boston to seize their stores of ammunition and arrest the patriot leadership. Two months later, on June 17, as a private awaiting his commission as a major general, Warren joined a thousand or more men at an earthen redoubt hastily constructed on a minor hill overlooking the British position in Boston. When thousands more British met this provocation with three massive frontal assaults, the Americans held them back until their powder was spent. Hand-to-hand combat ensued.

As their father took part in the Battle of Bunker Hill, Dr. Warren's four children remained in the company of Johnny and his three siblings, under the watchful eye of Abigail Adams. In the perceptible distance, as artillery exploded, the young ones did not know that this committed revolutionary was refusing to abandon the exposed redoubt. History would record his outstanding courage. For three years a widower, about to be wed a second time, the healer turned fighter stayed to the end of the battle and was shot through the head when the makeshift post was overrun. On that day, Joseph Warren's children became orphans.[32]

"My bursting Heart must find vent at my pen," Abigail wrote to her husband, then in Philadelphia, as she conveyed the somber news. "Our dear Friend Dr. Warren is no more but fell gloriously fighting for his Country." The war was so close that it threatened to reach their Braintree home, making the conveyance of mail uncertain. "I shall tarry here till tis thought unsafe," Abigail added when she reopened her letter two days later in order to confirm the martyrdom of her husband's intimate friend and her son's physician. "The tears of multitudes pay tribute to his memory."[33]

The sense of consequence, of loss, hung ominously over the Adams household and gripped John Quincy for years to come. He was a month shy of eight when his mother led him up Penn's Hill to hear the boom of distant battle and see the smoke rise. "Every rock and every pebble upon them associates itself with the first consciousness of my existence," he later said of that haunting prominence and the remembrance of Bunker Hill. In more ways than one, she helped him find footing. Toward the end of his life, he reflected somewhat bitterly, "My mother with her infant children dwelt, liable every hour of the day and of the night to be butchered in cold blood, or taken and carried into Boston as hostages." The Battle of Bunker Hill was too personal a memory that he could ever celebrate its anniversary with the revelry expected from the local citizenry. The day brought back the untimely death of the doctor who had saved one of his fingers from amputation and who had, before that, leaned on John Quincy's father to come out of the shadows and wear his radicalism on his sleeve.[34]

In June 1775, John Adams was at Congress in Philadelphia, several days' ride from home, as the news of Bunker Hill arrived piecemeal. The resisters had fought like hell against a professional army, bringing down some fifteen hundred of the enemy, including dozens of officers, setting the stage for a long and ultimately successful siege of Boston. Congressman Adams felt his remoteness. "Courage, my dear!" was all he wrote at first. His wife remained his chief correspondent at this watchful moment. He complained about the lack of intelligence from his male associates in and around Boston and reacted with ferocity to Abigail's reports: "Every year brings us fresh Evidence, that We have nothing to hope for from our loving Mother Country." He trusted the newly formed Continental army would be effective and preserve his family. "My dear Nabby, Johnny, Charly, and Tommy," he wrote, "I long to see you, and to share with your Mamma the Pleasures of your Conversation." By now there were four children: Nabby and Johnny were followed by Charles (1770–1800) and Thomas (1772–1832). They were learning to improve their handwriting and obtaining an understanding of the preferred forms of communication by poring over their mother's "letterbook"—a bound notebook in which people kept copies of their outgoing correspondence.[35]

Poignant Interlude

In December 1775, the oft-absent husband and father returned to Massachusetts, but the business of organizing resistance mounted almost at once. John met with Boston-area comrades, including General Washington. He was able to spend days, not weeks, with his family before setting out again for Philadelphia, where more months of political deliberations and war monitoring awaited. There was nothing even remotely romantic about the American Revolution as it was being experienced—as glory filled as it might appear in the retrospective imagination.

After Bunker Hill, he might have wished for independence, but Congressman Adams did not likely believe at the time that the United Colonies had the collective will to break from England. By December 1775, he was feeling more expectant. As of April–May 1776, he could taste it. Members of the New York and Pennsylvania delegations in Congress remained hesitant, and Adams played politics by putting firm but gentle pressure on the holdouts. On May 15, with confirmation that the king had hired Hessian mercenaries to fight in America, an officially printed broadside, which Adams authored, announced Congress's rejection of crown authority in light of its withdrawal of "protection" and its "cruel depredations" and intended "destruction of the good people of these Colonies." It was merely the preamble of a resolve, but in its assertive tone it was nearly a declaration of independence.[36]

In June, along with his fellow congressmen Thomas Jefferson and Benjamin Franklin, John Adams mulled over the legal instrument we know as the Declaration of Independence. This time, of course, it was Jefferson who was given the lead role in composing the document. Nevertheless, Adams proved its strongest champion when the declaration came to the floor and he earned the label that would first be applied to him in August: "the Atlas of Independence."[37]

The history-conscious Adams had recently purchased a new, large-size letterbook. He had been keeping a diary for over twenty years already, ever since graduation from Harvard in the autumn of 1755. In the midst of the Revolutionary fervor, he had not been as reliable as previously in recording his correspondence. Henceforth, as he told his wife, "I shall write more deliberately. . . . I shall be able at all times to review what I have written. . . . I shall know how often I write." And given the inordinate amount of time he was spending away from home, "I shall discover by this Means, whether any of my Letters to you, miscarry." It was wartime. Uncertainties abounded.[38]

In John Adams's life, work came first, family cohesion second. (He spent approximately one-half of the first twenty years of their marriage apart from his wife.) Yet he was a product of the culture of colonial Boston, which meant that family dignity was of constant concern. Later embarrassments would ultimately cost the parents of Charles and Tom Adams, whose lives were tragically shortened by a hereditary weakness for alcohol, which Abigail detected in her family line. On the other hand, there was never a moment in his exceptionally long life when the first president Adams ceased to glow with pride in contemplating the son whose political success matched his own. "John has Genius," he declared as early as 1776, when the lad was still eight. Equally committed to the cause of intellectual enrichment, Abigail Adams assured Johnny as he neared his teens, "These are times in which a Genious would wish to live."[39]

Although an irregular speller, Mrs. Adams oversaw the form that her children's education would take. She did so while tending to them through outbreaks of dysentery and mumps, known proximity to cholera, risky smallpox inoculations, and the various "Distempers" or "Stupefaction" arising in the colonial disease environment. As a result, Abigail had little time to herself. She lacked a Latin education but managed some French, which she was better at than her husband (as he readily acknowledged). She conversed with him easily and unabashedly on political subjects. Yet she knew her limits. One sign of her influence on Johnny is his early spelling, which copied hers: he wrote "cousing" for "cousin," adding a *g* as she tended to do. "With regard to the Education of my own children," she wrote to her husband in that critical year of 1776, "I find myself soon out of my debth, & destitute & deficient in every part of Education." (Both she and her husband spelled "depth" with a *b*.)[40]

Irregular spelling did not at any time diminish the strength of Abigail's message in her notes to John. On the eve of national independence, she transmitted a letter from Braintree to Philadelphia, bemoaning his "tedious absence," which placed child rearing exclusively in her hands for an uncertain length of time. "How many are the solitary hours I spend, ruminating upon the past, and anticipating the future," she wrote, "whilst you are overwhelmd with the cares of State." As loyal as she was to the Revolutionary cause and pleased by the increasing importance of her husband's role in it, she insisted that in home matters the children's progress "would be doubly inforced could they be indulged with the example of a Father constantly before them."

By now, Johnny was a couple of months shy of nine. Charles and Tommy were six and three, respectively. Taking three days in total to finish this particular letter (outbound mail service was not a daily event), she updated domestic conditions: "Johnny and Charls have the Mumps." The afflicted were in no danger of expiring—which she said directly. But she wanted her husband to appreciate the emotionally taxing work of keeping four young children healthy enough that she could devote the requisite amount of attention to the development of their minds.[41]

John and Abigail entered a poignant interlude in their correspondence during the summer of 1777. "Poor mortals pant and sweat, under the burning Skies," he wrote, amplifying weather reports. "Faint and feeble as children, We seem as if We were dissolving away. Yet We live along." It was his regular habit to ask about the children's education, knowing that his trusted law clerk and cousin by marriage, John Thaxter, was by now augmenting Abigail's efforts. "Let the Children write, when you cannot," he urged her, desirous of letters to ensure that no harm had come to anyone. "I am very anxious, but Anxiety at 400 Miles distance can do you no more good, than me." He conveyed his particular hopes for "Mr. John" (he meant John Quincy). "With his Capacity, and Opportunities, he can not fail to acquire Knowledge." Knowledge and virtue were partnered. "Let him know, that the moral Sentiments of his Heart, are more important than the Furniture of his Head." Here was an Adamsian construction—privileging morals while likening the acquisitions of a young and plastic mind to movable property.

If high-mindedness came first in the elder's prescription, practical fields of study were not far behind. John Adams wondered about his eldest son's preparation for a world in tumult: "Does he read the Newspapers? The Events of this War, should not pass unobserved by him at his Years." (At this juncture, it was Abigail who directed most of the conversation about current events.) Paternal counsel came with sample questions, reminders of the moral lessons obtained through study of past greatness and past treachery: "What Events strike him most? What Characters he esteems and admires? Which he hates and abhors?" John made clear to his wife that "modest" Nabby, their eldest, could get by with a less dynamic engagement with the forces of history. He had earlier told his daughter not to let it be known that she was picking up Latin and Greek, because it was considered "scarcely reputable for young ladies" to be too interested in that which lay in the province of the male of their species.[42]

In a letter written directly to John Quincy shortly thereafter, the absent father produced a list of European monarchs and governors whose activities he expected his son to study up on as his education proceeded. He opened this letter with a brand of fatalism unthinkable today:

> *My dear Son,*
>
> *If it should be the Design of Providence that you should live to grow up, you will naturally feel a Curiosity to learn the History of the Causes which have produced the late Revolution of our Government. No Study in which you can engage will be more worthy of you.*

In making book recommendations, he urged in particular that his prize student look for parallels in the experience of America and that of the "seven united Provinces of the Netherlands" (in their release from Spanish control). The Dutch Republic achieved its independence in the mid-seventeenth century, though its power on the world stage had since declined. Just three years later, in 1780, father and son would take their first steps in the Netherlands—the two of them, together—and would serve their country there, one after the next, in diplomatic garb. John Quincy's deepest study of the Low Countries would take place *in* the Netherlands, where he would take classes as a teenager at a prestigious university and outshine his father in learning the Dutch language. Until then, John Adams's exhortation to his son to heed the Dutch experience was pure prophecy. The letter ended with a blanket justification: "You will wonder, my dear son, at my writing to you at your tender Age, such dry Things as these: but if you keep this Letter you will in some future Period, thank your Father for writing it." One presumes he did.[43]

FEMALE PATRIOTISM

Abigail, more often than John, spoke through her favorite poets. Selected verses interlace her correspondence. She made it a family affair. When in 1784, John Quincy sent home a trunk containing commonplace books of "poetical transcripts," she wrote back telling him how much she valued his "little volumes." The commonplace book—collected quotations of published wisdom—taught the importance of well-chosen words. It is one of the ways John and John Quincy Adams mastered forms. Abigail told her son that she treasured his personal selections on two levels: they expressed a "purity of sentiment" that moved her; and more touchingly, they were keepsakes because the verses were written out in his own hand. Johnny wanted her to approve the literature he read, to let her see his character as a man of letters in training.[44]

The dramatic qualities of writing obviously mattered to the Adamses. Dramatic poetry expressed pathos—pity and poignancy—which was a principal means to register emotion in the eighteenth century. In the words of John senior, poetic language "naturally" vitalized the passions. It was for this reason that he remarked of the "great Shakespeare" (whom Abigail loved as much) that the bard's genius lay in his uncanny ability to explore "the Labyrinth of mental Nature."

The excitement leading up to the American Revolution automatically politicized language, and much of this was accomplished by putting into service the poetry and drama readers responded to. John and Abigail wrote with as much intensity as any others of the writers who took part in the cause, and they did so as their peers did, by recurring to pathetic suggestion. Beginning in 1765, we are able to see John's tone in newspaper pieces grow in stridency. Raising the specter of "domestic tyrants," he reached a higher level of engagement by quoting the most dastardly of home wreckers, Lady Macbeth, who had brutally murdered her own child: "Who 'had given suck, and knew / How tender 'twas to love the Babe that milk'd her.' / But . . . pluck'd her Nipple from the boneless Guns, / And dash'd the Brains out." The lawyer in him appealed to the common desire for justice in opposition to "imperious, unrelenting tyrants"; the student of poetry exposed injustices by appealing to the faculty of imagination.[45]

In the crucial years 1775–1776, Abigail peppered letters with vigorous passages from the Shakespearean tragedies *Coriolanus* and *Julius Caesar.* Quoting Brutus from the latter, she linked past and present and joined theater to real life. Brutus's choice was the same as the colonists': The "Tide in the affairs of Men" would sweep her countrymen in the wrong direction unless they had the moral courage to act. If they failed to assert their rights, they would be "bound in the shallows and miseries." She wasn't just reciting lines from act 4; she was situating Bostonians, including herself, at the center of an august drama.[46]

After Lexington and Concord and the military occupation of Boston by thousands of redcoats, she adopted several new identities, the most political of which was "Portia," a female patriot and women's rights advocate. She attacked the same moral enemies as her husband did, "tyranny, oppression, and murder," in equally rich language, rejecting any hope of reconciliation with Great Britain, once "she has plunged her Sword into our Bosoms." As an eyewitness to the suffering across the neighborhoods in and beyond Boston, she relied on her pen to capture the "heartrending scenes" before her. Public service suddenly loomed even larger than commitment to family for educated women, who would remain unfulfilled, and their men remiss, if they were excluded from the national stage. She reminded John, "If we mean to have Heroes, Statesmen, and Philosophers, we should have learned women." Their voices mattered. Her eldest son imbibed this lesson and at the time of her death in 1818 wrote in his diary of "an ardent patriot." The entire nation knew of John Adams's leading role in the Revolution, but John Quincy did not forget that "the earliest lesson of unbounded devotion to the cause of the Country that her children received, was from her." He made it a point to say, in this context, that she had "a warm and lively relish for literature."[47]

Men and women filled their letters with familiar quotations, because originality was not the requirement it would become. Published or unpublished, letters constituted a "performance" that involved impersonation—taking on an identity other than one's own—and liberally appropriating the words of others. This manner of impersonation was easily politicized. Revolutionaries looked to poetry and fiction for heroes and moral exemplars. "America is a theatre just erected—the drama here but begun," the playwright Mercy Otis Warren (no relation to the martyred Joseph Warren) wrote to her friend Abigail. Americans had to imagine a different country as they were inventing one of their own; they had to profit from the lessons bequeathed to them, whether from history or literature.[48]

From the mind of the past came new ways to experiment with civic identities. John worried that the American people were yet at a loss in the complex project of national character formation, with "no Idea, no Conception, no Imagination, no Dream, of the Passions and Principles, which Support

Republics." They could not engineer their ultimate escape from monarchy until the passions of the people were properly channeled through creative examples.[49]

For that reason, literary imagination and public drama were critical tools of both rebellion and nation building. Before he met his tragic death at Bunker Hill, Joseph Warren literally shed his colonial garb and donned a Roman toga when he stepped forward to deliver the annual Boston Massacre oration on March 5, 1775. That same year, Abigail and Mercy Otis Warren began exchanging letters in the shared guise of Roman matrons: Abigail was "Portia," the wife of Brutus; Mercy was "Marcia," Portia's half sister. In her satire, *The Group*, Warren gave a "Lady" a speaking role for the first time in American drama, and Abigail, writing to a London bookseller, quoted from that speech. "Portia" and "Marcia" similarly identified themselves as politically disinterested female spectators, able to judge men's morals from outside the political arena and qualified to deliver a stinging rebuke of male folly. As Abigail and Mercy insisted female patriots were meant to do.[50]

More than just a wife and mother, Abigail as "Portia" was a public advocate (or to adopt the language of contemporaneous critics, a "Stoick in Petticoats"), who illustrated "every manly virtue" without abandoning her understood obligations. In a heated newspaper exchange four years before Abigail chose her nom de plume, one unidentified New Englander who defended "women of merit" signed her opinion piece "Portia." During the Revolution, in rapturous prose, a Philadelphian recounted a dream in which she was carried to a celestial paradise of "female patriotism," where she encountered not only the historical Portia but Abigail Adams herself.[51]

Abigail's version of Brutus's wife, Portia, was a modern bluestocking—one of the female *salonnières* who hosted literary gatherings and highlighted female intellect.[52] This also explains why John and Abigail earlier reached out to Catharine Macaulay, famed English Whig historian and avid supporter of the American cause. The Whigs railed against royalist corruption and court politics that metaphorically "enslaved" the people. As a Whig, Macaulay celebrated a Roman-like citizenry imbued with stoical virtues. In a letter published in the colonies, she lauded the American "Ladies" for giving up "*Tea and Finery, for Homespun and Liberty.*"

John Adams was pleased to learn that Macaulay read and admired his

Boston Gazette essays of 1765, when they were published in England. Writing to the Englishwoman in 1770, he praised her as not only "one of the brightest ornaments of her Sex but her Age and Country." The *Gazette* pieces showed John at his most Whiggish, a man deeply disturbed by the way his fellows accepted their subordinate role within the British-American household. Alternately soothed and battered into submission, colonists quietly embraced the maxim that "Britain is the mother and we are the children." They unthinkingly accepted their dependence as something natural. Though not yet a leader, John Adams was racing toward 1776, in his own mind, when he came out of the political closet in 1765, chastising the colonists for their timidity, for consenting to a virtual slavery. Their fetters were personal, psychological. "We have been afraid to think," he scolded. "We have been told that the word 'Rights' is an offensive expression."[53]

His early radicalism came back to haunt him when, ten years after the *Boston Gazette* essays, Abigail applied Whig principles to demand rights for women. By the time he received his wife's now-classic letter of March 1776, urging the Continental Congress to "Remember the Ladies," John was caught in his own trap. He knew precisely where she stood as a woman with mature opinions on the nature of politics, that she wished for a more forward role in the cause of American independence. A year later, she would be telling Mercy Warren that she wished she could be a soldier. She had grown tired of being a "passive spectator" and envied men's freedom. Her husband felt she demanded too much. Social leveling in any form made him extremely uneasy. It always would.[54]

"Remember the Ladies" flowed from Abigail's assumption that the moment had come when Congress would be drafting a "new code of Laws" and that the men in charge needed a reminder to be more generous to women than their ancestors had been. "Do not put unlimited power into the hands of the Husbands," she urged. "Remember" appears twice, which suggests the tone of a biblical commandment. "Remember the Ladies" is followed by the graver warning "Remember that all Men would be tyrants if they could."[55]

John's treatment of Abigail's strongly worded letter was oddly inconsistent. He minimized her plaint and turned it into a joke. His peers had no desire to give up their "Masculine system," he said, before proceeding to deny such a thing as male authority: "We have only the *Name* of Master [emphasis added]." Men could not cede power over Abigail's "tribe" or they would find themselves at once subject to the "Despotism of the Petticoat." In this unnatural state, every American male would be unmanned: the newly named commander of the Continental army, George Washington, and "all our brave Heroes," would lose the will to fight.[56]

His wife's statement had evidently struck a nerve. A few months later, John wrote an urgent letter to James Sullivan, a political ally from Maine (then part of Massachusetts), on the drafting of a state constitution. He argued that granting females the right to vote would threaten the entire political order. If women could claim their right to a voice in government, it would produce a domino effect, and "insolent negroes" would disobey their masters, Indians would rebel against their "guardians," children and apprentices would ignore their parents' wishes, and poor men without a "farthing" might demand suffrage. He seemed to be arguing that the entire social order was founded on a "masculine system" of private power. And so, denying women their rights became for him a matter of necessity. It was 1776, and John Adams the revolutionary was making a Loyalist argument: all that women could hope for was their virtual representation, subsumed within the realm of a kindly domestic sovereign.[57]

Abigail and John never backed down from their positions. While she insisted on the worth of "learned women," he tried to smooth over their rift with a clichéd response: that behind every "great Character" was an influential female (safely contained in her home) possessing "Knowledge and Ambition above the ordinary Level of Women." Writing to Mercy Warren, Abigail was more adamant than she apparently was with her husband, wanting the pair of them to co-author a petition on behalf of women's rights. Mrs. Warren did not accommodate her.[58]

In 1776, Abigail was more egalitarian, and we might say more of a democrat, than her husband (though, as we shall see shortly, he was more invested in democracy at this time than he would be subsequently). In his wife's thinking, direct representation was an essential right needed for civil protection. If education could lift up common men, women should have no less of an opportunity to better themselves. She stopped short of petitioning the Continental Congress, and would not live to see her eldest son eventually become an outspoken defender of women's right of petition. Neither John nor John Quincy Adams was ever comfortable with female suffrage or coequality between the sexes, but they well knew that unimpeachable female voices were needed.

SYMPATHETIC COMMUNION

Domestic drama was a given in their world. The great crisis the Adamses faced in the summer of 1777 was Abigail's troubled pregnancy. By John's own calculation, they had lived apart for most of the past three years, in consequence of his greater devotion to "the Servitude of Liberty." British troops were marching south from Canada, threatening to seize Fort Ticonderoga, and there was little good news on other fronts. John Adams was a leading voice on the Board of War and sat at the head of numerous other committees in Congress. He was having an increasingly harder time defending that commitment to his wife. The most recent extended absence from home was six months and counting, and all he could do was to reassure Abigail, based on late intelligence, that while the enemy's movements were "a little misterious," there was "no Danger of an Invasion your Way." Her virtual widowhood could only be laid at his door: "The loss of your Company and that of my dear Babes for so long a Time, I consider as a Loss of so much Happiness."

This letter crossed in the mail with one she penned the next day. "I was last night taken with a shaking fit, and am very apprehensive that a life was lost." She did not wish to alarm him, but she wanted him "prepaird for any Event that may happen." He wrote again that week, before having read these pressing words, only to admit to his fears for the health of each member of their family. He recalled their friends who had died of dysentery, and it only intensified feelings of impotence. He knew, of course, that her pregnancy was far along, but that was all he knew at this point. In their world, the conclusion of a pregnancy was nothing to be taken for granted.

The day after her "shaking fit," the doctor visited and assured her she had no cause for concern. She had strong doubts; something wasn't right. With her husband far from home, she could not ignore the state of their farm. Cold winds had damaged the crop, and the cost of hired hands was steep. Her responsibilities did not end just because she was preparing to give birth.

On July 11, John Quincy's tenth birthday, Abigail's premonition proved accurate. Their daughter was stillborn. "It was an exceeding fine looking Child," the cousin/tutor John Thaxter advised the father, before the convalescing mother could pick up her pen again to tell John that her own life had been spared. "It never opened its Eyes," she wrote several days later of their "sweet daughter." Nabby "mournd in tears for Hours." Abigail was surprised that she herself had survived the ordeal.

A week after the stillbirth, as yet uninformed, the expectant father wrote, "My Mind runs upon my Family, as much as our public Concerns. I long to hear of the Safety and the Health of my dearest Friend." When Abigail's decisive letter finally arrived, ten days in transit, he allowed his full reservoir of feeling to pour forth: "Never in my whole Life, was my Heart affected with such Emotions and Sensations. . . . Devoutly do I return Thanks to God, whose kind Providence has preserved to me a Life that is dearer to me than all other Blessings in this World." Nabby's tears for the infant he would never see were "sweetly becoming" to him, but nothing could exceed "my Sympathy with the Mother."[59]

"Never in my whole Life" was not hyperbole. Abigail's mortal existence had been threatened. In consideration of the vast literature they read, we can understand the word "sympathy" as they did, in the dual context of bodily cohesion and heartfelt commitment. At this moment in history, among the educated, selfhood was viewed as a function of nervous sensations and fragile human connections. The sympathetic nervous system fed a sympathetic imagination (also known as "sensibility"), which grew in conjunction with the cultivation of moral refinement. Eighteenth-century life was agitated by a nerve-directed psychology that exceeds in intensity today's clinical readings of varieties of human behavior. John's "Emotions and Sensations" connected him to the defining atoms of personality. "Sympathy with the Mother," as expressed in private life, had a parallel connection in public life: the sympathetic union of interests and commitment that made the American Revolution possible. "Sympathy" projected an idealized communion or community.

For John Adams, the "spirit of 1776" was a unique embodiment of political sympathy. At a moment of ecstatic recollection, he described American independence by way of a musical-mechanical metaphor: "Thirteen clocks were made to strike together—a perfection of mechanism, which no artist had ever before effected." This Revolutionary sympathy uniting the original thirteen states would be put to the test in democratic politics ever after, and both presidents Adams would address the matter head-on, time and again. Could key indicators of political judgment—"conscience" and "reason"—prevail over less trustworthy "natural passions" common to their species? If not, how could political life be depressurized?

The sympathetic communion of the husband at the conclusion of a violent pregnancy had its obverse in war. "Resentment is a Passion," John Adams penned in 1776, "implanted by Nature for the Preservation of the Individual. Injury is the Object which excites it. . . . It is the same with Communities." An Adams never held a sentimental vision of society or state for long.[60]

DEMOCRATICAL BRANCH

While his wife flirted with the idea of female representation, John Adams pursued the idea of democracy as a crucial tool in fulfilling the would-be nation's bursting desire for independence. Few historians give Adams credit at all in imagining an enlarged role for democracy. Political scientists focus on his later writings, in particular *A Defence of the Constitutions* (1787) and *Discourses on Davila* (1790). However important they are, it is a mistake to start and end there. Neither his *Defence* nor *Davila* captures Adams's thinking in full.[61]

He was most optimistic about his nation's democratic potential in 1775 and 1776, when he argued for the viability of a "democratical branch" of government. A "Novanglus" essay he published in the *Boston Gazette* in March 1775 explained why the American colonies had never in fact owed allegiance to the British Parliament. Massachusetts had a charter that *predated* the British Empire, which only came into existence in 1701 with the union of England and Scotland. An imperial agreement occurred, but, according to Adams, the "American share of democracy"—the popular voice—had never been consulted.

Taking up a favorite theme, the mixed government of monarchy (king), aristocracy (lords), and democracy (commons), he contended that the English constitutional framework failed to include the colonies. The House of Commons was intended to represent every square inch of English territory, with representation based on population. America remained voiceless in Parliament. Adams did not stop with the one claim that the colonists were denied "democratical" representation under the imperial system; he drew upon a further measure: demographic growth. Twenty years into the future, America might have six million inhabitants, and in forty years double that number, justifying a thousand MPs. With its vast extent of inhabitable territory, America would soon enough dwarf the mother country in population. The "supream legislature," he taunted, would then have to be "translated, crown and all, to America." The royal throne moved across the Atlantic? How presumptuous, this John Adams! How ingenious! The House of Lords, in his scenario, would come to consist of "Irish, East and West Indian, African, American, as well as English and Scottish noblemen"; it would match the diversity of the future House of Commons, should America remain a dependent limb of the British tree. In Adams's reading of British standards, the "democratical" branch of government was the most important, insofar as parliamentary authority began with the people's consent and echoed the people's voice. Principles of representation followed native populations wherever they might roam over the political realm.

Ingenious thinking, yes. But not about to happen. So, why would Adams make such a far-fetched claim? His purpose was to say that the British government was not an empire but a limited monarchy; the British constitution made the government "more like a republic than an empire." A true empire was, effectively, a "despotism," whereas a republic was a "government of laws, and not of men." In reasoning that "Great Britain and the colonies must be distinct states, as England and Scotland were before the union," Adams pointed to the history of the two populous colonies of Massachusetts and Virginia. Were London to attempt to deny this coequal legislative system, "we shall be under a complete oligarchy and aristocracy." Because representation in Parliament was "impracticable," the only legitimate American form of representation was that which already existed in the various colonial legislatures.

According to Adams's mode of argumentation, it was democracy that doomed the Anglo-American empire. The British government could not claim to be at once empire and republic. Without a strong "democratical" branch, without home rule for colonial legislatures, the British constitution was not genuinely republican. The thirteen colonial legislatures were, in this way, the settings where legitimate popular voices and interests were heard and appreciated; where the essential *democratic* building blocks of American independence were laid.[62]

Adams revisited the argument when, in 1776, he drafted *Thoughts on Government,* a text that influenced the design of Virginia's state constitution and later Adams's own model for Massachusetts. He said that genuine representation required an assembly made in the image of the people: a "Representative Assembly should be in miniature, an exact portrait of the people at large. It should think, feel, reason, and act like them." Annual elections provided the safeguard that would accomplish this aim. "Where annual elections end," he wrote, "there slavery begins." Revolutionaries had to sweep away royal governors, parliamentary laws, and, finally, allegiance to a crown and an empire.[63]

Adams's remarkable language predated national independence. As he reviewed Jefferson's draft of the declaration in June, he told one of his Harvard professors that declaring independence would "arouse and unite the Friends of Liberty." By legalizing self-rule, the erstwhile colonies could "compleat their Governments," while state legislatures took necessary measures to prosecute war. By formally recognizing the popular voice contained in the makeshift institutions then in place, "our civil Governments" would "feel a Vigour, hitherto unknown," he said. Legitimately empowered, the people would be able to channel their democratic passions into the grand cause of *national* independence and *national* defense. No one could accuse this John Adams of a lack of commitment to democracy. Or of provincialism.[64]

In no small way, America already owed the headstrong New Englander for his active pen and voice. In the late autumn of 1777, he was commissioned by Congress to reinforce the diplomatic team already in Paris. As Johnny joined John, and the two sailed together to Europe in the early months of 1778, both would experience life under other forms of government, which they would inevitably judge in relation to their own.

TWO

WANDERERS

Eight years have already past, since you could call yourself an Inhabitant of this State. I shall assume the Signature of Penelope, for my dear Ulysses has already been a wanderer from me near half the term of years that, that Hero was encountering Neptune, Calipso, the Circes and Syrens.

—ABIGAIL ADAMS TO JOHN ADAMS,
April 10, 1782

The word abroad roused my attention, and I eagerly seized the Letters, the hand writing and Seal of which gave me hopes that I was once more like to hear from my Young Wanderer.

—ABIGAIL ADAMS TO JOHN QUINCY ADAMS,
November 20, 1783

On that first voyage, in 1778, father and son experienced heavy winds and a severe lightning strike, witnessed an attack on a British merchant ship, and were unable to avert their eyes from the amputation of a crewman's leg. The frigate *Boston* arrived safely at the French port of Bordeaux with both Adamses newly cognizant of the fragility of life.

In Paris, Johnny was enrolled in boarding school, where he studied French and Latin, dancing and drawing, as was required of any European gentleman. His father joined Benjamin Franklin and the Virginian Arthur Lee and contributed his opinions to the management of the wartime alliance of France and the United States. Their stay in Paris lasted a little more than a year, during which time John Quincy's father introduced the youth to bookshop haunting and theatergoing, both of which would become lifelong amusements.[1]

A pronounced bond between the two Johns took shape from the day they first set sail. Inspecting their assigned quarters, the elder recorded in his diary, "My Lodging was a Cott, with a double Mattress, a good Bolster, my own Sheets, and Blanketts enough. My little Son, with me—We lay very comfortably, and slept well. A violent Gale of Wind in the Night."

Just a few days later, on the open sea, the U.S. envoy wrote with uncommon feeling of the harsh conditions to which he was subjecting his boy: "To describe the Ocean, the Waves, the Winds, the Ship, her Motions, Rollings, Wringings and Agonies—the Sailors, their Countenances, Language and Behaviour, is impossible. No Man could keep upon his Legs, and nothing could be kept in its Place—an universal Wreck of every Thing in all Parts of the Ship." Seasickness overtook both of them: "I confess I often regretted that I had brought my son. I was not so clear that it was my Duty to expose him, as myself, but I had been led to it by the Childs Inclination and by the Advice of all my Friends."

By the child's inclination? How curious. Could the ten-year-old's voice already have mattered? Perhaps it did, given that the next words John Adams recorded speak to a father's pride: "Mr. Johnnys Behaviour gave me a Satisfaction that I cannot express . . . fully sensible of our Danger, he was constantly endeavouring to bear it with a manly Patience, very attentive to me and his Thoughts constantly running in a serious Strain." They would brave this storm together, and a good many more.[2]

As Abigail raised the little ones back in Massachusetts, she remained in the dark about the fate of her two Johns. To make matters worse, their return to America in the spring of 1779 took an inordinate amount of time. Waiting at Lorient, on the southern coast of Brittany, father and son rambled about the strategic port city for two full months until the new French minister to the United States arrived. Only then did their ship, a French frigate called *La Sensible,* set sail for America. Always given to expect that it would soon take to the sea, they had no time to establish any real connection to the strange coastal city. But for occasional dinners with the likes of the American naval hero John Paul Jones, bound for his next fight in English waters, the two were each other's constant entertainment.

Character Portraits

For a glimpse ahead at the variables involved in eighteenth-century globe-trotting, all we need to do is to present the Adams males' delay-filled itineraries in 1778–1779:

February 13, 1778, depart Boston on the *Boston;*
April 1, 1778, arrive Bordeaux, France;
April 8, 1778, reach Paris.

April 22, 1779, depart Saint-Nazaire, France, on *Alliance* for Lorient, France;
June 17, 1779, depart Lorient, France, on *La Sensible;*
August 2, 1779, arrive Braintree.

November 15, 1779, depart Boston on *La Sensible;*
December 8, 1779, arrive (unintendedly) in El Ferrol, Spain;
December 26, 1779, undertake overland route through northern Spain;
February 9, 1780, arrive Paris.

As we follow John and John Quincy on their life-changing journeys together in the late 1770s and early 1780s, it is the reading and writing material they carried with them, and preserved for us, that speaks the loudest. What they wrote of themselves (in their diaries) and to each other (in letters) ultimately reveals how they came to think of themselves as historical subjects.

Reading and writing was a man of the world's duty, but it was also a favorite pastime. Fortunately for the historical investigator, the eighteenth-century self was not content with prescriptive guides and formal tutoring. From the beginning of the century to its end, picaresque adventure novels held sway over many minds. Fiction taught, or at least commended, what we recognize as "democratic" skills: acquiring the means to judge the people one meets in life, and, when appropriate, unmasking their pretensions so as to cut them down to size. Here is where we come to understand the two Adamses' separately honed methods of critical performance.

The age of sail was consumed with adventure. For readers and writers alike, the vagaries of travel naturally combined with detailed observation of the human character to symbolize worldly engagement. Among the well-known titles that made the rounds and appealed to the Adamses were Miguel de Cervantes's *Don Quixote* (1605), Alain-René Lesage's *Adventures of Gil Blas* (multiple volumes, 1715–1735), and Laurence Sterne's *Tristram Shandy* (1759–1767).

The dubious heroes of these adventures were modest in pedigree, naive or roguish in disposition, and adept at navigating society. This was because they lived by their wits and saw the world literally. Picaresque novels were neither prim nor proper and should cause us, minimally, to reevaluate the influence of the Puritan past on John and John Quincy Adams. For the Adamses and for many others, novels went far to collapse differences in the outlook of Europeans and Americans; they were devoured by young men and women on both continents. As important, they help us grasp the comic side of book lovers in this generation. Exposing human foibles was an Adams specialty, and we can be certain that this trait did not spring from their heads independent of the books they consumed. When Adamsian wit was not a function of predictable spite, and when it was carried off with a picaresque flair, this is where it came from.[3]

We left our two adventurers, at the end of the previous section, in May 1779, shipboard, at the international port of Lorient. John Adams was reading *Don Quixote,* not long after Johnny had done so first. There, the departing diplomat was moved to diarize in a novelistic mode as he found himself ensnared by a fellow passenger, Hezekiah Ford, a garrulous Virginia clergyman of ambiguous political leanings who wouldn't let him be. His portrait of this whimsical character developed over a two-week period and achieved its ironic-satirical effect by selectively repeating Ford's own words and sinking the gossiper with gossip learned about him.

Adams saw right through the insufferable Anglican, who only bent Adams's ear because he wanted something from him. Time and again, Ford resorted to abject flattery by telling his trapped shipmate how much more popular he was among Parisians than his more famous colleague Benjamin Franklin. "F[ord] this Morning fell to talking," the writer confides to his diary, as he recounts the man's exact words: "Above half the Gentlemen of Paris are Atheists. . . . No Body goes to Church but the common People. I wish I could find one honest Man among the Merchants and Tradesmen &c." As the helpful man of reason in this picaresque episode, Adams quotes himself offering the parson ways to temper his speech if he should, as planned, report his findings to the Revolutionary leadership in America. "Oh! I am no Hypocrite," exclaims the self-righteous cleric, unaware of how much the man he addresses detests him for his hypocrisy. With nothing nice to say about anyone other than his momentary confidant, Ford urges Adams to book him passage on *La Sensible* to Boston so that they can break bread together for another six weeks. Reading the diary entry, we can almost see Adams rolling his eyes.

The "I am no Hypocrite" dissembler has regaled everyone who would listen with war stories that centered on his personal gallantry. It is moral vindication for Adams when he comes to learn Ford's secret from the ship's doctor. The fighting clergyman (a brave combatant only in his own mind) does not suffer from the rheumatic joints he routinely complains of, but is, in fact, syphilitic. "A Man of the Cloth—his Character is ruined," Adams tells his diary. Humiliating the parson with his pen satisfies.[4]

Adams the elder has equally choice words for the captain of this oddly peopled vessel, the *Alliance,* on which he was obliged to spend a good deal more time than expected or desired. Pierre Landais, though battle hardened, could not win the respect of his crew. He was "Jealous of every Body, of all his Officers, all his Passengers," Adams recorded. "He knows not how to treat his Officers, nor his Passengers nor any Body else.—Silence, Reserve, and a forbidding Air, will never gain the Hearts, neither by Affection nor by Veneration, of our Americans." The diarist was confident in his ability to size up any individual after only a short time. He had no problem finding the words he needed. "There is in this Man an Inactivity and an Indecision that will ruin him," he says of the captain, a man he felt deserved ridicule: "He is bewildered—an Absent bewildered man—an embarrassed Mind." The unstable Landais told his esteemed passenger that the men he commanded were putting on a show for Adams while disrespecting, even subverting, their captain whenever Adams returned to his cabin. The dialogue, this time, ends with Adams reading the captain's pathetic wounded heart: "This Morning he began: 'You are a great Man but you are deceived. The Officers deceive you! They never do their Duty but when you are on deck. They never obey me but when you are on deck.'"

Recurring to pop psychology, Adams concludes that Landais was "disappointed in Love," which is how to explain a proneness to feelings of moroseness. The captain exits Adams's narrative on the coast of France, only to reappear decades later, when he is recognized by the Massachusetts senator John Quincy Adams under the dome of the U.S. Capitol, of all places. Once again, the bereft Landais will come across, in an Adams diary, as grim and pathetic.[5]

The best example of John Adams's skill at portraying characters—indeed, the most picaresque of his writing—precedes the 1779 voyage by a good twenty years. At age twenty-three, he was thrown together with Parson Anthony Wibird of Braintree, seven years his elder. Tracing the minister's head, how it pointed forward, with the top half of his body tending in one direction, the bottom half in the other, Adams piles on description:

> His features are as coarse and crooked as his Limbs. His Nose is a large roman Nose with a prodigious Bunch Protuberance, upon the Upper Part of it. His Mouth is large, and irregular, his Teeth black and foul, and craggy. . . . His Eyes are a little squinted, his Visage is long, and lank, his Complexion wan, his Cheeks are fallen.

The picaresque novel *Gil Blas* opens with a brief description of the hero's uncle: "Figure to yourself a little fellow, three feet and a half high, as fat as you can conceive, with a head sunk deep between his shoulders, and you have my uncle to the life." In the riotous tale of *Tristram Shandy,* the "man-midwife" Dr. Slop presents similarly: "Imagine to yourself a little squat, uncourtly figure of a Doctor *Slop,* of about four feet and a half perpendicular height, with a breadth of back, and a sesquipedality of belly, which might have done honour to a serjeant in the horse-guards."

Like the authors whose spirit dominated the age, John Adams clearly loves the exercise of penning characters. He observes his neighborhood parson at prayer in his own home, goes home, and gives new life to Wibird's every movement:

> He raises on Knee upon the Chair, and throws one Hand over the back of it. With the other he scratches his Neck, pulls the Hair of his Wigg, strokes his Beard, rubs his Eyes, and Lips.

Wibird was a particular "type," a plain, pathetic bachelor of the eighteenth-century variety:

> When he sitts, he sometimes lolls on the arms of a Chair, sometimes on the Table. . . . Vibrates the foretop of his Wig, thrusts his Hand up under his Wigg, &c. When he speakes, he Cocks and rolls his Eyes, shakes his Head, and jerks his Body about.[6]

Touches of novelistic control muffle the moral conviction that otherwise carries John Adams's strong judgments. Adams did not think himself cruel or condescending. An unripe bachelor himself, five years shy of his marriage to Abigail Smith, he was not yet accomplished professionally when he mastered the art of the descriptive diarist. He'd known Wibird for a few years by this time, and they shared experiences as unattached young men in a modest outpost. Years later, confirming her husband's prodigious assessment of the man, Abigail Adams pointedly referred to Wibird as "our inanimate old Batchelor." The easily caricatured parson did not measure up to a picaresque hero, for he is the fool whom the hero outwits, serving as comic relief only.[7]

Like Adams's officious Virginia pastor, a landlord in *Gil Blas* proves "a busy prattler . . . ready to bother you impertinently about his own concerns, and, at the same time, with a sufficient portion of curiosity to worm himself into the knowledge of yours." And as in Adams's interview with Landais, characters in that novel must be "undeceived" on a fairly regular basis. So, it is meaningful that John would purchase for Johnny a 1756 Dutch-language edition of *Gil Blas,* along with a dictionary, when they arrived in Holland the following year; the father did so to encourage his son to learn a new tongue by reading a familiar text. Earlier, Thomas Jefferson had recommended *Gil Blas* and *Tristram Shandy* to a young man who solicited him for advice on building a starter home library; while in Annapolis, Maryland, in the early 1780s, he bought a copy of *Gil Blas* for his twelve-year-old daughter. Travel adventure was required reading for growing Americans, on the order of the works of Charles Dickens and Mark Twain in modern school curricula.[8]

Political stimulants are embedded in these eighteenth-century novels, if the reader chose to see them. Yet if there was a moral to any picaresque story, it was not didactic or demanding. The hero Gil Blas takes a lesson from a master of impersonation, a servant whose amorous adventures are managed through deception by quietly borrowing his master's clothes: "I dress myself up as a young nobleman, and assume the manners of one. I go to public places, and tip the wink first to one woman and then to another, till I meet with one who returns the signal. Her I follow, and find means to speak with her. I take the name of Don Antonio Centellés. I plead for an assignation, the lady is squeamish about it; I am pressing, she is kind, et caetera. Thus it is, my fine fellow, that I contrive to carry on my intrigues." The rogue's democratic pretensions enable him to counterfeit gentility, sabotage order, and confound social norms.[9]

The power of the picaresque style lies in its ability to combine the realism of human description with the narrative ease and mild irony that make the comic possible. The foolishness of humans is on display as they go about their daily activities, but arbitrariness and affectation are their greater sins. The adventure is about the hero's alternating fates: he goes from bad luck to good fortune. He is good-natured, and his vices are minor ones; he has a knack for success and rescues himself from untoward circumstances, one after the next. The message is plain: by perseverance, the wandering adventurer can, adopting one tactic or another, master even a foreign environment. The world is his school.

EMOTIONAL STATES

As wanderers, the world was now the Adamses' school, and the diary was the medium through which they would convey lessons learned from their wanderings. Hand-sewn personal journals became their constant companions through times of roughing it as well as in times of repose. The ocean voyage required a stoic sense of endurance, which all understood. Living abroad presented challenges, and feelings of dislocation could be soothed and sutured through introspection. The picaresque idiom gave their storytelling its irreverent tone—episodes of strange encounters peppered with revealing insights into the self. More than a travel narrative, then, the diary journal was a map of one's emotional state.

John Adams never tells us how he became an inveterate diarist. When he got hooked, in 1753, the practice of recording one's thoughts and activities day by day was certainly not new, but neither was it extensively practiced. In the colonial period, most diary records tended to be squeezed between the lines of a pocket almanac. Or else they were a clergyman's notes about sermons, with listings of marriages and baptisms performed; or soldiers' factual statements on movements and camp life; or a space in which a college student bemoaned reading assignments and expressed amusement at his classmates' social proclivities. The majority of these accounts, even when chatty, were not deeply personal. Until the nineteenth century, when it truly flourished, the introspective diary would not catch on either as an artifact of personality development or as a literary form. Unlike the practice of letter writing, for which a slew of orthodox guidebooks existed, there were few available models for a young person to turn to at the time either Adams embraced the discipline of diary keeping. As we have noted, it was the adventure novel that seasoned the medium of the diary and humanized the process of writing expressively.[10]

Altogether, John Adams filled fifty-one loosely bound volumes over the course of his life. After fits and starts, his son produced a like number, more comprehensive still—totaling perhaps as many as seventeen thousand pages. Their collective output is unmatched among major historical figures. John Quincy had one living model diarist only, his analytical, judgmental, censorious father. Relative to others of their time, these two demonstrated a conspicuous lack of inhibition in matter-of-factly setting down on paper both physical and emotional trials. Letters covered vast distances, which added to their emotional power, but scratchings in a compact diary carried a kind of spontaneity and candor that the familiar letter rarely matched.[11]

For nearly seven years, then, John and John Quincy would travel across Europe, seeing France, Spain, the Netherlands, and eventually England. Paris remained home base, from which Johnny would launch his own two-year excursion to Russia and back. Everything the pair saw and read, the names, occupations, and backgrounds of the people they met, filled their diaries.

Yes, it was a practice passed on from father to son. But not as easily as one imagines. During his first European tour, in the autumn of 1778, Johnny wrote home from Paris and confessed to his mother that he had yet to master the diary-keeping discipline his father endorsed. "My Pappa enjoins it upon me to keep a journal, or a diary, of the Events that happen to me, and of objects that I See, and of Characters that I converse with from day, to day, and altho I am Convinced of the utility, importance, & necessity, of this Exercise, yet I have not patience, & perseverance, enough to do it so Constantly as I ought." Perseverance was a lifelong Adams watchword. Young Johnny was berating his immature self, yet doing so with a level of maturity above what might be expected from an eleven-year-old. A year later, he would succeed in maintaining a diary, the first of many, finding the means to train an original literary voice. But there would be evidence of something else scattered across the brittle pages: the family curse—emotional inadequacy, to put it most succinctly.[12]

As clever as he was, and as eager as he appeared when he upbraided others for their weaknesses, John Adams could turn the microscope on himself at a moment's notice. While waiting for *La Sensible* to carry them home from France, and immediately after he had spent a scholarly morning with Johnny performing a joint translation of the "Carmen saeculare" (lyric poetry of Horace's from first-century B.C. Rome), John suddenly recoiled. This "great Man," as Captain Landais had so recently anointed him, got up from his studious pose, took one look in the mirror, and literally did not like what he saw. "There is a Feebleness and a Languor in my Nature," he recorded in terms comparable to his analysis of the Braintree bachelor Wibird. "My Mind and Body both partake of this Weakness. By my physical Constitution, I am but an ordinary Man. . . . My Eye, my Forehead, my Brow, my Cheeks, my Lips, all betray this Relaxation."

"Relaxation." Its eighteenth-century meaning goes well beyond any current definition. In the culture he knew, a man's physiognomy bore multiple meanings, and "relaxation" connoted the absence, revealed on the face, of a nature-given firmness and radiance. The squat New Englander was entirely convinced that because he was an ordinary-looking fellow devoid of natural charisma, his destiny would have been entirely unexceptional but for the "great Events" that happened in his immediate neighborhood when he was of the right age and temperament to become, momentarily, lionlike. His natural "Sloth, Sleep, and littleness" had been transformed into giant energy by external stimuli. But drilling down to the bedrock of him, at his flawed foundation, he remained anything but great.[13]

In between their first and second European tours, John Adams found himself back in Boston at a critical moment. It proved to be a stay of three months only, and he spent barely any of it at home with his wife and children. But he did accomplish something of lasting importance: the Massachusetts state constitution. Its text is an intellectual product, but for its main author it was the product of an emotional surge and a source of lasting pride. Unabashedly, he described his role in the state's constitution as "principal Engineer."

Foreshadowing the claims of the U.S. Constitution, John Adams's Massachusetts charter inscribed a "government of laws, not men," founded on the sovereignty of the people. He made it a point to rename the province what it remains to this day, a "Commonwealth," which harks back to an early modern English understanding of a society of independent freemen. John Locke held that a commonwealth was "not a Democracy, or any [exclusive] Form of Government, but any independent Community." The new state constitution of Massachusetts was hardly democratic: the qualifications for suffrage were based on wealth and property ownership. There was, on the other hand, an expectation of class mobility through education.

In this, Adams drew upon James Harrington's *Commonwealth of Oceana* (1656). The English political theorist determined that the state's health depended on the education of its youth. In his perfect state, every wandering young man was obliged to report on all he saw of other countries' governments, and anything else new or curious. John Adams's decision to bring John Quincy with him on official travel coincided with Harrington's prescription.

Adams acknowledged that the section of the constitution on education was his favorite part. It opens with a call for "The Encouragement of Literature, &c., Wisdom, and knowledge," echoing Harrington's plea for "schools of Good Literature." Adams's list of desired qualities to be imparted in the schools—humanity, industry, frugality, sincerity, "good humor"—can also be termed Harringtonian. It is worth noting that Abigail Adams quoted *Oceana* in 1778, invoking the familiar metaphor of the "ship of state," which held more than one meaning as she consented to her beloved ones' departure for Europe. Welcoming them home a year later, she could not have known that it would be several more years before the Adams family was whole again. The only intimacy they would have would be epistolary.[14]

On the eve of departure for their second, much longer European tour, John Quincy made an effort to fulfill the requirement set forth by his father. On Friday, November 12, 1779, in a large script, with apostrophes substituting for commas, his inaugural diary commenced. The now twelve-year-old wrote on the first page, "This Morning at about 11 o clock I took leave of my Mamma' my Sister' & Brother Tommy' and went to Boston." Ready to embark, he was complying with the year-old exhortation of "Pappa" that he begin to keep a record "of the Events that happen to me."

As early as the father's first diary, at age seventeen, one sees a person who incessantly pushed himself. A quarter century later, as John Adams pushed and prodded his eldest son, the son pushed back only infrequently. And then the father, by his own authority, began to yield, little by little.

That is the curious relationship we undertake to plot. The son emancipated himself incompletely. He did not feel the need to do more. At the age of twenty-one, thinking back, he would earnestly state (in diary form) that his legal coming of age "emancipates me from the yoke of paternal authority which I never felt, and places me upon my own feet which have not strength enough to support." We should add this caveat: An undeniable sense of duty to his father did nothing to inhibit growth in imagination, either at the tender age of ten, when he first saw Europe, or at eighteen, when he returned from Europe to study for Harvard.[15]

La Sensible

Late autumn 1779. They were again on board *La Sensible,* this time with Johnny's younger brother Charles in tow. Accompanying the boys was Johnny's cousin on the Quincy side John Thaxter, whose new role was to be that of John Adams's private secretary in France. It had been merely weeks since they'd disembarked. After one Atlantic crossing, the elder Adams was understandably confident that the well-armed vessel would carry them as safely back to Europe. It was too imposing a ship to awaken the guns of most British warships—something they had learned the hard way to steer clear of after that first voyage to France on the *Boston.*

John Adams had experienced choppy seas in more than one way. In Paris, on that first tour, a fractious American negotiating team was led by the legendary Benjamin Franklin. The former printer, now past seventy, was troubled by painful ailments and less than fully immersed in his official duties. Despite his reputation for mildness and charm, the Boston-born

Philadelphian clashed with the bright but irritable Arthur Lee, who, like Franklin, had been a longtime London resident prior to the war. The third member of the American deputation was the one John Adams was meant to replace, Connecticut's Silas Deane, a Franklin ally who carped about the dysfunction of the American delegation in his report to Congress. Deane would suffer disgrace as a result of financial indiscretions committed during his time abroad.

As a result of that first Paris assignment, Adams imagined himself as the only one who remained fresh and untainted, upright and collected. Compared with Lee and Deane, he was able to appear a voice of reason. At least, a handful of helpful friends in Congress had painted him this way during his absence. Anticipating his second posting, he looked forward to supplanting the compromised Franklin in managing the alliance with France and testing the waters for a negotiated peace with London. And that is where things stood, as father and son embarked for France. Franklin had gravitas Adams as yet lacked, but Adams was possessed with a sense of mission. Restraint was never his strong suit. The hero in this adventure stood against the odds. In his mind, he was more Hercules than Gil Blas.[16]

Headed out on a vessel he already knew from top to bottom, Johnny, age twelve, turned to his diary to describe his experience as a passenger on an armed ship in the midst of a war. He kept track of wind direction and the frigate's speed, categorized breezes as "fine," "fresh," and "middling"; reporting emotionlessly that the ship, mid-voyage, had been deemed "very leaky," he noted that a beam struck his head and "hurt me a little."

Until the ship landed, he was unaware of just how threatening the circumstances of the voyage were. *La Sensible* was off course and seriously distressed. After twenty-four days in open water, the crew at length sighted a ship that "hoisted Spanish colors" and led them into port at El Ferrol, a practical move in that the Bourbon states of France and Spain were common enemies of the British. Relieved to step onto dry land, John the elder soberly recorded, "The Leak in the Sensible, increases since she has been at Anchor, and every Body thinks We have been in great danger."[17]

In their world, shipwrecks were nearly as common as death in childbirth. No method of travel was deemed disaster-proof, and bodily health was never certain. By a parent's example, the young were taught fortitude along with resignation. It worked in this instance: Johnny kept his cool throughout the troubled voyage, seasoning his inaugural diary with touches of an ironic humor we might say he inherited.

A transatlantic voyage could take under a month or close to two. A loved one might learn only by return letter of a safe docking four months after sailing. Father and son reached port far from their destination, and Dr. Franklin would be wondering what had happened. No one would have known that the crossing had ended at a fortified port on the northwestern coast of Spain, where the ship had to be serviced over an extended period. In the unheralded town of El Ferrol, both Adamses' diaries struck the same peevish tone (the son's only slightly less irritated), by expressing minimal pleasure with their walking tour and even less with the Italian comedies they sat through. "A dull Entertainment to me," said the elder. "Much the same thing that we had Yesterday and the other day," said the younger, "except that a Farce was added to night, spoken in the Portuguese Language." At least they took pleasure in the Spanish chocolate drunk at breakfast.[18]

SPANISH CREEP

Preparations complete, the rocky road beckoned. They would not see Paris for two months; there was neither a guidebook nor even a plan. Hoping for the best, the father procured a three-volume dictionary and a Spanish grammar. He was rather too optimistic about his capacity to learn to communicate with the natives, having presumed Spanish easy for a Latin scholar to pick up. He was, on the other hand, impressed by his boys' facility for the language.

The father's Spanish journal mixes rich description with cold commentary. After seeing a Franciscan convent where veiled girls were prohibited from speaking and slept on the floor, he chided Catholicism for its many bad ideas and practices: "There is more intrigue in a Chapter of Monks for the Choice of a Prior than was employed to bring about the entire revolution in America." An Adamsian pose was always tart.[19]

The father worried about what lay ahead, and it reconfirmed for him how right he had been in refusing to bring the two Abigails, mother and daughter, along on the journey. "What Accommodations I can get upon the Road, how I can convey my Children, what the Expence will be, are all

Questions that I cannot answer," he jotted in his diary. "How much greater would have been my Perplexity, if the rest of my family had been with me."[20]

En route north toward the French border, conditions were brutal, accommodations crude, and the pace slow and exhausting. Johnny's writing captures their experience more matter-of-factly than that of his brooding, sleepless father. Johnny finds charm where John sees obstacles. Rickety chaises pass by: "Any body would think that they were as old as Noah's Ark." Through "prodigious mountains," they trekked, when "the Axletree of one of our carriages broke." From here, the party camped at a "Miserable Cottage" and, proceeding north, traded off between "calash" (a small, light, mule-led carriage) and individual mules. The unflappable son disembarked from the vehicle and walked.[21]

Of the same trials, his burden-bearing father wrote anxiously, "For the first Eight nights I know not that I slept at all and for the other eight very little." It took two weeks to stop himself from bemoaning Spanish "Sloth" and sleep-depriving "Swarms" of insects, marking the date in his diary when he finally found "clean beds and no fleas for the first Time." Physically pressed, John expressed a grim dissatisfaction with everything: "The Calashes are like those in Use in Boston fifty Years ago." Their seats were of old, stiff leather, and the harness was nearly busted. While his sons slowly adapted to life on the road, the elder Adams protested having to go on foot for stretches at a time. Of their unenviable lodgings, he scribbled on the spot, "We entered into the Kitchen, where was no floor but the Ground and no Carpet but Straw trodden into mire by Men, Hogs, horses and Mules." The little ventilation there was seeped in "through two holes drilled through the Tyles of the roof." Kitchen and stable abutted; a "fatting hog" lodged inside. "Smoke filled every part of the Kitchen, Stable, and all other parts of the House, and was so thick that it was very difficult to see or breath[e]." His nightmarish stopover among the "Family of Men and Beasts" commanded John Adams's pen longer than usual.

Johnny's pluckier diary account alternated moods. Learning how to observe people and places, he naturally ended up echoing his father's opinions, but the tone was less despairing. The sights and stenches of that memorable hamlet in the middle of Galician nowhere were equally impressed upon both. Days after John detailed the encounter, Johnny (presumably after spying his father's notebook) sketched, "We did once Lodge with the mules but not much better they shew us chambers in which any body would think a half dozen hogs had lived there six months. . . . We have not met with any place quite so bad as that but we have come very near." A new page opens with a rough correlation of the mountain people and their animals: "They are Lazy, dirty, Nasty, and in Short I can compare them to nothing but a parcel of hogs. Their cloaths are commonly of a dirt colour and their Breeches are big enough for to put a bushel of Corn."[22]

For the father, high sierra was the low point of a bedeviled journey; for the son, it was a chance to indulge an adolescent spirit of high adventure. As a novice diarist, Johnny takes things as they come, measures time without fear, and gives scant evidence that he considers his life in danger at any point.

They crept across northern Spain for weeks, along a serpentine route, before arriving at the cultured port of Bilbao, on the Bay of Biscay. At Bayonne, they crossed into southern France, after which both the journey and the journal keeping were more tempered; moving through land under cultivation liberated the pen wielders from dark thoughts. Neither *La Sensible* nor the mountainous roads of Spain would be displaced from memory anytime soon.

Low Countries

A break in the diaries occurs with arrival in Paris, where Johnny was enrolled in an expensive school—an added concern for his budget-conscious father. Father and son picked up their pens again during travels through the Dutch Republic, where John was to make diplomatic contacts and his boys were meant to acquire wisdom at a Latin school in Amsterdam. It soon became clear that his "too exquisite sensibility" was preventing Charles from adapting to Europe. In due course, he was sent home to Abigail; the traveling Adamses were once again a twosome.

It was the summer of 1780 when they rode through the Low Countries. John aimed to cultivate Dutch government officials so as to minimize Revolutionary America's reliance on France. He followed war news from America as it arrived by courier and learned that Charleston, South Carolina, had fallen to the British. But the event was expected and was not treated with disproportionate concern in his meetings with foreigners. Johnny received lessons in patriotism, learning from his diplomat-father that it was incumbent upon them both to convey the dignity of their largely unknown country.

The younger Adams acquired the Dutch language, though not proficiently enough to stay on the educational fast track. It was only through his father's good offices that he was able to enroll in courses at the prestigious University of Leiden, which was more than a day's carriage ride from "Pappa's house." The youth has a disarming way of describing his reactions; at his age, everything was new. Meanwhile, his father greeted the Europeans with fixed prejudices—his sorest point was what he saw of religious life—and he was occasionally left with so bitter a taste that he turned his criticism inward: "I could not help cursing the Knavery of the Priesthood and the brutal Ignorance of the People,—yet perhaps, I was rash and unreasonable, and that it is as much Virtue and Wisdom in them to adore, as in me to detest and despise." The stern, reprimanding tone he reserved for men of business (and the business of politics), and his abject disgust with the sins of humanity, did not infect his teenage son, whose mother reminded him by letter, "You my dear son are formed with a constitution feelingly alive."[23]

It is important to state that John Adams was more than the anxious, windy, scornful writer he can often appear. He was, better put, a peripatetic information gatherer. In the years 1781–1783, as he traveled repeatedly between Paris and the Netherlands, he obtained a great deal of knowledge of places and customs. He was still getting his feet wet (literally, too) at the time he began peppering his Dutch contacts with questions. "Before the Dykes were built," he noted in his diary, "there were frequent Inundations in Consequence of storms which are still frequent. It is supposed that the whole Country was originally level and covered over with thick and heavy Forrests of Woods. In great Storms, the Waves of the Sea threw up vast Heaps of Sand." Part of his purpose in recording questions and answers was to establish himself as a cultural-historical authority.

But that does not explain the psychological element that existed between the lines of his reports. As he rode horseback alongside a cavalry general, the two men exchanged intelligence about their respective nations. "In passing over the Spot of Downs," Adams wrote, "We saw three or four Hunters, Gunners, in search of Hares and Rabits and other Game, this being the Season of the Chase. The General seemed very apprehensive of these

Sportsmen that they would not keep a good Look out but might be so eager for their Game, as to be inattentive to Travellers and fire upon our Bodies. This was a fear that never occurred to me, and I never felt it after it was mentioned."[24]

The hunting incident serves as a symbol of John Adams's studied obliviousness. Registering his reaction to the Dutch general's caution was a way to proclaim his own courage. This was one of the ways he used the diary to write himself into scenes of action as a novelistic hero. Unlike the anxious jottings that accompanied his painful trek through northern Spain, when time was recounted as a slow, interminable march, he looked upon his prospects in heartier terms when he was in the closely connected towns of the Low Countries.

At fourteen, Johnny was pulled out of the University of Leiden in order to assume the conspicuous role of French interpreter on a diplomatic mission to St. Petersburg, Russia. That operation was being led by Francis Dana, a Massachusetts congressman who had been of their party on board *La Sensible*. Dana had endured the Spanish march with the Adamses, and Johnny would come to see his earnest elder as another father figure.[25]

The Russia they resided in was the empire of Prussian-born Catherine the Great, a so-called enlightened despot nearly twenty years on the throne when they arrived in St. Petersburg. This addition to an already remarkable résumé—another life-altering enterprise set in motion by his father—meant that Johnny would be exposed to more of the Old World than any other American of his time, his father included. John Adams was to remain in Holland, meanwhile, to continue pursuing an uncertain course: advancing his country's political and economic interests when the United States was in a battle for its survival. As frustrating as his job was, Dana's would be more daunting still: Catherine did not consider the United States worth her time.

The mission to Russia took the teen across Germany and Poland, where he kept up his journal and discovered an iniquitous world of penury and pauperism. Dirt was not the same everywhere, it turned out: the downtrodden people of the north of Spain maintained their struggle with the elements vertically; eastern Europe spread its even more accursed social subjugation horizontally. Russia was much the same. Extreme poverty lay before his eyes. His only anchor was Dana. The sunless stretch of time and space that divided centers of power at the far reaches of European civilization woke Johnny Adams to the reality of the world an isolated America measured itself against. He made do in far-off St. Petersburg, though the absence of boys and girls his age within the diplomatic corps meant that his classical education would suffer in this outpost, where he was destined to return as a fully accredited diplomat during the presidency of James Madison.

Time Measurement

John Adams was letting his son grow up at a tremendous distance from him. Though an exchange of letters was sometimes months in the making, the father expressed total faith in his maturing son's approach to life and learning. Upon arrival in the Russian capital in the late summer of 1781, Johnny let it be known that he was safe. He described St. Petersburg as "handsomer than Berlin"—which city his father had not seen and where John Quincy would return after fifteen years to assume a high diplomatic post (his second after the Netherlands) during the first Adams administration. What exceptional preparation for a diplomatic career all this was! St. Petersburg was visibly unfinished and would require, the teen judged, "another century to be render'd compleat." Time passed with oppressive slowness as temperatures fell.

It took three months before Johnny's letter from Russia found its way across twenty-four hundred miles of open country. In his reply, John commended the boy's improved handwriting, a key component for service as a diplomat's aide. John wrote, "Make it a Rule, my dear Son, To loose [*sic*] no Time. There is not a moral Precept, of clearer Obligation, or of greater Import. Make it the grand Maxim of your Life, and it cannot fail to be happy, and usefull to the World."[26]

They did not swear by time in the way we moderns do. John Quincy acquired his first timepiece in Paris, but watches were as yet ornamental status markers and not urgent reminders. Regimented time was simply not of their moment, and mechanical time was less personalized than it would come to be in the middle of the next century. Neither a timepiece nor a breathing being was, the elder wrote, "perfectly contrived and executed as never to go too fast or too slow." The mechanical was a practical reminder of all that becomes worn down with exposure to the elements. In their world, speed was almost not worth measuring. Indeed, people of their two generations were probably more attuned to aural sensations: both Adamses' diaries alert us to the peculiar substance of active conversations and, on travel days, church bells that woke them, reports of guns in the field, and the like.[27]

Needing visual markers of time, the traveling Adamses were keen letter copyists as well as regular diarists, employing written aids to memory wherever and whenever possible. They reviewed letters previously sent before following up with the next to the same, or another, correspondent. Their time was also measured in books. They recorded what they were reading; John Quincy did so in such detail that he often noted the number of hours spent and listed the pages or chapters read in the course of a given day, along with key observations of the book's author and his instant reactions.

The eighteenth century had no better, no more tangible time capsule than the diary. As a physical possession, it was the souvenir of an inward state, of a flourishing consciousness. In capturing impressions of time, it bespoke consistency in the midst of chaos and uncertainty—and ultimately, mortality. At this point, John Adams had been writing to himself compulsively for the better part of three decades. He recognized the diary form as a tool to reactivate the life of the mind and to revisit and renew the mental inspiration that accompanied movement and action.

Thinking is itself a constant process of temporal reorganization, so when we examine the father's and son's diaries, we glean not just testimony but an artful glimpse at the passage of time. A personal history becomes a course of commitment. The Adamses encouraged themselves to form good judgments and to acquire self-mastery; we see them reckoning with universals as well as particulars. The elder especially felt it was a crime to falsify history, that it was his job to tell it right. But even at this early stage in the son's diary-writing experience, John Quincy, too, reckoned with the immediacy of history and acknowledged its authority. The importance of these observations will grow as our narrative becomes more manifestly political.[28]

We dwell on the diary's function as a timekeeper and memory restorer, because it is how we open to more of the inner world of an eighteenth-century thinker, resourceful, energetic, and on the move. As much as the Adams family's faithfully preserved letters have intrigued Americans for generations, the diaries prove how close in spirit father and son were. From the age of twelve, Johnny clearly needed little outside encouragement to take up his father's intellectual habits—and to extend them.

Here is, perhaps, the best example of that bold claim: during the single month of February 1782, as a self-directed student in diplomatic exile recording the impossibly frigid daily temperatures in St. Petersburg, Johnny went through David Hume's eight-volume *History of England* in marathon reading sessions. He noted (competitively) how many pages he had just read. Once done with Hume, he immediately took up the more recently published multivolume history of England by the celebrated Catharine Macaulay, whose knowledge of the Adamses' world would only grow when she visited Boston the following year. Even as he was immersed in Macaulay, the teenager took time off to engage with Cicero's orations dating to the campaign against his nemesis Catiline. This was followed by Adam Smith's *Wealth of Nations*. By the end of March, Johnny was through all five (to date) volumes of Macaulay's history and was able to record, "Fine clear weather. Thermometer above 0." As in northern Spain, he bore all of these hardships without complaint.[29]

DESOLATE SHORE

"I want you with me." In the autumn of that year, on receipt of his father's appeal (it took months to reach them), Johnny and the luckless envoy Francis Dana plotted the youth's return to the Netherlands. At the end of October 1782, with a party of strangers, Johnny's carriage exited the Russian capital and trudged its way through exceedingly muddy roads. In destitute countryside, he was obliged to sleep out of doors in the carriage that bore him. Crossing Finland, on some days he was able to proceed no more than a few miles. Arriving in Stockholm on the evening of November 22, the intrepid fifteen-year-old wrote, "We found all the taverns in the town shut up and could not get one opened. . . . After having passed the whole night in the street, at last we found a publick house at the Swedish arms said to be the best in the city; but if it is the best is not good for much." He sought out the nearest bookstore and in no time at all discovered that strangers in Sweden were treated with uncommon civility and people of all classes acted with graciousness. He moved in polite circles and found it hard to take his eyes off the pretty girls.[30]

Wintering in Sweden was a spartan, yet manageable, experience. For John Adams, the months passed without word from his boy. The elder, who was at times fatalistic, found a way to endure. He waited as patiently as possible as Johnny ranged across wintry northern wastes. To his "widowed" wife (who joylessly marked each "anniversary" of their long separation), he conveyed the little he knew: "Our Son is now on his journey from Petersbourg through Sweeden Denmark and Germany, and if it please God he come safe, he shall come with me, and I pray We may all meet once more, you and I never to Seperate again."

Rather than stay on in Europe, or fear for his wife as she set sail for the Continent unaccompanied, he now devised a new plan. It was to drop everything and return to her: "And you may depend upon a good domestic husband, for the remainder of my Life, if it is the Will of Heaven that I should once more meet you." He felt pressure; this much is certain. In mid-February 1783, he at last heard from his son. To Abigail: "This Letter gave me great joy, it is the first I have received from him since he left Petersbourg, and the first News I have had of him since the Beginning of December, when he was at Stockholm. I have suffered extream Anxiety on his Account."[31]

The young wanderer did not exhibit much, if any, anxiety over his situation. The Swedish winter was never that desperate. This in January: "I set out from Udevalla all alone in a Slay for Gottenburgh. When I came to the third station I was obliged to Stop on account of the Storm. At the end of a couple of hours the Snow abated and I continued My Journey till about midnight." Alone in a sleigh, with fifty miles between the two towns on his itinerary?[32]

By early spring 1783, when they reunited at The Hague, John Quincy's growth in all respects impressed his father, to judge by letters sent to Abigail. The two years they'd lived apart made a father's heart ever fonder: he witnessed growth in circumspection greater than what might have been expected from a posting to isolated, autocratic Russia. Along with physical changes, which no doubt fascinated him, Johnny moved from child to apprentice to confidant and alter ego in a remarkably short amount of time. He would now assume the position of his diplomat-father's private secretary in Paris, where negotiations were ongoing to officially bring the Revolutionary War to an end. Who else in his cohort could relate such a wondrous claim to fortune? Indeed, he had no cohort.

As the eight-year-long Revolutionary War officially concluded, the former mother country reopened for business. Right away, father and son sailed across the English Channel to see what they'd been missing. They witnessed the opening of Parliament. They attended performances at the Drury Lane Theatre. They were treated to an intimate tour of the very "tasteful" (the father's diary description) Buckingham Palace. John Adams was deeply impressed with King George's extensive library.

Books that Johnny had acquired in St. Petersburg and London, some in Latin, others in French and English, made their way to Boston, where Abigail promised to keep them protected from the elements pending his and his father's return—"which I hope I shall live to see," she wrote, less melodramatic than the words must sound to modern ears. "And I please myself with the prospect of your growing into Life a Wise and Good Man." She could only guess, based on what she knew of the child he had been: "In your early days you had a great flow of Spirits and Quick passions. I hope you have acquired reason to govern the one and judgment to Guide the other." Based on what she knew of the proclivities of youth, she cautioned him against too much mirth: "Tis an old observation that empty vessels sound the loudest. I never knew a Man of great talents much given to Laughter."[33]

If Johnny remained cheerful and resilient, the father's increasingly erratic health was a major concern. Throughout 1783, he struggled. "I have great need for Repose," he wrote to Francis Dana from Paris in April, alluding to the "horrid Fever" he'd contracted in Amsterdam and never quite recovered from. He knew his fellow Bay Stater would understand his conviction that the only cure was to escape "Drudgery," sail home, and breathe "my native Air." That fall, while in England with his son, he was still feeling "feeble low and drooping." The moist English air did not appear to be helping, and as the year 1784 opened, further plans to explore England were cut short when an urgent dispatch from Congress informed John that he had to hurry back to Amsterdam to renegotiate the U.S. debt. National default loomed, and he was the only one with experience in the Netherlands who could get the job done. This time, as it turned out, he would be taking fate into his hands even more than usual.

In no shape to travel on his own, he had to be accompanied to The Hague by his devoted Johnny. They left London for Harwich, in Essex, and huddled together at a dilapidated inn beside the North Sea. For three fierce, storm-filled days, they waited, "without society and without books," to cross the water. Finally venturing into raging seas, their little packet vessel struggled to remain afloat. When they landed three days later, it was in fact on the Dutch coast, but a "desolate shore, we knew not where." Afterward, John senior wrote, dirgelike, of the Channel's well-known tendency to bring on seasickness: "a tremulous, undulating, turbulent kind of irregular tumbling sea that disposes men more to the mal de mer." Ailing, he feared he could go no farther than this nameless place. Sleepless, fitful, impaired by a "wasting sickness," he sighted no habitation but a poor fisherman's hut. "I thought it almost impossible that in that severe weather I could walk through ice and snow," he recounted. Attempting philosophical detachment, he assumed a somewhat nobler voice:

> As has been said before, human nature never knows what it can endure before it tries the experiment. My young companion was in fine spirits; his gaiety, activity, and attention to me increased as difficulties multiplied, and I was determined not to despair. I walked on, with caution and moderation, and survived.[34]

Johnny had quite possibly saved his father's life. The picture John paints of this particular crossing is the harsh reality to which every eighteenth-century traveler submitted; it commanded such phrases as "if ever we shall meet again" in letters home. He wrote, and not for the first or last time, of a squat, unathletic body ravaged by nature in one way or another. A still-determined man of forty-eight years, he refused to cut back on his wanderings; he had ambition enough to guide him through strange lands and backward communities, regardless of weather conditions. His son's struggles with preindustrial travel, already extensive, were just beginning.

Their shared ordeal in crossing the North Sea in 1784 was both a tale of daring and a moving demonstration of their interdependence. Over the years, John Adams would retell the stories of his harrowing adventures in Europe, to make the point that he had emerged undefeated, somehow favored by heaven. His definitive statement on the subject came in a letter to his wife years later that began with a reminiscence of the *Sensible* near disaster: "I have been mule carried and walked on foot over the Mountains in Spain—and after that nothing can come amiss." The North Sea nightmare was a close second, yet there was more: "I wish I had an exact Account of all the Voyages I have made between Harwich & Helvoet—and between Calais & Dover. . . . Did ever any Man make so many uncomfortable Journeys and Voyages? They have been enough to kill any other Man."[35]

Wherever father and son went in these years, their life on the road was one of improvisation. As it was in rugged Spain four years earlier, father and son were obliged to follow a zigzag course from the North Sea shore through to Rotterdam and The Hague. This time, the usual roles were reversed. The son was the more seasoned adventurer, veteran of a long retreat from Russia. He was as much in charge of their course as the compromised older man. For those critical days, the difference in their ages collapsed. Whether they were *père et fils*, or *frères d'aventure*, it is impossible not to recognize that an extraordinary relationship had formed.

THREE

ENVOYS

Is it my Vanity which makes me believe that the Dutch Negotiation has . . . carried Us tryumphantly to the End of all our Wishes? Without this the War would have continued for years.

—JOHN ADAMS TO JAMES WARREN,
December 15, 1782, after the signing of the Preliminary Peace Treaty between the United States and Great Britain

The foreign policy positions John and John Quincy Adams each took as president grew out of what they learned abroad, and this instilled in them a level of confidence few of their successors could claim. As a result of that nervy confidence, American stature in the world remained steady or rose during their single-term presidencies. This is not to say that their stubbornness always worked to their advantage. But their journeys—across thousands of miles of ocean and nearly as far in horse-drawn carriages, sleeping in hovels and dining in palaces—made their lives extraordinary. This was how agents of a young government learned to comport themselves on the world stage.

It is beyond obvious that their parallel careers in diplomacy accelerated the Adamses' political education and proved the readiness of both John and John Quincy to enter the "chief magistracy," as the U.S. presidency was also known in the opening decades of nationhood. Father and son stood toe to toe, time and again, with representatives of the world's dominant power, a self-satisfied, expansionist Great Britain. They repeatedly observed local conventions and continental manners. They studied and navigated institutions large and small.

Even before the 1783 Treaty of Paris confirmed American independence, the job of an American envoy in Europe was to advance commercial connections, convey American values, and convince foreigners of the positive moral character of an indebted, still unproven state. John Adams understood these things when he broke diplomatic ground in company with the world-famous Benjamin Franklin and the affable younger New Yorker John Jay. Barely a decade later, and still in his twenties, John Quincy Adams would accept the same facts of diplomatic life.

No aspect of the job was easy. American prestige was always on the line. The flow of information was irregular and periods of tedium were common. A conscientious U.S. envoy, keen on obtaining results, was hard-pressed to determine the extent to which his efforts were appreciated back home. To one as hypersensitive as John Adams—whether in France and the Netherlands or, after 1785, in Great Britain—such perceptions mattered. He could not know whether an act or opinion would be overturned. He was both independent and hamstrung, and understandably hesitant as to how far he should take any initiative. An inadvertent move might result in dismay or confusion back home, even a punitive rejection on return to the United States after recall.

From Paris, more than a year after the treaty was signed, with plenty to reflect upon, he summed up his experience in a letter to his congressman-friend Elbridge Gerry: "It is more agreeable, to be at home among ones equals, and to enjoy some degree of Respect and Esteem among those We feel a regard for, than to be admired by Strangers." Europe never ceased to feel foreign: "Among Strange Faces, manners, Languages, and looked on with Terror rarely finding a Person who dares to speak to one as has been my Case Mr Danas Mr Jays and others, for Years together is horrible. Oh! Tis horrible!" Allowing for conventional hyperbole, the cash-strapped, modestly attired emissary was saying that an American diplomat in a European posting would never be granted the kind of respect his titled European counterpart automatically received. "We cannot live in Character," griped John Adams. Looming over everything else was the modest reputation of the United States.[1]

Then there were the internecine feuds. From day one, he had to cope with colleagues in Paris who had preceded him, in addition to the condescension he felt from the representatives of stronger governments. A sense of disjointedness, resulting not just from conflicting personalities but from the unavoidable prolongation of news and official instructions from home, caused diplomatic tempers to flare within the U.S. negotiating team. John Quincy would face comparable conditions when he was forced to claw his way through times of even greater militancy—the long and disruptive Anglo-French wars that played out on the Continent concurrent with the rise of Napoleon.

The obvious parallel between the father's and the son's diplomatic careers is their signatures on treaties ending two successive wars with Great Britain, following which each went on to represent the United States in London at the Court of St. James's. History receives them as two who were rigid in their demands and not ready-made for the diplomatic arts. As dense and difficult as the father was known to be, the son (if we weigh anecdotal evidence) might have come across as even more chilly. But how else were relations with the formidable and exacting British to be managed? For decades after the Revolution, London was the most important diplomatic post to which an American could be assigned. The senior Adams's peripatetic journeying during and after the American War of Independence made him an obvious choice to serve as the country's inaugural minister to the former mother country. And by all accounts, he did a creditable job in London. John Quincy would take long and purposeful strides in his father's footsteps as minister to Great Britain thirty years later, from 1815 to 1817, after first leading U.S. missions in the Netherlands and Prussia (1795–1801), then as America's first ambassador to Russia (1809–1814). The amount of trust lodged in the two Adamses during their combined years of service in foreign capitals was sizable. While their nation might have been an insignificant player on the world stage, father and son did some of the heaviest lifting in setting a positive course for American diplomacy.

As we have seen in their personal lives, they habitually displayed an extraordinary tolerance of professional risk. During their years together in Europe, 1778–1786, they were on the front lines of contact with a most necessary ally, prerevolutionary France. Young John Quincy, who logged more miles in those eight years than his father did, grew up fast. He dined regularly in the company of transformative figures. He was on familiar terms with a young, soldiering marquis de Lafayette; an intimate of the erudite Thomas Jefferson; and a frequent visitor to the home of the illustrious Dr. Franklin.

The American press craved information about the Old World's nonstop conflicts. Even provincial papers covered political and cultural developments overseas as much as they featured domestic issues. Citizens of the new republic cast their eyes with a certain amount of awe to the fiercely competitive countries that the vast majority of native-born Americans had never seen, kingdoms with long histories that continued to chart the destinies of countless millions.

In these years, diplomacy probably mattered more than at any other time before the twentieth century. America's fiscal health, its maritime character, and the future of its commercial outreach were of the moment. Given this general understanding, U.S. representatives hammered out several key commercial treaties: the first, with France, was coordinated in 1778 by the diplomatic vanguard of Benjamin Franklin, Silas Deane, and Arthur Lee. In 1782, John Adams personally orchestrated recognition of his country in a treaty with the Netherlands while negotiating urgent loans with Dutch bankers. In 1785, the team of Adams and Jefferson reached a commercial agreement with Prussia. Commercial treaties with valuable but less strategic nations, such as Spain and Morocco, followed.

John Adams left an impressive record. Some might call it heroic. He certainly thought so. Yet the American envoy did not turn heads when he entered a room. He'd never develop the prepossessing attitude of a winsome figure on the diplomatic stage. He had to battle his way toward anything he accomplished. And battle he did. He was proud of his homespun American roots; he would not have wished for a different inheritance. Before the Revolution, when others still identified with metropolitan ideals, there was no part of him that could be described as a fussy Englishman. During years abroad, without attempting to change his Yankee demeanor, he attended formal events, sat through lavish dinners, drank and toasted, and conversed readily with Europe's best-educated citizens. He scarcely acknowledged enjoying such hearty moments. He did not style himself an art enthusiast, a lover of elite music, or an admirer of the agrarian idyll. No, John Adams was satisfied to be a modest representative of New England plainness.

Plain, yes. Except when it came to the mind's activity. He was sure of his insights and consistently wary of how he was being received. As a committee member in the Continental Congress at a time of emergency, he had worked agreeably with others. But over ensuing years, his patience with Revolutionary comrades dimmed, and he found himself trusting almost exclusively in his own motives and judgments. By the end of his posting in London, in 1788, he could be heard complaining that his job was "a species of slavery." A combination of setbacks and slights depleted his stock of munificence.[2]

The most dramatic element in his resistance to the ways of diplomatic Europe concerned the negotiation of celebrity. The very presence of Franklin, and the cult of personality that enveloped him, quickly came to symbolize the problem—nearly an existential one—of image over substance, and charm over discretion. If the United States was to fulfill its destiny, it could not elevate a slothful Franklin, who was well past his prime. Did the new nation stand for steady competence on the world stage, or was it just going to build marble monuments? In Adams's view, the puffed-up eminence Franklin projected served only to open America up to a French swindle. France, if an ally, placed its own interests first.

John Adams saw diplomacy as a living organism, an indivisible thing. It was a long-term investment, too. Which was why he disdained artificial measures of popularity. Franklin's combination of posturing and imposture, later to be replicated in the politics of personality surrounding the "men of the people" Jefferson and Jackson, was symptomatic of the larger issue: sustaining a national character. Hero worship substituted idolatry for results. A people that could not judge men would not know good government.

ODD CLANDESTINITY

The elder Adams did not enjoy any measure of success in his early dealings with the French, especially the comte de Vergennes, King Louis XVI's experienced foreign minister. He acquired active knowledge of the diplomatic arts and a specific understanding of Vergennes's style during that first, one-year-long European tour, during which time he studied up on French-authored books about statecraft and the laws of nations. As much as he valued French assistance during the Revolutionary War, he did not feel that the Franco-American treaty would or should bind the two nations forever. He could see a time when Anglo-American commercial relations would be restored and political enmity between the two culturally attached nations would soften. He held to the belief that his mission abroad was devoted to the long-term interest of American commercial ties with nations far and wide. In this way, he thought big.

During his second, longer stay on the Continent, following the demanding mountainous journey across northern Spain into southern France in the winter of 1779–1780, he insinuated himself into high-level conversations, initially attracting, and then losing, Vergennes's interest. Uncommonly forward in approaching the French foreign minister with his recommendations, Adams probably served only to stymie the development of a closer relationship with his country's principal wartime ally.

At the time of his arrival on the scene, Benjamin Franklin was the most practiced of America's diplomats. He was held in the highest esteem in Parisian circles. Indeed, Franklin's reputation for statesmanship was nowhere greater than it was there and then. Vergennes found Franklin as accommodating as he found Adams overbearing. The Philadelphian's calculation that you get your way by not offending people did not move John Adams an inch.

Franklin had been in France since the end of 1776. He'd busied himself cultivating the *beau monde* while tending to the pangs of gout and other ailments. If his diplomatic energies were compromised by age and infirmity, he certainly proved himself by pressing for a wartime military alliance, signed in February 1778, which committed France to "maintain effectually the liberty, sovereignty and independence absolute and unlimited" of the United States (Article II). Franklin's efforts brought the embattled Continental army of General Washington necessary funds and, before long, reinforcements.

The celebrity Franklin cultivated (and manipulated) ultimately took his image out of his personal control. The bestselling author, parodist, and self-parodist Laurence Sterne toyed with his readers on this very subject and serves as a fair analogue. "I wrote not to be *fed* but to be *famous*," he lectured a book critic after the opening portion of his titillating *Tristram Shandy* was published. In *A Sentimental Journey,* Sterne made himself indistinguishable from his narrator, the character Yorick. As a modern literary scholar observes of his method, "Sterne feigns self-revelation while revealing only that which his public already knows; he achieves the illusion of depth while mooring his readers forever at his surface." Something similar can be said of Franklin, the printer who understood the power of the press. Both Sterne and Franklin appreciated legend building and saw psychological advantages in giving shape to the public's reception of their script. Whether and to what extent either recognized the fact, cultic identity was an impersonation that the subject could contribute to but could not wholly control.[3]

Franklin's reputation in France was double-edged. He was feted and adored by many of the intelligentsia and nobility. Multiple versions of his image were reproduced and widely circulated. A mass-produced terra-cotta medallion was sold that captured him in the distinctive fur cap he wore while living in Paris. He dispensed with the fancy wig, dressing instead in Quaker linen and a plain brown suit. He caused a stir when he went to the palace of Versailles for an audience with the king, wearing his American costume. His defiance of the dress code led those in attendance to let out a loud cheer of support.

Beautiful, educated women hung about Franklin at salons and social gatherings; he gained the plaudits of French high society by dismissing his English enemy with a memorable bon mot. The British ambassador David Murray, Viscount Stormont, had made it his duty to spread vicious calumnies about Americans. Franklin countered Murray's false 1777 report of General Washington's humiliating surrender with one delicious line: "Non, Monsieur, ce n'est pas verité; c'est seulement un Stormont." (No, sir, it's not a truth; it's only a Stormont.) The timely quip was published in several American newspapers, wherein it was stated that the name Stormont had become, in French circles, a "cant phrase" for lying. Franklin's stormy relationship with the British diplomat took on a Shakespearean cast when rumors traveled back to Congress and reached Abigail Adams via the *Boston Gazette:* "The illustrious Patriot Dr. Benjamin Franklin has been assassinated in his Bed-Chamber, at the Instance of Lord Stormont. The Villain left him for dead; but one of the Doctors' Ribs prevented the Stab from being instantly fatal, and he lay in a languishing condition." The *Gazette* explained that the ship bearing the cited letter on the assassination attempt was about to sail, and the writer could not say for certain whether Franklin had survived his wounds. This dramatic scene had never taken place, of course. But it proves for us that Franklin's celebrity was of the sort that any story about him would be lapped up by gossipmongers.[4]

Though the scientist turned statesman made endless appearances at lectures, experiments, concerts, and the Paris Opera, his theatrical style also invited mockery—even from some of those who admitted to being fascinated by him. When Franklin asked Voltaire to bless his grandson, Benjamin Franklin Bache, an observer dismissed the exhibitionist act as "indecent puerile adulation." Meaner critics called Franklin a chameleon, seeing his attempts to win over the French people as a form of charlatanism. Adams recalled in 1807, when his late colleague was enjoying a return of celebrity, that King Louis XVI had mocked Franklin mania by engaging the finest porcelain maker in the country to design a pot with a portrait of Franklin's face on the inside. It was not just any piece of china but a chamber pot—a portable toilet, as it were—for the duchesse de Polignac. "When the King presented to the Duchess with his own hand," Adams wrote with satisfying sarcasm, he hoped "she might have the satisfaction of contemplating the image of her great philosopher and politician when she had occasion to look at it."[5]

John Adams was Franklin's temperamental opposite. Seeing himself as incorruptible, he worshipped an ideal of fame as merit that was unsought and free from manipulation. Though Adams was, like Franklin, a man of wit, his clever wordplay did not become known to the public and remained hidden in letters to friends and family members. The cult of personality surrounding George Washington would not attach to Adams either, of course, because it centered on military reputation, prowess on horseback, and an imposing physical appearance. John Adams could only hope that his cultivated judgment, his philosophy of history, might strike the public as profound.

He remonstrated against the blatant distortions of Franklin's image, though doing so was a losing battle. In composing his autobiography in the early years of the nineteenth century, the rejected second president would recite the famous meeting of Franklin and Voltaire at the Academy of Sciences, when the crowd egged the pair on, first to clasp hands, then to hug and kiss each other. For Adams, it was but "two Aged Actors" performing on a "great Theatre of Philosophy and frivolity." The public had already heard Franklin's prominent friend in the French government, Anne-Robert-Jacques Turgot, compare him to Prometheus, snatching thunder from the skies and scepters from tyrants. All such over-the-top Gallic praise struck Adams as patently ridiculous. The Franklin of French invention was hardly more than a jester or illusionist to Adams, a cheap commodity consumed as entertainment. Adams did not value Franklin's manipulation of a long-cultivated image to secure French support for the American Revolution. Adams didn't think like that. He hated political theatrics. The decorum that Washington perfected in his military and, later, presidential image would make far more sense to both Adamses in the 1790s. Franklin's faux "common man" delighted French audiences but also served as a reminder of how gullible the public could be.[6]

All theatrics aside, it was feared by some at the time (and has been confirmed by modern scholars) that Franklin lacked circumspection when it came to policing the flow of delicate information. His tendency to trust, prized by those who admired him, was also accompanied, as the historian Jonathan Dull has observed, by a "susceptibility to flattery," which his colleague Adams openly deplored. As the Revolutionary War pressed on, and the often-ailing Franklin conceded to France a determining role in directing bilateral relations, Adams grew hot under the collar. He would not stand for what he regarded as subordination to another power, even if that power held the key to America's victory over Britain. Of the two, only Adams recognized that the French wanted the new United States to emerge from the war both independent and weak.[7]

If Adams had his way, the larger-than-life Dr. Franklin would be known, after 1778, as no kind of American hero. It wasn't just a matter of personal pique. Adams had his own agenda. He contributed to diplomatic tension—or at least to diplomatic uncertainty—by publishing articles in the British press while the war, if still hot, had receded somewhat from its earlier boiling point. He both encouraged and cautioned his London readership, saying that Americans would gravitate toward France in the future only if the British ministry stubbornly refused to recognize the former colonies' right to be independent and equal. Battlefield reverses would not influence the envoy Adams, other than to stiffen his resolve. Since 1778, most battles were being fought in the South; the Continentals harassed the invaders without striking any permanently debilitating blows. Adams retained pride, though he rarely got positive news from the front. As the war entered its fifth year, the French comte de Rochambeau left for the American theater with more than five thousand troops, an event that promised to alter the balance of power—eventually. For some time yet to come, Adams remained in a stew. He wanted more from the Gallic ally.

Addressing the powerful comte de Vergennes, he complained that France's effort was not as substantive nor its attitude as hard charging as it had ought to be; the longer the war lasted, he feared, the more power the accommodationists back home would obtain. Vergennes did not take the bait. He was unable to decide where Adams stood—or even how friendly he was to France. Vergennes had no such worries with Franklin, to whom he directly complained about Adams, and Adams increasingly had a hard time separating his hatred for Vergennes—"vain, ambitious, and despotic"—from his hatred for Franklin. It was that pronounced discomfort which lost Adams a seat at the table, as it were, and led him to leave Paris with John Quincy, in mid-1780, to pursue stronger political and commercial relations with the Dutch.[8]

John Adams's Franklin problem was increasingly a visceral one. It had been swirling in his head for some time, never let up for long, easily rekindled, and sometimes reached a boil. Up-front and exacting in person, verbatim and literal in the ways of language, Adams did not have it in him to employ sly tactics or mind games to obtain desired ends. But that was precisely who and what Franklin was: a hustler, a hoaxer. It had almost always served him well. In a July 1782 letter to a regular correspondent, the Maryland-born, English-educated Edmund Jenings, a political insider who ranged about Europe in these years, Adams savaged Franklin: "F. must make himself a Man of Consequence by piddling." "Piddling"? His word choice was meant to denote an inferior mind, someone of trifling ability. Adams showed no compunction to soften his criticism of a senior diplomat who might have lost a step. In 1783, after nearly five years on the European scene together, Adams vented his spleen to James Warren, husband of Mercy Otis: "I can have no Dependence on his Word. I never know when he speaks the Truth, and when not."[9]

Their personalities were known, one to the other, since 1776, when Adams and Franklin worked together closely in the Second Continental Congress. Both served on the select committee that, with Jefferson, drafted the Declaration of Independence. Two months after that, they constituted two-thirds of an American delegation that conferred with British officials in New York, in an abortive attempt to find peace. It was en route to this conference that Adams and Franklin spent a storied night in the same room of a New Jersey inn, and the two fell to arguing over whether the window should remain open.[10]

In 1779, when the controversial ship's captain Pierre Landais was fretting at Lorient and attempting to involve the passenger John Adams in his ongoing dispute with the proud American naval hero John Paul Jones, it was Franklin whose communications with the rival captains were at the center of the issue of command and performance of duty. The dispute lengthened an already long delay in the Adamses' return voyage to America. Planting a dark seed in Adams's mind, Landais told his VIP passenger that Franklin was behind the whole operation and responsible for their present difficulties. This immediately struck Adams as a plausible explanation. He jotted in his diary his "suspicion" that Franklin would "prevent me from going home, least I should tell some dangerous Truths. . . . Does the old Conjurer dread my Voice in Congress? He has some Reason for he has often heard it there." Landais separately attested that an "exasperated" Adams "exclaimed very highly against" Franklin.[11]

Things had come to a pretty pass by the time Adams began laying out his thoughts to the Marylander Jenings, who was very much devoted to Adams. "Men of great Reputations may do as many Weak Things as they please," he growled. "To remark their Mistakes is to envy them." (Or, that's what people believed.) But Adams felt not the slightest twinge of jealousy toward Franklin; in fact, it was the other way around: "I Swear, I will affirm when and where I please that he has been actuated and is still by a low Jealousy and a meaner Envy of me." Referring to an unnamed person who had charged Adams with "clandestinely hurting Franklin," he reacted with annoyance: "I have done nothing clandestinely. I have complained of Franklins Behaviour, in Company with Americans so I have in Company with the French and Spanish Ambassadors, without any Injunctions or desires of Seccresy [*sic*]. This is an odd Sort of Clandestinity. That I have no Friendship for Franklin I avow." There are other instances in the life of John Adams where stinging character assassination can be found, but Franklin was a special target because of how the older man savored a fame he had ceased to deserve. By Adams's stern judgment, love of ease and dissipation constituted Franklin's years in France; if anyone deserved a reputation for his modest republican roots (as "nature's nobleman"), it was Adams. He had sacrificed his lawyer's income to serve the new nation's interest, while the septuagenarian was a moneyed man of influence and false modesty. Rubbing it in, Adams commented that Franklin's French was ungrammatical.[12]

Adams felt diminished in stature by what he convinced himself was a self-conscious refusal to trumpet his own hard work. While others in politics—notable among them James Madison—saw him as an insufferably vain character, Adams cast himself in letters as an unostentatious, underappreciated representative of American interests abroad. What bothered him most was that no one else would receive credit in Europe so long as Franklin remained on the scene, craving publicity without accomplishing anything. The old man's "insidious Manoeuvres" stood in the way of a diplomatic triumph that Adams could almost taste. Somehow, the old charlatan was the only American whom senior European officials trusted. Adams hated it. "His whole Life has been one continued Insult to good Manners and Decency," he charged in one of his unrestricted rants to James Warren. "I wish with all my Soul he was out of public Service, and in Retirement, repenting of his past Life, and preparing, as he ought to be, for another World." This was as close as Adams came to wishing Franklin dead. Assuming that others believed him to be jealous, Adams fought back by planting his truths in correspondence with influential friends and government officials and would continue to until the facts proved him right. Personal vindication would come. Or so he assured himself.

He communed with the discredited diplomat Arthur Lee, who on his return from France in 1780 paid a cordial visit to Abigail in Boston. In later years, Adams wrote of Lee, "His manners were polite, his reading extensive, his Attention to Business was punctual, and his Integrity without reproach." As another who suffered for his opposition to the singular celebrity, Adams felt he could speak to Lee uncensored of a "Dr. Franklin, whose System has ever been to sweep Europe clear of every Minister but himself, that he might have a clear unrivalled Stage." It was "galling," said Adams, to be subordinate to Franklin in the eyes of Congress.[13]

Adams knowingly took chances when he tried to expose a national treasure as a fraud. In the months leading up to the Treaty of Paris, he put his positions on record several times in letters to Secretary of Foreign Affairs Robert R. Livingston. Paris was not an unselfish ally; its government wished the United States limited success. It had placed roadblocks before him as he sought ties to the Dutch. It aimed to dictate America's posture in the eventual settlement with Great Britain. Adams would not let up until he had gotten across his warning to Congress: don't trust the French.

The language he used to make his points to Secretary Livingston was deeply personal. All of his distresses in Europe were caused by the "ill dispositions" of Vergennes, "aided by the Jealousy, Envy & selfish Servility of Dr. Franklin," who did the bidding of Vergennes instead of standing up for America. "You may be told, they have Confidence in Dr. Franklin," he noted of the French ministry. "It is not true—They never did." They used him as they pleased, "because he was always easy, quiet, never proposing any thing, never advising any thing, doing always as they would have him." Adams chafed at the thought that the Treaty of Paris would result in their century being renamed "the Franklinian Age, le Siecle Franklinnien."[14]

He never got past these feelings. Upon the man's death in 1790, Adams soliloquized, "Franklin is gone. Peace to his shade." He interrogated his own mind and reached a predictable conclusion: "I feel no ill will to his Memory—but I owe more to Truth than to his Fame; and I owe the Truth to my Country and Posterity." His conscience called out: "From the first to the last of my Acquaintance with him, I can reconcile his Conduct in public affairs neither to the Character of an honest Man, nor to that of a Man of sense."[15]

The record is inconclusive as to how much John Quincy picked up on, or at the time appreciated, the extent of his father's Franklin problem. But in later years, bent on correcting history's errata, he stood by his father's critique. William Temple Franklin, the illegitimate son of Dr. Franklin's illegitimate son, absorbed more of John Quincy's attention during their time in Paris. Temple, as he was known (the "Mr. Franklin" of Johnny's diary), was five years older and something of a ladies' man. He served as secretary to the treaty negotiators in 1783, a move made at the instigation of his grandfather. John senior was irritated when his own aide, the experienced John Thaxter, was passed over in favor of the unimpressive Temple, who was obviously being groomed for a senior diplomatic assignment, one that he would never receive.

Temple Franklin and Johnny Adams traveled in the same social circles, and on one occasion the latter wrote of him, "Mr. Franklin has been so long in France"—since 1776—"that he is more a Frenchman than an American: I doubt whether he will enjoy himself perfectly if he returns to America." Johnny was correct, insofar as Temple spent most of his life in Europe, where he used his inheritance to speculate in a number of financial ventures, always with mixed results. If John Adams lived to see his son succeed in spades as a diplomat, Franklin was wholly unsuccessful in paving the way for *his* favored offspring despite the considerable head start Temple received in the days when Adamses and Franklins were thrown together in Paris. Adding to his many complaints, the elder Adams was perturbed by the openness with which Dr. Franklin acknowledged his bastard line.[16]

But the worst aspect of the old man's character, according to John Adams, was Franklin's delight in his own fame. Everyone in their world had some charming story about the American polymath, but few knew anything of Adams's role in the French negotiations; he would say he was the hardliner that a fragile, fledgling, near-bankrupt republic needed. Just as Adams disguised little in his long reports to Congress, in his handwritten autobiography he squeezed between the lines of the manuscript—suggesting either a late addition or hesitation before committing the words—a mighty verdict on Benjamin Franklin for the eyes of posterity: "That He was a great Genius, a great Wit, a great Humourist and a great Satyrist, and a great Politician is certain." Wait for the shoe to drop: "That He was a great Phylosopher, a great Moralist and a great Statesman is more questionable." Adams's Franklin was a French tool. He was lazy. He was debauched. He was not to be trusted with affairs of state.[17]

Not surprisingly, the feeling was mutual. With Anglo-American peace around the corner in 1783, Franklin wrote to Robert Morris, the U.S. superintendent of finance, that the unpoliced mouth of John Adams was spoiling the American diplomatic effort. At issue was Adams's use of "extravagant and violent Language," spoken both in private and in public. "Luckily," Franklin qualified, this behavior was "imputed to the True Cause; a Disorder in the Brain; which tho' not constant has its fits too Frequent." To Franklin, whatever was wrong with John Adams was regarded, in Parisian circles, as a medical condition and accordingly discounted by his fellow diplomats. Thomas Jefferson related similar language to James Madison in a private communication of 1789, the year George III's mental deterioration was diagnosed and he became "the mad king." Before leaving Paris, Franklin had given Jefferson his characterization of John Adams: "Always an honest man, often a great one, but sometimes absolutely mad." To Robert Livingston, Franklin wrote similarly in 1783, "I am persuaded, however, that he means well for his Country, is always an honest man, often a Wise One, but sometimes and in some things, absolutely out of his Senses." One thing can be said about the Adams-Franklin rift: both men were consistent in their condemnation.[18]

Dutch Dealings

It was the capture of the South Carolinian Henry Laurens in the autumn of 1780 that elevated John Adams's role and lengthened his and his son's stay in the Netherlands, or United Provinces, as the country was known at the time. Congress chose Laurens, its past president, to manage bilateral relations; he was to solicit a $10 million loan from Dutch bankers. John Adams was expecting to greet Laurens in Amsterdam, until he learned that the envoy was captured on the high seas and made prisoner of the British. Laurens was languishing in the Tower of London, and fifteen months would pass before his release. Recognizing that "the said Henry Laurens has, by unavoidable accidents, been hitherto prevented from proceeding," Congress named Adams its agent and charged him with sole responsibility for negotiations with the Dutch. Seeming to confirm some of Adams's suspicions about the fickleness of the French ally, its minister stationed in Philadelphia reported to Paris that Laurens might have fallen into British hands on purpose. He had friends in Parliament from colonial-era associations and, one could surmise, took off for London bearing peace overtures.[19]

The Dutch, traditionally pro-British, were on the fence. Holders of British debt, they were toying with the idea of extending loans to the American rebels. As the longtime treasurers of the Continent, they had been at the height of their political and cultural power in the mid-seventeenth century and still entertained colonial ambitions in the East and West Indies in the late eighteenth. But they were a stagnant nation in 1780, and a vulnerable one.

John and John Quincy Adams first saw Holland that summer, traveling at leisure by canal boat. For a time, they were simply enamored with the culture. Adams senior, though hampered by the language barrier, enjoyed the adventure in diplomacy. "The Country where I am is the greatest Curiosity in the World," he wrote to his wife from Amsterdam. "This Nation is not known anywhere, not even by its Neighbours. The Dutch Language is spoken by none but themselves. Therefore they converse with nobody, and nobody converses with them." To the president of Congress, he wrote with equal patriotism and prescience that the modern world had seen two languages dominate politics and commerce: Latin, in the eighteenth century, had been supplanted by French. But French had yet to be "universally established," and Adams assured Congress that it would not come to pass. "English," he wrote, "is destined to be, in the next and succeeding centuries, more generally the language of the world."[20]

His tone was less flip as time passed, as his attempts to make sense of the Dutch Republic's political structure and decision-making process foundered that year and into the next. He encountered bankers, businessmen, and political figureheads without ever knowing for certain whether he was making headway in a two-pronged effort to obtain loans and secure diplomatic recognition. The Dutch were all business; they sought to conduct their business without interference or interruption. They were not keen on alienating the British, who had just declared war against them on the flimsiest of pretexts in a tactic meant to stay the hand of whatever government still existed among the Dutch.

It is no wonder that John Adams felt stymied. "I entered Holland a forlorn Pilgrim in 1780," he recalled in old age, "without a single line of Introduction." The nation's bankers would not extend the United States a loan unless and until their government granted it formal recognition. And even then, it would not be made easy. "The affair of a Loan gives me much anxiety and Fatigue," Adams wrote after a year's worth of entreaties to Dutch bankers.[21]

But the envoy was nothing if not persistent. He approached several tasks at once, and all with his trademark implacability. High on the list was his son's education—the totality of it. He sent Johnny to Latin school at The Hague and, after that, to the university in Leiden. Until the son left for St. Petersburg in July 1781, his father enlisted cultural translators who devoted themselves to the American mission. One, Charles Guillaume Frédéric Dumas, already sixty when Adams met him, assumed a kind of surrogacy, monitoring Johnny's education during those periods when the boy's father, as a peace negotiator, was obliged to travel the three hundred miles to Paris to keep tabs on the slow-moving talks with London's envoys—being the equivalent of his previous Boston-to-Philadelphia rides.

Dumas deserves his due. Born of French parents in a southern German principality, he settled in the Netherlands around mid-century. A classical humanist scholar and early enthusiast of democratic ideals, he acquired his fascination with the British-American colonies in the 1760s. Wishing to be a part of America's bright future, he was awestruck in the presence of Dr. Franklin (for whom he worked as a secret agent of sorts) and felt instantly comfortable in the presence of John Adams. He worked for very little pay and proved a most loyal subaltern throughout Adams's tenure in The Hague and Amsterdam. His wife served as hostess at diplomatic receptions. John Adams only *appeared* to be doing everything himself. Dumas was a partner, a clearinghouse for essential news, a booster, a momentum builder—an unsung hero within the Adamses' orbit. If Charles Dumas was a bit of a fabulist who lived vicariously through the Americans, he matters because he absorbed details, lifted spirits, and conveyed the ways of the Dutch to both father and son.[22]

Two cities, The Hague and Amsterdam, were the staging grounds for an American propaganda initiative, while peace negotiations with Britain remained stalled. "The permanent and lasting Friendship of the Dutch, may be easily obtained by the United States," Adams pressed Franklin in early summer 1782, "that of England never. It is gone with the days before the Flood." To his fellow diplomat and firmer ally John Jay, Adams expressed himself even more colorfully: "There is but one way to Negotiate with Englishmen. That is clearly and decidedly. Their Fears only govern them. If we entertain an Idea of their Generosity, or Benevolence towards us, we are undone." He said what he thought. "They hate us, universally from the Throne to the Footstool, and would annihilate us, if in their Power, before they would treat with us in any way. We must let them Know, that we are not to be moved from our Purpose; or all is undone." London was in no hurry to put the war officially behind, so Adams preferred to be in the Netherlands, where he could be more useful to his country.[23]

He sought out political friends in the Low Countries. And he read incessantly. A businessman from a Plymouth family Adams knew visited him on occasion and recorded that his accommodations contained "a fine library" and backed onto "a tasteful little garden." Wherever he went, book culture consumed John Adams. Most of the Dutch who stepped inside city bookshops did so to purchase writing paper, pen and ink, and perhaps an almanac but were unable to afford the high cost of literary and political works. But the upper crust could always find a rich selection of titles.

Among the literati, he talked up the American Revolution. The English-, French-, and Dutch-language volumes he acquired included a serialized treatment (in French) of the state of politics in the United Provinces, published in 1781. The author was Antoine-Marie Cerisier, a French-born Dutch patriot and occasional diplomat with strong pro-American sentiments. Cerisier insisted that the Continental army would never give up, that "robust" New Englanders, inured to hard farm labor, would rise to any challenge. The English nation was "blinded by pride over its prosperity," "proud of its own liberty & jealous of that of others." Adams and Cerisier formed a mutual admiration society. "His Pen has erected a Monument to the American cause," Adams wrote to Secretary Livingston.

To frustrate the ambitions of an overbearing empire required a united stand. A once-impressive commercial power, the militarily reduced Dutch could not contest London without plenty of help. "Above all," Cerisier pronounced, "European liberties depend on American independence." Sanctimonious Britain had declared war against the unpretentious United Provinces. The Dutch seemed ripe for Adams's message.[24]

On April 19, 1781, the American envoy presented a bold "Memorial to the States General," the governing body of the United Provinces, seeding the ground for a pragmatic alliance. He deliberately dated the proposal April 19, the sixth anniversary of the Battles of Lexington and Concord. Adams's text combined moral and practical argument, touting the "immortal Declaration, of the fourth of July," while pointing to the common form of government that the American and Dutch republics practiced. The American declaration was, he explained, "not the Effect of any sudden Passion, or Enthusiasm"—a word that connoted an overindulgence in emotion—"but a Measure, maturely discussed in some hundreds of popular Assemblies, and by public Writings in all the States." As to his other argument, "A natural Alliance may be formed between two Republicks, if ever one existed among Nations."

The United States and the Netherlands stood out at a time when monarchies prevailed in the Western world. There was also the fact that North American settlement was shaped by influences beyond that of English enterprise. Adams and his fellow New Englanders owed a debt of gratitude to the Dutch that they would not forget: "The first Planters of the four Northern States found in this Country [Holland] an Asylum from Persecution." The separatist Puritans had enjoyed "Protection and Hospitality" in the Netherlands for twelve years after feeling unwelcome in England. They remained safe there until the *Mayflower* voyage was conceived. To round out his appeal, Adams held out the prospect of a flourishing Dutch-American trade.[25]

He had taken it upon himself, largely unprompted, to hasten a comprehensive Dutch-American alliance. And he achieved unqualified success. One year to the day from the date of his memorial, the States General officially recognized the United States. Guaranteeing a paper existence to a not-quite-official proposal, Adams, with the assistance of Dumas, had the memorial bound and printed in three languages: Dutch, English, and French.

The Dutch, though early and influential colonizers of New York state, were not as well known to Americans as the French were. Their notable open-mindedness was an inheritance of seventeenth-century cosmopolitanism. Their wealth was the result of commerce and the steady development of an astute community of bankers. But the militarily insignificant republic ignored the militarization of institutional life in neighboring nations: it was enough, the Dutch believed, to be needed.

At this moment in history, the Great Powers of Europe—Britain, France, and Prussia—took note of internal troubles in the Seven United Provinces, from rising unemployment to simmering political contests that pitted the patrician class against the ruling house of Orange. Thirty-three-year-old William V, on the throne since the age of three, cared only to sustain the status quo and to reward friendly profiteers. As John Adams navigated its elite circles, the Dutch Republic faced an uncertain future.[26]

There is no question that Adams's initiatives had a major impact. But being who he was, insensitive to others' feelings, he gave offense to Henry Laurens, the long-detained envoy. On his release from an extended imprisonment in London, Laurens learned from the tactless Adams that his presence was no longer needed in The Hague; whatever business he might have thought he had there, Adams had taken care of it. Among its stipulations, the Dutch-American Treaty of Amity and Commerce codified the rights of neutrals in carrying on trade with nations at war. It invited each signatory to establish consular offices in the other's port cities. Congress had no expectations beyond these. John Adams had proven himself.[27]

Power Games

For much of the time that his father was engaged with the Dutch, Johnny was a full-time resident of the incomplete city of St. Petersburg. It turned out that his presence in Russia was unnecessary, because French translation was less in demand than his boss, the U.S. minister, had anticipated. Most of what Francis Dana knew of Russia had come from two histories he'd read that chronicled its government and society in the 1760s. It did not help that the projected League of Armed Neutrality, under Russia's aegis, did not develop as the American Congress had hoped. It frustrated Dana that Catherine the Great had no interest in extending herself to the Americans. In short, Russia was a complete diplomatic disappointment.[28]

Johnny remained cloistered for months. ("Stay'd at home all day," he repeatedly noted in his diary.) While he attended balls, saw plays performed in several languages, and enjoyed daytime outings with foreigners of all stripes, the affectionate Mr. Dana and the anxious father shared their concern over Johnny's minimal exposure to that body of literature a boy of his age was expected to absorb. Johnny borrowed from the "English Library" some volumes of Cicero and such modern titles as Samuel Richardson's extra-long epistolary novel of victimized womanhood, *Clarissa*. But he appears to have gained more in knowledge journeying back to The Hague than he obtained from his extensive dealings with the diplomatic corps in the Russian capital. Carrying with him secret correspondence from Dana to his father, Johnny wintered among the winning people of Sweden, whose government looked as favorably upon the United States as the Dutch did. The French minister to Denmark reported from Copenhagen that he had met with the wayfaring young American. "To judge by his way of thinking and speaking," baron de la Houze attested, "he has almost convinced me that men are born at the age of thirty in his country, although he can barely be sixteen."[29]

Back under the care of Monsieur Dumas, John Adams's model of scholastic excellence, Johnny slowly made up for lost time. His father hunkered down in Paris, finally pleased by the progress toward a respectable treaty. He wanted his son to read the New Testament in Greek. "Does he Speak the German?" John queried Dumas. "Has he lost his French or English or Dutch? It is time for him to think of a Plan of Life and a Profession to follow." He was approaching the age of sixteen, when these questions typically formed in an upwardly mobile American household.[30]

Despite his regular absences, when John Adams intervened in his son's education, he tried to reencounter the same texts himself. This activity added to the unending chore of composing diplomatic correspondence. He traced the currents of political life by studying the local newspapers, ever waiting on the next dispatch (by courier) from America. And he remained in daily conversation with himself. Comparing Dutch customs with those of France, he postulated (in his diary) that diplomacy could be learned the same way a man of science conducted a series of experiments, mixing disparate groups of people and observing their behaviors and reactions. He himself relied, as he wrote to Robert Livingston, on "private Friendship and simple Civility." The only requirement he had from his acquaintances in Europe was that they be "Friends to the United States."[31]

One experiment he performed was to observe the mitigating effect of a finely adorned dinner table. Business arose, and problems were smoothed out. When correctness mattered, a level of respect was maintained and polite conversation flowed. Whenever possible, he resisted kowtowing to moneyed power. Distinctions didn't have to matter. Until they did. The American revolutionary attended rich dinners and mingled with as many titled individuals (male and female) as men of commerce and finance. All were keen to analyze themselves, speaking of manners and modes and ways of impressing their peers. This was how Adams picked up on the sociology of diplomacy. He jotted ideas alongside the lists of names and associated foibles. Attendance at the theater was a form of social education as much as it was entertainment.[32]

Paris was close enough that he had been able to commute from The Hague whenever there was positive movement in bringing a parchment end to the Revolutionary War. Paying obligatory calls on the gouty Franklin, Adams built up what he thought was a strong case to present to Congress, that it should assign him greater authority. He would be satisfied with nothing less than supplanting Franklin at the negotiating table.

But Adams was not the only one to exhibit his displeasure with their diplomatic dance partners. His esteemed colleague John Jay of New York also disagreed with Franklin's approach and had his own problems with their French hosts, separate and apart from Adams's. "He says they are not a Moral People," Adams noted of Jay in late 1782. "He dont like any Frenchman.—The Marquis de la Fayette is clever, but he is a Frenchman.—Our Allies dont play fair, he told me." Both Jay and Adams felt the French would needle both sides in the negotiations to deprive the United States of the Mississippi River, while turning the entire Gulf of Mexico over to Spain.[33]

Whenever he brought up the battle-hardened Lafayette, barely out of his teens and a favorite of General Washington, Adams demonstrated his refusal to trust in any one European representative or any one European power. Lafayette had been dodging bullets on American soil since 1777, sailing home to France to promote the American cause, then recrossing the Atlantic for more action in 1781. "I enjoy his friendship," Adams wrote of the marquis, but "I see in that Youth the seeds of Mischief to our Country." The "applause" he'd already received "kindled in him an unbounded Ambition which it concerns Us much to watch." Adams saw what popularity had done to Benjamin Franklin. With his family connections, Lafayette could soon become a national political figure in France. Where, then, would his loyalty lie? "This Mongrel Character of French Patriot and American Patriot cannot exist long." Adams was a grumbler, but that's not all he was. He had been watching the behavior of the titled of Europe for long enough to issue a prudent warning.[34]

The decisive Battle of Yorktown occurred in October 1781. After considerable success in the South, the British general Charles Cornwallis had settled in there, at the peninsular point where the first English settlement had planted itself in 1607. He had with him some seventy-two hundred men and remained confident of regular supplies from the Royal Navy. He did not reckon on the French navy, which Vergennes had authorized the year before upon Lafayette's urging. Lafayette was in Virginia all the while, keeping watch on Cornwallis, before Washington brought his forces to bear. After a successful Franco-American siege at Yorktown, the British lay down their arms. They were not entirely beaten, still occupying New York, Charleston, and Savannah. But they were demoralized.

Was John Adams wrong when it came to the loyal Lafayette? Fast-changing events make the question moot. The French Revolution would significantly alter many other Americans' perspectives besides his own. While he occupied the vice presidential chair, the once unstoppable Lafayette would be sitting in an Austrian prison, shorn of his glory. Still, the larger lesson must be underscored again: Adams understood that the allure of fame made it hard for almost any man to avoid becoming corrupted. When the world stood up and cheered a man every time he went out in public, how could that not change him? Who should be entrusted with power? The moralist from tiny Braintree contemplated at length the mutability of human nature. The effect of what he was seeing in the decade of the 1780s would not fade in the 1790s, or at any time thereafter.

French duplicity would not cease to be a major preoccupation for him. To his old friend James Warren, Adams predicted that "the Confederation of our states" would become "an object of Jealousy to France" and that "Amidst all the Joys of Peace, and the glorious Prospects before Us, I see in Europe so many Causes of Inquietude." (He used the French word *inquiétude* to convey conspicuous concern.) As he gazed into his crystal ball, he cast himself as the last, best American patriot: "Our Country is a singular one. It is a Temple of Liberty, set open to all the World. . . . I never had thro my whole Life any other Ambition than to cherish, promote and protect it and never will have any other for myself nor my Children."[35]

Adams's reputation was mixed. It would always be mixed. As he reported home on the European situation, he continued to tout his own insights. He went so far as to claim that his efforts in the Netherlands were responsible for finally bringing London to accept American independence. "Without this," he boasted to Warren, "the War would have continued for years." Yet, he said, his former colleagues in Congress could expect to "hear of insinuations enough darkly circulated, to lessen me at home." Was he paranoid? Perhaps. "I care not," he concluded his desperate letter. "Let me come home and tell me [*sic*] own story." The Treaty of Paris was all but a done deal at the end of 1782, though it would not become official until a year later. In the interim, John Adams saw himself surrounded, suspect, and the subject of malicious gossip.[36]

He wanted to be in America and to launch a defense. If not the French, it would be Franklin whom he could expect to depress his accomplishments. Adams was confident that John Jay would back him up later, stateside, on the subject of Franklin's incompetence, but not even Jay, who distrusted the

French, shared the degree of pique Adams expressed toward Franklin. The old codger had exhibited great fondness for John and Sarah Jay's daughter, a toddler during their Paris years, and he had bailed Jay out when, as minister to Spain in 1781, Jay required funds. Franklin, plotting his return to America, thought of Jay as an ideal successor.[37]

LITTLE NEGOTIATIONS

The Treaty of Paris came as a denouement. Between April 1782 and August 1783, there were no major machinations, no decisive maneuvers undertaken by the American side. London was ready to move on and resume a profitable Anglo-American trade. That was pretty much all that mattered.

John and John Quincy had moved back to Paris not long after the latter's return from Russia. In chance moments, they conducted their share of touring, admiring art and architecture. Once terms of the peace were agreed upon, the elder waited for official news of his recall. It was not meant to be.

Independence was a given, but future U.S. relations with France and Spain, not just Britain, weighed in the balance. Adams and Jay were adamant, first of all, that the United States should not be closed in by a constricting border with British Canada north of the Ohio River. Second, the new nation had to be guaranteed perpetual access to the all-important Mississippi River. The U.S. negotiators were dead set on restraining future European designs on North America.

Adams was especially insistent on what might have seemed a minor point: letting New England fishermen dry their catch along Newfoundland's shoreline. They already had the right to fish in these waters. It was a matter of regional importance, but it related to larger concerns about Atlantic commerce. While Franklin and especially Jay acquitted themselves well in the final weeks of treating with their British counterparts, Adams stood his ground best with respect to territorial politics. Vergennes was not happy about his government's inability to exert real influence over the terms of the final treaty; he had figured out that any American polity would possess too much pride to accommodate itself to French priorities. All were tired of war.[38]

It is hard to imagine anyone in American history who had so practical a foundation in diplomatic procedure at so young an age as John Quincy Adams. He was a privileged spectator, able to record in his almanac on September 3, 1783, "Signature of the Definitive Treaty." (Congress ratified the Treaty of Paris early in 1784.) As anticlimactic as the event might have appeared to the main participants, his father's experience was rubbing off. Johnny Adams communed in Paris with fellow world travelers, foreign ministers, and men of letters. His social circle consisted of a multigenerational who's who of Europe. He attended theater with these luminaries and used his diary to pen critical reviews. The memory of all this would never fade, just as the Battle of Bunker Hill lived inside him for a lifetime. His father kept the seal he used on September 3, and it passed to John Quincy, who, for all intents and purposes, was serving as his father's personal secretary now.[39]

At the end of that year, father and son saw England together for the first time. It was no idle journey. The elder Adams might have protested his desire to return to the Braintree farm, but he was, in fact, entirely game for a new diplomatic appointment—to London. It was just too important to the nation, and to his needy ego, to refuse the post, if offered. He had once recommended John Jay for the position, conveying the necessary humility to Congress. But he had written to his wife, "I am soberly of Opinion, that for one or two Years to come I could do more good in England to the United States of America, than in any other Spot upon Earth. Much of the immediate Prosperity of the United States, and much of their future Repose, if not the Peace of the World, depends upon having just Notions now forthwith instilled in London." We hardly need to be reminded that this was the same man who had not long before railed against the British, "They hate us, universally from the Throne to the Footstool." Convinced that he was the only man for the job, he fretted all over again about the personal attacks he fully expected. "I think the British Court will be duped by the French and will entertain that dread of me, which neither ought to entertain, but which France will inspire."[40]

He shared everything with his wife. And the papers have been preserved. That is why the charge of pride sticks like glue to his historical reputation. To Abigail, he mused, "I hope it will be permitted to me or to some other who can do it better some Ten or fifteen Years hence, to collect together in one View, my little Negotiations in Europe. Fifty Years hence it may be published, perhaps 20."

When exactly would history be ready to view the papers of a contentious diplomat without prejudice or passion? He thought twenty years might be time enough for memories to cool. "The Situations I have been in between angry Nations and more angry actions, have been some of the most singular and interesting that ever happened to any Man," he reminded his wife, with yet another harangue of the French and Franklin on the verge of exploding from his pen. "The Fury of Ennemies as well as of Elements, the Subtilty and Arrogance of Allies, and what has been worse than all, the jealousy, Envy, and little Pranks of Friends and CoPatriots, would form one of the most instructive Lessons in Morals and Politicks, that ever was committed to Paper." It was almost as if the Revolutionary War were meant to be told, from beginning to end, as a story that centered on the visions and movements of one John Adams.[41]

He resumed his preferred role in directly overseeing—not just assigning—his son's lessons in the classics. They'd sit together over their breakfast coffee, reading aloud, making up for lost time. John constantly fretted that Johnny's education had been irregular; that it was, to a dangerous degree, self-taught, inconstant, and experiential. Tutorials had been administered to him by several different men. If he were to move ahead, it had to be in a proper setting: Johnny required structure and institutional belonging. He had to return home and prepare for Harvard.

Until then, his father wanted to have him situated in London. "Your principal Attention Should be to Parliament, and the Bar," he said to Johnny. "Your Stay will be short and you will not probably have another Opportunity of being much in London, for upon your Return I shall keep you very close to Business and your Studies." When push came to shove, the paterfamilias remained in charge.[42]

Clarissa's Cause

After all is said and done, how do we size up the style and effectiveness of the diplomat John Adams? Emotions colored his approach to foreign transactions—of this there can be no doubt. Beyond what he perceived as Franklin's passivity in dealing with Vergennes, the two "main attractions" from Revolutionary America clearly spoke in different diplomatic tongues.

Adams devoured histories of Europe, seeking inroads, while, if one listens to Adams, Franklin sat and perfected his pose.

In an odd way, both men sexualized the language of diplomacy. Franklin thought he'd win support from the French ministry by being courted like a virgin. He had no illusions that a fragile, untested United States could feign to argue from a position of power. By indirection, or as one scholar has described it, the "ability to coax funds out of the wealthier partner," the canny Franklin succeeded brilliantly. From 1779 to 1783, France lent the United States 21 million livres. Adams, of course, preferred the Dutch as partners. For him, a functional negotiation was conducted not by such coy approaches as his rival colleague resorted to but by seeking common ground and locating similar interests.[43]

His understanding of the French differed from Franklin's in many ways, some of them quite singular and even capricious. At a critical phase in the talks, while he was in Amsterdam, Adams read a newly published four-volume exposé on the private life of the late king Louis XV of France, grandfather of the reigning king Louis XVI, who was at this time not yet thirty. Louis XV had sat on the throne for nearly six decades before his death in 1774, presiding over France's catastrophic defeat in the French and Indian War (1763). Nothing "could have raised France out of that profound degree of Contempt, Misery and Debasement in which Louis the 15 left it," Adams wrote, "without the Seperation of America from Great Britain and her Alliance with France." In that respect, the French government *owed the Americans* for giving it reason to believe it possible to regain some of the advantages it had lost.

Reading the history of Louis XV led John Adams to a story with a moral that depreciated the diplomatic mode of the vaunted Franklin while boosting his own. In rediscovering *Clarissa,* Samuel Richardson's 1748 novel of seduction (another of the many titles he and his son shared), Adams reached an odd epiphany. The novel revolves around the dissolute character of the scheming Robert Lovelace, who succeeds in conquering the virtuous Clarissa Harlowe. In Louis XV, Adams saw an even more choleric version of the dastardly Lovelace. It appeared to him that the moral debasement Louis XV brought to France not only harmed France in the 1760s but lingered on after the monarch's death, affecting government and society into the 1780s.

Pursuing the parallel in his mind, Adams sought to justify his prejudices.

If America was the unsullied virgin nation, it did not have to follow the road Franklin had laid out. It should instead seize the moral high ground. It should take a firm stand and make it plain that French support for the United States was elevating France, helping it to recover its lost morals. In fine, virgin America could not allow itself to be duped by a nation that needed *it*. It should not succumb, Clarissa-like, before a French power broker. The United States was weak, yes, but so was the Dutch Republic. A Dutch Clarissa would have something more to offer, because she knew when to stand up. She'd negotiate from a mutually advantageous position, because she understood her worth.

In Richardson's novel, Clarissa commits suicide. Adams did not want America to be the English Clarissa.

To his ever-sympathetic correspondent Charles Dumas, he enumerated the four bold conclusions he had extracted from recent French history: "1. That France can never desert America. 2. That she ought to exert herself, with Zeal and that she will do it too. 3. That other nations, will do wisely to imitate the Example of France. 4. That the sooner they form Connections with America the more wisely they will act." He really believed that America had rescued France, and not the other way around.[44]

The letter to Dumas was penned prior to Yorktown, when France and America enjoyed a memorable day and forged a kind of camaraderie that was rare in the world. But as important as Yorktown was in cementing national pride, it was not the reckoning that concerned Adams the most. Statecraft consumed him, not warfare. A trial attorney by trade, he saw diplomacy not as tea-table conversation as practiced by Franklin (at least, the way Adams constructed him), a man who enjoyed watching women fawn over him. Adams confidently placed his own legacy next to Franklin's, on opposing scales, and the balance favored his own method, a more proficient brand of diplomacy—a robust forensic battle—a resolute mock war.[45]

That said, the Court of Versailles was not a New England courthouse. And there was more than one way to contend with the nations of Europe. Benjamin Franklin had, no doubt, lost some of his edge. But not everything had to be done Adams's way in order to guarantee the desired outcome.

FOUR

EXILES

One of the foreign Ambassadors said to me, You have been often in England.—Never but once in November and December 1783.—You have Relations in England no doubt.—None at all.—None how can that be? You are of English Extraction?—Neither my Father or Mother, Grandfather or Grandmother, Great Grandfather or Great Grandmother nor any other Relation that I know of or care a farthing for have been in England these 150 Years. So that you see, I have not one drop of Blood in my Veins, but what is American.

—DIARY OF JOHN ADAM, *Paris, May 3, 1785*

Once Dutch recognition of the United States was made official and a preliminary treaty with Great Britain had been put to bed, John Adams had initially thought that the most essential part of his diplomatic assignment was done. At the end of 1782, without waiting for the final Treaty of Paris, he had asked Congress for permission to return home. Congress never acted on his request.

He was left in limbo and torn in two directions. He'd grown ever more insistent that his own elevation to a lead role in diplomacy was utterly essential, in tenuous times, to the future health of his country. In accepting his own judgment as incontrovertible fact, he also pushed himself to place a time limit on his continued separation from his wife and their farm. In a letter to the family friend Mercy Otis Warren, he explained himself in a series of paradoxes: "The Times, Madam, have made a strange Being of me. . . . A Domestic Animal, never at home, a bashful Creature, braving the fronts of the greatest ones of the Earth.—a timid Man, venturing on a long Series of the greatest dangers.—an irritable fiery Mortal, enduring every Provocation and Disgust." This is the Adams image we recognize, the self-portrait proven to have had the longest and most enduring appeal: a lovable curmudgeon. "An humble Farmer, despising Pomp," he added to the mix of contradictions, "Proud as Caesar—But an honest Man in all and to the Death."[1]

The pungent character of this letter was meant not to disguise purposes but to convey frustration. Knowing what he'd sacrificed in removing himself from the American scene, he wrote to another in the months following, "I hope to be married once more . . . to a very amiable Lady whom I have inhumanly left a Widow in America for ~~Eight~~ Nine Years." (This included the time he had spent in the Continental Congress.) His lonely "widow" showered him with affectionate and increasingly nostalgic letters that he could not ignore. Praising his efforts toward achieving an honorable peace for the independent states, Abigail compared the man of modest expectations she had married to the "titled" statesman he had become: "I recollect the untitled Man to whom I gave my Heart, and in the agony of recollection when time and distance present themselves together, wish he had never been any other. Who shall give me back Time? . . . How dearly have I paid for a titled Husband."[2]

She was eminently entitled, too—to her opinion—which she was never reluctant to express. She worried in particular about the lack of adult supervision in Johnny's life: "I hope our dear son abroad will not imbibe any sentiments or principals [*sic*] which will not be agreable to the Laws the Goverment and Religion of our own Country. He has been less under your Eye than I could wish, but never I dare say without your advise [*sic*] and instruction." She had certainly not intended to forfeit influence over Johnny at the time of their second sailing, but that is what happened. During the husband's and son's interminably long absence, she'd alternated between gentle and firm negotiation tactics to persuade the senior diplomat to abbreviate his tour abroad. In the end, Abigail Adams seized the initiative, making the Atlantic crossing with their daughter, Nabby, before John could scoop up Johnny and arrange a return to Boston.[3]

SENTIMENTAL JOURNEY

The two Johns had been on their own and unsupervised by Abigail for too long, and her fears for her son's moral character are impossible to miss; we have abundant reason to suspect that Europe's allure conjured a salacious something to her. Johnny was a small child when she last cast eyes on him, and he was an intrepid traveler now, fully acculturated to his old-world surroundings, as European as he was American.

John Adams might have been a moralist, but he was not a dour one. He could parry sexual innuendo as well as the next man. In 1779, a dinner companion volunteered that there were two methods of learning French, taking a mistress and taking in a theatrical comedy, and he asked Adams which of these options he thought better. Adams smoothly replied that either method would succeed, but both at once was the surer bet. He was proud of his repartee and committed the anecdote to his diary.[4]

There is more to appreciate about his impulses, without resort to voyeurism, that is, without trying to speculate about the sex life of a plain and portly husband living apart from his wife for several years running. Masculine fortitude could be measured, in his world, in terms other than the physical. The fact is that both father and son prized their ability to read the human heart, and if not the most gregarious or festive of partiers, they were accomplished in this realm at least as far as formal gatherings were concerned.

If we return to the subversive power of good fiction in their lives, there is no doubt but that the elder Adams was a solid fan of Laurence Sterne's *Sentimental Journey Through France and Italy* (1768), a bestselling quasi-autobiographical novel that spoke broadly to the pleasures of life. Sterne's riotous script held a special power over the eighteenth-century mind, insisting that moral and sexual satisfactions were not mutually exclusive. If men could talk, without cringing, about going to war, the author (an Anglican minister) allowed that there should be nothing to deter one from openly addressing the natural act of procreation. Eighteenth-century readers of all stripes already had a boozy familiarity with sexual satire and broader caricature. Sterne merely proved that earthy reality could be a muse, that sensual contact was a kind of flight from ever-present death, and that recognizing these things did not have to ruin the emerging ideal of middle-class respectability.[5]

Sterne was just then at the height of his popularity among American readers. The gist of his flirtatious escapade through the same France the Adamses knew was told through his alter ego Yorick, who held that nothing so improved the world as the discovery of one's humanity in the company of others, especially strangers, and most especially winsome women. The author was an unabashed lover of the opposite sex, a fact that did nothing to debase his writing in Yankee eyes. In June 1779, while chatting with a French clerk about his frustrating wait for *La Sensible* to weigh anchor, John Adams joked that he had already been delayed "long enough to have made a Sentimental Journey through the Kingdom." The clerk attested to his love of the late author's spirited narrative, and Adams agreed: "Sterne was the sweetest, kindest, tenderest Creature in the World, and . . . there was a rich Stream of Benevolence flowing like Milk and Honey, thro all his Works."[6]

In the fall of 1783, en route to London, John Quincy was with his father in Calais, on the northern coast of France, where *A Sentimental Journey* opens. At the Hôtel d'Angleterre, where the pair stayed, "the master of the House," Pierre Dessin, announced himself "with a low bow" as the very same character who had welcomed "Yorick" to France. Johnny was tickled to be revisiting literary history, as his sister, Nabby, would be as well when she accompanied her parents to Calais a year and a half later. Abigail Adams would mimic the Sternean idiom in her correspondence with Thomas Jefferson. There was just enough subtlety in Sterne to appeal to a proper gentleman—or even to a proper woman. One did not have to subscribe to the bawdiness, the dissipation, or the leering eye to embrace the modest heroics of the generous-spirited traveler Yorick.[7]

We can assume that Johnny's susceptibility at a young age to the habits of Europe's wealthy and titled, whose sex lives were open and varied, made him less ignorant and less prudish than his father was at that age. At seventeen, with a bow to the pleasures of the flesh, Johnny set forth in his Paris diary, "Mr. Adams dined at the Spanish Ambassador's, Count D'Aranda, an old man 70 years of age who married last year a young woman of 20. Peace be with him!" Sternean drollery is recaptured in such lines as these.[8]

Apart from the episodic adventures of rogue heroes, eighteenth-century literature constantly reminded readers that theirs was an unfeeling world, save for the humane gestures that softened day-to-day encounters. If travel back and forth across the English Channel, or across the Atlantic, was by itself an unsentimental affair for two who were constantly reminded that they risked life and limb in service to their country, theirs was yet a family that appreciated the spirit embodied in Sternean gestures. For them, the Englishman Sterne unmasked falsity as he told essential truths.

John Quincy, at sixteen, might have been without guile, but he was far from being an artless provincial. In the spring of 1784, he was back in London and once more on his own, while his father continued to perform his duties in The Hague. With time to kill, JQA took in numerous theater performances and followed his dad's advice to bear witness to parliamentary debate. In reporting back on the proceedings, he demonstrated a maturing ear for oratory and a growing enthusiasm for the political arts. He did not have to be told that he was observing the best orators of the age.

It was then that he saw in the flesh a young man even more precocious than himself. William Pitt the Younger, who had recently become prime minister at the unheard-of age of twenty-four, impressed John Quincy as the "most pleasing speaker of them all," exuding ease, fluency, and distinctness. "I did not lose a word of what he said, and he was not once embarrassed to express his Ideas." William Wilberforce, also twenty-four, would much later stand at the vanguard of abolitionism. On the day John Quincy heard him, Wilberforce took his friend Pitt's side in debate, but his prowess as a speaker did not excite the young American enough to warrant any prediction as to the MP's future. Sizing up the movers and shakers of a Parliament his stateside contemporaries could only study from afar, the rising student of eloquence submitted his list of speaking attributes for his father's approval.[9]

FAMILY REUNION

When JQA was attending sessions of Parliament and soaking up knowledge of the British system, letters between father and son were but a few days in transit. John admitted he was jealous—rhetorically at least—of his peers whose European missions ended when the war did. "Happy Mr. Jay! Happy Mr. Laurens! in their Prospects of Seeing home," he told John Quincy. "I wish I had been wise enough, to have persisted in my Plan of going home too." But Congress had given him more to do, and Holland would remain his base for some time longer. Watching his colleagues sail home had, he said, "put me to sea, in an Ocean of Uncertainties, public and private." It was then that he beseeched his boy: "Come to me, and help me, for I must remain here now untill the Ladies arrive."[10]

Abigail's shipboard writings attest that theirs, like so many others, was a harrowing voyage. Seasickness lasted weeks; personal hygiene was all but abandoned. On hearing from his wife that she had landed safely in Britain, John replied from The Hague on July 26, 1784, "Your letter of the 23d. has made me the happiest Man upon Earth. I am twenty Years younger than I was Yesterday." He asked Johnny, whom, in words to his wife, he now called "the greatest Traveller, of his Age," to cross back over to England, purchase a coach in London, and bring the women to him.

When "Master John" appeared before her the following week—"O momma and my dear sister!" he exclaimed—Abigail was taken aback by how much he had changed. "I shall feel perfectly safe under his care," she reported back to her husband. John had just learned that Thomas Jefferson was due in Paris, bolstering the U.S. presence there; so, he changed his mind and hastened to London, where the family was finally made whole. On August 7, he left a terse comment in his journal: "Met my Wife and Daughter after a seperation of four Years and an half. Indeed after a Seperation of ten Years, excepting a few Visits." Johnny's older sister, Nabby, had her own take on their reunion: "Sure I am I never felt more agitation of spirit in my life." Save for two younger sons left in the care of relatives, the Adams family was reconstituted.[11]

They all left London for Paris the very next day. Over the next nine months, before her husband's reassignment to London, Abigail gave ample evidence that she was not impressed with French culture. Among the people she met, she was somewhat fond of the refined and indulgent marquise de Lafayette, but made few real friends. The one saving grace was the newly arrived American. Jefferson showed her unfeigned warmth, she felt. The tall, recently widowed Virginian had graciously sought her out in Boston on the eve of her journey. Obliged to wait for a later-departing vessel, he and his young daughter were unable to accompany the Adams women overseas. It was in Paris, then, that they found their rapport.[12]

ADAMS, JEFFERSON

Aside from the inimitable Dr. Franklin, John Adams's record in Europe was matched by none of the other leaders of his generation. His most notable ally in France, John Jay, was a close second. Jay was to take the place of Robert

Livingston in Philadelphia, as secretary for foreign affairs in the Confederation Congress. Otherwise, the only "competition" Adams faced was Jefferson, who was initially Jay's replacement and still wet behind the ears as a diplomat. Jefferson would succeed the exhausted Franklin as minister plenipotentiary at the Court of Louis XVI and remain five years, through the revolutionary storming of the Bastille, the state prison, in 1789.

The sweet-tempered Virginian changed the dynamic. He put a kindly, temperate face on the American presence in Europe. Bulldog-like John Adams would not have been described by anyone as amiable, but he certainly possessed an energetic wit. Jefferson appreciated Adams's toughness and did not find his testiness grating in the way others did. The two men, well matched at the moment of decision in 1776, when they collaborated on the Declaration of Independence, gamely accepted the postwar charge of shared responsibility for their nation's commercial growth and fiscal health. Adams might not have known how to suppress his dark and distrustful thoughts, but to Jefferson, at this time, he represented his country's interests with consummate skill.

Whether it was the calming effect of Jefferson's bearing or Franklin's sincere desire to smooth over his relations with Adams in the presence of family, the old man made for better company during his waning weeks in Paris, in 1784–1785. Jefferson gaily accompanied the now inseparable brother and sister, Johnny and Nabby, on their walking tours of Paris. Though he was famed as a student of language, the Virginian performed better on the page. Neither Nabby nor Mr. Jefferson spoke French with the facility of Johnny—not even close.

"Spent the evening with Mr. Jefferson, whom I love to be with because he is a man of very extensive learning, and pleasing manners," JQA recorded in his diary on March 11, 1785. His father wrote similarly a month later, anticipating removal to London: "Mr. Jefferson is an excellent Citizen, Philosopher, and Statesman, with whom I promise myself the most friendly and Cordial Correspondence, altho' I shall leave him with regret."[13]

These were their halcyon days, when the Jeffersons (father and twelve-year-old daughter) and the Adamses (father, mother, nineteen-year-old daughter, and seventeen-year-old son) overlapped in Paris. In the decade following, relations would rupture when politics set the two principals apart, but at the peak of their post-presidential retirement correspondence, John Adams wistfully recalled for Jefferson how, in Paris, John Quincy was "almost as much your boy as mine." Jefferson, proud of his alma mater, recommended that John Quincy attend the College of William and Mary instead of Harvard.

As evidence of the lasting impact this relatively brief period had on the Adamses, we have the anecdotal testimony of the son forty-five years later, when the second and third presidents were both in their graves. As a defeated president in 1830, alone and deserted and about to take his seat in Congress, JQA entered in his diary the pained lyric he still recalled from the light opera *Richard Coeur de Lion,* which he'd seen in Jefferson's company in 1785:

> *O, Richard! O, mon Roi!*
> *L'univers t'abandonne.*

> When I first heard this song . . . , it made an indelible impression upon my memory, without imagining that I should ever feel its force so much closer home.[14]

If the Paris interlude was an extended moment of relief and release, the entry of the cultivated Virginian into the reconstituted Adams family would make the later experience of disaffection all the more poignant.

Jefferson has been dubbed "nature's man" because of his belief in a positively malleable human nature. He was inspired by all he read about improvements in science and the arts. His friend Adams, eight years his elder, found it harder to imagine the male ego as invested in general improvement: for Adams, their less admirable natural predilections made men needful of considerable social constraints. Adams was self-righteous, gloomy at times, and sensitive to slights; any romanticism he upheld was purely personal. He did not encounter the sublime in the world he traversed. Jefferson was soft-spoken and intellectually stimulated by a language of nervous sensation. He was ruled by an aesthetic that Adams did not embrace: no one ever termed John Adams an Epicurean or a visionary. However, both couched their thoughts in the relationship between power and morals, and as diplomats they shared a deep concern lest other nations exploit America's weaknesses.[15]

One of the outstanding issues they worked on together provides a good example of a shared mind-set and the relative ease with which they communicated their respective ideas. The Barbary powers of North Africa maintained an ugly extortion racket, obliging the nations of Europe to pay protection money so that Mediterranean pirates left their commercial shipping alone. Over the course of many months, Adams and Jefferson debated the pros and cons of an aggressive stance, candidly discussing whether honor had a price tag, that is, how much national honor mattered in treating with a non-Western entity.

They had to partner, because neither was empowered to agree to terms unilaterally or to sign a treaty singly. Adams repeated for Jefferson his odd conversation with the "Tripoline Ambassador," who insisted that his nation was at war with America by dint of there being no treaty in place. "How," Adams posed, "can We preserve our Dignity in negotiating with Such Nations?" After weighing the relative cost in time and money to fight the several North African powers, he concluded, in the interest of American shipping, that the expedient measure of arranging payment made the most sense. Jefferson made it clear that he favored strong action. Despite distance and cost, he proposed that "it would be best to effect a peace thro' the medium of war." He said he believed that if the United States joined forces with Portugal and Naples, both of which had run out of patience with the "Pyratical states," the British, French, Spanish, and Dutch would all eventually see the value of joining their principled "confederacy."

Point by point, they argued a host of options. Adams expended more ink on the subject and was less sanguine than Jefferson as to the ease of defeating their seagoing enemy. Jefferson recognized his colleague's simpler solution as practicable, but he held his own for as long as possible, stating judiciously in the end, "The same facts impress us differently. This is enough to make me suspect an error in my process of reasoning tho' I am not able to detect it." At this moment in their relationship, the novice diplomat found he could not resist the elder's onslaught. No uncivil word ever passed, no overinvestment of ego was displayed, as Adams and Jefferson reasoned their way to a tenable solution.[16]

DIVERGENT LIVES

Americans of this era responded to European society in unpredictable ways. Letters that passed between travelers and their friends stateside tended to confirm the unsuitability of the Continent for young and shielded males; they were expected to find the comparative forwardness of European women initially shocking before succumbing to the freer attitude and sensual charm. American innocence was something of a cliché.

As a couple, John and Abigail would not shed the judgmental ways that attached to New England mores. They were tough nuts. While his parents "endured" the French graces, John Quincy remained open to the social pleasures of Paris because of his impressionable age. If his newfound companion Mr. Jefferson sent his daughter Patsy to a very proper convent school, he himself took readily to the insouciance and expressiveness of the French people.

That said, the Virginia widower and the elder Adamses subscribed to the aesthetic principle that mental pleasures were more permanent than physical ones. Thomas Jefferson and Abigail Adams found recreation in visiting English gardens together. They shared a taste for objets d'art, landscape design, and quiet neighborhoods. They bonded over the perfection of form. It becomes apparent that the cultural distance between educated southerners and their New England counterparts was less than it was to become in the next century, when the moral contest over the effects of slavery made their other differences sharper and their arguments increasingly severe.[17]

Major changes were coming. Johnny did not get to see England again with his father. He did not accompany his sister and mother when they were guests at the hotel in Calais that Sterne made famous. He did not cross the Channel with his family or bear witness when, on June 1, 1785, King George III officially received his father as America's first minister to the Court of St. James's. Instead, he acquiesced in his parents' wishes and returned alone to Boston. In mid-May, he "took leave of Mr. Jefferson," stopped by the Franklin residence one last time, bore up through a difficult farewell scene with father, mother, and sister, and went by cabriolet, several days ahead of the rest of his family, in a different direction. He kept his diary going as he moved along choppy, dusty, wearying roads; he found a room one night in a cobwebbed inn "where half-starv'd spiders feed on half-starv'd flies." He arrived at Lorient, a port he already knew well, and prepared for his next unsentimental journey.[18]

Altogether, Johnny Adams had been away from his native Boston for six critical years. Because father, mother, and sister would remain in England until 1789, he alone among them would be in New England when the nation obtained its ultimate governing instrument, the federal Constitution. He had to recommit to his roots, and it was not as automatic as one might expect. He was dragooned into reading even more intensively than he was accustomed to, because he was insufficiently prepared for the rigors of Harvard College. His practical-minded parents wished him to succeed as a lawyer, and he could not set aside their expectations easily. John Quincy's future was by no means settled. He would trade on the family name—he could hardly avoid that—but he still had to earn high grades at college and, after that, earn a living.

The intellectual journey from Paris, France, to Cambridge, Massachusetts, began uneasily. In consultation with his wife, John Adams sent out feelers from England to two influential contacts: Harvard's president, Joseph Willard, and Harvard Medical School's first "Professor of the Theory and Practice of Physic," Benjamin Waterhouse. Johnny would deliver his father's letters by hand. (Father and son had already established a close friendship with Waterhouse as a result of his years of study at the University of Leiden.) It was not the last time John Adams would try to intervene in the interest of his son's advancement.

The appeal to President Willard is carefully drawn. In anticipation of sending his largely French-speaking son back to the United States to train for a public career, John was defensive: "He has wandered with me in Europe for Seven Years, and has been for the last Eighteen months my only Secretary. . . . I shall part with him only with Reluctance." But the "necessity of breeding him to some Profession, in which he may provide for himself" persuaded him, in this standard construction, to recommend the boy for Harvard.

To the thirty-one-year-old Waterhouse, John wrote somewhat differently. He was forthcoming about his fears and unabashed in boasts about his son's talents. He knew Harvard's entry requirements were stiff for one who intended to take up the law: "He must undergo an Examination, in which I

Suspect he will not appear exactly what he is." John Quincy had squeezed in study amid travel, "without any Steady Tutor." He was "Aukward in Speaking Latin," and his Greek had suffered, too. On the other hand, "in Roman and English history . . . it is rare to find a youth possessed of So much Knowledge." He had translated Virgil's *Aeneid,* Tacitus's *Agricola,* "a great part of Horace," and some of Caesar's *Commentaries*. As for mathematics and geometry, his father was his teacher, which was both good and bad, as John Adams saw it. Listing the various texts they had used, he admitted that it had been thirty years since he had learned the same skills: "He is as yet but a smatterer like his Father."[19]

The lone voyager almost did not arrive at all. On the high seas, amid "squalls and thunderstorms" in the neighborhood of "the Bermudas" (in the Triangle, where, even then, sailors took particular note of strange weather patterns), uncertainty reigned. Through it all, Johnny maintained his diary. On July 4, 1785, he wrote expectantly, "I wish'd very much to arrive in America before this day, which is the greatest day in the year, for every true American." He knew the high seas, and he knew both the opulence and the impoverishment of the Old World. His frame of reference did not yet include much of America.[20]

He had already been at sea fifty days when he marked the national holiday. New York lay in the invisible distance, some days ahead, and Cambridge beyond that. When he finally reached dry land, he lolled about Manhattan for a while. When he finally met with Harvard's president, Willard, he was probably not shocked to hear that his Latin and Greek were subpar. But the youth carried the name of Adams, and so Willard put a plan in place: JQA would catch up to his peers under the tutelage of his mother's brother-in-law, who was a respected pastor. The returnee thus took his place in an unfamiliar household, thirty-five miles north of Boston, in Haverhill, near the New Hampshire border.

Meanwhile, so soon after the Treaty of Paris, London was not exactly friendly territory for Johnny's father and mother. But it strangely suited them both. To John Jay, in a statement presumably intended for liberal circulation, the senior American diplomat did his best to re-create the dialogue that took place at his royal introduction. John Adams spared no detail, highlighting the king's amusement in coaxing him: "There is an Opinion among some People that you are not the most attached of all your Countrymen to the Manners of France." To which, Adams replied, "That Opinion, Sir, is not mistaken." Speaking further, he said, "I must avow to your Majesty, I have no Attachment but to my own Country." The king, as Adams tells it, "replied as quick as Lightning an honest man will never have any other."[21]

The inaugural U.S. minister to Great Britain was profoundly moved by the singular character of what had just occurred, as anyone in his position would be. But there was otherwise nothing glamorous about John, Abigail, and Nabby Adams's arrival in London. The pleasure it might have afforded them was tempered by the tenderness all three felt in separating from their Johnny. Abigail wrote to her sister in Massachusetts, "You can hardly form an Idea of how much I miss my son." She reckoned she would soldier on, doing what was required of the wife of a diplomat (although she deeply resented the "Tory venom" she forced herself to read in London's newspapers). She took solace in the fact that the king had assured John, at the time of their interview, that his country had made a sound choice by appointing him. And if "News Liars" persisted in their criticisms, the protective wife would take to heart the treatment she received from the queen, who said to her directly, "I am glad to see you in this Country."

For her part, Nabby Adams wrote to her aunt that she had lost "a good Brother." She wished that he had been "induced to stay" but added unselfishly, "If he is to spend his Life in America it was time for him to go there, for by so long an absence and at so early a period of his life, he had never acquired or greatly lost just ideas of the Country, People, manners, and Customs." Nabby understood that America and Europe were so unalike that if Johnny had remained too long abroad he would never be happy anywhere else. (JQA had said the same about Temple Franklin.)

The reaction of Samuel Adams to the lad's appearance at his door was simply ecstatic. When John Quincy Adams hand delivered a letter from his father, the illustrious Revolutionary cousin answered sweetly, "The *Child* whom I led by the Hand with a particular Design, I find is now become a promising Youth. . . . God bless the Lad! If I was instrumental at that Time of enkindling Sparks of Patriotism in his tender Heart, it will add to my Consolation in the latest Hour."[22]

These were mixed blessings, because Johnny Adams was in exile. Or felt as much. He bowed to the necessity of reestablishing himself in America, but that did not mean he was ready to disconnect from his father, after they had grown to rely so heavily on each other. For one, he knew how much he was missing out on. Additionally, and no less weighty on his mind, he worried for his father's well-being, even if his mother and sister were present to tend to his needs.[23]

Their separation affected both, but in perusing JQA's diary for the immediate period after his return from Europe, one also sees a long-deferred bonding with members of his own generation. His coterie included a host of provincials, and his mind turned to the opposite sex. Almost from the day he disembarked in New York, the daily record is peppered with reports of what young female he finds "fair" and which "Miss" is a true "beauty"; on one particular day, he identified his teatime companions as "a number of ugly Ladies." Female "affectation" consumed and confounded the eighteen-year-old.

His time in New York produced some of the liveliest work of his pen to date. When one of his new acquaintances showed him her satire on "the young Ladies of the City," he passed critical judgment on the effort while allowing that it had prompted him to try his own hand at poetry: "I am trying to see if I can say something not so bad in the same way. And though I see I have no talent at all versifying yet like all fathers I have a partiality for my own offspring however ugly they may be." Over the next week, he tamely admitted that his versified product was "insipid."[24]

He was going through a phase, as we might say, awkward and giddy in the absence of adult supervision, balancing adolescent impulses with scholarly energies he could not long displace if he was to fulfill his parents' wishes and one day inherit his father's mantle. Eventually, John Quincy Adams's poetic effusions would go from insipid to inspired, his offspring multiplying in number and in beauty and presented to appreciative fans as gifts. But that day lay far in the future.

In a way, the uncertainty in his bearing matched that of his country, independent yet unformed. During the year leading up to his enrollment at Harvard, he continued (as he put it) "sketching Characters" in his diary so as to provide himself with a future reminder "of the opinion I shall have formed of the respective persons." Character sketches of women were the more elaborate and generally encompassed both physical attributes and capacity for intellectual companionship. He took interest in the pleasing countenance of one "very genteel" young lady who was marred only by a "little twist in the position of her eyes," and he added self-consciously, "She is sociable, but unfortunately I cannot be so with a stranger."

He dissected his own moods after each social encounter. He set down muted memoranda on the order of this ostensible appeal to the gods: "When our Reason is of variance with our heart, the mind cannot be in a pleasing State." His adolescent ruminations included the possibility of at once loving and despising another person. He wrote to buoy himself: "No Love can be permanent but what is founded on esteem; such there may be a temporary attachment to a person who we are sensible is wholly unworthy of it. And such must be I imagine, the conquests of a Coquette who though she may be beloved is esteemed by none." Something was stirring within, but as determined as he was, he did not quite name it.[25]

Nearly a year passed before word reached John Adams in England that his son was college-bound. He had reinterviewed with the Harvard faculty and demonstrated sufficient knowledge of the classics. He would enter as a junior (not uncommon at this time), his tuition waived in recognition of his father's sacrifice of ease and steady service to the nation. The long, intervening year before college had given the eldest son of John Adams time to think. He did not have to be told what was expected of him and matriculated at Harvard with sincere convictions. Slightly older than most of his classmates, he obeyed the rules, resisting immoderate drinking and the raucous behavior that many students of the time indulged in. Perhaps he'd sown a few wild oats during his gap year, dancing and learning to play the flute, but he'd come to accept that it was not enough to show up with a résumé that featured unprecedented exposure to the world. The chastened student took well to math, science, and natural philosophy. He graduated second in his class in 1787, prepared to follow in his father's footsteps, to seek a reputation by going into private law practice.

HOOKING TURGOT

During his time in London, given that first, most promising royal reception, John Adams made less headway than hoped for on behalf of his nation. He kept busy, which, for him, was never enough. Anglo-American relations lacked dynamism. He remained in exile, while others back home rose and led.

The independent wanderers were equally unsettled. If the younger required time to exchange contexts as he primed for college, the years in Europe disadvantaged the elder even more. He came across a mere handful of his former colleagues and had only secondhand access to internal American crises and political gossip. He had yet to meet either James Madison or Alexander Hamilton, two whose low opinion of him would be creating dire difficulties for John Adams in the not distant future. He inspected the newly completed text of the federal Constitution from his perch in London.

Despite these drawbacks, he read deeply in history with the aim of contributing his thoughts on the nation's political experiment. By publishing in London, beginning in January 1787, he announced a desire to resume his once influential role on the American scene. A course was now set. John Adams would see to it that his voice was heard, which would eventually lead his eldest son, in 1791, to shed what remained of political innocence and take up his pen in defense of his father's honor.

The treatise that the angst-ridden American minister to England decided to compose dwelled on urgent issues before his thoughtful countrymen in 1787: natural nobility, political wisdom, and good government. Three volumes appeared in rapid succession under the combined title *A Defence of the Constitutions of Government of the United States of America*. John Adams's work was available stateside throughout the critical period when the federal Constitution came up for debate across the states.

His philosophy of government came about as a function of his distaste for the political thinking he took notice of in France, though we are quick to add that his work was not pro-British either. As a diplomat, we know, Adams had never warmed up to the French. This was never a secret. He dismissed some of their best political thinkers as impractical men. In Paris, he was exposed to (but not attracted by) the liberal nobility who would dominate the scene in the first stages of the French Revolution. Philosophes whose well-publicized thoughts about human happiness helped hasten the king's overthrow symbolized for Adams the disruptive potential of political optimism. It is no less true that the slow denouement of those ponderous talks that yielded the Treaty of Paris caused Adams to lose faith in the titled Frenchmen whose vaunted "genius" impressed so many others. Of course, his discomfiture also left him appearing to many as a vain pessimist.

One of the central themes of the *Defence*—the portion that has received most attention over the years—concerns the putative failure of Europe's elites to comprehend the logic of American nation building. Adams's main target was the late French finance minister Anne-Robert-Jacques Turgot. Three years before his death in 1781, at the moment when the Franco-American alliance was forged, Turgot had written a letter to Dr. Richard Price in London. Price, who was a moral philosopher and a strong voice in favor of American liberty, appended Turgot's letter to a work that appeared in 1784. Its title must be spelled out for its full effect: *Observations on the Importance of the American Revolution, and the Means of Making It a Benefit to the World*. That is how John Adams came to the matter.

His problem with Turgot was uncomplicated. The Frenchman's prescription for building better republics (below the national level) leaned toward a unicameral legislature. Turgot did not seriously examine the bicameral option that Massachusetts established when Adams made productive use of his brief sojourn in Boston between voyages on *La Sensible*. But what really irked Adams as he waded through Turgot's uneven discussion was the powerful influence of Benjamin Franklin. Turgot had gotten an earful from Franklin, circa 1776, on the subject of Pennsylvania's unicameral legislature. While Franklin left Europe for good in 1785, his influence lingered on. Price's publication poured salt into Adams's open wound.

Adams had met Turgot once, in March 1778, just a couple of weeks, as it happened, before Turgot wrote his consequential (now controversial) letter to Price. The very idea of a French politico presuming to tell war-tested Americans how to manage their country chafed at John Adams. He had spent enough time in France to be convinced that its vast, ignorant peasant population, hampered by a servile "Romish" clergy and utterly unrepresentative, overbearing nobility, could neither prescribe nor properly value the quality of liberty Americans were already finding. Adams had not been in London long when he read Price's *Observations* and appendix, seeing Turgot's 1778 letter for the first time. He did not adopt an openly hostile attitude when the *Defence* was first published in 1787, but in reprintings after 1794 the subtitle announced the work in a more hyperbolic manner: *Against the Attack of M. Turgot*.[26]

What constituted an attack? For his part, Dr. Price obligingly pronounced America's superiority over his native land of Great Britain, where there were "abuses so gross as to make our boasts of liberty ridiculous." The United States was primed to become a "refuge to the world"; it was a place where "the way is open to social dignity and happiness." Praising the Massachusetts state constitution that John Adams had largely composed, Price noted that the Bay State was sensibly constructed so as to confine power to a proper number of popular representatives. "It has been often justly observed," wrote Price, with Adamsian certitude, "that a legislative body very numerous is little better than a *mob*." Adams had no beef with Richard Price.[27]

Turgot, communicating with Price in French, had written with incomplete information. He seemed to be saying that the United States did not need to construct a balanced government composed of an executive and a bicameral legislature (such that Adams was about to introduce in his home state). As Turgot imagined it, doing so would merely be to replicate the tripartite British system of Commons, Lords, and king.

Turgot's letter was imprecise, but it was respectful, certainly not aggressive. It concurred with Dr. Price's pro-American stance, declaring of the former colonies, "They are the hope of the world." On this basis, Adams should have seen Turgot's letter as reasonable and cautionary. On the other hand, Turgot did describe America in 1778 as a "jumble of communities," each with its own laws and "discordant" elements; it was, to Turgot's mind, something less than a "coalition," closer to a "copy" of the disjointed Dutch Republic. He did not see America as a properly fused nation in waiting.

Worse for Adams was that Turgot, a former French government official, crudely alluded to the retention in New England of the "rigid" and "intolerant" character of seventeenth-century Puritans. Adams penned margin notes in his copy of the Price-Turgot pamphlet, roundly dismissing Turgot's assessment: "This Letter is a mass of wild, inconsistent Reveries & Paradoxes." Of the unicameral/bicameral discussion, he wrote preciously, "Emptier piece of declamation I never read: it is impossible to give a greater proof of ignorance." The Puritan dig was one thing; there was no excuse for failing to appreciate republican theory as it concerned separation of powers.[28]

Historians debate to this day whether Turgot, who served King Louis XVI, was a greater admirer of enlightened despotism, constitutional monarchy, or republicanism. Yet aside from the Franklin factor, it is hard to explain Adams's extreme reaction to so minimal a critique. If he was not the "sometimes absolutely mad" character Franklin perceived, or a nervous critic acting out his martyr complex, then he was simply using Turgot as a "hook" in order to command the conversation and give further justification for his massive *Defence of the Constitutions of Government of the United States of America*. As one recent scholar has proposed, Adams "may have been thinking of opinions he had heard expressed verbally in Paris, but then chose to target Turgot because his letter was in print."[29]

The first volume of Adams's *Defence* was written over a period of mere months. It sprang from a relatively brief period of "Phylosophic Solitude" in London, during which Abigail spent time touring. She wrote to John Quincy upon her return, "Your pappa enjoys better Health than I believe he has for many years, reads & writes every Evening." And that must have been true, but John Adams clearly felt the urgency of the project. He tendered his resignation in a letter to Congress early in 1787, saying he felt he could accomplish nothing more of consequence as U.S. minister in London. Or, as his wife more colorfully put it, "England has wholy forgotten that Such a place as America ever existed."[30]

That tone is preserved in the *Defence,* which presumes to explain, from the author's firsthand knowledge, what Turgot, the French intellectual class, and the leaders of Great Britain could only distantly guess at: the intellectual sources and historical scholarship that stood behind the American state constitutions. Adams was intent on presenting evidence that the political class of his country was profoundly aware of the unique opportunities that lay before it. And he, John Adams, was not unwilling to admit to a desire to influence the next stage of constitutional deliberation. His son was at home, reporting to him on political events in Massachusetts, where he, as well, wanted to be.

In the preface to the first volume of the *Defence,* the only one of the volumes that found an American audience during the Constitutional Convention, Adams insisted that "the best and wisest prince" (meaning the national sovereign, chief authority, or architect of policy) had "an immense advantage in a free state over a monarchy." It was premature to propose that the United States move in a democratic direction; therefore, he placed his hope in "a senate consisting of all that is most noble, wealthy, and able in the nation," serving as "a check to ministers, and a security against abuses." A second body, "composed of representatives chosen by the people in all parts," would give voice to "the whole nation," communicating "all its wants, knowledge, projects, and wishes to government." This more democratic assembly would, Adams assured readers, answer the purpose of republican government by dignifying the popular will: "It excites emulation among all classes, removes complaints, redresses grievances . . . and gives full scope to all the faculties of man." The relatively small U.S. population made tolerance of this degree of popular expression feasible.[31]

Later in the text, Adams elaborates on the same principle in remarking that the natural bounty of America fed a hearty, free, and alert agricultural population. "The truth is," he writes, "the people have ever governed in America: all the weight of the royal governors and councils, even backed with fleets and armies, have never been able to get the advantage of them, who have always stood by their houses of representatives in every instance, and carried all their points; and no governor ever stood his ground against a representative assembly; as long as he governed by their advice he was happy; as soon as he differed from them he was wretched, and soon obliged to retire." Here we see, from a New England perspective, how democracy could, in fact, work.[32]

If only democratic rights were universally understood and easy to sustain. But because a tendency to corruption existed in every branch of government, Adams's first faith still lay with the mindful class of men he considered most trustworthy, who needed to congregate in a place apart from less exceptional minds—an upper house. "The rich, the well-born, and the able," he wrote, "acquire an influence among the people that will soon be too much for simple honesty and plain sense, in a house of representatives. The most illustrious of them must, therefore, be separated from the mass, and placed by themselves in a senate." Adams's practical concern about any across-the-board popular election boiled down to a single fact: "The multitude have always been credulous, and the few are always artful." Fancy speech could win votes or persuade common people to support bad ideas. Thus far, the states had proven themselves alert in this regard, which led him to project, "If men are now sufficiently enlightened to disabuse themselves of artifice, imposture, hypocrisy, and superstition," the public good would be protected.

As the inventor of a new political taxonomy, Adams saw himself as a successor to the political theorists Niccolò Machiavelli and Montesquieu, with a smattering of Michel de Montaigne on the human condition thrown in. Still, his first principles most often brought him into dialogue with the ancients: "The practicability or the duration of a republic, in which there is a governor, a senate, and a house of representatives, is doubted by Tacitus, though he admits the theory to be laudable." He had answers for Tacitus, whom he assumed would have been impressed with American political sentiments. Regarding Cicero, his preeminent model of statesman and philosopher for all ages, that man's "decided opinion in favor of three branches" was rooted in respect for the laws as "the only possible rule, measure, and security of justice" in a republic. "*Respublica est res populi*," Adams reminded readers. The republic is the people.

He noted hypothetically (and controversially, in light of accusations subsequently made with respect to his alleged monarchical leanings), "A simple monarchy, if it could in reality be what it pretends to be, a government of laws, might be justly denominated a republic. A limited monarchy, therefore, especially when limited by two independent branches, an aristocratical and a democratical power in the constitution, may with strict propriety be called by that name." Americans had enjoyed protections under the British constitution for a century and a half, and they knew, even as revolutionaries, what values it contained.

In the end, there was no contest between British and American models. "If Cicero and Tacitus could revisit the earth," he added dreamily, they would have liked what they saw of the amount of freedom exercised in America. The future beckoned. As he thought of the implications of all that was brewing in 1787, he took unusual license: "The institutions now made in America will not wholly wear out for thousands of years. It is of the last importance, then, that they should begin right. If they set out wrong, they will never be able to return, unless it be by accident, to the right path." It was a bold pronouncement, and one that arguably speaks to every modern generation.[33]

It is when he arrives at letter 25 in the body of the *Defence* that Adams condemns Turgot for having written an irresponsible prescription for the new United States. He yokes Turgot, the unknowing supporter of a naive unicameralism, to the imperfect reasoning of Franklin. Relying on Pennsylvania as his model, Turgot "was led to censure" the other state constitutions voted on in the period after independence was declared. Adams's condemnation reflects both reasonable concern and unreasonable fixation: first, his concern that the 1778 Franco-American alliance led too many Americans to accept too many French ideas too easily; and second, his fixation with an unabashedly pro-French Franklin. At least symbolically, the Philadelphian constitutes the subtext of Adams's critique. The subtitle of the *Defence* could have been: *Against the Attack of M. Franklin*.[34]

Turgot was dead in 1787, but Franklin was back home in his latest incarnation as a revered patriot, the octogenarian assuming a modest but not inconsequential role in proceedings at the Constitutional Convention. James Madison recorded Franklin's bright thought as delegates were signing the document and the old man sat pondering the stylized sun painted on the top rail of the convention president George Washington's mahogany chair. The "vicissitudes" of his hopes and fears had left Franklin for a time uncertain. "But now at length," he said, "I have the happiness to know that it is a rising and not a setting Sun." Similarly, the Maryland delegate James McHenry recorded in his diary that with signatures affixed, and as he emerged from Independence Hall, the pithy Franklin was ready with a quip for the ages. A woman approached with a question: "What have we got a republic or a monarchy—" "A republic[,] replied the Doctor[,] if you can keep it."[35]

People still tell these stories of Franklin at the Constitutional Convention. No one reminisces about John Adams's long-winded *Defence of the Constitutions*. Perhaps, though, they should, because the oft-disparaged work actually says a lot, of enduring value, on the subject of democracy.

ADAMSIAN DEMOCRACY

Volume 1 of the *Defence* is not a detailed defense of America's state constitutions, the overall title notwithstanding. Nor is it a line-by-line parsing of Adams's Massachusetts state constitution of 1780. What it did was to call attention to historical knowledge, drawing thematic examples from Plato's *Republic*, remote Swiss cantons of the Middle Ages, and political philosophers such as Machiavelli, James Harrington, John Milton, and John Locke. Adams's concerted plan was to deliver up a history of democratic theory, hoping to demonstrate to readers how to tell a bad government from a good one.

"Free government" is superior to even the most "virtuous prince," he begins. Free government allowed for the "collection of advice" from the people, offered "free access," and created an environment where all communicated "wants, knowledge, projects, and wishes." Active political engagement was a deterrent to abuses that came from self-aggrandizing factions of the "rich, the wellborn." Adams states it unequivocally: "There can be no free government without a democratical branch in the constitution."[36]

Here was the key: democracy required direct, fairly constant, and unfailingly accurate information from citizens to their representatives. Adams had embraced the precept in 1776 that representatives must mirror their constituents. He wrote something similar in the *Defence,* in asserting that representatives had to embody the "sense of the people, the public voice." He analogized: "The perfection of the portrait consists in its likeness." He strongly endorsed annual elections, and he praised the revolutionaries, not for leading, but for following the good sense of the people. How, though, was the popular voice to be heard? No verifiable solution followed. So far, the argument was abstract.[37]

If Turgot provided the hook for the three-volume *Defence,* another Frenchman assumed an equally important role in Adams's evolving thesis: the political historian Abbé de Mably. A letter from Adams to Mably was appended to volume 1. Mably had thought to write a history of the American Revolution, which in turn led Adams to identify the local institutions that had helped mobilize the movement for independence in his native state. Four institutions provided the training grounds for political dissent and political consent: townships (town meetings), schools, churches, and militia. It was the town meeting, Adams said, that most meaningfully schooled the people in the art of political communication. Here, "all the inhabitants acquire, from their infancy, a custom of discussing, deliberating, and judging of public affairs" so that they may "give instructions to their representatives." Local knowledge was the foundation for any kind of democratic system. The town meeting lay at the core of his faith.[38]

Not surprisingly, then, education held a position of prominence in the Adamsian method for improving democratic institutions. In the Massachusetts Constitution, he insisted that the state pay for the early education of all boys. He reiterated this proviso in the *Defence,* invoking an ancient Greek legislator, the little-known Charondas, who said that "all sons of every family" must learn to read and write at public expense. Adams could hardly have been more enthusiastic about his obscure reference: "This law alone has merit enough to consecrate to immortality the memory of this legislator and deserves to be imitated by every free people."[39]

Adams's state-directed education policy did not stop with the one example. He took up considerable space addressing Plato's theories of the republic. He had praise for Plato's idealized state of philosopher-kings and a guardian class that trained its sons to be geniuses, yet he understood quite well that Plato's republic was a dream. For it to exist, social fairness, or the general good, would have to be ensured. The state would have to countenance "no parties of poor and rich at war" and no hereditary favoritism. The vicious son of a guardian would have to be demoted to a lesser class.[40]

Plato helped the American political philosopher fashion a model of degeneration as he turned to the nature of corrupt republics. Wealth, Adams explained, was a moral disease that converted an ambitious republic (stage one), while it acquired strength through military prowess, into an oligarchy (stage two), "in which the rich bear rule, and the poor have no share in the government." Oligarchy becomes democracy once an "insatiable desire to be rich" consumes all members of that flawed society. The shift from oligarchy to democracy occurs when education is neglected. "Youth grow licentious," and a poor yet robust man learns to despise every weak, pampered, indulgent rich man, unfit for battle, whom he sees as "good for nothing." By this definition, democracy was a kind of unstructured, reactive form, prone to corruption as much as oligarchy was. While any republic was prone to corruption and required a balance among interests, free-for-all democracy was not a solution to anything. Owing to an inescapable trait of so-called civilized society, the tendency to fixate on acquiring personal wealth, democracy magnified resentments.[41]

Key concepts emerge from Platonic political theory. One is the idea, which Adams repeats elsewhere in the *Defence,* that wealth and avarice are driving forces in social psychology and that republics are unable to maintain justice or preserve rule of law where a gross imbalance exists in the distribution of land and wealth. As the political theorist Bruce Miroff has astutely observed, Adams believed that "once wealth and luxury became principal marks of distinction, avarice would corrode even the strongest republican structures." Wealth corrupted democracies (or democratic republics), because widespread economic inequality led inevitably to sedition and rebellion.[42]

It was axiomatic for Adams that in America's mainly agrarian society land was power. He borrowed from an odd assortment of sources, including the Old Testament, Aristotle, and Harrington, in reinforcing Plato's portrait of imbalance in wealth leading to imbalance of political power. If a man in possession of one hundred pounds had one servant, Adams mused, then a man with a hundred times that amount would control a hundred servants. He interpolated easily when applying the same theory to the distribution of landed property. Only if "the people" owned the majority of its land could a democratic republic last.[43]

Swiss cantons struck Adams as the most attractive model for democracy, and they resembled New England townships in many ways. Though not strictly definable as pure democracies, the cantons achieved widespread social equality. That of Glarus joined the Swiss Confederacy in 1352 as one of the original eight cantons, a citizen-soldier polity that was able to resist invading armies because of its isolated situation in the Alps. As Adams retold its history, he identified the one distinction in that society: subtle variations in the size of houses. Every home was built of wood, "those of the richest inhabitants only differing from those of the poorer, as they are larger." The inhabitants of Glarus were not taken with wealth or luxury, nor did they indulge their heirs. It was, Adams concluded, a government that guaranteed the "greatest happiness for the greatest number," producing an honest, dignified, and generous people.[44]

The next archetype in his Platonic examination of republics was the one that exploited people's natural weaknesses and fed greed. Here, the laws and constitution favored the rich—the first step toward a devaluation of education, expertise, and merit. According to Plato, democracy was prone to producing fragmented societies, wherein people indulged their senses and liberty turned to licentiousness. Everyone behaved in "whatever way he pleases"—individualism run amok. This society was, in fact, quite close to the consumer culture of our own day, with an impatient public that has to be constantly entertained. Its political leaders were chosen not in light of their talents or practical experience but for adroitness in flattering the masses, singing the public's praises. Reason and learning were supplanted by "boasting" and "impudence"; modesty and moderation dissolved into "stupidity" and "unmanliness." In a corrupt democracy, Adams concluded, there were no adults in charge and no respect for the law. Everyone mimicked the immaturity of youth.[45]

He was as wary of tendencies to oligarchic rule. Throughout history, oligarchies were run by prominent wealthy families. Just as Machiavelli observed, cunning princes manipulated family factions so as to stay in power. Even in his home region of New England, Adams saw how proud family lines promoted factionalism and posed a threat to political fairness. Nothing was a better breeding ground for aristocratic rule than Turgot's and Franklin's single-body assembly.[46]

In the United States at the time of Adams's writing, a competition for control of political discourse pitted Federalists against Anti-Federalists, those who praised the Constitutional Convention for producing a strong national system versus those who feared that the federal governing instrument had created a centralizing, not a liberty-granting, institutional arrangement. In this instance sounding like an Anti-Federalist, Adams opined that federal elections could weaken democratic republics, that voters needed to know candidates personally. He suspected that popular politics would be compromised when individuals ran for statewide office, and would become an even worse problem in nationwide elections. Imperfect knowledge opened the door to intrigue and deception: ambitious elites, unaccountable to their constituents, would use artifice—his phrase was "every popular art"—to advance the party's interest. Devotion to party would undermine the goal of genuine representation. The one with the "deepest purse, or the fewest scruples," he warned prophetically, "will generally prevail." Without a doubt, corruptibility lay at the crux of John Adams's political thinking. He regarded oligarchy and democracy as two governing systems equally subject to corruption, owing to ineradicable imperfections in the human character.[47]

Adams's combined enthusiasm for the republican form and his caution over the seeds of corruption planted in a representative democracy have been underreported during the last two centuries of intellectual history. In fact, his meditative critique instructs us that he was no mere curmudgeon. He was, rather, a severe student of government who refused to allow his nationalism to blind him to danger signs already present. His theory has merit. He saw that the most democratic instrument—the election—relied on the power of "show," whereby candidates invented public identities in order to acquire attention and impress voters. Political aspirants would always put image over integrity. What he had written to James Warren back in 1778, he repeated now, a decade later, in the *Defence:* too often, hard-core politicos were arrogant pretenders or crass peddlers—or both. "A Man must be his own Trumpeter," he lamented in the letter to his trusted friend. "He must dress, have a Retinue, and Equipage, he must ostentatiously publish to the World his own Writings with his Name. . . . He must get his Picture drawn, his statue made, and must hire all the Artists in his Turn, to set about Works to Spread his Name, make the Mob stare and gape, and perpetuate his Fame."

We see in these embittered lines John Adams's lifelong sense of his own incompleteness. He did not know how to separate himself from his political theory; he regarded himself as an underappreciated voice of honest ideas, surpassed in the public mind by men of intrigue for whom self-serving acts came easily. He knew how to advance himself the way these others did, as he stated directly to Warren, but he was held back by his scruples: "I would Undertake, if I could bring my Feelings to bear it, to become one of the most celebrated trumpeted, Admired, courted, worshipd Idols in the whole World in four or five Years."

But that was not all. As Adams saw it, a political climber was unendingly engaged in personal empire building: "He must get his Brothers, Cousins, sons and other Relations into Place about him and must teach them to practice all the same Arts both for them selves and him. He must never do any Thing for any Body who is not his Friend, or in other Words his Tool." This was precisely how he would come to view the tactics of his truest nemesis in the decade upcoming, the ever-intriguing Alexander Hamilton. "You and I have had an ugly Modesty about Us," he finished the fanfare, comfortable in unloading to Warren. "We have taken even Pains to conceal our Names, We have delighted in the shade, We have made few Friends, no Tools."[48]

You and I? Of the two of them, only James Warren of Plymouth, prominent in the early days of the Revolution, proved himself able to exist in the shade, private, secluded, and largely uninspected by history. Adams, of course, was being less than transparent. While he might have battled with his egoistic impulses, he invariably found ways to put forward his name. The *Defence* was his most ambitious self-advertisement to date.

FAMILY MATTERS

By analyzing Adams's perspective on political society, we see how he perceived dangers and why he insisted on the separation of powers into three branches. He had an abiding faith in political structures to contain the worst of human impulses, which in turn explains his reverence for the law and his view that state constitutions were the building blocks of civil society. Still, he could not entirely work out the corrosive problems he was able to identify. Legal checks on private power, self-interest, and family pride were never foolproof.

As for his critique of birth and breeding, his impatience with "illustrious families," and his concern about oligarchic tendencies, we must ask whether he bore in mind his own growing ambition for his eldest son. He had seen up close how inherited prejudice in favor of certain names allowed individuals to enjoy the affection of the public without giving them the necessary scrutiny. In Massachusetts, the name of Winthrop was still venerated a century and a half after the first of that name helped to found the Bay Colony. In every village across New England, familiar surnames filled important offices, generation after generation. Though Adams remained confident in Americans' continuing to scoff at frivolous aristocratic pretense, he was just as convinced about the potential harm that the power of family privilege posed. Those without a name had to work harder to secure political office, he said, and be "better at it" than the anointed offspring of distinguished genealogies.

Curiously, the *Defence* is written as a series of letters to Adams's personal secretary and new son-in-law, Nabby's Princeton-educated husband, William Stephens Smith. Why, in adopting the conventional mode of epistolary essay writing, he chose Smith as the recipient of his political wisdom, rather than his own son, is a mystery unless seen as necessary distancing. John Quincy had benefited from privileges granted by his father's diplomatic connections, by introductions to public characters across Europe. The father admitted that "wise men beget fools, and honest men knaves," but he also felt that by dint of a superior education parents could cultivate in their progeny a "likeness" in mind and heart. Conversely, vice and infamy, it was thought, could be passed down in families; the Adamses would rue the fates of John Quincy's younger brothers, Charles and Thomas, whose alcoholism finally defeated them. It is entirely possible, then, that the author of the *Defence* consciously redirected attention away from his biological offspring in order to center his thoughts on grand historical phenomena.[49]

Though he did not write the *Defence* to influence the Constitutional Convention, the first volume was widely read and praised. Franklin, of all people, advised Adams on the eve of the never-to-be-forgotten convention that his book was in "such Request here" that it is "already put to Press, and numerous Editions will speedily be abroad." Over time, many have claimed that Adams's *Defence* was unpopular from the moment of its appearance in the United States, a conclusion drawn on the strength of a single quotation from James Madison. The historian Eric Nelson has correctly quashed that myth, noting that even Madison, a critic of Adams, recognized the book's importance and admitted to Jefferson that it would be "a powerful engine in forming the public opinion."[50]

Not every idea in Adams's book was unique to him. Many in Philadelphia denoted the unicameral Pennsylvania Assembly as a dangerous precedent to be dodged at the national level. A prominent actor at the Constitutional Convention, Pennsylvania's James Wilson, subsequently a judge and political theorist in his own right, conceived the office of the presidency (in the *Defence,* the logic is applied to state governors) as a custodial position designed for the protection of the people against the aristocratic few. Had he been present, Adams would have been suspicious of Madison's initial design for the Constitution, which aimed to make the Senate the most powerful branch of government by placing in its hands an "absolute negative," or veto power. Adams wanted the veto to reside with the executive. At the end of 1787, he compared notes with Jefferson: "You are apprehensive of Monarchy; I, of Aristocracy." To be clear, none of the architects of the Constitution were any less committed than Adams to reining in the power of a political elite. The issue that divided them was where that power would be lodged.[51]

Adams parted company with Madison and Jefferson, and other Lockeans, when it came to their view that the fundamental purpose of government was the protection of property. Property was tied to wealth, the acquisition of *private* power, which Adams wanted separated from politics. His thinking began with an assumption about class conflict—not abstract rights. "In every society where property exists," he wrote, "there will ever be struggle between rich and poor." Unless all classes were fully represented, and independent of each other, "equal laws can never be expected," and the rich would find a convenient way to "fleece the poor." He could not be any more precise, or as farseeing, than that.[52]

Still, his argument for ostracizing the "few" in the Senate was imperfect. His own son wondered whether he would have supported the new Constitution had he been at home. To his cousin and Harvard contemporary William "Billy" Cranch, after closely reading the text of volume 1 of the *Defence,* JQA offered a number of critical observations. He questioned, in particular, the composition of the Senate: if it was supposed to be the aristocratic branch, then it should have been composed of men of the greatest talents and reputation. But it was not. The same kind of men were chosen for the House, which meant they shared the same class interests as senators and would work in tandem, rather than each acting as a check upon the other.[53]

Two months later, to the same correspondent, JQA expanded his argument. The House (being too much like the Senate) would not offer proper representation of the people; thus, there was "no democratical branch of the constitution." He found it in this way "impossible" for a congressional delegation of eight men to represent the people of Massachusetts in their entirety. They would be of the aristocratic part of the community, he said, matching his father's concern that cleverly arranged publicity would take precedence over ability, for only the best known among the elite would be able to attract sufficient votes from among a large population.[54]

A high-minded John Quincy Adams confided to the pages of his diary his real concern that the Constitution was "calculated to increase the influence, power and wealth" of those already greatly endowed with privilege. He imagined the birth of a new "aristocratic party" and thought that despite a lack of formal titles of nobility there would be inheritable distinctions in America. This fear was occasioned by the newly formed Society of the Cincinnati, a hereditary association of military officers who had served in the

Revolutionary War. JQA, his father, and Thomas Jefferson all registered the same deep suspicion about this emerging organization, even as the trustworthy George Washington served as its figurehead and presiding officer.[55]

The calling of the Constitutional Convention is understood by historians to have been spurred, at least in part, by the 1786 debtors' uprising in western Massachusetts known as Shays's Rebellion. But Shays's was not a catalyst for volume 1 of John Adams's *Defence*. Thanks to correspondents that included his eldest son, though, the diplomat-author was aware of the impact that this fairly isolated rebellion was having on political thinking across the United States.

In 1787, Captain Daniel Shays was as well known in the Bay State as the name John Adams was at the Court of St. James's. It was a time of privation, when large numbers of subsistence farmers—former soldiers—banded together in armed protests against farm foreclosures. They forcibly shut down courts that were issuing the foreclosure orders, and state leaders in Boston responded by calling out a few thousand militiamen. John Adams felt no sympathy for this extralegal resistance movement, afraid that the farmer-rebels would, if successful, destroy his precious state constitution. His complaints were tame compared with some others, though. His cousin Samuel Adams was in the thick of the controversy and had determined that the Shaysites were traitors.

John Quincy interpreted Shays's Rebellion through a similar lens as his father, while the Braintree-born John Hancock, the on-again, off-again governor of their state, was fortunate to escape the worst of the controversy. He waited out the crisis and slid back into the governorship by, in John Quincy's words, "pleasing the multitude." Adams the younger saw Hancock as an intriguer and an appeaser, and he hoped his father's *Defence* would deter ongoing efforts to do away with the Massachusetts Senate, which had already raised taxes well above prewar levels. Before long, the legislature in Boston reached a consensus that its hurting citizens in the western area of the state deserved leniency. Shays and his supporters were all granted pardons. The rebels had had their moment, and as things turned out, the hard-liner Samuel Adams went on to lose successive races for lieutenant governor and a seat in Congress.[56]

From the moment it was published, the *Defence* acquired a meaning beyond its author's original intent. Adams senior worried that the book would make him unpopular. It did, but not right away. When it came out, the *Defence* earned him greater respect from his peers. It was only in the 1790s that the positions he took would be successfully used against him, once the two competing political parties, Federalist and Republican, established themselves. Partisans of the Madison-Jefferson group would then be cherry-picking quotations to make Adams appear to be a lover of the British monarchy. In the late 1780s, everything was different. His text actually placed him closer in spirit to the Anti-Federalists who gave their attention to issues of right and social fairness and who recognized the permanent existence of class interests.[57]

The disdain for parties that grew in both John and John Quincy Adams may be said to have spawned under these conditions. It was not mere peevishness but rather their concerted constitutional study, that directed the actions they took when they veered from positions that the organized party closest to their worldview had adopted.

YOUNG HEIR

On July 11, 1787, JQA committed to his diary one of his more painful ruminations. It was his twentieth birthday that day, and he took stock of his meager accomplishments: "I am good for nothing and cannot even carry myself forward in the world." Like his father, he often sparred with himself in his private journals; otherwise, it should seem odd that these words of self-loathing came to him on the eve of his graduation from Harvard. Nor did he stop there: "These long years I have yet to study in order to qualify myself for business: and then—oh! and then; how many more years, to plod along, mechanically, if I should live, before I should really get into the world? Grant me patience ye powers!"[58]

Patience was not a constant in the life of either father or son. Of course, being the son of John Adams offered certain unambiguous privileges. Before John Quincy left college, he was chosen to deliver an oration, which the *Columbian Magazine* in Philadelphia saw fit to publish at the very moment that the delegates to the Constitutional Convention were completing their first draft of a federal government. In an address laced with dramatic pathos, the twenty-year-old graduate appealed to "generous souls" and praised "undaunted patriotism" while simultaneously warning against the widespread temptation of "luxury and dissipation" that characterized a misguided people.

The language he used, the message he chose to convey, was not particularly special. A good many commentators in the mid-1780s were expressing wariness about self-rule, saying that the states' post-Revolutionary promise was already being undermined by a slothful, free-for-all mentality. The voluntarily retired general George Washington predicted that with the British threat removed, "like a young heir, come a little prematurely to a large inheritance, we shall wanton and run riot until we have brought our reputation to the brink of ruin." A slew of newspaper writers looked about and saw rampant self-interest, soulless debauchery, and creeping tax resistance—a general lack of respect for the law. It went well beyond the Shaysites. In John Quincy's consensus rendering, "threatening clouds of sullen discontent" had appeared, and "indolent carelessness" had crept in, afflicting a host of citizens.

To read this compilation of hot-blooded language, one could easily conclude that a moral crisis existed in America prior to Washington's assumption of the presidency. The disillusioned son bought into the literary embellishment of the moment: current conditions, if unchecked, would produce an even worse America than if political tyranny had prevailed. In the ornamental style of the day, hyperbole oozed. In this case, it gave little indication of the supple mind or personal prospects of a future U.S. president.[59]

After attending her cousin Johnny's oration, Abigail's niece Lucy Cranch told her aunt that "Mr J.Q.A." resembled his mother: "I never saw the likeness so stricking [*sic*] as when he pronounced his oration. It was your mouth that smiled when he addressed the Ladies. It was your eyes that glistened." These words were more than simple flattery, one presumes. For Johnny's first ten years, his mother had maintained a privileged position in his life; through most of his second decade, the chief parental role was usurped by his father and other male surrogates. Still, Johnny must have retained something intangible, or gave off a spirit, that partook of the mother.[60]

At the height of his career abroad, the elder Adams momentarily thought of prioritizing his son's career over his own. Hearing only secondhand of John Quincy's 1787 graduation from Harvard, he registered how much he missed his son and considered recrossing the ocean so as to personally train him in the law. Upon further thought, he guided Johnny to the town of Newburyport, Massachusetts, and to Theophilus Parsons, a future chief justice of the state supreme court. Better for his son to learn at the feet of a practicing attorney.

John Quincy was plenty descriptive in his diary, but he was not the master of language that his father was at the same age. He adopts a similarly judgmental tone, but he does not as readily express the dry Adamsian humor that he would pick up later. There are suggestive instances, at least, that preview what is to come—notably an encounter at a tavern in Ipswich where JQA provides the blow by blow of a verbal duel between his law tutor and another man. "Parsons was witty," the diarist allows, "but strained rather too much for it." He had but grazed his adversary. "This kind of wit may I think be compared to a sky rocket, which spends all of its force in hissing, and then disappoints us with such a weak explosion that it can scarcely be heard." In his metaphor-laced accounting, JQA appreciates a facility for barbed humor: "Wit to be pleasing must I think be unexpected, like the lightening which flashes in our eyes."[61]

If the father wrote with greater abandon at the same age, the son would outlast the old man, keeping his pen busy until the end of his days. John Adams set aside his daily diary-writing habit when he turned his attention to the *Defence* and afterward never returned to his journals with the vigor of earlier years. Contrariwise, at the height of his own career in politics, John Quincy would launch into pages of commentary at a single sitting. Underscoring subtle differences between the two, the Adams family biographer Edith B. Gelles observes, "Unlike his father's youthful diary, John Quincy did not examine his soul and his spirit." Indeed, through the years, JQA stifled emotion better than the old man.[62]

But that's not the whole of it. At the moment of his introduction to the law, as he learned the ropes of courtroom procedure, and with an ocean still separating him from the eyes of judgmental parents, John Quincy Adams fell head over heels for one particular girl in his social circle, the blond, blue-eyed Mary Frazier. Their relationship had all the marks of an intense, unforgettable first love, reinforced by the suitor's ingenuous poetry. Johnny and Maria (as he called her) would last as a couple past the parents' return from Europe, but they would not be permitted to carry forward much beyond. Johnny's mother would see to that.

The lawyer in training confined his journal entries to a single line per day during the "limbo" years of 1788–1789, so what we glean of his state of mind rests on a certain amount of speculation. On the other hand, in the smattering of letters that cross between England and Massachusetts, the elder's tone is extremely affectionate. He evinces trust in his son's prevailing sense of right and consciousness of personal responsibility. It is altogether clear that he likes sharing confidences with John Quincy. The dangers they braved together were unbanishable from their minds; the exposure to books and ideas that formed so much a part of the fugitive moments they shared in Europe continued to find expression in letters. The matter of Mary Frazier was only a faint suspicion and not yet up for discussion.

FIVE

INSTIGATORS

An host of enlightened writers have arisen, in every part of the United States, to oppose the abominable heresies of Publicola.

—*FEDERAL GAZETTE (Philadelphia), July 1791*

The enlightened *writers, who have defended the principles of Mr. Paine, differ so essentially in the ground they have taken, that the one or the other would certainly have been charged with propagating detestable heresies, had not the end sanctified the means, and the object of defending Mr. Paine, reconciled the inconsistencies of their reasoning.*

—"PUBLICOLA," *No. 11, July 1791*

Publicola killed Tom Pain.

—THOMAS BOYLSTON ADAMS TO ABIGAIL ADAMS, *1799*

In late February 1788, John Adams had a farewell audience with King George III. That April, after one final trip to Holland, he and Abigail sailed home together. Everything he'd acquired amid travels was hauled back. There was furniture that the family would have to make space for at their Braintree home. More remarkably, the persistent bibliophile had acquired so many titles that it took his eldest son three days just to unpack all the crates containing books.[1]

When the Massachusetts legislature learned of the long-absent diplomat's pending return, it sent a formal congratulatory message. But when he resumed writing letters a few weeks later, John informed his daughter, Nabby, "in strict confidence," that he felt a lack of "esteem, admiration, or respect" from his countrymen. He fretted that his time overseas had removed him from consideration for a political office worthy of his abilities. He'd never take a job "beneath himself," he carped. He was in his mid-fifties. The law no longer appealed. A position in government was the only option he considered. As yet, there were no assurances.

On the other hand, as a father, he was gratified by any and all reports that touched upon the personal reputations of his sons, John Quincy, Charles, and Tom. "I am happy to hear from all quarters a good character of all your brothers," he told Nabby. "The oldest has given decided proofs of great talents, and there is not a youth of his age whose reputation is higher for abilities, or whose character is fairer in point of morals or conduct." His sources were not wrong, but they had not presented all the facts.[2]

Of the diversions John Quincy enjoyed in these years, nothing and no one compared to the Frazier girl. She was from Newburyport, in her midteens (that is, nearly marriageable) when she and her beau became acquainted. In the absence of his superintending parents, he was free to see her whenever he wanted. In a poem exalting Maria's qualities, the smitten boyfriend characterized her propriety: "Hers are the lasting beauties of the heart, / The charm which virtue only can impart." He designated himself in the poem "thy ardent lover."

Their courtship continued after John and Abigail returned stateside, but the Harvard graduate's still unformed career in the law presented a roadblock to marriage, and he knew it. He was forced to contend with his parents' expectations for him beyond the romantic scenario he had constructed for himself in their absence, and this was why he hid his relationship with the girl in Newburyport even as they pressured him to set up a law office in Boston. Passing the bar in 1790, J. Q. Adams began to make tentative steps toward establishing himself professionally, but the matter of Mary Frazier stood unresolved. Writing to a young male friend around this time, he mocked another of their acquaintances, a "gay, dissipated rake," for announcing his preemptive marriage to a woman of no consequence; the pair in question had been keeping company for three years. Without sufficient means, the so-called rake was "ready to sink into the dull, insignificant regularity of matrimony." Abigail Adams sensed what was afoot. "Never form connections until you see prospects of supporting a family," she lectured her eldest boy.[3]

Johnny stood up to his mother for a while, until a variety of pressures bore down on him. Maria had family demands of her own to contend with, compounding his. The couple parted, painfully and reluctantly, after a romance of more than two years. Twenty-three and lacking the means to move through life on his own, John Quincy wavered. Mary Frazier was the proverbial road not taken. His enduring memory of her was expressed with great sentiment when, in his seventies, he happened upon the grave of Mary's daughter. Inspecting the dates carved into stone, he could see that neither mother nor child had survived much past thirty. A young heart had been lost to him as a result of "distrust instilled into her mind by an envious cousin." One way or another, both of the young lovers had succumbed to outside pressure.[4]

Wherever she was, Abigail Adams worried, conventionally, about all of her sons. Her letters almost invariably contained the words "duty," "honor," "judgment," and "virtue" along with "temptation" and "vice." After England, she turned up the heat. It fell to John Quincy to monitor and restrain his playful younger brother Tom. "Watch over his conduct," she commanded. "Prevent by your advice & kind admonitions, his falling a prey to vicious Company."

In their century, "vicious" referred to depraved activity excited by base passion, to which the male of the species was often subject. Profligacy and debauchery went hand in hand; recklessness and extravagance were their deadly companions. Abigail's most uncompromising strictures involved the intertwined matters of amorous attachment and financial health. Again to her eldest: "As you never wish to owe a fortune to a wife, never let her owe Poverty to you. Misfortunes may Surround even the fairest prospects."

It was the defenseless Nabby who would shortly learn this lesson, her mother unable to stave off disaster. Shy of twenty-one, she had gotten married in England to William Stephens Smith, a Princeton-educated Revolutionary War officer and John Adams's secretary in London. It appeared on the surface to be a good match, and Nabby dutifully produced three sons in rapid succession as the couple settled on Long Island. Smith was the apple of his in-laws' eyes at the time of the wedding in 1786, but he turned out to be utterly vicious—in every sense of the word as Abigail understood it. The entire family suffered for his vulgarity and improvidence. Not only were Abigail Adams's darkest fears realized; she would live to bury gentle Nabby.[5]

Her Johnny was the only one of her three sons to gain in circumspection as the years proceeded. But even that measure of pride could not be ascertained from the vantage point of 1789–1790. As he joined the ranks of Boston attorneys, John Q. Adams occupied the lowest rung and had a very hard time making ends meet. His mother's axioms surged, letter by letter. She demanded regular updates and unremittingly weighed in with thoughts about "Humane [as she wrote it] Nature" and personal industry. Her tone was protective, but it was also no doubt taxing on him. "Make not haste to be rich," she reminded him. "Wealth suddenly acquired is seldom balanced with discretion, but is as suddenly dissipated." She was preparing him for a life she thought would be marked by mental strain and bouts of misfortune.[6]

One suspects that John Quincy had these exhortations already fixed in mind. Just before her letter came to hand, he told his first cousin and fellow attorney in training, William Cranch, that major decisions with long-term implications loomed. As his happy memories of Maria slipped away, he prepared to compete for business with men who looked at the son of John Adams with an uncomfortable mix of nepotistically tinged resentment and the common distaste for a young man's forwardness. JQA contrasted Cousin Billy's prospects with his own: "You will have no young rivals to rejoice at your failures or to envy your success; and you will not have the prejudice against you of assuming an higher tone than becomes you. All these disadvantages will probably be mine. But are not difficulties the test of merit?"[7]

Whereas Abigail poured forth warnings, John, with few exceptions, only ever approached his eldest boy with solicitous regard. He was an exceptionally eager, open, and charitable letter writer, as we know, but it is hard to find anything that compares with the straightforward tone of love and admiration reserved for John Quincy. "I Shall be very happy, my Son, to See you here, whenever the Journey may be most convenient," he wrote from the temporary capital of New York City in the summer of 1789. This was a few months after he was elected the first vice president of the United States. JQA remained in Boston.

John Quincy's father was too preoccupied with family finances to dwell on politics at this moment, and he tied his son to his own fate. "I must be pinched and Streightened till I die," he wrote melodramatically, "and you must have to toil and drudge as I have done. Do it, my dear son with out murmuring. This is entre nous." Between us. "I wish you to write me once a week," he pleaded. "I am my dear Child, with the tenderest Affection your Father."

Not only did he count on the endurance of their bond, we recognize as well his desire to invite John Quincy into the battles of his mind—and his battles with the world. We read edifying reminders of what matters in a man's world in John's letters, but there is precious little of Abigail's didacticism. John's sensitivity matched John Quincy's frustration as he weighed his prospects for success in Boston legal circles. The son regularly bemoaned the continued financial dependence on his parents. "I hope I shall not be much longer a burden to the kindest and most generous of parents," he told his father.[8]

His mother worried on a different level about his mental state. She told her sister Mary Cranch just after Johnny had paid a visit, "He appears to have lost much of his sprightlyness and vivacity. He says that the want of Buisness [*sic*] in his profession and the dismal prospect for the practitioners of the Law in Massachusetts, is the weight which depresses him, & that He should still be obliged at his age, to be dependant on his parents for a support. Altho these feelings are proofs of a good mind, and a sensible Heart, I could wish that they did not oppress him so much."[9]

To lift his son's spirits without shaving the truth, John recalled how it was for him at the same stage of life. "At the Age of 23, My son, I know by Experience, that in the Profession of the Law, a Man is not to expect a run of Business, nor indeed enough to afford him a subsistence. I mean to assist you, till you can do without my Aid." His language was unadorned whenever he addressed this son. Even in projecting "solemn advice," he was sure to give the underemployed attorney a big vote of confidence. And that is not all he was prepared to transmit to him. "I will give you the whole Management of my Estate, if you will take it," the doting father directed. "Yet I will not urge it upon you—perhaps it may interrupt your Studies too much." The need to read and improve was never far from his paternal considerations. "Above all Things keep up your Spirits and take Care of your Health."[10]

As a single young man, John Adams had been enamored of Hannah Quincy on a level only slightly less intense from how John Quincy felt about Mary Frazier. Without adequate means, he could not take the plunge into marriage either. The early years of his diaries show a proneness to despondency on a par with JQA. The difference was that a twenty-three-year-old

John Adams was not burdened with the apprehension his son knew as the likely beneficiary of nepotism. John Adams's father was not politically ambitious but rather a simple, respectable New England gentleman, nearing seventy at that time, and worn down. He had seen precious little of the world. There really was no legitimate comparison.

The son's emotional state remained a regular topic of conversation. The strong women of the family were as involved as the strong father was in seeking to understand him. Intimates noticed that Johnny's temperament had changed, that he'd become more impatient. One imagines the conversation that occurred between the child and his parents, as it was all reflected in his mother's correspondence. "He wishes sometimes," Abigail wrote to her sister Mary, "that he had been Bred a Farmer, a Merchant, or any thing by which he could earn his Bread, but we all preach Patience to him."[11]

Anxious watchfulness was the order of the day, well beyond the confines of the Adams family. The late historian of medicine Roy Porter explained, "One of the prime reasons people diarized so religiously was to keep track of physical routines, with a view, if necessary . . . to shaming themselves into mending their ways." As the young attorney resumed his regular diary the following year, he confessed, "I have now gone through another annual revolution in my progress to the grave, without advancing a step in my career."[12]

Some have termed this era the "age of reason," but it was no less the age of troubled nerves, when self-mastery required self-monitoring. The picture we paint, circa 1790, is certainly not the one history associates with the later politician John Quincy Adams, a supremely self-confident, methodical man with a forward posture and an uncompromising sense of right and wrong.

Circumstantial Pomp

John Adams flirted with the idea of service in the U.S. Senate (which was, until the twentieth century, an office obtained by votes in the state legislature). He even contemplated the job of chief justice of the U.S. Supreme Court. He did not openly proclaim for the vice presidency, just as George Washington did not campaign for president.

With a Virginian in the first position, a northerner was to be put in the second, for the sake of regional balance. Adams was known as a solid advocate of the new Constitution. Through some combination of tactfully circulated recommendations, nods, and posturing by influential men, his name was finally put in nomination. Each elector cast two votes, one for president, one for vice president. Adams received half as many electoral votes as Washington (69 versus 34), the remainder being split among numerous others. Adams was not pleased.[13]

If the eyes of the Western world were not all on New York, there were at least a few European capitals where highly placed diplomats expressed an interest in what was happening there. After Washington and Adams took their respective oaths of office on Wall Street—it was still a few months before the fall of the Bastille—the French ambassador to the United States, comte de Moustier, reported to Paris on a conversation he'd had with John Adams, late U.S. minister to Great Britain and newly installed vice president. Moustier wanted some assurance that in the event of an Anglo-French war America would show a marked preference for French interests. "Overall I had reason to be satisfied with the comments of the Vice President of the United States," wrote Moustier, "and it seemed to me that the little success he had had in England had served as a corrective for the bad inclination he has had toward France in the past. If he were to come to be impartial, we could not but be satisfied." Uncertain what the vice president's role in policy would be, the ambassador suggested a wait-and-see attitude: "I think it is wise to humor him not so much due to his influence in the Senate as because of the influence he can have on the President who unfortunately can scarcely avoid recourse either to him, to Mr. Jay or to both of them together in foreign policy as they are the only two who have any knowledge or experience in matters related to this."[14]

Because there were neither political parties nor presidential tickets, John Jay came in a distant third (after Washington and Adams) in the vote for president/vice president. He was named chief justice of the Supreme Court. From the start, the well-placed New Yorker was close to the administration, though not as a significant contributor to policy in spite of his experience as a diplomat and capable secretary of foreign affairs in the Confederation Congress. The one role given to Adams was a titular one: as president of the Senate, the vice president was able to cast a vote, but only in the event of a tie. He wrote to his Boston friend James Lovell that he saw his position as a "splendid pompous nothing." To John Quincy, it was that being "reduced" to a "mechanical" and "inactive" role was simply contrary to his character.[15]

President and vice president had had virtually no contact over the previous decade. Their relations were certainly amicable, but they were never close. Adams admired Washington's ability (despite his stiff formality). But there was no code of conduct in place for the second executive, and so Vice President Adams did not know how he was meant to comport himself. There was certainly a touch of irony in the fact that the first vice president found himself an executive interloper in the branch of government he distrusted most on paper, the aristocratically inclined Senate. Soon enough, he embroiled himself in a controversy that tested the proposition that a president of the Senate could take an active role in Senate debate, even if the federal Constitution had given no such direction or assurance.[16]

One of the first duties of the upper chamber was to draft a formal response to the president's inaugural speech to Congress, delivered on April 30, 1789. The House of Representatives had done its part five days after the event, mainly because James Madison was in charge. Madison had taken on a unique dual role, first helping the president draft his speech (as his one-man privy council) and then, as a leading voice in Congress, writing on behalf of the House its official reply to the same speech. The Senate would take longer—although a full week before the oaths of office were even administered, it began debate on what to call the nation's chief executive.[17]

In a long speech to the Senate, John Adams registered his thoughts on the unimpressive title of "President." A committee was set up to deliberate on the question of how the Senate should designate the elected leader of the Republic. Unaccountably, that committee disbanded, and a second was formed, simply to resolve this one, increasingly contentious issue. April bled into May. Should Washington be called "His Excellency," as some suggested, or "Elective Highness"? The most elaborate title came from the second committee: "*His Highness President of the United States of America and Protector of the rights of the same.*" A few continued to insist that the Senate, like the House, should stay true to the words of the Constitution and address Washington as nothing more than "President."[18]

Adams and the Virginian Richard Henry Lee, an ally from their days in the Continental Congress, stood with those advocating a grander name. In

Adams's mind, the grandness of the presidential title was an attempt to ritually strengthen the position of the executive vis-à-vis the aristocratic Senate, even if it should appear to be giving monarchical trappings to a republican. He worried, indeed, about the impression the chief executive would make on foreign dignitaries and ambassadors were his title to be artificially depressed for the sake of republican humility. And yes, he approved the idea of a glamorous title serving to elevate the national executive's stature over that of a state's governor; at this juncture, citizens tended to identify more strongly with state authority. Their minds needed to be enlarged to match the scale of the nation's ever-broadening territory. The rules that had governed them as colonies (or as states within the Confederation) had to be replaced.

He urged the Senate to consider the fact that "President" was too common a label. He made his point with a touch of absurdity, referring to "Presidents of Fire Companies and of the Cricket Club." The Senate became so divided and its members so angered that a postponement of debate was called. At wit's end, Adams burst forth with "What will the Common People or Foreign Countries, what will Sailors and Soldiers say, George Washington President of the United States, they will despise him to *all eternity*." After losing his cool, he alienated his colleagues by demanding that the Senate act alone, ignoring the work of a joint Senate-House committee. The effect was to invite a charge that *he* had come to embody the Senate's aristocratic pretensions. Adams soon enough came to regret his behavior, for he now had outright enemies in the Senate. When the country's newspapers got wind, he became an easy target. His reputation would henceforth be that of an antidemocrat, too long in foreign courts.[19]

His most unforgiving foe in the Senate was William Maclay of Pennsylvania, a prickly and self-righteous man, just slightly younger than the vice president. Unlike Adams, his political experience lay at the state and county levels. State pride came first for Maclay, who assumed Pennsylvanians to be morally superior in their embodiment of republican simplicity. Though himself a Presbyterian, he echoed the deeply held beliefs of Pennsylvania Quakers, who hated formality and admired plainness. Maclay found Adams's demeanor to be pompous and insulting and blamed Adams and Lee for the "idolatrous business" of the titles fiasco. He wasn't alone either. Pennsylvanians in the House of Representatives denounced Adams for his "Superlative Vanity."[20]

South of the Mason-Dixon Line, Virginians and South Carolinians formed a second anti-Adams bloc, where his behavior was labeled "odious." Much of their gossip sank to the level of adolescent banter. Thomas Jefferson's boyhood pal John Page, scion of an old and prosperous Virginia lineage, and Thomas Tudor Tucker of South Carolina turned their barbs into crambo, a rhyming competition, vying to see which of them could more cleverly make sport of the vice president for his "assload" of pride. The southerners seemed obsessed with Adams's appearance and aimed their jabs at his physical stature. Ralph Izard of South Carolina came up with the most memorable slur of all, "His Rotundity," which would return to haunt Adams during the election of 1800.[21]

When it came to the physical dimensions of leadership, neither Virginians nor South Carolinians could see past Washington, who stood imposingly three inches above six feet and displayed his dignity and serene republican majesty (paradoxically) in his every gesture. The Pennsylvanians, as well, took account of the relative height of the president and the vice president. Maclay, as tall as Washington, was dubbed "Your Highness of the Senate," and the Pennsylvania congressman Henry Wynkoop, an inch taller, was accorded the same mock title in the House.[22]

It was immediately clear that regional identity would continue to count in the national legislature. Some southerners who had seen the *Defence* found Adams "obnoxious" (to repeat the adjective Madison used in a letter to Jefferson in the fall of 1788). He was wrongly thought to have actively undermined General Washington as part of a "cabal" during the Revolutionary War; accused, too, of seeking offices for "private emolument"—an untruth that reveals the general suspicion among southern elites refusing to trust colleagues who lacked inherited wealth and position. Madison recognized the ambiguity of the vice presidency, an office "not at all marked out by the general voice." The president alone united the public.

For all of these reasons, a number of his peers immediately saw John Adams as a dubious character. Adams was all too aware of regional biases. His friend and former law clerk William Tudor pointedly expressed the double standard. "Had the Vice President been born on the other Side of the Potomac," Tudor wrote, "how greatly would his Foreign Services & American Merits have been estimated!"[23]

Congressman Madison declared that giving Washington a title would serve only to diminish his natural dignity. This was a leader who had no need for the artificial trappings of monarchy; character and corporeal display were sufficient to convey rectitude and fortitude. His most enthusiastic admirers insisted that the irreplaceable first president was so perfectly constituted as to possess everything a king did, without a "paltry" crown.[24]

Royal envy shadowed the entire congressional debate over titles. Many who ridiculed Adams were completely comfortable praising Washington in godlike language. Washington worship was nothing new, but at this moment it appeared to represent longing for a quasi-king. Adams inevitably became a foil, the antithesis of kinglike or godlike nobility. He was shown as clumsy, grasping, fat, and ungainly, nothing like the natural aristocrat.

Abigail Adams read these vicious satires. One chastised her for riding in a carriage, as though her unrepublican husband were compelled to indulge her weak, feminine, aristocratic ways. She marveled that the same people who railed against titles were converting Washington into a "Savior and God." In truth, Washington's royalist displays far surpassed anything the Adamses ever did. He took up residence with his family in the most elegant, freshly furnished mansion in the city and ranged about lower Manhattan in a cream-colored coach drawn by six horses. His inaugural procession to New York, from the moment he left his Potomac estate of Mount Vernon, was a finely orchestrated exhibition of public adoration. He made two grand tours through New England and the South during his first term. Which was precisely the point of it all. The "Republican Court" of George Washington featured levees, balls, soirees, and formal audiences. Only purists on the order of Pennsylvania's senator Maclay still longed for the Washington who had commanded troops in his "dusty boots."[25]

Villainizing Adams allowed his fellow Federalists (though the administration party was as yet unnamed) to deflect criticism from the elite political society they were forming. Adams had a markedly different perspective on all of this. He did not want power to attach to individual men, fearing a lust for power that would lead the most ambitious to use Washington to their advantage. To Connecticut's Roger Sherman, who had played a key role in shaping the Senate at the Constitutional Convention, he submitted his opinion that the "Aristocratical Power" would eventually "Swallow up" the "Democratical and Monarchical." Back in 1785, from his post in Europe, Adams had warned that "instead of adoring Washington, Mankind Should applaud the Nation which Educated him." We must remember that John Adams always put his faith in institutions over men.[26]

The base passions of greed, vanity, and love of fame were not only natural, he believed, but generally stronger forces than reason and modesty. He refused to adopt what he called an "affectation of modesty." While so-called Republican plainness could bind the nation together, still it behooved the federal government to use a "language of signs," in his words, to "attract the attention . . . and excite the congratulations of the people." Grandeur that stirred the spirit was not undue. Pomp and circumstance had its place. It instilled a fascination with government and a respect for government. To Dr. Benjamin Rush, Adams reasoned that titles might not be needed to inspire those who were already virtuous, but like the law itself respect for titles could check the darker impulses of "profligate" individuals.

This was not a pointless debate. Deference and hierarchy already existed, with nary a complaint about medals awarded for meritorious service in the ranks of the army and navy. It's just that no one knew what to do to get people to respect federal authority. One side was content to rely on an implicit moral regard for "natural" authority; the other side, which included Adams, opted for more explicit forms. Importantly for him, titles were meant as a carrot more than a stick. He did not distinguish between aristocratic elites and the democratic multitude, because he considered that both—that all—acted on the basis of similar psychological urges. His critics engaged in a different set of semantics, when they enveloped the popular desire for a surrogate king in a familiar vocabulary of nature and breeding. In the singular case of Washington, they functionally substituted intangible personal qualities (native excellence) for inherited pedigree. Neither side in the debate endorsed social equality. And in the end, the Senate resolved to go along with the House, at least for the moment, in addressing Washington as "President of the United States." Period.[27]

In March 1790, fresh from the titles debate and in the transparent testimony of his private correspondence, Adams composed a remarkable and revealing letter. Equally exhausted and wryly amused by what he described as twenty years of American newspapers "throwing out hints" of his low birth and obscure genealogy (the sum of which was reprinted in English papers as well), he detailed at great length the history of the Adamses of Braintree going back nearly a century and a half. The "industrious" clan had proven itself to be an "irreproachable" breed, descending to his generation. Less virtuous, he attested, were the famed lineages of colonial America, rich in government experience and at the same time more full of "Pride Vanity and Insolence on account of their Birth" than their counterparts within the English or French nobility. Adams found deeply dishonest all talk of equality among his peers, and specified the "Philosophical Democracies" promoted by those whose imaginations departed from political reality.

The upshot of all of this was that he, of all people, was the least deserving of the charge of abandoning republicanism. It was most absurd to suspect him of favoring aristocracy. His principles of government were "the same now as they ever were." He lived within his means. Unlike John Hancock or George Washington, he had never "dazzled" anyone because of wealth. He obtained no vote through false representation. He was the least likely individual ever to head a political organization—which was the next line in his defense against the implied suggestion that as a promoter of the aristocratic style he would somehow emerge as the "Leader of a Party." Ambition described others, not the popularity-averse John Adams.

His pen drifted from here to speculation as to what might occur if President Washington should not survive his term. On one point he was most insistent: he would have nothing to do with the vice presidency under anyone other than Washington. Furthermore, Adams vowed, he would yield the chief magistracy to the most worthy successor rather than try to fill Washington's shoes. But who might a proper president be, if not Washington? Sizing up his future competition, Adams mused, "Mr. Jay, Mr. Jefferson, Mr. Maddison. I know very well that I could carry an Election against either [that is, any] of them in spight of all Intrigues and Maneuvres. Yet I would not do it, if I thought either could govern this People. But I know they could not." So much for not putting on airs.

Surprisingly dismissive of his close ally Jay, Adams doubled down on his own sense of worth even as he insisted that high office held no allure ("public Life is not very agreeable to me"). Allowing himself to conceive, for the moment, that circumstances could suddenly convert him into "the Idol of a

Party" with Washington's demise, he made a knowingly ridiculous assertion: "I will at all Events quit the Country—if I spend the rest of my Days in a Garrett in Amsterdam." The colloquy closes with the pronouncement that he is wasting his breath on a subject that he can only pretend does not engross his thought: "Thank Heaven however the President is in a vigourous Health and likely to live till the Government has a fair Tryal." Vice President Adams would appear to lack introspection enough to perceive that his resort to strategic hyperbole only magnifies the unabashed pride and vanity that others saw in him.[28]

The long letter was to John Trumbull, Yale graduate and patriotic poet, who had studied law with John Adams in Boston in 1773–1774. While his former benefactor was in Europe, in 1782, Trumbull completed a popular lampoon of New England Tories called *M'Fingal.* During the spring months of 1790, while he and Vice President Adams were writing regularly to each other, the former poet obtained a new trust, serving as Connecticut's attorney general. He would spend most of the balance of the Federalist decade (1792–1800) in the state legislature, exercising his opinions.[29]

Thus, it was not Adams bursting forth unprovoked. Trumbull, a keen political observer, actively prodded his mentor to reveal himself. Acting in the shadow of the insurmountable Washington, frustrated by the titles debate, the easily tormented vice president was coaxed into putting down on paper an array of personal justifications. One of these related to his acknowledgment (and regret) that he had performed no military service. Speaking of himself now in the third person, as "V.P.," he indulged the righteous Trumbull: "In the Public service, he has escaped death in more shapes than any Man, not excepting any officer of the Army. He has escaped Death, in stormy Seas, leaky ships, threatening Diseases, Cannon Balls and private Daggers."[30]

One reason Adams reacted as he did is that Trumbull deliberately fed his ego in the course of drawing him out. Scanning the map, he described the vice president's detractors as a loud but isolated group arising from one particular latitude. They were "Southern Aristocrats, who suppose themselves born to greatness," but had been "eclipsed by merit" in the person of the vice president. In reply, Adams said that his New England detractors were more dangerous to him, owing to the worse passions inflamed by up close jealousy. He felt the pressure exceedingly.

But Trumbull did more than just feed the man's ego. Knowing how Adams fielded occurrences of character assassination—a mounting list in Adams's head—Trumbull pushed his buttons. He played the devil's advocate in questioning Adams's logic that some exaltation of public figures should be tried—because, Trumbull reminded him, the United States wished to differentiate itself from the Old World. What in Britain "dazzles the croud & sets them all agape," he said, "excites in our Yeomen nothing but envy, contempt & ridicule." And then, the kicker: "Let our Government be possessed of real strength—It will not need the aid of ostentation."[31]

Adams took the bait and took on Trumbull's lawyerly presentation of the countervailing logic as he would any personal affront. He was not campaigning for an American aristocracy in the British manner, he said. He merely wished to guarantee that foreign heads of state should see the U.S. president as an equal. Further personalizing, he compared his own imperfect reputation not to that of Washington, whom he genuinely respected, but to that of the popular, stinking-rich governor of Massachusetts, John Hancock. "The Number who worship splendor are greater than that of those who despise it," Adams wrote.[32]

Washington sacrificed ease to conduct war, but what had Hancock done? He was an aristocrat in the eyes of his Boston neighbors. As far as the public could tell, Adams and Hancock were mutually respectful, but that was not the whole story. They were really passive-aggressive competitors, each positioning himself for more. Though less than brilliant, Hancock had been handily reelected to the governorship time and again. He possessed *something,* though nothing close to what John Adams regarded as greatness.

The biography of the wealthy merchant and shipowner Hancock is less well known than his stylish signature. He was born, as Adams was, in tiny Braintree. They overlapped at Harvard as well. Hancock married a Quincy and then came into an extraordinary fortune upon the death of the uncle who raised him. His lifestyle was, therefore, not the result of his own entrepreneurship. Until the Revolution, he was a political protégé of Samuel Adams's; the two rebels parted ways, however, before the ink was dry on the Declaration of Independence. As a trial attorney, John Adams had defended Hancock back in 1768, when one of the latter's ships was seized by the British. Twenty years later, it was Hancock, as governor, who was the first to welcome the Adamses back from Europe. An even greater symbolic test would be upon them shortly when the Quincy crowd met to decide on a town name. As part of the 1792 reorganization, with the absorption of Braintree, the name "Hancock" would narrowly lose out to "Quincy." Plainly, the Hancock brand irked both the elder and the younger Adamses. Neither would have wanted to reside in any place named Hancock.[33]

As in his tense relationship with Benjamin Franklin, whose death at age eighty-four had recently occurred in Philadelphia, John Adams wished to be elevated over those, like Hancock, who worked less hard than he did. His feelings of resentment were nearly impossible to dislodge. He went so far as to claim to Trumbull that his detractors had nothing to fear from him, because he did not plan to outlive Washington (who was three years his elder). In retrospect, this sounds strange, knowing as we do that Adams succeeded Washington in 1797 and survived him by more than a quarter century, but the slash-and-burn method of his prose allowed for morbid thoughts to emerge and become almost a cosmic weapon: "Envy need not labour to prevent me from being President. There is no danger. The President is happily likely to live longer than the V.P.—and if it should be otherwise ordered, the V.P. has no desire to be P.—He would retire to his Farm with more pleasure than ever he accepted any public office." Far from any "fondness for the splendor of monarchical Court," he had only the desire to flee from the halls of power to the relative stillness of his modest Quincy homestead.[34]

MEET DAVILA

His emotions swung back and forth between the confessional and the wary or defensive. No one ever need guess at what John Adams thought about a passing political question or, more far-reachingly, the lessons of history. All was contained in his multivolume work, the *Defence,* which prioritized "balanced government," and in its opinionated follow-up volume, *Discourses on Davila*. The vice president was a restless man.

Davila was introduced to the American public in the pages of the *Gazette of the United States* in April 1790 and published in thirty-two installments over the next thirteen months. The dangers of democracy are written all through *Davila,* as is the counteracting tendency of people, in ages past, to prefer monarchical government. Adams was digging himself a deeper hole, as though being misunderstood were his actual aim.

But why Davila? Only the most highly educated of Americans would have understood. Enrico Caterino Davila was a historian of northern Italy who wrote in 1630 on the wars in France that he witnessed firsthand. As the French Revolution unfolded, Vice President Adams used the relatively obscure Venetian as a kind of trope, while modeling his own approach to human nature on Machiavelli's *Discourses,* which were, in turn, reflections on the Roman historian Livy. This chain of thought, developed across the centuries, animated not just Adams but a number of eighteenth-century political theorists. Inserting himself into their conversation, John Adams pronounced himself a philosophe.

Adams's Machiavellian turn does not have to be inferred. He embraced the Italian thinker with open arms. Niccolò Machiavelli lived a century before Davila; Adams generally refers to him as "Machiavel." Modern generations invoke the Italian in connection with his advice in the *Prince,* but to see Adams as "Machiavellian" in that way, as the proponent of a cold, opportunistic brand of politics, is to lose the more comprehensive eighteenth-century dimension to reading a sixteenth-century thinker.[35]

One can inspect John Adams's copy of the four-volume edition of Machiavelli's *Works*. As the avid reader opened volume 2 (at an unknown date), he underscored a few key words: "Those are much mistaken who think any Republican Government can continue long united. Differences and Divisions for the most part are prejudicial to republics." While some divisions could actually be turned to advantage, the "hurtful" differences, as Machiavelli explained, were "attended with parties and factions." Adams was reading and processing.

Historical models weighed heavily on him. In fifteenth-century Florence, the unselfish, faction-quashing Cosimo de' Medici matched "prudence and moderation" with public-spiritedness. As a natural leader who did nothing to "excite envy" and who never "transgressed those bounds of decency, which ought be observed by a modest Republican," he was both a Machiavellian and an Adamsian example of one who conducted state affairs with a superior knowledge of human nature. As Adams borrowed ideas from his copy of "Machiavel," he confirmed for himself that a worthy republic had to accord respect to the right characters.[36]

Contained in *Discourses on Davila* are some of Adams's most insightful writings on the relationship between emotions and politics. In addition to the Italian, he relied on a variety of other thinkers to explain not only the passion for power (and desire for attention) but also why it was that spectators (in our terms, voters) became enraptured with those seen as "great."

The politics of spectatorship was an eighteenth-century obsession that turns out to be surprisingly modern, too. Adams was convinced that education and merit would be less often rewarded in publicly held elections than would superficial measures—the traits that "glitter with the brightest lustre, in the eyes of men." What traits were these? Birth, riches, beauty, and unearned honors. Politics should be about the public good, but it almost never was. More likely, it was about being *seen*. Politics was about celebrity—an old theme of John Adams's.[37]

As he saw it, social beings were made to hunger after fame. "A desire to be observed, considered, esteemed, praised, beloved, and admired by his fellows" was, he stated in *Davila,* "one of the earliest, as well as keenest dispositions discovered in the heart of man." All political systems, including republics, accommodated these impulses. The mere act of striving to improve, to perfect one's talents, generated the desire for personal distinction. Self-improvement through the acquisition of knowledge and refinement of morals fed positive forms of ambition, of course, yet the same desire provoked the darker passions of jealousy, envy, and vanity.[38]

All the world was a stage, and for this very reason politicians mounted it. Genuine merit usually could not compete in the mad scramble; powerful men positioned themselves to display apparent advantages: "their taste and address, their wealth and magnificence," along with family name and inherited reputation. Were these attributes not enough to promote them, men would rely on "artifice, dissimulation, hypocrisy, flattery"—even "quackery and bribery"—to remain in the limelight. In Adams's *Davila,* celebrity offered built-in advantages. The spectator was hard-pressed to resist and to judge critically, rationally.[39]

Once again, as in the *Defence,* aristocracy was a key Adams concern. Aristocrats danced properly, played musical instruments well, rode as impressively, fenced dramatically, acted superior. Bearing a family name, the offspring of a celebrity "attract[ed] the eyes and ears of all companies long before it is known or enquired, whether he be a wise man, or a fool." Adams made it clear where he stood on the "irrational and contemptible" staging of family pride—and its opposite, the virtuous commoner's slow, deliberate path to respectability. He bemoaned the fact that human beings bore a tendency to look up in awe and obey those in society who commanded their attention.[40]

Obscurity was the plight of the majority. Though themselves unworthy of notice, they learned to identify with kings and queens and the associated "great" and somehow to live vicariously through these individuals' glamorous lives. "They feel a peculiar sympathy" for the powerful, Adams explained, so much so that when calamity befalls a celebrity, it "excites in the breast of the spectator ten times more compassion and resentment, than he would have felt, had the same things happened to other men." Adams repeatedly stated his belief (effectively a warning) that *even* in a republic, citizens were "obsequious to their superiors," prepared to accept rank, distinction, and social preeminence as if they were all deserved. Could republican merit compete with raw publicity? No. Elections did not have to be rigged to be susceptible to misdirection. Here was the guiding paradox: fame had a corrupting effect on human judgment, yet politics could not carry forth without the bright lights.[41]

Adams's Senate colleagues had their own agenda and did not care to consider the vice president's philosophy, nor did they particularly welcome his voice. If they believed that the Constitution permitted him no role in debate, then he would comply—or so he claimed. To the sympathetic Trumbull, he lodged his protest: "I have only occasionally asked a question or made a single observation, and that but Seldom . . . for I have no Desire ever to open my mouth again, upon any question. . . . To be candid with you, the situation I am in, is too inactive and insignificant for my disposition, and I care not how soon I quit it."[42]

He returned his attention to state politics. It was not the plantation lords but the "New Englandmen" whose antics most preoccupied Adams senior at this juncture. John Hancock remained a conspicuous thorn in his side. Though often bedridden, the Massachusetts governor hung on to his ambition. The Adamses (in this case JQA) did not let him out of their sights, insofar as Hancock had shown interest in becoming the nation's first vice president in 1788. He ultimately received several electoral votes, without posing a real challenge to Adams. While he nursed his painful gout—reminiscent of Franklin in France—and newspapers dropped hints of one sort or another, the young Boston attorney John Q. Adams kept his father apprised of political appointments. Hancock exercised the sly tactic of throwing crumbs to his rivals so that their state remained tranquil, JQA assured his father. The governor's chief backers claimed for him the "disinterested magnanimity" that adhered to President Washington—a character the Adamses knew he did not deserve.[43]

The vice president regarded his son as an astute interpreter of events. With each new report, he responded encouragingly: "Your Information on political Subjects is very Satisfactory, as it is given with that Freedom and Independence of Spirit, which I wish you always to preserve." Channeling his father's political theory, John Quincy bemoaned the fact that disinterestedness in decision making took second place to selfish advantage: "It is melancholy to observe how much even in this free Country the course of public events depends on the private interests and Passions of individuals." His father's prejudices had become his own.[44]

Still, paternal lectures on the virtue of patience continued to accompany exchanges of political intelligence. The son wondered when the day would come that his law practice freed him from financial insecurity. "Your Anxiety is too great," his father warned. "You have no right to expect and no reason to hope for more Business than you have. . . . Confidence in your Talents & Fidelity, must arise by degrees and from Experience."[45]

John and Abigail, now rarely apart, prepared to move with the national capital from New York to Philadelphia. Writing to Johnny, the frustrated father sighed: "It is to me a severe mortification that I cannot have more of your society: But Providence has ordered my Course of Life in such a manner, as to deprive me for the most Part of the Company of my Family." With almost insipid repetition, he went on to protest that the nation did not appreciate his many sacrifices: "I wish I had Served a Country possessed of more generous Sentiments that I might have been able to give my Children Some better assistance: but Complaints are Follies." It was not entirely clear what that better situation would have entailed. Writing, as he was wont, of their common fate, as he saw it, the elder concluded, "Ambition is a good quality, when it is guided by Honour and Virtue: but when it is Selfish only, it is much to be dreaded. I am my dear Child your affectionate[,] John Adams."[46]

The vice president retained his pessimism about American government one year in. State legislators looked covetously at members of Congress, exposing

"Passions and Heartburnings, which will end in Collisions." He would not retreat an inch from anything he had written since returning from England. The Republic was in existential danger: "The People have the Power to pull it down if they Will." Signs, to him, were ominous.[47]

He let Trumbull know that he'd come to learn more about the underhanded activities surrounding his own accession to the vice presidency. To ensure that he did not receive anywhere near the votes earned by Washington, the indiscreet Alexander Hamilton, along with interested others, had used back channels to carry out a letter-writing campaign to influence electors in the various states. Through a "lying manoevre," southern states were told that New Englanders would withhold their votes for Washington and that mismanagement of the process could actually make Adams president. Even Adams-friendly Connecticut took the bait, throwing two electoral votes to its sitting governor.

In artificially deflating the vice president (recall that Adams received 34 votes to Washington's 69), northerners and southerners were similarly duped, if one accepts John Adams's interpretation. To him, there was nothing accidental in what had happened. He was set up to be diminished in stature in the press, "insulted in Gazette or pamphlet at pleasure." His life was still being made miserable, and he smelled an ongoing conspiracy. "There has been more little malignity to me, than to . . . Benedict Arnold," he railed at no one in particular. "Whether this is owing to too much openness, or warmth, or too decided systems I know not." He presumed that his public mistreatment was a function of his habit of directness, along with his having put his political philosophy on the page for all to see. While his words sound pouty, Adams was right about Hamilton. But there was nothing to do for the moment. The antagonism between Adams and Hamilton would not come to a head until the end of the decade.[48]

So long his father's companion, JQA had learned to read the bilious language without overreacting.[49] But John Adams's combination of pride and pique was witnessed by a number of people outside Congress. An Italian count who met with both President Washington and Vice President Adams in New York in 1790 wrote of the dignified bearing of the former and then opened up on the latter: "Vice President Adams is the most pompous man I know and the most selfish that exists. What are they doing in France? he said to me the other day; I believe that they are madmen and that they did not understand my work [*Discourses on Davila*]. Well I'll go there myself and explain it to them."

It is hard to turn one's eyes from this kind of firsthand reportage. "God prevent his becoming President!" added the Italian. "The country would change faces in little time." It appears that an unfiltered John Adams could, on a bad day, create a really bad impression on someone. Or that he was oblivious to the ways in which a supposed virtue, honest emotion, could be read as noxious vanity.[50]

What political future could such a vice president have?

MEET PUBLICOLA

As the father battled to find purpose in what he supposed would be his final job in government, the son chided himself for deficient energy. He was not enjoying victories in court, and he was failing to show promise of becoming an expert at oratory, let alone a legislator like his father. The humility expressed in his diary, and in letters to his parents, was not feigned. He was frequenting lower-class neighborhoods of Boston and, for the moment, tempting himself with the kind of female company he could not introduce around.

Expectation hung about, weighed upon, John Quincy Adams. It might have been pressure to perform that led him to take up his pen pseudonymously. In a sarcastic and occasionally dismissive tone, he wrote, between early June and late July 1791, a series of opinion pieces for the *Columbian Centinel,* a Boston newspaper that was friendly to his embattled father's interests. He signed the eleven essays "Publicola" and kept his identity hidden.

His catalyst was the first American publication of Thomas Paine's *Rights of Man,* a spirited defense of the unfolding French Revolution that was explicitly critical of British hereditary government and aristocratic forms. The book was dedicated to the generally aloof and undemonstrative George Washington, who was no friend (but neither an enemy) to Paine. John Q. Adams resided in Boston and had no reason to involve himself in the business of a Philadelphia printer, other than that Secretary of State Thomas Jefferson had endorsed Paine's work in a very particular, very suspect way; it was featured right there in the opening pages. Jefferson had been in Washington's cabinet for a year and a half at this point, accepting the appointment upon his return from France. He had not been regarded as controversial in that station until he expressed his unabashed pleasure with Paine's latest offering. The appearance of *Rights of Man* meant, he wrote, that "something is at length to be publickly said against the political heresies which have sprung up among us." Everyone with an ear to the ground knew what this meant: Secretary of State Jefferson took Vice President Adams's *Discourses on Davila* to be antirepublican heresy. The vice president's son would not stand by while his father was hung out to dry.

One might call the *Rights of Man* controversy a perfect storm. The entire episode took off as a series of factors came together: the history of hurt as laid out in John Adams's letters to John Trumbull; JQA's protective instincts; and finally, the shock of the famously mild-mannered Jefferson putting pen to paper at an unguarded moment. It was not Jefferson's modus operandi to publicly criticize a colleague, though he did confide sensitive opinions in letters he believed private. He was more than a little perturbed when a thoughtless couple of lines in a cover letter to a stranger made the rounds in a number of newspapers. His close associate Congressman James Madison had lent Jefferson his own early copy of the London edition of Paine's pamphlet. Jefferson, as instructed, passed it on to a man he had never met who he presumed was the brother of a Philadelphia printer. Then he forgot about it.

When he saw that his remarks had been indiscriminately reprinted to sell books, an embarrassed Jefferson unhesitatingly apologized to the vice president, his fair friend of fifteen years' standing. "You and I differ in our ideas of the best form of government," he tried to assuage Adams, "but we differ as friends should do." The present misunderstanding would not have come about, he explained, but for the exposure of their differences to the public eye. Jefferson avowed that he had written the offending words merely "to take off a little of the dryness of the note," and he was "thunderstruck" to see what had unfolded as a result. "I was brought before the public without my consent," he underscored in the second of his letters of apology. He thought he was succeeding in putting out the fire elsewhere in the executive when he told President Washington that his vice president was "one of the most honest & disinterested men alive" *despite* his "apostacy to hereditary monarchy & nobility."

If true, it was quite an apostasy. Adams accepted Jefferson's explanation of being "thunderstruck" on seeing his throwaway lines come to light, but he still took umbrage. The author of *Discourses on Davila* most certainly did not perceive his work the way Jefferson did. "What Heresies?" he posed to Jefferson directly, tauntingly, telling his former comrade flat out that the two of them had never once entered into a serious conversation about forms of government. It was dead wrong for anyone to suppose that he had even hinted, in writing or in speech, that he favored "the Introduction of hereditary Monarchy and Aristocracy into this Country." As his ego commanded, he laid down a gauntlet before the Virginian: "I may safely challenge all Mankind to produce such a passage and quote the Chapter and Verse."

If Jefferson had erred, lying newspapers were making it worse. Adams lived long with his certainty and wrote to Jefferson more than twenty years later, with essentially the same thought in his head: "I will forfeit my Life, if you can find one Sentence in my Defence of the Constitutions, or the Discourses on Davila, which by a fair construction, can favour the introduction of hereditary Monarchy or Aristocracy into America."[51]

As Jefferson aimed to paper over an obvious slight, Adams was being himself a bit disingenuous. He believed that a concerted attempt was under way to remove him from office after one term and that John Hancock still wanted his job. No one would forget that in his constitutional role as president of the Senate, Adams had caused a stir when he recommended that Congress adopt artificial titles—calling the president "His Highness" so that citizens would look on him with awe.

Dr. Benjamin Rush of Philadelphia was a staunch friend to both Adams and Jefferson. A fellow signer of the Declaration of Independence, Rush would more than once interpose himself to restore cordial relations between the second and the third presidents. Throughout Washington's first term, he kept open lines of communication with the vice president. He wrote to Adams unreservedly that he considered republicanism and monarchy the deadliest of enemies and that any retreat from the former would point America unalterably in the direction of the latter. "I abhor titles and everything that belongs to the *pageantry* of government," Rush advanced. "I do not 'abhor

Titles, nor the Pageantry of Government,'" Adams replied, quoting Rush's words back to him. "If I did I should abhor Government itself.—for there never was, and never will be, because there never can be, any government without Titles and Pageantry."[52]

Rush reacted strongly. He wanted Adams to appreciate that monarchy and aristocracy were alike "rebellion against nature." One did not connect, even in a slight, symbolic way, "the *living* principle of liberty in the people with the *deadly* principle of tyranny in an hereditary monarch." Underscoring his point, the doctor struck where he knew Adams would feel it: "The characters you so much admire among the ancients were formed wholly by republican forms of governments."[53]

It was a lot to chew on. Rush echoed Jefferson's interpretation of their friend's "apostacy" from an unrestricted republicanism. Adams's very public failure to define "dignity" to the satisfaction of any then serving in government had clearly isolated him. In revolutionary France, Paine observed in his pamphlet, "rank and dignity in society" were meant to take "the substantial ground of character, instead of the chimerical ground of titles." And then: "The greatest characters the world have known have arisen on the democratic floor. Aristocracy has not been able to keep a proportionate pace with democracy." These were signs of the times, before the French Revolution turned to terror.[54]

Denial of an antirepublican bent was one thing. But Adams would not give Jefferson the slightest indication as to the true identity of the critic Publicola—widely assumed to be the vice president himself. Instead, he said that he "supposed" Publicola to be one who recognized Paine's work as "an Instrument to destroy a Man, for whom [Publicola] had a regard, [whom] he thought innocent, and in the present moment of some importance to the Publick, came forward." *For whom Publicola had a regard?* It was a sly choice of words. "I neither wrote nor corrected Publicola," Adams insisted. "The Writer . . . followed his own Judgment, Information, and discretion, without any assistance from me."[55]

Jefferson, in response, transferred all blame onto the still unidentified Publicola. He was thoroughly convinced, he said, that no one in the capital city of Philadelphia would have paid any attention to the "apostacy" comment had it not been for the meddlesome Publicola, who "thought it proper to misconstrue a figurative expression in my note." The writers who subsequently came to Jefferson's rescue, then, acted to "place the expression in it's [*sic*] true light." Others "hazarded a personal attack" on the vice president—"criminally" so, Jefferson added, somewhat disingenuously—on the basis of the belief that the senior Adams was writing as Publicola. For obvious reasons, Jefferson did not relate the opinion of Congressman Madison, who had recently guessed that John Quincy Adams was Publicola and had presented Jefferson with his reasoning. Except in quietly drawn correspondence, then, the son of the vice president was on no one's radar.[56]

Well, almost no one's. On July 27, 1791, a short squib appeared in the Philadelphia *General Advertiser*, edited by Benjamin F. Bache, a grandson of the late Benjamin Franklin. It went, "A writer in a Boston paper positively asserts that John Quincey [*sic*] Adams, the Vice President's son, regularly transmits the writings with the signature of Publicola to the press." But "transmits" is not exactly the same as a declaration of authorship, and this bit of intelligence did not succeed in eradicating the mystery; speculation persisted that Publicola was very likely the vice president himself. For his part, the mysterious Publicola did not drop any hints that begin to suggest the heady activities he was involved in during June and July 1791. Not even in his diary.[57]

And so it was that John Q. Adams entered the political fray as "Publicola," a Latin cognate of the Federalist Papers' "Publius," meaning, essentially, "friend of the people." His appearance in the *Columbian Centinel* was designed to mock the pretensions of the propagandist turned philosopher Thomas Paine while at the same time poking a bit of fun at the kindly Virginian he and his entire family had been drawn to in Paris.

The *Centinel*'s editor, Ben Russell, previewed the series by taunting readers that "the sentiments of MR. PAINE'S late pamphlet will be canvassed with as much freedom as is consistent with the reverence due to his character." In the first essay, Publicola professed an interest in contributing to a fair-minded conversation and then took a giant stab at Jefferson. "I am somewhat at a loss to determine what this very respectable gentleman means by *political heresies*," he posed, sounding very much like his acerbic father. "Does he consider the pamphlet of Mr. Paine's as the canonical book of political scripture?"

In the next essay, concentrating, as Paine did, on the distinctions to be drawn between French and English governmental forms, Publicola discussed the rule of law and the right to dissolve the social compact. "The people of *America* have been compelled by an unaccountable necessity, distressing in its operation, but glorious in its consequences, to exercise this right," he wrote automatically. But were the French actually at the point in their national political life where revolution was "absolutely necessary"? For Publicola, this was "a question, upon which the ablest patriots among themselves have differed, and upon which we are unadequate to decide."[58]

Paine's argument that constitutional change in England could profit from the French model was an idea that struck Publicola as irresponsible. It was to court mob justice: "The friend of humanity will be extremely cautious in how he ventures to put in action a tremendous power, which is competent only to the purposes of destruction." He warned against "blind imitation" of the French.[59]

A healthy debate about constitutionalism ensued in American papers, north and south, with counterarguments to Publicola appearing in a number of papers. One position Publicola consistently retreated to was a resounding defense of government under the federal Constitution. "Happy, thrice happy, the people of *America*!" he ended the eighth installment in the eleven-part series. Their "gentleness of manners and habits of virtue are still sufficient to reconcile their natural rights, with the peace and tranquility of their country."

Whether or not the younger Adams believed his own rhetoric, his editor, Russell, found himself in an other than tranquil editorial war with his counterpart at the *Federal Gazette* in Philadelphia. Russell defended his paper and its stinging series by asserting that "the pieces signed 'Publicola' have been written with calmness and decency." He then went after the Philadelphia editor Andrew Brown, reprinting Brown's intemperate language verbatim: "*Publicola* seems to have some talents, but perverted as they are, they are worse than thrown away."[60]

Among the respondents to "Publicola" was "A Republican" who hailed from Boston and wrote for the *Independent Chronicle*. He presumed that his rival essayist could not appreciate that a true "AMERICAN NOBILITY" would have to come from common ranks. "Who are *worthy* to be set up as a superior order of citizens?" he unloaded. "What individual has a *right* to expect, that his children shall claim a privilege to exercise authority over the children of other citizens?" The democratic impulse was alive and well in 1791, and so wary of any feint in the direction of "*pomp* and *parade*" that a true republican needed to assert the superiority of the U.S. Constitution to the unwritten British constitution, and the superiority of Americans, in all their simplicity, to Britain's "haughty nobility," as the writer reminded his readers. The irony in all such press-driven hyperventilation was the fact that the Adams family continued to live modestly and that the federal Constitution was close in design to that which John Adams had given to the state of Massachusetts several years before.[61]

Even JQA's sister got into the act. From London, where she, her husband, and the polemical Thomas Paine all resided at this time, Nabby wrote to her brother requesting the "Publicola" essays while claiming scant appreciation for the subjects they covered. Nonetheless, she had what she thought was encouraging intelligence: "Tom pain as he is called continues to Busy himself very much and to Court persecution in every shape—he has undoubtedly a party here but the Sensible and judicious People do not join him and I beleive he is falling off fast in the minds of that class of Persons."[62]

"Publicola" proved so effective that the British government, delighted to learn that the radical noisemaker Tom Paine was being torn apart by an American, turned to a respected London publisher and urged him to reprint the essays in book form. John Stockdale, who had produced John Adams's *Defence of the Constitutions* as well as Thomas Jefferson's compendious *Notes on Virginia,* was pleased to oblige. Yet, in doing the job, he made the common mistake of assuming the author to be the senior Adams and initially printed the title page with that designation. Once apprised of his mistake, Stockdale made the necessary correction, though some "John Adams" versions found their way into distinguished hands—such as the British Library. Stockdale next approached Vice President Adams about reissuing the *Defence,* with any additions or amendments the author desired to contribute. Unmoved, Adams replied to his publisher, "My 'work on Government,' as you are pleased to call it, has been so much neglected by Britons and so much insulted by Frenchmen, Irishmen and Americans, that it shall either be consigned to everlasting oblivion or be transmitted to posterity as it is." Always in character, John Adams.[63]

So, how much did John Adams actually target Paine? The answer is this: at least as much as his son did, though not in the public record. JQA undoubtedly heard his father say more than once that he considered Paine's celebrated pamphlet of January 1776, *Common Sense,* overrated and that its author, then a newcomer to America, did not deserve the credit he received (and would continue to get from history) for breaking the final resistance among members of the Continental Congress when they acquiesced in a final separation from Great Britain.

John Adams's stalking of Paine was a reminder of his belittling of Franklin during the negotiations in Paris. Always feeling his own accomplishments undervalued, he drew contrasts to the unwarranted celebrity of others. With Franklin and Paine, he found himself fighting the magnetic power of two men with transatlantic audiences. In 1793, once Paine had published part 2 of *Rights of Man* and was charged in Britain with seditious libel, Vice President Adams was able to inform his wife that the prosecuting attorney general at the trial "was pleased to quote large Passages from Publicola, with Some handsome Compliments: so that Publicola is become a Law Authority." Publicola's father sounded almost giddy in reckoning with the influence over politics that his son had surreptitiously acquired.[64]

SIX

EXTORTERS

It must ever be remembered that the Mob is a Part of the People, and I begin to fear the most influential Part. The Mob has established every Monarchy upon Earth—The Mob has ultimately over thrown every free Republick. . . . The Mob must ever be in the Power of Government—Government never in the Power of the Mob.

—JOHN ADAMS TO JOHN QUINCY ADAMS, *September 19, 1795*

I have received your favour of Septr: 19. . . . There are indeed situations in which, no service can be rendered without the assistance and support of popularity, but there are others in which it can be of no public advantage, and in that case popular opposition is nothing more than a danger to defy, or a difficulty to overcome.

—JOHN QUINCY ADAMS TO JOHN ADAMS, *December 29, 1795*

John Quincy held his tongue on political subjects for the next couple of years, save for communications with his father. The reason he gave for his lowered profile was the modest expectations he still had from his law business. "I have been really apprehensive of becoming politically known, before I could establish a *professional* reputation," he told his father late in 1792. "I knew that my independence and consequently my happiness in life depended upon this, and I have sincerely wished rather to remain in the shade than to appear as a politician without any character as a Lawyer.—These Sentiments have still great weight in my mind."[1]

The elder Adams, by contrast, did not let up. His otherwise spotty diary as vice president finds him in 1796 belittling the Paine blockbuster that succeeded *Rights of Man*, a broad critique of biblical authority titled *The Age of Reason*. "The Christian Religion is, above all the Religions that ever prevailed or existed in ancient or modern Times, The Religion of Wisdom, Virtue, Equity and Humanity," he wrote, "let the Blackguard Paine say what he will." To his second son, Charles, he wrote of Paine, "It is a Pity that his ridiculous 'Age of Reason': had not appeared before his ranting 'Rights of Man,['] that the poison concealed in it, might have been Suspected from the hateful Character of the Physician who prescribed it." John Adams was by no means a religious man, but Paine appeared to him boastfully antireligious, which meant, in effect, disruptively antisocial. And that irked him.

In 1805, permanently retired from government, he would write to Harvard's Dr. Benjamin Waterhouse of his disgust that their times were already being branded "The Age of Reason" when they had produced so much "Mischief." The prime culprit in all of this was, he charged, Tom Paine, "a mongrel between Pigg and Puppy, begotten by a wild Boar on a Bitch Wolf." If ridicule was an Adams specialty, this was one of his most colorful utterances.[2]

Enter Columbus

In the 1792 election, John Adams won a second term as vice president, though as with everything else in his political life the course of true grit did not run smoothly. He wrote to John Quincy at the peak of the campaign season, "The Utmost Efforts of my Ennemies have undoubtedly been exerted, and what success they may have had in Virginia and the States to the southward of it, is uncertain. New York it is expected will show their vain Spite against New England. It is not Antifederalism against Federalism, nor Democracy against Aristocracy. This is all Pretext. It is N. York vs N. England." Washington was unanimously reelected, of course, and while Governor George Clinton of New York received 50 electoral votes, Adams amassed 77, actually improving on his numbers from the 1788 election.[3]

Meanwhile, JQA was solidifying relationships in Boston. His law practice was finally on a firm footing and earning him a respectable income.[4] For the Fourth of July, in 1793, he was given a commensurate honor, being asked to deliver the keynote speech at the Old South Meeting House, famous as the site of much Revolutionary oratory. One local newspaper dutifully reported on the event, declaring that "John Q. Adams, Esq.," spoke before "a very numerous audience, whose countenances testified the sincerity of the universal plaudits." The speech itself was "excelled by none who have preceded him." The *Massachusetts Mercury* acclaimed JQA's classical prowess: "The eloquence and spirit of the composition, and the forceful elocution of the Speaker, excited such a *burst of admiration,* as would have flattered a CATO."

Cato the Elder did not come from patrician stock. He lived simply and rose in esteem in his community on the sole basis of his talents. Eloquent beyond measure, he defended his political positions admirably and served with distinction in the Roman Senate for years after his time as consul ended—which one may choose to see as an early projection of the second Adams's unique destiny. If the comparison to Cato was gratuitous at this stage in his career, it would one day prove prescient.[5]

When the vice president's son prescribed a course in patriotism on that Fourth of July, ten years had elapsed since signatures and seals were affixed to the Treaty of Paris. John Quincy Adams, a witness to that moment, held that "praise upon the fathers" needed to be inculcated in every student of American history. More than it was a call to arms, the Revolution was an appeal to future Americans to identify with the moral energy of the instant when the world witnessed an exhibition of "the feelings of injured freedom, the manners of social equality, and the principles of eternal justice." To be a republican, said the younger Adams, was to re-embody the Revolutionary spirit—here, he could not but have meant the courageous spirit of men like his father. The Fourth of July was for validating principles, not for raising fears of a political society coming apart.[6]

And yet the present could not be ignored. The obvious subtext on this Independence Day was the stark contrast between American and French Revolutionary zeal. The first was soundly argued, the second frenzied and depraved. For even if it was born of the same sentiments as the American Revolution, the French version had bubbled into a riotous soup. In 1789–1790, it had been greeted with guarded optimism in the United States as a mass movement that retained the authority of an enlightened liberal nobility and sought to enact social good. By the opening days of 1793, when Louis XVI was guillotined, the abstract talk about natural rights that helped bring on the French Revolution had yielded to political demagoguery and frightening levels of inhumanity.

As the violence increased in France, violence of thought increasingly powered American presses. The widening gap between the two political wings in the United States was already being defined on this basis. Federalism's call for a responsible, civilizing authority crept into a vocabulary that had earlier highlighted civil liberty and economic justice. An intense competition for control of Americans' collective conscience was under way. This is what caused John Quincy Adams to embellish his 1793 Fourth of July oration with dire warnings about French revolutionaries poised to "scatter pestilence and death among the nations."[7]

Yet another Anglo-French war erupted that year. The Washington administration announced that it would maintain a position of neutrality. Vice President Adams was already strongly associated with Federalist reaction against French ideas and popular politics, when the arrival on American shores of a new French ambassador, Edmond Charles Genet, stimulated even deeper resentments. Genet, who was not much older than JQA, insinuated himself into U.S. politics by directly encouraging American citizens to mount privateering expeditions and plunder British-allied vessels wherever they might find them. No less galling, Genet took liberties by pressuring President Washington into a pro-French stance, which deeply concerned the secretary of state: Jefferson, who was otherwise the best friend revolutionary France had in the U.S. government, called Genet's appointment "calamitous" and his treatment of Washington "indecent." Even Jefferson could not control the enthusiastic response Genet received from a large cadre of well-organized pro-French Philadelphians. President Washington had been forewarned by the senior U.S. diplomat in France, Gouverneur Morris, that Genet was something of an "upstart." But no one quite expected how much questionable activity he would start up.[8]

The younger Adams returned to print in November and December 1793 in the guise of "Columbus," writing once more for Ben Russell's *Columbian Centinel*. With even greater acerbity than Publicola displayed, Columbus condemned the French envoy. Genet had "made all the news-presses on the continent groan," he said, making such a spectacle of himself as to invite citizens "to indulge a smile at human impudence." In calling out the Frenchman's "repeated insults upon the first magistrate of the *American* Union, and upon the national government," JQA allowed that any U.S. citizen was free "to express without controul his sentiments upon public measures and the conduct of public men," but the same privilege did not extend to a foreign official residing in the country. In making direct appeals to the American public, Genet had crossed a line, rendering himself "obnoxious to every feather in the wing of wit, and every shaft in the quiver of satire." It was now open season on a French revolutionary who had become "the most implacable and dangerous enemy to the peace and happiness of my country."[9]

As it turned out, John Quincy's father knew a more circumspect Genet than the one he met in Philadelphia. As a diplomat residing in Paris, he had on more than one occasion enjoyed the company of the young man's mother and father in the course of carrying out his duties—the elder Genet having headed the translation section of the prerevolutionary Foreign Ministry. Though less instrumental than others in the administration in the push back against Genet, Vice President Adams had a clear perspective on the family. He told his wife he considered the younger Genet "destitute of all Experience in popular Governments" and "wholly ignorant of the Law of Nature & Nations." In person, he was "civil" enough, exhibiting "a flitting fluttering Imagination." But by no means did John Adams want his son to desist from criticizing Genet. Upon reading "Columbus," he wrote from Philadelphia to inform him that he appreciated the "maturity of Reflection and Elegance of Style" of the essays, and he reassured his eldest that President Washington had "formed the same Judgment with Columbus."

This interesting letter from father to son reflected the jitters being felt across the political spectrum. Vocal critics of the administration's neutrality policy who looked less unfavorably upon Genet channeled their energies into "democratic societies"—spontaneously organized groups of the disaffected that were fanning out from Philadelphia to cities and towns of varying size. President Washington was tormented by these political clubs, and Vice President Adams himself distracted by the phenomenon. Aiming to discover where Columbus stood, he turned it all into a big joke. "How does your Democratical Society proceed in Boston?" the vice president queried his son. "There ought to be another Society instituted according to my Principles, under the Title of the Aristocratical Society: and a third under that of The Monarchical Society and no Resolution ought to have Validity, untill it has been considered & approved by all three." The theorist of balanced government was mystified by it all, admitting that he did not know where things were heading. "Our People would do well to consider, to what Precipice they are running."[10]

Along with the provocations of Genet, a deadly yellow fever epidemic consumed Philadelphia in the summer months of 1793, killing thousands. In a retrospective on this nervous moment, John Adams, as an old man, suggested to Jefferson that the masses Genet awakened actually "threatened to drag Washington out of his House" and might have toppled the U.S. government had not the curse of the disease driven people away and shut down the town.[11]

Amid the rise of the bloodthirsty Jacobins, as French troops invaded Holland and food riots broke out in Paris, Washington began his second four-year term. Closer to home, slaves went free on the war-torn island of St. Domingue (the French colony of Haiti) as white planters fled to safety in the United States. The new Fugitive Slave Act, promoted by southern U.S. congressmen, allowed for the recapture of escaped human property by slave owners or their agents crossing into the North. Within Washington's cabinet, a power struggle swelled in intensity as the ideological war between Secretaries Jefferson and Hamilton came to center on their rival perceptions of the danger posed by so-called French ideas.

John Adams felt fairly helpless. The hardening of doctrine, the formation of factions, the organization of distinct parties (with scurrilous editors attached), combined to put a strain on everyone in government. The vice president was no unifier, having alienated key figures among the national elite by writing too much. As far as he was concerned, his countrymen had deliberately reduced his political philosophy to a caricature. He was willing to concede that the Revolutionary generation had turned on itself, that the collective mood had grown savage.

It was the younger generation that now claimed John Adams's declining hopes for the nation. He was only exaggerating slightly when he bade Abigail at the end of the year, "Your Children must conduct the affairs of this Country, or they will be miserably managed, for I declare I know of nobody but them or some of them rising up who are qualified for it." Charles and Tom Adams had graduated from Harvard and were lately admitted to the Massachusetts bar. For the moment, their father felt confident that the two younger sons would soon join the eldest in contributing to the national political conversation. If he wasn't thinking "dynasty" per se, he was as hopeful about their futures as he was disappointed in the actions of his peers.[12]

The eldest of his three boys was no less vexed than his father when it came to domestic fallout from the French Revolution. He saw neutrality—the middle course—as a sensible model to pursue. Refusing to set aside the Franco-American friendship of the prior decade, while admitting that he was "irritated" with the British, JQA told his father he believed the United States had "grounds of complaint against both with respect to their treatment of our commerce." It was best not to be too easily swayed by the instability within France when "the general disposition of the french ruling powers has been consistently favourable to us, and that of the british Government, acrimonious, jealous, and under the guise of false pretentions, deeply malignant." The father maintained a strong conviction that his eldest son was as reasonable as he was independent.[13]

John Quincy was gratified that "Columbus" had met with a generally favorable reception. At the same time, he reminded his father of his reluctance to say or do too much. "I cannot wish to be the rival of any candidate for public office of any kind," he attested. His motive in writing was simple patriotism. Genet and his "frenzies" had been dealt with, but the contention between parties that his father had condemned from the start of Washington's administration deterred him from seeking public office. "We can be ruined only by ourselves," he guided them both.[14]

His father had a plan for him and would not be deterred. "You must bustle in the croud[,] make speeches in Town Meeting, and push yourself forward," he exhorted as spring arrived in 1794. Of all the times for John Quincy to think of shying from public advocacy, it made no sense that he should choose this critical moment. John Adams knew his son's worth and wanted him to shine: "An erect figure, a steady Countenance[,] a neat dress, a genteel Air; an oratorical Period [that is, sentence], a resolute determined Spirit, often do more than deep Erudition or indefatigable Application." By practicing the art of address, he would, by alienating fewer important people, do a better job in politics than his father had.

But another part of him fully expected the pattern to repeat. "My sons according to all Appearances, must be content to crawl into fame and be satisfied with mediocrity of fortune, like their Father." Contradicting the faith in self-reinvention he had just expressed, he attributed to John Quincy, Charles, and Tom, all at once, "some Aukwardness in address" and "peculiarity of feelings" such that he himself owned (and owned up to). He was convinced of an ineradicable something in the Adams imprint. He then cautioned the son in whom he placed his fondest hopes, "You must not complain. The World will take Advantage of every murmur, and revenge itself on you for that superiority in some Things which it knows you possess." And then the kicker: "You must extort Admiration or you will never have it." Extort he would.[15]

A month later, the father repeated these concerns, this time directing John Quincy to re-familiarize himself with the particular section in *Discourses on Davila* wherein he wrote of the competition for public recognition ("Passion for the Approbation of others"). He had articulated his ruling conviction that worth ("*real Abilities*") was the underdog in any contest with artificially obtained popularity and privilege. John Adams derived "the whole Theory of Government, Despotic as well as free," from his observations about ambition. "Delicacy and Caution" should therefore be JQA's watchwords. "A Man must not commit himself," lest he "furnish his Rivals with stories to tell, of his Pride and Vanity."[16]

Here we have two of John Adams's most telltale letters to the grown-up Johnny. A Freudian might label the mass of advice he delivered as a form of "projection": the father has chosen to air his frustration with a world he judges to stand against him by imagining the son's self-rescue as the one way to rescue his own flagging spirits. To Abigail, during that same season, he said of the inheritor of his name and reputation, "All my hopes are with him: both for my Family and Country." Along with: "I have often thought he has more prudence at 27, than his Father at 58."[17]

John Quincy was his father's son—which is to say, his own man. No longer complaining about the state of his law practice, he grappled with his father's exhortations on the subject of public engagement. "You recommend me to attend the town meetings and make speeches; to meet with caucuses and join political clubs. But I am afraid of all these things.—They might make me a better politician, and give me an earlier chance of appearing as a public man; but that would throw me completely in the power of the people, and all my future life would be a life of dependence." His outspokenness impresses. "I would rather continue sometime longer in obscurity, and make some provision for Fortune, before I sally out in quest of Fame."

JQA did not yet wish to commit to the life his father had warmed to at a slightly later age. "If I can 'crawl into Fame,' like my Father," he wrote, "by serving so essentially the cause of Humanity and of Liberty, as he has done, I shall hardly breathe a sigh upon seeing any of the political Phaeton's leap at one bound into the Chariot of the Sun, to set the world on fire, and then be hurl'd to destruction for their plans."[18]

A phaeton, in the Adamses' day, was a horse-drawn carriage, but it was no ordinary story from Greek mythology that the son was conveying. The original Phaeton, son of Helios, demanded proof of his divine connection, asking for the reins to the Sun God's chariot. Granted the chance, he could not control the fire-breathing horses, and so fell to earth, destroying all in his path. His life was then taken from him by Zeus. John Quincy did not want to take the risk of succeeding to electoral politics in an untimely way, only to crash and burn.

In cognitive terms, we may say, John Quincy Adams was averse to accepting a diplomatic assignment in 1794. But an appointment to The Hague might already have been in the works when the father responded uncharitably to his son's denunciation of political ambition: "You come into Life with Advantages which will disgrace you, if your success is mediocre.—And if you do not rise to the head not only of your Profession but of your Country it will be owing to your own *Laziness Slovenliness* and *Obstinacy*."[19]

Vice President Adams was banking on his son's saying yes to Holland. And everything else.

Unsolicited Appointment

Diplomatic life ended for John Adams when he returned home and became vice president, a position with more symbolism than responsibility. For John Quincy, a diplomatic career was just around the corner, and all that he had soaked up in the previous decade was meant to be regarded as his apprenticeship. Despite his protests, the Boston attorney was about to take part in the same fight for national respectability abroad that his father had waged. Diplomacy would be his occupation for years to come, the most prominent feature in his résumé of qualifications for high office. It was that simple. Or was it?

First and foremost, it was George Washington who wanted his vice president's son named U.S. ambassador to the Netherlands. Because an appointment of this nature looked too much like an "inside deal," Vice President Adams wrestled within himself over his boss's resolve. He didn't want anyone to see how much *he* wanted it to happen. On the surface, John Adams kept his hands off while the matter remained under consideration, but we know that Secretary of State Edmund Randolph (Jefferson's successor) met privately with him, which leaves open the distinct possibility that the decision was made with some involvement by the appointee's father.

"You will have no young rivals to rejoice at your failures or to envy your success," John Quincy had earlier grumbled to his cousin Billy Cranch, and now the moment had arrived when just such a test lay before him. Taken completely by surprise, he was truly unnerved by the prospect of being talked into accepting the Dutch assignment. He noted in his diary, "I had laid down as a principle that I never would solicit for any public office whatever." His father insisted to him that he had "never uttered a word" in his son's favor, and that he should rest assured there would be no backlash: the Senate had approved the nomination "without a dissenting vote." Regardless, JQA considered himself unfit and diarized, "I was very sensible, that neither my years, my experience, my reputation, nor my talents could entitle me to an office of so much respectability."

In the end, he conceded that he had little choice. His persistent father rode up from Philadelphia, where the national capital sat, to Quincy, informing his son in person how surprised he was to learn what Washington and Randolph were up to—surprised, yes, but obviously delighted. "His satisfaction at the appointment is much greater than mine," wrote the son soon after. The younger would not have been as discomposed if he'd been consulted before the decision was "irrevocably" made. Even better, he breathed onto the page of his diary, "I rather wish it had not been made at all."[20]

In advance of departure for Europe, JQA spent weeks in Philadelphia, preparing. He met with President Washington and cabinet members. He watched diplomacy in action as the president entertained a Chickasaw Indian delegation. He dined with the French minister. Not insignificantly, he hired his brother Tom to accompany him to The Hague and serve as his private secretary there. He would pick up where his father left off in soliciting loans; Tom would discharge the duties he himself had undertaken for his father a decade earlier, after John Thaxter's departure.

Virtually succeeding his father as minister to the Dutch Republic, John Quincy did not, however, think of himself as the inheritor of his father's political ambition. He did not want elective office, and relying on a government salary was no one's idea of long-term financial security. Secretary of State Randolph told the new minister that the Dutch mission was "almost exclusively reduced to a pecuniary Negotiation," but the knowing John Adams took a different tack in wishing his son success: "The Post at the Hague is an important Diplomatick Station, which may afford many opportunities of acquiring political Information and of penetrating the Designs of many Cabinets in Europe."

The son bemoaned his fate precisely as his father had years before, when he'd left good prospects in Boston to his brothers at the bar in order to commit to a career in politics. What would he find on his return? "My juniors who are now just opening their Offices, or are yet students will then have reached the station from which I have departed. . . . [I]n returning to the bar I shall descend as much below the level of my ambition and pretensions as I have been by my present appointment raised above it." If entering the diplomatic corps was a promotion, it was a temporary one only. He calculated on a bleak future. Accepting the appointment his father wanted for him, John Q. Adams agonized.

He told his father just how he felt: "The idea of being many years absent from my Country; from my family my connections and friends is so painful, that I feel a necessity for fixing upon some period to which I may look forward with an expectation of being restored to them." How long could he stand to be apart from those he cared for most in the world? Three years—that was the time limit he decreed. As his sister said of him when they parted company in France in 1785, he repeated now: "It is hardly possible for an American to be long in Europe, without losing in some measure his national character." He feared becoming a kind of pariah, a man without a country. He did not want to lose America.

His more stoical father was of a different mind and recommended against establishing a fixed date of return. He encouraged his son to think ahead to the day he would resume a surer position before the bar in Boston. Hard work would pay off. Beyond that, he proffered some unexpected political advice: "Endeavour to obtain Correspondences with able Men in the southern & middle States as well as in the northern ones, and these will inform you & advise you." He signed off with a few tender words: "I am with constant Affection / your Friend and Father."[21]

The Adams brothers, John Quincy and Thomas, embarked from Boston on yet another highly risky ocean adventure. The twenty-eight-day voyage to England ended up being close in degree of danger to that of *La Sensible*. The *Alfred* was old, in a "flimsy crazy condition," as JQA wrote. But a considerable part of the danger the passengers faced was ascribed to the captain, whose "intellectual & convivial powers were below the level of mediocrity." Passing judgment in unambiguous language—that Adams specialty—seemed especially apropos in describing the man in charge: "He was liberally endowed with that self-conceit, and that exalted opinion of his own capacity which is so generally allotted to those from whom in reason it might be the least expected, and with an imperative, not to say an arbitrary tone, which naturally results from a station where authority is absolute and submission unqualified." It was his father's rank criticism of another absolutist ship captain, Pierre Landais, redux. Once more, a man's perverse pride, as much as a leaky hull, combined to reduce the already uncertain odds of survival. The intrepid J. Q. Adams, survivor of multiple travel mishaps, vowed this time, upon docking in London, to "avoid ever embarking in an egg-shell again to cross the atlantic."[22]

JAY'S TREATY

Before continuing to the Netherlands, this new pair of Adamses paused in London to deliver official state papers to the negotiator John Jay. JQA received a thorough briefing on the commercial negotiations "now on foot" (as his diary reads) between Chief Justice Jay and representatives of the British ministry. With his father's old comrade Jay, he attended the Covent Garden Theatre and witnessed the debut of a "Miss Wallis" in *Romeo and Juliet*. As a connoisseur of female beauty, he wrote, "Her external appearance has every thing to captivate. Young, beautiful, and amiable in the highest degree. But," he had to add, "her voice has hardly sufficient strength to fill the house." At intermission, the American endured a "thunder clap of loud applause" during a performance of "God Save the King." John Quincy mocked, in the privacy of his diary, the pretense of "pure Patriotism" that persisted in the hall for a good ten minutes. Without commenting on how any of the other Americans in his party behaved, he said that he rose with the rest of the audience to avoid making a spectacle of himself but considered himself "under no Obligation" to clap his hands. Back home, Federalists were accused of being subservient to British interests; JQA felt not the least enthusiasm for the British model.[23]

He had seen a lot of John Jay in Paris in the prior decade, during negotiations to finalize the terms of American independence. Now, an as yet untested diplomat, JQA listened to the man his father spoke so well of, enjoying "an hour of agreeable conversation" with the experienced envoy after a formal dinner. Picking up on the American delegation's mixed feelings about a treaty that was in the final stages of production, John Quincy concurred with the consensus view that its provisions were "much below the standard that I think would be advantageous to the Country," though they were, he promptly added, "preferable to a War." His father said precisely the same thing eight months later, after Jay's return to America. Congressional Republicans, led by James Madison, vociferously disagreed, totally confident that Great Britain had no thought of attacking its best customer for finished goods.[24]

War was not entirely beyond the realm of possibility, though, and the fledgling U.S. Navy was in no position to oppose its constantly expanding British counterpart. London was too stingy to grant the American merchant fleet access to its West Indian possessions, and British warships were already descending on U.S.-based merchant vessels on the high seas. The president's stated neutrality policy, of "friendly and impartial" relations with all, was a rhetorical device that would prove to be of long-standing value, but at the moment it was a stopgap measure amid Anglo-French warfare with Caribbean repercussions. Secretary of State Jefferson, before he retired at the end of 1793, had urged a tougher stand to compel the British to open to free trade. Seeing an uptick in anti-British sentiment on the streets of Philadelphia, Jefferson wished to "repress the spirits of the people within the limits of a fair neutrality," but he baldly mocked Hamiltonian eagerness to expose America's "breach" to "every kick" from Britain. Jefferson did not perceive in Vice President Adams a milquetoast who would stand with Hamilton in accepting "habitual insults" from London. Yet in Congress, JQA's father cast the deciding vote as president of the Senate, defeating a retaliatory measure that would have antagonized the British ministry.

"As a Treaty of Commerce this Treaty will indeed be of little use to us," John Quincy wrote. According to his extensive notes, one of England's most "conspicuous" opponents of American independence grandly assured Jay that Anglo-American friendship would be restored, and a "most liberal and amicable intercourse" would ensue. But when JQA visited his father's old friend Edmund Jenings, the Marylander long resident in Britain, that gentleman protested at length: all of England, "from the sovereign to the beggar," harbored an "inveterate hatred against America," he said, and King George was bent on one day restoring his dominion over North America. Speculation abounded. John Quincy hesitated. "When Mr. Jay asked me my opinions," the youngest of diplomats attested in his London diary, "I answered that I could only acquiesce" in a less than perfect treaty.[25]

No American considered the Jay Treaty, when it was made public in 1795, an ideal solution to any of the problems left over from the Revolution. London agreed to abandon all frontier posts in the Northwest, having been obliged to do so years earlier by the terms of the 1783 Treaty of Paris—a concession that was no concession at all. The United States agreed it would not pass any discriminatory tariff legislation (though London was under no such constraints) and would abide by the system in place, which accorded England first position among nations. The United States, obtaining marginally more access to Britain's Caribbean colonies, appeared to be otherwise abandoning an obvious cause: the rights of neutrals.

Jay's effigy was mangled, burned, and blown up in popular rallies in Philadelphia and elsewhere as Federalist politicos decried "mobocracy." Vice President Adams shared in the alarmed response but remained publicly silent. Despite his close association with Jay, he was not party to Washington's determinations during this period; Hamilton more or less commanded the president's full attention. When the Jay Treaty only narrowly passed the Senate, John Adams wrote to his son, "Poor Jay has gone through as fiery an ordeal As I did, when I was Suspected of a blasphemous Doubt of Tom Paines Infallibility, in Consequence of Publicolas Eloquence and Jeffersons Rashness."[26]

REVENGE EXCITES

Writing to his wife of the out-of-control French Revolution in late November 1794, the vice president lamented, "As Revenge excites Revenge, when will it Stop!" And again, three days later, redirecting his angst to the domestic scene in America: "This Country is to be the Asylum of all the discontented, turbulent, profligate and Desperate from all Parts of Europe."[27]

It is important for us to understand just how many were as convinced as John Adams that a spillover of French radicalism into America had to be guarded against. The Jacobins had not "exploded" onto the scene. A small group of intellectuals had joined together after the fall of the Bastille in 1789, attentive constitutionalists wary of royalist plans to undermine the Revolution. Their main ambition was to function as communicators of a political education. But in 1792, the Jacobin Society morphed into something larger and more dangerous as their moderate members lost control over the tenor of public debate and they became a band of ruthless authoritarians acting at the behest of the masses. A close observer, the ill-fated marquis de Condorcet, so-called last of the philosophes, emphatically warned what democracy unbounded looked like. He realized that the ordinary people in whose interest the French Revolution was launched did not yet understand the intellectual arguments in favor of humanistic government. The historian James Kloppenberg traces the contours of the Jacobin movement and says of Condorcet's timely warning, "The people distrusted everybody and wanted to judge everything by themselves. The pendulum of popular sentiment . . . could swing swiftly from forced impotence to delusions of omnipotence." Democracy unmediated was chaos unleashed.[28]

FACILIS DESCENSUS

In reenacting his father's former role in the Netherlands as a clearinghouse of European political intelligence, the new minister to that country, John Quincy Adams, took up America's interest. He would be his father's eyes and ears on the Continent for the next five years. Once the first vice president became the second president, the first son would remain his father's one truly dependable source of news abroad. JQA was now, more than ever, and in more than biological terms, an extension of John Adams.

Father-son correspondence in the waning months of the Washington administration, though as fond and expressive as before, functioned as a warning system. The fate of Holland, its golden age now a century gone, was intricately bound up in the ongoing Anglo-French War and continuing insecurity inside France. Before he heard from their son, Vice President Adams could only report to Abigail that "the News from Europe is enigmatical enough at present. The whole Theatre of Europe has been taken up, for years, with the Representation of a Tragedy of Errors. One knows not what is true, nor what is false: what is right nor what is wrong." His son's reports alone made sense of what otherwise seemed senseless.[29]

The "Tragedy of Errors," in its Dutch incarnation, involved democratic activism on the part of the "Patriots," who began to organize around the time John Adams ceased his work at The Hague, in 1783, and rose to prominence soon after John Q. Adams took up his post. Because the Dutch military was fairly impotent, the king of Prussia (related to the Dutch *stadtholder* William V by marriage) had, in 1787, dispatched forces against the democrats. The Dutch Patriots were anti-British, and many thousands of them took up residence in Paris once their movement started to fizzle. Things changed in early 1795, five years into the French Revolution, as the French-protected Dutch revolutionaries prepared to take over their country. The hapless William, Prince of Orange, fled to England.

JQA chronicled all of this in warm letters home. "The first and dearest of all my wishes is personally to give satisfaction and obtain the approbation of my parents," he wrote in June 1795, "and in a public capacity to justify the confidence placed in me by the appointment I now hold." This was a direct response to his father's exhortation, written two months before: "No Character in human Life requires more Discretion, Caution, and Reserve, than that of a Public Minister in a foreign Country." The young diplomat was gratified, he said, by the "kindness and indulgence" he received from his father. He missed him and reminded him repeatedly how much he counted on their periodic correspondence. Near the end of that year, he wrote, "The pleasure I receive from every new testimony of your approbation, is pure as it is exquisite, nor can there I think belong to the lot of humanity, a sensation more delicious than that of giving satisfaction to a Parent's expectations, when they have been founded upon a Parent's extraordinary tenderness and cares." The letters of 1795 were some of John Quincy's most effusive.[30]

Other than reaffirming his deep devotion, the son carried out the essential business of preserving, as he put it, "a chain of general intelligence relative to the most important political affairs of Europe." He did his job with the requisite amount of Adamsian scorn, calling out the confused Dutch activists as "a detachment from the old Patriots, whose principles they have abandoned altogether." The struggle between the revolutionaries and Orange loyalists was an ugly contest between one "wicked faction" and another. No one believed in anything anymore, save for the nonspecific "Rights of Man." An attempt was under way to constitute a new national government administered by a single assembly and predicated on universal suffrage. John Quincy declared the plan unrealizable, compressing his prognosis into a concise Latin phrase he knew his father would appreciate: "Facilis descensus Averni!" The descent into hell is easy! (The quotation is from Virgil's *Aeneid*.)[31]

A Franco-Dutch alliance was in the planning stages, and war with England was deemed inevitable. Paris was once again, by all accounts, "in a state of agitation." Complicating matters, France and Prussia, at war for the past three years, were rumored to be near rapprochement. This would be the Treaty of Basel: it raised tensions among nations formerly allied against France and at the same time foreshadowed the rise of Napoleon Bonaparte. JQA, watching from the traditional seat of government at The Hague, could do little. American ministers, by definition, held a "tolerably insignificant" position in Europe—even within the Netherlands, he averred. Yet something had occurred to suddenly change the reception he was getting: the "ill-will . . . covered with forms of decency" that he had coolly accepted in his first months there had unexpectedly yielded to a friendlier disposition on the part of Dutch power brokers since the armies of France had come through. "Personally my situation is far more agreeable than it was; but nothing is to be done"; that is, no official business was to be accomplished.

It was an odd thing to experience. "The Country is conquered," he summarized. And yet tendencies he observed among European affairs suggested to him that William V would one day be restored. "With him must come again the subserviency to the mistress of the Sea. In every political view this

Republic will in future be nothing more than a part of France or of Britain." America was blessedly separated from the jockeying for power. Neither the "mistress of the Sea"—Great Britain—nor the unruly French impressed John Q. Adams as superior to the United States in any measure but brute force.[32]

The French still generated the most disorder. The Terror was over, but the killing went on. "Former murderers are murdered with as little ceremony: the drowners are drowned," he advised his father. The British continued their own predatory activities. "On the strength of their maritime supremacy," they were "famishing their enemies into submission: and as they were unable to protect the Hollanders as friends they have concluded to starve them too. All neutral vessels laden with provisions bound for France or Holland are to be captured." British policy makers, like the privateers that patrolled at their behest, operated according to their own selfish pleasure. John Quincy made the point with another of Virgil's witticisms: "Trahit sua quemque voluptas." Each is led on by his desire.[33]

The Dutch continued in political "languor and imbecility," while the French squeezed from their northern neighbors the last gasp of public spirit. There was plenty of lip service yet being paid to beautiful notions of liberty and equality and as much crude invective being hurled at the House of Orange. A "spirit of turbulence" was kept alive in political clubs—"popular societies"—which were now "as numerous and mischievous here as they are elsewhere." In Rotterdam, "a mob of several thousand people assembled," demanding the arrest of members of the former government. Faced with this threat, the government panicked and consented to the formation of an ad hoc assembly. The sides continued to banter, but to no avail. JQA presented the details to his father so as to explain the effete condition of the Low Countries. It crystallized for him in the one Rotterdam confrontation. "In the rulers you see moderation, a regard for good principles," he wrote. Yet all cowered before the "popular will," as defined by the latest mob. Defiance took the place of just principle. Writing this to his father was preaching to the choir.[34]

Back home, George Washington remained obsessed with the local citizen gatherings that top Federalists disparaged as "self created" societies. Democratic groups wanted government to get an earful from the governed, and government was less than appreciative. By now, numbers of citizens were increasingly comfortable with the word "democracy," though it was still widely associated in the Federalist press with lawless Jacobins and the willful degradation of civil order.

The French Directory put the Terror behind and worked up a constitution. But John Quincy piled on as he revisited his father's critique of Franklin and Turgot. The French were loosely calling this, their newest product, a "*democratic* Constitution," the son reported home, adding parenthetically, "for they still give it that epithet without any scruple." The "*system of balances*" it contained was being spoken of with reference to Franklin—not John Adams, of course—as well as the moderate revolutionary figure comte de Mirabeau, deceased, and the philosophe Condorcet, a victim of the Terror. The French diplomat and power player Abbé Sieyès—"the *Great* Sieyes as one of my honest Dutch friends calls him"—separately proposed his own, improved model of a constitution, invoking the "elegant pleasantry" of Franklin on balanced government. JQA disparaged all French boastfulness as political, if not philosophical, naïveté. It did not have to be stated that it was his father who deserved credit for first proposing, and most convincingly arguing for, the eminently practical idea of a balanced republic. And he did it all, of course, a decade before the French Revolution.[35]

Appreciating his son's long dispatches for their cleverness as much as their content, Vice President Adams passed several of his letters on to President Washington. Telling John Quincy he had done so, he took the liberty to proffer more life advice while he had his son's attention: the elder Adams now calculated the optimum stay abroad in the diplomatic service as three years—unless named to a more coveted post than Holland. "I want your society as well as that of my other Children," he explained, "but I must submit to your and their Arrangements in Life." Whose arrangements? The father pushed his agenda: "I wish you to come home and be married after two Years. But you must return with the Spirit of a Stoick—a determind Spirit to bear any neglect, any Affront from your Countrymen without resentment." Figuring John Quincy would willingly return to the Massachusetts bar ("go obstinately to the Bar, . . . and attend patiently in your office for Business"), he cautioned him to expect to be passed up for advancement in favor of some "ignorant but chattering Coxcomb." Because when it came to making decisions, even the "wise & learned" could err in the same manner as an "indiscriminating Multitude." Those at the top were "at least as often wrong as the Mob." If you're an Adams, you trust that human nature is untrustworthy.[36]

John Adams harbored ambitions for his son and hinted that a more prestigious job might be his. The only two other American missions in Europe were Paris and London, and JQA preemptively rejected both: "I must assure you in the most unequivocal manner, that I have not the shadow of a wish for a more elevated rank than that in which I am now placed." On the one hand, he resented the British for their anti-American prejudice; on the other, he had no interest whatsoever in abiding the seesaw politics of revolutionary France. Of the two postings, he considered the English "an object of aversion" and the French "of indifference."

As he had done before in judging himself too young for his present position, he restated with more firmness of mind. He honestly believed that there were others more experienced and more deserving of plum posts, especially London. As an American obliged to confront the cunning of its diplomatic elite, the imperious treatment, the bullying manner, he knew his youth would not play well. He'd seen how smug the British were about maritime supremacy when he stood at John Jay's side. American commerce hardly stood a chance. It was not as if he had to remind his father about the character of Britain's representatives, but he did anyway: "Nothing will be conceded but to necessity, and every thing will be obtained that artifice, or cajolery can pilfer, or that insolence under all the forms of courtly politeness can extort." He was unready to engage with such people. "I have been accustomed all my life to plain dealing and candour, and am not sufficiently versed in the art of political swindling to be prepared for negotiating with an European Minister of State."[37]

Vice President Adams would not be reading these words right away, of course. In the interim, he weighed the wisdom contained in his son's evaluation of U.S. neutrality. It made good sense. As to John Quincy's interpretation of news filtering out of Paris, though, he reacted with a heavy shrug. The new cast of characters bothered him. "There is not a Man left in the Government of France whose Name I ever heard when I was in that Country." This did not bode well for the United States. Nor did it help that a nation he knew intimately, the Dutch Republic, was undergoing worse political upheaval. He fed his son the irritable commentary that is extracted in the epigraph to this chapter: "The Mob has ultimately over thrown every free Republick." To those icy words he added a critique of their own infant republic that he might have shared only with John Quincy at this fraught moment: *It was a bad idea to permit nonpropertied men to vote.* "It is humanity to those People themselves to exclude them from a Vote," he wrote, "for they never have it and Use it but to their own Disgrace, Remorse and Destruction." He'd felt this way, he said, since 1776.

In 1795, the designation of "party" or "faction" was an insult applied only to those who resisted a political writer's point of view. In describing organized opposition to the Washington-Adams administration as "a Party," Vice President Adams did not hold back before he had crossed a rhetorical line; now he thought an *appointed* chief executive, a *benevolent monarch,* might actually be better for the country than to stand by idly as unpoliced partisanship took over. His questioning view of human psychology returned in a flash to Adams's thoughts; his conviction as to the fragility of reason directed his pen. It told him that an unhealthy passion in politics fed the natural impatience of a volatile population and helped produce street mobs, whose unpredictability led to more bitterness and recrimination, recirculating in the bloodstream of a compromised electoral system.

Whether moodiness or fatigue or prudent good sense made him like this, John Adams divulged to his son the fears he was nursing with regard to America's immediate future. "The last hope of a Party seems now in a desperate Attack upon the President," he wrote. "A successful Attack upon that Man would be a Demonstration that Elective Executives are impracticable." His outburst was for the eyes of a trusted one, and certainly meant to be hidden from the public. No evidence exists that Adams conveyed any such sentiments to President Washington. "Be of good courage and of good cheer," he bade his son. There would be "clamour" in whatever the two of them did in the interest of their country. But the father concluded with a note of confidence, employing a pet name, "Publicola knows what a popular Clamour is."[38]

Near the end of two miserable terms as vice president, John Adams returned to reading Tacitus. The Roman historian "exerted the Vengeance of History upon the Emperors," he goaded, "but has veiled the Conspiracies against them, and the incorrigible Corruption of the People, which probably provoked their most atrocious Cruelties." Were the people always right and just? By now, John Adams had serious doubts. "Tyranny can scarcely be practiced upon a virtuous and wise People," he recorded in his diary, without crediting or discrediting anyone.[39]

For the eight years he served under George Washington, he regarded himself as "a target for the Archers," dodging multidirectional arrows. Whom did he fault for his predicament? There was plenty of blame to go around. Reflecting on these years from the repose of retirement, he told his old friend Benjamin Rush in 1813 that what he remembered most of his vice presidency was the abusive language hurled at him. Subject, as he put it, to "Misconstruction Misrepresentations Lies and Libel" from not one but two political parties, he felt "a nauseous fog" lift as he moved out of second position. Of course, he might have been conflating vice presidency and presidency when he wrote the above.[40]

Succeeding Washington to the presidency afforded him only a brief reprieve. He was unconvinced that the worst abuses were, by definition, committed by those at the top. The French Revolution had proven that citizens of the state were as prone to "incorrigible Corruption" as the ruling class. The people in a republic could become incendiaries as easily as a king could become a tyrant.

SEVEN

INTELLECTS

Regard me as a true-born Roman, liberally instructed by the care of my father, and inflamed with the desire of knowledge, even from my boyhood.

—SCIPIO AFRICANUS, *in Cicero's* Tusculan Disputations, *addressing the art of politics (ca. 54 B.C.)*

The institutions now made in America will not wholly wear out for thousands of years. It is of the last importance, then, that they should begin right. If they set out wrong, they will never be able to return, unless it be by accident, to the right path.

—JOHN ADAMS, A Defence of the Constitutions of Government of the United States of America *(1787)*

And how can a man obtain the confidence of a whole people in his moral character, or that knowledge of the human heart, which alone can establish his control over the will, without a profound investigation of the science of moral philosophy or ethics?

—JOHN QUINCY ADAMS, Lectures on Rhetoric and Oratory *(1810)*

To understand history better, you have to want to know more about *the ways of knowing the world* that were available to people in the past. That is how our study is framed, and why it now moves to the books and authors that exerted a significant influence on our co-subjects. Past wisdom made the prospect of American democracy problematic for the Adamses—that is, potentially uplifting and potentially perilous.

One outstanding characteristic shared by the presidents Adams was the mature pessimism of their Roman spirit, which was not despondency but a perspective culled from near-constant engagement with classical examples of human struggle. Far more than biblical lessons, it was reading Homer and Herodotus in Greek, and Cicero and Tacitus in Latin, that helped them assess the choices a public figure confronted. They viewed the course of human events through a classical lens, thereby becoming better versed in the temporal implications of personal ambition, the psychological dimensions of status seeking, and the dangers arising from popular credulity or ambivalence.

The skills the Adamses associated with public performance were, for the most part, Roman. Nothing was so idealized by budding national politicians in the early republic as an exhibition of the Ciceronian ethos, matching a pure, passionate expression of masculine friendship to the highest standard of eloquence. In the late eighteenth century, the Ciceronian model went far in establishing a man's character and reputation.

The trials once undergone in the Roman Republic were pressed into service by America's Revolutionary propagandists. Political angst was encoded in Latin, as pseudonymously labeled neo-Romans called attention to the importance of their message by dint of the adopted name: "Publius," of course, was the collective moniker of a trio of authors, Madison, Hamilton, and Jay, in *The Federalist*. Opposite them was "Brutus," who questioned whether the popular spirit was sufficiently accommodated by the elite men who drafted the Constitution. Hamilton wrote as "Tully," a shortened form of Cicero's middle name. "Sylvanus Americanus" (American Woodsman) rhapsodized the yeomanry of the country. Editorial use of the republican martyr "Cato" spanned decades of politically drawn letters. In defending his father's good name, John Quincy Adams made transatlantic waves as "Publicola."

The classical idiom literally constitutes the self-ennobling architecture of the United States, as any visit to government buildings in Washington, D.C., makes plain. Engaging with the history of Rome helped Revolutionary political thinkers navigate between ideal and practical formulations. Latin was, and is, the language of the law. Texts in the ancient language were at once tools and weapons in the Adamses' world: they excited the restless reader to see his time on earth as momentous while asking him to encounter his own humanity.[1]

But there was a danger. Deployment of the classics could encourage an elitist sensibility. When Dr. Rush disputed the elder Adams's definition of public dignity, he rubbed it in with a beautiful taunt. "Who are guilty of the greatest absurdity," Rush posed, "the Chinese who press the feet into deformity by small shoes, or the Europeans and Americans who press the brain into obliquity by Greek and Latin? Do not men use Latin and Greek as the scuttlefish emit their ink, on purpose to conceal themselves from an intercourse with the common people?" Elitism could be tied to an overemphasis on classical studies.[2]

It wasn't only the ancients who sharpened the Adamses' shared sensibility. To read the great thinkers of any age was to inhale a stimulant. When the second failed president Adams returned to Massachusetts from Washington in 1829, he started his post-presidential reading challenge with a biography of Voltaire, whose literary genius his father had attested to. It was John Adams's "ardent love of literature," the son reflected, that "raised him to distinction." His constant passion for reading "signalized the usefulness of his Life." As he approached Voltaire with his father's example in mind, JQA took heart in the fact that they both judged their life's value on "usefulness" rather than coarse measures of popularity.[3]

Attending the Continental Congress in 1776, John Adams brought along a good number of volumes from Braintree to assist in his daily habit of letter writing. In addition to political pamphlets purchased in Philadelphia, he kept close at hand the literature he most valued, which included William Shakespeare, the freedom-loving poet and political essayist John Milton, and the more satirical poet Alexander Pope, the last of whom was steeped in the classics and widely known for his translation of Homer. There were others, of course, but these writers in particular stood the test of time, conveying moral messages that could be republicanized. Asserting one's principles, communicating one's character, required backing from great writers.

PRINTED AMMUNITION

Books bound John and John Q. Adams together. They were insatiable readers who converted knowledge into energy. It was not in a casual way that the axiom attributed to Francis Bacon "Knowledge is power" became associated with enlightened thought. In the early American republic, books served as a form of ammunition.

Book collecting was a constant occupation. During their years in Europe, John the elder augmented the library his son would inherit by purchasing such breathtaking titles as a 1594 edition of Thucydides's *History of the Peloponnesian War* and a 1715 edition of Herodotus, the earliest of Greek historians. Their cousin and fond companion John Thaxter added to the growing collection with his presentation of a 1678 volume containing writings of the Roman historian Livy. Titles purchased in London, Paris, and Amsterdam that ended up in Braintree reveal an equal interest in classical thought and modern history. By 1788, the library at the Adams homestead had ballooned. Overflow titles sat in boxes. Shelves were fully stocked with works of political thought and ethics, law volumes, theological works, books on science and medicine, dictionaries and grammars—more or less in that order of significance.[4]

In 1789, as the incoming vice president, John Adams, found a house in Manhattan where he and Abigail would live during the first year of the Washington administration, he wrote home to his wife with the critical charge to withdraw essential books from the library before she took to the road. He did not wish to chance an accident that might ruin their most valuable acquisitions, so he settled on titles that were duplicates or else easily replaceable (such as Robert Ainsworth's Latin-English dictionary). In the postscript to his letter, restating his core concern with the ancients, John bade his wife, "Livy and Tacitus I would have sent, and a Plutarch in french or English, &c." If Livy was said to be the greatest of Roman historians, Tacitus was a lawyer and rhetorician as well as a historian; Plutarch, a Greco-Roman biographer. As to the "etcetera" in John's instruction, it went without saying that an Adams could not do without the prolific writer and ancient bibliophile Marcus Tullius Cicero, the Roman statesman par excellence—litigator, political thinker, orator, defender of a dimming republic, and model for humanist philosophy.[5]

John Quincy was just beginning to establish himself as a lawyer at this time. When he conversed with his father about living arrangements, he did not neglect the matter of access to books. To get ahead, he said, it made most sense to reside in Boston proper. "I shall request your permission to remove thither your law library, which is now at Braintree." In this manner, he'd have an edge over his peers with "such a collection of books around me . . . which few of the young gentlemen of the profession have."[6]

Two lifetimes of Adams diaries show us that books were more than tools of the trade. To a greater degree than his father, John Quincy, in a single week, could move back and forth between fiction and nonfiction. This is his diary entry for April 14, 1792: "For several years past I have endeavoured to vary my studies so that I might avoid in some degree the tediousness of a long continued application to one subject." He breaks down his day: "I have devoted the forenoon to those studies which are more immediately connected with my profession, and reserved the latter part of the day for mental amusement"—a manner of relaxation, he explained further, that surrendered his mind to "the commune vinculum [common bond] which connects every part of the moral world." Nothing held more cumulative value than that.

After he sailed back to Europe in 1794, John Quincy continued the family tradition, haunting booksellers and attending regular public sales. In the space of two months in Holland, in the spring of 1797, the accredited diplomat assigned to both Washington's and his father's administrations detailed what he read when he was not conducting official business: "Began this morning to translate the Annals of Tacitus." "Reading Rousseau's Nouvelle Héloïse." "Reading Rousseau's Emile. It deserves attention." A deputation, nondiplomatic in nature, was added: "Packed up a couple of boxes of books to the President of Harvard University, for the Library." At the University of Leiden, where he had once attended lectures, JQA cast eyes on rare books that the school librarian did not bring before ordinary visitors: "There are a number of antient manuscripts of the Classics. Among the rest an Homer more than 900 years old." This was his world, which he never forgot was a gift from his father.[7]

But let us not forget how old John Quincy was in the decade of the 1790s. His attraction to Jean-Jacques Rousseau tells us something more about the spirit of his late twenties: the famed French author promoted romantic love in ways that were unparalleled at the time. Nor, for that matter, was John Quincy's father a prig either, though common prejudice so asserts. It is assumed that because he did not take to French politics and politicians, the elder Adams did not warm to French literature and philosophy. That is not true. Beyond his esteem for the keen, skeptical Voltaire, John Adams recognized the power of Rousseau as a philosopher of liberty. The Rousseau titles that John Quincy gravitated to in 1797, however, were the novels of the 1760s that engaged with conscience, ethics, and emotions, toward training the human spirit to thrive in a cruel world. The emotion-laden, erotically framed epistolary novel *La nouvelle Héloïse,* with its plaintive plotline, tested the very concept of a pursuit of happiness. It said, on the one hand, that misfortune arises when desire dies and, on the other, that desire is worth pursuing only to the extent that it does not lead to self-deception. The second Rousseau title JQA tackled, *Émile,* experimented with means to self-sufficiency. It suggested that human nature could be changed—as the venerable John Locke commanded. Rather than accept religious orthodoxy as one's guide, *Émile* taught that virtuous conduct arose by listening to an "interior voice," which was in itself "divine instinct." Rousseau did not wholly embrace the antireligious creed of more radical French philosophes, and still France ordered his arrest and burned his books.[8]

If contemporary parables bound them to mundane literary modes, a contemplative manner tied the two Adamses to the distant past. John Quincy's above-cited diary entry of April 14, 1792, shows a twenty-four-year-old attorney balancing the categories of knowledge to avoid tedium. Still, he comes down on the side of Rome, "fully perswaded, that the clearest and most copious streams of science [at that time a synonym for "knowledge"] flow only from the fountains of Antiquity." After reflection, he affirms, "I have often determined to make myself a complete master of all the Latin classics." He had taken up both the histories of Tacitus and the orations of Cicero, vowing "if possible to understand them thoroughly in the original."

WHY CICERO?

In his *Autobiography,* John Adams recalled with immense satisfaction how, at twenty-three, he was encouraged by an esteemed Massachusetts attorney, Jeremiah Gridley, to pursue the life of the mind along with his professional career.

"What Books have you read?" Gridley posed.

"Many more I fear than have done me any good. I have read too fast, much faster than I understood or remembered as I ought."

"Do you read Latin?"

"A little sometimes."

"What Books have you lately read?"

"Cicero's Orations and Epistles."

Gridley gave him the best advice in the world, Adams thought: "A Lawyer through his whole Life ought to have some Book on Ethicks or the Law of Nations always on his Table. They are all Treatises of individual or national Morality and ought to be the Study of our whole Lives."[9]

John Adams expanded Gridley's advice to encompass mastery of oratory, and he put young John Quincy on a course toward oratorical excellence. Even Abigail got in on the act. When he was twelve and living in Paris with his father, his mother wrote to her Johnny, "It is not in the still calm of life, or the repose of a pacific station, that great characters are formed. Would Cicero have shone so distinguished an orater [*sic*], if he had not been roused, kindled and enflamed by the Tyranny of Catiline, Millo, Verres and Mark Anthony. The Habits of a vigorous mind are formed in contending with difficulties. All History will convince you of this." Cicero was always in the mix.[10]

It is hard for us to imagine a living, breathing Marcus Tullius Cicero or to see the relevance of any toga-wearing ancient to any single aspect of the modern world. For an Adams, however, the old Roman radiated a star quality that never dimmed. A warm note composed in January 1788 finds John recommending to the lawyer in training John Quincy an unambiguous course of study. "You should have some Volume of Ethicks constantly on your Table," he directed, repeating Jeremiah Gridley almost verbatim: "Socrates and Plato, Cicero and Seneca." But a pleader required the best in the realm of public speaking as well, which meant, first and foremost, Cicero and Quintilian, "and to read them with a Dictionary Grammar and Pen and Ink." It was the Roman poet Juvenal who wrote, "Studium Sine Calamo Somnium" (To study without a pen is to dream). And it was John Adams who quoted back Juvenal to his eldest son, as he coaxed him for the umpteenth time, "Preserve your Latin and Greek like the Apple of your Eye."[11]

John Quincy did not mind exhortations from his father. But he hardly needed the reminder, because diary entries show that he had been reading the works of Cicero for a good five years by that time. In 1790, as the son continued in his struggle to mount a career in law, the father (by now vice president) returned to his hobbyhorse:

> I now give it you as my Solemn Advice, to make yourself Master of the Roman Learning. Begin with Livy.—take your Book your Dictionary, your Grammar, your Sheet of Paper and Pen and Ink. Begin at the Beginning and read the Work through—put down in Writing every Word with its meaning as you find it in Ainsworth. You will find it the most delightful Employment you ever engaged in. . . . Cicero too, you should read in turn. . . . [M]ake yourself Master of every Sentence.[12]

Why Cicero? He was the best preserved and most accessible of the old masters of oratory, and not just a mover of hearts but the very embodiment of political courage. He aimed for compromise and conciliation but, when necessary, fought against greed and ruthlessness. There was seemingly no subject that Cicero did not address. Near the end of Washington's second term, Vice President Adams was at Quincy, at peace with the world (an unusual feeling for him), and noted gleefully, "I am reading a Work of Cicero that I remember not to have read before. It is intituled M. Tullii Ciceronis Si Deo placet Consolatio. Remarkable for an ardent hope and confident belief of a future State." (That meant life after death.)[13]

Cicero proved to be a lifelong commitment for both father and son. "He is the instructor of every profession," John Quincy declared, "the friend of every age." Indeed, while still living abroad in 1801, he decided, almost whimsically, to read Cicero in German. After a night's commitment to the text and its German commentary, he wrote, "I read it with much pleasure and I hope with some profit." On finishing the translation several days later: "I have seldom read a book with more satisfaction." That was the level of his commitment. As a U.S. senator during Jefferson's presidency, he "busied" himself with Cicero on "rhetorical invention" while preparing for a second career as the Boylston Professor of Rhetoric and Oratory at Harvard. The culmination of his public engagement with the Roman statesman can probably be dated to 1810, upon publication of his *Lectures on Rhetoric and Oratory*. The book, a summary of the popular course he taught at Harvard in 1806–1807, came out as the subject of rhetoric was becoming a thriving discipline across college curricula. In this still-readable volume, Professor/Senator Adams played up the works of Cicero at length. Much later, between his ouster from the presidency in 1828 and reentry into Congress in

1831, he reread *all* of Cicero in Latin. It took him, he informed his diary, two hours per day for ten months. He was by then sixty-three and saw fit to record that he was the same age Cicero was when put to death.[14]

It would be no exaggeration to call John Quincy Adams the most outstanding expositor of Cicero in the nineteenth century. Yet he was, at the same time, careful to qualify that he did not believe in blind worship of any ancient orator. He believed in American innovation. Eloquence had been "perverted," he said, by the despotic Caesars and subsequently buried in the "midnight of the monkish ages," only to arise again after centuries of neglect. In the hands of worthy Americans, eloquence was singularly poised to regain "her ancient vigor." Many alive at the time would have agreed. By restoring Cicero's art for modern purposes—or so Professor Adams embedded in his lectures—Americans would be able to acquire Ciceronian perspicuity and, if they did so, avert political dangers for as long as was reasonably possible.[15]

It is important to understand the hopefulness contained in John Quincy's Americanized Cicero. It rose from the quality of sincerity a Ciceronian ethos demanded of a republican. In a republican setting, self-knowledge—knowing one's limitations—was as important as possessing confidence in the exercise of power. As the Boylston Professor put it, "The eloquence of the bar, of the legislature, and of public solemnities, are seldom or ever found united to high perfection in the same person. An admirable lawyer is not always a popular speaker in deliberative assemblies." He was spinning language theory not for its own sake but to make any connection to the ancients politically relevant. "Eloquence is the child of liberty," he spoke committedly, "and can descend from no other stock." In the Greek Demosthenes and the Roman Cicero lay the "immortal" beginnings of a sincere and inspired brand of political speech. When it came to the Roman, JQA verged on hyperbole: "He presents the most perfect example of that rare and splendid combination, universal genius and indefatigable application." The "annals of the world" had produced no one superior.

Marcus Tullius Cicero, Rome's man for all seasons, embraced eloquence and action: the public man as a brilliant actor. All who learned Latin in the mid- to late eighteenth century took Cicero as their model of moral exposition. To the best educated of the Revolutionary generation, he was a standout among the ancients who bridged the dictates of good judgment (a personal value) and the art of good government (a public value). Professor/Senator Adams described his universality: "As a poet, a historian, a philosopher, a moralist, and an epistolary writer, the rank of Cicero is in the very first line." He was "what a speaker should be; what no speaker ever will be; but what every speaker should devote the labors of his life to approximate." Transcendently, Cicero was "the friend of the soul, whom we can never meet without a gleam of pleasure." Among the Roman exemplars, Cicero led in dignified expression.[16]

He was, as importantly, a dedicated statesman, embracing a principle of balanced government such that John Adams reintroduced in the state constitution of Massachusetts in 1779 and included in his *Defence of the Constitutions* a decade later. It was Cicero who first called for a republic that positively greeted institutional competition among monarchy, oligarchy (aristocracy), and democracy. Favoring popular election, he spoke out against tyranny. Drama followed Cicero. He lived through constant political disturbance, surviving numerous threats to his life before the sharpened blade of a political enemy finished him, just months after the assassination of Julius Caesar.[17]

JQA's worship of Cicero was strictly professional, though a gut affinity would have made sense, too. Attending Parliament at an impressionable age, commenting to his father on the oratory he witnessed, he was repeating the life of the young Cicero, who, as John Quincy remarked in his Harvard lectures, "frequented assiduously all the scenes of public speaking, and listened with eager avidity to the eminent orators of the age." Cicero traveled widely, honing his skills. He lived for years in Greece and strayed into Asia Minor for on-the-ground education. He was a wanderer.[18]

The elder Adams might have identified with Cicero's life story on a more personal level. A streak of Adamsian vanity emerges in Cicero, who believed that a busy political actor should always be a superior thinker, too. America's revolutionary and Rome's republican were equally proud of having arisen from provincial farms to achieve notoriety on Capitol Hill. John Adams successfully defended British soldiers accused of murder in the Boston Massacre, and Cicero made his bones as defense counsel to a man accused of murdering his own father. Both protagonists were scrupulous in avoiding partisan predictability—Adams, in repeatedly challenging consensus views; Cicero, in this instance, in pointing a finger at a close ally of the military dictator of Rome, and risking his future prospects. Both John Adams and his Roman model were outspoken civilians at a time when many other political figures rose to prominence on the strength of their military service. In Adams's case, this distinction framed his somewhat cool relations with George Washington, Alexander Hamilton, and other military men.

Like Cicero before him, John Adams was initially slow to turn to a life of public advocacy, yet was unstoppably involved in political life once he took the plunge. Both aligned themselves with the forces of order and stability and opposed radical moves. Cicero as consul, Adams as vice president and president, could not but personalize politics, undermined by supposed political allies. At a critical juncture, Cicero wrote to his best friend, Atticus, "You know I am right: it was not my enemies but jealous friends who ruined me." It is hard to think of any more Adamsian remark than that. When the members of his cabinet displayed a greater allegiance to Hamilton than to him, Adams became incensed. And of course, he early on convinced himself that even the world-famous Franklin was deeply jealous of him.[19]

Cicero was conservative in the main, identifying with aristocratic interests. But he was also ready and willing to deal with his popular opposition when doing so made practical political sense. Like John Adams. In private correspondence, too, Cicero had an Adamsian demeanor, as a thin-skinned man who could still make fun of himself. Plutarch said of Cicero that his "sarcasm . . . offended many, and gave him the repute of ill nature." The Roman consul had a strong sense of personal mission, was known to be subject to mood swings and bouts of depression, and second-guessed his own performances. Like the American lawyer-statesman, he dwelled on the impact his public statements had on his character and honor in others' eyes.[20]

The parallels can be hard to resist. Cicero's wife, Terentia, came from a wealthier family than he did, and she managed their property during extensive periods when he was absent. Unlike Abigail and John, though, the Roman couple grew apart and eventually divorced. Even so, Cicero's wife, like Abigail, was a strong-minded woman who took a considerable interest in politics and suffered along with her embattled husband.

It was Cicero's humanity—how approachable he still was—that the Adamses, father and son, found most appealing and beguiling. In the early years of his retirement, John Adams read for pleasure a three-volume biography of Cicero. A quarter century later, John Quincy described for his son Charles

Francis how real the ghosts of ancient Rome felt to him: "Every one of the letters of Cicero is a picture of the state of the writer's mind when it was written. It is like an evocation of shades [that is, ghosts] to read them." Marcus Tullius Cicero lived in what Americans knew as the late republic. The Adamses lived in what is today styled the early republic. A shared sense of moment connected otherwise distant lifetimes.[21]

MORAL SENTIMENT

In 1790, in another of the letters to his son at the start of John Quincy's public career, the relentlessly focused father gave his attention to the eighteenth-century Scottish philosophes whose ethical thinking influenced many of the American founders. "My dear son," he wrote, "There is a sett of Scotch Writers that I think deserve your Attention in a very high Degree. There are Speculations in Morals Politicks and Law that are more luminous, than any other I have read." Prominent among these "luminous" thinkers' writings, he named Lord Kames's *Elements of Criticism* (1762) and Adam Smith's *Theory of Moral Sentiments* (1759), along with the latter's *Wealth of Nations* (1776).[22]

John Adams was entirely smitten with the Scottish philosophes. "Luminous" was their penetration of the human condition. It was no coincidence, then, that he should combine book endorsements with an exhortation to Johnny to practice "liberal Philanthropy." The Scots' idea was to discover "the man within," reinforcing a Ciceronian command over the public square. To follow their rule was to exploit the "honorable" natural passion of sympathetic engagement with one's fellows. Arrogance and pride could be suppressed only through self-perception, reason, and conscience.

Kames called attention to negative phenomena such as the "infectious" emotions of fear and anger. He studied the human inclination toward harsh judgments (both inward and outward directed), observing, "A wicked or disgraceful action is disagreeable not only to others, but even to the delinquent himself. . . . The painful emotion felt by the delinquent, is distinguished by the name of remorse." Remorse was punishment granted by nature. In their diaries, the self-policing Adamses attested to its force.[23]

When a twenty-four-year-old John Quincy picked up Kames's *Elements of Criticism,* he discovered, he said, "dispositions inherent in human Nature." From Kames, he easily intuited, "The inquisitive mind beginning with criticism . . . gains imperceptibly a thorough knowledge of the human heart, of its desires, and of every motive to action." While celebrating the cause of knowledge through Kames, JQA berated himself at the same time for his persistent lack of focus: "I have read not a little this day, but without any connection, Law, Poetry, Oratory, History, Latin, French, English, heaped upon chaotic confusion in my mind."[24]

As with Cicero, the father's recommendation did not fail to resonate with the son. This was especially true in the case of Adam Smith. Smith offered a proper approach to living in modern, commercial society: to see ourselves as others see us, so as to prepare us to think of the public good. As Smith's modern biographer Nicholas Phillipson explains, the philosophe's power over late-eighteenth-century minds derived from his having identified the motive behind most human behavior: the constant need to have positive feelings reciprocated. It was, as Phillipson writes, "a simple observation with momentous sociological implications." Smith's contribution to Enlightenment thought was his investigation of two categories of compulsion: satisfying curiosity and engaging in imaginative understanding. He saw how people suffered for their delusions, notably in their "slavish admiration for the rich and powerful." Channeling Cicero and Rousseau at once, Smith struggled with the bleak tendency toward complacency. Where Rousseau wrote of civilization's corrupting influence and the individual's "enslavement" to others' opinions, Smith conceived a more comprehensive approach to ethics: "Man naturally desires, not only to be loved, but to be lovely. . . . He naturally dreads, not only to be hated, but to be hateful." To Phillipson, everything in Smith involves ethics and the human imagination.[25]

Tackling prevailing theories of moral sentiment forced upon John Adams an awareness of rational necessity. As early as 1770, looking to practice virtue without getting stepped on in public life, he found himself embracing the occasionally necessary lie. "Dissimulation," he wrote, was not always evil. "If it means only a constant Concealment from others of such of our Sentiments, Actions, Desires, and Resolutions, as others have not a Right to know, it is not only lawful but commendable." The logic went to his political impulses. "Because when these are once divulged, our Enemies may avail themselves of the Knowledge of them to our Damage, Danger and Confusion." As Adams penned in his diary, Smith published in *The Theory of Moral Sentiments*. There was "strength of mind" in "dissimulation"; one gleans this from the testimony of Cicero and "the judicious Mr. Locke." When dissimulation was "no more than Concealment, Secrecy, and Reserve," Adams construed, it was counted as "Prudence and Discretion."[26]

Indeed, Adam Smith defined discretion. He and his avid student John Adams believed in self-control and learned observation; they searched out "systems" that advanced philosophy and elevated political practice. The cultural anthropologist Ernest Becker wrote of Smith half a century ago: "The *Theory of Moral Sentiments* laid stress on the sentiment of sympathy which held society together. . . . *The Wealth of Nations* accented man's propensity to barter and exchange for accumulation and gain. But for Smith this two-sided picture was not in conflict; everything was under the sway of a higher regulative principle, the principle of justice as Smith conceived it."[27]

Where Becker reconciles two sides of Smith, we can reconcile two sides of John Adams. If he seems somewhat "conservative" in his political works, he does not abandon a theory of forward progress, and he certainly does not wish to reverse the cause of republicanism by recodifying the British system. He considered external controls necessary for those in society who lacked self-control, who could not police themselves as Smith's philosophy prescribed; only those schooled in enlightened mores could reach sound political judgments. If that is elitism, then elitism yoked together a disparate ruling group in the early American republic, well beyond the cadre of so-called conservatives.

Smith's legacy endured. Preaching masculine sensibility, the Scot retained power over the eldest son of John Adams, who at age forty-three wrote to his mother, "I met the other day, in reading Smith's Theory of Moral Sentiments a passage . . . which smote me to the heart, in thinking of my own children." He specified part 6, chapter 2, so she could follow: it was that the "tenderness" of a parent directed toward a child was "by nature" stronger than any other earthly relationship. One esteemed a parent, but one lavished affectionate feeling—well beyond a sense of duty—on a dependent child. "What is called affection is in reality nothing but habitual sympathy," wrote Smith, quintessentially. The psychological continuity he urged made sense to these Adamses, who knew viscerally the effects of long separations.[28]

Smith's main lesson in *The Theory of Moral Sentiments* concerned "self-command"—that which gave texture to personality. "Self-command" directed humans toward reasonable purposes and rational actions, making it an inherently political value. "Self-command" was required if "public spirit" (sympathy beyond one's immediate family) was to prevail. Thus, to Smith, the ideal public figure was "the man . . . who joins, to the perfect command of his own original and selfish feelings, the most exquisite sensibility both to the original and sympathetic feelings of others." Self-awareness led to discovery of new ways to promote the broadest public happiness. Lest the implications of these words be converted into modern populist notions, we need to state unequivocally that he did not mean ceding authority to the multitude. A Smithian conscience did not have to lead to full-blown democracy.[29]

Breeding Eloquence

Early in his diplomatic career, John Adams sought to advance the reputation of the United States abroad by translating the English language into a political weapon. His presence in the Netherlands in 1780 had given him ideas. In a boldly drawn letter to the president of Congress, composed in Amsterdam, he pronounced, "Eloquence is cultivated with more care in free Republics than in other Governments." His policy advice was unequivocal. "It is not to be disputed that the form of government has an influence upon language, and language, in its turn, influences not only the form of government, but the temper, the sentiments, and manners of the people." With the examples of ancient Greece and Rome in mind, he proposed the establishment, under congressional auspices, of "the American Academy for refining, improving, and ascertaining the English Language." Adams's logic was simple and straightforward: American English was bound to become "the language of the world."[30]

A generation later, in his *Lectures on Rhetoric and Oratory,* as Harvard's Boylston Professor, John Quincy Adams proclaimed that "men must be born to poetry, and bred to eloquence." He held that every tie to national literacy attached at the center of government. Once he became president, he quickly proposed a national astronomical observatory and a national university, and he famously championed the Smithsonian Institution. Taking his father's earlier recommendation the extra step, he insisted on national educational standards in support of republicanism.[31]

Here, the two Adamses owed a considerable debt to another eighteenth-century Scot, the Reverend Hugh Blair. Blair's *Lectures on Rhetoric and Belles Lettres* was first published in 1783, when father and son were transiting European capitals. The Scottish minister's nearly encyclopedic work on eloquence and taste had an immediate impact on scholarly discourse. John Adams endorsed it when John Quincy was a student at Harvard, recommending that he read it alongside Cicero and Quintilian.

Blair's *Lectures* fast became a staple text at the finest American colleges and engaged students from the birth of the Republic all the way to the Civil War. The author covered every kind of usage, every syntactical possibility, a wide range of tropes and metaphors—all illustrated with what were viewed as the most illuminating of English, Roman, Greek, and biblical antecedents. He anointed past genius while pointing the way to literary invention. Prescribing modes of power and persuasion in prose, he addressed conceptions of beauty in nature and in art at the same time.[32]

Blair praised Cicero for his self-awareness as a writer and a "swelling and musical style" that helped to carry his argument. And yet he did not treat every Adams favorite with the same degree of justice. One of John Quincy's peeves as he read Blair was the Scottish scholar's mistreatment of the poet Milton. "It is however remarkable," JQA demurred, "that [Blair] has placed Milton so low in rank among the Epic Poets." Milton was a favorite of the father's long before he became a favorite of the son's. At twenty, John Adams noted in his diary that the poet's "power over the mind" was "great beyond conception"; in 1786, in a patriotic flourish, he wrote to young Johnny that America's epic poets Timothy Dwight and Joel Barlow, the so-called Connecticut Wits, were such capable writers as to be inferior only to Milton's *Paradise Lost*.

Milton remained the standard of soulfulness. John Quincy would eventually look back on a lifetime's engagement with the poet and recall how, at the age of ten, he was embarrassed not to be seeing in the language of *Paradise Lost* the power his father perceived. It was not until the age of thirty that he fully realized its sublimity. In the days immediately following his 1797 wedding to Louisa Catherine Johnson, *Paradise Lost* was the first volume he turned to. When the newlyweds moved from London to Berlin, he was still drawing inspiration before bed from the "last book" of Milton's epic.[33]

In the father-son letter that praised Hugh Blair, John Adams also gave credit to the Englishman Thomas Sheridan, author of *Lectures on Elocution* (1762) and *A General Dictionary of the English Language* (1780). Like Blair, Sheridan argued for recognition of the "beauties" in speech and delineated the boundary between charm and flamboyance. Again, like Blair, and like John Adams, he believed that language carried with it the values of its national culture.

Blair and Sheridan were keen on the power of emulation (which marked their work as essentially conservative). They promoted the Adamsian credo: good conduct, honor, erudition, lofty dignity—or in Roman terms, *gravitas*. No contemporary could attain the universality of Cicero, but these two masters of syntax gave to the readers John and John Quincy Adams a sense of the heights to which a nation might rise when the power of language was harnessed. For all of these men, the dominant perspective on language was undemocratic. It flowed down from the literate elite, rather than flowing up from the democracy.[34]

II 4483 XXXIII 129

Berlin 25. November 1800.

My dear Sir.

Many months have pass'd since I received a line from you, or from my dear mother. From my brother Thomas I have no letter of a later date than July, and from the department of State I have but one dated since last February. Perhaps I am to impute the greater part of this seeming oblivion of my american correspondents to my own remissness during the last winter — For six months however I have scarcely suffered a week to pass without writing, and unless my letters should have been unfortunate beyond the common proportion of failures many of them, must before this have reached the United States — I have not written indeed directly to you since July, but I suppose most of my letters to my brother, written upon my tour into Silesia, have been perused by you, and have given you frequent information of our situation.

I have therefore been obliged to depend upon the accounts from America, contained in the public newspapers, and the private intelligence of some Americans in Europe — All these concur in representing the State of parties and the temper of the public mind in such a state, as to leave scarce a doubt but that a change will take place at the ensuing election which will leave you at your own disposal, and furnish one more example to the world, how the most important services to the public, and a long laborious life anxiously, and successfully devoted to their welfare, are rewarded in popular governments.

As I know that from the earliest period of your political life, you have always made up your account to meet sooner or later such treatment in return for every sacrifice, and every toil, I hope and confidently believe, that you will be prepared to bear this event with calmness and composure, if not with indifference — That you will not suffer it to prey upon your mind, or affect your health, nor even to think more hardly of your Country than she deserves — Her truest friends I am persuaded will more keenly feel your removal from the

head

J Q A Nov 25 1800

Letter, John Quincy Adams to John Adams, November 25, 1800. Reading American newspapers at his post in Berlin, the diplomat-son reviewed "the State of parties and the temper of the public mind" back home. Anticipating his father's loss of the presidency to Thomas Jefferson and a return to private life, JQA grudgingly acknowledged that the "popular governments" of the states were going to vote out of office one so "successfully devoted" to the nation as the industrious John Adams.

PART II

INHERITOR

Even as the father occupied the office of president of the United States, and the son resided abroad in a diplomatic capacity, the younger acquired a level of confidence that was to serve him for the remainder of his years on the political scene. In the summer of 1797, when his father had been in office only a few months, John Quincy was married without his parents' blessing. In the company of European leaders, he became his own man, enlarging upon what his father had been able to accomplish during their time on the Continent in the 1780s. President Adams relied heavily on his son's reports, and they meaningfully influenced the course of his conduct in office. Which is why the "Inheritor" part of the book opens, counterintuitively, with the father's presidency. Although the veteran revolutionary, sixty-one on assuming office, was to all appearances at the apex of his career, the torch had already been passed. And with the father's retirement in 1801, the son began to chart a wholly independent course in electoral politics.

EIGHT

Second President

You enquire whether France is to establish an universal domination over the whole Globe? by Land and by Sea?—Probably such is the design of her present Rulers; or rather it is their wish to ruin all other Nations as completely as France is ruined herself.

—JOHN QUINCY ADAMS TO JOHN ADAMS, *September 21, 1797*

The present situation of the affairs of France however, combining with the spirit which she at length finds roused in the United States, have produced a great and important change in her conduct towards us. . . . In proportion as our spirit of resistance has become manifest, theirs of oppression and extortion has shrunk back.

—JOHN QUINCY ADAMS TO JOHN ADAMS, *September 25, 1798*

Here is a curious parallel. John Adams was absent for the birth of his eldest son, and John Quincy Adams was absent from the United States for all four years of his father's presidency: for the election of 1796, for the March 4, 1797, inauguration in Philadelphia, and for his father's final day in the new Federal City of Washington, D.C., in March 1801. He spent all of those years in Europe.

During most of John Adams's presidency, the United States and France were on a collision course. John Quincy, stationed in Europe, more than once apprised his father that revolutionary France bore a "design" that threatened America. JQA was committed to no interest beyond his nation's—which, if there was any doubt before, was indistinguishable from his father's political interest now. The second president would rely on the young diplomat's dispatches as much as, if not more than, he relied on the other members of his administration.

The United States leaned heavily on the symbolism of Washington. Shortly after New Year's 1796, Vice President Adams was informed that the president would refuse a third term. Until that moment, he dared not envision his own succession to the highest office. "It must be kept a Secret wholly to yourself," he told his wife, with an eagerness he would have betrayed only to her. "You know the Consequence of this, to me and to yourself. Either We must enter upon Ardours more trying than any ever yet experienced; or retire to Quincy[,] Farmers for Life." If he came out ahead in electoral votes, the "Ardours" of the presidency would be his—theirs.[1]

Under the Directory, a collective leadership bent on conquering, the French continued to frustrate American statecraft. Republicans of the Madison-Jefferson school, predisposed to mollify their old ally, were known to Federalists as "the French party" and as such were considered dangerous to public order. From his station overseas, in close contact with rival factions in warring Europe, the younger Adams sometimes seemed more tenacious—more intransigent, even—than the elder.

The United States was reliant for its economic health on commercial relations with Europe, which were seriously threatened amid Anglo-French war. Meanwhile, Americans faced escalating dissent at home. John Adams did not cut the commanding figure of General Washington, but he did represent continuity in that he, like his predecessor, was known for firmness. To the critical public, his main competition—Jefferson—represented change, but what kind of change? The former secretary of state expressed fondness for revolutionary France on enough occasions that he gave leading Federalists deep cause for concern. Adams felt not an ounce of nostalgia for his days in Paris.

Now approaching thirty, John Quincy remained guarded and calculating. He knew firsthand the delicate nature of representing a young nation striving to abide by a policy of neutrality, of balance. Over the course of Washington's administration, he had only hardened in his public defense of his famously testy father—a man powerless in constitutional terms, as vice president, but controversial in all other respects. By 1794, George and Martha Washington had alike come to applaud JQA's talents, bolstering the ambitions of both parents on behalf of their offspring, though he himself was slow to accept his assigned political fate.[2]

The son had imbibed the main thrust of his father's political principles.

In *Defence of the Constitutions* and *Discourses on Davila*, John Adams roundly objected to French Enlightenment ideas about political equality. He considered these ideas to be fantasy, arguing that the world could not be governed without an aristocracy, without social differentiation in one form or another. It was owing to human nature that superiors and inferiors, alike prone to passion and intrigue, took to the political stage. If contending forces were to coexist, and avoid a violent showdown, there had to be a counterweight. The only counterweight John Adams could conceive in the competition between men with excessive power and men jealous of the ones in power was someone like himself—a leader without a band.[3]

As the 1796 contest began to take shape, the political landscape was easy enough to gauge, and Adams knew what had to happen next. He and Jefferson remained cordial on the surface, but their respective positions on the turbulence in France and its echoes in America were so diametrically opposed that Adams, to Jefferson, appeared unrepublican, and Jefferson, to Adams, appeared all too willing to keep dangerous company. "Frenchified" and "dangerous experimenter" were the loaded terms that stuck to Jefferson; "monarchy man" and "aristocrat" were used by unfriendly columnists to describe Adams. It was rumored that an Adams presidency could pave the way for monarchical succession, in the person of his eldest son.

The candidate Jefferson was a man John Adams once trusted and now felt a strong aversion to. To Abigail, he wrote, "I am at least as determined not to serve under Jefferson, as W[ashington] is not to serve at all." He expressed his resolve with his accustomed fervency: "I will not be frightened out of the public service nor will I be disgraced in it." To be second to Jefferson after eight years in Washington's shadow was simply untenable: if he lost, he would cede the vice presidency to whoever came in third.[4]

On September 5, 1796, approaching this decisive moment in his public life, John Adams ruminated on a particular anniversary. This was one date he recalled with precision: September 5, 1774. Twenty-two years had elapsed since the First Continental Congress convened in Philadelphia. He had been a proud member of that historic body. In his journal entry for the earlier September 5, he had marked the occasion with due deliberation, describing the delegates' walk from the City Tavern to Carpenters' Hall. The meeting room contained "an excellent Library," Adams noted at the time.

It may well be that September 5, 1774, was the day he first met John Jay of New York, whose "solid glory" he would celebrate after his colleague's steady contribution to the Treaty of Paris. It was also when he met up with Patrick Henry, a Virginian whose reputation for stirring oratory preceded him. In 1774, Adams recorded Henry's suggestion that the weight of each colony's vote should be determined before any other matter was taken up. The New Englander expected divided sentiment on this issue, and he was right. Twenty-two years later, preparing for the strong possibility that he would win the presidency, he had not worked out a means for competing interests (sectional or otherwise) to be balanced.

While in the minds of hopeful Federalists Adams appeared the likely successor to Washington, there was a southerner under consideration, too, and that was none other than Patrick Henry. His popularity, even now, was undiminished. The state he hailed from contained the richest depository of electoral votes. In dismissing as ignorant the charge that John Adams was "a friend to monarchy," one prominent Virginian cited chapter and verse from *Defence of the Constitutions* to certify Adams's republicanism and proudly announced, "I shall vote for Patrick Henry and John Adams." Though widely seen as the man who could best undermine a Jefferson candidacy, Henry peremptorily declared that he was not interested in national office, thus paving the way for Adams.[5]

Anything could happen and nothing was assured. The emotional force of the linked problems of the Jay Treaty fallout and U.S.-French animus was huge. America's wartime alliance with France, as fixed in 1778, seemed less noble now. A wariness of harmful connections to foreign capitals was the principal theme in Washington's Farewell Address, an influential text that was, for all practical purposes, written by Hamilton. To Madison and Jefferson, it was covertly partisan, associating the evils of "faction" exclusively with their support base.

How would Adams proceed? Perhaps, at this moment, the experienced diplomat did not himself know how, as president, he would interpret Washington's injunction. Everything was fluid. As he observed the activities of French officials in the United States, and their intense interest in the presidential election, he could not but mull over the likelihood of further French indiscretions that might lead to violent confrontation. He was ready for it if it came. He told his wife that given the popular French tendency toward

"Fire, Impetuosity, and Vehemence" in their national temperament, "Americans must be cool and Steady if they can."[6]

All the participants knew full well that the election was going to be close. The southern states held substantial power in the Electoral College (62 of a total 136 electoral votes), and Jefferson had a sufficient number of steadfast friends in the mid-Atlantic states to make it an uphill campaign for the Federalists. Adams's supporters had settled on Thomas Pinckney of Charleston, South Carolina, as a "running mate" to effect regional balance, though as yet electors voted for *two* individuals without prioritizing one over the other, and the formalization of a "ticket" would not become official until passage of the Twelfth Amendment in 1804. Pinckney had distinguished himself on Revolutionary battlefields; he had served the Washington administration in a diplomatic capacity in Europe, securing unimpeded U.S. navigation of the Mississippi and the right to deposit goods in Spanish New Orleans, which made him popular in the West. Historians have accumulated evidence suggesting that Hamilton exerted pressure on electors to leapfrog Pinckney over Adams; or, less insidiously, acted out of a belief that the likeliest Federalist to outpace Jefferson in vote getting would have to be another southerner. Whichever it was, John Adams was unlikely to see in Hamilton anything but the cold-blooded calculation he had witnessed him exhibit before.[7]

In the end, no amount of coordination could solve the logistical problems of the eighteenth century or see past the unsettling newness of the tangled process of electing a president. Not all electors recognized how crucial their second vote might be; as a result, Adams received 71 electoral votes, Jefferson 68, Pinckney 59, Aaron Burr 30, Samuel Adams 15. Others clearly threw their votes away. A number of Adams supporters failed to cast votes for Pinckney; some South Carolina Federalists gave their second vote to Jefferson instead of their native son. By three electoral votes—the slimmest of margins—John Adams defeated Thomas Jefferson. As stipulated in the federal Constitution, Adams became president. Jefferson, his chief opponent these days, acquiesced in the largely powerless vice presidency that Adams had lately endured. "The General of to-day should be a soldier tomorrow, if necessary," the vice president–elect wrote to his friend Madison.[8]

National Innocence

In his inaugural address, John Adams spoke of the American Revolution as a signature moment of character formation, when the "purity" of patriots' intentions, "the justice of their cause," and the qualities of "integrity and intelligence" combined to guarantee success in a time of trial. But this bright effort had merely "launched" the people of America onto "an ocean of uncertainty"; "zeal" and "ardor" had sustained them for a delicate, dangerous period, affording a "temporary preservation of society." Victory in war did not secure peace. A durable national government had yet to be instituted.

In this way, the address was something less than the public compliment Americans would come to expect at presidential inaugurals. It was clear to the second president that liberty could not be sustained without order. A desired form of government had been established, but its legitimacy was to be ensured only by "dissemination of knowledge and virtue among the whole body of the people." This was no easy feat, of course. Yet the inauguration of a president was also a time for imagining the perfectible, and certainly not a day on which to warn against an impending downfall. Therefore, as he proceeded with his address, President Adams pronounced his view of America's republican principles: "If national pride is ever justifiable or excusable," he explained, "it is when it springs, not from power or riches, grandeur or glory, but from conviction of national innocence, information, and benevolence." He described how, when in England, he read the federal Constitution with a sense of joy and satisfaction. He reiterated his "attachment" to and "veneration" of the document, saying, "What other form of government, indeed, can so well deserve our esteem and love?" After all, it aimed to balance competing interests, which was his main issue.[9]

He used twenty-three hundred words to make his case, to characterize the American nation in a way that echoed the language historians have since used to describe the annoyingly "Honest John" Adams himself. He projected a commitment to "purity" when he defined the just purposes to which good government was meant to be put. The "zeal" and "ardor" he invoked were qualities that presented a double edge, being understood at the end of the century as a proneness to compassionate engagement but also to outlandish prejudice. Most important, when Adams introduced the tripartite phrase "national innocence, information, and benevolence," he was praising human values: "innocence" meant lack of artifice; "information" bespoke a commitment to progress; "benevolence" stood for the uniform (Christian and secular) virtue of tolerance and forbearance.

John Adams's succession to the presidency produced the very first presidential "honeymoon," in view of the treatment he received from opposition forces. "Every body but Fools & knaves are charm'd with the Presidents speech," wrote his supportive sister-in-law Mary Cranch. The most virulent anti-administration newspaper, Philadelphia's *Aurora* (edited by a grandson of Benjamin Franklin's), allowed as how Adams deserved "a fair trial," because even as he had theorized about the natural human instinct to elevate and praise social betters, he was, in his person, more republican and less aristocratic in bearing than Washington. At about the same time, Madison and Jefferson deftly orchestrated the leak of a draft letter, never actually sent, in which the incoming vice president, Jefferson, assured Adams that he would cooperate fully. (It coyly reminded the president to keep an eye on "your arch-friend from New York"—Hamilton.) Adams was similarly warned by a dear friend, the middle-of-the-road Massachusetts Federalist Elbridge Gerry, to be wary of Hamilton and his pipeline to power through the devious Timothy Pickering, the secretary of state whom Adams had inherited from Washington. Jefferson, too, was on good terms with Gerry and imparted to that gentleman his conviction that Hamiltonians were "only a little less hostile to [Adams] than to me."[10]

While this was going on, the president's son, at The Hague, awaited definitive news. In his diary on Inauguration Day 1797, he wrote, "The day upon which the new Administration of the United States commences, and I am still uncertain what the Elections have decided."[11]

LOUISA CATHERINE

As John Adams was getting accustomed to the role of chief executive, his son was otherwise engaged. That is, contemplating marriage. Toward the end of 1795, at their well-appointed London home, he had set his heart on the second of the U.S. consul Joshua Johnson's seven daughters, Louisa Catherine. After New Year's 1796, he regularly broke bread with the family;

long dinners were punctuated by pianoforte and harp playing. Over the next eighteen months, much of which he spent in Holland, John Quincy kept his parents in the dark as he debated within himself whether or not to take the plunge. His intended was barely out of her teens when they exchanged portrait miniatures to gaze at adoringly during the months they were apart.

Anticipating Abigail Adams's reaction (for he was still, to her, financially unsettled), John Quincy alluded to "an highly valued friend" when he brought up the as yet unnamed Louisa. Announcing his engagement by letter, he was uncharacteristically ponderous, tongue-tied, pained, defensive. The language is tense: "Upon maturest reflection I have, though I own very reluctantly[,] concluded that I must not *yet* take upon me the incumbrance of a family." He does not sound at all happy, for he could not speak of passion to his mother as he might to a friend. When he put his foot down, he did so softly: "You may consider my choice as irrevocably fixed."

He placed his thoughts about a future with Louisa in a very particular context. It was clear that even now he had scars from the breakup with Mary Frazier. The episode remained unfinished business between mother and son. He wanted to say that he knew himself, but his mother had yet to be convinced.

As far as Abigail Adams was concerned, the earlier love affair was a major stumbling block on the road to emotional maturity. Johnny had been ill served by getting so serious so soon. Now, in making his intentions toward the Johnson girl known, he reminded his mother of a letter he had written to her the previous year—a vehicle by which to declare his personal independence. "The Heart," he'd written, "if it can choose again, its election must be spontaneous, without receiving any direction from the will." He wanted his mother to appreciate how he had come to see himself in his thirtieth year. "A marriage of *convenience,*" he stated for her benefit, was the appropriate recourse for a man of forty-five, not someone his age. Implicit in the argument was a rhetorical question: Could he not marry for love without marrying imprudently?

The word "romantic" was not understood by them as we understand it. "I hope you will not think me romantic," he said, eager to bring her over to his position. "The deliberate sacrifice of a strong passion to prudential and family considerations is indeed so widely distant from the orthodox doctrine of Romance, that there is not I believe a novel-writer of the age, who can get rid of such an incident without the help of a pistol." He defined "romance" as the story of an unfortunate lover who takes his own life rather than live without love. He was not that far gone with respect to Miss Johnson.

As if to announce his expertise in the amorous sciences, he dispassionately recounted the manner in which he and Mary Frazier had parted. There was no anger but "a mutual dissolution of affection: the attractive principle was itself destroyed. The flame was not covered with ashes, it was extinguished with cold water." The sober parties wished for the other eventual happiness with a deserving other. If breaking up with Maria was right, so was his choice of Louisa. But it almost didn't matter what he said. As soon as his mother sensed the seriousness of what was afoot, she immediately concluded that he was simply smitten by the outward allure of a female. So she did as before and impulsively issued a wad of cautionary advice. While Louisa, reared in Europe, spoke French as well as John Quincy, in Mrs. Adams's view she would be entirely unprepared for life as a New England wife. They should wait. Furthermore, as one who had been in the same position not long before, Abigail Adams was deeply concerned for the young, impressionable Louisa as the wife of a U.S. minister; she would succumb to the "dissapations and amusements" of life at a foreign court. In reply to all of this, her son assured her of Louisa's ability to resist foreign "allurements." He was writing more assertively now: "My friend has herself a delicate sense of propriety."[12]

The flow of correspondence between mother and child kept moving during the summer and autumn months of 1796. In a particularly waggish passage, he claimed that if he took her advice and waited until he was back in Boston and financially secure, "I should have been certainly doomed to perpetual celibacy." He'd already lost considerable ground by being absent from the United States for so long, he said. One only established a professional reputation through presence. As his father's experience proved, diplomacy kept one apart from the race for reputation where it mattered most. Almost parenthetically, the son added, "I have indeed long known that my father is far more ambitious for my advancement, far more solicitous for the extension of my fame, than I have ever been, or ever shall be myself."[13]

When John Adams, writing less frequently these days, got around to instructing his son, his subject was how to read the news from home that would soon be arriving in his lap. American newspapers reporting on the presidential election were undignified; partisan writers—"scribblers"—turned out petty, paltry editorials. "The Scribblers must have their itching, Scratched," wrote the candidate. "Poor Jefferson is tortured as much as your better Acquaintance [that is, John Adams himself]." He wrote knowing the election would be close: there was still a fair chance that JQA's honored father would be booted out of politics once and for all. "If I should be a private Gentleman next Year, I shall be a better Correspondent of yours than I ever have been, and my Farm will shine brighter than ever." Aware that his son was thinking about returning to the United States and striking out for the South, where his legal skills might be more in demand, the patriarch offered this conjecture: "If you become a southern Man, who shall I give my hill to?" He had settled on a name for his forty-acre Quincy property: "Peacefield."[14]

JQA a southern man? It sounds bizarre. In view of his later career, one understands just how uncommitted he was at this transitional time. He couldn't imagine being employed in government if his father was elected president—owing to ethical challenges—and it was certainly not likely to happen if Jefferson was the one to succeed President Washington. To his brother Charles, John Quincy speculated on what it might mean if he looked south. It was not a perfect solution, he well understood. Reckoning with the possibility of disunion as northern and southern interests further diverged, he promptly retreated to the position that one should at least accommodate "the general tenor of Southern politics" and "yield to their unreasonable pretensions" so as to avoid severing "the chain that binds us alltogether." If the Union collapsed, the older brother wrote fearfully, "we shall soon divide into a parcel of petty tribes at perpetual war with one another." His policy of accommodation was, in part, a reaction to affairs of the Old World as he observed them. "The state of American politics is far from being pleasant," he told Charles, "but in comparison with those in Europe they are still promising."[15]

Held back by his uncertainty about the future, JQA unpropitiously chose to pick a fight with his future wife, nearly bringing their wedding plans to an abrupt end. At a rash moment, he took issue with Louisa's bold suggestion that she travel on her own to The Hague and marry him there. Forewarned that President Washington wished to send him to Portugal, the young diplomat presumed they would be obliged to delay their nuptials, and for how long he could not say. But that wasn't all that weighed on John Quincy's mind. He reacted poorly to the mere thought that his betrothed was ready to seize the initiative. Apparently, he was concerned lest she turn into a take-charge wife. So he found himself suddenly agreeing with his take-charge mother instead, concluding that a period of proper Americanization would do Louisa (and their relationship) good and that they would both be better served, over the long run, if his fiancée was to accompany her family back to the United States and await John Quincy's eventual return. This is not what happened, however. Louisa proved her mettle, and he relaxed his grip.

She was eight years her soon-to-be husband's junior. She possessed ecstatic memories of a plush life within a prosperous family. In his loving daughter's eyes, Joshua Johnson was the handsomest man she'd ever known. She would recall, in later years, the "perfectly regulated" household with eleven servants that her father presided over as a "commission merchant" who, since 1790, doubled as U.S. consul. Looking back from the perspective of 1840, she regarded her younger self as one who bore the very traits her difficult husband and distinguished father-in-law noted in themselves: "Pride and haughteur were my predominant failings." In keeping with the standards of the day, Louisa Adams assured her children that their parents' courtship was proper, swearing "that I came pure and virtuous to his arms." A childhood free from disappointment was succeeded, in her role as Mrs. Adams, by "the disgusting realities of a heartless political life."[16]

It was Louisa, so young and so doted upon, who informed John Quincy by letter that his father had been elected president. What this would now mean for the young diplomat, whom the undiminished George Washington had favored, was not at all clear. JQA mulled. He preferred solitude these days, writing one night in March 1797, from The Hague, "Refused an invitation to a party for the sake of having an Evening to myself. Accordingly passed it at home," reading. Life went on in this vein for weeks on end: "Still contrive to make my self busy doing nothing.—Walk in the wood." Then, in May, two months after his father's inauguration, he embraced his fate, cryptically diarizing, "Determined upon a point very important to my self. Heaven grant it be for the best." The Johnsons were delighted to welcome John Quincy into the family, but as time neared for him to leave The Hague and return to the British Isles, he slept poorly.[17]

On July 18, 1797, in England, and just days before the wedding, he learned that his father had named him to the top diplomatic post in Prussia. President Washington had assigned him to Portugal, but in succeeding to the presidency, John Adams decided to redirect his son to Berlin. It would prove an astute move. Yet it was without the direct knowledge of either of his parents that he was marrying. The necessarily long interval between the dispatch and reception of letters made major life adjustments on both sides of the Atlantic hard to balance emotionally. As the son wrote home with final news of his personal decision, he also expressed, as he had three years earlier, extreme discomfort with the nepotism that went with a diplomatic appointment. His father replied aggressively in two letters, written days apart:

> By some Intimations in your Letter I understand that your Appointment to Berlin is not perfectly pleasing to you. I am a little Surprised at this. 1. Because your amiable Companion will I presume accompany you, and to her as well as to you I should Suppose Berlin would be preferable to Lisbon. 2. Berlin is Said to be the Athens of Germany, both in Learning and Taste abounding in Men of Science and Letters. 3. I should Suppose you will be more in the Way of Information and Intelligence, there than you would have been at Lisbon. 4. I think your health will be less exposed to danger, in Prussia than in Portugal. There are other reasons which I must leave to your Sagacity, to discover. There is one however, that I may mention. The great Characters and political Systems in the North of Europe, are not so well understood in your own Country as they ought to be.[18]

This would have been enough for most people, but for John Adams the enumeration of four solid reasons could always be supplemented. And so, in his next: "Your disapprobation of a nomination by the President of his own son, is founded on a Principle which will not bear the Test. It is a false Principle. It is an unjust Principle.—The sons of Presidents have the Same Claim to Liberty, Equality and the benefit of the Laws with all other Citizens." Almost as an afterthought came the following: "I congratulate You on your Marriage and give you my Blessing."[19]

On July 24, 1797, Joshua Johnson accompanied his soon-to-be son-in-law to the office where marriage licenses were issued. On a Wednesday, July 26, the couple was wed at Barking, in east London. Brother Tom was there to represent the Adams family at the lavish affair. John and Abigail learned of the event two months later, by reading about it in the newspaper.

All dined at a "splendid Country seat," the bridegroom jotted in his diary. "The day was a very long one and closed at about 11." The first reference to his wife after their nuptials was on August 6, when he wrote, "Mrs. Adams unwell, and could not go to Church." They would arrive, tempest tossed, in Berlin, in late October. John Quincy dwelled endlessly on his wife's physical state during their first year as a married couple. Serious illness and miscarriages plagued the twenty-two-year-old while her husband was away attending to public commitments. Take the diary entry for November 15, 1797: "Attendance upon a sick bed leaves no room either for action or reflection." It was an inauspicious beginning to a fifty-year marriage.[20]

The diplomat's diary bears out his father's supposition, in reverse: if Americans knew little of Prussia, Berliners knew just as little of America. Arriving at the city limits, JQA recorded the following: "Questioned at the gates by a dapper lieutenant, who did not know until one of his private soldiers explained to him, who the United States of America were." That said, the president's son profited from his father's reputation right away. Even before presenting his credentials, he was approached by officials and ministers of several nations, who told him that they had earlier been acquainted with his father at The Hague. They expressed "a disposition to render me any service."[21]

His father was right. Berlin at the end of the eighteenth century was, indeed, the Athens of Germany. Thanks largely to the liberal, enlightened rule of Frederick II, whose long reign (1740–1786) coincided with the intellectual and political ferment that gripped Revolutionary America, civil society thrived. Frederick's nephew and successor, King Frederick William II, did nothing to undermine Frederick the Great's programs. During his eleven-year reign, he practiced some censorship of the press—the number of independent printing presses in Berlin dropped by two-thirds—yet despite the upheaval in France after 1789, the Prussian king allowed for considerable openness. His General Code, enacted in 1794, guaranteed equality under the law irrespective of social class. He combined with the regional powers Russia and Austria to force the partition of Poland, acquiring territory that included Warsaw, promptly thereafter making peace with an armed and dangerous France, so as to avoid further costly fighting. And that is where things stood in 1797.[22]

This king died just as John Quincy was about to take up his post in Berlin. The throne passed to Frederick William III, who was barely older than the American diplomat and would reign for the next four decades. Informing his father that the king, while young, was a man with experience and judgment, Adams presented his credentials in December 1797, and His Majesty, according to JQA's daily record, assured him that he would be "very happy to maintain and renew the friendly and commercial connection with the United States." The American who shared a name with the current president gave notice that his government wished for him to take up the two nations' commercial treaty, and the king followed up by asking "how long my father has been President, and whether Washington has abandoned all connection with the administration of our affairs."

The Prussian king's query sounds odd, but should not. He was ill informed of all that emanated from Philadelphia, because, up to this point, the American republic had a high-level diplomatic presence in only a few capitals. Its interests were as yet of marginal consequence in the Old World; both its military and its economic reputation were weak. News from the United States was not high on the list of concerns, particularly in wartime. And because a peaceful transition from one administration to another was by no means an everyday occurrence to the European mind, it was natural for the young monarch to wonder why the world-famous general Washington would have completely surrendered the reins of government to another.

As for Prussia, John Quincy reported to his father that it was "little more than a nation of soldiery," the new king having himself been reared in the military. "There is in his manners a gravity approaching to harshness," the son observed, "but nothing that betokens weakness, indolence or dissipation." Standing in sharp contrast to the martial air of Prussian political men was Berlin itself, a center for enlightened culture, where politics were openly argued in literary clubs. Business thrived. Berlin was the one major German city where Jews were not forced to live in ghettos. With a population near 200,000, it was cosmopolitan and in all ways inviting. Relations with France were reserved, "suspicious amity without cordiality," his son wrote to the president confidently.

The safety of Berlin was, in part, why the son and daughter-in-law of President John Adams were there. He did not wish to worry about their well-being. The historian of Prussia Christopher Clark writes of the city at the close of the eighteenth century, "Christians and Jews, men and women, nobles, burghers, and artisans rubbed shoulders in this sociable urbane milieu. . . . It was courteous rather than courtly." As a crossroads of cultures, Berlin was the spot where the president's son might best serve as a clearinghouse of political news.[23]

Franco-Prussian relations were markedly better at this moment than Franco-American relations. John Adams had inherited as dicey a situation as any foreign policy pro in subsequent U.S. history would face upon taking the oath of office. France was predisposed to treat American sailing ships with no more solicitude than was ever expected of the British. Paris had clearly wanted Jefferson to win the election.

Despite previous hints at a mild wait-and-see attitude, Vice President Jefferson did not shy from joining James Madison in calculating an oppositional stance even before the Adams administration had developed a distinct personality. The "Virginia party," as it was constantly referred to by those who apprehended its reach, was on guard. If President Adams refused to see Jefferson as personally hostile, the hostility of two increasingly differentiated political parties made it difficult for any man to trust in another's goodwill. Too much was at stake.[24]

Entering office, the second president did not even have the support of two who had admired his talents since well before the Revolution. James and Mercy Otis Warren, old friends and long-favored correspondents from historic Plymouth, Massachusetts—she a poet, political satirist, and soon-to-be historian of the Revolution—were deeply devoted to Jefferson and the Republicans. As a fierce critic of the Jay Treaty, Mrs. Warren bemoaned "party malice" in general, unable to resist sneering at the Federalist Party. "They have got their treaty with dear England completed," she wrote to one of her four living sons. "Let them enjoy it."

What concerned her more than the Federalists' servile acceptance of British commercial power was the grim expectation that a fractured United States was spiraling toward war. "War, I dread as a Woman," she proclaimed. "I fear it as a friend to my country; yet thinking (as a politician)"—by which she meant a student of government—"I see it pending over this land." She strongly doubted that her lapsed friend Adams would do anything to reverse course and rescue the Republic.[25]

XYZ Affair

Before his wedding, and before removal from The Hague to Berlin, John Quincy had on a number of occasions enjoyed the company of Charles Cotesworth Pinckney of South Carolina. Pinckney was the erstwhile minister to France, whose credentials were not recognized by the topsy-turvy French government and who therefore lingered in Holland in 1797. This much was understood on both sides of the Atlantic: the French Directory, deeply disturbed by the Jay Treaty, needed to be assuaged that U.S. policy had not shifted so much that the government of Washington, and now President Adams, was cozying up to its abusive former parent. It demanded assurance that an imbalance in trade would not give Great Britain free rein on the high seas nor convert France into America's enemy.

From a French perspective, the Jay Treaty was a thorough repudiation of the 1778 Franco-American treaty of alliance, which had conditioned that nation's moral, as well as military, commitment to the American Revolution. As John Adams assumed office, the French were treating U.S. vessels with the same disdain for neutral rights that the British enemy exhibited. French seizures on the high seas greatly irked Federalists; if Franco-American war was to be avoided, skilled diplomacy was required. Without delay.

In June 1797, the younger Adams was at Pinckney's lodgings in Amsterdam, where he was treated to "interesting intelligence," as he classified it in his journal. It came in the form of a speech that his father the president had given before the House and the Senate the month prior, after ten weeks in office. Only an "extraordinary occasion" had made a joint session of Congress "indispensable," President Adams began this momentous address. While other nations were "desolated" amid war or "convulsed" with domestic chaos, America, separated by an ocean and "governed by mild and equal laws," had comparatively little to fear. Yet the nation's overseas commerce was being held hostage to European conflicts, and initial efforts to reassure the French and restore a friendly understanding had been rebuffed.

In the speech, he identified Pinckney as "the recalled American minister," without mentioning him by name. Notably, too, the president indicated that the envoy had been "threatened," dealt with dismissively, which was behavior wholly unbecoming in the relations between sovereign states. French interference in American political life, stemming from the Genet affair, wore a new pall. "I should have been happy to have thrown a veil over these transactions, if it had been possible to conceal them," John Adams said, as he outlined his position. "But they have passed on the great theater of the world, in the face of all Europe and America, and with such circumstances of publicity and solemnity that they can not be disguised and will not soon be forgotten. They have inflicted a wound in the American breast." Until further notice, diplomatic relations between the United States and France would be "suspended"; it was imperative to deal with "depredations on our commerce" and to guard against "personal injuries to our citizens," by attending to "effectual measures of defense," which lay primarily in the development of a stronger navy.[26]

The president was talking tough, yet he was not one to give up on diplomacy that easily. French privateers continued to torment American merchant shipping, when Adams sent three Americans to Paris. C. C. Pinckney would be joined by John Marshall of Virginia and Elbridge Gerry of Massachusetts, in the fair hope that these three committed envoys could prevent bilateral relations from further deteriorating. President Adams was thinking that they might discover points of rational agreement and succeed in resolving key differences.

Of the three, Gerry was the closest to the president and the least doctrinaire. Which was why Adams's cabinet uniformly opposed the nomination. Like the president, Gerry had resisted belonging to a political sect; he had reacted against the hardening of party organizations. But Gerry took the idea of political independence a step further than Adams, telling his friend in 1796 that he hoped for a "coalition of parties" if Jefferson was elected vice president. He suggested that Adams try to reach an accord with his vice president, somehow orchestrating a future Jefferson presidency based on Jefferson's agreement to remain loyal and supportive. The iconoclast Gerry liked Jefferson and hoped the Adams-Jefferson friendship could survive, but as the Adams administration got under way, he changed his tune and warned his old friend to remain alert lest Jefferson intrigue against the administration. He also cautioned Adams about his disloyal cabinet, telling him, for example, that Secretary of State Pickering had expressed the opinion that Adams was perennially unsuccessful at diplomacy.

Gerry was in the habit of speaking freely, and President Adams appreciated him for it. It was, after all, how Adams viewed himself. By excoriating "the British party" when he referred to the Hamiltonians, Gerry proved himself to be on the same page as Jefferson—and perhaps Adams, too. Gerry was neither pro-French nor pro-British but pro-peace. Adams had no doubt who Gerry was and how he saw his job when he named him to the French mission. Indeed, there was only one Massachusetts man less party-infected than Gerry, and that was Francis Dana, the generous-hearted mentor to fourteen-year-old John Quincy during his first stay in Russia; since 1791, he had been chief justice of the Supreme Court of Massachusetts. Perhaps because the president's cabinet, when first queried, gave Gerry a decisive thumbs-down, Adams offered his old friend Judge Dana the position. Once Dana turned it down (owing, according to his wife, to "nervous complaints"), he sent Gerry's name to the Senate. Gerry would now join C. C. Pinckney and John Marshall. Adams was thoroughly confident that Gerry, loyal to him since the Revolution, would act in America's best interest.[27]

John Quincy had his own strong, independent opinions, which he duly conveyed to his father and which sometimes directed the administration's positions. He was less sanguine than Gerry and closer to Pinckney's position at this juncture. In September 1797, for instance: "You enquire whether France is to establish an universal domination over the whole Globe? by Land and by Sea?—Probably such is the design of her present Rulers; or rather it is their wish to ruin all other Nations as completely as France is ruined herself. You say you hope they will not push us beyond our bearing:—I know not how much we can bear." Like Mercy Warren, he half expected a war between the United States and France during his father's term as president.[28]

Politically interested Americans in Europe at this time recognized the president's son as a facilitator, or at the very least a necessary way station. JQA had met many times in Holland with James Markham Marshall, who was only three years older than JQA and nearly a decade younger than his widely admired brother, the successful Richmond attorney John Marshall. Both were Federalists. In the Revolutionary War, James Marshall, not yet out of his teens, served under Alexander Hamilton at the Battle of

Yorktown; in 1795, he went to Europe as President Washington's envoy in an attempt to secure the marquis de Lafayette's release from an Austrian prison. He remained abroad, soliciting funds so that he could step up his land speculation efforts in northern Virginia.

John Quincy had very mixed feelings about this Marshall. "Our conversation almost learned," he wrote of their encounter, damning the Virginian with faint praise. "Young Marshall takes singularity for genius," he rubbed it in. "I have seen such men before—they always have a certain depth; because they exert their faculties of reason, reflection and observation. But they are never very deep because they depend too much upon themselves." Here was another example of an acid wit.[29]

The elder brother John Marshall was both personable and well informed. While ordinarily suspicious of Virginians, Abigail Adams reassured her sister that by all accounts John Marshall was "truly American." By speaking in favor of the Constitution at the Virginia ratifying convention in 1788, he became Washington's second-term choice for U.S. attorney general but declined the office. At the outset of his administration, John Adams took note of Marshall's unmitigated support and recognized him as a rising star in the Federalist firmament. The Virginian was finally persuaded to sacrifice his thriving law practice and agreed to serve abroad as the ostensibly moderate answer to C. C. Pinckney and a southern counterpart to John Adams's old friend Gerry. Marshall clearly favored the English manner over the French; he had taken a firm stand on the side of the Jay Treaty. He went to Paris, then, with "temperate firmness" in mind—his words. Knowing two of the three envoys already, knowing Marshall by reputation, and studying, day by day, the news out of France, John Quincy did not expect the trio's assignment to bear fruit and intimated the same to his father.

As expected, then, the mission of Pinckney, Marshall, and Gerry exploded when the three were barred from even gaining an audience with the French foreign minister, Charles Maurice de Talleyrand-Périgord, short of agreeing to pay a $250,000 bribe to three officials. The warring French insisted on a good-faith loan from the United States, to more than symbolize an anti-British bias. "When you were contending for your revolution, we lent you money," an unnamed woman, "well acquainted with M. Talleyrand," coaxed the envoys, who refused to deal further with "persons not formally authorized to treat with us." On learning of the incident, and of these outlandish demands, President Adams released diplomatic papers proving to skeptical Republicans that the snub was real and not a ploy by Federalists to court a Franco-American war; all he did was to replace the names of the French agents with the letters *X, Y,* and *Z,* thereupon announcing the "XYZ Affair." Citizens responded bitterly, adopting the stringent slogan "Millions for defence, but not a cent for tribute."[30]

President Adams was buoyed by the outpouring of public support. He received many hundreds of signed addresses, from every region of the country. For the first time since entering the executive branch as vice president, he was a popular figure. He could not appear in public without being met by exuberant cheers. He was lauded as the "virtuous successor of George Washington" and, as one paper reported, defended by average citizens in "affectionate terms." The first lady could not contain her pleasure, writing to John Quincy in April 1798 that the "Independent Freemen" of the country were expressing "full confidence in the wisdom virtue and integrity" of her husband, the "Chief Majestrate" of the nation.[31]

Affection from the people at large was gratifying when properly restrained; this was the president's modest assessment of the situation. In response to an address sent from Cincinnati, in the still underpopulated Northwest Territory, he took satisfaction in signatures. Better to gain a sense of the "Unanimity of the People . . . on the present Question with France" from local organizations, public gatherings, and earnest resolutions than from untrustworthy, passion-abetting newspapers. He had long valued the representative voice of the New England town meeting as the purest form of democracy, and that's what he saw this as—an honest barometer of public opinion.[32]

Adams personally answered the addresses, many of which (addresses along with his responses) were published in newspapers. His tone was as belligerent and moralistic as he considered his duty, in order to arouse the public against a dangerous regime. Answering the appeal of a Delaware militia, for instance, he warned of a "dishonorable Peace" and a "disgraceful surrender of our Rights." A united America, armed and ready for anything, would remove the remaining hopes of the French Directory that a strategy of "divide and conquer" could succeed in destabilizing the government. If he failed to deliver a firm response to the French attempt at bribery, he told the "ancient towns of Plymouth and Kingston" (Massachusetts), republican

America would become as "profligate" as revolutionary France. Moral surrender "would lay the foundation for employing our own Money in corrupting our own Elections." On his watch, incorruptible patriots stood guard.[33]

With the president's approval, Federalists in Congress responded to prowar sentiment by passing a series of bills that put the country on a war footing. It was this push that established the Navy Department, added a regiment of artillerists and engineers to the existing army, significantly increased the military budget, and granted the president the power to raise a provisional army of up to ten thousand men, not including volunteer companies. There were critics who saw an emerging trend, giving the chief executive too much "discretion" in nudging the country toward war, but Adams saw in his unprecedented popular approval a valuable new political weapon to be wielded in diplomatic negotiations.

From April through the summer months, Adams found himself embracing his surprising role as military symbol. In May, he appeared in military uniform, with a sword at his side, when he greeted twelve hundred young men who marched to the presidential mansion and offered him their services. Their display was the talk of Philadelphia, and so Adams continued the practice. Newspapers took notice. Artists went about refashioning his image. One famous caricature showed him in military dress, riding in a chariot. At first glance, it looks like Washington, but the facial features are clearly Adams's. Seated alone, he holds the reins, steering not a team of horses, but two rows of marching soldiers. He was, as provided by the federal Constitution, the commander in chief, head of both government and military. In a private letter to former president Washington, his successor disclaimed any expertise in the "martial arts," but out in the public he welcomed all military imagery and militant rhetoric for nationalistic purposes.[34]

The XYZ Affair continued to resonate. The insulted diplomat Marshall sailed home ahead of Pinckney, while Elbridge Gerry alone stayed on in an attempt to avert a war and to assist the president in any way he could. In May 1798, Talleyrand told Gerry bluntly that he believed his two colleagues had been insincere, having come to Paris under a guise, wishing only to prove that peace was impossible and war inevitable. For his part, Gerry understood both sides of the controversy: he was not seduced by the French minister, but he did acknowledge that Pinckney and Marshall might have come across as inflexible. The cat-and-mouse game continued.

James Marshall had returned to America earlier—in fact, just as his older brother was digging in his heels and resisting intimidation by the French. He appealed to Washington for a position as aide-de-camp in a prospective Franco-American war. (Washington had agreed to serve as commander on the condition that Hamilton was granted a generalship as well.) John Quincy might have had a visceral reaction to James Marshall, whom he considered less than meets the eye, but ex-president Washington apparently found him agreeable, and JQA's own father was impressed enough to name James to a federal judgeship on the D.C. Circuit Court when, at the tail end of his presidency, he named John Marshall chief justice of the U.S. Supreme Court.

Meanwhile, John Quincy had his professional duties to manage. The Prussian count Karl-Wilhelm von Finckenstein, now past eighty, had been John Adams's and Thomas Jefferson's counterpart in negotiating the first U.S.-Prussian commercial treaty. He was once again the principal go-between as the second Adams pursued a renewal of the bilateral agreement. These conversations with von Finckenstein were easygoing, regular, and informational. In July 1798, the Prussian "enquired whether I had any news from home," JQA noted in his diary when the count sought insight into President Adams's foreign policy. At this point, the president's son was himself uncertain; he would not even have known of John Marshall's safe return to Philadelphia. He only collected intelligence for his father and communicated the latest developments in as many countries as there were ambassadors in Berlin. He did not yet know how much his father leaned on his information in forming judgments. Indeed, JQA knew but one thing at this stage: the Adams administration's next move was contingent on the decisions taken in one continental capital, Paris.

ACTIONABLE INTELLIGENCE

All eyes were on the French. Napoleon Bonaparte had concluded his successful campaign against Austria, and the world nervously stood by as he changed directions and sailed to Egypt. "Relating to our situation with France," John Quincy could say to von Finckenstein, "an open rupture" still appeared likely. Talleyrand had repeated his assurance that the ruling French Directory "wished to live at peace with America." As far as the president's son was concerned, if Talleyrand was telling the truth—despite the "very hostile temper" apparent in earlier transactions—"peace would be preserved, because it was ardently desired by the American government."

He was correctly reading the intent of his father, who remained consistent throughout the crisis, despite pressure he received from his cabinet and from others. The president had prepared drafts of a speech asking Congress for a declaration of war, but he never delivered it, and he never gave it to his cabinet to consider. Unbeknownst to any American, Talleyrand was prepared to bring French privateering to an end so as not to drive a jittery United States into the arms of Great Britain.[35]

It is interesting that JQA and his father, an ocean apart, were, at this moment, among the least pessimistic of observers in predicting the behavior of Talleyrand's Foreign Ministry. "I have believed that pains were taken to misrepresent [Talleyrand] to Mr. P[inckney] while he was in Paris," the son wrote to the U.S. consul in Hamburg. Back in Philadelphia, the president, who knew Talleyrand as an avid speculator in American lands, likewise doubted representations he had heard of this particular Frenchman's inveterate hostility toward the United States. That said, the assumption did not eliminate all suspicion. Owing to the unpredictability of the increasingly militarized French Revolution, the two former allies were still much closer to all-out war than to resuming their formerly vigorous commercial relationship.[36]

Interesting, too, is that John Quincy Adams did not immediately recommend a course of action. He did not consider that his job. He did not minimize the insult to America's envoys when he conveyed news home; nor did the information he received lead him to support Gerry's resolve to remain in France to keep lines of communication open. "The manner in which the Commission to Paris terminated will soon be made known to you," he wrote to his father. "I know not what the remaining member [Gerry] has to say in justification of his conduct. If the only statements which I have heard of it are just, it has been dishonourable to himself and disgraceful to his Country."

The Parisian calculus was a complicated equation. Characterizations of Talleyrand aside, John Quincy adjudged the canniness of the French leadership, persuaded that they intended to cause as much harm to the Adams administration as they could. Their retreat from open hostility was "a design to lull us into security, and especially to divide the people of the United States from their Government." France appeared to be sending signals of accommodation to bolster the flagging fortunes of the party of Madison and Jefferson. To JQA, the French Revolution was, in reality, a friend to no country. His father was listening.

John Marshall received a hero's welcome when he landed in Philadelphia (aboard the *Alexander Hamilton*, no less) in the wake of his XYZ-scarred encounter. Carriages occupied by the town's leading citizens mixed with crowds on horseback to constitute a reception that, it was said, Washington alone had enjoyed before this. Pinckney stayed behind in the South of France only to expose a severely ill daughter to the good air. Of the three negotiators, Marshall was thus the one who profited most from the patriotic outpouring. Soon after, he would say no to a Supreme Court appointment, join a Federalist-dominated Congress, accept the secretaryship of state, and finally become chief justice—all in less than three years.[37]

President Adams was neither encouraged nor supported by his cabinet. Hamilton's handpicked appointees refused to believe that overtures from Talleyrand were credible expressions of anything. They urged instead that Congress declare war against France. Not all northern Federalists were swayed by the war party, however. Joshua Coit of Connecticut, Harvard class of 1776 and a nonpartisan advocate of fiscal restraint, rejected the intolerance and aggressiveness of the High Federalists, as the Hamiltonians were occasionally known. The representative from New London alienated them when he helped to organized intra-party resistance to war fever. At the same time, he voted along party lines to withdraw from Franco-American treaties in place since 1778. Marshall, too, was making the effort to transcend party; Vice President Jefferson attempted to gauge his mood, to see whether he might stand closer to Gerry than to Hamilton.[38]

As yet, President Adams was not interfering with his hawkish secretary of state, Timothy Pickering, the High Federalist who was unquestionably the most intense of the cabinet's Francophobes. Meanwhile, the retired Washington expressed concurrence with his successor's cautious foreign policy, a bolstering Adams no doubt appreciated. While agreeing to serve as commander of U.S. forces to repel any French invasion force, the first president had resolved "not to quit my private walks until the Army is in a situation to require my presence." Though he regarded the French leadership as an "intoxicated" crew, America's preeminent general did not think he would actually have to come out of retirement. He said he did not believe a "serious Invasion" would be attempted.[39]

Talleyrand did his best to keep Gerry positive, though his plan from the start was to delay any kind of official rapprochement with the United States until a successor to Adams—presumably the friendly Thomas Jefferson—was in a position to reevaluate Anglo-American and Franco-American relations at once. Not at all expecting the virulence of the patriotic response to XYZ, the French minister felt he had no choice but to dial down the anger. With Gerry itching to return home and acquit himself before the president, Talleyrand shrewdly dispatched Louis-André Pichon, a young official with close American connections, to The Hague. He was to confer there with the new U.S. minister. That was William Vans Murray, a former Maryland congressman whom Pichon had befriended during his time in Philadelphia. Murray was an Adams man, through and through, technically subordinate to Secretary of State Pickering but not beholden to him in the sense that Adams's cabinet was open to Hamilton's guidance.[40]

William Vans Murray and John Quincy Adams were in constant communication, and a meeting of the minds occurred. After Murray and Pichon began their talks, and Murray grew confident that Talleyrand's emissary—"a friend & a sincere one of the U.S."—was on a true mission of peace, he advised JQA to remain wary, and JQA told his father the same. The son's letter to his father echoed Murray, though it was cast in decidedly undiplomatic language. "It is no longer an overbearing and insolent Minister of external relations, attempting to dupe and swindle [the three U.S. envoys] by his pimping spies . . . dictating apologies and prescribing tribute." The French minister's tone had changed, yet John Quincy was unmoved. He perceived a system of intrigue that would not let up: "In proportion as our spirit of resistance has become manifest, theirs of oppression and extortion has shrunk back."

It remained the son's opinion that his father's friend Gerry was "not qualified for negotiation with such men as now govern France." Despite his tender age, he reckoned himself less vulnerable to a minister's cajolery than Gerry at fifty-four. "He was charmed with words: he was duped by professions: he had neither the spirit nor the penetration absolutely necessary for dealing with adversaries at once so bold, so cunning, and so false." Murray, too, surmised that Talleyrand's maneuvers were pure charade, and he told the president directly that what the French foreign minister mostly feared was an Anglo-American alliance.[41]

The well-intentioned emissary Elbridge Gerry arrived back in Boston that fall of 1798, while the president was at home. He found himself shunned by the same town that had sent him to Congress nine years before. It was as though he had betrayed his country. His wife had been forced to endure the kind of harassment Tories received during the Revolution, her ears offended by shouted obscenities and in one instance a bloody mock guillotine placed under her bedroom window. Gerry was under real stress.

Rumors of his apostasy originated with the High Federalists, of course, and in particular with Massachusetts's own Timothy Pickering, who would have succeeded in depriving the diplomat of his salary for his time in France after Marshall's departure, had not President Adams stepped in. When Gerry and Adams met at Peacefield, it was a sympathetic friend who quickly agreed that Gerry had done the right thing by remaining behind. So often generalized as a man of outbursts, John Adams, in most circumstances, rose above the common impulse. He was naturally suspicious of zealotry and could reason his way to war or reason his way to a negotiated understanding.

The president mellowed toward Gerry without letting down his guard. It was soon made obvious that Pickering and his allies saw the Gerry-Adams partnership as a stumbling block in their determined war preparations. When Adams referred Gerry's official letter of explanation for his conduct to Pickering, suggesting that Gerry be given a fair hearing in the public press, the secretary bared his teeth and insisted that Marshall and Pinckney knew better than Gerry what the French were up to. Adams did not press back. He held his cards close and waited.[42]

In February 1799, he finally resolved to deal with Pickering and sent a message to the Senate nominating Murray to assume primary responsibility for negotiations as the new minister plenipotentiary to France. Murray would carry out Adams's policy and no one else's. In that he and the president's son had built a confidential relationship in their overlapping stations, Murray and the Adamses successfully nurtured a transatlantic negotiating strategy capable of neutralizing the war party.

This marked the moment when President Adams unequivocally took charge of his administration. The staunch Federalist Harrison Gray Otis was a first-term congressman from Massachusetts whose extended family included Mercy Otis Warren. He happened to be on the House floor discussing the capture of French privateers when word arrived of the president's announcement of the Murray appointment. Otis, at one with the war party, stopped in his tracks. He had earlier prophesied, in dire strains, a French battalion marching through America's frontier, revolutionizing the South, and sparking servile war. The bill he was commenting on was mooted by the advent of serious peace talks, and he didn't know where to turn next. He remained respectful of, but somewhat disappointed in, the chief executive.

Merely demonstrating respect for John Adams was enough to induce Pickering to label Otis a weak-principled office seeker. Sharing the president's dinner table a few days later, the frustrated Massachusetts congressman, who was just two years older than John Quincy, listened to the president berate another of the dinner guests, fellow Federalist James Bayard of Delaware. Bayard feared that Britain would send its terrifying navy against the United States for having knelt before the French, and Adams barked at him that he had already taken on the British once before, when America was far weaker. "I know the power of Great Britain," he charged. "I have measured its omnipotence without treasure, without arms, without ammunition, and without soldiers or ships; I have braved and set at defiance all her power." War was something one did not forget. "Its horrors have been at our doors before." Bayard should know he was not afraid.[43]

The supremely confident President Adams derived actionable intelligence from the coordinated responses of his loyal operatives on the European scene, his son John Quincy and William Vans Murray. He governed from Philadelphia while his wife remained in Quincy, reporting on local reaction to his policies. Doing so, she sometimes fed their common taste for wit and wordplay, addressing him with a cheekiness intended for his amusement. As it was, political society in and around Boston did not know what to make of the independent president's turnaround regarding France, and news of Murray's mission was disorienting. The president's skeptics remained at a loss, "like a flock of frightned pigions," Abigail quipped. "Some swore some cursd."[44]

Mrs. Adams exuded a protective spirit, and it was she who most often shared good and bad news with their overseas son. She sustained his spirit when her husband was showered with public toasts; she reassured him that his time abroad was not being wasted and that everything he cared about at home was being attended to. John Quincy was unable to keep up with the whirl of her pen, but when he did have time to return the favor of a letter, he lavishly thanked her for presenting evidence of the public support his father was getting. Speaking their common language, he said, "Cicero tells one of his friends absent from Rome with Caesar in Gaul, that 'many have done the public and themselves, good service far from their Country,['] and many others have deserved nothing but disapprobation by staying at home." He doubted that his presence in Europe offered significant benefit to his country or would do much for his own prospects. Yet he also knew that the information he conveyed home bore weight in desperate times.[45]

The Adams and Hamilton wings of the Federalist Party—if distinctions could be precisely drawn—were at an impasse. William Vans Murray, as an Adams man, automatically came under attack from Hamiltonians. John Marshall, the man whose popularity soared the highest because of his resistance to Gallic tyranny, found Pickering too excitable and came to admire Adams's calm and moderation. In the months since Marshall took his stand on principle, the Quasi-war with France (as it has come to be known) was deprived of its fuel. Why step up bellicose speech, Marshall thought, and John Adams thought, when the French were eager to negotiate?

To supplement Murray's efforts in France, the president was persuaded by a number of Federalist senators to add to the delegation two elder statesmen: Oliver Ellsworth of Connecticut and William Richardson Davie of North Carolina. Murray termed the pair "exceedingly rude & raw"; they bad-mouthed him, and he naturally reacted. But as the French Directory ran out of steam, a new government dominated by Napoleon took its place and immediately indicated that it was predisposed to reduce tensions with the United States. Even if Ellsworth and Davie had wanted to fail in their peace mission, circumstances had changed that favored the pacific president. And yet Adams stopped short of replacing the Hamiltonians who remained in Philadelphia, running the government throughout the months when he repaired to Quincy. He knew they were covetous of power. But he would not take action abroad that he was unable to justify politically and ethically.[46]

An Intrigant

In one of history's ironies, the second president profited by war fever and faced internal opposition to a second term as a result of his peacemaking. Nevertheless, Vice President Jefferson implicated President Adams when he dubbed the current session of Congress "the reign of witches," owing to the administration's legislative move to stifle popular dissent through passage of the Alien and Sedition Acts.

Anti-immigrant frenzy followed from the political speech of Irish, Scottish, and Francophone radicals, a good bit of it heard on the streets of the capital. Immigrants were believed subversive of the country's interests. In Congress, the Federalist majority passed a series of repressive measures that accrued to the powers of the presidency. First, the Naturalization Act reset the waiting period for citizenship from five to fourteen years. Next, the Alien Acts authorized the president to deport all aliens he personally regarded as dangerous to security. Finally, the Sedition Act criminalized opposition to government policies or statements made that defamed officers of the federal government. Besides the newspaper editors who were targeted, tried, and convicted of raging at the Adams administration, the Swiss-born congressman Albert Gallatin of western Pennsylvania, instrumental in critiquing the economic theories of Alexander Hamilton, found himself (not for the first time) on the receiving end of unwarranted abuse because of his accent. "Gallatin is as subtle and as artfull and designing as ever," remarked Abigail Adams. A "Frenchman is a Frenchman," Harrison Gray Otis barked at the even-tempered Genevan. Even as some of his more outspoken Republican defenders went home, the naturalized American stayed to fight the hate. Vice President Jefferson did what he could from his perch at the head of the Senate to protect Gallatin (his future Treasury secretary). But the Federalists were having themselves a field day.

John Adams did not initiate or actively promote the Alien and Sedition Acts, legislation that would cause his administration to look bad in the backward gaze of historians. But he did sign the bills when they came to him, and he defended them. He'd always argued that the president, as defined in the Constitution, needed an unimpeded veto power, yet he never once resorted to the veto during his presidency. This fact alone proves that he backed the bills.

Abigail Adams was the member of the family whose language was most extreme in defense of the government's response to the "degenerate wretches, who Strive to create divissions and foment animosities." That was how she described the anti-administration press in a letter to her son. Writing to the U.S. minister in London, Rufus King, JQA indicated his approval of the Alien Acts, saying he supported any action that strictly limited the number of rebellious Irish coming to America, and especially New England. There were, he commented blithely, "too many of those people already."[47]

Back in Massachusetts, an Adams family favorite of twenty years' standing, Judge Francis Dana, weighed in. In notes he took when presiding at the jury trial of Abijah Adams (no relation), Dana wrote, "Sedition is the offence of endeavoring by advised and deliberate speaking or writing, printing and publishing, to spread abroad false, groundless, and scandalous rumours and reports touching the Constitution, Laws, or Administration of the Government, with an intent to excite and stir up an open and forceable opposition against them." Judge Dana concluded fearfully, "This Offence if permitted to have an uninterrupted course, most generally terminates in open Treason and Rebellion."

So, what had Abijah Adams done? Not a whole lot, because, as the bookkeeper at a Boston newspaper, he merely abetted his dying brother, editor of the *Independent Chronicle,* who was unable to stand trial. The paper had protested President Adams's policies and took particular aim at the nepotistic assignment of the chief magistrate's eldest son to a lucrative overseas post. Abijah Adams was found guilty of seditious libel in March 1799, and his paper was sold not long thereafter.

Part of Dana's reasoning about the case went this way: "That the genuine Liberty of Speech, & of the Press, is the liberty to utter & publish the Truth, is not to be confounded with a licentiousness in speaking & writing, that is only employed in propagating falsehood & slander." The *Independent Chronicle*'s charges were unprovable, and therefore amounted to slander.

Dana was confounded by the demonstrations of anti-administration sentiment that he personally witnessed. To him, it depended on "the good sense and true patriotism of the people at large whether their National Government shall be respected or become contemptible both at home and abroad." He feared there were citizens who had been so twisted as to identify more with the interest of a foreign power than with their own country. So, he was alarmed when he came upon a pole hoisted on the road outside the town of Dedham with a wooden board tacked on, an eagle painted in the center, and these lines:

LIBERTY & EQUALITY

NO STAMP ACT, NO SEDITION OR ALIEN BILL

DOWNFALL OF THE TYRANTS OF AMERICA

PEACE & RETIREMENT TO THE PRESIDENT

LONG LIVE THE VICE PRESIDENT & THE MINORITY

MAY MORAL VIRTUE BE THE BASIS OF CIVIL GOVERNMENT

The 1765 Stamp Act marked the start of colonial agitation against parliamentary oppression. To the dissenters of 1799, government had become as tyrannical as the rulers whom Dana had bitterly opposed when he sat in the Continental Congress. If not a reign of witches, it was, unquestionably, a time of commotion, caprice, and confusion. Along with a host of other New Englanders, Dana projected dire consequences from mounting social unrest.[48]

Friends and family shipped John Quincy bundles of newspapers at a time, which arrived with official dispatches. He therefore absorbed his news from America in rich spurts and perceived his homeland differently than all who were reading the news, local and national, with daily regularity. When all he saw was rampant hatemongering, he apprised his mother, "The spirit of party . . . has given to our very national character an odious aspect in the eyes of many observing foreigners." English newspapers had lately circulated a factual news item that needed no embellishment: two congressmen, a proud Federalist from Connecticut and a brash, Irish-born Republican from Vermont, had come to blows in the House chamber. The Vermonter would soon be imprisoned for violations of the Sedition Act after repeatedly insulting the president; he would win reelection from his cell. The English newspaper column making the rounds in Europe went with the tart headline "American Manners."[49]

Writing to his parents as the Fourth of July arrived that year, John Quincy was decidedly pessimistic, mulling over news out of Virginia. William Branch Giles, an easily agitated Jeffersonian whom he would come to know well a decade later, had issued threats that sent shock waves across the Atlantic. The diplomat-son read Giles's words and was incensed: "He avows the opinion that a separation from the union would be better than submission to the alien and sedition laws. . . . The example of talking about a separation rather than submit to this, that or the other law, which may be obnoxious in particular districts or States is dangerous—A separation is the greatest calamity that can befall us." John Quincy assumed that his mother and father were as alarmed as he was at what he branded treason. He reacted similarly to news of insurrections in rural Pennsylvania, not far from the capital, Philadelphia, where resistance to tax assessments on homes and property had arisen lately. Protests against the federal government would obviously work to the benefit of Jefferson and his party.[50]

Yet John Adams faced bigger problems within his own party. As election year 1800 approached, the prospect of campaign combat between a president and his vice president was to be less pronounced than the firefight on paper between John Adams and Alexander Hamilton—with their surrogates adding to the drama. Gouverneur Morris, a standout at the Constitutional Convention and Washington's intimate, wrote an insistent letter to the ex-president in early December 1799. He explained that High Federalists deemed Adams "unfit for the Office he now holds," and he listed the reasons why Washington should consider "fixing the Government" by resuming his presidency. But Washington died on December 15, the day before Morris's letter was received at Mount Vernon.[51]

John Adams had kept his enemies close long enough. The time had arrived when he would no longer put up with internal opposition, and he decided to remove Hamilton's proxies from the cabinet. As Secretary of War James McHenry tendered his resignation, the air between them was tense. McHenry put into writing his detailed recollections of their private conversation of May 5, 1800, and sent this transcript to the president for him to confirm. It captures the first president Adams as he was when his patience wore thin. His words were uncensored. At the conclusion of what began as a routine discussion, he broached a sensitive subject to McHenry: Hamilton's outright efforts to dissuade fellow New Yorkers from supporting Adams's reelection.

"I have heard no such conduct ascribed to General Hamilton, and I cannot think it to be the case," McHenry differed.

"I know it, Sir, to be so. . . . You are subservient to him, Sir."

Adams would have none of the secretary's disingenuous pose and confirmed his knowledge that it was McHenry (in concert with Pickering) who had "induced" Washington to foist Hamilton upon Adams as the top-ranking general in the new national army that was forming to oppose French forces that all knew would never actually launch an invasion.

"Even General Washington's Death and the Eulogiums upon him have been made use of as engines to injure and lower me in the eyes of the public, and you know it, Sir," Adams charged.

This purported statement would come back to haunt him.

"I have read very few of the Eulogiums," said McHenry, suggesting delusion on Adams's part.

But Adams balked, accusing McHenry of joining public praise of Washington to public praise of Hamilton—all of it being a sinister attempt to magnify the charismatic personality of General Hamilton.

"I cannot overlook your arrogant and dictatorial behavior to me," Adams upped the ante, relating a prior incident in which he'd discovered McHenry sowing discord.

And then came Adams's giant outburst:

"Hamilton is an intriguant—the greatest intriguant in the World—a man devoid of every moral principle—a Bastard, and as much a foreigner as Gallatin. Mr Jefferson is an infinitely better man; a wiser one, I am sure, and, if President, will act wisely. I know it, and would rather be Vice President under him, or even Minister Resident at the Hague, than indebted to such a being as Hamilton for the Presidency."[52]

The secretary of war was out, but Secretary of State Pickering would not go as willingly. In May 1800, when Adams requested his resignation, Pickering refused, forcing the president to dismiss him. Abigail Adams took up her pen and informed her son of the cabinet changes. "I could were it prudent, say many things to you which would satisfy you of the why, and the wherefore. Your own mind will suggest to you some." The collapse of civility within the executive branch represented a clear signal that her husband's, his father's, presidency was in jeopardy. "A Critical period is approaching," she said plaintively, "in which it is not improbable there will be a Change in the Chief Majestracy." On the same day she wrote to her son of the cabinet shake-up, the hostile Philadelphia *Aurora* took a stab at the administration by implying that Hamilton had been pulling the strings of McHenry and Pickering all along: "The Cabinet is not only disjointed but broken to pieces—*Timothy Pickering* has been dismissed, *James McHenry* has resigned—*Alexander Hamilton* has received a hint that his services will no longer be required."[53]

Pickering's pique had been steadily building from the very start of the Adams administration. As a holdover from Washington's second term, he believed that Adams would be in great need of his talents. When the new president revealed otherwise and began to rely on his son (and later on William Vans Murray) for critical information, Pickering grew testier and then downright bombastic. He tried to persuade Murray to stop sending reports to the president and to communicate solely through him.

There were instances when even Hamilton had a hard time getting through to the crusading secretary of state. In an attempt to bring Hamilton to an equally agitated condition as his own, Pickering went behind Adams's back and revealed to him details of the reports from C. C. Pinckney and John Marshall. In unfiltered instructions sent to JQA in Berlin, Pickering asserted that the French Directory was on the verge of taking over Europe and destroying Western civilization. He looked forward to "cooperative military efforts" with England, Pickering told Rufus King, and he actually said that he hoped the French would learn of America's new forward posture and guillotine the foolish peacenik Elbridge Gerry in retaliation. When President Adams requested correspondence relating to the XYZ Affair, Pickering ignored him in a crude effort to stall peace initiatives. Instead, he prepared what Adams called a "false and calumnious philippic" against Elbridge Gerry, which he'd intended to distribute as an official report. Reacting to his bothersome secretary of state, Adams announced that "Party rage" had no place in his administration.[54]

There was movement afoot outside the nation's capital, too. For an entire year, Pickering's source of energy, Hamilton, had been attempting to cajole prospective electors to replace the incumbent president with C. C. Pinckney. In one representative instance, in mid-1799, Hamilton knocked on the door of a likely presidential elector in Newport, Rhode Island, and peppered the surprised man with a series of reasons why he should change his opinion about Adams. The man protested that Adams was fair-minded, and Pinckney "too much attached to the British interest to be our chief magistrate." All Hamilton could say in reply was that Adams was unelectable.[55]

Lack of success in prevailing upon one Rhode Islander did not dissuade

Hamilton from his urgent mission. He made the political destruction of the president his highest priority. Yet Adams waited until the election year was well under way before making his move to rid himself of the enemy within. What tipped the balance? The thought of a military coup. He had evidence that an army was in the process of organizing, with Hamilton at its head, and that its design was his removal. JQA, in Berlin, had no idea just how threatened his father felt. He would know more in the spring of 1801, when he learned of the attack pamphlet Hamilton had authored, which left no doubt with anyone, anywhere, that the Federalist Party was broken.

In October 1800, as the election neared, Hamilton wrote an open letter to the president that he disguised as a logical, proportional response to problems facing the nation. With sham respect for the office of the presidency and manufactured concern for the workings of the government, Hamilton's "letter" carried its hostile tone for upwards of fifty pages. "Not denying to Mr. Adams patriotism and integrity, and even talents of a certain kind," it began, "he does not possess the talents adapted to the *Administration* of Government, and there are great and intrinsic defects in his character, which unfit him for the office of Chief Magistrate."

Feigning impartiality and a desire for exactness, Hamilton decided that some history was needed to document the case. Recalling the election of 1796, he explained why he had been moved to support Thomas Pinckney over Adams. The former revealed a mild temper, he said, whereas the latter was his emotional opposite, a man whose mind was marked by such "disgusting egotism," "distempered jealousy," and "ungovernable indiscretion" that they could not be overlooked. In Hamilton's judgment, Adams had refused to forgive those in his party who had given their support to Pinckney. "Against me," wrote Hamilton, claiming access to the president's delusional calculus, "his rage has been so vehement, as to have caused him, more than once, to forget the decorum, which, in his station, ought to have been an inviolable law."

From the time of his assumption of the presidency, according to his accuser, Adams displayed an "unfitness" for high office by allowing his imagined hurt to confuse him. At the time of the Murray nomination, "Mr. Adams had the option of a substitute far preferable to the expedient which he chose." Effectively, Hamilton's argument was that President Adams did not select the envoys *he* would have chosen. It was a rather weak argument, considering the gravity of Hamilton's charges. What it showed was Hamilton's signature method of flogging his enemies in print.

Because his cabinet preferred a different approach to France, the paranoid president could not but sniff "some mischievous plot against his independence." Under that false impression, in Hamilton's view, Adams dismissed Pickering without cause. More recent "gusts of passion" had alienated Adams from all but his secretary of the navy. Pickering, "justly tenacious of his own dignity and independence," did not have it in him to bow to the "imperious chief." And the dismissal of Secretary of War McHenry after their "long conversation"—transcriptions of which had by now circulated—brought John Adams's "indiscretions" to wide view. For Hamilton, it was obvious to all how "ludicrous" the president's reaction was to McHenry's remarks. "Wonderful!" said Hamilton. "Passing wonderful! that an Eulogy of the dead patriot and hero, of the admired and beloved Washington, . . . should, in any shape, be irksome to the ears of his successor!" One did not take Washington's name in vain, yet Adams could not stop himself from construing eulogistic tribute to the first president as an insult to the second.

Hamilton wished to make Adams appear the fool, perverse, even insane. The presidency was too much for one of his weak nervous constitution. The long-suffering Hamilton had experienced "a torrent of gross personal abuse" at the hands of the same John Adams in the conversation McHenry had repeated. Adams's unkind treatment of his "sensible, judicious, well informed," and now exiled secretary of war was the recourse of a sad, turbulent mind.[56]

An interesting sidebar deserves to be a part of this record. When contemplating the pamphlet, and collecting materials he might use to advantage, Hamilton had requested of John Jay, governor of New York in 1800, copies of letters Jay had sent that related to Anglo-French affairs and the Jay Treaty negotiations. He said they were to be used for "a public purpose," but that was all Hamilton said. Jay complied and then was disgusted by the use to which Hamilton put them in the pamphlet. Jay and Adams continued to regard each other highly, and when Adams read that Hamilton credited Jay's energies alone for the diplomatic success that America secured in the 1783 Treaty of Paris, he generously wrote to Governor Jay that the statement was "among the very few truths" contained in Hamilton's harangue.[57]

Obviously, the diplomat-son of John Adams could not have risen to defend the president in public, even if he had been in his native land and able to respond in time for the election. One who did was, ironically, a New York columnist who ardently supported Jefferson. James Cheetham wrote that he approved of Adams's character and thoroughly despised Hamilton, who was nothing more than a servant of British interests. Adams had "too much judgment and independence to submit" to Hamilton; this had irked the string-pulling former Treasury secretary to no end. Cheetham even came to Adams's defense with regard to Hamilton's unprovable opinion that John Jay had been more instrumental than Adams in securing American independence in Paris. The weakness of the Jay Treaty spoke to Jay's limitations, so Hamilton was not doing much of a job convincing anyone that he understood the inadequacies of President Adams. Indeed, Hamilton was more of a monarchist than Adams ever was or could be.[58]

Another who decided to respond to Hamilton was Connecticut's Noah Webster, a moderate Federalist. He who is mainly known to history for his 1828 *American Dictionary* was appreciated in 1800 for his editorship of a tart political newspaper published in New York called *American Minerva*. Webster was a graduate of Yale College. He had studied the law with Oliver Ellsworth and owed some of his success in Federalist circles to Hamilton's encouragement. His name does not appear on the title page; the author line of his short pamphlet reads simply, "By a Federalist."

In a tone as severe as Hamilton's, absent Hamilton's smarminess, Webster threw in the assailant's face the thinly disguised militarism moderates detected in him. The army Hamilton had been organizing, ostensibly to oppose a French threat, was more likely to be made available to put down supposed "domestic factions"—because the foreign invaders were not coming. Americans detested the idea of a standing army because of their experience living in the midst of a professional British soldiery on the eve of the Revolution. "Think not, sir," Webster wrote, "that all the monstrous schemes of daring ambitious men, to overawe and control the constitutional powers of our government, are either hidden or approved by federal men." As supreme commander of the new army, Hamilton would foist upon a supine citizenry a different government from the one they'd elected—government by force. Good Federalists would not allow this.

Next, the Yankee pamphleteer addressed the character issue that so consumed Hamilton. Lest the emphasis lie with Adams's passions, examples could be easily drawn from Hamilton's past to show how *his* passions had blinded *his* reason; *his* overblown self-regard had led him to suppose he knew what was best for everyone else in America. Was Adams the deluded one? posed Webster. Or was it Hamilton? A man who "disdains public opinion and overleaps all the ordinary maxims of prudence."

Hamilton had blithely accused Adams of inconsistencies in conduct. Therefore, Webster cited, chapter and verse, incidents from Hamilton's life. It was well known that indiscretion attached to Hamilton: private intrigue had elicited a humiliating pamphlet not long before, in which the former secretary of the Treasury brazenly confessed to an adulterous affair in the process of explaining why, while a cabinet member, he was paying hush money to a certain Mr. Reynolds. It was "merely" a blackmailing husband, and he paid the man from his own pocket, not by absconding with government funds. Concerned citizens could rest easy, the parsing attorney Alexander Hamilton rationalized. He expected to be received everywhere as a gentleman, an honest man who deserved the public's trust. Webster wasn't buying it.

Webster's tongue sharpened as he neared the end of the short pamphlet and addressed General Hamilton in the same tone in which Hamilton came at the president: "Your ambition, pride, and overbearing temper have defined you to be the evil genius of this country." As the author of a bestselling spelling text, a successful editor, and a future lexicographer, Webster found a decorous way to use politically acute language as he led up to a rhetorical question: "That the President is *unmanageable* is, in a degree, true; that is, you and your supporters cannot *manage* him; but this will not pass in this country for a crime. That he is unstable is alleged—pray, sir, has he been fickle and wavering in his opposition to *your* policy? If he has, the sound part of the American people will join in reproaching him."[59]

Webster's wit was quite nearly a match for the wit of an Adams. He was more than a match for the naturally combative Hamilton. And then there was Thomas Cooper, a lawyer and newspaper editor in Northumberland, Pennsylvania, with pronounced Jeffersonian leanings, who was convicted of sedition in April 1800 for libeling President Adams in a handbill. During his six-month confinement, his wife died; upon release, Cooper wrote an open letter to Hamilton, author of the most notorious attack on Adams, and asked why he, Hamilton, did not warrant prosecution under the same law.

As the "head of the party" that instigated the Sedition Act, Hamilton could hardly have intended it to apply only to men of the other party. "I have a right to try the experiment," Cooper adjudged, "whether *Republicanism* is to be the victim of a law, which *Aristocracy* can break through with impunity." After "tedious imprisonment" and payment of a substantial fine, he figured it was his turn, his "right to retaliate." He wanted Alexander Hamilton tried for the very same crime that had earned him a prison sentence. "You are worth trying the experiment upon," Cooper blasted with undisguised glee.[60]

Hamilton, of course, would suffer other consequences linked to a loose tongue and risky behavior. But that time had not yet arrived.

DUELING JACOBINS

Between 1796, when the campaign to succeed Washington lasted barely a hundred days, and the campaign of 1800, which spanned more than a year, much had changed. It was the drama of the campaign that most conspicuously changed, and the reason for that was the consolidation of parties, the birth of the two-party system. Furthermore, whether intentionally or not, campaigns were trending democratic: voices rose and more opinions circulated, to the degree that partisan bloodlust replaced civil argument, and persistent division reached the point where one side charged its opposition with treason. Not every election had to be this way, but 1800 announced the possibility that elections like it were in America's future, a lamentable feature of a fragile union.

Among the many opinions, charges, and countercharges that flew in election year 1800, it was not an immigrant editor or even an officer of the government who best described the phenomenon. It was the unhappy first lady of the United States, in a consummate letter to her eldest son on the vexing subject of party competition. The polarizing tendencies of organized political parties emanated from the U.S. Constitution itself. Formal parties were not prescribed—not even mentioned—in the Constitution, but formal competition was, in the manner by which president and vice president stood for office. No problem existed at the time George Washington was unanimously chosen as the nation's chief executive. It was his immediate successor, only narrowly elected, who ironically suffered from the structural deficiency—ironic, because of his clear desire that unbiased views and proven merit, rationally discovered, should settle the question of who became president.

Writing to JQA on September 1, 1800, Mrs. Adams began the long letter with a personal appeal. The six years since she had last seen him had brought regrets: "It is too long to be parted from those who have but a short leise of Life remaining to them. . . . You may Serve your country to more advantage at home than abroad." And yet, mincing no words, she immediately lamented the future she knew he would face stateside—it was to be no different from what his father had endured. However "disinterested" one's motives were, she said, "abuse and calumny," "Jealousy and Mortifications of various kind's," would continue to pile on; she'd watched helplessly as the "wise and just administration" conducted by the first two presidents failed to prevent an opposition force "rising up to over throw that System of political wisdom."

She did not yet state who or what was at fault, yet it had taken only half a paragraph for her to depersonalize the plea that her son abandon his European post and convert her petition into a structural critique of life under the federal Constitution. While she urged "moderation and œconomy" on John Quincy the young professional, she confronted the broader "fermentation," the seemingly ineradicable "political agitation" that enveloped the national community; a foul mood had descended upon the citizenry, substituting hate speech for the formerly mild sentiments expressed by a range of political actors.

The approaching election, as she saw it, hung on a single word. Recall the term "Jacobin," from the defunct ruling group that brought on the French Terror: it had come to be associated by Federalists in 1800 with mob-supported Republicans. As Mrs. Adams addressed her son in Berlin on "our State of parties," she expanded the range of meaning of "Jacobin." It seemed to her to work for *any* ruthless, absolutist, chaos-driven movement, not excluding the Federalist Party. Seeing a North-South split as well as an ideological one in the coming election, she packaged her critique into one trenchant line: *"I however see but little difference between French Jacobins and federal Jacobins as they are call'd[,] one are for democracy and the other would be for Monarchy if they dare openly avow it."*

Abigail Adams understood the problem of American politics. Campaign by accusation does not ensure political justice; it destroys it. By 1800, democracy and monarchy were two absolutes in partisan argument. In the Federalist idiom, the first was indistinguishable from violent protest and incipient anarchy. In the Republican idiom, the second was rule by the self-anointed, with "right" not open to debate and free speech and assembly denied.

"Democracy" was read as an absence of order and an excess of popular pressure on government. How did this happen? The short answer is through the rapid dissemination of partisan newspapers. They had become too powerful by the turn of the century, with Federalist papers lagging behind the burgeoning Republican press. For the sitting president and his deeply troubled wife, the press was exacerbating an already heated public discourse, and the damage done was quite considerable. Those whom President Adams regarded as hired hacks and scandalmongers were harbingers of doom, marking the beginning of the end of good government. Papers that spread slander and sedition, and called it "democracy," did not grasp what the mindful crafters of the Republic meant in the decade of the 1780s as "public opinion": ideas driven by forensic argument that were informative, not inflamed and doctrinaire. Just as an Adamsian chief executive was required to act as a neutral and impartial actor, a medium like a newspaper that shaped public opinion had responsibilities. It should have worked *against* factional party building by avoiding excess emotionalism.

John Adams knew what kind of chief executive he wanted to be, and yet conditions did not favor the outcome he sought. Two related questions suggest themselves: Why did he not seek the role as titular head of the Federalists? Why would he not choose to establish a moderate wing of the Federalist Party to counter the contemptuous Hamiltonians?

There was nothing neutral or impartial or transparent in heading a political party organization. It galled Adams to contemplate taking part in the wheeling and dealing that ended up rewarding private ambition (simultaneously allowing shrewd operatives to hide their motives). That was Hamilton and Hamiltonianism, which was, to Adams, reminiscent of nothing so much as old-style aristocratic intrigue. The Adamsian idea of republican government required the kind of transparency and impartiality he associated with the judge who sat at the front of a New England courtroom. That august figure was the very antithesis of an Alexander Hamilton.

Adams refused to lend his name to partisan organizing, but he did not kid himself: political parties were inevitable. He knew no way to answer his wife's plaint. Contending factions destabilized the nation—which further explains his acquiescence in the adoption of sedition laws. Nevertheless, only by remaining above party could he hope to minimize or modulate the abuses to which parties were prone. To have risen as the acknowledged head of a victorious party would have placed him in an unwanted role, and compounded all the Hamiltonian-tainted abuses he was witnessing.

John and Abigail Adams's common appraisal at the dawn of a new century leads us to a momentously unresolved question: *Does a representative democracy require parties?* The Constitution was written without any rules or regulations for, or restrictions on, parties. Parties are, therefore, what they say they are and what they want to be. We cannot imagine any politician today, even a declared independent, trying to get rid of the political party as a national institution. We cannot imagine what system would replace it. But that is what the political theorist John Adams mulled over and, in her consummate complaint, what his astute wife stared at straight on. They were not alone in wishing for a politics that de-emphasized the fashioning of national personalities in an environment racked by manufactured fears of compounding catastrophes. In the early years of the Republic, partisan organizations of any kind were widely seen as a hindrance to the development of a national political morality.

As Abigail Adams vigorously griped about the rise of democracy in the fall of 1800, she did not fail to get into particulars. Aaron Burr's active campaigning had almost magically turned the New York state legislature from Federalist to Republican. As a Princeton graduate, war hero, state attorney general, and active U.S. senator from 1791 to 1797 (ousting Hamilton's father-in-law, General Philip Schuyler), Burr had built an exceptional résumé. One of New York state's most highly skilled attorneys, he received thirty electoral votes in the presidential election of 1796, when he was barely forty. He was a Republican on the rise who capitalized on practical opportunities to bring about change.[61]

Because state legislatures named presidential electors, the large and ever-growing "swing state" of New York was bound for Jefferson's column as a direct result of Burr's canvassing for candidates. Referring to the Burr-Jefferson network by the decade-old nomenclature "antifeds" (Anti-Federalist), Abigail painted the impending election in terms of all-out political warfare: the enemy had its "troops" abroad, lining up voters, which was a bad sign for Federalists, who equated democracy with disorder. "We shall become sick of our popular Elections, after a few years more experience," she wrote to her son from her Philadelphia bunker. "We find that it is impossible to keep them free from cabal, intrigue, and bribery. It has been said, with how much truth I know not, that fifty thousand dollors were expended upon this very Nyork Election." The charges—leveled at Burr in particular—were yet another example of a rumormongering lack of substance, and even Mrs. Adams was unsure what to make of it all. As she apprised her son of "lies and falshoods . . . raised and circulated," she noted one that claimed "a coalition had taken place between the President and Vice President—and they had mutually engaged to support each other." In his diary, the incoming senator Gouverneur Morris, himself no ideologue, recorded the same rumor and used the identical descriptor: "It is said that Mr. Jefferson and Mr. Adams have made a Coalition."

Morris had paid a civil call on the president and Mrs. Adams a couple of days before recording these words, and yet he did not appear to doubt the latest rude speculation. An experienced British minister, Robert Liston, had been telling him that John Adams was a man like none he had ever met, whose "Imprudence" was "notorious." Morris himself had been bad-mouthed in America and across Europe by self-interested parties whose knowledge of his activities was scant; so he should have been on his guard. In his diary, nonetheless, he wrote that according to Jefferson the Republican Burr was to be named McHenry's replacement at the War Department. But Adams and Jefferson reunited? Thin threads of rumor and innuendo were woven together to form thick fabric.[62]

At the same time as the nation's first lady was writing to her son of the disagreeable state of American politics, John Quincy was doing his best to update his parents on the French Directory's undoing and the rise of Napoleon. He deplored "that hideous monster of democracy" (the French kind) and saw no end to turmoil on the Continent. From the relative calm of Berlin, and prior to receipt of his mother's impassioned plea, he expressed an ambivalent attitude toward a return home. His politically pinched father had already written that he wanted to recall him from Europe. John Quincy knew he could not accept a new appointment while his father was at the head of government (for the sake of appearances, minimally). But neither did he agree with his parents that he could establish a greater public character by resuming the practice of law in Boston. On his thirty-third birthday, in July, he told his mother precisely that. And so the matter would rest for what remained of the Adams administration.[63]

With any French threat abating, President Adams seized yet another opportunity to exercise his political independence—and independence of party—in advance of the 1800 election. The scenario that arose was already a familiar one in the Republic's short history. One John Fries of Pennsylvania had embraced the cause of two tax-resisting, German-descended citizens tossed in prison for refusing to pay a property assessment meant to help fund war with France. Adams called out troops to put down the hundreds of farmers Fries had assembled. Found guilty of treason, the rebel leader was sentenced to hang. But then the president reversed course. Forty-eight hours before the sentence was to be carried out, he issued a pardon of Fries and his accomplices.

In doing so, he rejected the advice of his cabinet, basing his decision on a careful review of the defense attorney's summarized opinion. He found treason law to have been misapplied in the case: at most, the accused were guilty of riot and rescue. Adams was more concerned about the precedent to be set if treason was applied to "every Sudden, ignorant, inconsiderate heat, among a Part of the People, wrought up by" partisan fury, as he put it in a letter to Benjamin Stoddert, the first secretary of the navy and the man responsible for managing the undeclared Quasi-war with France in the Caribbean.[64]

With Fries, as in the abortive Whiskey Rebellion of 1794, Hamiltonians proved themselves willing to settle for nothing less than full retributive justice. The same thinking led them to clamor for war against all Jacobins (foreign and domestic, real and imagined). Their modus operandi was to use extreme language to drum up support for decisive military action and uncompromising criminal prosecution. They urged the federal government to clamp down on every minor tax protest, seeing in any brand of local resistance the seeds of civil war. An established Federalist Party had become convinced that its enemies (terrorists and traitors) existed in large numbers and that on a moment's notice—inspired by a Fries, a Genet, or even a

Jefferson—these enemies were set to unleash the poor and disaffected and produce an epidemic of antigovernment violence. John Fries was just another convenient scapegoat; he was no traitor, as John Adams well understood. Or as Abigail Adams put it in her letter of September 1 to John Quincy, both parties created confusion with their embellishments and exaggerations. She saw the thousands of eager readers of the partisan press as willing "dupes" of extremists. Republican government could scarcely accomplish any good under such conditions.

Her problem was that she paid too much attention to the opposition press. Violent language was slung in a multitude of directions, and she absorbed it all. Still, she took solace in her husband's ability to maintain serenity. After decrying "French Jacobins" and "federal Jacobins," she ended her remarkable letter to John Quincy on a note of reassurance: "Your Father enjoys good Health and bears all this bustle with that calm Philosophy which conscious integrity imparts." Encircled by partisan extremists, he was the soul of good judgment.[65]

If the election of 1796 was close, the election of 1800 was closer. The incumbent, John Adams, was knocked out when the first votes were cast. But because the framers of the Constitution did not anticipate the formation of political parties, and gave each presidential elector two votes, Jefferson, the Republican choice, tied with his ostensible running mate, Burr of New York. The decision as to who would succeed Adams was consequently thrown into the House of Representatives and required thirty-six ballots before recalcitrant Federalists accepted that Burr was unwilling to be their tool. On February 17, 1801, James Bayard, the sole elector from the state of Delaware, put Jefferson over the top. In later years, Bayard gave conflicting reasons for his decision: a sense of urgency that Inauguration Day, March 4, should not pass without a solution; recognition of the public's understood preference for Jefferson; and, of more than passing concern, the possibility that Republicans might seek a military solution to the impasse.[66]

Jefferson would go on to label his election the "Revolution of 1800," a moment when the popular voice in America—a yeomanry more imagined than real—defeated an entrenched elite. It is true that a few states counted the popular vote for the first time, but it did not make any difference in the final outcome of the election. In 1804, the Twelfth Amendment would at last do away with the two equally weighted ballots, drawing a distinction from that year forward between presidential and vice presidential candidates and introducing the familiar party ticket.

Aside from the transfer of power from one political party to another, little immediate change took place in voting procedure. From the vantage point of the Adams camp, however, the election of 1800 spoke to the success of conspiratorial politics as practiced by unsavory individuals.

NINE

PARTY IRREGULARS

Having been the Object of much Misrepresentation, some of my Posterity may probably wish to see in my own hand Writing a proof of the falsehood of that Mass of odious Abuse of my Character, with which News Papers, private Letters and public Pamphlets and Histories have been disgraced for thirty Years.

—JOHN ADAMS, *opening section of* Autobiography, *begun October 1802*

I was and remain decided in the opinion that a work of this kind from you, would be extremely useful, both to your family and your Country. . . . As to the exhibition in their nakedness of other eminent men; it is one of the principal reasons for which I wished you to write—I am sure you will treat them all with perfect candour . . . , strip'd of all the disguises in which their own arts or the hopes or fears of others have arrayed them.

—JOHN QUINCY ADAMS TO JOHN ADAMS,
on the same subject, December 1804

John Adams lay much of the blame for his loss of the presidency on Hamilton. But he waited until after Jefferson's two terms ended to tell his side of things to the general public. That is when he composed a piece for the *Boston Patriot* and defended his sensible policy of negotiation with France, which a warmongering Hamilton had exploited for political gain. "Where," Adams posed, "was the danger of this negotiation? No where but in the disturbed imagination of Alexander Hamilton," who was "pleased to wield it as a poisoned weapon, with the express purpose of destroying."

Others might imagine him unnerved by his defeat, but the ex-president swore he was glad for a forced retirement. "Had I been chosen president again," he said, "I am certain I could not have lived another year." Why would he say that? Because the malice heaped upon him by Jeffersonian Republicans was more than matched by the malice directed his way by the conniving Hamilton and his obedient "satellites," as Adams called them. If the first president suffered the desertion of many of his fellow Virginians who had long boosted him, the second president faced a double-barreled threat from a "French faction" and a "British faction" in American politics. John Adams apparently considered himself the only unattached patriot active at election time.[1]

It is an oft-told story that the rejected president ungraciously exited the Federal City for the last time just as Jefferson was bathing in the glow of a memorable inaugural address abundantly supplied with appreciative, harmonious strains. The first president (and first first lady) to occupy the executive mansion in Washington, D.C., inhabited an impressively large palace that was a mostly empty shell, with freshly plastered parlors on the main floor, English crown glass windows, imported wallpaper, and, to the president's dismay, no vegetable garden. It was, in short, a construction site. The Adamses lived there for only a few short months. Abigail called the Federal City "a wilderness" and returned to Quincy three weeks before her husband. He stuck it out, cloistered within the unfinished residence, seeking solace from none of his peers. No one can know precisely what went through his mind as he quit town before dawn on Inauguration Day. In the note he sent to his successor after settling in at Quincy, he wished President Jefferson "a quiet and prosperous Administration."[2]

Still residing in Prussia as his father prepared to leave Washington, John Quincy Adams remained deeply saddened through the winter months after he was informed of the death of his alcoholic brother Charles. ("He was no mans Enemy but his own," observed the boys' mother.) Louisa Catherine felt unwell most days, and she took part in few outdoor activities. Haunted by disagreeable news arising from several places at once, her husband, by habit, continued to socialize on a daily basis.

These were heady times for the president's son. He was a fixture in Berlin's high society, which meant playing cards with an aristocratic lady at the home of a Prussian prince; taking walks with the British envoy Carysfort, a newly named baron who would soon join the House of Lords; chatting with the wife of a German general taken prisoner after the Battle of Saratoga who, until the Revolutionary War ended, lived in style with her husband down the road from Jefferson's Monticello. The month his father retired to Quincy, John Quincy—and Louisa, when she felt up to it—counted on the company of Carysfort and his lady, with whom they had grown quite close. The American diplomat would have to wait for the length of an ocean crossing to receive further word from the ex-president directly, but he pretty much knew his days in Berlin were numbered.[3]

From his own, independent procurement of intelligence from America, JQA had come to expect that the Republican victory would be even larger than it was. Federalism, as a system of administration, would have accelerated prosperity, as he told his father, but it was the Hamilton faction that lost all advantage by sticking to its absurd maxim "that a foreign war must be fostered for the sake of maintaining an army, and increasing the public debt." Short of presuming to tell his father what he should feel, John Quincy previewed in 1801 what his father would be saying in his later retrospective on the election: those who "at heart" took "the sincerest pleasure" at the incumbent's defeat were members of the Federalist Party. Using a similar tone, the son forecast Jefferson's political future: Republicans would fall to arguing just as the Federalists had. Jefferson's "friends and partizans" would come to feel "the same unacknowledged rankling in the breast, at his elevation, as those of the other party did at your's." Whether openly avowed or privately whispered, resentment toward the man at the top was to be an inevitable by-product of partisan activism.

The younger had turned advice giver to the elder. Aside from the "soothing consolation" he felt his father could expect from friends, he must prepare himself in defeat for anything and everything. Perhaps he would receive unexpected solace from fair-weather Federalists, or perhaps he would face a wave of democratic enthusiasm in "loud-mouth'd triumphs" from "avowed opponents." Over seven paragraphs, John Quincy Adams got a lot off his chest.[4]

He received another emotion-laden letter from his mother in early April 1801. It was written at the end of January, before she'd left Washington. She bade him act as a second father to Charles's young daughters, whom he had not met; their mother, Charles's widow, was the sister of Nabby's wholly unreliable husband Smith. Domestic joys were all too few for John and Abigail Adams. John Quincy's brother Tom, twenty-eight and unmarried, was dutiful but insecure, his financial prospects modest at best. John Quincy—so competent, so wise, so independent—was their saving grace. He was missed.

In the next breath, the wife and mother was venting her spleen at Hamilton's indecency for the repellent pamphlet he had published, which exposed "the falshood and malignity of the Anglo Federalist." From epistolary evidence, it may be that she felt the slings and arrows of politics even more than the defeated president. And, of course, she never minced words. A dream she'd recorded in 1797 symbolized the angst-ridden life of a protective political wife, absorbing some of the artillery aimed at her husband: "I was riding in my Coach, where I know not, but all at once I perceived flying in the Air a number of large black [cannon] Balls of the size of a 24 pounder. They appeared to be all directed at me."

When she turned from the ugliness of politics to the better prospect of a quiet life in retirement, the former first lady wrote expectantly of "the return of my dear Son to his family and Friends." She reassured John Quincy that his father was in good spirits, "beyond what you could imagine; he has the consciencious*s* [*sic*] of having served his Country with pure intentions; with upright views and from the most disinterested motives." The couple would not retire rich, she added, though they were "free from debts, or embarassments of that nature." While their circumstances demanded "a strickt oeconomy," modest living perfectly suited the Adamses. "We have been a scatterd family," she observed, repeating the main thrust of the letter. "If some of my Children could now be collected round the parent Hive it appears to me, that it would add much to the happiness of our declining Years."[5]

No Repentance

President Adams recalled his son from Berlin to save his successor the trouble. JQA received this instruction around the time he read his mother's January letter. On April 12, 1801, Louisa gave birth to their first child, whom they named George Washington Adams. The ecstatic new father told his brother Tom, "President Washington was, next to my own father, the man upon earth to whom I was indebted for the greatest personal obligations." To this he added with Adamsian wit, "I know not whether upon rigorous philosophical principles it be wise to give a great and venerable name to such a lottery-ticket as a new-born infant—but my logical scruples have in this case been overpowered by my instinctive sentiments." Lord and Lady Carysfort served as the child's godparents, and the Prussian king even redirected traffic away from the new mother's street so that she could rest and regain her strength, a sign of the American couple's popularity at court.

After inoculating George against smallpox, John Quincy and Louisa departed Germany in June 1801 and arrived in Philadelphia in early September. Now a resident of that city, with a small legal practice, Tom Adams met them at the dock. Louisa was, by her own account, "a poor broken consumptive creature" at this point, and her condition evidently shocked her soft-hearted brother-in-law. The ocean-tossed couple, late of Berlin, dined with the celebrated Dr. Benjamin Rush, a family friend of long standing, who attended the ailing Mrs. Adams.[6]

During their weeklong respite from travel, Louisa Catherine attempted to regain her health, and John Quincy spent time with Tom's old friend from Harvard and present roommate, Joseph Dennie. He had begun publishing a new literary and political magazine called the *Port Folio,* in which John Quincy's descriptive travels through Silesia were already being serialized. While on shaky ground in 1801, the *Port Folio* would become increasingly an organ of anti-administration fervor as cocky Jeffersonians became comfortable with power. Dennie's turn to invective would give an embittered Abigail Adams occasional delight and prove enough of a threat to President Jefferson that he eventually had the editor prosecuted for seditious libel. The irony, surely not lost on any of the Adamses, was that Dennie's principal patron was the notorious Timothy Pickering, whose star had understandably faded, in Dennie's mind, as the Adamses' rose.[7]

The involuntarily retired president was very much on his son's mind during the Philadelphia stopover. John Quincy could hardly wait to get home to Massachusetts. For the first time in four years of marriage, a tenacious husband and a weakened wife parted, so that the recalled diplomat could reunite with his parents. Louisa hurried in another direction, to the neighborhood of Washington to see her own extended family. Morbid thoughts nearly overcame the young woman, and her father did not even recognize the pale creature who showed up at his front door.

John Quincy's homecoming was, as he wrote, a moment of "inexpressible delight." After putting Louisa on the Baltimore stage, he'd gone on to New York City, where he looked up Vice President Aaron Burr and other politicos before pushing on to the residence in Quincy now known as Peacefield.

After seven long years away, he arrived at night on September 21, 1801. John and Abigail welcomed their boy with "tenderest affection." John Quincy went walking with his father, taking in the mass of improvements made to the land. His father put him right to work, not on the farm, but inspecting and arranging decades of private papers. The ex-president had a new agenda: to tell his history of accomplishment. Naturally, his dutiful son agreed to help lay out the story. But before John Quincy could even think of embarking on the project, he first had to reverse direction and travel back to Washington "to bring home my wife."[8]

He found Louisa, along with son George and his in-laws, in good spirits. The couple visited President Jefferson and Secretary of State Madison, meeting the new president's as yet obscure private secretary, the former army captain Meriwether Lewis. Then John Quincy and Louisa paid a call to Martha Washington at Mount Vernon, presenting the babe who bore the name of her late husband. After paying respects and carrying out social duties, the couple proceeded north, accompanied part of the way by Joshua Johnson, Louisa's father, who took sick in what would prove to be his final illness. To make matters worse, both Louisa and George were ailing again. "I cannot describe my suffering of both mind and body," she recorded. At Philadelphia, Dr. Rush looked in on her once more. In New York, the young family stayed overnight at the home of sister Nabby, which eased the journey somewhat. Louisa gushed. Nabby was not merely an affectionate sister; she possessed "persevering fortitude; uncomplaining sweetness, and patient resignation, with the Christian devotion of a Saint."

John and Abigail did not set eyes on their fragile daughter-in-law and grandson until just before winter came on. Of the two, it was the ex-president who proved the more attentive. He was certifiably enamored of Louisa. "The old Gentleman took a fancy to me," she wrote. Abigail, on the other hand, gave one look and adjudged her not long for this world.[9]

The cycle of welcomes among the extended family in and around Boston produced feelings of inadequacy in the newest Mrs. Adams, which was only worsened by stories Louisa heard of her husband's passionate attachment to Mary Frazier. She had known nothing about John Quincy's first love until he finally narrated the story of the relationship on the voyage from Europe. Then, compounding her certain knowledge of the impending death of her father, Louisa was made to feel inferior in the company of one so strong and opinionated as her mother-in-law: "I hourly betrayed my incapacity; and to a woman like Mrs. Adams; equal to every occasion in life; I appeared like a maudlin hysterical Fine lady, not fit to be the Partner of a Man, who was evidently to play a great part on the Theater of life." Tom Adams knew, and no doubt the young couple did as well: Abigail and John were upset that their first son's first son was named after the first president and not the second.[10]

None of this appears to have dampened the spirits of John Quincy. He moved his little family into Boston and enjoyed his improved status in local political circles. Whether a result of his ministerial positions in Europe or the residue of goodwill being expressed toward his generally underappreciated father, the source of his newfound sense of calm is not clear. It was not to last.

In 1802, and not for the first time, JQA came to the defense of his father. This time, it was in the pages of Dennie's *Port Folio*. Thomas Paine had been welcomed to the United States by no less a figure than President Jefferson and had charged that the ex-president was "of a bewildered mind." In his printed counterblow, the ex-president's eldest son denounced Paine as both troublemaker and "blasphemer," who, after dishonoring himself in England with repeated praise for the topsy-turvy French Revolution, had returned "to try his luck, once more, in the American lottery." It was Publicola's rebirth: "Spirit of Jacobinism and Infidelity where wilt thou lead us!" To any who would listen, an undiplomatic John Q. Adams contemptuously called out the rascally Paine.[11]

When the good citizens of Quincy assembled to honor John Adams on his sixty-seventh birthday in October of that year, the honoree responded graciously but still defensively on the subject of his legacy: "During the Period when I was President of the United States, I see nothing of any Consequence to repent or regrett. Some measures were the Effect of imperious necessity, much against my Inclinations." Rationalizations followed, and then a doubling down: "Let me add one observation more. Under the Continual provocations, breaking and pouring in upon me from unexpected as well as expected quarters, during the two last years of my Administration, he must have been more of a modern Epicurean Phylosopher, than I ever was or ever will be, to have born them all, without some incautious expressions at times of an inutterable Indignation." Not enough? "I have no other Apology to make to Individuals or the Public." He predicted "National Greatness," concluding his statement before the citizens of Quincy with tribute to "A Union of honest Men." He did not speak of Jefferson.[12]

Meanwhile, John Q. Adams was becoming a fixture among Boston intellectuals. He now held a seat in the Massachusetts State Senate and sought but failed to win a seat in the U.S. House of Representatives. By all appearances, he was not greatly disappointed in the latter result. It meant that father and son would enjoy each other's company for a sustained period. It had been close to a decade since they were able to do so. Rounding out the months of diversion, Louisa, in the summer of 1802, was finally introduced to her husband's first love, the stunningly attractive Mary Frazier, now engaged to be married. The discomfort she'd felt dissipated. Even Abigail Adams mellowed a bit, to Louisa's great relief.[13]

That autumn, the ex-president Adams was none too excited that the rogue journalist James T. Callender, who had written a vulgar pamphlet defaming Adams in 1800, had now suddenly turned on President Jefferson, his erstwhile benefactor and a man he believed he had helped to elect. It was a sign of the times, for John Adams, that the power of democratic speech, in the wrong hands, could reach wider and have more of an impact than the official acts of the duly elected. John Quincy was not terribly disturbed to find the sitting president placed under a microscope for questionable personal behavior. Unlike his father, he wanted to see the Virginia aristocrat squirm.

Callender was an immigrant from Scotland, more than once prosecuted for his forwardness, and now a disappointed office seeker who interpreted Jefferson's refusal to award him a lucrative federal job as a slap in the face—and an invitation to take the president down a notch. He had gone after Hamilton, whose extramarital activities made him easy prey; his hit job on Adams, *The Prospect Before Us,* was a murderous piece of political propaganda. As a candidate, Jefferson did not find fault in either of these two works. But now he was on the hot seat, because when Callender appeared in Washington armed with demands, he was denied an audience with the new president. Rebuffed, he hinted to Meriwether Lewis that he was "in possession of things which he could and would make use of." Subsequently, the bold immigrant introduced to history a Monticello slave named Sally Hemings, explaining to newspaper readers far and wide that folks in Jefferson's neighborhood were aware that the president and "black Sal" were lovers. Callender had America talking.[14]

John and Abigail Adams had known Sally Hemings. As the teenage maid to Jefferson's younger daughter, Maria, she had slept under their roof in London. They certainly knew that she was not exactly "black," in the parlance of their day, being three-quarters white but nonetheless a slave on the basis of her mother's legal status. John Quincy was already back in the United States in 1787, when Hemings had arrived in Europe, and so he could not have had a precise picture of her in his mind when he contributed lighthearted verse regarding Jefferson's presumed sexual conquest in the pages of the *Port Folio*—the authorship of which Jefferson might well have recognized.[15]

John Adams was disinclined to speak for attribution on Jefferson's expedition along the sexual frontier of race relations, and we cannot be certain that he accepted Callender's assertions as readily as his wife and son seem to have. "What Shall We Say," the ex-president wrote to a Dutch intellectual. "The Editors of Newspapers, have no Check, and yet have Power to make and Unmake Characters, at their Will; to create and uncreate Constitutions, to erect and demolish Administrations. When a few scribblers, all foreigners, whose origin history and Characters nobody knows, have more influence than President Senate, the Peoples own Representatives, and all the Judges of the Land?" Here was an early critique of tabloid journalism.[16]

Critical Thinking

Personal financial issues took precedence in the spring of 1803. John Quincy was living in Boston, practicing law, and just elected by the Massachusetts state legislature to a term in the U.S. Senate, when he and his father faced a serious and sudden financial crisis. They both had a sizable percentage of their net worth held in a London banking firm that failed. John Quincy's property and (because it was used as collateral) his parents' were both in jeopardy of being seized. As soon as he learned, he rode out to Quincy to deliver the shocking news. "They felt it severely, but bore it with proper firmness and composure," he wrote, praising his parents for their sturdiness while accepting his share of responsibility. "I feel myself in a great degree answerable for this calamity, and of course bound to share largely in the loss." He would not take his place in the Senate before autumn, so there was time to commit himself to the family financial crisis.[17]

He conceived a means of drawing funds from Holland to meet urgent needs, but that plan backfired, and the house in which he was presently living remained at risk. As he looked for an investor to cover the amount (plus interest) owed on the Dutch loan, he tried unsuccessfully to sell an insurance policy he owned. In the days following, adding to the general misery, he found his mother ailing; plus, the physically fragile Louisa was pregnant again and suffering from headaches.

Rescue came when John Quincy received assurances of financial support from relatives on his mother's side. Still, money problems remained, and he would have to monitor business closely for some time to come. He kept to his schedule throughout, "reading assiduously" at his office, boning up on case law. In the snowy month of April 1803, his evening reading was an eclectic mix: a history of Columbus's West Indies expeditions, *Essais* of Michel de Montaigne, with their constant quotations from the ancients. Night after night, he read Shakespeare aloud to "the ladies"—moments Louisa said she adored. He recorded an afternoon walk with his father "over the hill" of the Quincy property. On another occasion, father and son met up in Boston and walked about the Common.[18]

John Quincy's world, for the moment, was Boston and a family that touched off existential woes (with occasional repose). He would relocate to the nation's capital when Congress reconvened, an eventuality he accepted but did not especially yearn for. For hard-core New England Federalists, the change to a Republican administration augured genuine evil: southern men with poor judgment were suddenly dictating the political agenda. "Washington is not paradise but purgatory, where I fear, sinners are made worse," wrote Fisher Ames of Massachusetts, who saw the writing on the wall as Federalist voices fell silent in most other parts of the Union. Though willing to abide John Quincy Adams as a representative of his section, Ames feared where his stubborn independence might lead. "John Q. Adams" was, he wrote, notoriously "unmanageable."

In a rare instance of two U.S. senators being named from the same state at the same time, JQA's Massachusetts colleague was none other than the Salem native Timothy Pickering, his father's former U.S. secretary of state and sworn enemy. "There was a degree of ascerbity [*sic*] in his manners altogether repellant," said Louisa. While some old Federalist hands referred to the second president as "queer," Pickering was one of those who doubted his sanity. A close watch on Senator-elect Adams was called for, if you were one of the High Federalists.[19]

We have seen how a prickly manner of engagement passed from father to son. Now, as he reentered politics, John Quincy began to suffer from hemorrhoids, a condition that would continue to plague him for the rest of his life. Even as he made his way into the august body of the national legislature, he confided to his diary that he felt himself forever drifting toward "indolence" and "idleness," that no matter what honors came his way, he could not escape mediocrity. Marking his thirty-sixth birthday on July 11, he wrote with "sorrow to think how long I have lived, and to how little purpose."

It is hard to know what inner compulsion so often led to this refrain. He was one of the great bibliophiles, blessed with that love of learning his father imparted. The inner life he cultivated gave ample evidence of purposeful living. Once he opened a book, he kept on through to the end, whether or not it excited him. He was, if nothing else, driven to see every task to completion. He was, endlessly, a doer. In Boston, he regularly attended meetings of the Natural Philosophy Club (mainly composed of old Harvard friends); he dutifully appeared at public ceremonies; he dined with visiting politicians and professors. Hours each day, he sat with book in hand. And yet, John Quincy Adams somehow still regarded himself as an aimless, negligent, unrealized soul.[20]

Aside from the periodic self-recrimination, we mostly see his critical focus projected outward and his ego soothed by finding limitations in the works of celebrated others. As he turned the pages of the Englishman William Winterbotham's sympathetic four-volume *History of the United States* (1794), he recorded fugitive thoughts in his literary commonplace book. The oft-cited "Speech of Logan" drew his particular attention. The Mingo chief was a tragic figure in Revolutionary lore. In 1774, he found that his family had been slaughtered by whites, and he delivered a sublime oration lamenting the severing of his bloodline. In his well-known, well-thumbed *Notes on Virginia* (completed in Paris and published in numerous editions since 1785), Thomas Jefferson first popularized Logan's plaintive speech and its culminating sentiment: "There runs not a drop of my blood in the veins of any living creature." It was all part of Jefferson's protest against the renowned French naturalist the comte de Buffon, who charged that North America's environment supported a degenerated species. To make his case, Jefferson listed comparative weights of European and American animals. "Mr. Jefferson's tables," JQA noted to himself, "are very plausible, but . . . ," and then he went into a tear detailing what he thought was illogical in Jefferson's geographical distinctions. Buffon's positions were "erroneous," Adams concurred, "but Jefferson's mode of refuting them is equally wrong."

And that was just part of the problem. Jefferson lauded Logan's speech as an example of oratorical skill equal to that of the ancient Demosthenes. Adams agreed that Logan's passion and pathos were real, but in the Indian's words, he insisted, there was "scarcely one original idea." His study of rhetoric gave him an edge over Jefferson, he figured: "The drop of blood may be original, and is a good thought. But the idea has too fair a complexion for a Mingo Chief: it is an European idea. To compare such a shriek of feeling as this with the Orations of Demosthenes and Cicero, shows but little knowledge of them. The cackling of a hen, when robb'd of her chickens, might as well be celebrated for its eloquence." JQA wrote all this for himself; its value for us lies in the Adamsian tone of criticism, dismissive of President Jefferson's reputation for erudite thinking.[21]

The elder Adams was of a similar bent. He had always been disgusted by political sleight of hand, and especially libelous politicking. Jefferson might not have bested him without the benefit of Hamilton's sinister actions. Jefferson had not done it alone, because candidates did not succeed on their own. The former president wished it were different, but he could not fight human nature. Since the time of the Revolution, he'd consistently dismissed all ostentatious tributes used to puff up men who stood for office. That's just what he saw happen with Jefferson in 1800, though he did not necessarily attribute to his opponent the artificially constituted persona that worked to make Thomas Jefferson greater than he was, that got the "mob" to gape, to bathe him in glory and perpetuate his fame—beyond the fact that Jefferson let it happen. The younger Adams was far less forgiving than the elder. He seized every opportunity before him to detract from Jefferson's more or less Franklinesque good fortune in securing and sustaining popularity.

On July 4, 1803, in Boston, Louisa gave birth to a second son, and this time the couple remedied the earlier oversight by naming the boy John after his grandfather. "I recovered very slowly," she recalled, "but as soon as I could crawl came out to Quincy to see Mrs. Adams." The next month saw ninety-degree days, which JQA dealt with by going down to the wharf each morning for a swim. His mother slowly recuperated from a fall down the stairs but was laid up now with "a large and highly inflamed tumour." She urged him to tarry a while longer instead of returning to Boston. The old man took his son out riding, and together they surveyed the lands that remained in the parents' name, then rode on to several other farms that were being conveyed to the two remaining sons. Abigail, who handled more of the family portfolio, delineated how she and her husband would distribute stock among Nabby and the late Charles's children. JQA then sat and read "some of the correspondence in Papa's works"—a project he would have to put on hold.

It becomes clear that Abigail was in such pain as to be convinced that she was on her deathbed. The distinguished Dr. John Warren, younger brother of the Revolutionary martyr, came out to Quincy and called the tumor "in the highest degree" life threatening. Presumably, this is why Abigail and John were determined to update John Quincy on their wills and physically show him how they had sectioned off the Adams property as a final bequest. For the next several days, the son was unproductive, because he could not stop thinking of his mother's desperate condition. All he did was read, and that "without system or profit." Then Mrs. Adams, against all odds, began to recover, and John left her side to join their son at a Harvard function.

In early fall, father and son toured the orchards of the Quincy farm. Attempting to restore order, JQA sorted through his collected correspondence covering the period since his return from Europe two years earlier. For safekeeping, he placed these papers (along with his by now twenty-seven volumes of personal diaries) in trunks in his father's office. Then he closed up his home in Boston and prepared to embark on a career in Washington. His parents, meanwhile, persuaded his brother Tom to close down his unpromising legal practice in Philadelphia and return to the fold in Quincy, where they could watch over him.[22]

"Hyper" Politics

The Adamses' private world was in transition, and the concept of democracy was, too. Jefferson's election shook up a good many already agitated people.

Part of the issue was Jefferson's caginess. His professed reluctance to engage in "collisions of opinion," as he once put it, was nullified by his prompting of younger allies to do his dirty work. But that was not the only cause for concern. The French Revolution was the great disrupter that still led the defenders of order to equate democracy with Jacobinism. Three years into Jefferson's presidency, the displaced second president was responsive enough to reverberating waves of anti-Jacobin panic that he felt impelled to write to his son of what he could not purge from his mind: "Strange, unknown, mysterious Persons have been running about the State of Massachusetts, for Eight Years past, offering themselves as Schoolmasters and even as Labourers by the Month or by the day, and preaching Republicanism extolling Jefferson, and clamouring down the Federalists and the Federal Administrations."[23]

Call it discomfort. Call it confusion. Reverberations were strong following the changeover in administrations. Despite his wife's trenchant commentary of 1800 on Federalist "Jacobins," John Adams retained at least a modicum of respect for men who continued to believe that a latent, insidious, French-style democracy might spring to life on American shores. Edmond Charles Genet, the French radical whom his son, in the guise of "Columbus," mauled in print ten years earlier, had found asylum on Long Island and was married to the daughter of the Republican governor, George Clinton. That fact was not lost on the ex-president. Destabilizing democrats, men with allegiance to no community ("unknown, mysterious Persons"), lay in wait—what we might, in modern parlance, call "sleeper cells."[24]

Those who would not abide a Jefferson presidency embraced rough language. Hireling journalists could be as vile as Callender, and "anti-Jacobin" Federalists decried each new incarnation of print-world democracy. Observing the ever-enlarging cadre of pro-Jefferson newspaper editors, one inventive critic in 1802 branded the profession a "demonarchy," emphasis on "demon." The following year, a New Englander who opposed Jefferson wrote evenhandedly that whether it was Jefferson's "sable amours" or Adams's "Toryism," the viciousness of partisanship threatened the institution of the presidency.[25]

How, then, to disengage "democracy" from French ideas and give it less of a partisan color? Many were trying. Even before Adams's defeat, thoughtful political columnists probed conditions of factionalism while keeping emotions in check. A typical article of 1800, titled "What Is Democracy," set out to show that democracy wasn't always "odious." As proof that the word, the concept, simply meant lodging sovereignty in the people, the author quoted *Defence of the Constitutions*. If John Adams could be seen defending democracy—praising the union of the states when he wrote that "Governments more democratical never existed"—there was no need to hold up the Jacobin bogeyman. A "true American . . . *must be a democrat*," this writer concluded.[26]

But contrasts continued to matter, and definitions would not be forced. "Democracy" still felt hot to the touch. Federalists thought in terms of opposing forces and judged the election of 1800 as a struggle between "republicanism" and "democracy." In claiming republicanism exclusively for themselves, Federalist partisans defined their preferred government as one guided by "principle and reason," "benevolence and moderation," and they branded democracy an "empire of passion, caprice and madness." There was not much wiggle room when conversations contained near absolutes.

Jeffersonian partisans claimed republicanism, too. When not minimizing the differences between "republican" and "democratic" forms of government, they positively identified *aristocracy* as democracy's natural enemy. With Jefferson's victory in 1801, they wrote, "Aristocratic federalism" was on course to expire; as a result of "elective franchise," a democratic sentence had been executed upon a moribund form. The New World was coming into its own.

Thus, two doctrinaire parties called out the other's "dangerous doctrines." The anti-Jacobin "democracy as tyranny" image hung on, because resistant Federalists could only conceive of a democracy that empowered *demagogues*. One Federalist newspaper found a determined slogan: "Elections are brothels." Jeffersonians countered by proudly insisting on their supporters' open-mindedness. According to their democratic principles, the mere act of thinking (and voting) for oneself made one a "convert to democracy." The language wars continued unabated.[27]

While capable of sudden outbursts like the one he made to John Quincy about "unknown, mysterious Persons . . . extolling Jefferson," John Adams refused to absolve his side of electioneering sins. To his son Tom in 1801, he asserted that Federalists and Jeffersonians indulged alike in an "extravagant spirit of democracy." Let us take note of the slipperiness of the concept: John Adams's conception of "democracy" at this moment implied fearmongering political activity. Coining new terms frequently helped him get his message across. To Tom, he explained it this way: "Hyperfederalists will afford nourishment and Countenance to Hyperrepublicans." So as to restore their viability as a political ideology, Federalists needed to build on more "liberal" principles, with less smugness and a "less selfish Policy"—by which he meant less aristocratic tendencies. It was the only path he saw to a "purer Morality." Political morality.

The moralistic political independent John Adams took personal pride in having refused to hire "Libellers" to slander any of his opposition. Neither did he accept that democracy, *as he understood the form,* would ever countenance bribery as a means of obtaining power—whereby the party with the "largest purse" could "plunder the people" to refill its coffers. For this reason, he considered many leading Jeffersonians to be *faux* democrats, neither true idealists nor true enemies of aristocracy. Here, the Republican governor Thomas McKean of Pennsylvania, whom he knew well, was the perfect foil—a man whose electoral success, in John Adams's view, had nothing to do with any "enthusiasm" for democratic principles. According to Adams, McKean was an opportunist who won his office by machination and subterfuge, by understanding "Management of the People" of his state "better than any of the Federalists." Adams acknowledged that self-styled democrats were the more effective party leaders. They actually possessed a better sense of popular feelings and opinions than the Federalists did. To label them incorrigible puppeteers was far too simplistic. He was a realist trying to map the political field without sticking to labels.[28]

John Quincy Adams likewise rebuked the "unlimited democracy" of Federalist scare sheets. It was an absurd construction. Even more than his father, though, he placed the lion's share of blame for the ills of partisan wrangling on the southern states. The planter set were *faux* democrats, he wrote to his brother Tom, "holding in one hand the rights of man, and in the other a scourge for the backs of slaves." Across the states, the leaders of factions tried to paper over their hypocrisies with furious rhetoric and inflated attacks on their opposition. The two Adamses could not have been less charmed by the current state of partisanship.[29]

The Adams family hung together. In a long letter home at the end of 1800, John Quincy had complimented his father unblushingly, describing his diplomatic management style as that of a model republican, especially in the way reconciliation with France was handled. As a worthy successor to Washington, John Adams had balanced national honor with good sense, acknowledging the weakness of the United States without "cringing" before a foreign power. "You were the man, not of any part but of the whole nation," who stood firm, applied "cool and equitable reason," and held fast to the highest ideals of republican governance: moderation and benevolence. Putting the nation above party, he put logic before ideology.[30]

That did not mean the ex-president was to be silenced. Once he resumed life as an ordinary citizen, he retained an attitude, as we can see, and could not but react to changes in his immediate political neighborhood. In 1804, when the son had just embarked on a Senate career, the father found himself affected by losses to Republicans in state elections in Massachusetts, and fumed, "Democracy is Lovelace, and the people are Clarissa." He took his metaphor from Samuel Richardson's popular seduction novel, *Clarissa,* in which Robert Lovelace schemes to obtain what he wants from a woman. The people had been beguiled, lied to, and finally deflowered by democrats. Yet after this rhetorical flourish, he knew he would be remiss if he did not again diagnose the failings of the Federalists: they were never capable of seeing any position taken by the opposition as reasonable, when some of those positions actually were. Their stubbornness allowed them to be outflanked whenever Republicans placed respectable men with "conspicuous" names on the ballot in Massachusetts—men like his old friend Elbridge Gerry. The party behind Jefferson grasped human behavior better and exploited the force of—Adams said it—"popularity," far more effectively than the Federalists. If they were to have a future in government, the Federalists had more to learn, and not much time.[31]

By 1806, he would throw in the towel, having reached the conclusion that party loyalty was all that mattered anymore, on both sides of the partisan divide. Public oratory was, he said then, useless, "for every Man in our public assemblies will vote with his party, and his nose is counted before he takes his seat." He seriously wondered whether modern democracy bred "contempt of Wisdom and Virtue," endangering the public square. If the "art of lying and libeling" was put in charge of the political process, unsuspecting citizens would deliver their votes to "fools and knaves."

Obviously, the deflated defeated president was more than a little perturbed. The "public" in "republic" was under attack. In civic assemblies, where the strongest arguments were meant to be aired to good effect, intelligent speech was giving in to the sensationalism of partisan ravings and petty insults. He dissented from this brand of democracy. And thought little could be done to arrest the trend.[32]

SENATOR ADAMS

The acrimony and confusion John Adams reacted to was amplified in the echo chamber of a rapidly expanding newspaper industry. It seemed unlikely that John Q. Adams would improve much on the fractured republic that his father's "moderate" administration of government could not rectify. On October 21, 1803, he took his seat in the U.S. Senate. The Louisiana Purchase had just been voted on. More than 800,000 square miles of added territory made the scope of congressional activity immediately greater than it was before.

The first matter Senator Adams would hear debated concerned the election of president and vice president—what would become the Twelfth Amendment. It was meant to correct the constitutional flaw that had made John Adams president and his principal opponent, Jefferson, vice president. The amendment's implementation in 1804 meant, first of all, an acceptance of organized political parties, which the framers of the Constitution had failed to anticipate: henceforth, presidential and vice presidential candidates would run as a ticket. Ironically, it would be the second Adams alone who would become president, in 1825, on the basis of the Twelfth Amendment's provision that in the case of multiple candidates and no clear victor by majority vote, three finalists would compete in a vote among House delegations.[33]

The new senator from Massachusetts followed protocol and formally called on the senior officers of the government. Seeing Secretary of State

Madison, he met with difficulties in getting some of his expenses in Europe reimbursed. But both he and Louisa came to respect and appreciate Madison's combination of wit and gravity. While scoping out the capital scene, JQA found a good-natured guide in a fellow Bostonian: the sixty-three-year-old Samuel Allyne Otis, his father's friend from days of yore and, for some years now, secretary of the U.S. Senate. A younger brother of the distinguished writer Mercy Otis Warren, Otis had rejected a legal education in favor of business. During the war, he managed clothing purchases for the Continental army. As more than the average witness to history, he stood beside George Washington at Federal Hall, in New York City, in April 1789, and presented the Bible, resting on a small cushion, on which a U.S. president took the oath of office for the first time. Like the Adamses, the Otises knew American history in personal detail: Samuel's sister Mercy, now estranged from the Adamses, would shortly publish a multivolume history of the Revolution; it would lead to yet another episode of Adamsian distress, with "honest" John Adams all too ready to reignite the fury of times past in a strained effort to answer an author's retrospective belittling of his contributions to the nation's founding. But none of that had happened yet; Mrs. Warren's *History of the Rise, Progress, and Termination of the American Revolution* was not quite ready for the world to see.[34]

Like his father, nothing was to deter John Q. Adams from his appointed destiny. Engrossed in the business of governing from day one, he quickly sized up his Senate colleagues, spoke with little hesitation, and made a mark. More than once he introduced legislation when he knew it had as much chance of passing as a "feather against a whirlwind," as he himself put it; he did so simply in order not to have to call himself a "coward." He would soon determine that the federal government was constituted in such a way that most legislative initiatives emerged from the House of Representatives.[35]

By the end of his first month in the freewheeling, mud-strewn national capital, he established his routine. Up at seven. Note taking and letter writing for two hours. Breakfast at nine. Completing the process of attiring himself, he'd walk at a healthy clip of eighteen minutes per mile for the two-and-a-half-mile distance between his lodgings and Capitol Hill. The Senate began debate at eleven, ending sometime between two and three o'clock. On days when it adjourned at two, he attended debate in the House chamber. Home for four o'clock dinner, he passed the time "idly" with his family. He turned in at eleven with his mind still on the public's business—more so, he wrote, than "suits my comfort."[36]

After regarding herself as a duck out of water in New England, having spent her entire life up to that point in Europe, Louisa adapted to life as an American politician's wife with surprisingly little discomfort. Whatever was courtly in the practices of U.S. senators and resident diplomats merely reprised her first years in Berlin as the wife of the president's son. This does not mean that she adapted to the Jeffersonian style. Whether in sympathy with her kindly father-in-law or on the basis of her English upbringing, she unabashedly labeled the third president a "demagogue," finding Jefferson, in person, to be a man whose conversation had its charms but who was otherwise "ungainly ugly and common." She judged there to be "a sort of peering restlessness about him"—of the many descriptions of Jefferson, this one was unique to her. On the other hand, much as she tried to despise Vice President Aaron Burr, he was so unfailingly decent—"quite handsome and his manners were strikingly prepossessing"—that she found it soothing, one time when they sailed north together, to see him lovingly holding her baby John in his arms.[37]

In this phase of his political evolution, Louisa's husband plainly disliked, and unreservedly disparaged, Thomas Jefferson. He devoted an entire page of his diary to the details of a moral lapse in Jefferson's past, which James T. Callender exposed in 1802 in the course of printing his Sally Hemings revelations. In 1804, the story still had legs, and John Quincy outlined how it was that "Mr. Jefferson attempted to debauch" the wife of a neighbor, Colonel John Walker. The aggrieved husband would not rest until the sitting president issued a public apology for the incident, which had occurred years before the American Revolution.

John Q. Adams was simply unwilling to overlook Jefferson's imperfections. Not long after he reported on the so-called Walker Affair, he brought several members of Louisa's family to a dinner with Jefferson, after which he noted his impatience with the Virginian's penchant for relating stories of his time in Paris. Senator Adams listened closely as Jefferson repeatedly shaved the truth for the ostensible purpose of adding entertainment value. The president was off his game, according to JQA. His lies were not just transparent; they were, at times, truly pathetic. "He loves to excite wonder," the senator noted with contempt. His "large stories" included the claim of having properly learned Spanish on his voyage to France in 1784 by reading *Don Quixote* with the aid of a Spanish grammar text. "His genius is of the Old French School," John Quincy noted of this Jefferson, with a cleverly worded mixed message about the nature of that genius: "It conceives better than it combines."[38]

The adventurous youth, the boyfriend of Mary Frazier, had become, after foreign assignments, marriage, and fatherhood, a noticeably grim figure. His abruptness of tone is perhaps easiest to spot in his Jefferson commentaries, but it reverberates elsewhere, too. Still resolute and reactive, but testier than before, he was willful and opinionated like his father, but with less of the sardonic wit to offset the tone of criticism; thus, in temper, he appeared more like his rule-bound mother.

In the middle months of 1804, Abigail Adams had her own run-in with Jefferson. After learning in the newspapers of the untimely death of Jefferson's gentle daughter Maria, she initiated a flurry of correspondence—altogether seven incisive and penetrating letters. The child she had boarded, and adored, in London, who was but nine years old at the time, had succumbed at Monticello at the age of twenty-five, weeks after giving birth for the second time. Having lost her own son Charles a few years before, Abigail said she knew "how agonizing the pangs of seperation" were when a child was taken so young. She signed her condolence letter, "her, who once took pleasure in subscribing Herself your Friend."

Jefferson's reply was predictably gracious, and he took the opportunity to express his appreciation for the character and commitment of Abigail's husband. While their "political reading" had led them to different conclusions, which their respective parties exploited, it was a "rivalship" neither of them had invited. "We never stood in one another's way," Jefferson tried. Thinking his soothing approach would be received as it was intended, the famed stylist of language wrote, "I have thus, my dear Madam, opened myself to you without reserve. . . . I feel relief from being unbosomed."

The response Jefferson received from this unexpected correspondent could hardly have been to his liking. The former first lady refused to leave well enough alone. She said she could not understand Jefferson's flirtation with the "serpent" Callender in 1799–1800, when he was libeling her husband the president. But she took strongest issue with Jefferson's actions on succeeding to that office, in removing her son John Quincy from the remunerative, nonpolitical position he briefly held as bankruptcy commissioner in Boston. That felt personal to her.

In his next, Jefferson protested his innocence. He had up to that moment no knowledge whatsoever that JQA had even been appointed to the office, and so he bore no responsibility for the decision to replace him. She accepted the explanation. But Jefferson went on longer than he might have in explaining his understanding of executive authority, and Mrs. Adams felt impelled to contest several of his points. In the end, what began as a thoughtful review of a broken friendship ended in a forensic stalemate. The drawn-out exchange took place over a six-month period, unbeknownst to the former president and, we can presume, unbeknownst to the new senator Adams as well. When his wife finally showed him the letters in November 1804, John Adams scrawled by her signature on the last outgoing missive, "I read the whole. I have no remarks to make upon it at this time and in this place."[39]

During the summer of 1804, as Aaron Burr took the life of Alexander Hamilton, and as letters from Jefferson arrived in Quincy, JQA was living with his parents, which certainly makes it odder that his mother would have been hoarding Jefferson's letters to her. Nevertheless, it appears that this is what occurred. Louisa and the children remained with relatives in Washington, while John Quincy, so as to occupy himself between congressional sessions, took turns reading the laws of the United States and Alexander Pope's translation of the *Iliad*. He rode often into Boston with his father, where they occasioned to dine with Samuel Allyne Otis and other old friends. At the end of September, after father and son attended the funeral of the longtime Harvard president Joseph Willard, JQA's first cousin William Cranch, his Harvard roommate and these days chief judge of the Washington, D.C., circuit court, urged him to exchange his Senate seat for the presidency of Harvard, and he was not the only one to make this recommendation. Juggling Thucydides with "the curious case of Marbury and Madison," as laid out by Cousin Cranch, JQA attended several sessions of the Massachusetts Supreme Court.

He was not all business, however. Mixing the serious and the satirical on his regular reading list, he paired *Transactions of the American Philosophical Society* with the seventeenth-century mock-epic *Hudibras,* a quixotic parable about the English Civil War. Always one to review his daily schedule at regular intervals, he noted his healthy habit during the months at his boyhood home: "Rise between Six and Seven—Breakfast soon after—Read till noon. Walk about half an hour, dine—Read untill dark—Walk again, a half an hour. Pass the Evening untill 9 in conversation with my father, and read a little poetry or something as light before going to bed."[40]

It was not all quiet intellectualism and family meals, either. Before departing Boston for Washington in mid-October, Senator Adams left a pile of newspaper essays he wrote that were critical of the Virginia-led Republican Party. Writing for the Boston *Repertory* as "Publius Valerius," he protested the ongoing Republican attack on the federal judiciary, which was clearly inspired by Jefferson. And he mocked those (especially the prominent Boston Republican Perez Morton) who gave the president their uncritical "adulation" and "unmerited flattery" and credited Jefferson with policies that were actually begun during the Adams administration or had not yet accomplished enough to be heralded at all.

New England had been "the dupe of her own good nature," Publius Valerius contended, for it had failed to guard its interest against a Virginia-led government. In the fourth and final installment of the tart, exacting series, JQA took a stab at southern slavery, using Jefferson's phrasing in *Notes on Virginia*. Stationed in Europe in the 1780s, Jefferson had deplored the masses of population living in urban squalor; he compared the phenomenon to "sores" on the human body. Here, the younger Adams wrote severely: "If this comparison be just[,] the slaves of our southern neighbors are abscesses of the deepest and most dangerous matter to our national body." And thus, he reasoned, the three-fifths clause, artificially assigning population to slave states for the purpose of adding representation, was a bad, unrepublican system, serving only to extend "avarice and cruelty."[41]

At the moment these essays were being seen by the public, their pseudonymous author was back in Washington. Restored to his wife and children, he was effusively entertained by the same national executive he was criticizing in print. Jefferson received J. Q. Adams at the President's House on the same day the senator arrived in town, and they discussed, according to Adams's notes, "impressments by the British frigates upon our Coast"—a subject they saw eye to eye on—as well as a subject that Adams looked upon less approvingly: "the trade carried on by some of the merchants with the Blacks at St. Domingue—This he appears determined to suppress." Jefferson the Virginian was queasy about a republic run by former slaves and would take no steps to formalize relations. But neither, it should be said, was any Adams prepared as yet to stand up in any meaningful way to the unholy institution of slavery.[42]

CONTROLLING *CUPIDITATES*

J. Q. Adams, when much younger, had sat in Parliament and listened to the giant orators of the age. He was not easily impressed, and the talents exhibited by his fellow members of Congress in 1804, in print or in speech, did not elicit any great praise from him. He was, however, harshest on his own performances. In his personal journal, he reserved year's end for a thorough exercise in self-criticism—opposite the way other people inaugurate each new year with hope-infused resolutions.

"I have been a severe student all the days of my life," he wrote, as he questioned the social value of his reading. "An immense proportion of the time I have dedicated to the search of knowledge has been wasted on subjects which can never be profitable to my self or useful to others." He did not elaborate, but targeted his haphazard method: "I have been tempted to abandon my books altogether." John Adams, who passed on a critical eye to his son, had never gone this far in self-abnegation.[43]

As Jefferson waltzed into a second term, the younger Adams continued to nurture doubts. In taking up causes that few, if any, of his colleagues agreed with, he exceeded his father's reputation for perversity. "I took a large part in the debate," he penned to himself, "and indeed an exclusive one on the side I advocated. . . . I felt most sensibly my deficiency as an extemporaneous speaker. . . . It is slowness of comprehension, an inability to grasp the whole compass of a subject in the mind at once. . . . An incapacity to form ideas properly precise and definite, with the rapidity necessary to give them uninterrupted utterance." The most common of plaints became evidence of a defect peculiar to himself. "Sometimes the most important details of argument escape my mind at the moment when I want them."[44]

He decided to share this lingering self-doubt with his formidable father: "I have never in my gloomiest moments considered my situation as of so trying or severe a nature, as was yours during the whole period of our revolutionary controversy." The son was not just admitting that he could never be the legal standout John Adams had been in his prime; he was saying that no matter how much he read, how hard he studied, how long he prepared, he considered himself an inconstant public speaker, painfully ill suited for a career in the law. "You had the advantage of a great and powerful consolation, which totally fails to me—and that was the honour and profit which you never failed to derive from your profession." He wrote self-effacingly to the man he most admired, "I have had experience, and acquired self-knowledge enough to be convinced that from my profession, neither profit nor honour will ever derive to me—Not that I reluct at any toil of mind or body—Not being conscious that the dread or aversion of labour is among my deficiencies—But that from both natural and adventitious circumstances in my composition and life, the Bar is not my element." A hardworking lawmaker with strong, independent opinions chose this moment to spurn the profession he was trained for.[45]

He well knew that the patriarchal advice giver would not let such dire statements go unanswered. With the combination of encouragement and sternness he had always reserved for this one child, John Adams reminded his senator-son how far he had already come in impressing those of his peers who were not still caught up in envy or prone to artless gossip. Given the prestige JQA had duly earned *on his own,* he could have "a place in the most honorable and lucrative rank at the Bar, whenever you please to take it." John Adams was unwilling to accept that his son harbored real distaste for the practice of law: "Men must brave Adversity: and be modest in prosperity. If they cannot, or will not be rich and popular they must submit to be poor and obscure." Though disquieted, he concluded the letter sweetly: "I am, my dear Sir, with the tenderest concern for your health, your affectionate J. Adams."[46]

The first few months of 1805 saw the most incisive father-and-son exchanges in a decade. The elder found it hard to resist putting pen to paper, writing week by week. Though as self-assured as his son was self-questioning these days, he could still fixate on the particulars of his failed presidency. Beginning with his ordinary pique—"I wish that both Parties would let my name alone"—he reached cosmic conclusions about the new century: "How are passions to be allayed, and the People to be united? I know not. I believe they will have their Course. We know [not] what that Course is and have reason to dread its bloody and cruel Catastrophy, as well as its Consequences unfavourable to Liberty."[47]

John Adams, in his seventieth year, staged his American drama in nearly Shakespearean terms. Four years after he was cast out of Washington and the drafty President's House, with his son having now taken up the family cause in the same Federal City, he was back to writing the national morality play. His script incorporated the tremors he sensed beneath the fragile foundations of government. The curtain rises, the peace of a continent hangs in the balance. Humanity is to be tested throughout. Washington's presidency, act 1, scene 1, contains the seeds of conflict, threatening violence. His own unsteady term as president, act 1, scene 2, shows hatreds intensifying. Sometime in act 2, prospects will appear even more bleak. There will be war. A seer appears. It is John Adams. Will all end as Shakespearean history or tragedy?

Adams senior took his cues from writings that had long spoken to him. Once again, Cicero held answers, or at least provided a language in which answers could be discovered. Comparing Cicero and Shakespeare in their devotedness to understanding human impulses, he copied into the next letter he wrote to his son a long paragraph from *De officiis,* or *On Duties*. Cicero had composed the short book in the last year of his life, when it was clear that even with Caesar dead and buried, the republic was done. Quoting Cicero at length (and in Latin), the elder Adams noted that the "Splendor of the First Magistracy," whether an elective presidency or an imperial crown, held an allure too great to be resisted. Whether in civil or military dress, power was beguiling. Caesar was brilliant, yet he succumbed. For the ex-president, balanced government was never more important than it was in the wake of his defeat. He imagined his son as one of few voices with any chance of arresting the downward trajectory of American politics.

Marking time, John Adams had no doubt as to where he stood. It was where he nearly always stood. MISUNDERSTOOD. When it mattered, when constitutionalism was in vogue, he'd written extensively on government and on the lessons of history. He was rejected as a sage. He was rejected as a seer. He was pushed aside as an irrelevant antiquarian with wayward prescriptions, his thoughts on monarchy and aristocracy deemed reactionary. But they were not wrong. Of that he was certain. If his ideas were to reemerge in a palatable form, his son would be their messenger. Senator Adams had to be vigilant. He had to speak up and be heard and overcome his self-loathing.

And so the retiree let his words flow. Cicero's issue with the corrupting nature of power was John Adams's issue, too. A Jefferson, so fulsome in his invocations of a bright democracy, could not be trusted any more than the grasping Hamilton, because geniuses and bibliophiles could be turned toward monomania almost as easily as despots. To rescue the future, the old man reminded his son of the two universal elements in favor of his argument for sensibly balanced government: "1. That in all Ages and Countries, Liberty Property and Safety have been in proportion to the perfection of the Ballance. 2. That without some ballance, there never was or can be any Liberty but such as depends upon mere Will, either of a Prince, a Senate or a Multitude."

He stuck with his mantra and laid it on thick. "Limitations must be set, and without a ballance there can be no limitations. Liberty has no other Chance upon this Globe but in a ballance." The ancients had tried it all. "When the Ballance was broken, all their Liberties were lost." Good government alone could "overaw[e] and control these *cupiditates,*" he lectured. *Cupiditates*. Lusting for power.

Feeling even more unappreciated and irrelevant than usual, Adams senior believed that nothing he had said or done had ever truly mattered to his countrymen and that the definition of liberty he had fought for in the Revolution—systemic restraint against a power grab from above or below—was a matter of ambivalence in the new century. If he did not say so outright, he was impatient to have his son do the impossible and do something to change the tenor of politics.[48]

TEN

SHAPE-SHIFTERS

In short Sir, Gravity himself could not keep his countenance at the nauseating littlenesses, which were resorted to for proof of atrocious criminality; and Indignation melted into ridicule, at the puerile perseverance with which nothings *were accumulated, with the hope of making* something *by their multitude.*

—JOHN QUINCY ADAMS TO JOHN ADAMS,
March 8, 1805, complaining about the partisan character of arguments used against Associate Justice Samuel Chase at his impeachment trial

The Senate upon the Tryal of Impeachment, is a Sacred Trybunal of Judicature, and the Principles, the Passions and Predjudices of Party Should have no Influence in their decisions. . . . If the Spirit of Party intermingles in the least in these Impeachments and Expulsions, the Man convicted or expelled is immediately taken up by his Party, put upon the compassionate List and returned again to Congress.

—JOHN ADAMS TO JOHN QUINCY ADAMS,
December 14, 1807, reflecting on partisanship and the possible ejection from the Senate of Ohio's John Smith

The Constitution was being tested. The Declaration of Independence was being tried. With a further hardening of the party system, matters of life, liberty, and collective happiness were theory no longer. In the final months of Jefferson's first term and at the start of his second, because of a single, prominent judicial controversy, exercise of power (broadly speaking) became the dominant issue before the nation. It inevitably affected the entire U.S. Congress.

The man at the center of this controversy was Justice Samuel Chase of Maryland. He was a signer of the Declaration of Independence and a staunch Federalist, though he voted against the Constitution at the Maryland ratifying convention in 1788. Nominated to the Supreme Court by President Washington in 1796, he had vocally embraced John Adams's candidacy that year; he supported prosecutions under the Alien and Sedition Acts; and he sentenced to death the tax-resisting rebel John Fries, a sentence set aside by President Adams. After 1801, Justice Chase roundly criticized Jefferson's administration from the federal bench.

Owing to a penchant for fiery pronouncements, Justice Chase became the first and only high court appointee ever to face impeachment. His trial took place in the Senate in 1805. At issue, ultimately, was that spectacle of political life known since early in the eighteenth century as the "spirit of party." Both John and John Quincy Adams regularly denounced it, and now that Republicans had won majorities in both houses of Congress, party orthodoxy sounded different. Could a Court that did the bidding of the Federalist Party be deemed partisan? What about a party in power that removed a judge on specious grounds? Did partisan pronouncements from the bench constitute "high crimes and misdemeanors"? Adding to the immediate drama, the outgoing vice president, Burr, the indicted murderer of Alexander Hamilton, presided over the trial in the same position previously held by John Adams: president of the Senate. To the surprise of his many and sundry naysayers, Burr successfully blasted the spirit of party with his extraordinary fair-mindedness at this emotion-laden time.[1]

John Adams followed press coverage of the Chase case and eagerly awaited the trial's outcome. He adopted a vocabulary all his own as he reminisced about "the Friends of honest impartial Government" who were, by his own subjective definition, the men who approved of his now-discredited brand of leadership. They, like he, were subject to "the Deviltry of Hamilton and Company," as much as they had suffered at the hands of radical newspaper writers. There was no room for moderates.

The damage was done. Federalism was largely beyond repair, as ensuing elections would prove. As the "Federal Faction," in John Adams's particular idiom, imploded, those who advocated a dangerous democracy—bold Jeffersonians like the outspoken Virginian William Branch Giles—made their way to the podium. How do you like your democracy now? John Adams asked his son to ask Giles, the senator who was doing Jefferson's dirty work and publicizing the case against the offending associate justice.

Senator Adams could not quite stomach Giles. In his diary, he dismissed the man as a furious partisan who could not be controlled. Acknowledging that Justice Chase was ill advised to politicize his courtroom, JQA felt he had done nothing of real substance to warrant a Senate trial. Still, Giles did his utmost to lower the bar for what constituted an impeachable offense. So, what was it that mystified Senator Adams? Out of doors, Giles was consistently kind and respectful toward him, but within the Senate chamber he was an attack dog, and two political beings could hardly have been more different.

The long-running soap opera of a Senate trial provoked several reports from the son to the father. After Chase's acquittal, JQA gave a damning appraisal of the entire Jefferson administration. He wrote to his father of "the strong stimulus of political animosity, aided by all the perverse ingenuity of party spirit," that infected the seventy shameless Republican members of the House of Representatives who had sanctioned this lost cause, before the generally more reasonable, equipoised Senate went on to find the prosecution wholly unjustifiable. The cause of judicial independence was safe. A grave danger had been decisively averted. With an air almost of smugness, JQA took a jab at his father's sly successor: "President Jefferson is reported to have said to a member of the Senate, that Impeachment was but a clumsy engine to get rid of Judges—His warmest friends in both houses of Congress, are I believe by this time tolerably well convinced of the same thing—I do not imagine they will very soon attempt to ply it again."[2]

The Massachusetts senator did not expect any cooling of passions to happen overnight. But he also had a reverential view of the body in which he sat. He believed he had succeeded in allowing justice to unfold in the Chase impeachment trial without making known his investment in the outcome: "I felt myself under an obligation to impose absolute silence upon my pen, and as far as human infirmity would admit, upon my tongue." In his idealized view, U.S. senators should always be "discreet" and in such instances as an impeachment trial "observe a dignified and unaffected silence" afterward, preserving an air of gravity and grandeur. Nevertheless, the spirit of party lingered on. As he pointed out in the next letter to his father, if Chase had escaped the clutches of Republican partisans, "the Spirit which impelled to the prosecution . . . is so far from being subdued or abashed" that the "violence" of party was likely to reemerge in some other form.[3]

HALCYON DAYS

The previous year saw tensions rise in John Quincy's marriage, when he left Louisa and their children to return to Quincy for several months. It proved to be a onetime-only experiment, for, soon enough, he saw how much he missed his wife. He wrote sexually charged letters and enclosed a particularly suggestive John Donne poem—"Your gown going off, such beauteous state reveals"—to reassure her of his devotion.

The couple repaired what was wrong between them. In years following, though he continued to demand the final word on most matters, they spent far less time apart. Money remained tight in 1805, but the summer and fall passed in pleasant reverie in New England. JQA returned to the study of Greek. At his father's house, in anticipation of taking on the Boylston professorship at Harvard, he revisited Aristotle on rhetoric and Cicero's *De oratore*. On quiet evenings, he recited poetry and modern short stories to "the ladies" of the house.

His unfailingly sweet sister, Nabby, was there. His financially pressed brother, the affectionate Tom, was on hand, too. Tom, newly wed, was headed for the Massachusetts legislature when he joined the gathering at Quincy. One could argue that the Adams clan was never as close as they were at this moment. Louisa's siblings were also welcomed to Peacefield and spent a considerable time on the property. While the Johnson clan had suffered greatly as a result of the financial collapse of Louisa's late father, they were all otherwise well taken care of at the sprawling property of a Georgetown relative by marriage. The Adamses, for their part, were never rich, but their physical and financial health alike was gradually becoming more stable, promoting contentment for as long as the noisome state of party politics was not on everyone's minds. It might be optimistic to characterize any epoch of life at Quincy as "halcyon days" for the Adams clan, but this season comes close. At least, it can be asserted with confidence that Washington, D.C., was never the place where happy memories resided.[4]

Domestic life ironically had its high points under a Jefferson administration. As John Quincy and Louisa Catherine returned to the national capital, they left their children behind in Quincy. A typical father-son letter opened with grandfatherly tenderness and cajolery: "My Exordium must inform you that George is and has been a long time in perfect health. John has been as plump and gay and hardy and hearty as you could wish him." Though wary of political correctives, he relied on "Grandmammas Remedies."[5]

In diverging from political matters, the elder Adams satisfyingly described his humble way of life and the manageable acreage he farmed. He contrasted this with an elite Virginian whose political success far outdistanced his own—and it wasn't Jefferson. "But what a Miniature picture of a Lilliputian Plantation, would Six Acres and four Acres and three Acres and two Acres appear in Comparison of President Washingtons which as Mr Lear [the first president's aide] informed me employed five and thirty Ploughs in continual motion all the year round." "The Old Gentleman," as Louisa liked to refer to her father-in-law, still found hyperbole to be an effective literary strategy. The moral, if one existed, had something to do with economy of scale. "General Washington was a wise man from his Youth, took good care of himself and married a rich Wife; whereas I was a Simpleton from the beginning, took little care of the main chance and married a Girl as poor as myself." The ex-president Adams preferred the self-effacing route to express pride in commonness and personal industry. No southern nabob could beat him at that.[6]

En route from Boston to the Federal City, Senator and Mrs. Adams fell in with two prominent Philadelphians, John Vaughan of the American Philosophical Society and Benjamin Rush of the University of Pennsylvania. Dr. Rush sat JQA down and assured him that very recently President Jefferson and Secretary of State Madison had spoken of their high regard for him; it was Jefferson's intention to entrust him with a foreign appointment. The senator was caught off guard. When Rush proceeded to suggest "that I might govern myself accordingly," JQA refused to cave—or, perhaps better put, acted to save face. He allowed that he felt "obliged" to the pair "for their good opinion" of him and that he would never "sollicit" the president for a post, nor "refuse it merely because the nomination should come from him." As intermediary, Rush judged the response to be satisfactory and said that "a disdainful refusal was the only thing which would deter Mr. Jefferson."

If nothing more, this quaint diplomatic dance offers a quick preview of John Quincy Adams's later abandonment of the Federalists. Completing his testament to political independence, he gave Rush to understand that "without being rich, I possessed the means of maintaining my family, without feeling the necessity of any public station." It was a statement of modest republican pride to match his father's unpretentious contrast with the large farmer George Washington.[7]

Then, one day in December 1805, en route to his seat in the Senate chamber, JQA, now in his thirty-ninth year, spotted a familiar face at the entrance to the Capitol. Captain Pierre Landais was still recognizable after twenty-six years. They had last seen each other on shipboard at the French port city of Lorient in 1779, when John Quincy was not yet thirteen and the indecisive captain was daily complaining to John Adams about the crew's refusal to give him the respect he felt he was due.

At the U.S. Capitol stood two intrepid survivors of a tempestuous world. The senator still remembered the frigates *Alliance* and *La Sensible* and referred to those times in his diary as "the American war." He wrote, "Captain Landais this morning gave me a history of his life since that time, which has been various and full of adventure." He was still demanding respect, this time by marching to the seat of government and petitioning the House of Representatives to compensate him for "his share" of British prizes taken as a privateer in the service of the Continental Congress. John Q. Adams was a member of the other branch and was not moved to involve himself directly. When the House finally took up the Landais case at the end of 1807, every detail John Adams recorded in his wartime diary, beginning with the captain's rivalry with John Paul Jones and his communications with Benjamin Franklin, was dredged up again. It was ancient history, though the United States was a young country and British seaborne depredations remained the order of the day.[8]

Despite all the places he had lived, and all the titled men and women who had welcomed him and his captivating wife, John Quincy Adams did not seem to boast a life "various and full of adventure." It was the sort of thing he disliked about Jefferson. This Adams was a lawmaker who felt no love for the law, an advanced student of rhetoric and oratory who constantly disparaged his own public performances. He did not go out of his way to make friends in Washington, and he did not wish to owe Jefferson for any favor that man might think of bestowing. Fortunately for him, it did not come to that.

The elder Adams remained active by devoting the bulk of his time to the family farm. From 1805 to 1812, he served as president of the Massachusetts Society for Promoting Agriculture. When John Quincy was teaching at Harvard in the summer of 1807, after Congress had adjourned, father and son dined elegantly with the trustees of the agricultural society. It was one day before Louisa and John Quincy celebrated their tenth wedding anniversary. She was eight months pregnant.

There was nothing simple about Louisa's pregnancies. The year before, she had stayed with her sisters in Washington and suffered through a pregnancy that ended in stillbirth. JQA was at Quincy when this occurred. His pained letter on receiving her news is a remarkable artifact of a prickly man's compassionate side. It bore the same tender sentiment his father had revealed in 1777, when he was in Philadelphia as Abigail endured a similar personal crisis. Addressing Louisa as "my dearest and most affectionate friend," an overwrought John Quincy described what he felt when her letter came to hand. "I hurried hither to the retirement of my own chamber, where I could indulge the weakness, which the bitterest of sorrows is forbidden to discover to the world. . . . If the tears of affliction are unbecoming a Man; Heaven will at least accept those of gratitude from me, for having preserved you to me." Whatever else he was, he could not bear the thought of losing her.[9]

Together in Quincy during the summer of 1807, the expecting couple went on evening walks. John Quincy tended to George's education, reading to his six-year-old in French; other evenings, he read the engaging essays of Sir Francis Bacon to his wife. On August 18, Louisa went into labor—it was the one and only birth her busy husband was able to attend. Their infant appeared void of life for the first half hour, upon which, in Louisa's words, "the Child had recovered the play of his lungs, and my husband had witnessed sufferings that he had no idea of." JQA entered in his diary, "By the Blessing of God, I have this day a third son." The infant was baptized by the Reverend William Emerson (father of Ralph Waldo Emerson) as Charles Francis, given the names of his father's late brother and the still surviving Massachusetts jurist Francis Dana, who had been so instrumental in young Johnny's development in St. Petersburg, Russia, in the early 1780s. Of the three sons, Charles was the one who would not meet a tragic end, who would not disappoint.[10]

Chesapeake Affair

In the aftermath of the Chase trial, Congress's attention turned elsewhere, and foreign policy became a significantly greater focus for the administration. While in Fourth of July oratory and in the pages of their magazines,

Americans touted their "mild" form of government and their advantages over the Old World, this was the age of Napoleon, and they could not escape its vagaries. Because it was a seafaring age, trade with the warring, as well as neutral, nations of Europe engaged America's interest. Commerce was the young republic's lifeblood, and threats to that commerce were ever increasing. Already, unwanted contact with Barbary pirates had resulted in American warships being sent to the Mediterranean. The aggressive foreign policy of Jefferson and Madison began to make sense to Senator Adams.

Toward the end of 1805, the "Old Gentleman" retracted some from his customary opinion sharing. He decided that he should write to his Washington-based son about planting and plowing and let the busy senator manage political affairs for the both of them. It would be "ridiculous," he wrote, for him to be weighing in on pressing issues at this stage of life. Though keenly aware that "the World is in Commotion and great Events are Struggling for Birth," he was too far from the political mainstream to come up with viable solutions anymore. He was, he confessed, entirely out of ideas. And so he turned the page, literally. "Now for my Pleasures," he enticed his son. "I have read the Six first Volumes of Gibbon, the three Vol. of Middletons Life of Cicero, and now I am Seriously Studying Tacitus, by comparing him Word for Word with Murphys Translation; and am Surprized to See how many more Words he is obliged to Use, than his Author. He gives a faithfull Idea of the Sense: but the Grace, the Brevity and the Pomp of the original are wanting, and I fear must never be expected in English."

Their epistolary conversation had often recurred to these subjects, as would the revived Adams-Jefferson exchanges in subsequent years. JQA happily took the bait, disagreeing with his father as to the superiority of Murphy's translation while applauding his energetic reengagement with Tacitus. They were in their element discussing the ancients. As it was, the son returned to Rome even more often than the father, when he assumed, concurrent with his senatorial duties, the Boylston Professorship of Rhetoric and Oratory at Harvard. Recalling how recently, and how gravely, he questioned his skill as an orator only adds to the mounting evidence of Adams family unorthodoxy.[11]

It was now that the son reached an acute moment in his disapprobation of both President Jefferson and his congressional colleagues. John Quincy

Adams was *of* the Federalists but not unimaginatively bound to a faction, as his putative allies were. Those who had betrayed the intelligence, evenhandedness, and practicality of Adams-friendly Federalism adhered to an ill-tempered cronyism now. Meanwhile, Jefferson's stalwart supporters, with insurgent strength, were on a do-or-die mission to box into a corner all suspect New England Federalists.

John Adams could not resist telling his son that he believed Jefferson's administration was making matters worse and taking party spirit to new levels by making executive appointments serve narrow party aims. Why not privilege competence over sycophancy? The power of appointment should not be a party loyalty litmus test, yet it was being practiced, he said, "with more Severity than it was by the Federalists."[12]

If it wasn't predictably so before this, at the end of John Quincy's first two years of Senate service, father and son jointly recognized that the two of them, in their respective careers, stood largely alone among political men. John had never looked up to anyone else as a political mentor or political boss; John Quincy had no model but his father. Neither man would march in lockstep or surrender independence. In practical terms, they knew how to work with others toward a definable legislative goal. But expectations from self and from others had made the first Adams appear vain and irritable in the eyes of colleagues and was making the next appear cold and callous—anyway, not known for tact. Popularity did not interest JQA. He had become, in a word, grumpy.

When the ex-president did communicate with his son about politics, it was most often about conditions overseas. He was in favor of armed neutrality and expressed his opinions with appealingly provocative humor. Returning in his mind to their time in Paris: "Do you remember the Motto over the door . . . where the illustrious and immortal Franklin and the obscure and mortal John Adams lived together as American Ministers to the Court of Versailles. I think it was 'Si Sta bene non Se move.'" (If you cannot move, stand.) One imagines that on reading the setup, JQA knew an incisive payoff was coming. Perhaps he smirked. And then, "While our Government were allowed to maintain their Neutrality we stood well. But when the Republicans Sacrificed me to Mr Jefferson and Mr Talle[y]rand, and the Federalists Sacrificed me to Mr Hamilton and Mr Pitt, all went wrong and here we are."[13]

It was personalized, of course, but the point—"all went wrong"—was well taken. As a nation built on Atlantic shores, America held up a mirror to England and France. It could never quite act for itself apart from heated assessments of those two eternal rivals. The father maintained that whether it was the Republicans' pro-French tilt or the Federalists' subservience to Britain, either posture left the United States weak. What was next?

One might say that John Adams was the first to anticipate another spiraling into war with Britain over captures on the high seas. He wanted the United States to back up its diplomatic talk with defensive action, by outfitting privateers to counter any power that preyed on American shipping. Father to son again: "Jealousy of Commerce, and Envy of maritime power in any people but themselves is a very strong passion in an English Bosom. It is seated and rooted in every fold of every English heart. I have been so sensible of it, all my Lifetime that I always expected it would occasion another War with Us. When I was in England I saw it in a Stronger light than ever." As a forecaster, he wasn't always right in every detail, but he had a remarkable talent for sending a shaft into the heart of a matter. "If she forces us into a War she will find an Enemy very different from that of 1775! our Confusions will be very great, but she will suffer most in the End."[14]

His senator-son was certain to keep him in the loop as to the temper of Congress while Napoleon achieved victories and Britain continued its bullying of foreign merchant vessels. He left the predictions to his father, unsure "whether in the terrors we are assuming against Great Britain, there is not as much or more of vapour than of substance." As Jefferson and Madison considered nonimportation as a form of commercial retaliation, even the administration's cotton-exporting southern allies were not on board. "All the *quakerish* Members of both Houses, are averse to anything that looks even by a squint, towards energy," JQA noted scornfully. "Being for Peace all the world over they begin to discover that these measures may give Offence to Great-Britain, and they think the only course to be pursued is negotiation."[15]

It took the *Chesapeake* Affair to cause indignation against Britain to escalate. In June 1807, outside Norfolk harbor, an American frigate bound for the Mediterranean suddenly came under fire from the fifty-gun *Leopard*. There were numerous American casualties, and when the unprepared captain of the *Chesapeake* offered to surrender, a British party boarded and searched for deserters.

Official inquiries ensued. Newspapers stoked resentment. The New York *Public Advertiser* immediately ran the headline "War!" and declared the country "ripe and prepared for any thing that may promise revenge." For JQA, this "new outrage from a British armed ship" was a "disgrace" that had to be addressed promptly. The Boston *Repertory*, to which JQA had previously contributed, ran a judicious story about the national humiliation, posing one question: "What will be the consequences?"[16]

As the crisis broke, Senator Adams, in Boston, did not react as a partisan of any sort. Instead, he sought to convene a town committee, to share perspectives. Doing so, he took a turn that was to prove significant. Disappointed after his Federalist associates "utterly discouraged" any kind of discussion, he noted that southern Federalists were expressing open resentment toward the British in town meetings across the Carolinas and Georgia. At the site of the incident, the Federalist *Norfolk Gazette* disapproved of northern Federalist reticence. JQA was disenchanted enough with the political mood that he turned down an invitation to celebrate the Fourth of July with young Federalists in Boston—"I know none of them"—and found himself sitting down with local Republican lawmakers. Among this crowd was the independent-thinking elder statesman Elbridge Gerry, the Adams intimate who had thrown his support to Jefferson in 1800.[17]

Elsewhere, another drama played out. The former vice president Aaron Burr sought to recoup his fortunes in distant corners of the Union, where land speculation and tales of lawless adventure abounded. He'd paid visits to a smattering of Federalists as well as to mainstream Republicans, senators and ex-senators, moneyed men and military types; the combination led to rumors of a nonauthorized Mexican invasion. In the context of Burr's alleged imperial ambitions, which President Jefferson took to be conspiratorial, one sitting senator, the Ohio Republican John Smith, was hard-pressed to detach his name from the New Yorker's.

Burr's drawn-out treason trial ended in a "not guilty" verdict. It turned out that rumor had far outpaced any evidence of illegality. Senator Smith, on the other hand, succumbed to pressure, a fair portion of which was prompted by Senator John Quincy Adams, who chaired the committee investigating him. When the Ohioan's expulsion from the Senate failed by a single vote,

Smith acceded to the wishes of the majority in the legislature of his home state and resigned his seat.

John Quincy Adams was unlike most in the Federalist Party when he took the Jefferson administration's side both in railing against Smith and in looking askance at Burr. Adding to the irregularity of this political season, John Adams's son-in-law, John Quincy's brother-in-law, William Stephens Smith (no relation), was acquitted in federal court in New York of the charge of recruiting on behalf of the Venezuelan filibuster Francisco de Miranda. President Jefferson was convinced that Federalists had somehow saved the latter Smith from conviction.[18]

From the fall 1807 congressional session forward, Senator Adams expressed deep concern over the implications of the *Chesapeake* Affair. He continued to lean toward the administration as more intelligence arrived that revealed a hardened British policy on maintaining maritime supremacy in a time of war. Britain's war with Napoleon had simultaneously resulted in an increase in seizures of American merchant vessels. This led Jefferson and Madison to urge Congress to adopt an embargo, a drastic means of declaring America's rights as a neutral by ceasing all exports to England and France.

New England Federalists staunchly opposed the embargo, but Congress passed the measure easily. John Quincy Adams voted with the Republican majority. In going against the interest of his section, in sacrificing a regional economy that relied heavily on its commercial connection to England, he knowingly committed political suicide. To a trusted Federalist, his cousin Josiah Quincy, he explained his "late conduct" in Congress. Cousin Quincy replied that the act was "too pure," because the dishonorable Republicans would never reciprocate—would not "value" him. JQA answered bluntly that it didn't matter to him "whether they valued me or not," because he had no expectation of receiving better treatment from the Republicans. "My character such as it is must stand upon its own ground," he told Quincy; he was concerned for the integrity of the "Union." What more brilliant declaration of Adamsian backbone could there be?

When Senator Adams justified to his father his assent to an "unlimited" embargo, he elaborated, "We had no other alternative left, but this or taking our side at once in the War—I do not believe indeed that the Embargo can long be continued—but if we let our ships go out without arming them . . . , they must go merely to swell the plunder of the contending parties."[19]

This was a concise explanation of strategic considerations that motivated him to vote with the administration. Either the United States found means to preserve national integrity on the high seas or its productions became regular "plunder" for European belligerents. The long-serving diplomat and son of a diplomat knew what he had to do at that moment.

Receiving the letter just after New Year's Day 1808, the ex-president answered in a strong voice while confessing to his own irrelevance. "My great and good Son," he wrote with unblushing pride. "The distance between Us, the total retirement in which I live and the Want of Facts, render a Correspondence between Us, upon public affairs of very little use to you, though it is a great pleasure to me. The Storm that has agitated the Elements for twenty Years in Europe"—Napoleon was still exhibiting his military prowess—"must be drawing towards a Conclusion, and the last blasts may be the fiercest of all." Though he went into no more detail than this, whenever John Adams pondered Anglo-American relations, 1775 was never very distant in his mind. He'd said it often enough. Shock waves emanating from Europe were heading for American shores.

As to his son's personal situation: "I think it is clear, plain and obvious. You are supported by no Party. You have too honest a heart, too independent a Mind and too brilliant Talents, to be Sincerely and confidentially trusted by any Man who is under the Dominion of Party Maxims or Party Feelings: and where is there another Man who is not? You may depend upon it then that your fate is decided." This was how John Adams saw himself in his son. "You will be countenanced neither by France, Spain or England," he went on. "You will be supported neither by Federalists or Republicans." This, too, we have seen before but never as starkly written. Standing alone was a family trait.[20]

In advance of James Madison's successful run for the presidency, the "Old Gentleman's" accumulated nationalism took full flight. "Mr Madisons bias towards the French has always been too great but I never suspected him of Corruption. On the contrary the bias of all the Federalists to my certain Knowledge, even of my friend Mr Jay is too Strong against France and in favour of England." To his son, John Adams poured forth: "If I were Alexander the great and had absolute Power like him I would declare War against England France and Spain all at once and Soon have the Floridas and Mexico too, and have Commerce by Sea at least by captures." He had the broad contours of the Mississippi River valley in mind. "It is ours," Adams senior proclaimed, "and We must defend it."[21]

It was the opening of Jefferson's last year as president, and Senator Adams had the green light from Peacefield as he veered sharply from his high-toned Federalism. He was now in a cautious but increasingly well-defined alliance with both the third president and his secretary of state (and putative successor). He obviously alarmed many former colleagues when he spat at "party spirit," consulted his inner compass, and switched sides.

The Adamses' world was turned upside down, and not for the first time. JQA's estrangement from New England Federalists would, of necessity, lead to the loss of his seat in the Senate. He was firmly committed to the Republicans now—to the political party that had unseated his father. More remarkable still, the "Old Gentleman" wholeheartedly concurred with the decision reached by his self-exiling son.

There was a certain poetry in this fateful decision. As a Federalist who ended up an outsider to the Federalist Party even as he remained within it, the son was the second coming (and going) of his father. The other common denominator was one of personal enmity, set in motion yet again by the overbearing Timothy Pickering. There was no longer a Hamilton to contend with, owing to that unfortunate duelist's early demise, and Federalism without the Adamses fell once more into the lap of "Tim Pick," as he was sometimes referred to by antagonists that included the Adamses. And yet, beyond an attachment to the foreign policy subscribed to by James Madison, neither John nor John Quincy Adams had anything positive to say about the Jeffersonians and their democratic rhetoric: switching sides had no relationship whatsoever to a theory of democracy.

One way to explain the switch is that their allegiance to each other—father to son, son to father—somehow eliminated all other publicly exhibited forms of allegiance. The son's empathy for his abused father fed his own brand of iconoclasm, while Madisonian reasonableness opened the door to cooperative statecraft. The conversion might not have happened if the more ideologically driven Jefferson had formulated a foreign policy without the mitigating influence of Madison. The father-and-son turnabout had happened in stages, yet it happened fast by any measure of political time.

In Massachusetts, the ex-president predicted that the votes were there for a Republican to be chosen to replace his son in the Senate. He was wrong this time; a Federalist was chosen. But what matters more is the interpretation he gave for his son's rejection by both parties, and the company this would place him in: "You will be numbered among the dead like Jay . . . and an hundred others of the brightest Geniuses of this Country"—all men of firmness and principle, in John Adams's view, who were prominent in the 1790s but refused to kowtow to Hamilton. "You ought to know and expect this," he lectured his son, "and by no means to regret it.—Return to your Professorship but above all to your Office as a Lawyer devote yourself to your Profession and the Education of your Children." It was to be a fitting end of JQA's career in politics. Or so the family patriarch believed.[22]

MRS. WARREN

Adams the younger might have derived gratification from his demonstration of political backbone, but a narrative history of the Revolution in three volumes, published in 1805, made the year 1807 a tiring and contentious one for the senator's father. Upon finishing the work in question, John Adams became obsessed with the need to explain himself to its nationally known author—his and his wife's once dear friend Mercy Otis Warren of Plymouth. The book bore a grand title, too: *History of the Rise, Progress, and Termination of the American Revolution*. Adams's problem with Mrs. Warren's tome was a matter both of wording and of implication. Simply put, he conflated her history with the efforts of those men who had done everything possible to destroy his reputation while he held political office.

Mercy Warren mentions the name of John Adams for the first time in chronicling the year 1774. He is introduced in the text (alongside several others opposing "present ministerial measures") as "a barrister at law of rising abilities; his appearance on the theatre of politics commenced at this period; we shall meet him again at still more dignified stations." Samuel Adams, by contrast, is on the scene several years before his cousin's appearance and possesses "a quick understanding, a cool head, stern manners, a smooth address, and a Roman-like firmness." If Samuel was inherently noble, John was merely the occupier of dignified stations and, rather than a featured player, more like an unavoidable presence in the narrative.

Warren's biases were part of her story. As an adherent of the politics of

Thomas Jefferson, she credited Virginia as much as Massachusetts for advancing key elements in cross-colonial cooperation. Nor could she resist a dig at Colonel Timothy Pickering, long before he grew into the inveterate enemy of the two Adamses. Pickering's Salem militia was, she states, slow in arriving on the scene of the British retreat from Concord to Boston in April 1775. "Whether Mr. Pickering's delay was owing to timidity," Warren speculates, "or to a predilection in favor of Britain, remains uncertain." Nothing she would ever say about John Adams was more damning than that.[23]

She commends John Adams for his active stance amid deliberations over the Declaration of Independence: "He rose with a face of intrepidity and the voice of energy, and invoked the *god* of *eloquence,* to enable him to do justice to the cause of his country." He next appears, if only briefly, as a diplomat in Paris in 1778, an adjunct to Benjamin Franklin, and "disgusted" by his early recall by Congress the following year. In his second tour, situated in a secondary post—the Netherlands—Mrs. Warren finds Adams well suited, "vested with ample powers." There, he "exercised his discretionary powers with justice and ability." She places emphasis on his greater comfort with Dutch than with French ways and highlights his "judicious," self-generated memorial to the governing body of the United Provinces seeking recognition of his country: "He was everywhere cordially received as an American, respected as a republican, and considered in the light of an ambassador from a new and great nation."[24]

At the end of a long discussion of his triumph in the Netherlands, she takes liberty in detailing the character she knew so well, at least in those years: "Regular in his morals, and reserved in his temper, he appeared rather gloomy in a circle; but he was sensible, shrewd, and sarcastic, among private friends." Sarcastic, indeed, though it could be said that the quality she was referring to was his form of witty wordplay. Sarcasm, as such, was a literary convention of the age; it was not strictly defamatory or inconsiderate of the hearer's sensibility, as it tends to be today. There was, however, no nuance in the least in Mrs. Warren's very next comment: "In France he was never happy: not beloved by his venerable colleague doctor Franklin; thwarted by the minister, the count de Vergennes; and ridiculed by the fashionable and polite, as deficient in the *je ne scai* [*sic*] *quoi,* so necessary in highly polished society."[25]

The author's overall assessment of Adams's skills was less than friendly:

"a statesman of penetration and ability; but his prejudices and his passions were sometimes too strong for his sagacity and judgment. . . . After Mr. Adams's return from England, he was implicated by a large portion of his countrymen, as having relinquished the republican system, and forgotten the principles of the American revolution. . . . Pride of talents and much ambition, were undoubtedly combined in the character of the president who immediately succeeded general Washington." By the end of volume 3, she leaves John Adams a monarchist, overtaken by the "splendor of courts and courtiers." It was an unfair generalization, and one that would also attach to the second president Adams in an age where the idea of democracy was celebrated with rhetorical flourishes.[26]

The offended subject wrote the first of his letters to the author on July 11, 1807, after finishing the greater part of three octavo volumes. He could identify, he claimed, factual errors he was eager to correct "in the spirit of friendship," attaching documentary evidence, chapter and verse, to show her the light. He acknowledged the plausibility of her remark that his "passions and prejudices were sometimes too strong for his sagacity and judgment." If true, she needed to understand that any such imperfection was no reflection on his motives, which were directed solely toward the public good; he was saying to her that he was man enough to accept criticism. What made him resentful, however, were her insinuations: yes, a certain quantity of "erratum" was to be expected, but "unfounded" allegations (as he saw them) required his principled denial. To wit, "I have never deceived the people, Mrs. Warren, nor any individual of them."

Her response, on July 16, was to assure him that she had composed her history "with impartiality," "with truth and candor." She expressed surprise that he felt justice had not been done to him in the work. Having drawn a picture of John Adams and his Revolutionary compeers as they were when they enacted history, she expressed the opinion, delicately put, that "the character of man is never finished until the last act of the drama is closed." Perhaps she hoped that such language would temper his response. For he had promised her "further commentaries," and she awaited these, limiting her rebuttal and leaving it up to him whether he felt the need to "indulge in retaliation."

She did not have to wait many days before his next installment arrived. And retaliate he did. As the letters droned on, Adams painted himself more and more as victim, not just of her pen, but of political arts as practiced by the men who made him a one-term president. He never sought revenge against anyone—perhaps she was not aware of this commendable aspect of his character: "Have I ever done any thing in opposition to Mr. Jefferson's government?" Point by point, he quibbled. He disputed her statement that he related to the Dutch better than to the French: "Conversation is more gay, more sprightly, more good-humored, more entertaining and instructive in France than in any country I ever saw." (He adjudged this characterization of him as a "satirical sneer.") As he cited every offending page, his sentence constructions grew increasingly labored. He obsessively picked apart the problematic areas: a line here, a phrase there. "Pride of talents." "Much ambition." Reading the charges, he sought to reclaim his honor as a gentleman: "I have never sacrificed a principle, nor even concealed an opinion, from a motive of ambition or an affectation of popularity." He accused her of having "personal motives" in attacking him, which he supposed had something to do with his not having rewarded her family with federal patronage.[27]

Clearly, John Adams wished to write his own history of the American Revolution. After wading through his tenth letter, Mercy Warren ended the debate—if debate it was. She was shocked by what she called "your exertions to insult and affront a woman of my age and standing in society." She was in her eightieth year and still showed that she could dish it out as well as he. "There is a meanness as well as malignancy in striving to blast a work that many of the best judges of literary merit that even yourself have been acquainted with in America have spoken of in a manner very flattering to the author. Nor has your correspondent ever been charged with a want of veracity until you have unkindly done this." His "intemperate passions" in the letters made it impossible for further communication to amount to anything. "As an old friend I pity you," she said.[28]

Two months after the Adams-Warren exchange began, three days after the final letter was sent from the Warren home in Plymouth, comes this entry in the son's diary, absent any elaboration: "Read my father's letters to Mrs. Warren."[29]

John Adams was expressing feelings of personal betrayal, of course, but it was more than that. Her take on history was, as he informed the author directly, a partisan effort designed "to cry up Jefferson as the great republican." What irked him most was his impression of her naïveté about democracy. She held, in a strict Jeffersonian sense, to a theory that democracy was based on the right of voters to choose their representatives. Adams felt otherwise, bringing back to mind the host of outrageous lies and libels that had circulated during the 1800 campaign. Had he not been accused of scheming to anoint his son-in-law, Smith, as the king of North America and to marry his son into the royal family? He was sure to remind her of these things. Did she not remember how the opposition claimed he would outlaw all religions except Presbyterianism? That pitiful ploy was put into service in the state of Pennsylvania, solely to prejudice German voters against him.

In the gullible South, misrepresentations reached new levels of absurdity. There were the sexual smears: it was rumored that President Adams had prevailed upon one of his envoys to France, C. C. Pinckney, to procure a pair of European prostitutes for the chief magistrate's personal pleasure. When he tired of them, he returned the used merchandise on borrowed government funds. In repeating some of the ugly stories that were spread about him, Adams wanted Mrs. Warren to see how easily corruption took hold in an unpoliced democracy. "Artifices," "fabrications," "electioneering passions"—manipulated emotions—only debased a republic.[30]

Mercy Warren's opinion on the 1800 election focused on other factors entirely. She considered Adams's defeat to have been of his doing, and no one else's. Her husband, James, who knew John Adams as well as any man, honestly believed, as a "large portion of his Countrymen" did, that the second president acquired monarchical leanings in England, just as the Republican newspapers were reporting. Before her multivolume history was even published, one Boston newspaper exploited the rift between the Adams and Warren families, claiming that he deserted his old friends when he abandoned his former political principles. When, in 1805, the Philadelphia *Aurora* revisited the elections of 1796 and 1800, the gadfly editor William Duane insisted that Adams's 1796 victory was hollow, that he was elected on the basis of *Washington's* reputation, not his own. Moreover, Jefferson's overwhelming reelection in 1804 proved he'd earned the "affections of the people," which Adams had not done. The party line that Warren and Duane subscribed to went this way: "Mr. Adams had indeed, taken such an honorable and conspicuous part, in the early period of the revolution, that even many whigs could not believe that a short residence in Europe could have so soon corrupted him."

John Adams believed that the Warrens actually started the hurtful rumor about his "corrupted" political heart. He might have been right. Her history gave credit to Jefferson and Jeffersonianism for completion of the Revolution and its democratic promise. Doing so, she exiled John Adams from the grand saga: he was a traitor to the spirit of 1776; or, to quote Thomas Paine, a "counterrevolutionary." If Republicans had decided to write Adams out of their history, Mrs. Warren's work can hardly be regarded as impartial. Neither she nor her discomfited former friend could claim disinterestedness.[31]

PICKERING AGAIN

In the early months of election year 1808, the most visible power broker in the Senate was William Branch Giles of Virginia. Five years John Quincy Adams's senior, he hailed from Amelia County, southwest of Richmond along the Appomattox River. He had gone north, as James Madison did, to study at Princeton, and returned to Virginia to study law under George Wythe, who had trained a young Thomas Jefferson. Throughout the 1790s and early years of the nineteenth century, when he served in the House, and from 1804, when he occupied a seat in the Senate, Giles was an archetypical Jeffersonian. If unsung in most historical treatments, he was, nevertheless, a real force in Congress for many years.

As Jefferson's and Madison's embargo rattled the New England merchant class, Giles and his fellow Republicans in Washington enjoyed a position of strength. The same Senator Giles who had led the charge against Associate Justice Chase three years earlier now cozied up to the independent senator from Massachusetts, doing his best to take advantage of his colleague's exposed position. On January 16, 1808, Giles gave Adams a ride home in his carriage. Four days later, Adams was invited to "consult" with the Republicans of the House and the Senate at a weekend meeting in support of James Madison's succession to the presidency. In his diary, JQA underlined "Republican," presumably to remind his future self of the moment when he responded positively to overtures from the other party.[32]

As Giles was lining up support for a continued embargo, he was simultaneously serving in an official party capacity as one of two congressional "managers" pushing Madison's candidacy. In an enviable position politically, he buttered up Adams shamelessly. The loose transcription of their conversation in John Quincy's diary cited Giles insisting that whenever his Republican friends queried him about Adams's political character, he "uniformly told them that he believed that I considered every public measure as I should a proposition in Euclid, abstracted from any party considerations, and that was the reason why he thought that since we have been together in the Senate there were perhaps no two members who so often voted together as him and me." Giles knew what Adams wanted to hear: that he was independent and couldn't be bought. JQA was that transparent.

Giles openly admitted that he was trying to steal from the Federalist column. He also acknowledged, as he was clearing the air with Adams, that he was simultaneously coaxing James Bayard of Delaware, a moderate Federalist, in the same direction. Bayard was generally thought of as easygoing and collegial, but he also had a reputation for gambling and drinking. And he had lately singled out JQA—in a disparaging way. He'd belittled his fellow senator's forensic abilities when showcasing his own.

Adams reacted predictably to the implication. He immediately seized the moral high ground, assuring Giles that whatever Bayard might have wanted in exchange for his support, he himself did not desire any favor from any Republican. He was alone with Giles after one productive committee meeting, when the Virginian flashed a wry grin and alluded to Bayard's "ill humour" that day. Adams completed the sentence self-servingly: ". . . and he seems to me to be laboring under a violent internal struggle, between his fear of deserting his own party, and his wish to join yours." Feeding Adams's ego, Giles proceeded to narrate the "history" of Bayard's awkward "overtures" to the administration party, which his auditor took in eagerly. Senator Adams did not disguise his joy as he related a picture of the queasy Delaware Federalist squirming.[33]

Giles was obviously proud of the success he was having getting through to the less doctrinaire Federalists. But he never entirely figured out how the mind of John Q. Adams operated, and he could not say that he had ever talked Adams into anything. In 1825, after John Quincy Adams was elected president, and appeared to him more "Federalist" in outlook than he had in many years, Giles was poised to become the next governor of Virginia. He conferred with an eighty-two-year-old Thomas Jefferson about life in Washington. Jefferson said that then-senator Adams's revelation to him of the New England Federalists' betrayal of the nation was something that remained etched in his mind—as did his recognition of JQA's "rectitude and patriotism." The issue he recalled was how far the Federalists would go in conducting secret talks with British representatives.

Despite having made his support of the embargo clear to all, Senator Adams actually had less direct contact with President Jefferson during the second term than he had in the first, when they stood at a much greater political distance. But as Giles recalled events in 1825, he reminded Jefferson, "Mr. Adams first intimated to you his intended change of politicks through me." Giles had exhorted Adams not to be content to use him as an intermediary but to meet with Jefferson face-to-face at the President's House. So, Adams did just that, explaining to Jefferson "that propositions had been made by certain British agents, to many leading federalists in the Eastern States, in the event of war between the U.S. and Great Britain, to separate New England from the rest of the States, and to enter into an offensive and defensive alliance." This was treachery.

In Giles's and Jefferson's common understanding, Adams was invited to the table at the precise moment that old-line Federalists were cozying up to the British plan. JQA had been "consulted on its feasibility, and urged to unite with the approving federalists." He obviously identified strongly with his section of the country, but, according to Giles, "his love of country, became shocked at the proposition, and he had resolved to abandon a party, who could be induced to countenance the treasonable prospect."

Jefferson and Adams met repeatedly on this matter. Each time they did, Adams reaffirmed his noninterest in "official preferment" or "personal aggrandizement in any form." So, when one Massachusetts senator came under attack from another—the ever-spiteful Pickering—William B. Giles stood before the Senate and gave a speech in defense of the discredited Federalist J. Q. Adams. "That transaction," Giles intimated to Jefferson, "turned out to be the most eventful of his whole life." Whether the younger Adams would have agreed with Giles's assessment of the "transaction" remains doubtful. But the moment was, clearly, a turning point.[34]

On learning of her son's active participation in the Republican caucus, and his expressed preference for Madison, Abigail Adams felt betrayed. She remained deeply disapproving of Jefferson's conduct, which she attributed to an unwholesome kind of personal and political ambition. It colored her thinking. That her son would even contemplate joining the Republican side—the news came to her from friends of his, not from him—sank her spirits. It "staggerd my beleif," she promptly wrote to him.[35]

Abigail's husband did not blink, even as he found a way to satisfy still-hurt feelings of abandonment and abuse by projecting Madison as another one-term president. He wrote to his son four days after his upset wife did, "He will be turned out as I was." (John could be as transparent as Abigail.)[36]

The foreign policy John Quincy Adams embraced that turned so many Federalists against him was a policy that clearly wasn't working. It was crippling the South as well as the North. The singular sage of Peacefield put in his own two cents. "The Embargo tingles in every Vein," he informed his son. "The Clamour against it will grow louder and louder and every Man who voted for it more and more unpopular with the Party who oppose it." He doubled down on the warning his son had delivered to Jefferson as New England secessionist talk wafted in the air: "We may be more disposed to War among ourselves, for what I know, than we are to fight with any foreign Power. The present humiliation of the northern States cannot long endure, without producing Passions which will be very difficult to restrain."[37]

It is no exaggeration to say that a giant gulf separated the two U.S. senators from Massachusetts. Senator Adams recognized, much as his father did, that the embargo could not remain in place much longer. Jefferson and Madison would not stand in the way of its repeal. But they all believed it was the best way to forestall war while efforts continued toward eliciting an apology from London over the *Chesapeake* incident—which was step one in the larger project of seeking to negotiate a retreat from the island empire's abusive maritime operations. Senator Pickering, on the other hand, met with a principal British envoy in Washington and proffered a separate Federalist policy toward the great nation whose values he and his urbane fellows shared.

Pickering's sixteen-page public letter on the course of Anglo-American relations was addressed to his state's governor and to his constituents. In it, he termed the failing embargo "a measure pregnant with incalculable mischief to all classes of our fellow-citizens," and he described the *Chesapeake* Affair that started relations on their downward course as a simple British attempt to recover some deserters—nothing very dramatic and certainly not an unprecedented action. The Jefferson administration wished to "excite a war pulse," he insisted. Toward that end, it had sought to raise an "artificial fever." The embargo was a gross overreaction, and the British position entirely reasonable.[38]

Two days after receiving a copy of Pickering's letter, with no time for writing other than evenings, Senator Adams jotted in his diary, "It may cost me my eyes; but I cannot remain silent." Aware that Pickering's piece would be widely read, he felt impelled to respond. This was as his parents—both of them, at this point—wished. He finished his letter at the end of March 1808 and rendered it in the same format Pickering had adopted, except that JQA's was addressed not to the governor but to Harrison Gray Otis, a member of the Massachusetts State Senate whom he knew all too well: this Otis was the Harvard-educated son of Secretary of the Senate Samuel Allyne Otis. In the open letter, Adams defended his conduct in Washington, sensitive to the fact that the Massachusetts legislature elected its U.S. senators and was the requisite body to which he should convey his argument. His political future hung in the balance.[39]

He adopted a nationalistic tone and contended that by caving to British power, Pickering was ignoring that country's aggressive acts. The November 1807 Orders in Council defended the confiscation of American property taken from its neutral merchant ships, which were to this day "detained in British hands." It was not mere "pretence," as Pickering charged, that led the administration and Congress to authorize an all-out embargo; it was a measured response to a grave national insult, a "temporary expedient" that made excellent sense.

Adams went on to criticize the parochialism of Pickering and his Boston-based faction. Their "antagonizing appeals" were, he said, designed to "distract" the people of one state while producing "asperities and rancors" of a partisan character that might spiral out of control. If Pickering was successful in diverting attention from what really mattered to citizens, "the great concerns of the nation would degenerate into the puny controversies of personal altercation."

The letter was strongly worded but coolly composed. JQA affected aloofness from all petty sniping, but the fact was that his beef with Pickering and friends reflected his father's legacy as much as his own ego. The "asperities and rancors" John Adams was forced to endure from state-level, intraparty protests constituted one subtext to the letter. The second president's moderation in the years 1798–1800 had been undermined when irresponsible rumors of French threats to American security made him unpopular in his own party.

Tom Adams independently came to the very same conclusion. He gave his Washington-based brother an up-close perspective on Boston political gossip, saying that "the freedom of remark in which some Gentlemen have indulged upon the course you have pursued" was "full of reproach and very much in the style formerly used towards your father upon his continuing to treat with the French Government in 1799." And then: "I need not add that it has proceeded from the same sources and from a similar policy." The men of the Adams family were in full alignment. Weighing the present state of affairs with Great Britain, Senator Adams echoed the ten-year-old opinion of his father: that the United States needed to grow its navy and, for the time being, arm merchant vessels as a show of resolve. This was the way to preserve neutral rights and to uphold national honor, short of war.[40]

JQA's strong response to Pickering did not overturn opinion in Massachusetts Federalist circles. A pamphlet following on the heels of the publication of Adams's letter proposed reconsideration as to "whether the Honourable Senator has not been overrated as a scholar" and, owing to his pedigree, "flattered, admired and trusted beyond his merit." This brutal pamphlet, produced by Hamilton's protégé William Coleman, claimed that "Mr. Adams's party, the Jeffersonians," were planning to circulate 100,000 copies of the long letter to Otis "across the United States." Coleman parsed and nitpicked with little shame and less restraint, repeatedly pointing out where "the learned Professor" fell short of established standards of rhetorical expression ("the violent separation of the pronoun *which* from its antecedent"). Coleman took a fair stab at the younger Adams's temperament, identifying him as "a gentleman who hardly suppresses his ill-humour" toward a colleague. Adams would "violate established principles of decorum" merely to serve as a "mouth-piece" for his new Republican friends. They were all the "obsequious servants" of an imperious Jefferson, who had forced the nation to swallow the ill-considered embargo.[41]

By mid-spring 1808, Massachusetts Federalists organized to force Adams from the Senate. Wishing to serve out his term (set to end in February

1809), the nominal Federalist made appearances in and about Boston, but to little avail. In early June, in a move apparently undertaken to embarrass him, both the house and the senate of his state considered early nominations for his U.S. Senate seat. The "no confidence" vote was followed by a majority instruction that he vote against the embargo on his return to Washington. Gossip held that Madison had already struck a deal with Senator Adams, promising a foreign post in exchange for his support in the impending campaign. Under such circumstances, he did what was called for and resigned his seat. John Quincy Adams was no longer a Federalist. In the national election that fall, to no one's surprise, James Madison won the presidency. It was clear now that save for tiny Delaware no Federalist could secure electoral votes outside New England.[42]

Adams's acceptance in Republican circles was such that on the eve of Madison's inauguration rumors were floated that he would be named secretary of state. There is no indication that Adams himself believed that would happen. Jefferson's hardworking Treasury secretary, the western Pennsylvanian Albert Gallatin, had served the administration as faithfully as Madison himself and felt he had earned the post. The honor went instead to Jefferson's intellectually unexceptional, administratively challenged, but nonetheless politically well-connected navy secretary, Robert Smith of Maryland. When the War of 1812 came, Smith would already be gone, and JQA somewhere else entirely.[43]

ELEVEN

Distant Companions

I never was afraid of the reproach of being ambitious. . . . When I came to Russia, my motive doubtless in the opinion of many was Ambition—But there were not wanting persons who thought I was sent here for the express purpose of putting me out of the way. . . . I knew that [the posting to Russia] was not agreeable to you, and that Circumstance alone was enough to take away all pleasure from it.

—JOHN QUINCY ADAMS TO JOHN ADAMS, *July 21, 1811*

Shall you retire, and divote your Life to Science, Litterature and publish your Studies from Time to Time? With all my heart, You would do as much honour to your Country and Service to Mankind in this Way as any other. But this I know to be impossible. Your Nature cannot bear it.

—JOHN ADAMS TO JOHN QUINCY ADAMS, *February 19, 1812*

It is unclear which foreign capital the earlier rumormongers expected John Quincy Adams to be offered in return for his support, but the post he ultimately accepted from President Madison—St. Petersburg, the capital of imperial Russia—did not possess the charms of Paris nor the book culture of London. While it was viewed as the most European of Russian cities, St. Petersburg, young by European standards, was raw: still under construction and prone to flooding.

JQA had spent an entire year there as a youngster, toward the end of Catherine the Great's long reign, when he served as French interpreter for Francis Dana, the American envoy, still alive and well, and of whom he remained eternally fond. At fourteen, he had found St. Petersburg a place of inadequate stimulation. It was four hundred miles northwest of Moscow, icebound for half the year, and too far north to experience a real summer, even as daylight prevailed for almost nineteen hours in the second half of June.

Needless to say, the illness-prone Louisa Catherine Adams was little desirous of relocating there. But her husband wanted what he wanted. John Adams's strong doubts when his son accepted the assignment, which he expressed to his son directly, elicited a weak rationalization after the new minister had completed his first year's residence there. "I knew," John Quincy wrote to him, "that it was going straight away from the high road of Ambition, and so far as related to political prospects, retiring into obscurity." But, he still insisted, with an air of formality, a higher duty dictated his course of action: "The Constitutional Organ of my Country had assigned this to me as my proper Post—I saw no reason sufficient to induce me to refuse it."[1]

In truth, the diplomatic life appealed to him, regardless of any of the rogue complaints that appear in his diary. He knew he might in time return to the national stage. Furthermore, he did not believe President Madison was trying to get him out of the way. Madison did not resort to such tactics, a new Boston newspaper contended. The *Patriot* began its twice-weekly publication just as Madison's inauguration was set to take place, and it proclaimed that the fourth U.S. president entered office without having made an enemy. "During his whole life, it is believed, there is not a single act for which he can be reproached as a man or as a citizen," assured the Republican editor, David Everett, an experienced, well-positioned writer with roots in central Massachusetts. No "improper motive" had ever been assigned to the slight but sturdy James Madison.[2]

Heaped Upon

John Quincy Adams attended Madison's inauguration on March 4, 1809, and was present as well at a ball that evening attended by the outgoing president, Jefferson. "The crowd was excessive," Adams wrote in his diary, "the entertainment bad." He had returned alone to Washington and was earning his living at the bar. He argued before the Supreme Court on behalf of the defendant in a case that concerned the disposition of Georgia lands. On March 6, as his case wrapped up, Madison called Adams in for a meeting and said he would nominate him for the Russia post. How long would he be expected to remain abroad? the ex-senator inquired. For an "indefinite" period, returned the president, perhaps three or four years. It would turn out to be twice that—the entirety of Madison's two terms.[3]

A few days after their meeting, John Quincy booked stagecoach passage north and ruled the roads out of Washington worse than he'd ever seen them. Arriving home after ten days, he found his family generally well and knowledge of the president's offer to him already widely disseminated. A writer in the *Boston Gazette* immediately pounced, accusing both Adamses, father and son, of enriching themselves through government appointments, each having returned from Europe "with a pretty fortune."

It wasn't true, of course, but the *Gazette* was not interested in fair play. The son, in particular, since his return from Berlin, had not been "six months without holding some office of high *honor, profit, or trust,*" the story went, and now, "*both parties* seem to vie with each other in favoring him." The writer, signing his name "SPARTACUS," made noises about the Adamses entertaining ideas of a hereditary presidency. John Quincy wrote directly to the editors of the *Gazette,* asking "SPARTACUS" to reveal himself in order that he might know to whom he should pen a thoroughgoing response for publication in the pages of the newspaper. He received an evasive, sarcastic reply mumbling something about journalistic ethics.

Meanwhile, the *Anti-monarchist and Republican Watchman* delighted that the Adams family were "converts" from Federalism. "Is not this proof of itself sufficient that our cause is just," the article smugly surmised. What greater loss to the ranks of the Federalist Party could there be than the desertion of the Adamses? A more skeptical *Massachusetts Spy* contrived a scenario in which John Adams could have become so distraught over the Republicans' ascendancy at his expense that he conspired with his son in 1805, just after Jefferson's reelection, to keep their family in power through any means necessary. If the embargo presented itself as a "plausible and speedy pretence" for the perturbed pair to advance themselves, the son's failure to retain his Senate seat gave them their just deserts. "Ah Messrs. Adams," this critic oozed, "you ought to have known that honesty is the best policy." Instead of the son sitting imposingly in his Senate chair and the father enjoying "otium cum dignitate" (ease with dignity) in his retirement years, the younger was left "dancing attendance upon a set of upstart Jacobins," while the elder was obliged to maintain close connections with "the most virulent and contemptible" of his former "revilers."

In response to the general uptick in Federalist abuse of the Adamses, David Everett printed an unequivocal "COMMUNICATION" for readers of the *Patriot,* publicly shaming those responsible for their "indecorous and insulting manner" toward the Adams family. Extremists had proven themselves all too willing to sacrifice "every man who dares openly avow his approbation of the general government, and his disapprobation of that of the British." But nothing was as bad as the "violent and slanderous aspersions heaped upon that venerable patriot and statesman, JOHN ADAMS." Whether or not occasioned by such attention, John Quincy noted in his diary at the end of April, "We seldom go to bed much before midnight."[4]

And so the transition in government marked a transition for John and John Quincy Adams in their double-barreled recurrence to writing for public consumption. As Jefferson retired from active political life and rode home to Monticello, his worthy predecessor began publishing with renewed purpose in David Everett's paper. Over the next few years, he would present a labored, lawyerly, and generally compelling defense of his administration, though laden, especially in the early pieces, with personal animus.

Possibly forewarned of the second president's project, the New York Federalist Gouverneur Morris, who never much cared for either father or son, wrote in confidence to a political friend, "As to the Mr. Adams's, old and young, Nothing from them surprizes me. Could either of them learn a little Humility he would be in the Road to Wisdom; but so long as they beleive themselves the Alpha and Omega of America, no Letter of the Alphabet can be touched without making them wince." Morris, known for his caustic humor, would do nothing to offset the elder Adams's reputation for intemperance, and he saw little hope in the old man's efforts at redemption: "Attempts to recall him within the Pale of Propriety would be about as prudent as to spur a lifeless Horse."[5]

The first flurry of John Adams's "letters to the printer," in April–May 1809, reestablished him as a major figure in the struggle to win independence. With extended autobiographical reflections, he documented his role in the Revolution, his wartime service in Europe, and his part in forming the new government. In the introductory piece, he took perverse pride in the fact that he was "never a favorite with the *leading men* of the Federal party."[6]

The villain in John Adams's story was the late (and not everywhere lamented) Alexander Hamilton. In the words of the aggrieved one-term president, orthodox party members found his most "unpardonable sin" to be actions taken to secure peace with France in 1800. Hamilton, the brains of their operation, convinced his people with "dogmatical assertions" that demonstrated a complete refusal to distinguish between "jacobinism and neutrality." Largely ignoring British mistreatment of the United States, Hamilton "panted" with the greatest ardor for war with France. Adams (according to Adams) saved much blood and treasure by averting a pointless war. "Peace with France," he momentously declared in his eighth letter, "produced demonstrations of the prejudices, passions, views, designs, and systems of parties." Implicit in this statement was his utter confidence that no American statesmen other than the Adamses, father and son, could be said to have exhibited, thus far in the Republic's history, an honorable rejection of the hardened party system. They stuck to their guns and followed reason rather than succumb to partisan passions.[7]

Also in April 1809, in the same Republican newspaper, there appeared the anonymously authored *Review of Works of Fisher Ames*. Ames was a leading Federalist congressman from the state of Massachusetts who died at age fifty, on July 4, 1808. The author of the series, barely disguised, was the outgoing senator John Q. Adams, whose point in writing was to prove that a few New England secessionists, with dishonorable purposes, were fiddling with the Ames legacy. John Quincy Adams was disgusted by all that had forced his removal from the Senate, and his bile came out in the Ames series. Father and son might have been spectacular grumps, but they were secure in the knowledge that they had good cause to be that way.[8]

While he lived, Fisher Ames was an unapologetic elitist who reacted viscerally to Jefferson's populist rhetoric. But that was as far as he ever went in actively opposing the first Republican administration. "Scarcely was he cold in his grave," Adams the younger wrote for the *Patriot,* "when his name was doomed by his friends to stand before the public, responsible for the assertion that on the most momentous questions at issue between Great Britain and us, she was *right* and we were *wrong*." Ames was many things, but he was not disloyal. The outgoing senator's goal in authoring the series was simple enough: to detach an old-school Federalist from the unnamed Federalists who wished to wield Ames as a cudgel in order to undermine

Madison's defense of the nation against Britain's ongoing designs to cut off American access to foreign markets.

In Adams's view, Fisher Ames had entered public life with good intentions, but he erred grievously when he "connected himself with Hamilton . . . in a manner which warped his judgment and trammeled the freedom of his mind." In Congress, he'd joined a cohort that exaggerated the French threat and "lived in a perpetual panic, that America would finally be only the last morsel left for the voracious maw of the monster Bonaparte." Adams considered Ames a man of mental endowments who took the twisted path he did due largely to the tubercular condition that eventually killed him. Dispirited and slowly dying over a period of ten years, he allowed his fevered imagination to get the best of his reason: "The disease which was undermining his constitution, without impairing the splendour of his fancy, affected the tone of his nerves."

Opposing the acquisition of Louisiana in 1803 (which Adams supported as he began his term in the Senate), Ames had said, "Our country is too *big for union;* too *sordid for patriotism;* too *democratic for liberty.*" Four years later, it became: "A REPUBLIC wears out its morals almost as soon as the sap of a white birch rots the wood." Ames was colorful, to be sure, but to hear the younger Adams present it, "these ideas were part of his disease." In his own evolution as a national political actor, Adams had come to see the "fanatical idolatry of Britain" as deeply unpatriotic and Federalist dogma as a kind of pathology. By publishing his political letters, he insisted, Ames's so-called friends had produced a false tribute to a respectable man and had done it merely to raise the level of "violence and intemperance" that was driving American political discourse as Madison took the reins of government.[9]

The two Adamses had simultaneously reached the point of refusing to write guardedly. They could hardly deny their hauteur, and they were content to reenter the public sphere as members of an exclusive sect, a defensive partnership. Within the family, there lived a devil's advocate, Abigail Adams, who remained discomfited by it all. She still did not want her son accepting an appointment from the party that engineered her husband's defeat.[10]

But a new reality had imprinted itself. John Adams was a good deal more suspicious of the British in 1809 than he had been as president, a decade earlier. His stern son went further, deploying Anglophobic language in the manner of a Jeffersonian Republican of the 1790s. British intransigence was obvious to all who participated in American statecraft. The nation was drifting toward war.

On the morning of July 4, 1809, father and son met up in Boston and were side by side at the Old South Church as the day's festivities began. But only the younger Adams joined the march across the Charles River Bridge to Bunker Hill for the next phase of the daylong celebrations. Early evening, he visited briefly with the "young Republicans" of the town and rejoined his wife for rooftop gazing at a Boston fireworks display that left fiery embers in his backyard. His official commission arrived from the secretary of state the next day.

Minister Plenipotentiary

On July 11, his forty-second birthday, JQA reflected on the year past. He could not overlook the "persecution which the combined personal enemies of my father and myself, had unrelentingly pursued." He put things in their proper perspective: "I have now just received an appointment of great trust and Importance, totally unsolicited, and confirmed by every vote in Senate, excepting my personal enemies, and two others, who voted not against me but against the mission." He meant those who thought the posting of a full minister to distant Russia to be a waste of money, when a low-level commercial consul would do just fine.

He had reached his decision despite objections from his mother, father, and wife. To his brother Tom, he turned over his legal and financial affairs. Then he arranged for a good many of his books to be stored until his return at the newly established Athenaeum library. And he finalized arrangements for the publication of his Harvard lectures—the *Lectures on Rhetoric and Oratory*.

On August 5, for the fourth time in his life, John Q. Adams embarked from Boston on a voyage to Europe. It was aboard the *Horace* this time, a vessel owned by one of his friends, William Gray, whose son Francis was accompanying the Adamses in order to learn the ins and outs of international commerce. This time, it would be eighty days before the party reached its destination.[11]

The *Horace* stopped along the banks of Newfoundland before proceeding across the Atlantic. There, JQA penned a flurry of political letters, including one to William Plumer, resident of Epping, in southern New Hampshire. Plumer had been a fellow Federalist U.S. senator, an independent who took the same political turn as JQA did, at the same time, and who would soon become the governor of his state—as a Madisonian Republican. Like JQA, he'd kept a careful diary during his days in the Senate, and was desirous of writing a history of their times.

The Adams-Plumer correspondence settled on their common desire to reverse trends. Objecting to a "spirit of party" never "so virulent," JQA fantasized a "congenial spirit" in its place, immune to "the infectious vapours of faction." He seemed to believe that Plumer and he might one day combine to effect an alteration in the political climate. But he was also realist enough to know that regional prejudice would always be hard to shed. Chief Justice John Marshall had recently completed the fifth and final volume of his *Life of George Washington,* well received in Federalist circles but flawed to John Quincy's mind. "I see a little too much of the Virginian in Marshall," he told Plumer, reckoning the southern slant unavoidable. He accepted that Plumer's history would correspondingly exhibit a New England bias, but still suggested to his New Hampshire ally that he draw upon the ex-president Adams's diplomatic papers: "My father, I am sure will be happy to see you at Quincy, & to furnish you any material in his power."[12]

Given the relative isolation of St. Petersburg, John Quincy thought long on the appropriate titles to carry with him on the extended voyage. Among these, he packed Adam Smith's *Theory of Moral Sentiments* in his trunk. It was a momentous book in the age of Enlightenment, one that his father had pointedly recommended to him back in 1790. One passage so struck John Quincy that he would repeat it to his mother in a letter from St. Petersburg: "A father is less apt to be attached to a child, who, by some accident, has been separated from him in its infancy, and who does not return to him till it is grown up to manhood. The father is apt to feel less paternal tenderness for the child; the child less filial reverence for the father." At the time, he was worrying about the two young sons he was leaving in Quincy, George and John, because he and Louisa brought only Charles, their youngest, along on the journey. Without doubt, the father of three was recalling his own early separations from one or another parent during impressionable years.[13]

John Adams was forlorn. "You and your Family are never out of my

Thoughts," he wrote during the first year of separation as he kept his son close in symbolic ways. "Our Reading has been all about Russia," he said of his wife and himself, after they had finished a life of Catherine the Great. He passed on fan mail, too. A reader he did not name had written a congratulatory letter to the Adams family, saying he was unable to put down JQA's *Lectures on Rhetoric and Oratory:* "I have read it three times over, and could wish that it had a place in every house in the United States, and that its Principles pervaded every American Bosom."[14]

That reader was, in fact, Richard Rush, son of Dr. Benjamin Rush. As in the case of John and John Quincy Adams, Rush the son would prove at least as adept as his father at navigating political seas. A prodigy who graduated from Princeton at seventeen, in 1797, he was shortly to become a Madison intimate, then U.S. attorney general, and eventually secretary of the Treasury under the second president Adams.[15]

A nostalgic John Adams lamented the loss of the once-regular weekend visits from John Quincy. He repeatedly reminded his son that his allies back home considered him "more necessary here than in Russia." He convinced himself that JQA was his mirror image, as he recalled the homecoming of 1788, after his years of service in Europe: "When you return you will find as I did, they will not know what to do with you. To make you a great Man will be dangerous, and to make you a little one will be impossible."

There were tricks of the political trade that John Adams had failed to master, and he hoped John Quincy would profit from his mistakes. "You have made an Impression upon our Nation that never can be oblitterated alive or dead," he wrote supportively. "But it is a Thing that requires great delicacy, Self Government and Reserve, which it is to be hoped you will preserve or Acquire, though your Father never could."[16]

John Quincy Adams was the first full-time U.S. minister to Russia. As such, he was eager that the two neutral powers, territorial giants, could find common purposes and act upon them. Anglo-French competition was a given, even in the absence of war. With Napoleon poised to conquer more of the Continent, there was real urgency: JQA had seen en route to his post several American vessels stalled in the Baltic—watched by the Danes, on orders from the French, and unable to dock in St. Petersburg.

President Madison did not give his minister a checklist of the goals to be attained, but this did not mean that the challenges before him were minor.

Russo-American commerce was already of consequence and growing annually. JQA hoped to honor the Madison administration by gaining an ally that would echo Washington's calls for the protection of neutral commerce. He did not take long to solicit this kind of support from his hosts. It only helped his damaged reputation back home that the merchant vessels on whose behalf he lobbied were largely owned by New England Federalists.[17]

Russia was in all respects a strange environment, and not simply because of the cold winds and sub-zero temperatures that the diarist daily recorded. Somewhat amazingly, Adams's lifelong habit of long walks persisted despite these conditions. A keen observer of local customs, he rode out by sleigh to "the frozen flesh market in the open Square near the Monastery of St. Alexander Nefsky" on a special day when the people stocked up on meat for the balance of the long winter. He sensed the heartbeat of the city and learned survival techniques. He studied the personalities of those who made up the diplomatic corps, jotting down snippets of conversation in increasingly vivid journal entries.

Social engagements held at the "Palace of the Hermitage," where he and Louisa took in the priceless art collection, sometimes lasted long into the night. The luxurious costumes and pageantry they witnessed struck Louisa most. "All this was too much like a fairy tale," she wrote. Yet for half of March 1810, her husband was bedridden, fighting a persistent fever and leg inflammation. His eyes suffered as well, and it was not until early April, three feet of ice still covering the river, that he was able to read the latest installment of his father's autobiographical letters to the *Boston Patriot*. The diplomat had chosen a hard life. Evidence of this fact surrounded him constantly.[18]

Mail delivery was a continuous problem. Periodically, he would receive a box of newspapers sent from the State Department. Whenever word reached him that a U.S. vessel was about to return home, he wrote long and arduously to take advantage of the opportunity. He worked especially hard at pleasing his mother, who he knew was anxious and had been the most critical in the family of his decision to serve the Madison administration; he recorded receipt of a letter from her dated three and a half months earlier.

On August 5, 1810, he marked in his diary the first anniversary of his departure from Boston. "The year has flown swiftly away," he said. "The opportunity to do essential good has not yet occurr'd." Reading an old issue of Washington's paper of record, the *National Intelligencer,* he could not suppress his anger at a Norfolk, Virginia, congressman who quoted liberally from his *Review of Works of Fisher Ames* on the floor of the House, without acknowledging the source. No one noticed. The incident drove him to stay up past midnight rereading the *Review,* a copy of which he had carried across the ocean.[19]

In diplomatic terms as well as every other, the view of the world from St. Petersburg was unique and irregular. Napoleon's unstoppable progress dominated the news, which led JQA to a wrong forecast: he thought that Anglo-American relations would mend themselves. But he was in the same boat as his fellow diplomats: their conversations bespoke a frenzied quest for reliable information. Adams regularly consulted with Russia's minister of foreign affairs, Count Nikolai Petrovich Rumyantsev (Romanzoff, in Adams's rendering), a former minister of commerce. The topsy-turvy French Revolution had resulted in "the greatest excess of Monarchy," as Adams characterized the current state of affairs, and yet Rumyantsev, the tsar's most trusted minister, seemed largely unconcerned about Napoleon and where he might strike next. At an official function, the American minister witnessed an awkward exchange as Rumyantsev and the French ambassador drank toasts to the health of their respective heads of state. As the months went by, Adams and the count continued to share opinions freely, agreeing at least on the importance of strengthening U.S.-Russian relations.[20]

Since 1799, the Russian-American Company had been developing trade and, in competition with the British, sought to colonize Alaska and the Pacific Northwest. Count Rumyantsev, the most active promoter of Russia's North American settlements, kept the dream alive in the second decade of the nineteenth century, when the United States had no presence in the Pacific beyond John Jacob Astor's short-lived fur trading post. Rumyantsev and Adams spoke of Alaska and points south primarily in terms of Anglo-Russian competition north of Spanish California. But, on any given day, they were more likely to be advancing hypotheses as to how Russia and America might seek mutually profitable solutions to the "embarrassed state of commercial affairs" in war-torn Europe. Without any solicitation from the American, Count Rumyantsev, "Chancellor of the Empire," presented Adams's recommendations about "neutral navigation" to his boss, Tsar Alexander I.[21]

All eyes remained on Napoleon. Celebrated and feared, he was a phenomenal figure, and his military exploits were closely followed. Everything about him piqued the interest of the diplomatic corps. At a ball hosted by the French ambassador not long after his arrival in Russia, with 130 guests present, Adams was seated at dinner beside a young Russian officer whom the tsar sent on "special missions" abroad. "He has been the whole of the last campaign with Napoleon," Adams's diary reads, "constantly the companion of his table, and sleeping in his tent." He had been Napoleon's intimate through "eight pitched battles" that included crossing the Danube and routing some 150,000 Austrians at Wagram. Taking advantage of the opportunity, Adams inquired of his dining companion whether Napoleon was "subject to the epilepsy," as he had heard somewhere. Not to my knowledge, the officer replied. But then, to Adams's prurient delight, "casting his eyes on both sides, as if fearful any body might hear, he said 'Il a la galle rentrée.'"

He had just been told that the emperor Napoleon suffered from the mange, scabies, with sores around the genitals that resembled the symptoms of syphilis. The condition was chronic and contagious, with transmission among bodies of soldiers during long campaigns far more common than it was within the general population. Adams now had it on good authority that the emperor slept little and daily dealt with his itchy, hard-to-treat (albeit nonvenereal) sores. The conqueror was as yet childless, newly divorced, and looking to get remarried. Tsar Alexander's younger sister was a prominent contender for the honor, which would presumably cement a Franco-Russian alliance. When the match did not occur, Russia's situation and Napoleon's fortunes both changed dramatically. As America went to war with Great Britain and Napoleon's invasion of Russia began, Adams would remain close to the action.[22]

Of psychological as well as political import in the most distant post in which a U.S. minister plenipotentiary could possibly have found himself, John Quincy Adams and Tsar Alexander I, ten years his junior, grew fond of each other, if not precisely friends. It most likely began at a ball in May 1810, when Alexander made a point of dancing the polonaise with Louisa Catherine Adams. (His eye for women has been remarked upon by many.) After this episode, she denoted her husband as "a marked man everywhere for great ability and statesmanship and already so distinguished by the Emperor [Tsar] and his Minister." That fall, Alexander once again singled out Louisa, when he extended a personal invitation for her to attend theater at the Hermitage; she acknowledged herself "the only *Lady* of the Corps Diplomatique" to be so honored. In January 1811, on the tsar's express orders, the Adams party was admitted to the Winter Palace by the entrance reserved for the imperial family. There, Louisa and Alexander engaged in friendly (unceremonious) banter, moving beyond the stiffness of most imperial encounters.

Because John Quincy walked for exercise whenever possible, he often met up with Alexander along the banks of the river Neva. When their paths crossed, the Russian ruler invariably asked about Mrs. Adams, whose absence from social events was felt. When she gave birth to a daughter in August 1811, the tsar followed the progress of mother and child. In a letter from home, the former envoy John Adams wondered how his son got on at diplomatic dinners and dances. One thing he knew about royal functions: "The Expence of these would have built Ships."[23]

Though he had all the powers necessary to perform his diplomatic duties, the American minister was of a rank below ambassadorial, which his European counterparts did not quite understand. To his father, JQA confided that the imperial court of Russia required a certain outward performance that the young American republic, by refusing to name ambassadors, did not present. A French associate had told him directly, "Princes should send Ambassadors, possessed of large fortunes of their own, and willing to spend their own income as well as their salaries for the credit of their Country."

The Adamses' modest fortune obviously precluded any such display. Still, John Quincy was confident that America's dignity had not suffered. He credited his father for setting a standard and imparting that confidence: "I have here an example under my eyes, and as I remember a certain axiom of diplomatic skill, which I first learnt from you, and which consists in a certain vulgar adage—such as 'Cut your Coat according to your Cloth' I have made up my mind to put myself at ease with the qu'en dira t'on [gossip], and go to honest Plutarch for the answer of the Priestess to Cicero when he consulted the oracle of Delphi." Father and son had their own language, built on years of reading the same books, that provided allegorical means of conveying truths: according to Plutarch, when Cicero visited Delphi and asked how he could fulfill his ambition and become illustrious, the

"Pythian priestess" instructed him to adhere to his own mind, not the opinions of the masses, to guide him forward. And that is how America's minister plenipotentiary resolved he would behave as well.[24]

Yet in terms of self-presentation, John Quincy Adams was, in fact, a different sort of diplomat than his father had been in the 1780s. The elder, while posted abroad, held others at a distance and was altogether wrapped up in his Americanness. Not so his European-reared son, who adapted quickly and was friendlier toward his foreign peers. Only the British officials he met in St. Petersburg seemed to find him poor company.

For a while, it looked as if Tsar Alexander might be the linchpin in moving the United States and Britain to end a mutually unprofitable war, officially begun in June 1812 over the paired issues of impressment (the kidnapping of sailor-citizens) and the incitement of Indians in American territories. War hawks in Congress imagined a second war for independence, but once it was declared and there was no Bunker Hill or Saratoga to sustain martial flights of fancy, continuance of a costly war found far fewer boosters. Enter the tsar, whose potential for greatness was ever a matter of conjecture. Napoleon, an erstwhile ally who turned his armies on Russia during Adams's residence there, said of him, "It would be difficult to have more intelligence than the Emperor Alexander: but I find that there is something lacking in him and I have never managed to discover what it is." The Austrian Empire's eminent foreign minister Prince von Metternich, who helped arrange Napoleon's marriage to an Austrian archduchess, later described the elusive Alexander as "a strange combination of masculine virtues and feminine weaknesses. Too weak for true ambition, but too strong for pure vanity."

To outsiders, the young tsar had an honorable ambition. He embraced (at least in theory) "the rights of man," which made him a timid democrat in the same sense that the enlightened Thomas Jefferson—another of the tsar's eager correspondents—was a timid abolitionist: thought and action clashed. The same autocrat who in 1804 proposed to the British that they help him transform all Europe into a league of states founded on liberal humanist principles carried out repressive militaristic policies with respect to the internal affairs of his country. John Quincy appears to have been genuinely impressed with him, yet historians all remark on Alexander's erratic moves, his impulsiveness. From the tsar's perspective, the American minister probably appeared a safer foreign representative to listen to than a suspicious

European neighbor would be. Conversing in French, the two men gravitated from small talk to philosophical conversations about ideas of political organization. A chance conversation between Adams and Alexander let Adams know that France and Russia would soon come to blows.[25]

When word reached him that Congress had declared war, Adams immediately recognized that he would have to remain longer in Europe and that his two eldest sons would be prevented from joining him there. In September 1812, he and his wife had to face the loss of their infant girl. Baby Louisa Catherine was "as lovely an infant as ever breathed the air of Heaven," the father wrote in his diary. "Nothing can fill the dreadful void in my heart," wrote the grieving mother.[26]

Communications were compromised by war, but father and son did their best to keep the flow of long letters current. JQA assumed his father was thinking as he was about a divided Boston, where Pickering types were still holed up. "Whenever we have a War with England," said the son even before the news had reached Russia, "we shall have to contend against an internal struggle of the same Spirit—God Grant that it may be suppressed without blood!" He anticipated reports from Quincy on local resistance to what was now being called "Mr. Madison's War."[27]

The ex-president remained nonplussed by congressional doings. With wry, almost gallows humor, he wrote to his son, "It is hoped that Congress will not be driven from their Seat and their General with his Armies be hunted from State to State, and from mountain to mountain like flocks of partridges, as We were for many years in the revolutionary War." The history was too well known to ignore, and the 1814 torching of government buildings in Washington would only confirm the old man's half-formed fears. But what he was really thinking, and could not hold back in 1812, was the desire to see his son stand up to the mistaken crowd of Anglophile New Englanders: "You ought not to be absent from your Country. She bleeds and groans, and too many of her Northern Sons have no feeling for her."[28]

During that tragic September, JQA unloaded in his diary: "The English talk much about their honour and National Morality, sometimes without meaning; but generally with a mixture of hypocrisy and of self-delusion." Louisa recorded a dream in which their infant was restored to her, "in full health," "all life and animation." Her father returned from the dead as well. But then her sleep vision shifted, and the scene presented "vivid flashes of

Lightning"; terror took her. Somehow, across the sky the words formed: "Be of good cheer thy petition is granted." It was not long after this that the tsar, through Count Rumyantsev, broached the subject with JQA of his mediation of the Anglo-American conflict.[29]

America's war with England and the land war in Europe appeared equally unnecessary. When JQA first arrived in Russia, Alexander and Napoleon were on decent terms; the French had at that point been at war with England for three years. As a relatively bloodless Anglo-Russian war drew to a close, Franco-Russian relations soured over which of the two nations would control Poland. With more than half a million troops, Napoleon invaded Russia; in mid-September 1812, Napoleon entered Moscow. He expected Alexander to offer terms. He was wrong. Vast numbers of peasants descended on St. Petersburg, there to be trained to combat the French invasion force. Napoleon's vulnerabilities became clear to the diplomatic corps in St. Petersburg as the French retreat began.

Writing to the man who best understood him was ever a balm for John Quincy Adams. Since setting foot in Russia, he had sometimes gone several months without a line from any of his countrymen. He never stopped feeling the oppressive power of wartime restrictions. "We have lived in eventful times," he recalled for his father, "but in the course of my life I have no recollection of a moment so full of portent as the present." John Adams assigned the greatest share of blame to London for what appeared to him as everlasting conflict. Writing to an admirer around this time, he put it succinctly: "Great Britain appears to me to have been the principal aggressor and the original disturber of the human race for the last half a century."[30]

In that chaotic year of 1812, he tried imagining John Quincy living nearby, engaged in the tranquil pursuit of knowledge. "But this," the father was forced to admit, "I know to be impossible. Your Nature cannot bear it." After their son's first year in St. Petersburg, Abigail Adams had taken the unusual step of writing directly to the president, urging his recall. When a Supreme Court justice died, Madison offered the position to John Quincy, who turned him down. He gave as the reason his wife's physical condition, which precluded travel. But there was more to it than that. He had his eye on high office and presumably saw a jurist's charge as a dead-end job.[31]

His stubborn independence did dismay John Quincy's parents. John Adams bemoaned the fact that he was not willing to trade Russia for a less strenuous existence. The old man looked back on his own imperfect life and projected defeat and public dismissal for his similarly formed son. "This Nation will not cease to irritate and torment you," he stated dismally, "till they force you out, that they may have the pleasure of insulting and abusing you." He wanted him home and recognized that no amount of persuasion would succeed. Perhaps that was what his dour prediction really meant.[32]

As the year 1813 opened, John Q. Adams was in the middle of his fourth Russian winter. He took walks, sometimes before breakfast, other times before dinner. He reread Cicero (in translation, this time) and the sermons of Laurence Sterne. He plunged ahead with Voltaire's *Essais sur les moeurs* and *Philosophie de l'histoire,* though he found "ludicrous," "disgusting," and "contemptible" Voltaire's undisguised attacks on Christianity. He was having young Charles Francis read portions of the New Testament. "Sorrows," he said indefinitely, "absorb many of my hours."[33]

His letters on politics were as dark as his father's. In particular, the phenomenon of the militarized state irked him. "We live indeed in an age," he wrote home, "when it is not lawful for any civilized Nation to be unprepared for or incapable of War.—Never, with an aching Heart I say it, never did the warlike spirit burn with so intense a flame throughout the civilized World as at this moment—Never was the prospect of its continuing to burn and becoming still fiercer, so terrible as now."[34]

Britain's chief ministers were altogether too optimistic that New York's DeWitt Clinton would defeat Madison in the election of 1812. Again to his father, JQA opined, "They believe that if Mr Clinton is the new President, . . . Peace is to be asked for on such Conditions as they shall chuse to dictate, and the *maritime rights,* of man-stealing [impressment] and so forth are to be sanctioned forever—Anxiously as I sigh for Peace, I *need* not say to you that it is not for such a Peace as that." He believed that London was enjoying a string of "good-fortune," adding to its natural "pretensions"; he thought "the folly and the disasters of the French Emperor" would make things worse. He was right. Napoleon's setbacks allowed Britain to turn its attention to the prosecution of its war with America.[35]

In 1783, John Adams was recalled from the Netherlands to help conclude the Treaty of Paris. In 1813, after the tsar's offer to mediate Anglo-American discussions was set aside, John Quincy Adams was recalled from Russia to negotiate with British envoys in the neutral site of Ghent, Belgium.

LITERAL COMPLEMENT

"My dear Son," began the letter from John Adams in April 1813. "I have Official Information that Mr Bayard and Mr Gallatin are joined with you in a Negotiation of great importance and no little difficulty, nor less hazard to your Reputation. What the Result will be I know not: but I need not Say to you that you cannot decline a Share in the Business. Your return to me is the first Wish of my private heart: but I am not yet So Selfish as to hope for the gratification of my Inclination at the Expence of your honour, or the Interest of your Country." He reported on the war at home: "Our Frigates have won Laurels, which they can never looze: but how soon they may be compelled to Submit to Superiour force or reverse of fortune, cannot be foreseen."[36]

Twelve whole months passed between the dispatch of the above letter and the day JQA actually left St. Petersburg on the long journey to Ghent for direct talks with the British delegation. Napoleon had abdicated his throne and gone into exile, bringing the long continental war to an end. "With this prospect of a general Peace in Europe," John Quincy wrote in his diary, "I commenced my journey to contribute if possible to the restoration of Peace to my own country." He dined with his wife and six-year-old son, "embraced them and committed them to the Protection of a kind and gracious Providence," and parted from them for what would prove to be eleven months, though at the time he anticipated returning to St. Petersburg before winter blew in. He prayed for "presence of mind and fortitude." He felt the weight of the assignment "incessant upon my heart."

As he departed Russia on the *Ulysses,* he drew a comparison to ancient Odysseus, whose nightmarish wandering in some way resembled JQA's own history of tempest-tossed travels on the high seas, and then to make it all poetically consonant, he crossed the North Sea on a vessel named the *John Adams*. The solitary wanderer wrote to his father from the port city of Reval (in present-day Estonia), finally concurring with the prescription long since conveyed by his parents: "It is my own opinion as it is yours that I ought to be at home—and although I am not yet recalled from the Mission to Russia, I flatter myself that this new Charge will ultimately furnish me the opportunity of returning home." He used the occasion to give an accounting of the books he had bought in St. Petersburg, taking pride in the bargains he'd found and happily conferring a compliment on his father: "Of all the libraries that I have ever seen, it has not been my Fortune to meet with one better selected than your's." No one would have been surprised by the next sentiment: "My Passion for Books has not in the smallest degree subsided."

He noted that the diplomatic schedule made it harder to indulge in pleasure reading. But, he clarified, "I am not like Dr. [Samuel] Johnson who said he learnt every thing he knew from *conversation.*—I hear nothing in Society but *Talk*—Politics—the Weather—Dancing—and the Card Table—This is the Circle of social Conversation which I am accustomed to find—Half an hour of reading gives me as much instruction, and more amusement than I should derive from a Century of all this." Whatever the nature of his ambition, he could always conceive of happier days surrounded by family and with a less mobile library.[37]

In August 1814, when JQA wrote to update his father on the talks in Ghent, he was preoccupied with the fact that his effort as a negotiator was the literal complement to his father's work in an earlier era. "The eyes of mankind are turning with great and increasing interest towards us," he wrote nervously. "We shall be brought again to the trial whether we can maintain the Independence atchieved and the Union founded by our fathers."[38]

President Madison was itching to find a resolution to an expensive war plagued by difficulties in the recruitment of men to fight it. Before it became known that London had rejected the tsar's offer of mediation, and absent Senate confirmation, he had dispatched the negotiators James Bayard and Albert Gallatin to St. Petersburg. They spent half a year there, during which Adams wrote in his diary of Bayard's dispiritedness and constant complaining and Gallatin's dutiful study of the Russian language. Bayard was the Delaware senator who had revealed himself to be an Adams adversary in the Senate in 1808. The Swiss-born Gallatin was honest, frugal to a fault, and so vital a secretary of the Treasury under Jefferson that he continued in the cabinet under Madison. Known for solid research and dispassionate judgment, he'd opposed the embargo for pragmatic reasons, proving correct in his assessment.

The American delegation held its first meeting with the British commissioners on August 8, 1814, as the U.S. Capitol itself was about to succumb to a fiery British onslaught. Gallatin accurately predicted that the administration should be wary of an attack on New Orleans, "our most distant and weakest point." As negotiations proceeded, the triumvirate of Adams, Gallatin, and Bayard were joined by Jonathan Russell, former U.S. chargé d'affaires in London, and Henry Clay of Kentucky, the once and future Speaker of the House, a strong-willed statesman ten years Adams's junior, whom Madison considered the hardest bargainer of the bunch. If the combined firepower on the American side implied strength, it remained throughout the autumn that the British side felt its bargaining position was stronger than it had been since the start of the war.[39]

As the lead U.S. diplomat, Adams faced as his counterpart a British vice admiral, Lord James Gambier, along with Henry Goulburn of the Colonial Office; the more senior British negotiators were at the Congress of Vienna constructing a post-Napoleonic order. The American side declared its principal issues to be free trade and impressment of U.S. seamen—an end to British bullying activities on the high seas. The British side, concerned with the Americans' continental ambitions, pressed a plan to create an allied Indian state in the western Great Lakes region; or, if not an Indian buffer zone, then some other credible "barrier . . . against which neither party should encroach." JQA's diary catalogued everything.

London was intent on redirecting America's westward push. It had to safeguard Canada, which the Madison administration ostensibly sought to annex to the United States. Facing plausible British arguments about Canada, Adams took a hard stance. "I answered that the Conquest of Canada had never been the object of the War" but had been subject to invasion only "in consequence of the War, as they themselves had invaded many parts of the United States." There was no trust established in the opening weeks of negotiation. Adams felt the other side's unsuppressed "bitterness and rancour against the Americans and the jealousy of their increasing strength and population." No one knew as yet of "the taking of Washington City" and burning of government buildings.[40]

Within the American delegation, the clash of egos was at times pronounced. In Adams's increasingly long-winded diary entries, Clay and Russell were prone to express themselves in loud, angry voices, whereas Bayard got under Adams's skin less than he had when they were senators. Gallatin, if at times given to frustration, almost always adopted a prudent approach to the problems that arose. Easily perturbed by morally suspect gestures, Adams revolted against Clay's after-hours routine of gambling and drinking well past midnight. Adams himself rose most days at 5:00 a.m. and continued his habit of solitary evening walks of up to two hours.

Gallatin came closest to being a peacemaker among his associates. A few weeks into talks, a note from the British commissioners reached them and was read aloud. Bayard pronounced it "stupid"; Clay thought it deserved no more than a half-page reply; Adams saw the value of responding at length and with substantive arguments. Gallatin proposed to subject the note to detailed analysis and to respond exclusively to the matters that they chose to regard as meaningful. And that is what "the mission," as Adams labeled this disparate group, agreed to in the end. But then the next note from London was even more "overbearing and insulting," he recorded. Dealing with it caused friction among the Americans. Adams admitted his culpability: "I cannot always restrain the irritability of my temper." He began noting Bayard's "open heartedness" and wrote of a building respect, one for the other. It was Clay whose emotionalism received most attention in the diary, Clay who sang the praises of Kentuckians while belittling the people of Massachusetts. Clay's pushiness combined with a "scornful sneer" in one instance where Adams surprised himself by managing to contain his anger. "A soft answer, turneth away wrath," he recited. "I have not always a soft answer at my own command." He recognized his own surliness, grew accustomed to being outvoted by his fellow commissioners, and dealt with situations by going off on therapeutic walks.[41]

By mid-October 1814, a more accommodating atmosphere emerged within the mission and across the negotiating table. Oddly, the sack of Washington, which became known on the first of that month, did not raise the temperature. It turned out that the city's destruction was viewed in British government circles as a rebuke to American aggression in Canada, a singular lesson taught rather than a sign of further humiliations to come. A short time after, news of the bombardment of Fort McHenry, in Baltimore's harbor, and the repulse of British forces there, further muddied diplomatic waters.

The U.S. side refused any territorial concession whatsoever. London relented on its agonized attempts to constitute an Indian buffer state. But it would not agree to a complete return to prewar borders: parts of Maine had been taken, and the British were loath to give them back. The Americans retreated on the point of exacting a statement about impressment: the once paramount issue would be of lesser import because the British navy no longer needed to contend with a French adversary on the high seas.[42]

On October 25, JQA paused in detailing the negotiations to mark in his diary, "The day of Jubilee, of the marriage of my parents"—their fiftieth wedding anniversary. He picked up his pen and wrote a letter to his mother: "My dear father can look back to all the succession of years since that time, with the conscious recollection that it was a happy day . . . and may that gracious being who has hitherto conducted you together through all the vicissitudes of an eventful life, still watch over you!" On conditions faced at Ghent, he was less sanguine: "Of Peace, there is at present, no prospect whatever."[43]

Two days later, he wrote to his father and explained the problem. The British were running out the clock, waiting to see if an event along the U.S.-Canadian border might compel the American side to make some meaningful concession. "The situation in which I am placed often brings to my mind, that in which you were situated in the year 1782[,] and I will not describe the feelings with which the comparison, or I might rather say the contrast, affects me." The similarities were there, but vague: "I am called to support the same interests, and in many respects the same identical points and questions."

A different balance of power existed in 1814 compared with 1782. At Ghent, the British were operating from a position of relative strength, and France was, at long last, out of the picture. JQA had no massive surrender to hang his hat on, as had been the case after the Franco-American victory at the Battle of Yorktown in October 1781, which effectively announced the end of British military operations in America. John Adams was even able to return to the Netherlands during slow months in the negotiations, and while he might never have gotten over what he saw as Benjamin Franklin's incompetence, he was able to leave his capable ally John Jay in place to monitor Franklin until an end to Anglo-American wrangling was finally in sight. John Quincy Adams had nowhere else to go: he fought an uphill battle across the negotiating table, finding himself at odds, at one time or another, with each of his negotiating partners. Nor did he quite know what the latest thinking was in Washington (or wherever the government's leaders were huddled in the wake of Washington's destruction). The diplomat-son did not hesitate in conveying to his father the degree of his anxiety: "How far it may be the interest or the policy of our own Country to continue this game of chance, and to keep us here as puppets to move according to the chapter of Accidents, it is not for me to determine." Plus, he would be spending the long winter away from Louisa and young Charles.[44]

Something began to wear the British down after this, and it was not just the unshakable pose of the American commissioners. Financial considerations dictated against further prosecution of the war. So, on December 1, Admiral Gambier announced to the Americans that his instructions were altered; he was glad to report "much fairer prospects for success" than when the two sides had last met. The issue now was merely fishing rights for New Englanders in Canadian waters.

JQA's stubborn refusal to give in raised an awkward possibility: that his fellows would sign a peace accord without his concurrence. Gallatin wanted the treaty to leave the matter of the fisheries for future consideration; Bayard resisted outright rejection of Adams's position, but he was the only one. Clay went so far as to confer with Goulburn, the most anti-American of the British negotiators, assuring him that the United States would never risk war to benefit the interests of its fishermen. In the end, though, Adams got his way, when Goulburn uncharacteristically folded his hand. He explained in a letter to his father that the honor of New England had been at stake, that he could not turn his back on his native province. To the son's subsequent satisfaction, his father let him know that the fisheries clause conformed to what he had fought for in the earlier Treaty of Paris: "Your Country itself knows not and never did know the Importance of the Fisheries." He had done his father proud. Months later, still ruminating on what was, to everyone but New Englanders, of little weight, he thanked his father again: "You have impressed upon me with the energy peculiar to yourself, and with the wisdom, in my situation so essential to me, the duty of supporting our rights on this important question." Fishing rights in Canadian waters.[45]

On December 24, 1814, the treaty was signed, with neither side truly profiting. The conditions that prevailed in 1812 were restored. To his father, JQA related in detail the several ways in which he had reengaged with the

Treaty of Paris by adopting a strong position on America's territorial integrity. And then he went a step further, coyly revising what his diary undeniably revealed as the irascibility of his colleagues and himself: "I have great satisfaction in saying that our harmony has been as great and constant as perhaps ever existed between five persons employed together upon so important a trust—Upon all the important questions we have been unanimous."[46]

Repaire d'Horreurs

He was not coming home. Not yet, anyway. As soon as he affixed his signature to the Treaty of Ghent, he asked his wife to meet him in Paris, expecting either to receive an appointment to London or to return to America. In either case, he would not be traveling back to St. Petersburg to lead Louisa and Charles to safety.

In early 1815, the icy waters impassable, Mrs. Adams packed up, sold off what she could, and traveled overland through territory scarred by the recently concluded war. Conditions throughout the journey were far from ideal: aside from the frigid weather, here was a woman without a husband (though accompanied by two armed servants) moving across international boundaries as the exiled Napoleon was staging his return to Paris. From her carriage, she observed unreconstructed towns and battlefields, exhausted populations, and "women unprotected." She paused in Berlin, a city she adored, where she and her husband had lived a decade and a half earlier.

After forty days on the road, Louisa and child arrived safe at the Hôtel du Nord, where a seemingly unruffled John Quincy received them on the evening of March 23. It had been a somewhat typical day for him: he'd looked in on his colleagues Gallatin, Russell, and Bayard, visited with the marquis de Lafayette, and attended the theater. His reunion with Louisa is announced in the diary nearly as an afterthought, making it hard to fathom how, in spite of all he knew of the world, he had expressed little concern as to what might befall his family on a cross-continental journey. Years later, rationalizing on behalf of her husband, Louisa appended a moral to the tale of her wintry trials: "If my Sex act with persevering discretion, they may from their very *weakness* be secured from danger." Either John Quincy trusted in providential protection or he simply refrained from exposing his fear for her.[47]

England now beckoned. Imitating the career path of his father before him at the end of the earlier Anglo-American war, the diplomat Adams received word, in early May, of his appointment as minister plenipotentiary to Great Britain. While Clay prepared to resume his illustrious career in Congress, JQA's other Ghent partners, Gallatin and Bayard, were named ministers plenipotentiary to France and Russia, respectively. Bayard refused the appointment; he would cross the ocean and die at home in Delaware within days of his arrival. Gallatin took the better part of a year to finally accept Paris. He sailed home in the company of Henry Clay, was reunited with his wife, and entered into extended talks with President Madison and Secretary of State James Monroe over his future prospects. Gallatin, Clay, and the former minister to France William H. Crawford of Georgia all wished to succeed Monroe at State, when Monroe succeeded Madison. While Crawford would settle for Gallatin's old job at Treasury, John Quincy Adams was to receive the most coveted cabinet post in the Monroe administration. For the moment, though, the American diplomatic family in Ghent, their past disagreements tempered by success, parted ways.[48]

Overshadowing everything else, a resurgent Napoleon ended his career once and for all, at Waterloo. The world appeared suddenly altered. Before assuming his post in London, John Quincy wrote to his father, with some trepidation, that "if Napoleon should be destroyed, and France again restored to the Bourbons, England will again be the dictatress of Europe." Indeed, France's diminished stature was the reason why Gallatin waffled on taking up the president's offer of Paris. If London was the only important diplomatic assignment in 1815, it was not in all ways attractive. Thirty years earlier, John Adams had braved postwar anti-Americanism in London, and now his son prepared mentally for the animus he rightly expected to encounter.[49]

With volcanic prose spewing from patriotic writers on both sides of the Atlantic, a paper war was to take the place of military conflict in Anglo-American affairs in these years. The political satirist, patriotic essayist, and popular storyteller Washington Irving, a native New Yorker, sailed to England in 1815 and spent a number of highly productive years there. In one of his early sketches, "John Bull," Irving offered a lighthearted portrait of England's bumptious, plainspoken, unsentimental personification: "He cannot hear of a quarrel between the most distant of his neighbours, but he begins incontinently to fumble with the head of his cudgel, and to consider whether his interest or honor does not require that he should meddle in the broil." Irving, known for his polite charm, was yet keenly attuned to the urgency in outsiders' perception of an immodest British government. "All that I wish," the author concluded, "is, that John's present troubles may teach him more prudence in future." John Bull, that is.[50]

Anticipating their son's move, John and Abigail had seen fit to send grandsons George and John to be reunited with their parents and youngest brother in London. John Quincy and Louisa Catherine arrived in the city where they'd first met and found happy quarters in the countryside, at Ealing, several miles from the center of the city. Louisa's modern biographer has called the three-story brick structure "the happiest home she and John Quincy would ever know." It was named Little Boston House. There, George (fourteen) and John (twelve) got to know their brother Charles (eight), who, even now, was the most like their father, having been exposed to European ways and a European education. The elder children, thoroughly American, proved hard to handle and resistant to the intense immersion in the classics that John Quincy favored. Their grandmother Abigail, as grandmothers are wont, adopted a liberal "let boys be boys" approach and warned her son, "You must not look for old heads on young shoulders." Continuing his ritual long walks in the early evenings, John Quincy brought his wife and three boys along with him. In the mornings, before sending George off to school, he subjected him to lessons of his own devising.[51]

Back in Quincy, John Adams nervously awaited word. "We are at our Wits ends for News from you. . . . We are equally anxious for your Lady and your Son." Now in his eightieth year, John Adams had lost none of his tartness or insouciance. He wrote of being relentlessly pursued through the mails by citizens of all stripes who bore opinions about his long career that they felt obliged to convey to him directly. "I continue to receive Strange letters, some anonimous, others with respectable names of Persons who never Saw me, Some of admonition, Some of instruction, Some of Applause and Some of reproach." Presuming John Quincy had been as hounded through the mails, he asked, "What Shall We do with these Insects that buz about Us? Their Bite in former times tingled: but I am grown almost as insensible as a Boston

Dray horse in September." He acknowledged himself an oddity, and one who no longer fretted as he once did over reputation. He was housebound more than he was out and about, but his mind focused with the same intensity as ever.[52]

Old John Adams missed his loved ones but was fully prepared to embrace fate. Putting his most unmannerly thoughts on paper somehow connected him with his son. He despaired of understanding Europe in the nineteenth century and testified to it anecdotally: "The Baron de Stael, said to me once in a confidential Tête a Tête 'Qu'est que c'est, que L'Europe? C'est un Repaire d'horreurs.'" (What is Europe? It's a den of horrors.) The elder's unapologetic epistolary attitude ranged from ruminative to abrupt. And in the end, "On the brink of the Grave, your Father and Mother enjoy more health, Strength and Spirits than they have any right to expect; for which they never can be too gratefull."[53]

In June 1815, John Quincy was finally able to send him a comprehensive report. The sons had arrived; the family was whole; the American minister's reputation had been established on firm ground. Britain's powerful foreign secretary, Lord Castlereagh, was impressed with his intellect. John Q. Adams was actually in a good place.

One issue still on the table was the disposition of forces in the Great Lakes region. Adams senior had dealt with the same problem during negotiations in Paris in 1782, when he tried to talk the British into a complete demilitarization of the border. Unlike the Atlantic Ocean, where the British reigned, the United States had the upper hand all along the Great Lakes border with Canada; its naval presence was formidable. In broaching the subject, JQA concurred with Castlereagh that it made most sense to move discussions to Washington. There, the acting secretary of state, Richard Rush, and Britain's U.S. minister, Charles Bagot, reached agreement on the precise number of vessels each side would maintain. It was the first modern instance of a reciprocal disarmament of naval forces.

A thornier problem for John Quincy Adams was finding means to cooperate with London in putting an end to the international slave trade. One hopeful (yet vague) clause in the Treaty of Ghent related to joint efforts to suppress smuggling operations. Castlereagh and Adams took it up. Discussions stalled once it became clear that any American acceptance of the principle of inspections at sea would leave open the possibility that British naval officers would again be boarding American vessels, this time looking for chained cargo instead of defectors, but any hint of the impressment issue rendered this well-intentioned conversation moot for the time being.

JQA was unable to solicit a single statement from the British government relating to the principle of neutral rights. Without that, there was really nowhere to go in broadening Anglo-American understanding. Castlereagh made it clear that he wished to conciliate the late American enemy (if for no other reason than to pay down the national debt), yet it was too soon for a thoroughgoing shift in policy. Adams took heart in the foreign secretary's body language.[54]

Then, another letter from Peacefield. Something had changed in his father's tone; the words read differently. John Adams sounded listless, mopish, lost: "I feel so uneasy, on your account, that I want to write to you, every hour. But I am become so great a Coward, that I dare not write any thing to you. I never take my Pen, but with the utmost Anxiety, last I should hurt your Feelings, embarrass your Employments, give you unnecessary solicitude for your Country or excite a useless gloom on the prospect before Mankind." He had spoken of his premonitions before; the letter made no predictions, but it expressed helplessness.[55]

Fortunately, the slump did not last. Soon enough, the octogenarian resumed his familiar synopses of the political mood, adding tangential barbs and Sternean jabs at the world and calling this turn of mind the "pedantic reflections of old age." One thing did not improve: the contrarian saw no end to mankind's wars. "Son! I can write to you in no other Stile. If Superstition and Despotism are about to reassume their Empire, it will be the Reign of Anarck. It will be worse than the Crusades, the Wars of the Reformation, or the French Revolution." When John Adams let loose the commas of complaint, he was usually protesting an immovable force or raising a demon that he could not exorcise. "This World is a Church militant and a State militant," he blasted.

The postscript marked the writer's recognition that the recipient of his ranting language deserved a tad more reserve: "If you should summon up Spirit and decision enough to live at Lodgings till Spring and then return home with or without leave as I did: give yourself no concern relative to an establishment. Come to my House, which is large enough for such Phylosophers as We are, with all our Families, till you have [time] at leisure to arrange your Affairs. Be assured it will be the most joyful part of my Life to receive and enjoy you all with open Arms." Imagining a repeat of his own unilateral decision to abandon his post in London in 1788, he reached out to John Quincy to do something daring.[56]

These yearnings grew stronger month by month. He presumed his son agreed that there was no longer an advantage in remaining abroad. He was only guessing, because the correspondence was entirely one-sided at this point. Then, in a long letter of August 31, 1815, John Quincy did his best to respond to the general tenor of his father's last *sixteen* letters.

If John Adams was misguided as to the state of human affairs, his son was only marginally less so. Even before JQA had received his father's worst laments about the fate of the Atlantic world, and despite the moderation he found in Lord Castlereagh, he, too, conjured the possibility of a third "war for independence," giving voice to similar fears with respect to Britain's penchant for going to war. It was, he told his father, America's "interest and policy to avoid as long as possible a new War with England—How long it will be possible I know not. . . . [T]he danger is that they will plunge the Nation headlong into a War with us, because it is against us only that they will be able to stimulate the National passions to the tone of War." He was a wary diplomat, situated as he was in the lion's den. Demonstrating the currency of this feeling back home, Henry Clay stated with unmitigated contempt, "That man must be blind to the indications of the future, who cannot see that we are destined to have war after war with Great Britain."[57]

In his letters, John Adams had recently acquired a habit of mixing politics and diplomacy with thoughts on religion and philosophy. These days, he had more on his mind than prognostications about terrestrial or corporeal affairs. Reaching out to select correspondents, he made stinging allusions to religious disputes in times past that had shattered the political world. He was seeking to understand the human condition on a deeper level; he was reading at length, and thinking long and hard, about the enduring intellectual debate "between Spiritualism and Materialism," immortality of the soul versus materiality of the mind.

Why this, and why now? Owing to the friendly conspiracy of their mutual friend Dr. Benjamin Rush, in 1812, John Adams had reengaged Thomas Jefferson in a regular correspondence. By 1816, it had come to encompass politics past, public opinion, ancient Greek theories of the good life, and the nature of God. In the fall of 1816, the "Old Gentleman" wrote first to Jefferson, and then to his son, about the spiritualist-materialist controversy. He coaxed Jefferson to respond to his theory of grieving over death, its private uses and public abuses; he coaxed his son, between appeals to hurry home, to read books on "Hindoos" and to oblige him with his thoughts on alternatives to orthodox forms of Christianity: "What is the Truth? Surely it exists; and as Surely, it may be found. Let Spiritualists and Materialists, dispute, till they tell Us, What is Spirit?"

Jefferson weighed in dutifully on the elder's questions. The conversation advanced month by month. The two ex-presidents were deists, prepared to question the divinity of Jesus and the reliability of the New Testament. But not John Quincy, whose faith, as his father well knew, made him less of a skeptic. Their kinsman and, from 1805 to 1813, congressman, Josiah Quincy, portrayed JQA as one whose "moral character" was founded on "religious principle." But for the moment, the son sidestepped argument as best he could by playing into his father's good humor: "I think I shall neither commence champion of Orthodoxy, nor as your old friend Franklin used to say[,] of any man's *doxy*."[58]

The second and third presidents were only slightly less comfortable when the conversation turned from religious philosophy to a review of their past partisanship. Both agreed that it was high time to bury negative emotion. They concurred, for one, that Napoleon was "a cold-blooded, calculating unprincipled usurper" (Jefferson) and "a Military Fanatic like Achilles, Alexander, Caesar, Mahomet" (Adams). And when Adams lauded Cicero's thoughts on government, Jefferson termed the same Roman honest, industrious, and the "first master" of style.[59]

Not surprisingly, it was Adams who more readily infused emotion into their communication. He unabashedly recurred to his old plaint of being misunderstood by the citizens at large; misunderstood, perhaps, by Jefferson as well. He insisted on revisiting what he meant when he wrote of the natural human tendency to respond favorably to aristocracy: his opinion was not in the least an endorsement of inequality but simply a recognition of it. Jefferson put forward the notion that there were, qualitatively, good and bad aristocrats: natural (owing to virtues, talents, beauty) and artificial (owing to birth and wealth). Adams felt the distinction didn't matter. He thought Jefferson too trusting in the human capacity to evolve and improve.

"I dislike and detest hereditary honours," he told Jefferson, lest any doubt remain from the slander-filled 1790s. John Adams remembered all too well the humiliation he suffered for suggesting a grander title for Washington than "President."

But he wanted to make a larger point: that political corruption was not exclusive to the aristocratic or monarchical form, nor was the republican form immune. Jefferson's natural aristocracy of talent could be corrupted. America might be a hundred years away from its first despot, he mused, but the impulse Jefferson associated with specific forms of government was in fact a part of nature. However social inequality was understood, competition for power produced factions; jealousies led to ruthless acts. The people were similarly defenseless against the "rapacities" of cunning politicos and the cool allure of celebrated names and demagogic public speakers. Even in a democratic-leaning polity, elections were opportunities for the venal to grasp power.[60]

Strong Impressions

His entire career had been fixed on dislodging falsehoods, which explains why the ever-unsettled John Adams was positively entranced with Unitarianism as it rose in popularity among his fellow New Englanders. The grouchy wise man loved to assert things, that his words might provoke a thoughtful reaction from any of his trusted correspondents. Nowadays, he bellyached about the recovery time with each ensuing illness, and as his eyesight began to fail, he gamely called himself "half blind." But nothing changed in the essential honesty that characterized the father-son relationship. When he prodded John Quincy with his conviction that Jesus was no more than a man inspired by God, John Quincy replied with what made *him* comfortable: "My hopes of a future life are all founded on the Gospel of Christ."[61]

Father and son had anti-Catholicism in common. JQA joked crudely with regard to the absurdity of the virgin birth. For laughs, he reproduced the sales pitch he'd heard at Christmas from the vicar in Ealing: "whosoever doth not keep the Catholic Faith whole and undefiled: without doubt *he shall perish everlastingly*." Even so, the father wielded the freer pen and could slip an exclamation (or several) between quieter paragraphs: "An incarnate God!!! An eternal, Self existent, omnipotent omnipresent omnicient Author of this Stupendous Universe, Suffering on a Cross!!! My Soul Starts with horror, at the Idea, and it has Stupified the Christian World. It has been the Source of almost all the Corruptions of Christianity." The son was never as worried about the damage that might yet be done to society by religion: "Is it conceivable that the driveling dotards of this age can bring back the monkeries and mummeries of the twelfth Century? Oh no!—Europe is tyrannized not by Priests, but by soldiers."[62]

In fact, when they argued matters of theology, father and son never seriously quarreled. They alternated between earnestness and sarcasm. Wit was an idiom that had always bound them. They entertained each other as impatient intellectuals as much as they shared a self-image as political outcasts. That said, the son grew increasingly pious in the pages of his diary, which his father would not have seen. Louisa had been reared in a loving household that introduced her sequentially to Anglican, Catholic, and Unitarian practices, and she seems to have had no trouble accommodating herself to her husband's preferences, especially when he began coaching his sons in how to profit from their reading of Scripture.

When fresh out of Harvard, John Quincy had asked, somewhat predictably, "If we cannot know God, then what is the meaning of life?" The older he got, the more he adored the Bible for its literary merit and its centering moral influence. To his "dear and ever honoured father," he wrote in the prolific letter-writing year of 1816 that it was only through deep study "that the mind of man can arrive at the idea of a God." It was his father, though, who contributed the pithiest line in the exchange: "Let the human Mind loose. . . . Superstition and Despotism cannot confine it."[63]

All may be equal in the eyes of God, but John Quincy and Louisa Catherine Adams did not appreciate the reduction in class status that they felt during their stay in England. They had become accustomed to special privileges throughout the years in Berlin and St. Petersburg. In England, they had to adapt. And so they did. At a high society dinner at the country seat of a British lord in June 1816, JQA sat next to Sir James Mackintosh, a man of his approximate age who was at work on a history of the Glorious Revolution of 1688. Mackintosh had been informed that Benjamin Franklin, before leaving London in 1775, remarked that "he lamented the Revolution that was to Separate the Colonies from Great Britain." He asked John Quincy whether Franklin's words were "sincere" and whether other American statesmen had similarly regretted the need for so drastic a course of action. "I told him I did not believe Dr. Franklin wished for the Revolution," JQA penned in his diary. "Nor Washington." Sir James followed up by asking whether there were leaders who had wished all along for a revolution. "I said, perhaps my father—Samuel Adams—and James Otis."

What is curious is the "perhaps" that he inserted here. If the American minister was simply offering an honest opinion, would he not have known for certain whether his father had shared Franklin's and Washington's regrets or stood firm at the side of Cousin Samuel? No one better understood Boston's role in the struggle that led to the Revolution. He knew how his father wished to be remembered. And yet . . .

As he segued back to American politics in letters to his father, a warm, positive tone emerged. He had learned that the newly elected governor of Massachusetts was John Brooks, a physician by profession. When young, Brooks had led militiamen at Lexington and Concord and rose to be a general in the state militia. From the early 1790s, he was a Federalist stalwart. But on taking office in 1816, the old warhorse disappointed the most ardent of his Federalist patrons by exhibiting a moderate, harmonizing sensibility. "I always entertained a very respectful opinion of Genl: Brooks," said John Quincy. At first fearful that the governor might "condescend to some compromise of principle" and ally with the anti-Madison forces (who, as recently as 1814, considered severing New England from a southern-dominated Union), he felt relief. Reading Boston newspapers, he perceived that Governor John Brooks could not be bought.

A statement on the maturing character of his own patriotism followed. "The longer I live," JQA wrote, "the stronger I find my national feelings grow upon me; and the less of my affections are compassed by partial localities—My system of politics more and more inclines to strengthen the Union." America had to be united if it was to navigate increasingly hostile seas. Whether a states' rights agenda originated in the North or in the South didn't matter to him: he regarded states' rights as unwise and defeatist. The War of 1812 had amplified the "national character," he observed, but it had simultaneously "multiplied and embittered our Enemies."

The younger Adams was seeing effects of "the late War" up close. "Royalists every where detest and despise us as Republicans," he apprised his father. "Wherever British influence extends it is busy to blacken us in every possible manner—In Spain, the popular feeling is almost as keen against us as in England." The question he posed nervously was not rhetorical: "How long will it be possible for us to preserve Peace with all Europe?" The circumspection conveyed here succinctly captures the state of mind he would bring to U.S. foreign policy as secretary of state in the very near future. "May our Country be always successful," he preached to his father, "but whether successful or otherwise, always right. . . . The truth is that the American Union, while united *may* be certain of success."

John Adams responded with his customary mix of pride and skepticism: "One hundred Years hence, your Letters and Writings will be Sought, with infinitely more Avidity, than those of Mary Queen of Scotts, or The Ministers of Queen Elizabeth." He himself had written tomes on government that, to his mind, no one paid any attention to, work that he felt would disappear completely from the annals of history. Maybe his son, an as yet unsung genius, would rescue the family honor.[64]

If only his Johnny would come home. Letters between Quincy and Ealing always contained discussion of the children's upbringing and education, and barely hidden between the lines was that plea. Things finally came to a head as the old man boiled over: "I can not bear the Thought that your Sons Should be educated in a foreign Country." The issue of their education was a small part of what troubled his soul. "I have long desired to write you Seriously my Sense of your Situation: but conscious of my Incapacity to judge, I have hitherto postponed the Subject. But of one thing, if I am not absolutely Sure, I have a Strong Impression; and that is that you will be wrong to remain much longer in Europe." JQA replied soothingly: "Your advice to me with regard to my children must in all cases have the greatest weight." He needed say no more. They wanted the same thing.[65]

Soon after, it became clear that Secretary of State James Monroe would succeed to the presidency. Barely masking his excitement, John Adams conveyed the latest rumor to his son: "The Newspapers, throughout the Continent are announcing to Europe and America, Somewhat imprudently, that you are recalled and to be made Secretary of State. I know not whence this comes: but whether true or false, I hope it is true."[66]

The father's wish was granted.

PEAS PARCHING

The Adamses arrived in the City of New York on August 6, 1817, where the incoming secretary of state was honored at a banquet attended by some hundred prominent citizens. In his diary, John Quincy revealed mixed emotions: happy to be in his native land and anxious about the "cares and perils" he was about to confront. From Manhattan, their party headed north and arrived in Quincy on August 18, the tenth birthday of Charles Francis Adams.

"[I] had the inexpressible happiness of finding my dear and venerable father and mother in perfect health," JQA squibbed in the diary of that day. The family's safe return was, for his father, "one of the most uniformly happy days of my whole long life." The next day, John and John Quincy paid a visit to their Quincy cousins; Abigail and Louisa investigated tutoring prospects for sixteen-year-old George, to see how long it would be before he was ready to matriculate at Harvard. Under discussion was the unavoidable fact that the boys' parents would be residing in Washington City for half the months of the year throughout their adolescence.[67]

Before John Quincy journeyed to Washington, the Adams men attended a grand public dinner in Boston. It would be their last shared happening for a long time to come. Father and son were joined by two hundred celebrants, including many of John Quincy's old friends, a couple of governors, notable jurists, and one former secretary of war. The honoree hobnobbed with the War of 1812 naval hero Commodore Isaac Hull, attended Harvard commencement, and shook hands with his former academic colleagues. He was so sought after on the eve of his departure that he had to refuse Governor Brooks's invitation to dine together.[68]

Washington, D.C., at this time was noted less for majestic boulevards and more for its stagnant pools of muck. It had yet to be rebuilt since the British set public buildings ablaze three and a half years before. The secretary of state, meanwhile, had lost his hair, as Gilbert Stuart's portrait of him shows. He'd passed his fiftieth birthday on a "boisterous" day in the mid-Atlantic. "I have lived half a century," his diary reads simply.[69]

Taking up his post in September 1817, John Q. Adams found himself surrounded by southerners. The Virginia-born Georgian William H. Crawford was, like Adams, a former U.S. senator. He was the U.S. minister to France during the time of the Ghent negotiations and nearly swayed Republicans to promote him over Monroe at the party's caucus. This made Crawford a supremely self-confident secretary of the Treasury. John C. Calhoun was a Yale-educated South Carolinian, a compelling orator for six years in the House of Representatives prior to joining the administration as secretary of war. His apparent lack of warmth in social situations made him somewhat like Adams. Before approaching Calhoun, Monroe had offered the War Department to Henry Clay, but the hard-charging Kentuckian would abide nothing less than the office Adams now held and consequently refused to cede his powerful position as Speaker of the House. Meanwhile, the Adams-friendly Richard Rush, acting secretary of state until JQA's arrival in town, took his place as minister plenipotentiary to Great Britain.

In the early American republic, all contenders for the presidency understood that secretaries of state occupied the pole position: Jefferson, Madison, and Monroe had all performed in that distinguished role before acceding to the presidency. John Quincy Adams would prove, once again, how central, how influential, the office could be. Prior to his own elevation to Madison's cabinet, Monroe had thrice gone abroad as a diplomat: to France, in 1794, at the behest of President Washington, when his job was to reduce French fears that the United States was cozying up to Britain; his second tour was to France again, in 1803, to help finalize the Louisiana Purchase. Three years later, he traveled to England as an envoy representing Jefferson and Secretary of State Madison. His charge this time, like John Jay's a dozen years before, was to reduce Anglo-American tensions by negotiating a mutually respectful treaty.

In none of these missions was James Monroe particularly successful. To his credit, he recognized that John Quincy Adams possessed talents he did not. A brave junior officer in the Continental army, Monroe was something of an upstart when he broke into politics as a result of his association with Thomas Jefferson, who had trained him in the law. By all accounts, Monroe had a tendency to brood, and no one ever called him brilliant. An irritable partisan of the 1790s, ambitious beyond his natural endowments, he somehow evolved into a lackluster president. He was the last of his kind among the presidents: an active participant in the Revolutionary War, dressed in the old style, with a somewhat rigid manner shaped by colonial society. But having hired on an expert cabinet, he managed them expediently from an intellectual distance. Monroe, it seems, aimed to preside in the manner of Washington, to be a ceremonial leader and a mediating one, deriving policy from consensus within the executive branch. To judge by the volume of their correspondence, he also relied on advice and support from the ex-presidents Madison and Jefferson.[70]

Before he had been at his desk one month, before Congress had even convened, John Quincy received a letter from his father containing premonitions of death. The line from Luke "Now lettest thou, thy Servant depart in peace" was, as the old man was quick to say, a "hackneyed" phrase, but he felt it fit. Feelings of mortal excitation were nothing new to John Adams, but for some reason, at nearly eighty-two, a "delightful family scene" at Peacefield had moved him to take up the subject of his own mortality. He finished unburdening himself on this question and went directly to his fears for the secretary of state. "'Political Calms' cannot be of long duration in this Country." Republican governments were "Greenhouses and Hotbeds of Ambition. . . . Eternal and incalculable Competitions will grow out of them as naturally and necessarily as Grass and Corn grow in a rich deep Soil well Sunned Watered and cultivated. Storms must arise." He'd assumed the same stance with Jefferson the year before, when he insisted that competition for power produced factions and that jealous, cunning politicians attached to republics as much as to monarchies.[71]

In his reply, John Quincy offered assurance that he knew what he was up against. He was sufficiently thick-skinned and had reentered the world of politics as his father's son, fully aware of all contingencies. It shouldn't have been necessary, but he recounted the nature of his dismissal from the U.S. Senate a decade earlier: "You know that in my own person I am not without experience of the vicissitudes of public favour and displeasure—That I have once gone through the process of being discarded with signal marks of disapprobation by those whom I had most faithfully served, and of being abandoned at the critical hour, by those upon whose friendship I had the strongest claims." His alienation from the New England Federalists in 1808 pretty closely matched his father's alienation from the Hamiltonian Federalists in 1800. In another spark of commiseration, the elder penned one of his more endearing epiphanies on their oddly conjoined careers one month later: "Never were two Peas parching in the Same fire more alike."[72]

Bringing structure to the State Department, Secretary Adams was obliged from day one to sift through piles of requests for federal appointments. "Sturdy beggars for Office" presented him with unwanted homework. "I 'sit with sad civility, and read,'" he told his father, quoting from a poem by Alexander Pope. And what did he have to read? "Quires of Vouchers and Testimonials, and pathetic Narratives, with which they support their claims to office." His commiserating father upped the litany by insisting that he'd had it worse. "I Sat with Sad Civility and read, and often with more excruciating Civility heard the dolorous Representations of Misfortunes, Distresses, Wants of Wives and Children, of aged and helpless Fathers and Mothers of Idiot or mad Brothers and Sisters; of Services Sacrifices, of Wounds and Sickness of Skill Ingenuity Experience Talents Virtues and Merits and all this Some times from the most worthless of Mankind." Everyone, it seemed, expected a government handout. "When I was President my Patience was So often and So Severely tried that it was Sometimes found Wanting." John Adams acknowledged his reputation for incivility, but to him the worse "distemper" had to do with outrageous expectations and an embedded selfishness that he, once again, believed universal and "incurable."[73]

As an executive, John Quincy Adams did not have time to dwell on personnel matters. The greatest concern for U.S. foreign policy at this moment, and for the balance of the Monroe administration, were the colonies of Spain, which at the time included East Florida as well as South America. Spain's collapsing empire had created a vacuum in many places: war was under way in Venezuela, and resistance movements had arisen in Colombia, Peru, and Bolivia; meaningful actions had been taken in Ecuador, Uruguay, and Chile. By the time Adams took over at the State Department, Argentina and Paraguay were already completely independent. As he kept abreast of the news, his father voiced support for the various popular movements, writing, "Our national Sympathy with the Patriots of South America is natural and inevitable."[74]

The secretary of state naturally concurred. He and Secretary of War Calhoun were inclined to grow the military (but not to use it) and to take political advantage of Spain's weakness. Adams, in particular, kept a close eye on Europe. He would walk softly enough in South America so as not to invite an aggressive response from across the Atlantic, where one or another nation might intervene, ostensibly on Spain's behalf, and then come to blows with the United States. Adams saw dangers where his colleague Clay salivated over possible opportunities. Adams knew Lord Castlereagh well enough to hedge his bets, uncertain of the British response to a more forward U.S. posture. He could not but recall the twisted course of the French Revolution after its initial burst of hopeful energy. "We have ardent Spirits, who are for rushing into the conflict, without looking to the consequences," he wrote to his father with a sense of drama. Race and slavery added a dimension of uncertainty. "Spain on the one hand by her mode of negotiating provokes us to take a part against her, and the Colonies by the irregular and convulsive character of their measures, and by their internal elements of the exterminating war between black and white, present to us the prospect of very troublesome and dangerous associates—and still more fearful allies—Such are the ingredients of the cauldron, *which will soon be at boiling heat.*"

He was the only significant member of the administration to resist recognition of the new republics to the south. For Adams, neutrality had its benefits. Plus, privateering involving U.S. citizens was rampant in the region, which created potentially explosive conditions that needed to be controlled before naval power was extended south. Monroe agreed with his deliberative secretary of state that it made sense to focus on obtaining from Spain the section of Florida not yet under U.S. control and delimiting the entire southwest border.[75]

Over the next year and a half, Adams secured his enduring reputation as a giant among statesmen. The months did not pass easily, though. Urgent affairs of state prevented him from stealing time to help his father cope with the catastrophic loss of his partner of more than half a century. When, at the age of seventy-three, Abigail Smith Adams died, John Quincy was unable to immediately leave his post to perform his filial duties in person. And when he could finally be spared to return home, the grieving son was obliged to wrestle with yet another unanticipated family emergency—the decline of his brother Tom.

With his daily habit of walking distances, John Quincy kept remarkably healthy. Others of his intimates were less fortunate. While he was abroad in

1813, he lost his sister, Nabby, to breast cancer. She was forty-eight and living in New York as the beleaguered wife of a presumptuous, financially reckless, deeply self-centered former Revolutionary War colonel. Racked with pain, Nabby took a physically demanding stagecoach ride from New York to Quincy, just to die in her parents' arms. Five years later, it was Abigail Adams, too worn down to overcome typhoid fever. She had already outlived two of her four adult children.

Having spent six weeks in Quincy during the summer of 1818, John Quincy was back in Washington when his mother's end came on October 28. One month prior, she'd appeared perfectly healthy to him. Once he took leave of his parents, word of her rapid decline came in successive letters from his sons, now seventeen, fifteen, and eleven. "I have probably no Mother on earth!" JQA diarized. "Gracious God! Support my father in his deep and irreparable affliction!" Abigail Adams was a force of nature. "She had been fifty-four years the delight of my father's heart."[76]

To his stricken father, JQA wrote of the release that his faith told him came with life's conclusion. "My Mother, I humbly hope is a Spirit." He pressed: "Let me hear from you, my dearest father; let me hear from you soon." The father, as always, obliged. "My ever dear, ever affectionate, ever dutiful and deserving Son," he opened the letter. "The bitterness of death is past. The grim Specter So terrible to human Nature has no Sting left for me." He counted backward, then forward: "The Separation cannot be So long as twenty Separations heretofore. The Pangs and Anguish have not been So great as when you and I embarked for France in 1778." John Adams planned to slip away before too much longer, joining his wife in death. He underestimated his own endurance.[77]

John Quincy's one remaining brother was not in a position to care for their father. A good companion at key moments in his own life, Tom was a fair, but not a particularly accomplished, attorney. Now forty-six and a father of six, he had proved himself a less than dependable earner. Amid his financial descent, he drank—not to the extent of his late brother, Charles, but to an unhealthy degree nonetheless. He became a drain on the family when he was most needed. As John Adams approached the final decade of life, eyesight fast disappearing, his remaining hopes were pinned on one extraordinary son.[78]

John Adams exchanged sentiments with his comrades in arms. He reconnected with the chronically ailing John Jay as each coaxed the other to get out and about. "I too am feeble and confined to the house the greater part of the winter," Adams said, "but I hope to crawl out like a turtle in spring." And to Jefferson: "If the Secretary of State can give satisfaction to his fellow citizens in his new Office it will be a Source of consolation to me while I live: though it is not probable that I shall long be a Witness of his good Success or ill Success." He'd always assumed it would be Abigail who buried him, not the other way around. But even now, as a widower, his words of foreboding could not speed up the dying process.[79]

Ill Intent

JQA's first full year at State had been especially fraught. In spring, Major General Andrew Jackson conducted an illegal invasion of Spanish Florida. Jackson interpreted his orders from the administration to protect Georgians from cross-border incursions by Seminole Indians flexibly. He seized the Gulf town of Pensacola and marched east, intent on reducing any site where Indian collaborators might be living. Secretary of War Calhoun had instructed him to stop short of provoking a war with Spain. But the incendiary general—Napoleon of the backwoods, someone dubbed him—did not stop at humiliating the toothless Spanish. He went so far as to execute two British subjects he believed to be in league with the Seminoles. Jackson viewed himself as an avenger, boasting to his wife, "I have destroyed the babylon of the south, the hot bed of Indian war & depradations of our frontier." He was not one to be overly concerned that he might create an international incident and embarrass the administration.

After the facts were known, President Monroe was of two minds in considering what the government's posture should be. Jackson was a scene stealer whose biography featured both heroics and histrionics. Why should he be credited? Why should he not be dismissed? Adams stood alone among members of the cabinet in protecting Jackson from becoming a casualty when Congress met to grill him. During hearings that lasted weeks, Henry Clay warned against the combination of ambition and intemperance exhibited by Jackson, and he decried "military despotism."

Ultimately, Monroe listened most closely to Adams, who insisted that

Spain's inability to monitor Florida affairs and restrain the Indians had made action necessary. The president was less inclined than Secretary Adams to accept the degree of violence practiced by Jackson as a fair application of administration policy, but he decided against punishment. He rationalized in a letter to his mentor Jefferson that too strong a censure of Jackson would have "convulsed" those parts of the country where the Tennessean's exploits were most prized.[80]

In early 1819, Spain ceded Florida to the United States in the Adams-Onís Treaty (also known as the Transcontinental Treaty). It drew a long boundary line demarcating the territories of the United States and Mexico, at least for the time being. Over the course of several months, Adams strong-armed the Spanish minister, Don Luis de Onís, into accepting American terms. In fact, before Adams's departure from England, Castlereagh had already given him a preview of Spain's willingness to satisfy American demands in return for a nonintervention stance regarding South American insurgencies. Castlereagh had said that Florida could be had easily if the United States accepted the Mississippi River as the western end of its reach. Adams was keenly aware that Britain wanted to keep its options open in North America. This explains what predisposed him to excuse Jackson's questionable (and possibly unconstitutional) moves, while many others in Washington City openly questioned Jackson's judgment and feared his zealotry.

A few naysayers later held that Adams could have secured all of Texas, avoiding future fighting with Mexico. Yet history accepts his move as sagacious: he pressed a good bargain by establishing a line of control all the way to the Pacific. Spain now recognized American authority across the Louisiana Territory, north of Texas. The Adams-Onís Treaty favored an expansive Union.[81]

Until 1819, the issue that would eventually tear apart the Union—slavery—still lay dormant. In that momentous year, Missouri applied for statehood as a slaveholding state, and a battle raged in Congress as to whether the federal government could make statehood conditional on the timely disappearance of slavery there. As secretary of state, Adams was not directly involved in the national debate, but it stirred him to think more about the persistence of a despised institution. Early in 1820, he wrote, "The Missouri question thrills in every Southern nerve. It is yet in a state of chaos in my mind." He spoke with Secretary of War Calhoun, his esteemed colleague from South Carolina, who could describe the features of race enslavement from firsthand knowledge. To Adams's utter horror, the intellectually supple Calhoun defended the practice of confining blacks to "menial" activities as an effective (if artificial) means of lifting ordinary white men above those whose laboring condition was bleakest. "What can be more false and heartless," Adams logged in his diary, "than this doctrine which makes the first and holiest rights of humanity to depend upon the color of the skin?" If no political solution sprang from the epiphany, the sentiment was nonetheless manifest and the logic entirely plain. Race prejudices were almost universal in America, but a slave state could maintain itself only by diabolical lies. Slavery was an inheritance and also a pathology.[82]

At the time, the United States comprised twenty-two states, eleven free, eleven slave. Missouri would be the first state formed from the Louisiana Territory. Although Speaker Clay argued noisily against the restraint of Monroe and Adams in other policy arenas, he proved himself a conciliator with respect to the Missouri crisis. When he forged a compromise over slavery's extension west, Missouri entered the Union as a slave state, Maine (formerly part of Massachusetts) as a free state, thus maintaining a numerical balance between slave and free states.

The compromise appeared to most observers to give a slight edge to slaveholders. Adams, without claiming the power of prophecy, recorded in tremulous tones, "If slavery be the destined sword of the hand of the destroying angel which is to sever the ties of this Union, the same sword will cut in sunder the bonds of slavery itself." Supposing that a "calamitous" civil war would be required to defeat slavery, he took a dramatic breath and proclaimed, "As God shall judge me, I dare not say that it is not to be desired."[83]

At this point, two slave state figures were in the ascendant. Secretary of the Treasury Crawford appeared to Adams as the probable front-runner in the bid to succeed Monroe as president. But Speaker Clay was also in the mix, and it was he who bothered Adams more. "Clay's conduct has always been hostile to me," he observed. "From the time of the Ghent negotiation I have been in the way of his ambition." The Kentuckian supported anti-administration candidates in his home state and made it his business to paint Adams as a foe of western interests—"working like a mole to undermine me."

And yet, in the prideful manner of his father, JQA told an inquiring member of Congress from upstate New York, "I had never been unfriendly to him." Like his father, he saw himself as a consistently well-meaning participant in public transactions and at the same time a victim of others' machinations. Like his father, he could not imagine having caused offense or fed gossip. While his temper was at times volatile, he had never, to his mind, done anything to warrant the deviousness of Clay.[84]

But how honest was Adams being with himself? Did he really deny his own cunning? He wanted to advance his political reputation no less than Clay. He wished it known that no other American had sat across from leading representatives of foreign nations as much as he had or in as many distant locations. He did his best to put on paper every bit of proof of his hard work, wisdom, and thoroughness. Those he counted as friends were meant to judge him on his human virtues. He did not know how to be any more expansive, gay, or convivial, to reach out, to attract. Indeed, he was not Clay, who embodied all of those adjectives and who was featured in countless tales of magnificent posturing, which made him striking as a politician. John Quincy Adams did not know how to compete with such a formidable personality.

One of JQA's public performances did stand out, however. On the Fourth of July 1821, in his role as secretary of state, he delivered a thrilling and memorable oration. It served as a reminder of the moment when his presidential father became suddenly popular for standing up to the arrogance of a French regime long since overthrown.

To be an American in 1821 was to feel liberated from lingering questions about national endurance. The United States was no longer being "degraded by a rankling resentment," as JQA recognized, having been himself instrumental in raising America's reputation after two wars with Great Britain. In uplifting strains, he promoted America's rank among the nations of the world. He testified that the first generation, now receding from view, had bequeathed to its children a stable society. "The cause of independence is no longer upon trial," he celebrated. All that the growing country required was a reinfusion of positive energy from its rising youth.

The original of the Declaration of Independence was kept at the State Department. It was his to hold, his to read from ceremonially. The text did not resonate with hostility, he said. No longer was the Fourth of July an occasion on which to recall the separation that had occurred. America was a nation apart. It was on a proud trajectory, civilizing its wildernesses. What made it special was an "inventive genius" that good soil supported. "Her glory is not *dominion,* but *liberty,*" he professed of the personified America. "Her march is the march of the mind." John Q. Adams's America would advance the cause of peace through unconventional measures of strength; to wit, an expansive state need not be a warring state. His was a confident vision, foregrounding what would become the crux of his nationalist program as president. It defined national purposes in a national language, something even the protectors of states' rights were not resistant to on this, the forty-fifth Fourth of July.[85]

The next year, turning fifty-five on July 11, 1822, JQA recorded that "the five most laborious" years he had known were those that commenced on his attaining the mid-century mark. His job placed many demands on him. Of the arduous events occurring since his return from Europe in 1817, "the severest" was still the passing of his mother. Everything else that preyed on his mind was a buildup to the long-anticipated election of 1824, when the presidency would pass from the hands of a Virginian for the first time since John Adams left Washington in 1801. The possibility of his winning the presidency was never far from his thoughts. Nor did he disguise it very well in his dealings with officials of the government. He pestered Monroe in cabinet meetings, most plainly during the spring of 1822, as he took up a labored defense of his résumé that resulted in a book of personal writings, which he compiled without help and sent to his father.

The manuscripts in question related to the negotiations at Ghent and Adams's compulsion to answer charges leveled at him by one of the former commissioners there. Jonathan Russell was a Massachusetts man who had lately won a seat in Congress. He favored Henry Clay's presidential ambitions. At a critical juncture in the negotiations, according to Russell, he and Clay had momentously opposed Adams, Gallatin, and the late Bayard, who were inclined to sell out the West by allowing Britain free navigation of the Mississippi. Adams's singular obsession with the fisheries issue was (allegedly) part and parcel of this rude division arising within the American delegation. The point was that Adams had promoted the New England economy over the national interest.

Adams was thoroughly convinced that Russell knew otherwise. His "intriguing and caballing" were designed to aid Clay and stop Adams from becoming president. Adams could have let a newspaper columnist take up his case but chose instead to compile documents—a hefty counterweight to the thin file his accuser had assembled.

Russell's ammunition stemmed from a single communiqué he had written from Paris at the end of 1814, which he did not discuss or share with Adams. Pointedly, though, it was addressed to the then–secretary of state, Monroe. JQA noted in his diary that Russell's motive at the time must have been to impress a Virginian who worked for another Virginian (President Madison), because he knew how valuable the Mississippi was in the strategic calculus of westward-gazing southerners. The junior negotiator wished to score points with Madison and Monroe, "to recommend himself . . . and to give me a secret stab." Reviving the highly prejudiced letter eight years later was obviously meant "to decry my chances of popular favour in the Western Country." Adams suspected Clay was behind Russell's action.

Secretary of State Adams—candidate Adams—went immediately on the warpath. When he met up with Russell in Washington, the new congressman earnestly denied ill intent, and Adams refused to believe him. He minced no words, announcing to Russell, there and then, "Of private and individual intercourse, the less there is between us from this time forward the more agreeable it will be to me." In the newspaper skirmish that ensued, competing interpretations of Ghent were offered. Adams apprised his father that it was not only "the defence of my own character" that commanded him to go public but also a desire that posterity should have reliable "elucidations of the real character" of the transactions at Ghent. If Russell was no more than Clay's cipher in advance of a presidential campaign, the compulsion felt by John Quincy to tell his story borrowed its emotional character from the saga of John Adams versus Benjamin Franklin in Paris.

Even after he made his case in the press (in multiple installments), Adams could not let go. He got his hands on newspapers from Kentucky, looking everywhere for Clay's fingerprints in the commentaries he took in. He repeated the worst of what he read to his patient wife: "It says *if the Secretary* [of State] *were President* and the British were to claim the navigation of the Mississippi to-morrow, he would be obliged to grant the claim." While off visiting in Philadelphia, and in consultation with supportive friends, Louisa urged restraint upon him. She even expressed pity for her husband's hapless accuser: "Your best friends are anxious that you should . . . take as little notice of him as he merits." To persist, she said, "would look like torturing a poor reptile, already crushed beyond recovery." A friendly Massachusetts newspaper recognized Russell's claims for what they were: "a shaft aimed at the popularity of Mr. Adams," constituting tabloid nonsense.

Adams eventually listened to his wife and his political allies. He reassured her that he would publish no more on the subject, but he could not sign off his letter without licking his chops and declaring once again that Russell had brought his misfortunes upon himself. After a single term in the House, Jonathan Russell went back to a life in obscurity, whereas John Quincy Adams became president.

All of his friends felt he had turned up the heat a bit too much and had been almost predatory in his takedown of Russell. Not so his father. John Adams would not disparage his son. "You have been laid under the necessity of doing all that you have done in self defence," he wrote, "against an attack as unforeseen as it was unnecessary and you have defended yourself with great ability and I think with sufficient moderation."[86]

And why not? Like his father before him, John Quincy Adams had taken to a newspaper to outline the extent of his positive activities in negotiations that brought an American war with England to a close. The only difference was that the father waited until a decade after his presidency ended to publish in the *Boston Patriot* and the son acted swiftly in order to preserve his chance of becoming president. He relied on the most influential Washington, D.C., newspaper, the *National Intelligencer,* to distribute his rejoinder to Russell, convinced he had to set the record straight if there was hope of his becoming the second president Adams.

TWELVE

SIXTH PRESIDENT

The multitude of my thoughts and the intensity of my feelings are too much for a mind like mine in its ninetieth year—May the blessing of God Almighty continue to protect you to the end of your life as it has heretofore protected you in so remarkable a manner from your cradle.

—JOHN ADAMS TO JOHN QUINCY ADAMS, *February 18, 1825*

My father had nearly closed the ninety-first year of his life A life illustrious in the Annals of his Country and of the World. He had served to great and useful purpose his nation, his Age, and his God. He is gone. . . . The time, the manner, the coincidence with the decease of Jefferson are visible and palpable marks of divine favour.

—DIARY OF JOHN QUINCY ADAMS, *July 9, 1826*

John Adams had the good fortune to live long. He held on to witness, in his waning days, the hopeful beginnings of his son's presidential administration. No other president has departed this world under such circumstances. A story passed down to the next century maintained that a courier from points south arrived in Quincy after midnight, bearing the dramatic news of John Quincy Adams's election. Roused from slumber, the former president dressed himself and sank into his easy chair in order to receive the all-important message. Hearing the intelligence that his son was elected, crusty John Adams, "overwhelmingly anxious" about the fate of the son, "cried like a child."[1]

The old man harbored no illusions about political competition. The infighting his generation knew had carried over into the next. Therefore, he no doubt took solace in one extraordinary result of the election of 1824 that no one could have predicted: the reconciliation between his son and JQA's rival Henry Clay, who together formed a team that set U.S. foreign policy on a confident course. As the presidential campaign got under way, the likelihood of an Adams-Clay axis emerging appeared no greater than for the first president Adams to have found a way in 1800 to reconcile with the haughty Hamilton or the disagreeable Pickering. On this basis, then, John Quincy did better. Yet for all his efforts to reconcile contending forces, the sixth president experienced a single term in office no more successful than his father's.

ADAMS BALL

More than two decades had elapsed since his father lost reelection, and yet the second Adams did not know how to organize a campaign for president any better than John Adams had in 1796 (when he won) or 1800 (when he lost). Relationships with select newspaper editors bore fruit, but he was not skilled in, nor inclined to practice, the once objectionable, and now advancing, art of campaigning for office.

By dint of his service as Monroe's secretary of state for two terms, many assumed that Adams held the inside track in 1824. The competition, however, was stiff. Until 1823, when the very active and personally popular Georgian William H. Crawford suffered a paralytic stroke and temporarily lost the use of his voice, the Treasury secretary was seen by many as Adams's chief rival. Also until 1823, in refusing President Monroe's appointment to a foreign mission and taking a seat in the U.S. Senate instead, no one saw General Andrew Jackson, a successful racehorse owner, coming on strong from the outside.[2]

Adams probably lacked the ability to appear coy under any circumstances, but his aggressiveness during the unequal contest with Jonathan Russell in 1822 might have been the moment when he truly made his intentions clear. What he regarded as a matter of preserving his honor as a patriot was most likely read as the thin-skinned reaction of a man looking for public attention for reasons that could easily be inferred. Directly after putting the Ghent documents into a book and sending them to his father, he told his wife all that was on his mind.

The gist of his confession was this: he could not change even if he wanted to. There were well-wishers who had been good enough to inform him that unless he mended his manners, unless he came across as less of a bulldog and more a model of grace and affability, he would never be president. "Well, and what then?" he pursued the internal argument. "There will be candidates enough for the Presidency without me—and if my delicacy is not suited to the time, there are Candidates enough who have no such delicacy. It suits my temper to be thus delicate—do they call it aristocratic hauteur, and learned arrogance? Why so be it."

He could acknowledge his touchiness. He was aware that some in politics found him fussy and fastidious. He knew all too well that his mood occasionally turned sour. The one thing that consumed him was: maintaining dignity. In this, he would not bend.

He took a dark turn. To Louisa: "You think I am panting to be President, when I am much more inclined to envy Castlereagh the relief he has found from a situation too much like mine." The formidable Lord Castlereagh had recently taken his own life by cutting his throat. "I implore the mercy of God that I may be never so deserted of him as to seek relief in the same manner—I have reliance upon God, and therefore while possessed of my Reason, I shall never cut the thread of my own life."

With this, he resumed his familiar stance as an Adams: the unflagging patriot, the selfless servant, the honest soul who could not help but believe he deserved it all. "If I should tell you that I *dread* infinitely more than I *wish* to be President, you would not believe me [emphasis added]—But suppose it for a moment to be true—How could you advise me to act? Will you say it is very easy? Decline publicly to be a Candidate? No. That would be political suicide. It would be to distrust myself and my Country."

Yes, it would be political suicide; the lethal metaphor was intense because of Castlereagh. But what did it mean to trust his country? For JQA, it was to bank on the electorate's recognition that he possessed the right credentials (more than superficially) to earn the presidency. He wished to be the consensus choice of informed citizens.

Though he maintained an outward neutrality, President Monroe was inclined to see Adams as his successor. Yet Adams did not know how to line up the right kinds of political friends, in and out of government, and get them to do his bidding. To Louisa at least, he spilled onto the paper everything he was thinking and explained why he judged himself the most accomplished member of the Monroe administration—including Monroe: "All that will be worth telling to Posterity hitherto has been transacted through the Department of State." JQA mentioned advantages gained with respect to Britain, France, Spain, and South America, all of which were "obtained, I might confidently say, by me."

He had shown his stiffened resolve on countless occasions, and no one could interpret this facet of his personality as well as Louisa. But as relates to his greatest ambition, one statement he made to her fourteen months earlier sums up perfectly his thought on deserving the chief magistracy of the Republic. "There is not another man in the Union," he said, "excepting the Presidents past and present, who receives or continues to receive from the people of this country indications of esteem and confidence more distinguished and flattering than I have." How he construed "the people of this country" in a way that was not reducible to the raw subjectivity, the wishful thinking, of a grasping man is less clear than the unfeigned conceit embedded in this unusual admission.[3]

There is something actually bitter and agonizing lying behind the candidate's words, when we understand that whatever favor he enjoyed came *despite* his unsociable qualities—which he readily acknowledged. For her part, Louisa reassured him of what she knew: that his "coldness" proceeded from "modesty" and that others did not know the real John Quincy Adams as she did. Again, he owned up. "I am certainly not intentionally repulsive in my manners and Deportments," he reminded her, thinking of what he had to do to become president. "But I have no powers of fascination—None of the honey which the profligate proverb says is the true fly-catcher—And be assured my dear friend, it could not be good policy for me to affect it—The attempt would make me ridiculous because it would be out of Nature." He was almost saying that he would be content if a cult of personality enveloped him, because he would not then have to persuade anyone (or himself?) of the existence of active admiration from among "the people of the country."[4]

When the purpose-filled secretary of state arrived back in Quincy on the afternoon of August 25, 1823, it had been two years since his last visit home. The presidency was not all that was on his mind. "I was deeply affected at meeting him," he wrote after the encounter with his still-alert father. "His eyesight has grown dim, and his limbs stiff and feeble. He is bowed with age, and scarcely can walk across a room without assistance." Though taken aback by the change, a wave of fondness caused John Quincy to seek out the great portraitist Gilbert Stuart, the gifted if disorganized son of a Rhode Island snuff grinder; his work was prized in Europe, and yet he was pleased to reside in the town of Boston. Stuart had taken the image of John Adams as president more than twenty years earlier, and George Washington before that. "Time has wrought so much change on his countenance," JQA reflected. "I wish to possess a likeness of him as he now is." Stuart promised to oblige him and to complete "a picture of affection, and of curiosity for future times." The former congressman and newly elected Boston mayor Josiah Quincy, an Adams relative, later commented, "Stuart caught a glimpse of the living spirit shining through the feeble and decrepit body."[5]

On September 9, 1823, father and son learned of the existence of a pamphlet reprinting letters that passed between John Adams and a distant relative named William Cunningham in the early years of the century. The letters had been coaxed out of an embittered Adams prior to his reconciliation with Jefferson. They upbraided the third president for his "mean thirst of popularity" and served no present purpose other than to make the ex-president John Adams look petty. Adams had prevailed on the man to keep the letters from public view and gave them no further thought. But when Cunningham picked up a gun and took his own life in May 1823, the letters passed to his less than scrupulous son, a Jackson partisan, who decided to release them so as to bring unwanted attention to the elder Adams and somehow sink the presidential hopes of the younger—"to blast my reputation and my father's," JQA swore to himself. Still fixated on Jonathan Russell, he wrongly presumed Russell to be connected to the Cunningham letters. Whoever the instigator was, and whatever the intent, he proclaimed, "Here I am, sound mind and limb, neither better nor worse for the Cunningham correspondence." The second and third presidents were oddly gratified by this rude intrusion into their tranquil times. "Hideous phantoms" such as those raised by Cunningham could not mar their restored friendship, an animated Jefferson wrote to Adams. "How generous! How noble! How magnanimous!" Adams reacted to Jefferson's fine sentiment.[6]

And yet this same Jefferson was all along quietly supporting the candidacy of William Crawford. He referred to the Adamses, father and son, less charitably some months earlier, as part of a long letter to the South Carolinian William Johnson, a sitting justice of the U.S. Supreme Court: "Mr. Adams's papers too and his biography will descend of course to his son, whose pen, you know, is pointed, and his prejudices not in our favor." Without doubt, Jefferson wrote differently to northern and southern friends. He could not but see the younger Adams as the candidate of the northern states, and despite the sober statesman's long years honorably advancing the Madison-Monroe agenda, JQA would always be, for Jefferson, insufficiently weaned off the Federalist mother's milk.[7]

The Crawfordites of Georgia were not to be duped by any of the professions of John Q. Adams. The *Georgia Journal* explained their native son's support of the Quasi-war in 1799 as a patriotic impulse and not, for a minute, evidence of a Federalist bent. Nor was the second president to be hailed for guarding against the French, for he had merely carried on the policies of George Washington in standing up for the national honor. The biggest problem for Georgians in differentiating their man from either Adams was the fact that the younger Adams's candidacy was being abetted by his former cabinet colleague John C. Calhoun of neighboring South Carolina. Nothing could justify Calhoun's "protruding such a man as J. Q. Adams on the stage."

In the Crawfordite construction of the contest that impended, the second Adams was an untrustworthy European-bred northerner with unrepublican views. A litany of accusations were lobbed at him: "His opinion was quoted as authority in England"; he had "endeavored to introduce into this virgin republic a code of Etiquette suited only for the meridian of St. James"—the aristocratic district of London. At Ghent, he "jeopardized the West for the Fisheries," and most recently he "trammeled Missouri with restrictions to create a sectional party of whom he was to have been the chief." Adams had so long fought under the Federalist flag that he was to be found "straitway guilty of tergiversation [that is, equivocation] to obtain office." Georgia was taking no chances.[8]

Before returning to Washington that fall, the harassed secretary of state spent a quantity of time with his largely sedentary father, taking the carriage out, though it "over fatigued" the old man. Nevertheless, at the father's insistence, they visited one of their Adams kin and examined the will of a great-great-grandfather who died in 1694, and then the will of the original John Quincy, who died in 1697. They borrowed a funeral sermon preached in Braintree upon the death, in 1737, of another Quincy. "I read it this evening to my father," JQA recorded. As he reached his eighty-eighth birthday, John Adams was newly interested in where he fit into family history.[9]

Resuming official duties after a satisfying visit home, John Quincy could not help but mix with politicians who eagerly probed him about his intentions. In March 1824, Senator Ninian Edwards of Illinois was slated to travel to Mexico as a diplomat, when he met up with JQA, who somehow could not resist querying Edwards as to whom he considered most presidential. "He declared to me his conviction that it was the attack of Jonathan Russell upon me and its consequences which had brought me up as a candidate for the Presidency." Did Adams not see the flattery in Edwards's remark?[10]

His early entry into politics was being revived for the purpose of discrediting him. Publicola's identity, unknown in 1791, was exposed in 1823 for all to see; it was meant as evidence of a secret and embarrassing past knocking down republican principles. Back in 1791, readers of the series had assumed that Publicola was John Adams, then vice president. Only a few figured out that it was actually the son, then in his early twenties. Publicola was now in his late fifties and living in a very different world. Was time irrelevant? Was the French Revolution no longer studied? Who would believe that he subscribed to the same political views now as he did then?

The doubters didn't care to distinguish. How, they asked, could a so-called apostate from the Federalist Party be the fit inheritor of the Republican mantle? To some of his New England Republican neighbors, JQA's "aristocratical and monarchical opinions" were even stronger than his father's ever were. Despite service to Madison and Monroe, he had never *publicly* abandoned his former principles. In the words of one critic, "The Chief of this nation must be sought for from among those republicans, whose fidelity to the constitution, and whose love for a simple, economical republican government are undoubted."

Were they to have access to the complete record, including letters over the years to his father, wife, and brother Tom, his censurers would have had a hard time justifying the charge that JQA held "aristocratical and monarchical opinions." He considered Napoleon's reversion to hereditary titles farcical and was keenly aware of the failures inherent in a system that allowed dreadfully stupid offspring to inherit power. As in his father's case, expressing interest in studying the character of a form of government, as a political scientist, did not amount to an endorsement of same. Furthermore, again as with his father, his time abroad ultimately made him feel *more,* not less, American.

Among his New England supporters, it was a comfort just to know that the second Adams was trusted by presidents beginning with Washington, who had sent him abroad to represent the United States when he was yet in his twenties. As to Publicola, all he really did was to "respectfully" confront a popular writer in Tom Paine and to "boldly, fearlessly, and independently" defend constitutional principles.[11]

Boston's *Independent Chronicle* reported that "enemies of Mr. Adams are finding fault with his father, for having received a friendly letter from Mr. Jefferson." The nation knew of this particular letter, because it was deliberately leaked to the press by its recipient; it was Jefferson's "generous," "noble," "magnanimous" letter of the previous autumn, and it was publicized so as to show the former presidents rejecting all attempts to revive the hostile terms of a generation-old debate that would serve no purpose other than stopping JQA's political momentum.[12]

There was talk of a possible Adams-Jackson ticket, and it was not just talk. Aware of Crawford's, Clay's, and even Calhoun's efforts to advance their presidential chances, Adams conceived an uncharacteristically self-serving social event in the nation's capital. Guided by the Tennessean's modest presence on Capitol Hill, he must have been insufficiently attuned to the extent of Jackson's presidential ambition as well as the extensive planning of his well-placed publicists, when he and Louisa hosted a gala party for the new Tennessee senator on the evening of January 8, 1824, the ninth anniversary of the Battle of New Orleans.

Estimates range between seven hundred and eleven hundred persons in attendance at what was billed as a "demi-publick entertainment" at the Adamses' fine (but by no means extravagant) home. One attendee noted that the secretary of state owned a "shabby blue coach" and cared little for opulent display. In a silk dress and plumed Spanish hat, Mrs. Adams stood out among the guests, "promenading the rooms" before disappearing into the growing throng. According to reports, the gala orchestrated at her husband's behest was "as splendid an assemblage of beauty and fashion" as the nation's capital had ever seen. It was the most democratic means J. Q. Adams could come up with to advertise himself as a nationalist without promoting his candidacy obscenely.

In the perfume-rich air, beneath walls adorned with mountain laurel, a navy band played. Firsthand accounts commended Mr. Adams, though an unnatural master of ceremonies, for his "republican plainness." As a human specimen, one could not but notice that he had a head "polished like a mirror," his "eye and brow penetrating, with a slight expression of asperity." The unexciting host did not inspire more than that.

It was Jackson, of course, who stole the show. When his name was announced thirty minutes or so after festivities had begun, all turned and gazed in the direction of the smiling "Hero of the night." The general's usually sallow face wore a pleasing ruddiness, and as he made his way past a line of ladies, partiers witnessed "a fine image of Mars in the presence of Venus." Belying his reputation for brutality, he exhibited "urbanity" and "affability," according to one who became quickly caught up in the excitement. Jackson was shown to advantage: a fittingly stern leader of men, capable of chivalrous regard.[13]

"Every day brings forth a new rumour," Mrs. Adams entered in her diary in advance of what became known as the "Adams Ball." After that night, questions only multiplied. Crawford's health was problematic, and no one could accurately predict where his supporters would turn, should his condition worsen. Many newspapers, north and south, thought Adams the likely beneficiary. Louisa herself was so depleted that she absented herself from Washington in June and traveled to a spa in Pennsylvania. Her self-regulated husband, as fit as ever, habitually walked over to the Potomac, tossed his clothes, and took morning swims that might last an hour and a half. Yet his health and hardiness were never mentioned in electioneering literature.

Truth is not always visible. Or reported. Reputation can be doctored, and former glory retains its sheen. This was how Jackson held the advantage. Adams and Jackson were both born in 1767, but it was Jackson whose supporters kept alive the legend of his masculine prowess, despite his actual physical frailty in 1824. He was said to be much at ease conversing with females, yet even political admirers who marveled at his naturalness and gallantry acknowledged his frequent misuse of words and awkward pronunciation. For those less entranced with the poorly educated soldier, the obviously uncharismatic Adams warranted "the nation's honor" in view of his deep moral conviction. Would moral principle matter at the polls as much as the other's storied exploits? Of the four candidates, only Adams had refused to engage in the practice of dueling—though this distinction ultimately mattered less in 1824 than it would in the Victorian age. Adams attended a birthday dinner for the remarkable Senator Jackson in March. Newspapers from Massachusetts to Georgia were still floating the idea of an Adams-Jackson ticket in May.[14]

Pursuant to a joint resolution of Congress, the secretary of state sent his father two facsimile copies of the signed Declaration of Independence in advance of the Fourth of July 1824. The original remained in safekeeping at the State Department. Three years earlier, he had read it aloud, solemnly, before proclaiming, "A nation was born in a day." Now, in dispatching the facsimile to Quincy, he reported to his nearly blind father that the rolled-up documents he was receiving were "copies as exact as the art of engraving can present of the Instrument itself, as well as of the signatures to it." He put his own signature on the accompanying letter beneath a statement marveling that "after the lapse of near half a century, you survive to receive this tribute of reverence and gratitude from your children" (a figurative expression that happened to be true in this case), the children having become "the present fathers of the Land." Secretary of State Adams sent a facsimile of the declaration, and the exact same accompanying letter, to eighty-one-year-old Thomas Jefferson.[15]

Positive patriotic emotion could not be sustained indefinitely in an election year as combative as this one. On the final day of August 1824, before departing for Quincy, Secretary Adams thundered in his diary at the "bitterness and violence of Presidential electioneering." He believed he held the advantage and that Jackson might at some point be persuaded to withdraw from the presidential race, but he was manifestly nervous. Trying to decide how to combat newspaper slander, Adams waffled. "It does not surprize me," he wrote, "because I have seen the same species of ribaldry year after year heaped upon my father, and for a long time upon Washington." The "First of Men" was not immune, so why should he expect anything different? He could intellectualize all that confronted him in 1824, but he recognized that someone of his temperament could never be "wholly insensible" to public assaults. (Jonathan Russell understood how that played out.) "I have finally concluded to take a Month of Holiday to visit my father and dismiss Care," Adams told his diary. Politics smelled of slander, and personal politicking held no allure.[16]

Arriving in Quincy, he found his venerable father in a weakened state. John Adams could neither read nor write. Still, the son remained reasonably upbeat, attesting to a memory that had not lost its elasticity, judgment that remained sound, and a desire for talk that had not abated. After a day devoted to conversation, John Quincy concluded, "His mind is still vigorous but cannot dwell long on any one subject." Helpless in most respects, John Adams still possessed the fortitude his son had always admired in him.

While rummaging, John Quincy discovered the diary his mother kept during and after the 1784 voyage to Europe, when she reunited with husband and son after five years apart. The son's nostalgia was, as nostalgia generally is, equal parts heavyheartedness and, he observed, "pleasing . . . recollections." He walked alone in the "burying-yard" among the granite markers where his ancestors lay entombed, and he noted to himself which of those stones had been erected by his father.

Home visits were meant as a reprieve, time away from public business. John Quincy refused a public banquet in his honor at Faneuil Hall in Boston, professedly because he did not want to appear solicitous of popularity. He rationalized to himself, and suggested as well to his political friends, that if he agreed to be feted in Boston, it would be reported that he had generated artificial enthusiasm for his candidacy. Better to err on the side of caution and display the necessary humility.[17]

After only eighteen days at home, he took to the road again. Politics were unavoidable. He might not have been able to stomach campaigning, but it would have made no sense to have absented himself from Washington when the votes were being counted.

REPRESENTATIVE DEMOCRACY

His arrival in Philadelphia in early October happened to coincide with the appearance of the marquis de Lafayette, who had been touring the United States over the past year. It was the triumphal return of the most famous volunteer soldier, the last living major general to have led troops of the Continental army during the American War of Independence. In late August, the Frenchman paid his respects to John Adams at Quincy, and now, barely a month later, he had the company of John Quincy Adams over several days.

Lafayette was accompanied by his son, who, like JQA's eldest, had as first and middle names "George Washington." They attended religious services, a humane prison facility, and the Pennsylvania Hospital, where Adams studied the physiognomy of patients. He was entranced by one particular "lunatic" who seemed perfectly sane and who asked after the health of his father. More revealing of the presidential candidate's supposedly cold personality was his behavior on board the vessel that carried their party to Washington: the reputedly aristocratic Adams refused comfortable quarters and slept on a hard bed, surrounded by undistinguished travelers, in a "vast dormitory" on deck. He rejected the entreaties of George W. Lafayette to exchange places. "If there be any aristocracy in American manners," wrote Lafayette's private secretary, Auguste Levasseur, certain "great officers of the government" do not subscribe to it.[18]

At Baltimore, they all attended a lavish ceremony at Fort McHenry, scene of the dramatic defense ten years earlier, when the noted Maryland attorney Francis Scott Key, temporarily trapped on a British ship in the harbor, saw bombs bursting in air. The tattered flag from that day in 1814 was hoisted anew for the occasion. Symbolism abounded. Levasseur noted that Adams was deeply moved by the morning ceremony, which took place under a tent that Washington had used during the Revolutionary War. There, too, he saw Charles Carroll, eighty-seven, one of the three surviving signers (along with Adams and Jefferson) of the immortal declaration. Back in the nation's capital, Adams went right to business, starting with a meeting of the cabinet. On the agenda were preparations for the official welcome of "the Nation's Guest" (as General Lafayette was then popularly known) at the rebuilt President's House.[19]

As the fall election approached, Adams's diary betrays surprisingly little interest in political wrangling. As late as mid-December 1824, he claimed that the probability of his election was not "sufficient" for him to be giving serious consideration to naming the individuals who would constitute his prospective cabinet. Henry Clay had other ideas, when he engaged him in dinner conversation during the Lafayette fete. As on occasions past, Clay proved himself a formidable speaking talent, touting progress in arts and learning in America since the Revolution. Adams heard from a reliable source that "Mr. Clay was much disposed to support me, if he could at the same time be useful to himself." Something was brewing.[20]

In January 1824, the *Columbian Centinel,* a Boston newspaper, correctly predicted the three candidates who would vie for the presidency in a post-election House vote: Adams. Jackson. Crawford. In December, once the electoral votes were tallied, no candidate had won a majority. Adams stood at 84, trailing Jackson, who had 99. Crawford was a distant third, with 41, 4 more votes than Clay, who, as fourth-place finisher, was constitutionally excluded from the runoff.

Under the terms of the Twelfth Amendment, each state's delegation in the House of Representatives was accorded, collectively, one vote. Each state's determination was, therefore, to be set by the majority vote within its congressional delegation (the size of which reflected the number of electoral votes accorded to the state on the basis of its population). The candidate who received the votes of a majority of the states would become president.

Adams wished he didn't care, but he did care. He was proud. He was also resentful of those who doubted his republicanism and belittled his achievements. On January 9, 1825, Clay informed him that he would deliver to Adams the three states that he'd won, which he succeeded in doing. When the House voted on February 9, Jackson's plurality of votes did not matter. Adams was president-elect.

He walked into a minefield, willfully, it would seem, because it only took Adams a short time to place Henry Clay at the head of the State Department, a move that exasperated Jacksonians, who smelled a "corrupt bargain." Those two words would haunt the Adams administration from its first day to its last. Why JQA did what he did has preoccupied historians for ages, though perhaps the best explanation is the least complicated: an Adams did not do what was merely expedient or tamely accord with the public mood; he did what his own mind told him was in the nation's best interest. Clay understood politics as well as any man in America; he had been prepared to lead the State Department eight years before, when Monroe opted for Adams instead.[21]

The Virginian who gave the oath of office to John Quincy Adams on March 4, 1825, was John Marshall, the Federalist whom the first president Adams had appointed chief justice of the Supreme Court in the waning days of his administration. When JQA took the oath and became the sixth president, the reconstructed U.S. Capitol was topped by a brand-new, bowl-shaped, copper-covered wooden dome that Abraham Lincoln would replace with today's grander, white-painted cast-iron version. The Federal City that John and Abigail Adams had found to be a marshy wilderness in 1800 was at last a commercially viable city. The President's House, painted white, had by now received its enduring name (if only informally). The park out front was newly designated Lafayette Square, honoring the Revolutionary hero's recent visit.[22]

John Quincy Adams's White House was an imperfect structure. The president himself had put up with many far worse accommodations in his travels, but the nation's new first lady was rather displeased by the condition of the executive mansion. To her son Charles, she said it was "a matter of wonder" to her how "a Lady of so much delicacy" as Elizabeth Kortright Monroe could have inhabited so undistinguished a house, which lacked even the comforts of a "mechanic's" abode. To prove her point, she opened the place to all who wanted to see what splendor the supposedly aristocratic Adamses enjoyed. That, she presumed, would "correct the absurd and preposterous notions" the public believed about the first couple. Mrs. Adams set aside her pique long enough to bid of her third son, "Present my best love to your Grandfather."[23]

When he delivered his inaugural address, the second president Adams spoke glowingly about the founders as a collective. He recited a portion of the Constitution's preamble. He pointed to "the blessings of liberty" that Americans, "in their successive generations," were meant to enjoy, and he gave thanks to the few surviving "forefathers," his own father (unmentioned) being one. The rest of these "eminent men" were gone, having seen the American people through "a most eventful period in the annals of the world."

Returning to the intergenerational theme, the sixth president took forward strides. It was John Quincy Adams, of all people, who for the first time in a presidential inaugural address abandoned the pejorative association of political democracy with unsteadiness and unpredictability. "If there have been those who doubted whether a confederated representative democracy were a government competent to the wise and orderly management of the common concerns of a mighty nation," he pronounced, "those doubts have been dispelled."

In all, it was an oratorical performance that faithfully adhered to the Ciceronian ethos, removing the self in favor of the nation as a moral community. As he kept his father's unheralded presidency out of sight and out of mind, John Quincy Adams candidly acknowledged his disadvantage in entering office under the most intimidating kind of political circumstances. Having failed to win an outright majority of the vote the previous fall, he admitted that he was no equal of the first five chief executives: "Less possessed of your confidence in advance than any of my predecessors, I am deeply conscious of the prospect that I shall stand more and oftener in need of your indulgence." He meant it. As a compromised choice, he came close to predicting his own political fate as he implored the electorate to "discard every remnant of rancor," to yield up "the badge of party communion" in favor of selfless appreciation for the "talents and virtue" of those who prove themselves worthy of the public trust.

It was too much to hope for, but that is what inaugural addresses typically aim at: healing internal division and asking citizens to abandon the usual disposition to view politics as a zero-sum game. In his memorable inaugural address of March 4, 1801, Jefferson had sought to collapse party distinctions by optimistically proclaiming, "We have called by different names brethren of the same principle. We are all Republicans, we are all Federalists." When it came his turn, John Quincy Adams invoked the disquieting phrase he and his father had recurred to often, since the 1790s, by stating his wish for an end to "the collisions of party spirit" through a renunciation of partisan entanglements, party fusion—that is, pressure to conform.

The political ideals of the American republic strain to harmonize with political reality. The inauguration of a new president is the one ceremonial instant when they almost do. Privately, Jefferson seemed convinced that the opposition would gradually melt away, though by 1825, after sixteen years of Madison and Monroe, he succumbed to the vestigial fear of a resurgent Federalist bogeyman. John Q. Adams, coming into the presidency, reckoned that "geographical division" was the cause of long-term national political dysfunction—indeed, its most dangerous manifestation. He used the occasion of his inaugural to warn against complacency in allowing dormant North-South competition to reawaken, rightly understanding that it would harden party antagonisms. He appealed for "magnanimity," for munificence, which was like praying for a miracle.[24]

In his address, the second president Adams made no direct reference to his father, lest it provoke dynastic associations from nasty newspapermen.

But on that very day, an orator in Braintree felt no such compunction. He pronounced the election of the son of John Adams to be an implicit acknowledgment that the second president had been terribly mistreated by a brash, unformed republic. America in 1800 was yet a "self-conceited, flaunting youth," prone to acts of "folly." It had maligned its necessarily "firm father," the "venerable Sage of Quincy," whose "efforts for the Public Good were ungenerously requited." His son's rise was proof that a more mature America would get everything right: "The faithful page of history will carry his fame, as a wise and efficient statesman, down to remote posterity—and with it, will convey the unequivocal expression of a nation's regrets for their unkindness, in the fact that she has elevated to the same post of labor and honor, the eldest son, and noble emulator of the father's worth."[25]

Overrun with letters requesting lucrative federal appointments, the new president took his time. Nor did he show his hand. As a result, even some friendly representatives expressed concern that the second president Adams would revert to the effete Federalism of the first. The Connecticut congressman (soon-to-be senator) Samuel A. Foote, a supporter of Adams, wrote to verify that the president was not going to give federal patronage to any unreconstructed Federalists who opposed the Madison administration during the War of 1812. Nutmeg State Republicans were concerned because old-line Federalists somehow construed the inaugural address to work in their favor. The letter from Foote was a reminder to JQA that the last bastion of tory Federalism should be allowed to die and disappear. Their betrayal of the nation while at war was, Foote underscored, "of too recent date to be forgotten." Fears such as these proved unwarranted.[26]

On December 6, 1825, in his first annual message, President Adams announced an ambitious prescription for nation building—structural and cultural improvement all at once. While his program proved much too forward thinking for his historical moment, it constituted the "big idea" for which his presidential administration is remembered. His cabinet was made up of disparate elements, men who did not feel an automatic allegiance to the man they served. Three were left over from Monroe's administration, another a Crawfordite. Nor did the Adams cabinet hold out much hope that the new president's program would be realized. They were sensitive to the political price Adams would pay for being perceived as an illegitimate president—with feet of clay, or "our Clay president," as the critics sneered.[27]

Despite past arguments and stark differences in their personalities, Adams and Clay collaborated well. Theirs was an arrangement oddly reminiscent of Jefferson's partnership with his trusted secretary of state, Madison. But neither his judiciousness nor his improved relationship with Clay would help Adams implement any of the plans laid out in the annual message. Congress took in its report on the state of commercial relations with Europe, sales of public lands, and management of the public debt, but it rejected the rhetorical pageant that no one but John Quincy Adams was ready to stage: federally sponsored roads, canals, and other advanced engineering projects; a national university more or less on the model of the great European temples of learning; an astronomical observatory (the Old World boasted 130 such "lighthouses of the sky" and America not one); and broader encouragement of invention. The sixth president's unwanted initiatives were airily described in the press. The Enlightenment ideal of human improvement fell flat as a political motivator, either because the ideal itself had lost the magic it had held in the prior century or because John Q. Adams was the wrong symbol for progress or both.

Whatever the members of the Nineteenth Congress might have thought of him, the second president Adams articulated an agenda in his first annual message that befitted a nationalist. He understood that a purposeful improvement plan could not emerge piecemeal from the individual states. It would have to be undertaken by an enlarged, and highly competent, federal government. He saw no reason why the United States should accept as given the position of inferiority still accorded it by Europeans, and he said it boldly: "While foreign nations less blessed . . . are advancing with gigantic strides in the career of public improvement, were we to slumber in indolence or fold up our arms and proclaim to the world that we are palsied by the will of our constituents, would it not be to cast away the bounties of Providence and doom ourselves to perpetual inferiority?"[28]

Coincident-Decease

It was the moment of one generation's final fade-out and its successor's self-realization. But was it too soon for an accounting of the Adams legacy?

As his father entered the presidency and his parents moved into the

White House, George Washington Adams, the eldest child of John Quincy and Louisa Catherine, was twenty-four years old (the age his father was when he entered the lists as Publicola). He and his younger brother John had been shuttled from one place to another throughout their youth, a point George underscored in an autobiographical sketch he worked on during the topsy-turvy months of presidential transition.

"Few men have been blessed with a youth or childhood possessing advantages like mine," he opened the sketch. Advantages, yes, but a feeling of strangeness, too. He was born in Prussia and brought back to Quincy as an infant, where he spent most of his formative years away from his parents. "Could my youth have been passed with them," he says somewhat ominously, "its present results would have been probably very different but it was not to be; my Fathers public employments imposed duties which compelled him to be often absent from his children and left him, when with them little time for their instruction."

George was Harvard educated (class of 1821), less self-demanding in his studies than either his distant father or his nearby grandfather—though aptitude was not at issue with him. His penmanship was beautiful and balanced, suggesting, at the very least, an attention to appearance. In recalling his youth, he said he understood why his parents acted as they had; it was by necessity that he grew up without them. He and brother John had been left with their "venerable relations," the Cranches, who died within days of each other in 1811. "My thoughts were under the exclusive sway of my imagination," George said of this time in his life. Sent next to Atkinson, New Hampshire, to live with a great-aunt, he indulged "a singular taste for that mental excitement which calls forth the painful passions and shakes the inmost feelings for narrations of crime, tales of terrible depravity, mysterious horror; and supernatural powers." His occult taste was offset, he notes, by a "gayer taste for wit and satire," which seems to put him solidly in the Adams camp.

He was not bitter. He intellectualized the course of human events. It was not his father's fault that war with England was declared in 1812, keeping the family apart that much longer: "Political events affect the fortunes of individuals." Nevertheless, the fact remained that George Adams reached the age of consent without parents. He was keenly conscious of what it meant. On the plus side, he saw a good deal of the family patriarch, his doting grandfather;

it was through the retired president's influence and guidance that he came to care about his/their history.[29]

On the Fourth of July 1824, George's holiday oratory found its way into print. His mother wrote to his father in advance of the event, "I hope George will acquit himself handsomely on the fourth as I am sure it would gratify his Grand father very much." It must have, because the *Independent Chronicle and Boston Patriot* confirmed that "the oration at Quincy, by Mr. George W. Adams, was eloquent and interesting. There is something in the associations connected with Quincy, well calculated to awaken the eloquence of the orator."

With his grandfather in attendance, George demonstrated a facility for language hardly less distinguished than that of John and John Quincy Adams before him. Humbly, he resisted any urge to place his immediate family at the center of discourse, according that honor to another son of Quincy, the late John Hancock. In George's rendering, it was the patriot's rejection of moneyed privilege that most distinguished him. Hancock owned "every prospect of pre-eminence under the ancient aristocratic system." Yet he turned from the "glittering bait which courted him" to do something for others. "Liberal, charitable, generous, his fortune was his country's." In his closing, offering up praise to the Revolutionary generation, George reached the obligatory crescendo: "The majority of that vigorous race have gone to brighter climes; a few, alas, how few! remain to greet this morning." One can only imagine how John Adams received these lines. "Blessed by the sight of national prosperity beyond their fondest hopes.—the rest we trust are joined again with Washington, above the reach of time."[30]

It was the respected *Columbian Centinel,* continuously in print since 1790, that gave the most emotional picture of George Adams's entry into public life: "The presence of the HON. JOHN ADAMS, the venerable grandfather of the Orator, excited feelings that pressed upon the heart, and awakened sensations in the soul much easier conceived than expressed." And to top it off: "It seems to be the universal prayer, that he might live to see another citizen of Quincy the first magistrate of this great nation."[31]

Those prayers were, of course, answered the following winter. Like John Quincy before him—when his father was vice president—George Washington Adams remained in Boston in the year 1825, hoping to get his law firm on firmer footing. He continued to enjoy the company of the first president Adams.

In August 1825, according to George's diary, the son and namesake of Boston's mayor Josiah Quincy, who was the same age as George, came to him with a discovery. Josiah had retrieved a manuscript in what he recognized as John Adams's handwriting. He and George "ran up" to the ninety-year-old's room and asked about it. "It proved to be his minutes of the trial of Captain Preston for the Boston Massacre," George wrote excitedly, "no account of which has ever been published." In 1770, John Adams had been co-counsel with an earlier Josiah Quincy in the most famous of pre-Revolutionary murder trials, standing for American guts and moral resolve by defending those who had fired on fired-up colonial youths, with deadly results.

George and Josiah knew precisely where they stood in a favored genealogy. A rising generation of biologically connected families with Revolutionary surnames lived surrounded by symbols. Their surnames were place-names. Papers in their possession went back to the country's earliest settlements. Their access to a gloried past was unique, which was why George was predisposed to set down in his diary any speck of wisdom given to him, spontaneously, by his grandfather. On the subject of "ambition as an instrument by which greatness is acquired," John Adams was still quotable. "There can be no great mind without intrepidity and humanity," he exhorted George.[32]

As the year of national jubilee approached—the fiftieth anniversary of American independence—the national mood took a sentimental turn. On June 17, 1825, on the fiftieth anniversary of the battle, the cornerstone of the Bunker Hill Monument was laid by the marquis de Lafayette in a lavish ceremony. This was capped off by a momentous address from a giant of the rising generation, Congressman Daniel Webster. Born in 1782, as John Adams was in Paris negotiating an end to the Revolutionary War, Webster was nourished on stories of Revolutionary exploits. At the Bunker Hill event, he faced an audience in the thousands, at the front of which sat "the Nation's Guest" himself, alongside a few dozen survivors of that dramatic battle. Animated by the scene, Webster told his hearers, "We need not strive to repress the emotions which agitate us here." Three generations occupied the same space.[33]

History was not lost on George W. Adams, because it enveloped him.

His father the president wrote as often as he could. When able to leave Washington, and repair to Quincy, he regularly met up with George, who lived and worked in Boston. Aboard a steamboat outside New York, headed back to Washington, the president penned a sonnet to the comet he and George had observed together and sent it to his son. Their personal relationship noticeably deepened that year.[34]

The days were long for President Adams. He was too busy to devote more than a few minutes each day to his diary; it became a short digest barren of personal reflections. As 1826 opened, his son George served as chief liaison between the current and the former presidents. John Adams's thoughts were on ironing out financial affairs; John Quincy leaned on George to fathom the patriarch's intention for disposing of some "woodland" that he wished JQA to purchase. Property matters were complex.[35]

On the morning of July 4, 1826, the jubilee of independence, George was in Boston as his grandfather conversed with the Reverend Peter Whitney, ordained in 1800, who was set to give a Fourth of July oration in Quincy later in the day. Asked to contribute a "sentiment," the second president replied, "Independence forever." George came out to Quincy, and reached his grandfather's bedside that afternoon, but only after John Adams could no longer speak and was barely alive.

His younger brother Charles, aged eighteen, did not yet know about any of this. He was in Manhattan on the day of jubilee, accepting the compliments presented to his family from celebrants at a public dinner he attended. He would subsequently realize that at "about the time" John Adams and Thomas Jefferson "had ceased to breathe," he was in the company of people who were drinking to their health.[36]

The deaths of Adams and Jefferson took place five hours apart on this fiftieth Fourth. The perfectly timed exit of the second and third presidents—partners in the heady days of June and July 1776 and friends for longer than they were foes—was a chance event that would have struck any generation as mathematically near impossible. But for the founders' filial offspring, keen on commemoration, the deaths of Adams and Jefferson on this already exceptional Fourth of July went beyond mathematics. The country had been given a sign.

Owing to the nature of communications in 1826, the so-called double apotheosis sank in gradually. In the North, citizens got word of Adams's death first; in the South, it was Jefferson's. JQA learned of Jefferson's death on the sixth. He made note in his diary of a "striking coincidence," as it regarded Jefferson alone. He meditated on the appropriate form of official mourning: the only precedent was Washington's death in 1799. For the moment, he did not think a presidential proclamation was called for: Jefferson's passing "should be noticed" as part of the annual presidential message in the last month of 1826.

As yet unaware of his father's fate, the president knew from a letter his brother Tom had sent mid-June that the ninety-year-old was fast fading. Hoping for one final interview, he set out from Washington a few days after the jubilee; he got only as far as Baltimore when he found out that he was already too late. After he reached Quincy, he noted in his diary the unimaginable odds of the two political warriors ending their lives on that particular day; it was "unparalleled in the history of the world," he wrote.[37]

As the days went by, wishing Louisa were with him, he sat in his father's house and answered letters of condolence. To New York's mayor, Philip Hone, he shared his correspondent's sense of marvel at the two presidents' "co-incident decease." To his secretary of war, the Virginian James Barbour, he was mindful of the possibility of a preternatural communication, or that, perhaps, a higher calling was shared by two minds separated by hundreds of miles on the fiftieth Fourth. "It is among the remarkable incidents of that day," wrote the presidential son, "that it retained its power over the minds of both the men, to whom it was so momentous, and occupied the last of their thoughts upon Earth. We can not perhaps without presumption, attribute special incidents of mortality to special purposes of Providence."

The "co-incident decease" meant something more to John Quincy Adams. Henceforth, the national holiday would be bittersweet. "The house of feasting must be also the house of mourning," he said. Independence Day was at once a day of civic education and one of festive activity. Others would register its unexpected new lesson, but not on the same order as the surviving president Adams. The double apotheosis repaired whatever residual discomfort remained in his mind over what Jefferson had said and done in the past. In the national consciousness, memories of Adams and Jefferson were indissolubly connected. "Those whom God has joined in death," he told Secretary Barbour, "let no man put asunder."[38]

Eldest Sons

For a time after his father's death, President Adams remained preoccupied with matters of personal import. He promptly requested of Gilbert Stuart a second portrait of his father, copied from the canvas of a couple of years earlier, so that he could hang one in Quincy and one in Washington. He brought George with him to probate court for the reading of his father's will. They met up with George's brother John, and together listened to the resounding eulogy given at Faneuil Hall by Congressman Daniel Webster, one of the many joint eulogies on the deceased presidents that the current president would be obliged to sit through during his time in the Boston area. Not all would please him so much as this one.

"This is an unaccustomed spectacle," the seasoned orator began. "The tears which flow, and the honors that are paid, when the Founders of the republic die, give hope that the republic itself may be immortal." As he proceeded, it became clear that Webster was framing history so as to give equal weight to Adams and Jefferson, notwithstanding the Boston venue: "They have been so intimately, and for so long a time, blended with the history of the country . . . that the death of either would have touched the strings of public sympathy." With concurrent deaths, a living connection to the past was decisively cut.

The eulogist was a celebrated trial attorney, a performer whose grim face bore the classic imprint of dignity. Before his career played out, he would become a lion of the Senate and a proactive secretary of state. In solemnizing the life of John Adams in the presence of those who knew him best, Webster presented a detailed political biography of a man of constancy and purpose, of moral directness and moral energy. Recalling an "unabated love of reading and contemplation," he observed, "No man ever beheld more clearly, and for a longer time, the great and beneficial effects of the services rendered by himself to his country." John Adams had lived to see the Republic embarked on steady seas. With his own son at the helm. "Auspicious omens cheer us," intoned Daniel Webster, "Great examples are before us."[39]

In Quincy, and able to reflect, the president spent time reviewing "deeply interesting" letters written by his parents to the late Dr. Cotton Tufts that dated to the late 1780s. He read through the papers of his great-grandfather and namesake, John Quincy, too. As gifts, he arranged for a number of souvenir rings to be made, along with "trinkets" containing strands of his father's and mother's hair. In a nostalgic frame of mind, he took George outside, and they gazed up at stars.

The eldest son became his constant companion. They rode into Boston and back; they took strolls through the family's garden and orchard. JQA was directly replicating the emotional bond he'd forged with his own father. He spent a night in bed beside his son and initiated a roving conversation about his post-presidential plans to build a modest monument to his father, publish a full-length biography of him, and establish an educational institution in the second president's name. Convinced that George would make a fine assistant in these enterprises, the president tried not to obsess on his fears.

He had premonitory tremors with regard to George's well-being and spelled these out in his diary: "I had another long conversation with my Son George in which he opened to me the state of his own mind and feelings, with the most confidential Sincerity—His heart is pure; but his imagination outruns his judgment . . . , his temper tending too much to despondency; to which his present feeble state of health contributes." George lacked the thick skin the first son of an Adams required to navigate the world.[40]

During his weeks at home, the president held an interview with the Reverend Peter Whitney. Though he'd never joined the congregation of his Adams ancestors in all these years amid his many residences abroad, he resolved to do so now and take Communion. Anticipating the day when he would be "gathered with my fathers here," he wished to put his own life in order. Execution of his father's will was taking up too much of his time. Surveys had yet to be made of land willed by the deceased; precise boundaries remained uncertain, though on some portion the very first American railroad would soon pass.

He was obliged to depart for Washington before the probate judge ruled. But he made it a point first to obtain from Whitney a copy of the sermon he preached at the burial so as to have it published. He made arrangements to place chests containing the collected papers of his father and mother (and his own, prior to 1809) in a secure vault in a bank in Boston. He went with George to inspect plans for the Bunker Hill Monument, the quarried granite for which was to be transported on the new railway that he rightly saw as the harbinger of a transportation revolution. Having earlier purchased a portion of the family lands in order to establish a fixed annuity for his father, he was hoping that the property would provide for his own financial security in a retirement he convinced himself lay only two and a half years down the road.[41]

He continued to ruminate on the intricacies of life, from his own pending "exit from the stage" to the health of his eldest son, which he called "precarious." George's psychological crisis was so "painfully predominant" in the president's mind that it had become a "serious obstacle" to his retirement plan. "Among my earnest wishes," he wrote, "is one that George should soon connect himself judiciously in marriage." He begged for normalcy.

For a man of ambition who had ambitions for his offspring, each encounter with his children presented, as he put it, "foretastes of discouragement." As he headed out after three months away from the seat of government, the diarist of near half a century was at his most wistful: "I left for the last time the dwelling House of my father in which he had chiefly resided for nearly forty years; and entirely for the last twenty-five—I left it with an anxious and consoling hope of returning to it as to my own." He had become a patriarch more restless than the patriarch whose loss he was mourning.[42]

Trap Doors

On October 19, as he landed at Baltimore, President Adams found his son Charles waiting for him with carriage and horses. They rode six hours from there to the Capitol, where a giant procession was under way. With the business of government resuming, this was the day set aside for the official celebration of the lives of John Adams and Thomas Jefferson. JQA arrived on Capitol Hill to find a large assemblage of gentlemen and ladies awaiting him; it included members of his cabinet, military officers, and members of the city's religious community.[43]

The orator of the day was Attorney General William Wirt, a holdover from Monroe's cabinet, a longtime student of oratory, and perhaps most significant at this moment the biographer of the Revolutionary firebrand Patrick Henry. John Quincy's father had playfully taken on Attorney General Wirt in 1818, after the biography appeared, contesting the presumption that Henry, a Virginian, had singularly spawned the spirit of 1776. To John Adams, it was a native son of Massachusetts, James Otis, who deserved at least as much historical notice as the Virginian for his Revolutionary oratory: "If I could go back to the age of thirty-five, Mr. Wirt, I would endeavor to become your rival—not in elegance of composition, but in a simple narration of facts, supported by records, histories and testimonies, of irrefragable authority." The heroes of his rival work would have included some lesser-known names, plus others that still resonated: his onetime co-counsel Josiah Quincy, "the Boston Cicero," who died prematurely in 1775; the martyr of Bunker Hill, Dr. Joseph Warren, another of his good friends; Francis Dana, the Boston attorney who was young John Quincy's surrogate parent in Russia; and most generously, Mercy Otis Warren and her husband, James, the latter of whom had survived the Battle of Bunker Hill. Adams personally admired Patrick Henry and attested to his integrity and "daring enterprize," but he was not bowled over by the exaggerated claims contained in Wirt's biography.[44]

When first approached to deliver a joint eulogy, Wirt protested that he had never met John Adams. He knew Jefferson all too well and adored him. How, he asked, could he possibly muster equal enthusiasm for both founders? Hearing of his humble protest, First Lady Louisa Adams soured on Wirt and told her husband how she felt. There was talk about enlisting the D.C. Circuit Court judge William Cranch, an Adams cousin, to share the rostrum with Wirt in the House chamber and deliver the Adams half of a dual eulogy. President Adams seemed entirely unperturbed by the controversy.[45]

In the end, Wirt agreed and did a creditable if fairly unemotional job with the giant he referred to as "the sage of Quincy." Taking the two together, he pronounced that "Jefferson and Adams were great men by nature. . . . They were heaven-called avengers of degraded man." He dressed Jefferson in quasi-divine garb, claiming for him uncommon wisdom "flowing from his heart with that warm and honest frankness . . . , with his silver locks hanging on each side of his honest face." His Adams was "venerable," a "perfectly honest man," but otherwise drained of color in this portrait. Wirt's unbalanced eulogy lasted for two and a half hours and received, according to the president, "apparent universal approbation." Louisa Adams was right in doubting Wirt's equanimity. Or perhaps it was Wirt who was right all along to have acknowledged his insufficiency up front. Daniel Webster he was not.[46]

Politics returned that fall. In places where congressional elections were held, candidates were identified as "the administration ticket" or "the Jackson ticket." There was never a doubt who was slated to rival the incumbent president in 1828. Thoroughly prepared for dismissal after one term, JQA was trying to make peace with himself. Talk of the "corrupt bargain" between Adams and his secretary of state lingered on, and in a replay of the ambush John Adams met with in the late 1790s, surrounded as he was by a Hamiltonian cabinet, John Quincy Adams was forced to endure, three decades hence, the defection of his vice president. By 1826, Calhoun had already switched sides, allying with Jackson, which caused President Adams to appear all the more like a sectional rather than a national figure. The world was against him, he told his wife. And yet, like his father before him, the stalled sixth president proved reluctant to dismiss from federal offices those who did not support him. It would have been beneath him to do so.[47]

The artist John Trumbull (not the same of that name who studied law with John Adams) was in the process of hanging his large Revolutionary paintings in the restored Capitol Rotunda, including the famed *Declaration of Independence,* with a squat but erect John Adams front and center. The children of the founding generation were forming their civil religion. Yet the second Adams was no longer feeling the nostalgia he'd experienced in Quincy. Politics hung heavy. The pressure was getting to Secretary Clay, when, in mid-November, he asked the president's permission for time off to go to New York. It was for needed rest, he said, and he would do his best to avoid crowds. Once Clay returned to Washington, Adams learned that his most senior cabinet officer had soured on the Chesapeake and Ohio Canal plan that the president wanted Congress to endorse. Though Adams made a "most earnest and emphatic recommendation," the engineering project was shot down. Governing required consensus, and he did not have anything close to consensus, even in his own cabinet.[48]

Despite setbacks, this indefatigable man, the sitting president, rose between five and six o'clock each day, walked from the White House to the Capitol and back, and returned "in time to see the sun rise from my northeast window." He built his fire and read newspapers for an hour and a half and finally paused to eat breakfast. From ten in the morning until five in the afternoon he was at his desk on the second floor, receiving visitors. At the close of his working day, the steadily self-monitoring, manifestly unpopular president dined, usually with Louisa, and then returned to his desk to attend to state papers and correspondence. Finally, he wrote a paragraph or a page in his diary and at 11:00 p.m. went to bed.

This was his routine. But as the final month of the year 1826 opened, he wrote with dread, "The days of trial are coming again." The Nineteenth Congress was about to convene its second session. It meant having his thoughts, and occasionally meals, interrupted by congressional delegations or unannounced visitors; it meant abiding the slow torment of debate over legislation. He was president; he felt disempowered.[49]

The precocious Edward Everett spent an evening in conversation with the president in early December. Because his older brother Alexander had served, for two years, as private secretary to JQA in St. Petersburg, he was long known to the Adams family. The younger Everett was now a thirty-two-year-old first-term congressman from Massachusetts, his brother the chief U.S. diplomat in Spain. Congressman Everett was unique among Americans in having traversed much of the same European landscape as John Q. Adams, earning a Ph.D. (the first of his countrymen to do so) at the prestigious German university of Göttingen. Next, as a Greek scholar teaching at Harvard—Charles Francis Adams was one of his pupils—he had engaged the retired Jefferson in a wonky epistolary exchange about the beauties of that ancient language. Enthusiastic about the program for internal improvements laid out in the first annual message a year before, he was a confirmed Adams partisan—a label few others so openly embraced.[50]

Their conversation that evening turned to a very long letter Everett had seen. It was a political communication of 1824 from an eighty-year-old Thomas Jefferson to the rising senator Martin Van Buren of New York, and it contained a piece of intelligence that President Adams found irresistible: Jefferson eagerly explaining his past behavior and stating that the "federal party" could not legitimately claim George Washington as one of theirs. This last notion piqued Adams's interest. Everett promised to get hold of Jefferson's letter and submit it to Adams for his "perusal."

It had now been five months since his father's death. The awkward dance that John Adams and Thomas Jefferson performed would henceforth be in the hands of historians. But as the president gave thought to someday writing his father's life story, he could not pass up opportunities to obtain new insights into politics past. Jefferson's letter to Van Buren was long, and it featured a tortuous logic of historical self-justification. On Washington and the party that claimed him, the third president's words, which Everett was only able to paraphrase, were these: "The truth is that the federalists, pretending to be the exclusive friends of G[enera]l Washington, have ever done what they could to sink his character, by hanging theirs on it. . . . Genl Washington was himself sincerely a friend to the republican principles of our constitution. His faith perhaps in it's duration might not have been as confident as mine; but he repeatedly declared to me that he was determined it should have a fair chance for success."

Jefferson thought in black and white, wholly convinced that the Federalist Party had plotted to "subvert" (his word) republican government, redirecting it back to a more British, even monarchical design. As president, Washington had done his best to keep the republican experiment alive and was, whether he knew it or not, a Jeffersonian. John Adams, in this construct, was neither for nor opposed. The convictions he held were of secondary value: Jefferson treated the first Adams as impotent before the Hamiltonian onslaught, merely a bridge between the first president and the third.

When it came to historical revisionism, John Q. Adams, at the end of 1826, exhibited curiosity but no urgency. His journal entries suggest emotional detachment, even from evidence of Jefferson's foibles. If the past did not sting, it was probably because the present looked so unpromising. Which was, in a very real way, owing to the opposition he saw coming from Senator Van Buren and Vice President Calhoun. Jackson's vanguard in Washington was operating in concert with the Tennessean's home state publicity network.[51]

On the last day of the year, halfway into his term, the embattled president issued a two-fisted Adamsian axiom for his depressive son George, who had recently been elected to the Massachusetts legislature. "Never yield to any party your own well considered sense of right," he urged. "*Beware of Trap doors.*"

FATHERLESS PRESIDENT

John Quincy Adams respected Henry Clay's perspective on Latin American affairs, which took up a considerable amount of national debate during the second Adams presidency. Adams and Clay wished to take a lead role in fostering stability in the Southern Hemisphere, mainly by seeing that the environment was unfriendly to all European powers and solicitous of U.S. interests; we would exercise leadership in the region as Spanish influence receded. To commit to such a policy was the natural next step in consequence of JQA's long labors as Monroe's secretary of state. But an unfriendly Congress harassed the president and his successor at the State Department.

A Panama conference, organized by Simón Bolívar, took place in the summer of 1826. The American envoy, Congressman John Sergeant of Pennsylvania, arrived after the proceedings had come to an end, thanks in large measure to stalling tactics in Congress. Antislavery pretensions among the new governments of South America alarmed southern U.S. politicians, which further muddied the waters. In the end, the administration failed to secure by treaty anything resembling an amicable understanding of the future direction of hemispheric relations. Volatile matters involving Cuba, and especially Mexico and Texas, were left for future administrations.[52]

Was there any chance at all for an Adams administration after 1828? Reelection became a topic of conversation between Adams and Clay at the end of 1826. Clay intimated that "friends of the Administration—Eastern, Northern, and Western"—considered it critical to arrive at a comfortable consensus as to a vice presidential running mate, rather than wait for speculation to take form: it should be someone with cross-sectional appeal. Clay allowed that his own name had been put forward and that he had in turn—with unassuming directness, we might imagine—raised the name of Secretary of War James Barbour, the Virginian, as a credible alternative. Adams noted in his diary that he'd be content with either as vice president.[53]

He could be a stubborn advocate and insistent doer, as when he attempted to reframe the role of the federal government in advancing internal improvements, or he could be accommodating and nonpartisan, as when he gamely accepted the consensus candidate as a running mate. Facing life-and-death decisions, braving storms and near shipwrecks, he showed he had guts. With everything else weighing on his mind at the close of 1826, an unexpected threat materialized after a court-martialed assistant army surgeon named George P. Todson made plain to more than one person that he was prepared to kill the commander in chief for refusing to restore him to his rank and position.

Adams recorded the warnings as he received them. This doctor he had never met, a convicted embezzler, "fancied he should redeem his character by Revenge." Todson considered the evidence "clear and palpable" that a broad-based conspiracy against him went all the way to the top. He "avowed . . . his determination to assassinate me," Adams took note, his handwriting revealing no sudden disruption. He consulted with Secretary of War Barbour, who confirmed that there was no cause to dispute what the army had done. The president was well known for his solitary morning walks, leaving the White House before the dawn's light. It was then, he figured, that Todson would most likely strike. Yet he did nothing to forestall his would-be attacker. And then he wrote for his own eyes, "I am in the hands of a higher Power."

The aggrieved man appeared before him on December 16, 1826, to contest the court-martial face-to-face. In the unprotected White House, Adams stood firm, despite what he'd been told about Todson's state of mind, and advised the man that he required solid proof of unfair treatment; otherwise the court-martial stood. Todson lingered in Washington for a time, making repeated demands, but nothing he said or did succeeded in wearing down the president's resolve. John Quincy Adams had withstood abuse before this. He could be difficult, but sometimes being difficult served him well.[54]

He was a survivor. Yet so much else had occurred to shake his confidence that he began exhibiting noticeable signs of strain. The state of Georgia was behaving with savage determination in putting pressure upon the Indian population within its borders; the Jacksonians were organized and sniping at him from every angle. Meanwhile, the fatherless president never stopped worrying about the health and emotional well-being of family members.

The youngest son, Charles Francis, was yet another Adams diarist committed to a critical perspective on the world around him. The nineteen-year-old recent Harvard graduate gave a stark appraisal of his president. "My father has unfortunately such a cold manner," he confessed directly, at a loss to understand how political supporters could look past it. By contrast, he found it easy to appreciate the ways of his "lofty and yet cheerful, decided and yet gentle" grandfather. In life, John Adams had had "a stout, well-knit frame, denoting vigor"; "his eye was mild and benignant, perhaps even humorous," his presence "grave and imposing, on serious occasions, but not unbending. He delighted in social conversation." Charles was not blind to his grandfather's excess of pride, for which he had a well-deserved reputation; nor did Charles doubt the powerful sense of honor and duty that motivated his father. The youngest inheritor drew deliberate distinctions between a grandfather whose political pique had abated, and a father whose alienation and ill humor were very much tied to politics present.

Growing up when he did, Charles held a view of "the people," that amorphous depository of genius in a political democracy, that was less censorious than his father's. Perhaps that explained why John Quincy Adams was deprived of even the calculated warmth that a public man needed. Whatever had hardened him could not be offset now. It is quite possible, too, that, at this point in his life, Charles, like the voters, did not get to see the softer side of John Q. Adams, who composed a heartfelt sonnet to his late father on what would have been John Adams's ninety-first birthday. It opened,

Day of my fathers birth. I hail thee yet
What though his body moulders in the grave
Yet shall not death the immortal soul enslave.[55]

THIRTEEN

SURVIVING SON

More than 60 years of incessant active intercourse with the world has made political movement to me as much a necessary of life as atmospheric air—This is the weakness of my nature.

—DIARY OF JOHN QUINCY ADAMS, *March 23, 1841*

From March 4, 1801, through July 4, 1826, John Adams had twenty-five full years to mull over his political past, store the immense written record of his life, and wonder, in his predictably acerbic way, whether the world would even care to remember him. His eldest son, chief caretaker of the public memory of John Adams, never got around to completing his founding father's life story; that job was to be undertaken by Charles Francis Adams and subsequently improved upon by Charles's even more famous son Henry.

The season of eulogies on the life of John Adams lasted into the spring of 1827, when Judge William Cranch, the president's cousin on his mother's side, delivered a nearly three-hour-long speech to an audience that comprised females and males equally. Having sat through a number of these eulogies already, President Adams appreciated his cousin's conscious effort to draw upon unique materials—notably Jefferson's letter of condolence upon the death of Abigail Adams. It "affected every hearer," JQA observed, and "more than once moved me to the very borders of manhood." Reminding the history conscious of the essential character of John Adams, Judge Cranch began the process of legacy building in a formal biography he published the following year: "He was not a man to be led or driven. He was as independent as he wished his country to be. He never would go the whole length with the party; yet all their sins have been laid upon his head." John Adams couldn't have said it better or more concisely.[1]

As Congress blocked initiatives and his vice president undermined him, John Q. Adams gave more of his thought to personal matters. He refused to abandon the idea of entrusting his and his father's papers to his eldest son. But as smart as George was, he was also inconstant. Although placed under the tutelage of no less a luminary than Daniel Webster in 1827, he gave less of himself to building a career and more to socializing. He indulged in drink and devoted himself to women his parents would hardly have approved. His father went so far as to urge him to weigh the contributions of his upstanding grandfather, whom George knew as well as he knew his own father. Before long, George ran into money problems and had a child with a chambermaid.[2]

The spring of 1827 brought further recriminations from the administration's all-too-numerous detractors. JQA made mention, in his diary, of "hatred and division," "odious misconstruction," "the bitter and rancorous spirit of the opposition"—virtually the same vocabulary his father's supporters used in an earlier era of partisanship. The sixth president noted that there had been "four or five challenges to duels" in the last session of Congress—though, fortunately, "all ended in smoke." He masochistically scouted the newspapers, noting abusive language directed his way. This came to mind on the same day that the persistent George Todson appeared before him again, asking for a "remission" on the cash payment demanded of him as part of the guilty finding in his court-martial trial. Here, the president could finally do something for the forsaken doctor. The next day he received a polite letter from the thankful man, "a flattering Latin quotation from Cicero."

Todson had interrupted Joseph Anderson, comptroller of the Treasury and former Tennessee senator, who was busy assuaging the president's feelings by reminding him that Andrew Jackson owed him for his career. The upstanding citizen John Q. Adams had been "ill requited" for his service to the backwoods general. Jackson would not be in the position he was in—likely successor to Adams—had Adams not saved his military career in 1818. JQA was all that stood between Jackson and dismissal after the Florida incursion, when as secretary of state he strongly defended the general's use of excessive force. In the current mood of the country, however, the president felt he had to temper his speech, lest his words be turned on their head. "I can never be sure of writing a line that will not some day be published by friend or foe," he said. He opted to reduce the output of his personal correspondence, quieting his political opinions. It wasn't a confident strategy.[3]

His heart was often tested. One day in the spring of 1827, a northern Virginia woman presented herself before him and begged for leniency for her seventy-three-year-old brother, who had been sentenced to hang for murdering a man after an argument. The oddity of the case—the advanced age of the convicted man—resulted in the trial being reported across the nation. Mr. DeVaughn was one with an ungovernable temper who shot his victim at close range over a "trifling matter." The Alexandria jury needed only ten minutes to convict. "He now stands upon the awful brink of Eternity," a Washington paper imparted, "sustained by the faint hope of Executive clemency."

The president listened to the distraught woman at considerable length. "Her tears and sobs and supplications deeply affected me," he wrote. "Her story told in untutored language was itself moving. I scarcely dare think of it." Whereas Charles Francis did not understand how anyone could enthusiastically embrace his politically clumsy father, this reaction to the sister of a killer reminds us that the second president Adams was imbued with a very human kind of moral vitality that he did not readily voice. He was a good listener, certainly not insensitive to the pain of others—or, for that matter, the just rights of oppressed Indians—but in cases of this nature he took limited action because of restraints placed on his power to reshape the world around him. In short, he followed the law.

The sixth president was not a hard-hearted man, just an opaque one. In listening to a sister's tale of woe, he contemplated the condemned man. "Must he be hung? All this and more I heard, and while it wrung my heart, I resisted every impulse to comfort her with hope. . . . My duty was of the most painful kind." Before the woman got up to leave, she accepted "that it was not in my power" to grant the relief she sought.[4]

He might have been the highest executive in an expansive nation, but he tended to reflect his modest means. His bold ideas, those projected in the first annual message, collapsed, because America was not yet ready for massive investment by the federal government or for a president who did not know how to channel his respect for the public into something with popular appeal. And that is the ultimate tragedy of the presidency of John Q. Adams.

ELECTIONEERING MATTERS

The "corrupt bargain" charge was so deftly deployed by the opposition press that when the garrulous John Randolph of Roanoke brought it up in the U.S. Senate, Secretary of State Henry Clay challenged the uncensored Virginia planter to a duel. During a debate over the Panama Conference, Randolph, a longtime House member recently elected to the Senate, described the Adams-Clay alliance as "the coalition of Blifil and Black George," or "the puritan and the black-leg." The two were characters in Henry Fielding's picaresque novel *Tom Jones,* and the clear implication was that the piratical Clay was a dishonest gambler.

Randolph, a small-government champion, had always seen politics as blood sport. This dandyish, almost comical tormentor, constitutionally frail and with a high-pitched voice, nurtured a hatred for the Adamses dating to the years when the "Vice-Regal carriage" of John Adams nearly ran his brother off the road in Manhattan. This symbolic personal affront dating to Washington's presidency allowed the old-fashioned Republican to magnify the mirrored outlooks of both presidents Adams into proof positive of their unrepublican leanings. "The days of John Adams have come again," Randolph said in the spring of 1826. "It is now exactly twenty-five years since [he] fled like a thief in the night from the Palace—who then believed that the son was ever destined to occupy it?" On the floor of Congress, Randolph likened the second Adams to a seventeenth-century British monarch when he deemed him "the evil genius of the American House of Stuart." Adams registered Randolph's rancor, but he did not regard honor culture in the southern manner and chalked it all up to the vulgarity of the political scene.

The Randolph-Clay duel was fought, then, over the implication that the Adams administration was immoral and illegitimate. The odd, fatalistic Virginia senator and the determined cabinet secretary from Lexington, Kentucky, met on the banks of the Potomac, marched their paces, aimed, and shot. No damage was done to either in the first fire. "This is child's play!" Clay cried out, demanding a second shot. His next bullet tore through Randolph's coat but missed flesh. Randolph fired into the air, announcing that he had no intention of doing physical harm to the offended secretary. Honor restored by the chivalric code, both men returned to work. "We are happy to state, the affair ended in *smoke,*" commented the *New-York Mirror*—the same metaphor JQA used in his diary when categorizing an unreasoning, duel-heavy Congress that had no interest in enacting his agenda.[5]

The duel might have been good fodder for the press, but the fact remained that tension levels rose as the verbal abuse of political men convulsed Washington. While Congress fought with itself, the veteran diplomats Adams and Clay did all they could to extend America's participation in hemispheric deliberations. Uncharacteristically, Europe was enjoying an era of peace; the possibility of European intrigue in the Americas could not be ignored. It would only harm U.S. interests to be relegated to the sidelines when the future of the young South American republics was still at issue. The president remained statesmanlike in his communications, though his prudence and tact fell flat before an obstructionist Congress. His administration was at an impasse.

If the Virginia dynasty of presidents was a thing of the past, so was the notion that sectional grievances could be suppressed. Adams was somewhat heartened by the knowledge that the political class contained a good many who were nervous about a President Andrew Jackson. The frontier-bred battler was prone to disregard the law and was likened, at times, to the military usurpers Julius Caesar and Napoleon Bonaparte. When Henry Clay publicly labeled Jackson a "military chieftain," this was precisely the reputation he had in mind.

As the election of 1828 loomed, the well-organized pro-Jackson, anti-Adams coalition dug in its heels. In the critical state of New York, the self-made political "magician" Martin Van Buren built up a machine with long tentacles, called the Albany Regency. A former Crawford backer, Van Buren had swung to Jackson of Tennessee in the blink of an eye. When the New Yorker got around to writing his autobiography, this hard student of politics and energetic purveyor of party loyalty sloughed off the Adamsian idea that "party spirit" was an evil spirit and instead embraced organized parties as a legitimate, even desirable facet of a democratic society.

Some of the worst anti-Adams language came out of New York state. The *Albany Argus,* a Van Buren vehicle, assailed the president's character in such a way as to permanently malign the Adams brand: like father, like son. When Secretary of War Barbour accepted a diplomatic assignment to

England in the spring of 1828, President Adams named as his successor the New Yorker Peter Porter, a War of 1812 general and recipient of a commendation "for gallantry" from Congress. As Porter took up Adams's cause in the New York press, reaction was swift and severe.

Porter claimed, incongruously, that Adams was of the Jeffersonian school of republicanism. It didn't take much to provide contrary evidence. For one, there was "Publicola," the authorship of which Adams had still not publicly avowed but which his friends continued to praise. His "attachment to a privileged order," dating to "Publicola," matched him to his father's, not Jefferson's, political thinking. And his association with Madison and Monroe? If anything, he proved himself a serial apostate.

According to the *Argus,* John Adams had somewhere stated that President Washington was "saved" by the anti-French writings of his son. It was not Hamilton or Pickering, or anyone else, but, somehow, a young John Q. Adams who had "turned the tide of sentiment" against the French Revolution. For the *Argus,* "effusions" in praise of John Quincy Adams were patently ridiculous.

The same columnist played off Washington Irving's popular character Rip Van Winkle. "Were a partisan of the 1790s," after having "rested in peace" for a generation, revived in 1828, what would he say to the second President Adams? He'd say, "You bear in your bosom a heart of frost and fire, cold to generous emotion, but burning with malice." So long abroad as a diplomat, "you did not share in our arduous struggle to overthrow the power of your father." And, most cruelly, "In the dark days of 1798, emphatically called by the republicans of that period the days of the 'reign of terror'; in the days of alien and sedition laws . . . where was John Quincy Adams?" In short, "You are no republican." Publicola left the United States, and Publicola returned.

According to the *Argus,* President John Q. Adams was overrated as a literary scholar, as a diplomat, and as a moralist. Elected to public office only once (as senator from Massachusetts), he remained on the public dole from 1809 forward: "He has had but *one* object, his own *self-aggrandizement.*" The final insult cut deepest: "You have made no sacrifices for a country, from whose treasury you have been supported through life. . . . The nation has gained nothing from your experience."[6]

In 1823–1824, when the second Adams made voters aware that he wanted to serve as president, he hoped to be elected on the basis of his known strengths, and that alone. He held that the former party affiliations of officeholders would not disqualify them in an Adams administration; he would not fire anyone who could do the job well. All that mattered was competence and a commitment to the country's advance. He did not need yes-men.

Van Buren scoffed at such thinking. In his sturdy lexicon, a party stood for something. It created bonds based on commonly held principles; it sought to collapse sectional distinctions. In giving greater structure to an emerging, semiofficially named Democratic Party devoted to Andrew Jackson, Van Buren pragmatically restored the old alliance between the Virginia planter interest and New York Republicans, taking slavery off the table (as Jeffersonians had done in the earlier period). Jacksonian Democrats would largely succeed by adhering to this playbook: party loyalty made the party powerful. Making matters worse, many of the New York newspapers that opposed Jackson were fans of the native son DeWitt Clinton; they were at best lukewarm toward the incumbent president, Adams.[7]

There were numerous echoes of 1800 in the tone and tenor of the election of 1828. Martin Van Buren reprised Aaron Burr's deft politicking of seven election cycles previous, encouraging New Yorkers once more to feel comfortable taking a backseat to a southern president. Van Buren was by no means the only activist who took history as his guide. There was one who bore the surname Hamilton. He was James Alexander Hamilton, third son of the fallen Federalist, one of the new Jacksonians.

This brings us to a poignant interlude in Adams historiography: a battle between sons over their fathers' legacies. It did not escape JQA's notice that once again a Hamilton stood against the reelection of an Adams. To no less an Adams hater than Timothy Pickering, the forty-year-old James A. Hamilton wrote of the man he was so pleased to serve: "His intercourse has been much greater with men than books. . . . He possesses an independent spirit, and great confidence in his own powers." Jackson, indeed, had something in common with James's father: near-absolute confidence in his own powers, and the presumptuousness to do as he saw fit so as to see his will enacted.

The sixth president was unlikely ever to forgive the elder Hamilton's peevish pamphlet of 1800 that attacked a sitting president from his own party; its barefaced, scheming coldness just could not be explained away. Yet once these two proud sons of founders engaged in a challenging (but also civil) discussion of Alexander Hamilton's involvement, not long before his death, with a cadre of New England Federalists who wanted to secede from the Union, a kind of truce crept up on them. Evidently, not everyone with a genealogy to defend was filled with the same partisan venom.[8]

JQA would eventually understand the change under way when he reentered Congress as an ex-president. But as an embattled chief executive in 1827–1828, he was prisoner of a new style of politicking that he was powerless to resist. In *Inquiry into the Origin and Course of Political Parties in the United States,* published long after Adams was dead, Van Buren wrote extensively about Adams's abilities as well as the failings he perceived. He respected John Quincy Adams the man, and despite diametrically opposed politics that respect grew over time. "Notwithstanding the occasional fierceness of our political collisions," wrote Van Buren, "I have never heard of any unfriendly expression by him in respect to myself personally."

Van Buren was more Jeffersonian theorizer than Madisonian pragmatist in his political retrospective. As such, he came to believe it was the second Adams's centralizing policies that allowed an effective opposition to coalesce. "He was by nature truthful," the New Yorker wrote, "if at times blinded by prejudice." The prejudice he had in mind was intellectual. Too genteel in his authorial pose to attribute Adams's electoral defeat in 1828 to hyped-up resentment over the "corrupt bargain" of 1825, Van Buren held that the New Englander's main problem lay in his reading of the Constitution. Here he tried to match up JQA's theory of government with John Adams's writings of the late 1780s. "Van" was misguided—because he took the easy route. All he could muster for his argument were selections from a Jefferson biography of the 1850s that defended Jefferson every step of his public career and habitually placed John Adams in a negative light. And it went like this: The senior Adams adopted an "incoherent" position in favor of British forms. That shift in ideology alarmed Jefferson. Regrettably, the antidemocratic seed sown by the father was harvested by the son.

Conflating two generations of Adamses, Van Buren quoted directly from *Defence of the Constitutions:* "The proposition, that the people are the best keepers of their own liberties, is not true; they are the worst conceivable. . . . They can neither judge, act, think, or will as a political body." This statement had come to stand for Adamsian doctrine, at least for Van Buren, who was careful to soften the charge (as he did in his assessment of JQA) with praise: "John Adams was in every sense a remarkable man" who possessed "intellectual materials sufficient to have furnished many minds respectably." To sum up, then, Van Buren conflated the constitutional theories of father and son, extolled their honesty as human beings, and certified that they did not share the slain Hamilton's "absorbing preference for monarchy." But neither were they real republicans.[9]

There were certain politicians whom Adams watched with an eagle eye, and Van Buren was key among them. In 1828, campaigning strongly, the opportunistic New York senator emphasized in speeches how John Quincy was as "aristocratic" as his father before him. Adams and Van Buren put on a performance, as professional politicians sometimes do: Van Buren shored up his alliances in a journey to the southern states, then stopped by the White House on his return north for a casual meeting with the man he was hell-bent on unseating. Thereupon, Adams labeled Van Buren "the great electioneering manager for General Jackson."[10]

He himself had no electioneering staff to speak of, though Henry Clay and Daniel Webster did what they could to take the case for Adams to the press. It did not help that the president's personal secretary was his unexceptional middle son, John. John Adams II, as he is known to history, did the best he could to serve the administration, but his only notable performance was a well-publicized dustup with an especially antagonistic Washington journalist. With his son of no use in matters of public outreach, the president did his job serviceably well but remained remote from the voters.

There is, however, a perfectly ironic postscript to the sassy story of the sixth and eight presidents. In 1848, seven years after departing the White House as the first disappointing one-termer not named Adams, Martin Van Buren made another run for the presidency. It was not as a Jeffersonian or Jacksonian Democrat this time but under the banner of the short-lived Free-Soil Party, which opposed the extension of slavery westward. His running mate that year was none other than John Quincy's youngest son, Charles Francis Adams.

An explosion in partisan journalism overspread the states in election year 1828. Press organs competed with one another in creative mudslinging. In sheer numbers, and in terms of circulation, the partisan press undeniably worked in favor of the Jackson campaign. This war among rival newspapers was something not seen since the election of 1800. The editor Isaac Hill of New Hampshire, formerly an outspoken supporter of JQA, announced his conversion to Jackson when he publicized the "fact" that during his tenure in St. Petersburg, Adams had "procured" for the libidinous tsar a shapely American virgin. Not to be outdone, the former Federalist Charles Hammond launched the *Cincinnati Gazette,* which savaged Rachel Jackson as "a convicted adulteress" and called Andrew Jackson's mother "a common prostitute."

It went downhill from there. In a memo to Congress, John Adams II listed as a public expense the purchase of a billiard table for the White House. The president's enemies milked this obvious impropriety for all it was worth. A billiard table? Such were the trappings of the aristocratic household. In truth, President Adams had used personal funds to pay for the billiard table, but the mistaken memo item lost no currency even after the official correction was made. Adding insult to injury, the president learned that his own postmaster general was working to elect Jackson. Amid all this mayhem, Adams joylessly signed the patchwork Tariff of 1828, or "Tariff of Abominations," as it was soon dubbed, for it altogether satisfied no one section or economic interest.[11]

If Adams profited at all from the no-holds-barred techniques of the campaign, it was in the narrow sense of halving the number of rude accusations he had to absorb, because he shared that dubious honor with his designing secretary of state. The reactive Jackson probably hated Clay more than he had ever hated any other political or military rival, and there had been many. Yet Jackson did not have to lift a finger, because the pro-Jackson press hurled the epithets for him.

A so-called democratic style of electioneering had emerged. When it wasn't a name-calling contest, it was a chaotic showcase of constructed personalities. Who was the real Adams? The real Jackson? And did it even matter? Men's imagined attributes were haphazardly invoked in the partisan press so as to convince voters of the steadiness of one side and the moral corruption of the other side. Adams attempted to come before the public with cautious, well-reasoned policy positions. The more limited Jackson did not take positions, but wafted above; he was, ironically, almost nonconfrontational in 1828. John Quincy Adams and Andrew Jackson, like the earlier Adams and Jefferson, by dint of who they were in print, simplified the process for voters. Adams and Jackson were born in the same year, but it is hard to imagine two more dissimilar candidates for the presidency.[12]

In the end, Jackson won handily: 178 electoral votes to Adams's 83. The South and the West were solidly in the Tennessean's column, save for Louisiana, where his imposition of martial law after the Battle of New Orleans and his high-handed treatment of French-descended residents presented a different understanding of "the Hero's" political personality. It was not entirely surprising that the unpopular incumbent received no electoral votes south or west of Maryland. Adams's running mate was Richard Rush, son of Benjamin Rush, a capable Treasury secretary who had reduced the national debt by 70 percent. But Rush could not even deliver his home state of Pennsylvania.

This historic election had a number of nervous echoes. The South Carolinian John Calhoun, who had assumed the vice presidency under Adams and remained in office even after becoming disenchanted, became Jackson's vice president—a strange move never to repeat in U.S. history. But arguably, the most idiosyncratic result of the election of 1828 concerned the most coveted cabinet office: State. After Clay helped Adams past Jackson to reach the presidency four years earlier, by deftly maneuvering among congressional delegations, he was awarded the office of secretary of state. It had been a stepping-stone to the presidency for Jefferson, Madison, Monroe, and JQA. Senator Van Buren helped win New York for Jackson, almost singlehandedly bringing back the Jeffersonian North-South coalition, and was named by the victorious Jackson to the very same office.

John Q. Adams, the first U.S. president to be inaugurated in pantaloons and not Revolutionary-style breeches, was honest, fearless, and, even at sixty, committed to a taxing daily exercise regimen. Yet he was dismissed by voters as "sedentary"; he was, reputedly, a throwback to old and discredited ideas. The aloof Adams was no kind of politician. That said, he was often misjudged. He might not have had a catchy slogan to symbolize his political identity, but neither was solemnity the same as passionlessness.

Perhaps it was his fatalism that best characterized him at this moment. Almost from the start, he resigned himself to a one-term presidency. Yet he did so without a reduction in effort, energy, or, for that matter, creative engagement with his surroundings. He tended personally to the White House gardens, digging and planting with his own hands. Always thinking of improvement, large and small, he oversaw the importation of seeds and saplings from across the globe; he had trees planted along the still sparsely populated route he walked to and from the reconstructed Capitol. He was quietly productive. The times demanded something other than quiet competence.[13]

His generosity was real, and his resentments were just as real. Like his father before him, he refused to attend the inauguration of his popular successor, a man whose talents he openly disparaged and whose temperament he roundly denounced. He thought Jackson represented the "rabble," non–property owners newly allowed to vote. There was no way for Adams—or Clay as his surrogate—to sway such people from the crude belief that Adams symbolized entrenched power and Jackson liberty.

John Quincy Adams lived an unpretentious lifestyle. Virtually no one in America understood that. He was painted with a broad brush as overly refined and glaringly effete. And the charge stood; indeed, it appears to have stood the test of time.

According to the convenient formula history resorts to, it is said that with the defeat of the second president Adams and the inauguration of Andrew Jackson as the seventh president, one age ended and another began. Whether or not the arbitrary division of American history into eras is truly reliable, we will concede that something new was in the air. Jackson headed the Democratic Party. National Republicans (the party of Adams and Clay) had not yet acquired a collective name, but as of this moment, the so-called second party system—Whig versus Democrat—was being ushered in.[14]

3:40 A.M.

It was meant for George W., the eldest, to carry on the Adams tradition. If he failed, the youngest, Charles F., would have to step in and fill the vacuum, because the middle child, John Adams II, though more of a charmer than most Adamses, possessed the least talent. All three brothers had overlapped at Harvard, yet none had managed to approach the standard set by their father and grandfather. George and Charles finished in the bottom half of their class, and John was expelled in 1823 for bad conduct.

As the second president Adams became the second ex-president Adams, George was still the repository of his hopes. Before Charles—intellectually speaking, a late bloomer—proved himself a superior money manager and competent editor of the Adams Papers, the eldest son remained the chosen one. George was clever but had a depressive disorder of some kind and a reputation for carousing. In one instance, his father, as president, admonished him for his "Licentious life." Spurned by his fiancée-cousin (on his mother's side), who took up with his brother John (who married her), George had managed to get the family maid pregnant.[15]

Still, George and his father shared a passion for poetry. John Quincy did not forget how dependent he'd been on his own parents in the early years of his legal career, and he did all he could to accommodate the spending habits of his eldest. He never gave George any reason to believe that life was devoid of purpose. There was something pointing the boy in a downward direction that could not be laid at the feet of his parents. Even as he was turned out of office, the president allowed himself to hope for a reprieve from the family's history of private misery.

It was not to be. George's father was fated to experience something like what George's grandfather had experienced in losing his connection to the earlier Charles, a hapless son who drank himself to death at the turn of the century. In both cases, the end came at the moment when the father was sinking politically. Coincidences compounded. They were not happy coincidences.

It was early June 1829, three full months after his presidency ended, that an unresisting John Q. Adams finally put his affairs in order and left Washington. His son John was with him, while Louisa remained at the home of one of their friends. ("We parted with anguish that I cannot describe.") As he headed for Boston, by way of Philadelphia and New York, George's body washed up on New York's shore. The eldest son had disappeared into Long Island Sound off the side of a vessel called the *Benjamin Franklin*. Out of Philadelphia, the ex-president engaged socially with his fellow steamboat passengers, unaware of what had befallen George. He had to find out from a paragraph in the *New-York Morning Herald*, a copy of which he picked up shipboard.

What followed was pure romantic angst. "I wrote to my wife the tidings of melancholy consolation," he penned in his diary with apparent stoicism as he learned that his son's body was to be interred, for the time being, north of Manhattan in Eastchester. After a night at the City Hotel, he proceeded along the Eastern Stage Road to the place where George was to be put to rest; that is when and where the shock hit as the bereaved parent stood next to a mahogany coffin and prepared himself to look upon poor George's remains. He had second thoughts only after he tried lifting the lid and found that it had been screwed shut.

At that moment, someone handed the ex-president possessions found with the body, which included a pocket watch frozen in time as George went into the water: 3:40 a.m. Seeing the watch dial, the grieving father let his mind drift into a dark place. His diary: "No language can express my feelings on remarking the point of time at which the hour and minute hands of the watch had stop'd. Oh where at that moment was the Soul of my Child?"[16]

The last significant political rumination in Adams's diary prior to receiving the news of his son's death concerned his own political autopsy. He was taking his last horseback ride for exercise in Washington before heading north and met up on the road with none other than Martin Van Buren. "We stop'd and exchanged salutations," Adams noted. "Van Buren is now Secretary of State. He is the manager by whom the present Administration has been brought into power. He has played over again the game of Aaron Burr in 1800 with the addition of political inconsistency, in transferring his allegiance from Crawford to Jackson. He sold the State of New York to them both." Jackson's new top aide was not gloating, but that isn't exactly how the defeated president saw it: "Van Buren is now enjoying his reward. . . . His pale and haggard looks shew that it is already a reward of mortification."

What could be more revealing of a man's spleen and spite? Adams was choosing to interpret Van Buren's physiognomy in the manner most consistent with his own wish fulfillment: that he who gained power unscrupulously should be unscrupulously treated ever after. With a wounded man's vain hope, he added to this diary entry a Latin phrase, "Nec lex est justia ulla" (Nor can there be a more just law), leaving off the second half of the phrase because it was implied: "Quam necis artifices arte perire sua" (than that the contriver of death should perish by his own invention). He wanted to pronounce a moral, and he wanted it to be that the "Little Magician" Van Buren should find his own political hell.[17]

On the same day, Adams immersed himself in the newly published blockbuster biography of Christopher Columbus by Washington Irving. He had arrived at the episode where the Genoese admiral was subverted by his hitherto most deserving and technically most skilled subordinate, Martín Alonso Pinzón, who stood at the helm of the vessel *Pinta*. In Irving's treatment, which cast Columbus as a moral exemplar of the George Washington variety, Pinzón was his Benedict Arnold. He deserted Columbus in the New World to search for gold that would benefit himself. Separated from Columbus on the return voyage to Spain, Pinzón arrived in port just after Columbus had already received a proper hero's welcome. Pinzón thought he would be the one to make it back first and that he would be the honored one. He was crushed. Within a year, "broken in health," Pinzón was dead.

Something in this story moved Adams greatly. He could barely resist drawing comparisons to the betrayal he'd suffered at the hands of depraved political operators whose greed was responsible for taking the country dangerously off course—the infraction committed by Pinzón. John Adams, at the end of his presidency, was able to identify a "British" party (Hamilton's), a "French" party (Jefferson's), while he stood alone as the one who was purely American. Arriving at the same moment in his own unhappy career, John Quincy Adams felt a similar kind of moral victory over an intractable Congress that refused to adopt his policies and act in the nation's best interest.

Of Pinzón, Adams had this rueful observation to make: "The glory that he might have shared and the disgrace that he did incur, his mortification contrasted with the triumph of Columbus, [left behind] a dishonored name while that of Columbus brightens from age to age." Irving's message when it came to the humiliated mariner was that history should not forget his positive attributes or focus exclusively on his tragic impulse. Before jealousy of Columbus's superior position corrupted his mind, he was masterful.

Irving and Adams agreed that there could be only one Columbus or Washington. But the lessons of history did not stop there. His diary shows that JQA regarded the malignancy of mortal envy in the same way his father had. The Pinzón episode "led me into a train of meditations upon human Nature," he wrote. "Many Pinzons there are of the human species in all ages—and how few Columbuses in any age." In the end, Adams proved to be less sanguine than Irving. The flawed Pinzón was like most of the political men Adams knew who had too little heart to go with the grandiosity of their ambition.[18]

Charles Francis Adams, whose relationship with his father was not without serious bumps in the road, wed happily in early September 1829. The ex-president was pleased and could not resist commenting that he was fortunate to have a daughter-in-law—Abby, short for Abigail—who shared a name with his beloved mother. Louisa did not attend her son's wedding, because, for her, it was too soon after the loss of George to indulge in such merriment. For a wedding gift, JQA gave the couple the excellent Gilbert Stuart portrait John Adams sat for in his final year.

His time of romantic angst continued. Two months later, George's coffin was brought north to Quincy and reinterred next to the remains of Nabby Adams. Charles saw dejection—a "quiet sadness"—in his father's visage. The "Old House" of the two presidents Adams (Peacefield) was being defined as a final resting place for defeated statesmen. Tending to young trees and chickens was not enough to make up for political death.[19]

Militant Self-Righteousness

The survivor would not allow his name to be disposed of that easily. He could have remained in Quincy, as his wife clearly preferred, but he was not ready to embark on his father's biography in any real way, though he'd expressed his intention to do so. The second president Adams had not behaved in the manner of conventional politicians before, and at sixty-two he was not ready to succumb as his father had and spend his post-presidential years engaged in self-vindicating writings.

Instead, he would act. And on more than one front. He ran for a seat in the House of Representatives in the fall of 1830 and was elected. Though "counteracted by a double opposition, federalist and Jacksonite" (as he wrote in his diary), his win was nothing short of a landslide. Not content to confine himself to the political realm, he spent a good amount of his spare time writing poetry. In April 1831, still months from officially taking his seat on Capitol Hill, he completed a historical epic of the twelfth century. *Dermot Mac Morrogh* is the tale of the conquest of Ireland by Henry II of England.

But it is, even more, a morality tale, which the congressman-poet dedicated to "the young men and women of my native country."

JQA's diary entry for the day he finished *Dermot Mac Morrogh* mingles creative catharsis with the usual self-doubt. Of his personal "Poetical Power," he judged, "it is an important question whether I should throw this, and almost all the other verses I have ever written into the fire." He had busied his mind performing translations in the past, but this, the product of two months' labor, was his first invention of any length to be considered for release to a critical public.[20]

The first president Adams is known to history for morally constructed positions on the history of governments and the character of the American people. The second president Adams was even more zealously inclined in this direction, and especially now, in this phase of his life. The historian Paul C. Nagel termed the early period of his post-presidential political career the start of a "militant self-righteousness."[21] In the preface to *Dermot Mac Morrogh,* Adams explained, "History, as it should be written and read, is the school of morals. . . . It is a narrative of a few prosperous voyages and multitudes of shipwrecks." One wonders whether he considered his presidency a "shipwreck," because surely he was wishing (and expecting) right now that Andrew Jackson's would be.

The virtually unknown *Dermot Mac Morrogh* centers on the uncontrollability of one man's passions; in Adamsian language, it is "license" or "licentiousness." The lusty Dermot is captivated by the wife of a rival prince, which results in a series of alliances and amoral warfare. There are no moral heroes in Adams's retelling of a philosophical history that, he insists, David Hume related improperly when he artificially made the inconsistent conqueror Henry II into a man whose character appears far greater than that which he actually possessed.

Adams offers up his own religiosity—the foundation of human morals—before embarking on the substance of the tale:

Divine religion! bliss of man below,
Thou link of union between earth and skies;
Nurse of our virtue, solace of our wo[e],
Lore of the learned, wisdom of the wise,
. . . .

Oh! How canst thou behold such deeds of shame,
Such crimes accurst, committed in thy name?

In his design to teach his fellow citizens the timeless values of "conjugal fidelity," "genuine piety," and "devotion to their country," Adams blames both the historically obscure Dermot and the "young, lively, tender, thoughtless" wife who, "though link'd in wedlock to her spouse," thought "more of her beauty, than her marriage vows." It was a familiar trope: male ambition, female vanity.

It is worth recalling Abigail Adams's near obsession with Alexander Hamilton's adulterous affair with Maria Reynolds in the 1790s and her detestation for that man's unholy quest for personal power in attempting to take down her husband in advance of the election of 1800. John Adams did not react as she did to Hamilton's moral failures, and yet it does seem to be an Adams family trait to disparage political men with a pronounced inability to control their moral selves.

Dermot Mac Morrogh was not explicitly an attack on the Jackson administration, but its pietistic appeal to vanquish all "unprincipled ambition" could easily be read that way. Because of the prominence given during the 1828 presidential campaign to the bigamous union of Jackson and his late wife, Rachel, a reader could assign a specific contemporary context to the stanza in which Adams contrasts the "'Thou shall not covet' precept" with tyrannical Dermot's "lascivious eyes." The poet's message is completed in the couplet: "The knee can bend, the tongue devoutly pray / And yet the heart the foulest vices sway." A few stanzas later, Adams reminds the reader, "Ages pass, and human lusts remain." It requires even less of a leap to see a Jacksonian echo in this characterization of Dermot: "The fiercest passions, still his breast control'd; / Reckless of feelings other than his own."

There were always "artful" villains; there were always "dupes":

Whoever studies the historic page,
And reads the record of recorded time,
Shall find in every realm, in every age,
The same return of error, vice, and crime—

The uneducated mind, poor at discernment, invariably bred "a wild confusion" as historical events spun out of control. Yet even in accepting human nature, Adams refuses to abandon his hope that "a God of justice" reigns. Opening the fourth and final canto of *Dermot Mac Morrogh,* he made clear that he did not look upon ambition as an automatic vice:

Teach not your children then to shun ambition;
Nor quench the flame, that must forever burn:
But, in the days of infancy, their vision
To deeds of virtue and of glory turn:
Of man, their mortal brother, the condition
To mend, improve, and elevate, to learn.[22]

These arresting lines were well calibrated as an idealized self-description, if not a transgenerational family motto.

Outside his versification, John Q. Adams made no effort to disguise how he felt about Andrew Jackson. There would be no reconciliation on the order of his father's with Jefferson. JQA so detested his lean and hungry successor that he craved every tidbit of information that highlighted the seventh president's inept political maneuvers. One unpromising change immediately stood out: after it was thought that Jackson would continue Adams's policy of retaining in federal office any who performed their duties honorably, the Democrat reversed course and replaced many in federal jobs with loyal political appointees. The practice became known as the "spoils system"—a form of patronage to coincide with the return of a paranoid style in partisan activity.[23]

Freshman Congressman

Upon his election to the House in the fall of 1830, Adams confided to his diary, "My election as President of the United States was not half so gratifying to my inmost soul." What drew him back to Washington politics was, at bottom, a sense of personal pride. He had tried out scholarly reimmersion but needed more. He wanted to be where he could defend himself and reestablish his prestige after the nastiness of the late presidential campaign.[24]

Returning to Washington in December 1830, the ex-president waited nearly an entire year before the first session of the Twenty-second Congress began. A fair portion of those intervening months was spent ruminating on politics past. Even the old Adams-Jefferson rift reopened as word reached him that Martha Jefferson Randolph, surviving daughter of the late founding father, had gone to Boston to visit a married daughter who now lived there. Mrs. Randolph was disturbed by Louisa Adams's failure to call on her and wondered whether politics was at the root of it. After this, in his position as living interpreter of the Adams-Jefferson correspondence, JQA was approached—one might say taunted—by North Carolinians who were revisiting a matter of history that the deceased presidents had sought to put to rest: Mecklenburg County, North Carolina, believed that it deserved to be credited for its May 1775 Declaration of Independence, in standing up for a United States a full year before the five-man committee in the Continental Congress assigned Jefferson responsibility to draft the nation's official birth certificate.

Adams had read Jefferson's brief autobiography, along with a cleansed version of his collected letters, published in five volumes in 1829 by his eldest grandson, Thomas Jefferson Randolph. The account of Jefferson's formative years was "not boastful," Adams allowed, but there were "no confessions," to wit: "Jefferson by his own narrative is always in the right." Adams found this disturbing, given that Benjamin Franklin had already shown in his celebrated autobiography a willingness to expose flaws.

JQA was obstinate in sizing up Jefferson's praise for college instructors who pointed him toward a suspicion of clerical authority. Their instruction had, Jefferson wrote, "fixed the destinies of my life." The pious John Quincy agreed, saying that "the mysteries of freethinking and irreligion . . . *did* fix the destinies of his life" and that "loose morals necessarily followed." For this Adams, but not the elder, Jefferson's bad traits could be laid at the feet of faithlessness: "If not an absolute atheist, he had no belief in a future existence." Jefferson the freethinker was proof of Jeffersonian "insincerity and duplicity." JQA's Jefferson was a confessed libertine: in his diary, Adams named the neighbor's wife who had spurned a young, unmarried Jefferson's awkward advances. Interestingly, Adams cared so much about this matter that he refused to accord Jefferson even the level of forgiveness he granted the (as legally constructed) bigamist Jackson.

This degree of animus toward Jefferson is rare in the extant Adams record, and coming now, five years after Jefferson and John Adams were dead and buried, it shows the persistence of the past in the mind of the sixty-three-year-old freshman congressman. Disappointed that Jefferson did not get around to a self-defense of his presidency, for the revelations it would no doubt have brought to the younger Adams as a prominent player in that administration, the sixth president found a way to reverse course slightly, when he credited the third president's "ardent Passion for Liberty," his "Patriotism—the depth and compass of his understanding—the extent and variety of his knowledge."

To JQA, Jefferson's saving grace was his Revolutionary love of liberty. Jefferson was, of course, largely responsible for the Declaration of Independence, the language of which John Quincy Adams adored and eternally defended. But as JQA brought his moral balance sheet up to date, the Virginian's "infidel philosophy," his "burning ambition," his "treacherous and inventive memory," led to the unwarranted "treatment of . . . my father," which exposed "perfidy" of an epochal dimension—reminiscent of the annals of ancient Rome. In sum, the second Adams considered Jefferson a world-class deceiver. The ousted president might have set aside the planned biography of his beloved father, but the past kept catching up with him. Indeed, he relived it practically every day.[25]

Also at the end of 1830, the congressman in waiting caught wind of a history of more recent vintage that was in the process of being rewritten. It was said that President Monroe had stood alone against the censure of General Jackson in 1818 after he exceeded his orders during the Florida invasion. Of course, this was not the case: it was the well-articulated legal argument of Secretary of State John Quincy Adams that actually prompted Monroe to go with his gut and remove the stigma from the professional combatant who now occupied the White House.

There was more to the story, a lot more. It was the season of nullification in the nation's capital. Vice President Calhoun had recently become a South Carolina sectionalist in reaction to the 1828 protective tariff that increased the cost to consumers of British-manufactured textile products. Exporters of cotton considered the tariff detrimental to their economy, and a radical faction of South Carolina legislators declared the right to nullify that act of Congress within its own borders. The argument went that because the states had originally created the Union, the states could act as they saw fit to protect themselves when the federal government overstepped its authority. Over the winter of 1830–1831, as he made his position known, the tall, humorless

John Calhoun felt he had to move from the boardinghouse where he lodged, because, as Adams noted in his diary, the company of Senator Hugh Lawson White and Congressman James K. Polk, Tennessee allies of the president who resided there, was "no longer acceptable to the Vice-President."

Implausible as it sounds, Adams soon found himself aligning with Jackson in opposing Calhoun, the turncoat vice president they had in common. The onetime presidential candidate William H. Crawford had devilishly revealed to Jackson, not long before, that Calhoun, as Monroe's secretary of war, wanted to censure the general for his aggressive actions in Florida, and that Jackson's putative enemy, John Q. Adams, had been the one most sympathetic to his position. This was news to Jackson.

There was no end to political dogfights, especially for Jackson, who always insisted that he have the last word. One day in early March 1832, after the House had adjourned for the day, Richard Mentor Johnson, a Democratic congressman from Kentucky, asked Adams to join him for a walk. Johnson broached the delicate subject of Adams's coolness toward his successor. Jackson wished to reconcile, no longer believing the stories that Adams was responsible for newspaper columns that insulted his late wife. Convinced that Jackson possessed "dispositions entirely friendly" toward the New Englander, Johnson wished to serve as go-between in restoring the presidential pair to a state of greater civility and personal harmony. Adams made up his mind quickly and rejected the overture.

Though nullification placed Adams and Jackson on the same side, in nine of every ten votes he cast, Adams would register his opposition to the new administration. At this point, he was concerned with the tariff only insofar as it produced sufficient revenues for the government so that investment in internal improvements—a national system of roads and canals, mainly—might be enacted. Jackson picked and chose which bills he would back, based on political self-interest, and he refused to move ahead on federal support for improvements, which Adams and Clay (now in the Senate) strenuously championed. The reason for Jackson's reluctance, Adams insisted, was a fear that improvements to interstate communication would only bring economic progress and greater political solidarity to the commercially adaptive northern states while further consigning the slave South to its backward position within the Union.

Clay had a personal investment in the outcome of this issue. In 1832, incensed after Jackson vetoed internal improvement that serviced his hometown of Lexington, Kentucky, the former secretary of state gave the presidency his second of three tries. Like JQA, he was defeated soundly by the gaunt yet indomitable Tennessean.[26]

ATRABILIOUS DREAMING

One day in March 1832, as he sat at his desk in the House chamber, a letter was delivered to John Q. Adams by hand. It was from his son Charles, and it concerned JQA's "dear and amiable brother," Thomas Boylston Adams. Tom's death could not have come by surprise to any of the extended clan. Able and engaging in his younger years, by the 1820s he was dependent on family. Having turned to drink, he went into a slow downward spiral, leaving behind a wife and six children.[27]

John Quincy worried, too, for his son John, who lived in Washington. A good-looking young man, John was not the hearty specimen his father was. In January 1833, Congressman Adams, his wife, and their second son were all under the weather at the same time, when John was "copiously bled." His father the inveterate diarist, who did not make a habit of recording dreams, produced in this instance an explicit entry in his "line-a-day" summary that departs from the rest: "Dreams of disease." In the long-form entry, he elaborated: "Dreams of a man to whom life becomes a burden—atrabilious—My wife—my son, myself, in sickness and in sorrow." ("Atrabilious" was a synonym for "gloomy" and "dispirited.") In October 1834, with Congress in recess, word reached him in Boston that John was gravely ill. Louisa felt too weak physically to travel, and the sixty-seven-year-old father went immediately, unaccompanied, to see his child.

On board the steamboat *Benjamin Franklin* to New York—very likely the same vessel that George Adams had fallen or jumped from five years earlier—he chatted with a motley group of passengers. Some, including a Quaker preacher, were known to him; others had met him on one or another occasion, though he did not recall them. As they weighed in on issues of the day, the passengers' conversation touched on the divinity of Christ as well as the scourge of slavery, "prospects of universal emancipation, and the intellectual capacity of the African race." The congenial group stayed up past midnight. This was a form of democratic exchange John Quincy Adams embraced.

When, days later, he finally reached his son's home, it was nighttime, and he was fatigued from the journey. The cheerless father climbed the stairs, only to find that the thirty-one-year-old sufferer "had no consciousness of any thing on Earth." JQA's daughter-in-law of six years—Louisa's niece and the mother of two young daughters—was bedridden. She "burst into tears" at the sight of her father-in-law as he told her lovingly that he would be a father to her and her children. The next morning, as another John Adams took his final breath, the well-practiced mourner turned to God, as was his custom, and reminded himself that full compensation for the pain experienced in life would be provided in the hereafter. "My dear Son had been in a declining and drooping state of health more than three years," he recorded wearily.

John Quincy Adams the politician appears in the historical record as a fighter, unconquerable in spirit. But he was, equally, a pious sufferer. Turning to his diary as he prepared to bury another son, he took what little solace he could find in the cruel fact that he had "kissed his lifeless brow yet warm" in the hours before death came. The night after the funeral, adding forebodingly to the tragedy, a fire broke out in the house of the frantic widow. Though smoke filled the upper chambers, the home was saved through prompt action. "My spirit is awed even to superstitious terror by these menaces of divine chastisement," wrote J. Q. Adams, direct descendant of the credulous folk known to history as Puritans.[28]

FOURTEEN

STANDARD-BEARER

I have no communion with any Anti-Slavery Society, and they have disclaimed all confidence in me. But I sympathize with all their aversion to Slavery.

—DIARY OF JOHN QUINCY ADAMS, *November 4, 1846*

Charles Francis, the youngest son of Louisa Catherine and John Quincy Adams, was the one sibling who remained intact and would survive to uphold the family legacy. A future U.S. envoy to Great Britain—the third in as many generations of Adamses—he would be kept busy for years as editor of the family's papers, because his father, post-presidency, still had a lot to prove.

As JQA's second career in Congress opened, Indian policy and slavery came to occupy center stage. First, a little background: Major General Andrew Jackson had executed Indians, without trial, during the 1818 Florida invasion. As secretary of state at the time, JQA was, by all outward appearances, unperturbed by these events, prioritizing, as he did, the U.S. position with respect to Spanish colonial regimes. He well understood that Georgia's political leadership regarded the social status of Indians as akin to simple tenants on their land, barely better than slaves. As president, JQA temporized, making a concerted attempt to stop the state of Georgia from acting unethically toward the Creek nation, while supporting voluntary removal of the Cherokees. Even this mild push back caused land-hungry Georgians, protesting federal interference, to reject Adams and welcome the compulsory removal plan of his successor.

Congressman Adams entered Congress too late to have a vote on the Indian Removal Bill of 1830, the first major legislative initiative of President Jackson. By then, Adams regretted his former ambivalence. He listened with interest as his former attorney general, William Wirt, presented arguments before the Supreme Court in favor of the Cherokees, and he decided to make himself a thorn in the side of Jackson and all southern whites whose menacing behavior toward Indians had amped up. Adams presented pro-Cherokee petitions before the House, one of which, sent from New York City, contained thousands of signatures. Seeing the futility in opposing removal, and having convinced himself that the original Americans were already on a one-way highway to cultural extinction, he soon backed down, though not without expressing outrage at the injustice. At the same time, his Whiggish—that is, morally suffused, open-minded, improvement-oriented—posture did not prevent him from voting with the Jackson Democrats to authorize funds to resist Indian violence.

He had found that he could become an outspoken critic of Democrats' perverse moral posturing by posturing himself. It was a somewhat doubtful balancing act: on the one hand, he championed the Native underdog, serving as a source of moral authority; on the other, he did not sacrifice himself or spearhead any effort on behalf of Indian rights. He saw his activities as indeterminate and merely as a stopgap measure.[1]

Slavery was a very different matter, facilitating a more intensive brand of political posturing. Once again, the South was his primary target. News out of London affirmed for him that the end of slavery was near, as the accumulated efforts of British abolition groups finally bore fruit in direct response to an island-wide slave rebellion in Jamaica at the end of 1831. Tropical plantations where slaves far outnumbered white colonists were obvious breeding grounds for a kind of misery and violence that was no longer to be tolerated. Adams noted, "The abolition of Slavery, will pass like a pestilence over all the British Colonies in the West Indies; it may prove an Earthquake upon this Continent." There was no justification for the continuation of slave labor in the U.S. South. When Alexis de Tocqueville queried him about the heat and the suitability of different races for certain kinds of labor, Adams had a ready reply: "The Europeans work in Greece and in Sicily, why should they not in Virginia and the Carolinas?"

When Parliament's Slavery Abolition Act was finalized in 1833, creating short-term indentures, it simultaneously freed Caribbean slaves and opened Canada to black fugitives from the United States. On its heels came the

American Anti-Slavery Society, founded in December of that year, which would keep the issue in constant, plain sight. Its strongest voices proclaimed from Boston. Congressman Adams, attuned to the Christian principles that animated the antislavery movement, monitored abolition activity while maintaining his independence.[2]

BRAGGART MENACES

The slavery issue shadowed, and eventually came to dominate, all congressional debate. A cadre of reform-minded men and women, born at the start of the century, would carry to the floor a crusading ideology that established the moral identity of their generation. But as of the early 1830s, their time had not yet come. John Q. Adams's generation still held the reins, and it did not take long for him to stand out as one of the most formidable members of the House of Representatives.

Over the remaining seventeen years of his life, the ex-president carved out a unique place in history—less as a defender of national interests and more as a spokesman for his native section. The father had weighed in on political matters as "Novanglus" (a Latinization of "New England") in the lead-up to the Revolution; the son, reared in the courts of Europe and often blamed for it, significantly reclaimed his "Pilgrim" roots during the final chapter of his political career.

Though we choose to emphasize the regional bookends in our story of father and son, it was, in fact, an all-encompassing history of the Republic that directed JQA's political refashioning in the years following his father's death. When he mustered the intellectual resources he needed to tackle hypocrisies on display from the ardent defenders of slavery, the second Adams channeled, first and foremost, the philosophical strengths of the founding era. In spite of his personal animus toward Thomas Jefferson the man, John Q. Adams, in his mature years, often invoked the Declaration of Independence as the cornerstone of American values. He developed an "originalist" argument in an effort to rewrite the nation's constitutional destiny; that is, his sectional agenda required a nationalist logic.

He was more than ready for conflict. He might have held the highest office in the land at one time, but the former title gave him little cover: he knew the kind of vitriol to expect from southerners. Congressional debates increasingly brought forth personal attacks, and some outlandish charges of treason were hurled at him. He received profanity-laced letters and occasional death threats (which he took seriously). Yet he quickly came to relish the political battles he waged and was pleased to take on the role of watchdog in Congress. To encounter *this* John Quincy Adams is to realize how much it mattered to him that he was no longer in the executive branch. As congressman, he viewed the political landscape differently than he had before. He was in the belly of the beast, evaluating democracy as an active player in America's most visible deliberative body.[3]

The House of Representatives was the most publicly oriented branch of the federal government. It was designed to be. The representatives who made waves and garnered the most newspaper coverage were those who understood political combat as a democratic war of words and symbols. That is why Thomas Jefferson, a wordsmith without equal, served Adams's purposes so well. In sparring with southern colleagues, he achieved the rhetorical effect he sought by invoking the rhetorical Jefferson. Doing so was almost a form of revenge against that other Jefferson, the one who succeeded as a *symbol* of democracy but who actually muddled the concept. Insofar as Jefferson was a hero to Andrew Jackson and Martin Van Buren, JQA knew of no better historical model to embrace when taking on hubristic slaveholders and dishonest (merely rhetorical) democrats. By featuring natural rights theory and presenting slavery as its outright opposite, Jefferson's Declaration of Independence undermined the positions of those who claimed to be Jefferson's political offspring.

Every bit of Jeffersonian thought had given way to the demands of sectionalism by the 1830s. And this thing called Jacksonian democracy was worse, because it thrived on visceral appeals and violent imagery. The spoils system it spawned rewarded the loyal rather than the principled, which was antidemocratic. By the end of John Quincy's career in Congress, sectional politics would reach the point where southerners, knowingly or unknowingly, abandoned the sage of Monticello altogether. In 1845, a decade after he battled Adams in Congress, James Henry Hammond of South Carolina would actually repudiate the sacred declaration by denouncing Jefferson's abstract notions of equality as "ridiculously absurd."[4]

At first glance, Adams's recovery of the Declaration of Independence as an antislavery instrument may not appear radical, or even that surprising. But in the larger scheme of things, he aimed to establish the text as the equivalent of a social contract—the Revolution's social contract—representing at once a break with the past and a guiding law. Thirteen years before the Constitution, it endowed citizens and residents of the new country with inalienable rights that held precedence over the privileges that come with owning property. Again and again, as a late-in-life congressman, the second Adams was to reiterate Jefferson's logic, backing his younger congressional adversaries into a corner. They knew better than to contest his intimate knowledge of the founders and the founding.[5]

His thinking on slavery began to crystallize during the Missouri controversy of 1819–1820 while serving as Monroe's secretary of state. He kept his opinions to himself at that time, but in his impassioned diary notations on congressional proceedings, and in his private discussions with Secretary of War Calhoun, he began to sketch out key parts of a constitutional theory. He was taken by how adept the members of Congress from slave states were as they bullied their colleagues and obliged them to acquiesce in southern demands. He later insisted that southern "Hotspurs" (referring to Shakespeare's tantrum-prone rebel) were always ready to resort to lordly histrionics, erecting a united front to silence opposition. Their threats of "dissolution of the Union, and oceans of blood" led northern politicians to "sit down quietly, and submit to the slave-scouring republicanism of the planters." The frustration Adams felt as he recorded these words cannot be missed. But it was early. It was only 1819. Still, he coined a term for the undemocratic southern attitude he'd observed: "masterdom." He saw a "domineering spirit" burst forth in response to the mere mention of slavery restriction (let alone abolition) in the presence of slavery's defenders. He actually found their obstructionism pretty simple: southern elites aimed to "govern the Union as they govern their slaves." He was ready for these "braggart menaces," he said.[6]

Without embracing abolitionism directly, Adams acknowledged the corruption of the Constitution in the deals made over the years with powerful slave owners. As his legal argument developed, he found that slavery violated the most basic principle of free government, "consent of the governed"; no one in America ever consented to be a slave. In the history of mankind's wars, slaves were defined as captive "enemies," but according to the 1793

Fugitive Slave Act, they were property to be returned to their masters. All in all, the Constitution's three-fifths compromise, awarding slave states additional representation on the basis of the unfree black population, was a Faustian bargain that necessarily rankled New Englanders. Adams bristled at its dubious calculus: that slaves were "persons not represented themselves, but for whom their masters are privileged with nearly a double share of representation." The pact with slave owners was "vicious," and it betrayed the American Revolution's first article of faith.[7]

He determined that the Missouri crisis had its roots in Jefferson's first administration. He'd supported acquisition of the Louisiana Territory when he first entered the Senate in 1803, but he later had misgivings. It came at a steep price, he thought, "not of money, but principle." The purchase gave unequal advantages to what he identified at the time as the "slave-holding sections" (South and West). And it hurt New England. The persistence of slavery as an American institution meant that Congress condoned the "right of conquest," the right to govern without asking consent. What was true in the theft of Indian lands was even more evident in the treatment of African Americans as a conquered race. By annexing land under the terms of "colonized dominion," conquest gave slavery a permanent legal haven. Louisiana was bad precedent. Too much of the United States, in Adams's view, remained amenable to slavery.[8]

So, how do we connect the declaration to John Quincy Adams's legal theory? Adams held that the nation's official birth certificate possessed all the power of a fundamental law. In his 1821 Fourth of July oration, in Washington, he tested the theory, according the document its literal revolutionary function: "It demolished at a stroke the lawfulness of all governments founded upon conquest." Again, the critical issue was consent versus conquest. Of America as a whole, he sounded out, "Her glory is not *dominion,* but *liberty.* Her march is the march of the mind." In this moment of clarity, he reminded his hearers of the personified Liberty: "She has a spear and a shield; but the motto upon her shield is Freedom, Independence, Peace. This has been her declaration . . . , her practice." Five years later, in the poem he wrote on his father's birthday, just months after the coincident deaths of the second and third presidents, he praised John Adams and the patriot generation for breaking the "oppressor's chain" and enacting a future promise that "not a slave shall on this earth be found!" He wished that it were so.[9]

But as he departed the President's House in 1829, the second Adams well knew that the living declaration had hit a roadblock. The Revolution embraced the "natural rights of man in society" to alter government, but the dictates of economic advantage were as blatantly obvious as the racial limitations placed on equality. Jefferson had subtly endorsed sectionalism on coming into the presidency, when he described the role of the federal government as "encouragement of agriculture, and of commerce as its handmaid." Handmaid? In subservience to agriculture? For all practical purposes, Jefferson's first inaugural address revealed the far greater value he assigned to the agrarian interest in America—the slave-owning South. So grossly imbalanced was Jefferson's theory that JQA concluded (bitterly now) that the perspective it reflected "could only have originated on a tobacco plantation." The danger to the nation, once again, lay with that ugly thing, "masterdom."[10]

In developing his constitutional critique, JQA consciously divided Jefferson in two. The rhetorical Jefferson had authored the consummate declaration, while Jefferson the Virginian was handcuffed by slave culture. Adams was sure that Jefferson's love of liberty was sincere, even "ardent," but the Virginian often had to keep his beliefs hidden. Jefferson understood "the gross inconsistency between the principles of the Declaration of Independence and the fact of negro slavery," and, crucially, he made no attempt to justify the ownership of human beings.

In this way, Jefferson appeared to the second Adams superior to the likes of John Calhoun, who had come to see slavery as a positive good. In a conversation with Adams during the Missouri crisis, Calhoun had insisted that the subjugation of slaves actually created a greater degree of equality among white men. This was patently untrue, of course, because elite southerners despised poor whites with a passion. Yet the developing myth of racial solidarity allowed men like Calhoun to reassure themselves that the South's system was preferable to the commercial society of the North.

Jefferson had once been a bona fide revolutionary, an unmitigated idealist. With eloquence, he had sought in his draft of the declaration to decry slavery; yet in the main, as JQA noted with sublime awareness, Jefferson "had not the Spirit of Martyrdom." His half-hearted attempts to end slavery were either mistimed, subtly withdrawn, or published after he was in the grave.

This sense of the tragic, of a missed opportunity, exposed Adams's own inner struggle. One naturally wonders whether his long public silence on slavery led him to acquire some greater measure of sympathy for Jefferson and a life riddled with contradictions. Perhaps it did, though nothing concrete emerges in the diaries. At any rate, on reentering Congress, something changed, and John Quincy Adams stood poised, ready to speak his mind and invite reactions. With little to lose anymore, he developed a pugnacious style on the floor of the House. He made it clear that he was going to address slavery in ways that would get him into trouble. His "vivacity and energy of manner" were "astonishing," reported a Columbus, Ohio, paper; others around the country concurred.[11]

NULLIFYING SOPHISTRY

It was the nullification controversy, 1830–1833, that brought slavery's inherent contradictions to a head. Nullification (under the banner of states' rights) proved to Adams that those who condoned slavery refused to disavow the outmoded right of conquest and the regressive feudal ideas inherent in colonial empire. He brought to bear a combination of legal acumen and his unique personal connection to the nation's founding, as he took on doctrinaire southerners.

States' rights theory was aimed at redefining the original social compact of the United States. Behind the clamoring over tariffs—the apparent substance of the nullification debate—Calhoun's idea of state sovereignty sought to turn the clock back to the Articles of Confederation that governed the Union before 1789. The articles, in turn, had borrowed from the feudal British custom the idea that sovereignty resided in the state and was not lodged in the people—nor derived from the rights of man, as the Declaration of Independence momentously held.

Thomas Jefferson had introduced the concept of nullification in the late 1790s, in response to the first president Adams's willingness to go along with the Sedition Acts. But in 1830, the aged James Madison, who had avoided the political fray for years, broke his silence and publicly condemned Calhoun's illogical theory. It was inconceivable to Madison that an extreme minority could dictate to the majority: a state's ability to nullify legislation passed by Congress would, he said, "overturn the first principle of free Government and in practice necessarily overturn the Government itself." The threat could not be any clearer.[12]

Adams, too, was impatient with the "sophistry of nullification," as he denoted it. In an oration he delivered in Quincy on the Fourth of July 1831, he elaborated on Madison's principle. Seizing on the centrality of the declaration in American political life, he forcefully argued that state sovereignty was a "hallucination" founded on the same idea that Parliament had earlier subscribed to. British colonial power—and sovereignty—had been based on force, violence, conquest, dominion, and subjection. In 1776, the thirteen colonies were not declared sovereign *states,* Adams insisted. The word "sovereign" was not even to be found in the declaration. And states' rights were not human rights. If one state could nullify a law of the land, then that one state was effectively being granted absolute authority over every other state.

Nullification was a ploy, waged in the spirit of "masterdom," which stripped the northern states of *their* rights, so as to undermine what Adams termed "free debate." The nullifiers of South Carolina put forth a concept of sovereignty at odds with the republican notion of deliberation and at odds with the democratic principle of majority rule. As a feudal remnant, nullification was "incompatible with the nature of our institutions."[13]

In May 1833, after South Carolina vetoed another tariff law, Adams took to the House floor and restated his view of the connection between slavery and nullification. It was a rousing speech, triggered by the obnoxious words of Representative Augustin Clayton of Georgia. Alluding to northern industry, Clayton had chosen a poor metaphor when he marked slaves as the South's "machinery." In his jaundiced view, "a white man in a factory was no better than a slave"—whereby northern labor was "slave labor."[14]

Three days after hearing Clayton, Adams tore into the South's faulty logic. Most important, he said, the federal government was not the enemy of the South. It never had been. Since the Constitution became the law of the land, representation favored the South by counting slaves. Adams looked around the House chamber and took note of the fact that slave owners enjoyed a political advantage of twenty or so seats. By contrast, he said, "looms and factories" had no votes in Congress. Insofar as tariffs were used to fund the federal government, free northern laborers subsidized the military, which helped to put down slave uprisings. What better example was there? Though he did not mention by name Nat Turner's 1831 rebellion, its more than symbolic effects were fresh in everyone's minds. Federal troops, eleven companies in all, had been deployed to suppress the slave insurrection in Southampton County, Virginia. Northern state courts complied with the fugitive slave law. The South received abundant federal protection, at the expense of competing interests outside the South.[15]

As chairman of the House Committee on Manufactures, Adams co-authored a report that was even harsher in tone. It called out the abuses of the southern political class, and it avowed the humanity of men and women in bondage. They were productive workers, "of flesh and blood, and bone and sinew." Nor was it lost on Adams that landed men in feudal aristocracies held "real cultivators of the soil" in "oppressive servitude." The historical parallels fit all too well. The fact that southerners devalued labor itself only convinced Adams that royalist impulses attached to the quasi-feudal planter class. In short, there was nothing at all democratic about nullification in support of the slave economy. Meanwhile, an entrenched class of southern oligarchs continued to infiltrate all branches of the federal government. In a diary entry of 1835, Adams remarked that slave owning had become, for southern voters, a prerequisite for the presidency.[16]

His speeches before Congress were at times satirically drawn. In one instance, he spoke of the threat of disunion by recurring to *The Adventures of Gil Blas,* the comic novel he and his father had enjoyed so well during their European adventure. In an episode, the hapless hero stops to count his money and sees a hat in the road before him. A voice comes from nowhere, asking him to drop a few coins in the hat. Gil Blas assumes it to be a "poor mendicant" but soon discovers that it's a sinister someone, hidden in the bushes, with a blunderbuss pointed at his head. The moral of the story was only slightly subtle: nullifiers were pretending to be the injured party when they were anything but. They dressed up their political logic in the language of victimhood while at the same time threatening violence. Subterfuge. Extortion. That's what Adams saw. One New Hampshire newspaper said of his speech, "It fell like a thunderbolt among some of the slave-holding gentry of the South."[17]

As to theories of conquest, Adams never lost sight of the disruptor-president himself. Rigid, defiant, imperious Andrew Jackson was a pivotal figure in the ever-darkening portrait of a blustering, conquering, slave-protecting not-real democracy. As early as 1830, as an incoming congressman, JQA predicted that the Jacksonians would find some excuse to conquer Mexico by force of arms. But it was Jackson's use of the presidential veto that more directly caught Adams's attention. In his first year as president, Jackson vetoed three of four bills on internal improvements, flouting what Adams described as the "great reserve" of his six predecessors, who, combined, had rejected only four acts of Congress. Autocratic behavior came easily to the plantation-owning president. Adams likened him to an "overseer" (literally, a slave driver), asserting masterdom over the whole nation.

In Adams's view, Jackson's arrogance was fed and fortified by the blind devotion of his followers, who received his denunciations with "rapture," according to one prickly diary comment. It was not hard to figure out that the seventh president's power rested on his combined "military services" and "personal popularity," neither of which John Q. Adams could boast. The "Old General" was heroically cast, the first presidential hopeful to be propped up by an inspirational campaign biography that sold a larger-than-life personality to voters. Congressman Adams dug deep to find the source of Jackson's power, which by 1835 was unambiguous: he had placed in perfect alignment the demands of western land speculators and southern slaveholders. Indian removal and the opening of public lands for sale worked in conjunction with the larger goal of conquering territory to expand the slave system.

Talk of democracy was the smoke screen that hid the real engine behind party politics: material wants, new lands. Jackson's cult of personality camouflaged the conquest imperative. "This is the undercurrent," Adams confirmed for himself, "with the tide of democracy at the surface." In another diary entry, almost in disbelief, he wrote, "Slavery and democracy, founded, as ours is, upon the rights of man, would seem incompatible with each other. And yet, at this time the democracy of this country is supported chiefly, if not entirely, by slavery." He could say it no plainer.[18]

TEXAS DEBACLE

By 1836, the year the Alamo's defenders were martyred and the Republic of Texas was born, the year the anti-Jacksonian Whig Party held its first national convention, Adams had abandoned what caution and decorum remained in his political speech. With another election year facing the country, he bemoaned the age of Jackson. At least Jackson the man was "daring," he acknowledged; his unfit party merely tagged along. There was nothing remotely like personal appeal in Jackson's chosen heir, the equivocating Martin Van Buren—to JQA, a puppet of the master class. To win the presidency, he'd had to (1) defend states' rights; (2) reprove abolitionism; and (3) protect slavery. For the first time in American history, slavery lit up a presidential race.[19]

Texas independence in the spring of 1836 gave Adams an even stronger platform on which to attack the forces of slavery and conquest. Many southerners were already arguing that Texas belonged to the United States under the terms of the Louisiana Purchase. They called it "a land of slavery," with a future in cotton and sugar production; it simply required "a constant supply of slave labor." The popular position was to see Texas as a blessing for the nation, land that could be annexed without a war.[20]

Adams rejected such logic. In speeches on the floor, he repudiated outright the argument that the federal government had no right to interfere with slavery. First, the federal Constitution itself had stipulated that the slave trade would end in 1808. It had the right to interfere, to supervene. But the larger solution lay with Congress's war powers. Adams used the example of slaves' emancipating themselves or joining an enemy in a time of war. If it was beyond a master's ability, or a state's power, to restore domestic peace, would Congress then have no right to interfere? Yes, most definitely it would, starting with the work of negotiators who were bringing this hypothetical war to an end by treaty. The federal government had a role to play in protecting or ending slavery, "from the instant that your slaveholding states become a theatre of war—civil, servile, or foreign."

Adams meditated at great length on the future of Texas. Antislavery Mexico was agitated, and antislavery Great Britain was eyeing the area, too, for commercial opportunities that a direct political relationship would strengthen. Despite the ardency of southerners' desire to realize slavery's expansion west, slavery in Texas was not ensured yet. The federal government was waiting in the wings, alert, involved. Adams lectured his congressional colleagues that Texas independence, so called, was "a war of aggression, of conquest, of slave-making," that involved the U.S. government. Mexico had abolished slavery a decade before. Which was why Adams charged that Texas was a war of *re-conquest* and *re-enslavement*. He minced no words.

National defense was a matter of prime concern. Once the U.S. military entered Texas, as he predicted it would at some point, Washington automatically became an interested party. (Abraham Lincoln would apply legal logic similar to Adams's when, as a war measure, he issued the Emancipation Proclamation, freeing slaves exclusively in those seceded states that remained in rebellion after January 1, 1863.) And so, Adams argued, making America safe for slavery was a dangerous pursuit beyond the purview of any one state. Was not the land taken from Native Americans enough to satisfy land hunger? "Are you not large and unwieldy enough already?" he posed, no doubt scanning the assembled representatives as he spoke. "Do not two million of square miles cover surface enough for the insatiate rapacity of our land jobbers?"[21]

These were stern words. It was a powerful speech. Linking westward expansion of slavery to Indian removal in the southern states at this charged moment—May 1836—put a spotlight on impulses that flew in the face of human liberties. Once Mexico and Great Britain had done away with slavery, Americans could no longer claim to carry the banner of liberty where they went. If, as Adams predicted, the United States was to conquer more of Mexico—cynically undertaken with "freedom, independence, and democracy, upon your lips"—it would be a bloody affair without a moral basis. "I do not think it possible to keep the question [of slavery] out of Congress," he concluded.[22]

He had succeeded in putting slavery at the center of the Texas debacle. Though President Jackson had endorsed the idea of the "reannexation of Texas" (suspiciously claiming it as part of the Louisiana Purchase), the ordinarily impulsive chief executive was forced to proceed more slowly once resistance to annexation gained political momentum. That his close friend Sam Houston, former governor of Tennessee, was now president of the Texas Republic, made Jackson's Whig detractors wonder whether the president himself had helped bring about the plot to separate Texas from Mexico's dominion. Adams was convinced that Jackson would recognize Texas as an independent nation, a prediction that came true on the day before Jackson left office in March 1837.

The activist congressman from Massachusetts was not finished with this subject. On June 19, 1836, he tried to add an amendment to the bill to admit Arkansas as a state. In a midnight session (actually, at five in the morning), he moved to insert the following words into the bill: "Nothing in this act shall be construed as an assent by Congress to the article in the constitution of said State in relation to slavery and the emancipation of slaves." It was a ruse, as well as an act of mockery, to shame colleagues who wished to avoid any mention of slavery. JQA's nuisance amendment would have restricted not just slavery but emancipation as well. The uncomfortable language sparked a "fiery" debate that lasted over three hours. He described the ensuing scene in his diary—one colleague "drunk with whiskey" and another "drunk with slavery," both lashing out at him directly. To no one's surprise, his fire-breathing amendment failed to get the requisite number of votes.[23]

Nine days later, the ex-president Madison died, and the ex-president Adams was asked to deliver a eulogy in Boston. He made it an unusual speech, offering up a detailed political history of Madison's career, resisting the overblown rhetoric found in most eulogies of the great men of the era. Adams thought to include negative reflections on a founder he genuinely admired. "There were circumstances in the Life of Mr. Madison," his diary reads, that could not be passed over "in silence." He meant the flirtation with nullification in the Kentucky and Virginia Resolutions of 1799, initiated in concert with Jefferson in opposition to the Alien and Sedition Acts, which history had already begun to use to tarnish John Adams's reputation. The son felt compelled to vindicate his father, and the New England character, and at the same time (as his diary explains) "expose some of the fraudulent pretenses of the slaveholding democracy." How would he reclaim Madison from the slaveholding Democrats of the tortured present?[24]

In some ways, the eulogy of Madison reads more like a legal brief than a memorial. Adams went to great lengths to distinguish the views of Jefferson from those of Madison. While chastising Madison's Virginia Resolution as a "party measure" (to unseat President John Adams), he insisted that Madison did not endorse Jefferson's nullification doctrines, that he "disclaimed them in the most explicit manner at a very late period of his life." Of the two Virginians, Madison was the better man, his mind "tempered with a calmer sensibility and a cooler judgment."

Adams closed the eulogy by citing a speech Madison gave at the convention to revise the Virginia state constitution (1829–1830), in which the fourth president challenged the consensus in place by speaking to the "condition of the colored population." This was clearly a difficult subject in Virginia. Slavery had produced a conflict between "the rights of persons and the rights of property," Madison acknowledged. It was "due to justice; due to humanity; due to truth; to the sympathies of our nature in fine, to our character as a people, both abroad and at home; that the colored part of our population should be considered, as much as possible, in the light of human beings, and not as mere property." As legal subjects, nonwhites had "an interest in our laws."

No wonder Congressman Adams highlighted these words. Madison had always looked to the future. He wanted his Virginia audience to recognize that slavery did not reflect the true character of the people. Rights of property did not trump all other rights. As for his commitment to self-evident truths, Madison, in plain language, sided with justice and humanity. The Father of the Constitution decried states' rights as a retreat to the old confederation. It was left for Adams, in his eulogy of Madison, to reclaim the high ground: "A confederation is not a country."[25]

Outgeneraling Generals

On the same day in the spring of 1836 that he launched into his speech against Texas, Congressman Adams seized a moment to ask colleagues whether he was being "gagged." The Speaker of the House was refusing to let him speak. He used the word "gagged" intentionally, referring to the controversial action being debated in the House that permitted it to reject antislavery petitions—*all* antislavery petitions.

James Henry Hammond of South Carolina had instigated the gag rule a few months earlier. "What, sir, does the South ask?" he'd posed dramatically, alluding to libel and slander laws and the circulation of subversive abolitionist literature. Congress "ought to be a sanctuary, into which no such topic [as slavery] be allowed to enter."

Hammond was a slaveholder not by birth but by marriage. Nevertheless, he was one who fully embraced the idea that slavery was a positive good in bringing tremendous wealth to the South. Like Clayton of Georgia, he thought of slaves as "operatives." And as a South Carolinian, he used the logic of the nullifiers to declare that if Congress took any action to legislate on the subject of slavery, it would be the first act in dissolving the Union. He went so far as to send a warning to any abolitionists who dared come south that they would meet a "felon's death."

Hammond's position on the threat to southern slavery had the backing of the outgoing president, Jackson, whose 1835 annual message called for Congress to devise a law that severely punished any who sent such ("incendiary" was his term) antislavery materials through the mails. Postmaster General Amos Kendall adopted a policy of states' rights with regard to the kinds of materials that were unauthorized: states could use their own laws to protect themselves against dangerous speech.

After Hammond's outcry, the House of Representatives placed the petition issue in the hands of a special committee, headed by a South Carolinian. Its members drafted a resolution, which passed easily, stating that the House would table "petitions, memorials, resolutions, propositions, or papers, relating in any way or to any extent whatever to the subject of slavery." Broadly worded, the new restriction did not just forbid the reception of petitions on slavery; it allowed for the censorship of the speech of House members.

Hammond took a deliberate swipe at Adams. He called the Yankee's attempts to defend the general "right of petition" as nothing but "slang." He meant that the House had no intention of hindering the speech of *legitimate* petitioners, but in his construction antislavery agitation was an *illegitimate* use of the right of petition. Hammond assumed that any antislavery petition was invalid, because it demanded a hearing on a subject over which Congress had no power: ending slavery. An antislavery petition might well incite slave rebellions; they were tinder for treason. Hammond claimed that it was the intent of abolitionists to "subvert the institutions of the South." Of course, this was twisted logic if not a knowing lie. Indeed, Hammond's speech was supremely ironic. It revealed that southerners of the 1830s were actually hoping to revive the punitive measures of the Federalist Congress of 1798, by treating "incendiary" antislavery publications as a new kind of seditious libel.[26]

With no apparent consciousness of the connection, Hammond and his supporters went about retooling the moribund Federalist game plan. Just as early Federalists blasted the democratic societies of the mid-1790s for fracturing the country, southerners now rebuked antislavery societies as disloyal entities. Both groups wanted to be immunized against inflammatory political speech, and both believed good government would fall apart if legal restraints were not enacted. It is more than a little curious that both High Federalists and planter-politicians referred to the activist opposition as "barbarian"—that is, a bloodthirsty, unrepresentative minority whose radical protest threatened civilized society. In each instance, the aggrieved expected deferential treatment.[27]

In the end, Congress avoided the historic mistake of the Federalists by refusing to pass a law to prosecute abolitionists, though that is what President Jackson had openly wished. But the South did give sanction to reactionary mob violence when the antislavery printer Elijah Lovejoy was murdered in Alton, Illinois, in 1837. Adams publicly condemned the atrocity, insisting that the suppression of speech in the House—the menacing censorship of the gag rule—derived from the same spirit that would condone Lovejoy's murder (demonstrating, too, that pro-slavery violence was not confined to the slave states).

The gag rule remained in force until 1844. It meant that the House would not officially receive, or read, antislavery petitions. Southern politicians thought that the gag rule served a larger constitutional strategy of propping up states' rights, but its real function was to curtail free discussion. To make the U.S. Congress a "sanctuary," as Hammond demanded, was to build a wall between its powers and the laws of the states.[28]

As Adams fully appreciated, southerners had changed the very meaning of the petition. This broad and inclusive right had become subject to a political test that could be applied to any man or woman, organization, printer, or officeholder who dared to bring the issue of slavery before Congress. Clothing antislavery speech in the dress of seditious libel—taboo, criminal, and inflammatory enough to dissolve the Union—stripped antislavery petitions of any claim to civil protection. It also recognized that abolitionists had learned to exploit the tools of democracy: they published newspapers, held conventions, funded itinerant speakers, and worked to shape public opinion with slogans and disturbing images of scarred slave bodies.

The gag rule put the petitioners' messenger on notice. Representatives such as Adams were not just being browbeaten by their bombastic colleagues; their speech was being policed and their rights removed. In defiance of this practice, the congressman from Massachusetts used parliamentary maneuvers to make sure that the issue of slavery came to the floor of the House. When an effort was made to drown out his voice, he rose above the tumult, his cheeks reddening, as he declared of the gag rule, "I regard this resolution as a direct violation of the Constitution of the United States, the rules of this house—and the rights of my constituents." The gag rule went beyond petitioners' rights. Taking a stand in the most democratic forum that existed in the United States, John Q. Adams aimed to shame contemptuous southerners for abusing the democratic rights of everyone else.[29]

Gagging had symbolic resonance in American popular culture at this moment. The most famous visual example was engraved in 1834 and pictured Henry Clay with needle and thick thread, sewing President Jackson's mouth shut. The Kentucky senator dominates and physically restrains his pained quarry, and a piece of paper pokes from his back pocket, on which is written, "Cure for calumnies." As for Clay's former boss, a lithograph of 1839 shows Congressman Adams lying prostrate, worn down, his body stretched over a pile of his vaunted petitions, among which are an abolitionist newspaper, the *Liberator,* and a resolution to formally recognize the Haitian republic. "Abolition Frowned Down" features Waddy Thompson, a congressman from South Carolina, leaning over the floored Adams. He stares at him maliciously while declaring that any discussion of slavery must be "indignantly frowned down." Two cowering slaves off to the side appear in need of protection from the southern patriarch. As for J. Q. Adams, two separate attempts were made to censure him for raising the petition issue (in 1837 and 1842), and both failed.[30]

Louisa Catherine Adams had as little patience with southerners' antics and referred to them as a "puppy in fits." Her husband gave the pro-slavery carnivores plenty of red meat, more than once setting off a pack of enraged southerners by presenting petitions from a variety of justice seekers: slaves, free blacks, white women, and even a disunionist who did not wish to be the citizen of any Union that countenanced slavery. In 1837, JQA started a protracted debate by waving a Fredericksburg, Virginia, petition in the air, and asking whether the Speaker would allow it. It was from twenty-two slaves. The uproar that ensued lasted for more than three hours and was reported as an "extraordinary scene" in which the "whole South" was set "aflame." Cries came from the floor: "*Expel him, expel him!*"

Representatives urged one another to "vindicate the honor of the South." The ex-president, now just another congressman, remained perfectly still throughout. When he finally spoke again, it was to correct his colleagues for misapprehension: he had only asked if the petition could be presented, and yes it was from slaves, but it was a petition of a particular character. He did not, for the moment, offer more detail.[31]

That same day, he'd asked to present a petition from nine women of Fredericksburg. Someone spoke up, saying he understood that these were mulatto women and women of ill repute. Adams feigned ignorance and insisted that the "virtue" of the supplicant was not an issue in petitioning. He had no idea whether the petitioners were "colored women," he said, because the petition itself did not indicate color or condition. So, he asked whether right of petition was limited to freemen of the "carnation" (by which he meant white). Over the course of the debate, he roguishly turned the question on its head and faulted the chivalrous South for producing so many slave children that looked like their white masters. He mocked his colleagues for knowing—after all, how could they have known?—that the females petitioning through him were prostitutes. The word for his tactic did not exist at the time, but let it be said that John Q. Adams was being snarky.

As he listened to resolutions seeking to punish him for his insults to their proud body, Adams finally explained to his fellow congressmen that they'd jumped to conclusions based on groundless fears. Their censure resolution would have to be reworded, because, as he put it, "my crime has been for attempting to introduce the petition of slaves *that slavery should not be abolished.*" More reaction. He was trifling with them. Or perhaps he was too senile to realize that a hoax had been perpetrated.

Yes, it was a hoax! But he knew that it was. Virginia slaves petitioning Congress to protect the institution of slavery? The culprit might have been a slaveholder; that's what Adams suspected. He merely took hold of a document and deliberately deployed his legal stagecraft, thriving on misdirection and baiting a restive audience. His adversaries went ahead and made fools of themselves. They convicted him absent the facts.[32]

Then he added fuel to the fire. Slaves *did* have the right of petition, he proclaimed. He waited for the shoe to drop, as he knew it would. A congressional resolution passed, maintaining that Adams had "given color to the idea that slaves have the right of petition," to which he replied coyly, "I had given color to the idea, that the right of petition is confined to no color." His purpose was to expose the absurdity that *any* reason could be given to withhold the right of petition or censure a congressman. Abolition aside, any petition that insulted the feelings of members, or caused a stir, was too dangerous to be heard. "What," he inquired in his retrospective on the day, "have the feelings of the House to do with the free agency of a member in the discharge of his duty?" Was the ex-president an "enemy to the union" merely for presenting a petition?[33]

The rascally congressman saw to it that his constituents heard about his speeches and read his detailed thoughts in their local papers. "What is the South?" was among the questions he posed in this forum. Southern congressmen wished to present their section as subject unfairly to outside interference. Adams returned an explicit counterargument. The South consisted, he said, "of masters, of slaves, and of free persons, white and colored, without slaves." Which, if any, of these classes of people would be harmed by a petition from slaves? Not the slaves themselves, of course, they of the "producing class"; nor would the free people, white or black, be offended. In fine, the master class did not represent the *whole* South. Abridging the right of petition so that only they could be safely heard was shortsighted, to say the least. Establishing the precedent of denying petitions would too easily become a partisan tool and "the exclusive possession of the dominant party of the day."

Southern sectionalism remained a festering issue, of course, but in JQA's mind, it was something quite specific, part of a poisonous inheritance, an unjustifiable ideology predicated on a big lie. The source of the present contaminant was the distortion of meaning being given to founding documents. To Adams it was all fairly simple: one either sided with the Declaration of Independence and the U.S. Constitution or with masterdom. He took a new tack in condemning the defenders of states' rights: "We are told that the national government has no right to interfere with the institution of domestic slavery in the states, *in any manner.* What right, then, has slavery to interfere in the free states with the dearest institutions of their freedom? . . . with freedom of the press? with freedom of speech? with the sacred privacy of correspondence by mail?" How could the essential rights of life, liberty, and the pursuit of happiness be bestowed selectively? How could one favored class, the master class, overtake the rights of everyone else?[34]

All in all, his obstinacy paid off. With each countermeasure, he won new admirers for "outgeneraling the generals," as a Portsmouth, New Hampshire, newspaper claimed for him. Facing down the combined power of a clamorous opposition, he'd found loopholes allowing him to forward petitions. In order to deny a new petition from Congressman Adams, more discussion was needed to justify its exclusion. The more discussion there was, the more opportunity he had to catch supporters of the gag law off guard. Despite his advanced age, he remained always a step ahead of his detractors. One Massachusetts newspaper editor referred to the petition campaign as the "crowning act of his life."[35]

Adams won the battle when the attempt to censure him died. In one respect, and one only, the House bested the old Harvard professor of rhetoric: it left out of Congress's official *Register of Debates* some of his most capably reasoned arguments, many of his cleverest barbs, and the bulk of his longest speech. Which is why he went on to publish the whole as a pamphlet, under the clear title *Letters from John Quincy Adams to His Constituents of the Twelfth Congressional District in Massachusetts: To Which Is Added His Speech in Congress, Delivered February 9, 1837.*[36]

MOCK DEMOCRACY

With changing times, Adams's views on race departed from those of his father, who never seemed emotionally troubled by race prejudice and tended most often to intellectualize it. JQA shared his mother's deep revulsion toward the sexual practices of masters. Even in 1819, watching the Missouri crisis unfold, he worried that a full-scale interracial apocalypse was to result:

blending the two and bleaching the black, eventually to form a different kind of white race. He does not explain the resulting pigmentation with any precision, but the portrait he left us shows his general discomfort.

The possibility of Texas annexation contributed to his fear of slavery's unchecked population growth. The southern section of the Republic, as a slave breeder's paradise, was a veritable "nursery" for slaves, he wrote. By 1838, he was openly calling the domestic slave trade "internal piracy." To view this truly existential problem from a legal-constitutional perspective that Americans understood, normalizing a trade in human beings was at least as shameful as turning a blind eye to the hated regime of British impressment; both were concessions to a corruption of civil liberties. The United States went to war over impressment.[37]

Prior to the 1830s, at least in his public statements about national policy, JQA had never been especially sensitive to the injustices Americans of color suffered. In the Senate, during Jefferson's presidency, he did not see any urgency in keeping slavery out of the Louisiana Territory just acquired from France. As secretary of state, conducting negotiations with the Spanish minister, he did not press Monroe to bar slavery from Florida. As a negotiator, he argued fiercely that London was bound to compensate Americans for slaves who fled to the British side in the War of 1812. His public face betrayed no antiracist leanings.

In actions, his father was the more engaged in issues involving race. As a young attorney, John Adams took on the cases of several men whose slaves were suing for their freedom, and in each instance he lost. But he did openly express his hope that the Supreme Judicial Court of Massachusetts would see fit to end slavery in his state. Over the course of the 1790s, he watched as the Haitian Revolution unfolded and did not pass judgment on the viability of a republic of liberated slaves on the basis of the racial background of its leaders or its people. As chief executive, he took a decidedly progressive turn. Through a formula advanced by Secretary of State Timothy Pickering (whom he eventually fired for political subversion, of course), John Adams carried out a pragmatic, race-blind policy in support of diplomatic and commercial engagement.

Jeffersonians tended to believe that the Adams administration was acting out its hostility toward the pro-slavery South with its Haiti policy. The avowed abolitionist Albert Gallatin, then a Pennsylvania congressman, warned that politically inexperienced Africa-descended people were unlikely to be successful in self-government. Alexander Hamilton expressed his deep concerns to Pickering. President Adams moved cautiously out of concern for the British reaction to an increased U.S. commercial presence in the Caribbean, but nothing race-related slowed his hand. The president's son, then in Europe, agreed at the time that a full engagement with the former French colony was due and that a "close alliance" between the United States and independent Haiti made sense. But the time was not ripe for a serious discussion of the future of slavery in the United States.[38]

In the 1830s, Americans of the northern states did not support the abolition movement in significant numbers, but they could see that slave owners dominated the presidency, all branches of the federal government, and the Supreme Court. The master class engaged in what Adams called "mock democracy" and "double dealing." Slaveholding politicians would not speak honestly about slavery, and they stole the speech of those who could. Slavery was built on piracy, on kidnapping. It eroded the very idea of inalienable rights. That was what animated John Q. Adams now.[39]

In a rare moment, writing to an abolitionist in 1837, he explained why defense of a slave's right to petition was sacrosanct for him. It was because his father had helped to write the Declaration of Independence. The son of John Adams believed that no matter what was said of it in latter days, that sacred script could not be limited to people with white skin. The slaveowners' "new school of servile philosophy" debased the very notion of "rights of man" and was equally "abhorrent" to the "self-evident truths" set forth in the declaration. It was more than bittersweet longing that returned Congressman Adams to 1776; he was chagrined by the moral deterioration that had taken place with the disappearance of his father's world, and most transparently in the cruel policies toward unrepresented peoples in the presidential administrations of Andrew Jackson and Martin Van Buren. "In the treatment of the African and native American races," he wrote trenchantly, "we have . . . degenerated from the virtues of our fathers."[40]

With the petition campaign, Adams became increasingly attached to all things New England. In the *Letters . . . to His Constituents,* he addressed his readers as "Sons of the Plymouth Pilgrims." While recalling the founding as a time of greater humanity, he was seeing Massachusetts of the present day as the last stronghold of liberty. At an 1838 reception organized by the ladies of Hingham, just east of Quincy, he defended a woman's right of petition, trusting that it would be "maintained in Massachusetts if nowhere else." In 1841, he recalled the pride those of his generation felt when the first national census was taken in 1790, and Massachusetts "stood alone in the return of the word 'none' upon the column under the head of 'Slaves.'" When enemies in Congress tried to expel him for the second time—to the point of accusing him of treason—he defended himself as a son of New England. Like the people in his district, he declared, "I come from a soil that bears not a foot of a slave upon it. I represent here the descendants of Bradford, and Winslow, and Carver, and Alden—the first who alighted on the rock of Plymouth."[41]

As it happens, his father's memory was undergoing a revival during the period when JQA was doing some of his most serious damage to southern pretensions. Daniel Webster's glowing eulogy of Adams and Jefferson acquired a second life, as Webster, by now a long-serving U.S. senator from Massachusetts, was reaching the peak of his renown. Ensuing generations were to recite as part of patriotic catechism his ecstatic words, supposed to have come from the mouth of John Adams, and spoken in defense of the declaration before it passed Congress. A portion of that mythic speech went like this: "Sink or swim, live or die, survive or perish, I give my hand and my heart to this vote. . . . But while I do live, let me have a country, or at least the hope of a country, and that a free country." Like his heroic father in 1776—at least as John Adams was being remembered—the son had returned to the theme of defending embattled freedom in lofty strains.[42]

The editor of the *Richmond Enquirer* had other opinions, arguing that the second Adams was literally "mad." There were those in the South who lamented his having besmirched his family's name. Pressing on with his "abominable multitude of Petitions," the prodigal son had sapped the strength of the America "which his own father so nobly contributed to establish." Other Virginians had nothing good to say about either Adams. They remembered the father as a member of the "British Party" of the 1790s.[43]

When Henry Wise of Virginia stepped forward in January 1842 to urge the censure of his colleague Adams, he painted both father and son with the same brush of Toryism. Congressman Wise, nearly four decades younger than Adams, was known for his short fuse, and Adams chose to provoke him. It was known that Wise took part in an infamous duel a few years earlier, acting as a second when a congressman from Maine fell dead. Adams accused Wise of having entered the House with "his hands and face dripping with the blood of murder." As Wise taunted him back, another sturdy New Englander entered the fray. A former Federalist, now Whig congressman, Leverett Saltonstall, rose in the defense of the Adams clan. Without the "illustrious father, and his equally illustrious relative, Samuel Adams," there would be no nation at all, Saltonstall reminded the members. The Adams men were sometimes "rash," and likely "pertinacious," but such qualities were needed "when a great principle was to be maintained at great cost." Southerners' attempts to censure JQA for his ridicule of the slavery regime served the collateral purpose of questioning the New England origins of the Revolution, if not the region's legitimately democratic tradition. To be an outlier was to invite trouble, and JQA, post-presidency, issued an open invitation to any and all. An admirer wrote in 1839 that he found it odd that so skilled a statesman joined no organization. His isolation, his aloofness, made it easy to accuse him of undemocratic leanings.[44]

But the iconoclast could not be had. Adams went to lengths to pronounce his reluctance to support immediate abolition. In a published letter of 1839, he took the American Anti-Slavery Society to task for expecting slave owners to voluntarily surrender their property. He disliked the American Anti-Slavery Society, because, as he put it, "every man who enters into a political association, must leave not only his opinions but his common sense at the door." Adams said things, as one astute editor recognized, that were "little calculated to win friends from any quarter." He was often found "voting in a party of one."

The end of the overseas slave trade and colonization (that is, resettlement of freed slaves outside the United States) had only served to increase the value of domestic slaves. This is why JQA did not have to reach deep to find the right vocabulary when he designated Texas as a nursery for "slave breeding." He knew, as a seasoned politician, that immediate abolition was impossible without the consent of owners and indemnity for their losses. But abolitionists had no intention of reimbursing slave owners; anyway, payments would be too large ever to be undertaken. By the very nature of government, slavery could end only upon the consent of slave owners, state legislatures, and voting majorities, and if not by these means, it would end in war.[45]

Was he now the voice of doom? His enemies called him a "flaming abolitionist," but he wasn't that. He was stubborn in pursuit of legal logic and occasionally passionate on matters of natural rights. It is just that he refused to identify with a single camp. He roundly disavowed party affiliation and let the public know that he had not taken any part in a presidential "canvass" since losing reelection in 1828. Following the contest between the incumbent president Martin Van Buren and General William Henry Harrison in 1840, he acknowledged his thorough disgust with the ongoing style of campaigning. He wrote with unprecedented cynicism that if military service was not, by itself, "the direct and infallible path to the Presidency," it had to be coupled with demagoguery and the quasi-military "art of party drilling." Harrison, the putative Whig, had been an Indian fighter and war hero, whereas Van Buren was a "drill master" enforcing party loyalty. Ideas weighed less than the distractions of political theater, whether in the form of folksy orations from Harrison or the "riotous democracy" that entertained prospective voters with parades and free food and drink. Adams did not join movements; he thought and spoke for himself, for those who elected him, and for intelligent republicanism.

What measure of man stood at the helm did not so much matter to Adams anymore, because either way party ruled. There was only so much he could do to highlight the inherent problems of party culture. As an outlier, he assumed his days were numbered. When he delivered his Madison eulogy in 1836, he took literary license, but he might have been expressing a deeper sensibility, too: "He who now addresses you has but a few short days before he shall be called to join the multitudes of ages past." He harbored too many larger and larger doubts about the present. He belonged more and more to the past. Yet he felt obliged to weigh in on the present while he lived in it. Congress was his platform and he took it.

There was already, at this time, an organized public relations element in national campaigning, even before the modern concept of "public relations" was understood as such. Song and symbolism. Politics of personality. Adams had witnessed it in 1828, when he was beaten by the overestimated lowbrow Jackson. Post-presidency, he regarded the division into national parties as a sinister tool to co-opt thought and, in the case of southern Democrats, a crude weapon for those who would "purchase auxiliary support for slavery from the freemen of the North." The language he used was explicit. He would not compromise on language.[46]

On matters of race, active participation in House debates made him re-evaluate his more tentative beliefs of a former period. He had moved beyond the legal position he took as a secretary of state, when he allowed himself to perceive a categorical difference between English impressment of American sailors and American trafficking in slaves. As late as 1829, in an unpublished treatise on political parties, he was still describing the British practice of "man-robbing" and "kidnapping" as somehow worse than enforced race servitude. Ten years later, he saw what slavery and impressment had in common, that both were forms of piracy. If impressment was an "anomaly in the British Constitution, utterly incompatible with their boast of freedom," he could now admit that the slave trade left a similar stain on the Bill of Rights. Slavery was strong in the 1830s; the domestic slave trade, a form of kidnapping, was protected by law. Slave smuggling continued apace. He would not ignore what was happening.[47]

Amistad Case

Many of his concerns received a full hearing when he stood before the Supreme Court in 1841, arguing in the famed *Amistad* case. He spoke in defense of several dozen Africans, originally taken in Sierra Leone, brought to Cuba in 1839, and placed on board the Spanish schooner *Amistad.* The captured men took over the slave ship in Cuban waters and demanded to be returned to West Africa; they ended up instead on the coast of Connecticut. There they were imprisoned for having murdered the captain and a crew member of the Spanish vessel. Where would they be sent? Even as murder charges were dropped, President Van Buren placated his southern constituents by authorizing return of the slave mutineers to the Spanish government in Cuba. A federal court in Connecticut disagreed, ruling that the Africans had been enslaved illegally.

JQA was drawn to the case for the same reason he cared about petitions. In a letter published in 1840, he described the Africans in terms that recalled the impressment issue: they were stolen, shorn of their rights, treated as political prisoners. And they suffered an added burden: "They knew nothing of the Constitution, laws, or language of the country upon which they were thus thrown, and accused as pirates and murderers, claimed as slaves of the very men who were their captives, they were *deprived of the faculty of speech* in their own defense." They were deprived of speech in the way Congress was intent on ignoring the voices of antislavery petitioners.[48]

Adams knew that to win in court, he had to avoid converting his pleading of the case into a frontal assault on slavery. He would identify a more rhetorically appealing villain to frame his drama: the unpopular Martin Van Buren. The eighth president had abused the powers of his office in his apparent indifference to the plight of prisoners. In Adams's construction of the case, the president proved himself willing to compromise law and to engage in "trickery" to hide his maneuvers. Along with Secretary of State John Forsyth, he indulged the Spanish slave traders; instead of ensuring impartial justice, the two leading government executives had shown "sympathy for the whites, and antipathy for the blacks."

To make one of his key points, the artful Adams drew from the popular novel *Gulliver's Travels*. The title character had come upon a nation of beings ("not exactly human") with a unique way of exposing lies: they said "the man has 'said the thing that is not.'" The secretary of state, in this case, repeatedly "said the thing that is not." Forsyth ignored the Africans when they insisted they were not slaves. He ignored the fraudulence of the papers presented by the Spanish. The Spanish minister claimed that the Africans were "Spanish property" and murderers, and the administration refused to allow any court to investigate these questionable claims. Van Buren had even attempted to employ naval officers to transport the Africans back to Cuba before the case had gone through the appeals process.

Showing his hand, Van Buren had sought to circumvent—to subvert, in fact—the judiciary. Secretary Forsyth wrote to the Connecticut district attorney that the president did not want *any* judicial tribunal to hear the case, stating that "vessel, cargo, or slaves" should not be taken out of federal control. The U.S. attorney general Henry Gilpin had to conceal Van Buren's real intent, which was to hand over the slaves to Spain to be prosecuted for murder.

Adams exposed the ugliness of the government's ruse. The thrust of his argument thus centered on political ineptitude, which he hoped might appeal to Jacksonian appointees on the Court, who already harbored distrust for the New Yorker Van Buren. The president should never have displayed such utter disregard for the right of habeas corpus—protection from improper detention. His personal interference was, Adams wrote, an exercise of "arbitrary and unqualified power"; he was behaving as though he alone were qualified to decide the Africans' fate. The congressman from Massachusetts understood that no major legal principle was at stake. The U.S. president merely wished to appease the Spanish for material reasons; he would protect the interests of slave owners and ensure that extradition applied to any fugitive slaves who might escape to Cuba. This wasn't justice, Adams contended, but a commercial transaction, a quid pro quo, a promise to deliver lost property.[49]

Addressing the high court, he could not resist pointing to the two copies of the declaration that hung on the wall. Nor could he resist turning President Van Buren into the former king of England:

> I will not recur to the Declaration of Independence—your Honors have it implanted in your hearts—but one of the grievous charges brought against George III was that he had made laws for sending men beyond seas for trial. That was one of the most odious of those acts of tyranny which occasioned the American Revolution. The whole of the reasoning is not applicable to this case, but I submit to your Honors that, if the President has the power to do it in the case of Africans, and send them beyond seas for trial, he could do it by the same authority in the case of American citizens.[50]

The dramatic gesture was meaningful. Adams had been asked by an antislavery group to take up the Africans' cause. By defending their right to live out their lives as free men, he presented himself not as an abolitionist—he well knew that Chief Justice Roger Taney of Maryland was a slave owner—but as a child of the American Revolution.

John Q. Adams was not pleading for a body of enslaved people to be set free; they already were free. Preparing the case, he made a special trip to the Library of Congress in order to reread a favorite speech delivered by James Madison at the Virginia Constitutional Convention on December 2, 1829. Standing before the justices of the Supreme Court, and inspired by Madison's reasoning, Adams attacked Spain's minister for tripping over the essential contradiction of slavery: *that slaves were both persons and property*. He expressed his particular disgust that the surviving thirty-six men, women, and children had been "lumped" together, as he put it, denied their rights as individuals, and considered cargo. They were recognized as persons in order to be punished, to satisfy bloodlust. If they were turned over to the Spanish as "assassins," which was what the minister demanded, then why should the children—"infant females"—be returned? It was because they were considered merchandise.

Adams argued that officers of the executive branch of the U.S. government, whether intentionally or not, were in violation of core principles enshrined in the declaration. The president pretended not to see; he was amenable to the idea that the federal government actually allowed the re-enslavement of free men and women. (We hear an echo of JQA's disgust at the thought of Texans' reinstituting slavery where Mexico had forbidden it.) Were the Africans returned to Havana, it would be solely "to appease" vengeful slave traders. "Is there a law of Habeas Corpus in this Land?" Adams asked sharply. The Court should refuse to surrender to "the demand of despotism." The attitude he adopted in court was one of cool control, yet exuding deep disquiet. "Has the 4th of July, '76, become a day of ignominy and reproach?"

Nearing the end of his presentation, he waxed nostalgic about a prior instance when he stood before the justices of a different Supreme Court. It was in 1809, arguing a property case—the poetic opposite of what he was doing in 1841, standing in defense of human dignity. Feeling his age, he recalled each of the former justices by name, listing their accomplishments. And then: "Where are they all? Gone! Gone! All gone!"[51]

By a 7–1 majority, the Supreme Court ruled that the Africans aboard the *Amistad* were not, and had never been, slaves. They would not be handed over. John Quincy Adams had performed brilliantly, justice was served, and American slavery remained a protected institution where it continued to exist.

Constitutionalist Party

At seventy-three in 1841, Congressman Adams remained a constant thorn in the side of his southern enemies. He pestered, he badgered, he constantly upped the ante. He clearly enjoyed taunting them. Battling the likes of Henry Wise of Virginia, he knew how to touch a nerve, whether it was in tarnishing southern armor over their code of chivalry or exposing hypocritical statements brought on by their racial fears. Wise, for one, admitted to his concern that the influential, unpredictable former president might push for diplomatic recognition of the black republic of Haiti—completing the work his father had begun as president.

JQA's final decade in Congress featured more concentrated competition between the two major parties, Democratic and Whig. Yet Adams was not a Whig per se. He could never be so confined. He agreed with the party's essential belief that the federal government had a significant role to play in improving society. But by the spring of 1841, when Vice President John Tyler inherited the White House after William Henry Harrison's untimely death a month into his presidency, Adams was stewing. It was of little consolation to him that the sturdy Daniel Webster was now secretary of state. JQA unreservedly despised "His Accidency," as the mediocre Tyler was known. Yet another sectionalist Virginian, he was neither a political Whig nor a model of erudition. In diarizing, Adams loosed a string of insults for the "slave-breeder" president: "a political sectarian of the slave-driving Jeffersonian school, principled against all improvement, with all the interests and passions and vices of slavery." The Whigs had made too many political compromises with southerners for Congressman Adams's taste. In 1844, JQA did not even actively support the presidential bid of the Whig candidate, his former secretary of state, Henry Clay, because Clay owned slaves. No one owned John Quincy Adams's opinions.[52]

The political climate was intense, animated, and above all unstable. On Capitol Hill, there were out-and-out brawls to be seen and deadly duels to read about. Members carried pistols and daggers. Prostitutes openly plied their trade in the halls of Congress. Clay even assigned a special section of the gallery to that "abandoned" class of women so they could hear his speeches. In stark contrast, like his father before him, J. Q. Adams donned the robe of the stodgy and exacting schoolmaster. Instead of the birch, commonly used to whip young students into shape, he used his tongue to chastise those who failed to meet his righteous standard. Henry Wise dubbed him the "hissing serpent from Braintree." Which was, no doubt, fine with the second of the unloved Adamses.[53]

Neither could John Q. Adams rest his pen. In 1842, a new pamphlet he authored made the rounds. *The Social Compact* denied Jacksonians exclusive claim to the democratic ethos, historicizing democracy and clarifying its evolution in conjunction with party competition. Democracy was not, he claimed, the child of either Jefferson or Jackson—though history had already resolved to misattribute it to them. Democracy, he held, was another name for "representative government." Effectively a protest against consensus history, *The Social Compact* was of a piece with "Publicola," as well as John Adams's *Defence of the Constitutions*. A popular man did not make democracy any more real.

Yet instead of defining what democracy was, Adams took time to explain what it wasn't. The word "democracy" does not appear in the Declaration of Independence, nor in the federal Constitution, nor in the Massachusetts Constitution. Democracy was but one element within America's "mixed government"—to repeat his father's philosophical touchstone. Adams wanted it known that, short of promoting democracy, Jackson's party was actually composed of "obsequious champions of executive power," acolytes of a warrior-based cult of personality who wallowed in a fantasy view of the glamour of conquest. Which was decidedly *not* democracy.

The Massachusetts congressman thoroughly despised the current political cant. Jacksonians had concocted their so-called democracy and cast it as—here Adams satirized them—"the government of the *whole* people and nothing but the people; that no fraction of the people, not the purest, not the strongest, not the wealthiest, not the wisest, no—the whole people, man, woman, child, born or unborn, foreigner and native—the lunatic, the lover and the poet, all must govern—and that is Democracy."

To his mind, the most accurate name for an American political party that honored the nation's founding principles would not include the word "Democrat." So, where would he want to make his political home? There was only one way for JQA's statement of belonging to conclude, if he was to go to his final resting place content. "Were I permitted to select a name for the party to which I should wish to belong," he wrote, "it would be that of Constitutionalist; meaning thereby faithful adhesion to the two Constitutions, of the United States and of the Commonwealth. They are the fruits of the wisdom and valour of our forefathers matured and modified by the experience of more than threescore years." The most he would say for democracy was that it was "oxygen or vital air," essential for life, but combustible and deadly in combination with other elements.[54]

THE END

On July 11, 1847, Congressman Adams marked his eightieth birthday. His health was poor. On the occasion of their fiftieth anniversary, two weeks later, he'd presented his wife with "an elegant Bracelet as a memento of the occasion," as Louisa noted in her diary. "The day passed most quietly according to our own desire." Their son Charles Francis and daughter-in-law Abigail celebrated with them a few days after.[55]

The times were bittersweet. The congressman, his voice softer than it had been, dated his certain approach to death to the end of 1846, when he'd suffered an attack in Boston and lapsed into an insensible state ("a suspension of bodily powers") that lasted days. With his partial recovery and return to Congress, he chose a macabre heading for journal entries in the year 1847: "Posthumous Memoir." His mordant wit was well known, especially within the family. But did his wife know he had done this?[56]

She meditated on her mortal flesh no less than he, expressing the "fluttering uneasiness" of her heart at the end of 1847, anticipating a fatal attack. She sought solace in religion as she updated her will. Louisa Catherine Adams would outlive her husband by four years, despite abundant doubts on her part as to her survival prospects at the time of their jubilee anniversary. John Quincy remained wry and wary. "Thanks to Almighty God that I am yet alive," he scribbled on November 6, 1847. "May I be ready to surrender my soul at His call whenever it shall come." He kept going to work on Capitol Hill, urging territorial restraint in an atmosphere favoring immoderate expansionism.[57]

Though he did not quite expire while seated, we can report that Congressman John Quincy Adams died at his desk. It was Monday, February 21,

1848. He had gone to church the day before. On the fateful morning, he jotted a few lines of poetry for an admirer. It was otherwise to be a rather ordinary day in Congress. A reporter for the *National Intelligencer,* a Washington newspaper long friendly to Adams, gave the blow by blow: "Just after the yeas and nays were taken on a question, and the Speaker [Robert Winthrop of Massachusetts] had risen to put another question to the House, a sudden cry was heard on the left of the chair, 'Mr. Adams is dying!'"

Since March 1845, the president of the United States had been James K. Polk, a former Speaker of the House and a political disciple of his fellow Tennessean Andrew Jackson. He and Adams did not have much in common. The debates over Texas had finally ended, and the Lone Star State joined the Union as a slave state. Mexico severed diplomatic relations with Washington, and boundary disputes between the two nations intensified as Polk assumed office. Adams's warnings over the years had not made enough of an impression.

Whigs protested the march to war. Adams accepted that he would be called unpatriotic for opposing the southwest extension of "manifest destiny." Of course, it did not stop him from voting his conscience. At Polk's instigation, Congress declared war on Mexico in May 1846. Its outcome was never in doubt. "War for the right can never be justly blamed," Adams pronounced. "War for the wrong can never be justified." He was reelected to Congress that year by one of the largest margins of his post-presidential career.

Even as he turned eighty, he would not give up on dipping his withered body in the Potomac, where, as president, he used to walk from the White House regularly, at the break of day, and swim for a good hour. If he had represented anything in his life, it had to be willfulness and resolution. And none of that changed, even as he neared the end.[58]

So, on February 21, 1848, as the octogenarian congressman fell across the left arm of his chair, David Fisher of Ohio, who occupied the next seat, stopped his fall. But there was little that could be done for the venerable son of the Revolution. The House, collectively in shock, promptly adjourned, and the sufferer was attended to. At first, they moved him to the Rotunda, but a crowd formed, threatening to undo the dignity of the scene. News was brought to the Senate chamber, and the veteran Jacksonian Democrat Thomas Hart Benton of Missouri rose. "I am called on to make a painful announcement," he said. "A calamitous visitation has fallen on one of [the House of Representatives'] oldest and most valuable members. . . . Mr. Adams has just sunk down in his chair, and has been carried into an adjoining room, and may be at this moment passing from the earth." Benton moved for the Senate's adjournment as well. Government ceased to function while the sixth president began to die under the watchful eye of colleagues.

His own father's death had been recorded as a sensational event without precedent, because of the exquisite timing—because of the unique day on which it occurred. But the son's final moments were drawn out according to the precepts of the romantic age, and for the benefit of the living generation, which relished deathbed scenes in literature. Lying down in the office of the Speaker, the dying man briefly regained the use of speech and, according to Benton, "uttered in faltering accents, the intelligible words, 'This is the last of earth,'" adding soon after, "I am composed."

Death would not take him for another forty-eight hours, but we are instructed that "I am composed" were his last words. Had he died on Washington's birthday, more dramatic language might well have been summoned, but he denied his eulogists that trope and gave in on the day following, February 23. His wife was by his side, though she proved unable to muster the energy to attend his funeral.[59]

Newspapers carried reports on the return of his body by train to its final resting place in Quincy and the somber affair that took place in Boston's Faneuil Hall, draped all in black. Lightening the mood, a local correspondent recounted a scene he witnessed at a slightly earlier session of Congress, when two rustic Virginians were peering over the House balcony, hoping to glimpse their local congressman, while noticing a "shiny-headed old man" with "watery eyes and hunchy shoulders" whose pathetic appearance they could not resist mocking. "Guess he ain't no great shakes," said one of the Virginians. "He ain't got no papers on his desk." The time came when he gained the Speaker's attention and rose from his chair. Everyone in the chamber suddenly turned their attention his way, "anxious to catch every word," as they did with no other representative. "Je-hos-ophat," the rube exclaimed when informed that the "hunchy" oldster was J. Q. Adams, "Old Man Eloquent" himself.

Less colloquially, the *Wisconsin Democrat* recalled the insults Adams had received as president while noting how in his last years "all parties listened to him with a respect and reverence which he never received when he was occupying the highest dignity in the world." The *Emancipator* remembered him in the same words that had been used to characterize his father in 1826, as "the venerable and venerated sage of Quincy," whose "self-sacrificing devotion to humanity, to freedom, to the true principles of republican liberty" were legend. In the *Southern Patriot*, a South Carolina newspaper, "the habits of Mr. Adams" were praised as "pure, simple, and unostentatious even to awkwardness. . . . No one ever was more industrious. . . . He was one of the most prolific writers of the age." There was something distinctive about him that produced a general curiosity. He was known, even in Charleston, as an early riser, fond of swimming, a man who, rather than prevail on servants, "made his own fire." It was understood that his well-maintained cache of letters to and from eminent men and women would be a treasure trove for lovers of history.[60]

In recognizing his patriotic parentage, those who delivered eulogies of the last president to have personally known each and every one of his predecessors also affected to have observed his excellence and moral goodness at close range. A Boston preacher assured his congregation, "He was a tried and enduring friend," and he described the deceased, for the record, as not merely "the son of one of the patriarchs of the revolution" but himself "the friend of Washington." One of the first to eulogize John Quincy Adams, the Massachusetts senator John Davis, reminded his listeners what no one needed to be reminded of: "His father seemed born to aid in the establishment of our government, and his mother was a suitable companion and co-laborer of such a patriot. The cradle hymns of the child were the songs of liberty."[61]

The eulogist Nathan Lord, the president of Dartmouth College, reached deep as he compared Adams's relatively serene passing to the "momentary paralysis" that seized the nation's heart when Washington died in 1799, and "a father, a deliverer" was entombed. The country at that time experienced a singular "agony," because it was still in its "infant State." The death of John Quincy Adams was only different because it constituted the removal of someone who had come of age along with his country. He left behind a different America, one that had grown into its "lusty, independent manhood." Lord, trained as a clergyman, explained the underlying emotion that abounded: "We lament, but with a mingled feeling of remorse for our own errors, and of admiration at his exalted virtues." Fearless John Q. Adams fought for justice.

What struck the eulogist was how highly insightful the second Adams was. He saw what was happening to his country and spoke out often. But it was clear that his fair "warnings and remonstrances" were going unheeded as the United States lost its way. The departed statesman was special because he still adhered to something old—a spirit—that was intensely moral. "The aim of Mr. Adams was to be right and wise; right in his principles, and wise in his application of them; in which consists all true morality." This Adams was a flawed man, Lord allowed: "He could be impetuous and unyielding; but he was not obstinate or malignant. He could be impatient and angry. But he was not resentful." This was ultimately what distinguished him from the more ordinary politicians of the mid-nineteenth century. True dignity.[62]

No one was quite the Adams intimate that his eulogist Edward Everett was. The Harvard valedictorian of 1811, subsequently a graduate student in Germany, Everett was nearly as erudite as John Q. Adams himself. By 1848, the fifty-three-year-old had served as a Massachusetts congressman and governor and as an ambassador to England; he would at length be named secretary of state. Everett was proud, he said, to have been a close associate of the second president Adams, "possessing his confidence" during the four years when he held the nation's highest elective office. In transmitting his panegyric to posterity, Everett acknowledged his onetime student Charles Francis Adams (the two of them were married to sisters) for providing him with unpublished material not available to others who proposed to give John Quincy Adams a fitting spoken memorial.

Everett spoke at Faneuil Hall, where so many Revolutionary memories lived on. A two-story structure built by Peter Faneuil as a gift to the city in 1742, the market house had succumbed to fire in 1761 and was rebuilt, with a third story added at the time of Jefferson's presidency. Despite its less than ideal acoustics, it had served as a meeting place for patriots since the Revolutionary era and bore a historic character.[63]

Those in attendance would all have felt these connections. As a prelude, Everett retold the progenitor's story first: "John Adams perceived, perhaps, before any other person, that the mother country, in depriving France of her

American colonies, had dispossessed herself of her own." He said this with a special kind of transmission of spirit in mind. When John Quincy Adams was born, "he received the first parental instruction from one, to whom the United Colonies had already begun to look for encouragement and guidance, in the mighty crisis of their fate."

The theme of national destiny gave Edward Everett the wind for his sails. "It would be interesting to trace, in the opening mind of the child, the effect of the exciting events of the day." Every important episode in the birth of a nation was "brought home to the fireside at which young Adams was training, by his father's daily participation." This, we know, was an exaggeration, but it seemed necessary and useful as the eulogist launched into yet another overblown notion: "It may be fairly traced to these early impressions, that the character of John Quincy Adams exhibited through life so much of what is significantly called 'the spirit of seventy-six.'"

In Europe with his diplomat father, he was "the favored child," in Everett's rendering, aided at a distance by "the counsels of the faithful and affectionate mother." Through regular proofs of an extraordinary self-discipline, he rose in the estimation of all until President Washington himself stepped in and overruled his vice president's "over-delicacy" by insisting on the appointment of the young man to a senior position within the diplomatic corps.

Everett, himself a classical Greek scholar, trumpeted JQA's erudite Harvard lectures. Next, he recalled the demanding negotiations at Ghent and how, "in happy coincidence with his venerable father's career," the son served as U.S. minister in London. Mainstay in Monroe's cabinet for all eight years, he attained a special status: "The office of Secretary of State is, at all times, one of immense labor; never more so, than in the hands of Mr. Adams." It was Monroe's presidency, but Adams did at least as much to make it successful so that history should reckon among his achievements "the substantial fusion of the two great political parties."

The second Adams presidency should have been an equal success, because it was, "in its principles and policy, a continuation of Mr. Monroe's." If a "formidable and harassing opposition" had ruined its promise, Everett reckoned that with the passage of time it had come to be viewed by non-supporters as "honest, able and patriotic." JQA's "Herculean powers of thought and labor" could not be denied. Despite failure to win reelection, the one-term president remained unfazed. The eulogist hinted at insider's knowledge: "Mr. Adams, I doubt not, left office with a lighter heart than he entered it." As to the ex-president's remarkable decision to enter Congress in 1830, "he was conscious of his capacity to be useful."

It was typical for him to remain on the House floor late into the evening, when most members had gone home. If he had refused to break for lunch, he would gnaw on a piece of hard bread extracted from his coat. There was something stoical in this portrait: a man "blazed forth . . . with a fervor and strength which astonished his friends."

Adams the antislavery activist was undeterred by all opposition and heedless of the violent reactions his strong stance tempted. Instead, he commanded reverence and won appreciation for his generosity of sentiment. "It was impossible not to respect the fearless, conscientious, unparalleled old man."

He had seen the end coming about a year before his final collapse, when, taking a walk in Boston, he suddenly suffered a "palsy," an impairment in the muscles. Once he recovered from the shock of it, he noted in his diary—and Everett repeated—"From that hour I date my Decease, and consider myself, for every useful purpose to myself and fellow-creatures, dead." As he reached a crescendo in his address, Edward Everett integrated the late president's best qualities: "His perception was singularly accurate and penetrating. . . . His argumentative powers were of the highest order, and admirably trained. . . . His memory was wonderful. Every thing he had seen or read, every occurrence in his long and crowded life, was at all times present to his recollection. . . . He had, withal, a diligence which nothing could weary."

Everett would not have wanted to conclude without recalling the philosophical writings of Greece and Rome. Even as president, John Quincy Adams filled his time with Cicero, "his favorite author." In addition, Shakespeare, Milton, Dryden, Pope, were "stamped upon his memory." As a politician, he was a "singular mixture" of progressive and conservative values. Thus, perhaps even more than he resembled the first president Adams, he was a Washingtonian. By this, Everett meant a capable judge of right.

As to faith, "no man laid hold, with a firmer grasp, of the realities of life; but no man dwelt more steadily on the mysterious realities beyond life." The second Adams read the Bible almost daily. He attended services faithfully. Everett had inspected the diaries. He knew of the man's desire to engage with the sacred. "He remained, till the end of his days an inquirer after truth."[64]

In March 1848, a little-noticed commentary of the life of John Quincy Adams was published in a recently established newspaper in the bustling city of New Orleans by an as yet obscure New Yorker—until late a writer for the *Brooklyn Eagle*—who had recently arrived in the Crescent City. The dyed-in-the-wool Democrat Walt Whitman was a tremendous fan of President Polk and a good friend of the editor John O'Sullivan, who had recently coined the phrase "manifest destiny" in his *Democratic Review.* Still several years from publishing *Leaves of Grass,* his immortal book of poetry, Whitman was a writer of inoffensive pieces about local characters until he treated his new southern neighbors to a sharply worded critique of the second president Adams a month after his death.

"The People and John Quincy Adams" was a kind of anti-eulogy. It began by protesting the claims of those eulogists in the northern states who held that Adams was insufficiently appreciated by the people at large and who rationalized at the same time that "his administration was overthrown because it was too honest." For Whitman, "the mass of the people" were nearly infallible; ipso facto, their coolness toward the sixth president was a sure sign that *he* had not quite measured up.

John Quincy Adams was, said Whitman, "a virtuous man—a learned man—and had singularly enlarged diplomatic knowledge; but he was not a man of the People." And why had he failed to achieve personal popularity? He was not formed to generate enthusiasm. "He was 'a gentleman of the old school,' no doubt; but the old school, with all its polish and grace, had its sources too near monarchy and nobility to be entirely free from their influences." For the poet of democratic enthusiasm, "master minds" were "*radical* minds that went to the roots of things." And that was not the Adamsian mind.

Good riddance to the "old school," then, was Whitman's message to his bold contemporaries. Of course, he was not dismissive of the founders by any means, only stingy in delimiting the great names of that generation who deserved to be celebrated. "Some spirits there were, of that age, towering not only above it, but above the ages yet to come. They need no eulogium." (He was thinking mainly of Washington and Jefferson.) "History will in due time give places to the men of the first three score years of our republic's existence. By her stern fingers, swayed from no passion or party, there will doubtless be formed various grades—not so much that some need a lower station, as that others deserve a higher." He did not speculate as to where John Q. Adams would end up on the scale of history.[65]

The election of 1824 was the most democratic election up to that point, and arguably the most convoluted one in U.S. history. The political cartoonist David Claypoole Johnson etched the quadrennial "Foot-Race" that pollsters and politicos to this day glibly term a presidential "horse race." The celebrated contenders, J. Q. Adams, William H. Crawford, and Andrew Jackson, lurch forward, as the ex-president John Adams cheers on the front-runner, his own offspring. "Hurra for our son Jack," he exclaims, while a fan of the hero-general issues a "Hurra for our Jackson." There is nothing noble about the footrace, as a motley group of spectators place wagers on the outcome.

Ad Consummandum*

Romances will never be written, nor flattering orations Spoken to transmit me to Posterity in brilliant Colours, No Nor in true Colours. All but the last I loath. Yet I will not die wholly unlamented.—Cicero was libelled Slandered insulted by all Parties.

—JOHN ADAMS TO BENJAMIN RUSH, *March 23, 1809*

This Nation will not cease to irritate and torment you, both with Flattery and Reproach till they force you out, that they may have the pleasure of insulting and abusing you. If you were capable of eternal Taciturnity in Publick, and incessant confidential Correspondence and Secret Intrigue in private, you might Arrive to the hight of Reputation of Washington or Franklin: but what is all that worth?

—JOHN ADAMS TO JOHN QUINCY ADAMS, *February 19, 1812*

Pay attention no longer to the vulgar herd. . . . Let what others say of you be their concern. Whatever it is, they will say it anyway.

—MARCUS TULLIUS CICERO,
De re publica *(ca. 52 B.C., manuscript rediscovered in 1820)*

To understand the presidents Adams best, we have written their histories in tandem. As critical thinkers, they shared a library; as political actors, they manifest a similar antiparty awareness; in observing human imperfections, their exacting manner was complementary but by no means identical. (It would be absurd to try to collapse their two personalities into one.)

* To sum up.

The first Adams never ceased pointing out the cruel ironies of history. He flatly distrusted motives and judgments, and when he broadcast his insights, he willfully set himself above his fellows. He was, as charged, a vain man. The second Adams was equally stubborn, equally driven, equally disputatious. He, too, refused to witness in silence the defective conduct of men who chose a political life. But as the one more freely bound to his religious faith, especially in the years after his father's involuntary retirement from politics, John Q. Adams did not give up trying to promote remedies for moral lapses and poor political judgments that beset the nation.

The irrepressible presidents Adams were products of a culture that led wandering minds in a search for useful knowledge. As avid readers, letter writers, and diarists, they took the past as their province. A preoccupation with history spawned two inexhaustible critics who documented the excesses they saw in unchecked democratic posturing and democratic pretense. Which makes them memorably combative.

Our initial investigation into their wandering minds led us next to their earthly wanderings, where we found the elder an audacious negotiator and the younger an incomparable globe-trotter. What they learned could not be contained, even in the ever-expanding personal journals they kept. "Travel is fatal to prejudice, bigotry, and narrow-mindedness, and many of our people need it sorely on these accounts," wrote Mark Twain near the end of *The Innocents Abroad*. "Broad, wholesome, charitable views of men and things cannot be acquired by vegetating in one little corner of the earth all one's lifetime." Twain's lines seem entirely apropos here. It is not merely reading matter that informed the two Adamses' thinking, though reading while abroad made a better America more imaginable for them. Wandering had long-term effects: it conditioned their trust in institutional solutions; and it fed their repugnance for unthinking types whose prejudices caused them to dismissively label entire groups of people instead of sifting through, and reasoning through, differences.

Europe produced judgments, positive and negative, about men and women of inherited wealth and power to whom they were daily exposed. A sustained immersion in distant capitals did not suck either of them in; we must underscore that they did not venerate any old-world political form. Their contemporaries were wrong who charged that any displeasure they voiced with regard to Thomas Jefferson's or Andrew Jackson's brand of democracy should be regarded as an illegitimate embrace of aristocracy. That bugaboo attaches to both father and son, for no good reason. It was the easy route for anti-Adams partisans in campaign literature and one-sided histories. It should be seen, with one backward glance, for what it was. Europe added to their inner lives but did not alter their essential personalities. In fact, foreign postings were extended opportunities to exhibit an unwavering nationalist passion.

There is another way to put this.

John and John Quincy Adams struggled surprisingly little in striking a balance between their New England provincialism and the age-old protocols that prevailed in European diplomatic circles. They never curried favor to gain acceptance. Adams bluffness, or Yankee hardheadedness, defined their relationships abroad no less than it was manifest in national congresses in which they both played important roles. In short, they studied the world without abandoning the moral geography of America.

If travel swelled their heads, it was owing to (as official correspondence shows) the pride each took in his position as the dutiful vanguard of a dignified U.S. foreign policy. John and John Quincy Adams did not feign humility; neither "plain John Adams" nor his European-reared son was "common" when he communed with others of the wandering set. In 1795, as he was preparing to embark, without his father, on his first tour abroad as a U.S. diplomat, John Quincy wrote to his sister, Nabby, of being "once more scattered about the world" and said that he and his father were destined to live the life "of wanderers, beyond the common lot of men." Beyond common. They experienced the worlds contained in their libraries on a level beyond mere sedentary amusement. This is, arguably, what led them to become instigators—another of the terms we use to designate their shared experiences and attitudes.[1]

HERO WORSHIP

There's a reason why, despite John's farmer persona, despite John Quincy's years as an endurance swimmer, despite the danger-fraught wanderings of both, they were not mythologized as Jackson the frontiersman was or Lincoln the log splitter would be. The inner heat that sparked the Adamses' political activity was of a skeptical nature. Their detached erudition did not appear forward-looking, or even, at times, American, because it was cautionary rather than invigorating. John Adams captured his own karmic condition succinctly in a post-presidential letter to his son: "I have always been a Prophet of ill, and punished Accordingly."[2]

Of those most closely connected to the presidents Adams, even the foremost chronicler of their public papers and personal writings, JQA's son Charles Francis, confirmed the public's dark appraisal of the lineage. When his father was president, Charles weighed in with an almost cruel curiosity, in characterizing supporters as "more impelled by a sense of his merit in the performance of his duty than by any art of personal popularity." The sixth president, and for that matter the second, would likely have construed (had they seen it) Charles's diary entry in a favorable light. The self-diagnosing Adamses understood that success was doubtful when knowledge went unaccompanied by glad-handing skills. But they could hardly change who they were. "These thoughts have often occurred to me in connection with my father," Charles proceeded. "I have still more wondered at the peculiar and astonishing merit of his political abilities which in this democratical government have been able to form so complete a counterpoise." How could a personality so unwelcoming have gotten this far? "The people are," Charles wrote unabashedly, "more led by the winning graces of a flattering demagogue than by the more stern and serene character of the unbending statesman." This was just what his father and grandfather had been saying.[3]

While the general image of JQA that descends to us is the cold fish that his son Charles confirms for us, that is not all there was to him. Not by a long shot. When the *Amistad* case was before the Supreme Court, a reporter covering the stolid congressman witnessed a telling—otherwise unrecorded—incident in his life. In view of the Capitol, Adams's Irish coachman was violently thrown from his seat atop the carriage after the horses took fright, crushing him beneath the wheels. The passenger's face revealed unmistakable "mental anguish" as he tried unsuccessfully to save a man's life. Plodding along with his books, the reporter acknowledged, Adams was conventionally taken for a "walking encyclopedia"; sitting in his seat in the House of Representatives, he struck a pose like a "marble statue." But in witnessing his humanity, one was able to draw a truer picture of the man, to attest to the essential sweetness of this Adams at a moment of "domestic affliction." Following the coachman's death, Adams asked to be excused from his scheduled argument before the high court; he hoped the next session could be delayed so that he could attend the poor man's funeral. This was not a "cold-hearted, affectionless man" but one brimming with the "tenderest sympathies."[4]

The reporter was an avowed abolitionist, which obviously colors his story. But we are bound to engage with his report, and others like it, in the context of the media's self-anointed role—yes, even then—as image makers. They affected an ability to discern a living person's essential nature, which should make every biographer suspect who seizes upon the low-hanging fruit of political stereotyping. It is true that JQA's enemies consistently portrayed him as a "worn-out politician," or as a silly old man, and then there was the simplistic claim that he retained, even in the 1840s, aristocratic pretensions that attached to his father as a perennial member of the "British Party."[5]

It is hard to know precisely why, but the Adamses remained where nature had placed them: on the short side of manly stature and, for no particular reason, quoted insufficiently relative to the quantity of good writing they produced. As to their paired reputations for personal honor, we must note that rectitude is itself apolitical but also devoid of the raw material of so-called greatness. That is probably why John and John Quincy Adams descend to modern times as two who were out of step with what Walt Whitman, in his poem "To Foreign Lands," called "athletic Democracy." Without a tribe of cheerleaders, they could not be associated in the public mind with the electric expectations of a warmly embellished republican empire.

Andrew Jackson died in 1845, and eulogists galore celebrated the "orphan hero" for his "vigor and boldness," his "indomitable spirit." The Massachusetts-born-and-bred historian George Bancroft, speaking in Washington City, declared Jackson to have been, from the start of his political career, "modest, bold, determined, demanding nothing for himself, and shrinking from nothing that his heart approved." Arguably, no one did more than Bancroft to enshrine Andrew Jackson as the intrepid "Old Hickory," a man as impetuous as American democracy. To Levi Woodbury, former U.S. senator and Treasury secretary, and another New England native, Jackson was somehow "a fit statesman for the stormy and responsible dangers of a republic!" Even in "*the very tempest of his passion*," said Woodbury, "he was remarkably wary and watchful." Martin Van Buren praised his "immoveable nerve," comparing him to Napoleon in their shared "impetuosity" and eagerness to seize the offensive. "In some instances, he may have misjudged," allowed the New Yorker, "but his impulses were always honest, and sustained by public approbation." How different the Adamses' combined reputation for stodginess. Their incorruptibility was passed over; their nerviness was discounted. They could not compete with a larger-than-life battlefield hero or, for that matter, the humane-sounding Jefferson, whose heralded connection to the masses never failed to resonate.[6]

Far from finding forgiveness, "Old Man Eloquent" remembered Jackson as one whose murderous tendencies were exceeded only by his vengeful spirit in the realm of politics. John Davis, who held sequentially the jobs of U.S. congressman, Massachusetts governor, and U.S. senator during Andrew Jackson's presidency, was so disgusted by the fawning behavior required of the men with whom the would-be sovereign surrounded himself that he wrote in 1834 of Jackson's treatment of his office, "the more arbitrary the measures become the less the laws, the constitution and the principles of civil liberty are regarded."

Jackson's belief in his own omnipotence far outstripped his engagement with ideas. Demanding fealty from aides as he expected "due subordination" from his troops, he alienated many of those who had helped to make him president. Furthermore, nothing he said or did as a two-term president concretely improved ordinary lives or delivered democratic social reform. Bluster alone survives of Jacksonian democracy.[7]

History hardly cared. The presidents remembered as proponents of democracy had their noble faces placed on currency. The Adamses rarely caught a break. In 1846, the year following Jackson's death, while John Q. Adams still sat in the House of Representatives, a political writer with a pro-Jefferson genealogy decided to reprint a critique of the first Adams administration written in the first decade of the century. In prefatory remarks to a biased treatment, the editor painted a picture of the Adams temperament in vogue when the Democrat James Polk sat in the White House: "It appears, throughout Mr. Adams's administration, that his imagination was disturbed by the *goblin* of *Democracy*. The same uneasy ambition which characterized him in public pursued him even to his retreat. Envy and jealousy seemed to have burned in his bosom, and he conceived the Herculean project of prostrating the reputation of Mr. Jefferson, and of raising himself and his family on the ruins of democracy."[8]

On the ruins of democracy? To claim as much is to give either President

Adams more power than he ever held. Neither John nor John Quincy publicized his differences while Jefferson held office in a way that could be termed "prostrating" a "reputation." Yet it may be said rightly that both Adamses perceived flaws in Jefferson's logic and identified in him a rich capacity for rationalization that modern historians have only begun to focus on in earnest in recent decades.

Because they were less given to the smooth-talking, consensus-building activity of their party-identified peers, the Adamses would never receive the kind of free publicity Jefferson and Jackson could count on. It also helped the southern presidents to have supportive others constantly on hand to do the promotional work they needed done. The Virginian and the Tennessean both used others with canny efficiency, and neither wrote for the press. Where Jefferson crafted exquisite public statements, Jackson, as the most intellectually wanting of the early presidents, employed speechwriters: he latched onto an idea, and someone smarter prepared the address or proclamation. The Adamses probably shouldn't have griped about any of this, but it was hard to resist, given what they knew: that the Jackson image, like the Jefferson image before it, camouflaged two flesh-and-blood individuals who could be small-minded and cold-hearted. Hero worship always conceals.

The Adamses wished, almost innocently, that sincerity would play a demonstrable role in the life of the Republic, to supplant that hero worship. They wanted it more widely known to citizens how the government functioned, how real work altered the trajectory of foreign or domestic issues, leading into or out of war. The elder Adams was thoroughly disgusted that Benjamin Franklin, the first national celebrity, stole the show, when, from his perspective, Franklin contributed less than he and Jay to the Paris negotiations in the early 1780s. The younger Adams observed the power of ideology in Jackson's elevation, perceiving a force that operated apart from reality; the symbol who might have proved himself in war had little inkling how to govern effectively.

How should it have been, then? In a democratic republic, no one individual, even a president, is to be deemed above the legislative function. A statesman's positive acts deserve recognition; yet, it is too often the legend as constructed that steals the public's attention. To an Adams, Franklin and Jackson were mock actors. Even the salvageable Jefferson was persuaded by the fanciful stories he told of himself.

While history has dismissed the presidents Adams as sore losers, they in fact were more capable of transcending electoral loss than those whom history credits for greater accomplishments. The first president Adams reconciled with the man who defeated him, whom he had called, at various moments, "cunning" and "a party man." Not only did he come to "forgive" England after independence, but he was magnanimous in his desire to forgive individuals who had slighted him, asserting that all he had needed was a sign from them: he would have been happy to forgive "Alec Hamilton and Tim Pick" if he "could perceive a Symptom of sincere Penitence in either." (There is obviously some caustic wit along with actual intent here.) Though his son had no desire to shake the hand of a regretful Andrew Jackson, the second ex-president Adams showed humility by reentering Congress, proving himself, issue by issue, as one among many.[9]

Jefferson was less forgiving and constantly self-justifying. Despite his famously mild exterior, he almost never found a need to apologize, or retracted a hyperbolic pronouncement, or altered his political ideology when the facts contradicted him. His merciless persecution of Justice Samuel Chase and the vice president he squeezed out of the Republican Party, Aaron Burr, are just two prominent examples. Jackson, for his part, acted high-handedly throughout his life, exhibiting little if any sense of restraint in office. He, like so many other southern politicians of the era, praised the little man, while acting solely in the interest of the plantation economy and the planter elites. Democracy, so called, was a triumph of platitude over substance. And yet it was John and John Quincy Adams whom history demeaned as mulish and obdurate.[10]

So, how should we treat the Adamses' notable exclusion from the "club" of two-termers: Washington, Jefferson, Madison, Monroe, and Jackson? A simple answer, in macro-historical terms, would be that the South was more committed to a southern chief executive than the North was skeptical of sectional bias on a president's part. More to the argument of the preceding chapters, the explanation lies in the success of the broad brush that painted the presidents Adams as antidemocratic. The Adamses and those who backed them did not do enough to convincingly contest their typecasting.

Representations of democratic uplift gave new stimulation to American celebrity. Throughout John Quincy Adams's mature years, American literature was permeated with romantic theories of natural genius and sublimity of character. Heroic narratives reached multitudes. How could his father and he compete? Raw attributes of individual exertion concentrated attention on the frontier saga and "nature's nobleman." It began with the Benjamin Franklin myth and would eventually bring forth the Horatio Alger myth. Adamses were industrious, whereas democrats (ironically) wanted life that was majestic. In the middle decades of the nineteenth century, when political parties were concretely organized, ideological distinctions proved to be of less interest to readers—presumably voters, too—than stirring tales magnifying human experience. Individualism supplanted moral didacticism, foreshadowing an ever more disorderly future for the nation writ large. An Adamsian worldview became increasingly irrelevant.

The democratic populist impulse attracted a rising generation. Biographers wrote more like novelists. Pictorial description enlarged. As more people marched confidently into the unknown, an immoderate, entrepreneurial national press stepped up its role in reconfiguring historical models, abetting an insidious cult of personality. The Jefferson image (literary), the Jackson image (action packed), accepted a world in flux that fed dreams. The presidents Adams did not sell dreams, let alone democratic dreams. They fought a losing battle with historical memory, which made them virtual exiles from their own historical moment and damaged their combined legacy.[11]

Party Purposes

At the close of the second Adams administration, and just days before the inauguration of a successor, the *National Journal* announced that a major book on the John Quincy Adams presidency was in the offing. The as yet unwritten book was to be authored by a State Department clerk, with the sixth president's blessing; its express purpose was to goad history into seeing the outgoing administration in a favorable light. According to the prospectus, the John Q. Adams presidency "existed throughout a period of popular excitement so general, that its acts have been regarded rather as objects of attack and defence, than as the operations of a great Republic through its constituted organs." The failure, in other words, lay not with Adams's ideas, policies, or leadership but with flaws inherent in the democratic process. That meant parties. Owing, one can only conclude, to a lack of response among prospective subscribers to the volume (without which a publisher could not afford the investment), the project was dropped.[12]

All that remains of the promised volume is an unpublished manuscript in the hand of John Quincy Adams that the Massachusetts Historical Society retains, which was meant to be used by the intended author, one Philip R. Fendall. The text consists of JQA's thoughts on the evolution of political parties in the United States and ends before the 1824 presidential campaign begins to heat up. While it is only the second Adams who contributed directly, *Parties in the United States* is a testament to father's and son's common denigration of partisan tactics.

The presidents Adams were consumed not just with "party spirit," or partisan fervor, but with parties themselves. They wrote about them incessantly. The father targeted three outstanding sins associated with parties: (1) as factions, they ultimately served private interests, and were therefore often driven by greed and fame; (2) they exploited the cult of celebrity, selling candidates by "trumpeting" (his word) fake talents; (3) relatedly, they were so stuck on the Washington image that they made it a standard for all others, focusing on gestures, going so far as to praise Washington's silence as a "gift," and privileging the superficial—mere public performance—over words of import. As a result of the prejudices built into the party system, voters turned men of wealth, or men with recognizable family names, into idols. To do so was to ignore the real requirements for good government: established expertise and beneficial public service.

The satirical power of the elder Adams—a wordsmith superior to Jefferson, if deft and pointed satire is the measure—nails the problem of George Washington. In a letter of 1807 to Benjamin Rush, he gave an ironic rendering of the many anecdotes that circulated about Washington, which Adams had heard from members of Congress on the eve of the Revolution, when the need to bolster confidence was great. From the general's "Bravery and good Council" to his "Equanimity" and "Self Command," each was a fable with a moral and bore little resemblance to the living Washington, whom Adams and Rush knew. His flattering promoters praised Washington for "an Handsome Face." Adams, ingeniously: "That this is a Talent, I can prove by the authority of a thousand Instances in all Ages." Next, "A tall Stature, like the Hebrew Sovereign chosen because he was taller by the Head than the other Jews." "An elegant Form." "Graceful Attitudes and Movements." "A large imposing Fortune consisting of a great landed Estate left him by his Father and Brother." The ironic list reached ten items. "I have made out ten

Talents without saying a Word about Reading Thinking or writing," Adams enjoined his friend and frequent correspondent. Parties gave the lie to language when they redefined the word "talents" in promoting a candidate.[13]

The second Adams tackled the same issues, because the nature of party politics did not improve between the first (Republican-Federalist) and second (Democratic-Whig) party systems. It began as JQA saw up close how Jefferson outdid Washington in marketing an image. Eight years in office gave Jefferson and his victorious party time to maximize his personal influence over the narrative of his time. His will became "almost dictatorial," JQA noted just after his own failure to get reelected in 1828. Jefferson exploited the old perceptual division between Whig and Tory, between democrat and aristocrat, between Republican and Federalist. His branding strategy consisted of denying party, denying that the taxonomy he developed required an implacable enemy, denying the tactical element in his zero-sum game of eliminating the competition.[14]

JQA readily admitted that the Federalists had signed their own death warrant. They had relied on shrill spokesmen such as Fisher Ames to "preach hatred" (his words), rail against everything democratic, and belittle the people. They refused to conceal their contempt for republican institutions. Hamilton was their artful ringleader who controlled the party by associating his name and imprimatur with Washington. Were it not for John Adams, he would have marched the United States into a war with France. When Hamilton died, the party lost its mastermind and could no longer scheme; that's when everything fell apart. The Republicans failed to learn from the Federalists' demise. In 1812, Jefferson's handpicked successor, Madison, nearly lost reelection to DeWitt Clinton of New York, because Madison was not adept at, nor even inclined toward, image building.

As the second Adams beheld with ever-growing concern, state and sectional interests always threatened to fragment party. By the time Jackson came into office, all that was left to national political contests was the struggle of sections. Those who were eventually branded the "slave power" advanced the Jackson image for their own purposes, ushering in a new era of craven fabrications and empty rhetoric. To further their own narrow interests, these latter-day political manipulators did for General Jackson what John Adams earlier saw his Revolutionary cohort do for the first "man of the people," General Washington—telling confidence-building stories and feeding a glib new form of celebrity worship to an equally gullible audience, with benefits accruing to party.

As the late historian Ralph Ketcham wrote, parties have to stand for something in order to thrive. But not only that: "Their main purpose is often to gather enough support, to seem all things to all people, and to clarify some issues and obscure others, in order to win elections." This is the crux of the dilemma that the two Adamses perceived. It was impossible for parties to be truthful, because parties were driven by the need to win at all costs.[15]

From the time of his *Thoughts on Government* (1776), John Adams emphasized the need for local knowledge so that voters carried their wishes to their representatives. For him, it was the town meeting, not the power-engrossing party system, that expressed the will of the people best. He waged an oratorical war against the British Parliament when the colonies were deprived of their voice. There was no democracy when people's voices went unheard or were ignored.

The second Adams saw a similar problem as the country moved westward, and especially when annexation of Texas was under consideration. Southern masters were still being granted a "double share" of representation in the House of Representatives, and in the Electoral College, because of voiceless slaves and a flawed calculus of representation. Tyranny over the voiceless was no longer about the British, as in 1776, or the Federalists, as in 1800. An aristocracy that stole the right to speak from others ruled now. Northern Democrats made room for slaveholders in their party because of a common greed for western land. They resorted to a mishmash of ideologies simply to win elections. JQA properly identified the marriage of "wild democracy" and "iron-bound slavery" as Democrats did everything possible to rig the party system in their favor in preparation for the election of 1844, the last national contest he would live to see. Party had become what John Adams early on predicted: a vehicle for moneymaking, for amassing personal wealth. Greed finally eclipsed even the manufacturing of fame in a presidential nominee.[16]

HISTORICAL AMNESIA

The past has an insistent voice, though it speaks in many dialects and delivers different messages at different times. Some aspects of an earlier American political culture seem familiar, especially those that recall today's broad-based critique of the rowdy mass media, a ubiquitous social network, and celebrity culture. But most of the parallels are indirect.

Yet we perceive, unequivocally, that the two Adamses associated the cult of personality with manufactured partisanship—masses of committed people surrendering their capacity for critical thinking to an unwavering party orthodoxy. It was a subject of discussion in many places, but for the two of them it especially chafed and long festered. Because it generally worked against them. We must register the fact that key politicians in the post-Revolutionary period, each with a vested interest in legacy building, took up the "history of parties" in their later years: the same phrase was adopted by such rival interpreters of partisan worship as Thomas Jefferson, John Quincy Adams, and Martin Van Buren. None could resist envisioning a "history of parties" that would command the market, justify their life's work and core beliefs, and serve as a medium of influence in future generations.[17]

American political life remained a subject of intense interest as the nineteenth century proceeded. The agonies of the founding era were only gradually displaced. But the day arrived when the wounded egos, the tone of impatience, the violence of language, were all smoothed out so as to construct a common genealogy with patriarchs worthy of the Old Testament. Historical amnesia set in, and the superlatives flew. The founding fathers gazed down on their grateful children and grandchildren. They felt no more pain as they watched democracy become a fixed ideology.

The truth of democracy's claims to fairness, or equality under the law, is another story, of course. But the essential theory that the United States was designed to be a government propelled by popular consent is beyond dispute. The presidents Adams might have been accused, at times, of favoring something else, something less consistent with mainstream belief, but they never backtracked on the democratic mantra of "government by popular consent." Their discomfort was not with representative democracy but with an overindulgent popular democracy. The distinction is an important one.

Their critique concerned the need to assure a judicious mixture of powers so that reason and restraint would always outweigh and outlast personal popularity. If one wants to define that impulse as conservative, then they were conservatives. But it strikes us that a better description of their larger goal in fostering democratic debate is this: they sought to advantage a system that secured national dignity and national respectability, that rewarded informed self-possession rather than demagoguery. The shared ideal of father and son was to build a system that warranted pride and that extended human happiness, one that honored expertise and promoted goodwill.

The general impression history retains is that the "elitist" presidents Adams were obstinate enemies—rather than astute observers—of assertive democracy. We hope this book has changed that misguided generalization. It serves no constructive purpose to reduce men, women, entire lives, entire generations, to symbols or to make father-son presidents emblematic of a single idea. But this is what happens, constantly. In the temperamental theater of American memory, the reputations of our supposedly best-known historical actors rise and fall, "trending" in one direction or another according to the needs of the reigning generation. As the unloved Adamses have reminded us, founder hagiography is highly unreliable, if not wholly illusory; the evasiveness of historical truth obliges us to reexamine inherited judgments. If truth is absolute, it is also absolutely unstable in human hands.

The Adams story does not end with the two we have featured. Among the direct descendants of John and John Quincy Adams were several other Harvard men whose attainments were notable. Charles Francis Adams (1807–1886) managed his father's and grandfather's libraries and their masses of personal papers, and the attractive Stone Library he built on the family's property remains a prominent feature of the Adams National Historical Park today. During the Civil War, he served honorably, like his father and grandfather before him, as the chief U.S. diplomat in England. By the time of America's centennial celebration in 1876, Charles Francis was doing his utmost to avoid showiness, playing down familial connections to moments of glory.

Charles's son Henry (1838–1918) was a major American historian and a heralded memoirist. True to the family name, he exhibited personal pride and public purpose, experiencing a painful loss when his wife inexplicably ended her own life. In 1880, he published (anonymously) the successful if disturbing *Democracy: An American Novel,* which involves the pettiness and moral failings of self-serving elites who eat at the heart of national politics, and a president who is limited and corruptible. Henry's brother Brooks (1848–1927), an iconoclast like his grandfather and great-grandfather, authored *The Law of Civilization and Decay*. His conspicuous effort (some six hundred manuscript pages) to publish a biography of their presidential grandfather, John Quincy

Adams, was stopped in its tracks by Henry, who could not stomach its hagiographic qualities. Brooks was the last of the Adamses to reside in the "Old House" of John Adams, the second president.

Brothers Henry and Brooks were both accomplished citizens of the ripened republic. They had two older brothers, John Quincy and Charles Francis junior, who, though mildly burdened by their names, also fared well in life. But when Henry and Brooks realized that no astonishing brilliance was appearing in the generation that was arising as theirs began to fade, they conjectured that the Adams temperament of days gone by required a concentration of genius in only one family member *per generation;* the siblings of the second and sixth presidents had all either underperformed or self-destructed. Charles Francis, the father of Henry and Brooks, was the only one of John Quincy's three sons to succeed. So it appeared to them that the family's impressive qualities were being watered down as a generation of Adamses came of age with several brothers of comparable intellectual worth and moral balance.[18]

The Exceptions

The educated class to which the Adamses of Quincy belonged was an exclusive Boston-area fraternity with clear-cut sources of requisite knowledge. John Adams, progenitor of this brood, dutifully followed the rules it prescribed. He scratched his way toward recognition and reward.

Members of the social set to which he aspired could easily veer into snobbery, convinced that they had earned the right to judge others. Peckish John Adams became that classic snob, assured of his deservingness. But then something happened. He was rejected by his peers who saw his political tomes as pretentious. Indeed, he was not permitted to live down *Davila.* His son John Quincy might have been less invested in confirming his superiority over others, at least as a young man. But that had to change once he entered politics, because an Adams never did anything halfheartedly.[19]

John Adams's modern biographers have tended to portray him as a crusty, testy, truth teller. Gilbert Chinard's *Honest John Adams* (1933) started this trend, and the majority of chroniclers since were most comfortable situating him in Revolutionary times as the most awkward, yet committed, of the founders. When Benjamin Rush wrote to him in 1808, complaining about America's becoming a "bedollared nation," and then, hyperbolically, entertained the fantasy of erasing his name from the declaration he had signed in 1776, Adams replied sublimely, "How can a Man repent of his Virtues?" For both John and John Quincy, the Declaration of Independence was sacred and undeniable, which was why, in this instance, the elder Adams refused to repent what he saw as his own "Benevolences" and demanded the same of his friend Dr. Rush.[20]

What father and son shared as advocates and would-be opinion shapers was a quality we might call, admiringly, *a beautiful antagonism*. They saw no point to a life mired in complacency. Others played it safe or went along to get along. Not they. Father and son maintained a rich, revealing two-way correspondence, uncollected for posterity to marvel at the way the Adams-Jefferson correspondence has been over the years. But it should be, because the Adams-Adams letters are no less kinetic.[21]

The people of America want what the Adamses can't give them, and they want it even more than they want giant historical personalities. What they want is to feel in an almost visceral way the founding promise of democracy, ill defined as it is. Our age conflates "democracy" with its constituent qualities, two perfectly American yet wholly ambiguous nouns: "liberty" and "freedom." These three words presuppose a political republic constructed on an ethical foundation. The most favored over the lifetimes of the two presidents Adams was "liberty." For the citizens of the early republic, it was associated with the qualities of moderation and decorum, which it no longer is. Liberty was a value unceremoniously prized, quietly cherished.[22]

It was not obvious to the candid student of government John Adams that republics always did a better job than old-world monarchies at educating citizens. The American patriot's catechism makes it hard to admit the possibility that the United States at any time had legitimate competition abroad. That's because Americans have long been conditioned to regard their history the way the propagandist Tom Paine lectured us: as a uniquely blessed, intrinsically superior polity, righteous and deserving. Was there another kind of patriot?

In fact, the seeds of modern-day American exceptionalism sprouted early in the language of republicanism and knee-jerk critique of monarchy, aristocratic haughtiness, and political centralism. The uncompromising exceptionalist faith has dubiously erected a collective self-confidence, reassuring citizens that theirs is a national culture with exportable values, that they are moral exemplars armed with a quintessentially decent, transformative political vision that makes America deserving of its accrued power. What exceptionalism really ever meant, though, was extraordinary freedom, opportunity, and advantages for some, only some.

History is devalued by any article of faith that is unsubstantiated. Just as rags-to-riches stories were not the norm when the Republic was in its infancy, localism was stronger than we'd prefer to admit, and states' rights tendencies contested federal patronage of improvements and services, arts and education. In Europe, it was the opposite: kings and queens and royal societies underwrote signature projects, actively cultivating a cognitive elite. So, in boasting the moral superiority of their republican form, America's leaders and literati remained reactive: they were for a very long time intellectually dependent on London, Paris, and elsewhere, monitoring new ideas and passing them on to the rising generation. Even an Anglophobic Jefferson, post-presidency, sent abroad for a superior faculty who would set the curriculum and train future educators at his embryonic University of Virginia.[23]

A different article of faith propelled John Adams: the belief that institutions were only as good as the characters who exercised authority within them. Projecting from Europe in the years 1785–1787, when he composed his *Defence,* he was altogether convinced that divisions among the players in American politics made pursuit of the republican ideal as useful as ghost hunting. Superior characters, immune to faction, had not emerged, and did not appear likely to in the future. For seemingly good reasons, then, an element of paternalism infused John Adams's political analytics. He wanted at least one governing body (the Senate) to feature men with strong, capable, reasoning abilities (meritocracy) and to provide stability (the six-year term). It always came back to a superior education in political ethics as the means of lessening self-seeking and extending leaders' concern for society writ large.

John Adams was not credited for his fair-minded approach to Platonic theory, for projecting the historical moment when democratic idealism ran headlong into human selfishness. According to Plato, if laws favored the rich, and education and true merit took a backseat, liberty turned to licentiousness. Adams warned similarly in his *Defence* of individualism run amok;

he saw reason supplanted by "boasting" and "impudence" as a desirable modesty in public servants turned to indecency and self-aggrandizement. In a corrupt democracy, Adams told us two and a quarter centuries before the internet, an adult could be made to degenerate into the immature character of impressionable youth. A society of such individuals would lose its honest democratic character.[24]

These analytics were made clear—to his political detriment—in *Davila,* published in the second year of his vice presidency. A cursory reading of the text revealed to colleagues such as Thomas Jefferson, and old friends like the Warrens, that Adams, as a thinker, was outside the mainstream of republican thought, which was just then as ecstatic as it would ever be in praise of individual liberty. For his part, the author of *Davila* felt his words were being twisted and that an informed philosophical treatise, historically based, was being forced into an ideological prison where it did not belong.

We and others have judged that John Adams acquired his reputation as a crypto-monarchist, a retrograde thinker, because of his non-PC (to risk anachronism) refusal to play to the crowd. In *Davila,* his straw men of history were thickly presented as strong personalities whose self-promoting behavior came to the fore during their years as government administrators of one kind or another. He held that the most remarkable trait in a political character was "the *passion for distinction,*" as he wrote early and often in his text. "A desire to be observed, considered, esteemed, praised, beloved, and admired by his fellows" was, he continued, "one of the earliest, as well as keenest dispositions discovered in the heart of man."

Would Jefferson and the Warrens deny reality? Adams made the apparent mistake of defining political ambition without presuming that the American republic would escape old-world ills. He made readers squirm who had felt confidently exempt from his prophetic concerns. "The national attachment to an elective first magistrate, where there is no competition, is very great: but where there is a competition, the passions of his party, are inflamed by it." It did not matter whether someone's position was lowly or exalted; all craved distinction: "Wherever men, women, or children, are to be found, whether they be old or young, rich or poor, high or low, wise or foolish, ignorant or learned, every individual is seen to be strongly actuated by a desire to be seen, heard, talked of, approved and respected, by the people about him, and within his knowledge." That universal enticement to reputation and renown had to be considered most dangerous at top levels of government: "In proportion as men rise higher in the world . . . , the effects of these passions are more serious and alarming," John Adams philosophized, to the discomfort of his peers.[25]

The son of John Adams derived his political philosophy over a longer span of years and from a somewhat more empirical understanding of political affairs. As a U.S. senator when the Federalist Party was in decline, he saw something manifest in the "airy vivacity of youth" and something else in the "grave and dignified energy of years and station." For him, solutions lay in the stirrings of principled debate, in the educability of sensible citizens moved by astute politicians. This was the one way a representative democracy could succeed: the right ideas had to sway the most people.[26]

The Adamses came of age when political actors could still envision a representative democracy that did not rely on the two-party structure. Fact: No allowances for organized political parties were made by those who framed the Constitution. Yet before George Washington's first term had ended, Federalists and Republicans vied with each other with a vehemence not vastly different from the Whig-Tory divide of Revolutionary times. The rival parties were first referred to, in an effort to disguise their permanence on the political landscape, as "interests," but they quickly organized and maintained coordination, establishing friendly newspapers to promote a national agenda. Eventually, to maintain a sense of their viability, the distinction was made between parties ("governed by *Principles*") and factions ("governed by *Men*").[27]

As we have tried to convey, there were few who resisted the hardening of parties or who saw, as the Adamses did, that independence of party promoted a superior brand of statesmanship. The father implanted in the son what he imbibed from Cicero on the ethic of a wise republican. "Virtue clearly desires honor, and has no other reward," said the Roman consul. "What riches, what power, what kingdoms can you offer such a man?" None, truly. "If universal ingratitude, or the envy of many, or the hostility of the powerful, deprive virtue of its proper rewards, yet it is soothed by many consolations, and firmly upheld by its own excellence." What was Ciceronian was Adamsian, too.[28]

The presidents Adams were a party of two. This is ironic, of course, because how can an individual be a perennial outlier who has assumed legislative and diplomatic roles repeatedly, who has held state and national positions and served with distinction in all? An explanation lies in the compulsive need, passed from father to son, to stand firm even at the cost of public office; moreover, it was to keep motivated, to engage in deliberative persuasion, to expose inaccuracies. The call to practice Ciceronian virtue, to deserve leadership, to meet with envy from lesser men, to suffer ingratitude and take solace in one's own pursuit of excellence—this was the willful mission of both presidents Adams. Restless, doubt driven, maladjusted pedants, they were sticklers for intellectual honesty, and they made it hard for others to live up to their refashioned Ciceronian calling.

In Shakespeare's *Richard II,* the banished Mowbray, loyal aide to the king, recites, "The purest treasure mortal times afford / Is spotless reputation: that away, / Men are but gilded loam or painted clay." In *Othello,* the ill-fated Cassio laments, "Reputation, reputation, reputation! Oh, I have lost / my reputation! I have lost the immortal part of / myself." Upon which the scheming whisperer Iago makes his own case: "Reputation is an idle and most false / imposition; oft got without merit, and lost without / deserving." A certain ambiguity persists here, then. In an Adamsian polity, reputation could be secured only through a lifetime of learning, through honorable intent and public mindedness. But no such republic of virtue existed. Lack of introspection on the part of zealots inevitably sacrificed peace to political violence.[29]

Fickleness of reputation remained a sticking point for the Adams pair. Not only did they suffer for their principles; there were, contrarily, those who enjoyed reputations that were not deserved. The first Adams recurred to his maxim that only a properly balanced government protected earned reputations. JQA took his father's philosophy the next step: democracy that toyed with reputations resulted in social chaos. Before he left the United States for The Hague on his first diplomatic assignment, still in his twenties, he penned in his diary, "Perhaps there has never been a period in the history of mankind, when Fortune has sported so wantonly with Reputation." In revolutionary France, national "idols" had become, in a moment's time, "victims of the popular clamor." The second Adams found it deeply disturbing that mediocre individuals were suddenly being brought to prominence through revolutionary activities. When Cicero warned against public violence, he pointed to the disregard of merit that a wanton populace, without models of moral excellence to look up to, were prone to carrying out. "There can be nothing more horrible than that monster which falsely assumes the name and appearance of a people," wrote the Roman consul. An unmanageable multitude will only defy law and abandon justice.[30]

Whither Democracy

In the final decade of his life, John Quincy Adams authored a number of grandiose pronouncements on the destiny of America and its people. In a public lecture delivered in several cities, he was most effusive, building on popular tropes of stages of human development, from savage hunter to pastoral herder, and simple agriculturalist to the civilized form that existed in the 1840s. His tone was upbeat, almost poetic. His theme concerned the rise of a genteel culture that incorporated pastoral versions of "tenderness" and "contemplation" into a God-fearing nation that possessed a symbiotic rural-urban character. As scriptural messages wafted over an appreciative populace, a supervening government authority could step in as required to help iron out conflict on the self-fulfilled continent.[31]

When *The Social Compact* came out in 1842, a steady broadening of the franchise had already given democracy the appearance of solidity. This led the surviving Adams, resentful of the claim of Jacksonians that an emerging democratic ethos was their doing, to set the record straight. To any American who used the word "democracy" to describe the current government, he urged caution: democracy was, and would always be, limited, because "perfect self-government" is impossible. Rampant self-interest made perfect self-government impossible.

His father's well-drawn 1780 Massachusetts Constitution was, he states explicitly, "the work of the democracy," after which he says, paradoxically, "but there is no definition of democracy, which can claim it." Perhaps this is owing to the fact that it was a Revolutionary document. Less than 10 percent of the former British colony voted on it. The amended constitution of 1821, refashioned under the eye of the still living John Adams, could again claim that the convention framing it acknowledged its powers as "derived from the whole people," but this time it was in the hands of a greater number of "qualified voters," over two-thirds of whom approved the convention's work. Property qualifications for voting were gone; payment of state or county tax sufficed.

So then, was the 1821 constitution democracy? Not really. Rousseau had established that the social compact could be constituted only by "unanimous consent." America had not been so constituted. With a modern exercise of political logic, Adams held that democracy could not even be defined as universal white male suffrage (a "government merely of numbers," he called it), when "the whole people" was exclusive of the majority who were not white males. There were "the people," and then there were "the people capable of contracting," a subset of the whole people. The male head of household represented an entire family and was the only qualified voter. There was only ever "representation." To claim that democracy is inclusive is to conceal the fact that government recognizes hierarchies: if broad suffrage does not democracy make, and popular sovereignty is a legal fiction, then *representative government*—which counts interests—is as close to real democracy as America gets.

Without a "fraudulent perversion of language," neither his home state of Massachusetts nor "this great confederated Union" could be termed a democracy. Instead, the United States was that "mixed Government" his father had outlined all those years ago, a compound of three standby forms: democracy, aristocracy, and monarchy.

To hammer home his point, Adams brought into his argument as keen a reference as he could have drawn, words spoken in Washington, D.C., on March 4, 1801, the day his father ceased to be president: "We are then as Mr. Jefferson forty years ago said, all federalists, all republicans—but not all *Democrats,* no more than we are all Aristocrats or Monarchists." He was doing an awful lot of parsing, but his science of politics did make sense.

What's in a name? The first two political parties had both desired to be known as Republican, he reminded his readers. They were quick to "stigmatize" their opponents by calling them odious names—anything but Republican. "The struggle was long and acrimonious for the name of Republicans," Adams recalled. In 1801, key members of Jefferson's "anti-federal" party reacted against the new president's determination that "we are all"—including those who voted for John Adams—"republicans." That's when they supposedly opted for what was until that moment an odious name: "Democrat."

He was just about done with his *Social Compact*. Post-Jefferson, Democrats wanted it understood that the word "democracy" meant "the *whole* people and nothing but the people," "eternal justice ruling through the people." By this rather naïve redefinition, citizens were meant to believe that there were no longer any exclusions, any qualifications: that democracy encompassed everybody. It may have sounded good and desirable, but it was patently absurd. Because, as he had already shown, not all people had a voice.[32]

And today? When we consider the meanings embedded in the Declaration of Independence, modern defenders of the democratic spirit remain trapped in universals. The presidents Adams resisted universals to a greater extent than their political peers. Critical thinking allowed them, and allows us, to challenge the convenient myths on which our national philosophy is based. Democracy is not simply counting heads. Democracy is not simply majority rule. When industry lobbyists buy legislators' votes and donors are awarded cabinet positions, government will ignore those citizens it doesn't care about and discriminate against the groups it worries about. No one should think that such an outlook is democratically inspired.

In the Adamsian construct, America cannot justly call itself a democracy.

Let's go a step further. "All men are created equal," "endowed with inalienable rights" are but the buzzwords of an oft-recited fable. Words do not advance cooperation between haves and have-nots or defeat influence peddling. Aside from the Christian conceit that souls are all equal before God, "created equal" has no transcendent meaning. "Created equal" is only true to the extent that human beings agree on a particular division of power. The hallowed concepts of "freedom" and "equality" are, logically speaking, contradictory, because true equality must limit the freedom of the relentlessly ambitious individual. "Inalienable rights," to be pursued, must always apply to those who have the most to lose under an evolving governmental regime—and who determines that? Laws and morality are functions of culture, which develop over millennia. Societies define "justice" not in universal terms but in terms that satisfy the psychological makeup of the ruling elite. This is, practically speaking, the actual scope of Jefferson's beautifully rendered preamble. America was born of bright ideas, but no guarantees.

On its best day, democracy is a promise. It supposes that all citizens are entitled to equal protection under the law and an equal chance of feeling free to test one's talents in the marketplace of ideas and commerce. It does not promise to heal the prejudices we have inherited from past generations that block the realization of our democratic promise. Democracy, to the extent it is practiced, does not eradicate the advantages given to those who have exploited opportunities through nepotism, inheritance laws, and the tax code. Ours is not a leveling but a rule-making polity. Representative democracy only aims to secure, to keep safe, to prevent extremism. At its most benevolent, it calls for inclusiveness. But it does not seek to be truly fair.

Neither should democracy be imagined as a promoter of the godliest of rights and responsibilities. The Republic of the American founders derived not from a democratic deity—the declaration's softened, life-giving Creator—nor, though some would still dispute it, did it arise from the God of the Old and New Testaments. The Republic grew from the critical musings of a select number of thinkers who wished to reorganize hierarchical systems and amend conditions where disproportionate power drove politics. They were not true radicals; they only sought to moderate social imbalances a little bit at a time. As it has been promoted historically, democracy is a desired tendency, a hopeful direction, an imagined order, a means toward finding agreeable outcomes. If we define democracy as an established system of government in which unfettered self-expression at the voting booth is strong enough to check the power of an elite financial bloc, then America does not have democracy. As inequality grows and intensifies, the Republic is compromised.

We know how democracy is denied. It occurs as myth supplants truth. Brooks Adams affirmed his grandfather's superiority over Andrew Jackson on this very basis, when he wrote of Jacksonianism as "the degradation of the democratic dogma." Jackson pretended to favor the rights of the modest white man but in fact saw to it throughout his career that only a minority—politically privileged loyalists—received the best available frontier land. Brooks Adams held that JQA was the real democrat, for he did not spout a rhetoric of rugged individualism, recommending instead a federal government duly empowered to expand infrastructure across the states; government would demonstrably support the public without playing favorites.[33]

First, John Adams warned against a democracy that merely stirred up passions. Next, John Quincy Adams campaigned for national standards. If Democrats embraced a democracy that sounded beautiful while promoting some and excluding many, Adamses aimed for something different: enacting a theory of smart government. *That* is their true legacy.

The Adamses were never surprised by what they found. Cicero warned of failure in government when "popular error" ceded power to the most visible, which could mean the already ambitious and overconfident, if not those most comfortable (materially) and most detached from the national mien. Benevolent despots are anomalous in history. A tendency to "flatter" demagogues and to reward with political power the advantaged—rather than the wise—is an old problem, universal in scope, which Cicero understood and ruminated on at length. In the United States, as elsewhere in the world, voters entrust their happiness and security to others. It's a simple fact.

Democracy was meant to overcome defeatist tendencies. It is presumed to guard against rule by those who disregard the rights and interests of the many. The Adamses never swallowed that Jeffersonian bromide; they saw the allure of power pervert as many reputed democrats as self-acknowledged elitists. Their studies of moral philosophy and world history produced in them unsentimental ideas about human psychology. If there is a twenty-first-century lesson to be taken from our study of the two presidents Adams and the contentious character of democracy, it has most to do with the obstinacy of those who indulge in wishful thinking when greater circumspection (and honest introspection) would do us all good. The danger of complacency, the danger of blind pride, exists as the state tilts toward injudicious acts while mollifying, in soft words, the credulous mass of citizens. Say what you will of John and John Quincy Adams, they were onto something when they observed that the errors of the people threatened "government by the people."

The lives of the presidents Adams speak to the present in pointedly critical ways. Their honest diagnosis of the political scene, repositioned and reconditioned for our present, has social as well as institutional implications. In ideological terms, it is neither liberal nor conservative; it has no dog in that fight. It embraces education that produces expertise. It espouses a philosophy of government in which the expert's commitment to public service exceeds all private pecuniary motives. It expects the state to solve key problems that ordinary people—that is, the will of democracy—might not be equipped to debate.

If the United States were a democratic society, it would look structurally different than it does. People would understand that they had, close at hand, the power to arrest the accumulation of preponderant power by a favored few who transgress upon the common good with relative impunity. Isn't the historical evidence presented in these pages enough to get us to admit that it is at the very least premature to assume anything close to unified devotion to our noble-sounding democratic principles? Shouldn't we stop bragging about "American democracy" and find a more plausible interim label?

For those who wrote the American republic into being, democracy was a form of government prone to turbulence and therefore feared. That was the understanding John Adams tapped into when, in 1814, he wrote, "There never was a Democracy yet that did not commit suicide." The objectives of democratic society are clearer today. Yet fears of turbulence are as fixed in political language as is the inbred antagonism of the two-party system. We readily admit that concepts of democracy and popular government are as elusive in the real world as the declaration's rhetorical evocation of human equality.

The conduct of politics as we presently experience it differs from the early American republic only in scale. Privilege and power operate in ways so monstrously large that the Adamses could never have imagined us. Our politicized court system has made campaign funds solicitation and influence peddling (effectively, bribery) the law of the land. Money in politics is so blatant that it ruins any chance of democracy. In that "more perfect union" rhetorically envisioned, divergent views do not paralyze, elected representatives are not covetous of power, and there is no such thing as a partisan donor class; big business does not have a built-in advantage over the best ideas or the broader public interest.

Beyond these iniquitous practices, an Adamsian would ask why elected leaders of the twenty-first century are marketed according to their imagined (that is, poll-tested) qualities dictating what they should and shouldn't say. In the interest of encouraging greater political honesty, the modern Adamsian would argue that personal charisma should not substitute for proven judgment, a sense of fairness, breadth of knowledge, and administrative command.

When it comes to quelling "party spirit"—the tribalism of bloc voting that the Adamses sought to counter—American history has settled thus far on one particular kind of party nonidentifier. He is perceived as strong and independent and electable because of his military career. Generals have bested conventional politicians in numerous instances. The war heroes

George Washington, Andrew Jackson, William Henry Harrison, Zachary Taylor, Ulysses Grant, and Dwight Eisenhower have all served as president (those who survived their first term won a second). But strong military men are not democratic idols; they are monarchical idols. So, once again, how democratic have American impulses been over time? Not nearly what the national ideal assumes possible or proclaims as having been realized through elective franchise.

In Quincy, Massachusetts, the long line of Adamses remain fixtures in their former community. With their wives, John and John Quincy lie in a cool crypt, a few feet apart, one floor below the still active United First Parish Church. From the family pew, one stares straight at busts of the presidents Adams, each created by an American sculptor—Horatio Greenough and Hiram Powers, the most accomplished stone carvers of their respective generations.

Under the second president's bust, the inscription reads, in part,

Beneath these walls
Are deposited the mortal remains of John Adams

After that:

He pledged his Life, Fortune, and sacred Honour
To the Independence of his Country

And farther down:

On the Fourth of July, 1826,
He was summoned
To the Independence of Immortality,
And to the Judgment of his God.
This House will bear witness to his Piety,
This Town, his birth-place, to his munificence;
History, to his Patriotism;
Posterity to the depth and compass of his mind.

The sixth president's monument was set up on the opposite side of the pulpit by his able son Charles Francis. The long inscription begins,

Near this place
Reposes all that could die of
JOHN QUINCY ADAMS

And below his date of birth, the following:

Amidst the storms of Civil Commotion
He nursed the vigor
Which nerves a Statesman and a Patriot,
And the faith, which inspires a Christian.
For more than half a century,
Whenever his Country called for his labors,
In either Hemisphere or in any Capacity,
He never spared them in her Cause.

Then comes an accounting of JQA's accomplishments. And finally, the inscription reads,

A Son, worthy of his Father.

Chronology

30 Oct. 1735	John Adams (JA) born, Braintree, Massachusetts
22 Nov. 1744	Abigail Smith Adams (AA) born, Weymouth, Massachusetts
1755	JA graduates from Harvard College
Oct. 1764	JA and AA are married in Weymouth
July 1765	First child of JA and AA, Abigail "Nabby" Adams, born
1765–1766	Stamp Act sparks resistance to parliamentary authority; JA joins cousin Samuel Adams in protest
11 July 1767	John Quincy Adams (JQA) born, Braintree, Massachusetts
March 1770	Boston Massacre; JA defends British soldiers at trial
May 1770	Second son, Charles Adams, born
Sept. 1772	Third son, Thomas Boylston Adams, born
1774	JA in First Continental Congress
April 1775	Battles of Lexington and Concord
June 1775	Battle of Bunker Hill
1775–1777	JA in Second Continental Congress
1776	JA authors *Thoughts on Government;* signs Declaration of Independence
Feb. 1778	JA and JQA sail to Europe, reside in Paris
Aug. 1779	JA and JQA return to Boston on *La Sensible*
Oct. 1779	JA drafts Massachusetts state constitution
Nov. 1779	JA and JQA sail back to Europe on *La Sensible*
Jan./Feb. 1780	JA and JQA escape dangers, on sea and land, travel north through Spain and arrive back in Paris
Summer 1780	JA and JQA travel together to the Netherlands

April 1781	JA publishes "Memorial to the States General" requesting Dutch recognition of the United States
July 1781	As secretary/translator, JQA travels to St. Petersburg, Russia, with Francis Dana; JA tangles with Vergennes in Paris, returns to the Netherlands
April 1782	Owing to JA's efforts, Dutch recognize American independence
Oct. 1782	JA back in France to help finalize Treaty of Paris
July 1783	JA and JQA reunite in the Netherlands, return to Paris
Sept. 1783	Treaty of Paris officially ends Revolutionary War
Oct. 1783	JA and JQA travel to England, attend session of Parliament
Jan. 1784	JA and JQA make harrowing trip from England to The Hague
Summer 1784	JA and JQA are reunited in Europe with Abigail and Nabby
1784–1785	Four Adamses in Paris, joined by Thomas Jefferson
May 1785	JQA sails home to Boston
June 1785	JA begins serving as first U.S. minister to Great Britain
Jan. 1787	Volume 1 of JA's *Defence of the Constitutions of Government of the United States of America* published
May–Sept. 1787	Constitutional Convention held in Philadelphia
July 1787	JQA graduates from Harvard College
Aug. 1787	Volume 2 of *Defence of the Constitutions* published
Jan. 1788	Third and final volume of *Defence of the Constitutions* published
April 1788	JA returns to Boston
April 1789	George Washington inaugurated, JA becomes vice president, settles in New York City; JQA opens Boston law practice
Sept. 1789	JQA visits JA and AA in New York, observes Congress
May 1790	Serialization of JA's *Discourses on Davila* begins
Spring 1791	Thomas Paine's *Rights of Man* appears in the United States
June/July 1791	JQA publishes "Publicola" newspaper essays; their author wrongly assumed to be JA

FEB. 1793	JA reelected vice president
NOV./DEC. 1793	JQA publishes "Columbus" essays
JUNE 1794	President Washington names JQA minister to Netherlands
1794–1795	Traveling between The Hague and London, JQA confers on Jay Treaty
MARCH/APRIL 1797	JA inaugurated as president, names JQA minister to Prussia
JULY 1797	JQA marries Louisa Catherine Johnson (LCA) in London, assumes diplomatic post in Berlin
SPRING 1798	XYZ Affair rocks Adams presidency
JUNE/JULY 1798	Alien and Sedition Acts pass Congress
1799	JA dispatches peace mission to France
AUG. 1800	Alexander Hamilton writes scathing pamphlet attacking JA's character
DEC. 1800	JA loses reelection
MARCH 1801	JA retires to Quincy as Jefferson is inaugurated
APRIL 1801	JQA's first child, George Washington Adams, born in Berlin
SUMMER/AUTUMN 1801	JQA sails back to Boston, resumes law practice there
APRIL 1802	JQA elected to Massachusetts State Senate
OCT. 1802	JA starts composing autobiography
MARCH 1803	JQA elected to the U.S. Senate (serves until 1808)
JULY 1803	JQA's second son, known as John Adams II, born in Boston
AUTUMN 1804	Jefferson reelected president
1805	JQA named to Boylston Professorship of Rhetoric and Oratory at Harvard, concurrent with his service in the U.S. Senate
JUNE 1806	JQA delivers inaugural lecture as Boylston Professor
JUNE 1807	*Chesapeake* Affair intensifies anti-British sentiment
SUMMER 1807	JA disputes Mercy Otis Warren's history of the Revolution
AUG. 1807	JQA's third son, Charles Francis Adams, born in Boston
1807–1809	Embargo in place, JQA defends Jefferson-Madison foreign policy

1808	JQA supports Madison candidacy, forced to resign from U.S. Senate
MARCH 1809	JQA named U.S. minister to Russia by President Madison
SPRING 1809	JQA's *Review of Works of Fisher Ames* marks his defection from Federalism
1809–1812	JA serializes self-vindicating autobiographical material in *Boston Patriot*
1810	JQA's *Lectures on Rhetoric and Oratory* published
AUG. 1811	Ill-fated daughter born to LCA and JQA in Russia
JAN. 1812	JA resumes long-stalled epistolary relations with Jefferson
AUG. 1813	Death of Nabby Adams in Quincy
1814	JQA participates in peace talks in Belgium
DEC. 1814	Treaty of Ghent signed
FEB. 1815	JQA named minister plenipotentiary to Great Britain; LCA and son Charles travel on their own to meet JQA in Paris
MAY 1815	Sons George and John reunite with JQA and LCA in London
MARCH 1817	JQA named secretary of state by President Monroe
AUG. 1817	JQA arrives back in United States, never again to travel abroad; son George enters Harvard (graduates 1821)
OCT. 1818	Death of Abigail Adams
1819–1821	JQA negotiates Transcontinental (Adams-Onís) Treaty with Spain
AUTUMN 1820	JA participates in Massachusetts Constitutional Convention
SEPT. 1821	Charles Francis Adams enters Harvard (graduates 1825)
DEC. 1824	JQA second in electoral votes behind Andrew Jackson, ahead of William Crawford and Henry Clay; presidential contest must be decided in House of Representatives
FEB. 1825	House votes, JQA elected president
DEC. 1825	JQA's first annual message delivered to Congress
4 JULY 1826	JA and Jefferson both die on jubilee of American independence
1827–1828	Charles Francis reads law in the offices of Daniel Webster

Nov. 1828	JQA handily defeated at polls by Andrew Jackson
June 1829	Death of George W. Adams.
Nov. 1830	JQA elected to House of Representatives
July 1831	JQA disputes nullification in Fourth of July oration
Dec. 1831	JQA takes his seat in Congress
Mar. 1832	JQA's brother Tom dies
Oct. 1834	JQA's son John dies
1835–1836	"Right of petition" tested in Congress
Sept. 1836	JQA delivers eulogy of James Madison
1841	JQA argues before Supreme Court in *Amistad* case
1842	JQA publishes *The Social Compact*
1846	JQA opposes entry into war with Mexico
23 Feb. 1848	JQA dies in Washington

ACKNOWLEDGMENTS

When we were first testing the idea of a book that encompassed the Adamses' dissent from democracy, our dear old friend Joan Witkin asked, "Do you mean 'descent' or 'dissent'? Because it works either way."

We have a number of such clever friends. Fellow historians have offered their informed perspectives on the long eighteenth, nineteenth, and twentieth centuries. First on our list is David Waldstreicher, whose rich insights carry special weight with us. Rosemarie Zagarri helped us contextualize relations between Adamses and Warrens. And we have profited from the good ideas of Matthew Dennis, Douglas Egerton, John Ferling, Leigh Fought, Edith Gelles, Amy Greenberg, Christoph Hanckel, Annette Kolodny, Nancy MacLean, Greg and Anna May, Alexis McCrossen, Johann Neem, Barbara Oberg, Peter Onuf, Lizzie Reis, Bethel Saler, Alan Taylor, and Maurizio Valsania.

At the Massachusetts Historical Society, where Revolutionary America enjoys a blissful afterlife, we are deeply grateful to Sara Martin, editor in chief of the Adams Papers, and to Sara Georgini and Dan Hinchen. We appreciate, too, the excellent scholarship of Richard Ryerson, former editor in chief of the Adams Papers, whose comprehensive book *John Adams's Republic* (2016) is just the latest reminder of how an expert draws from founding-era texts, many of which are now digitized online. Same goes for Melanie Miller, editor of the Gouverneur Morris Papers, whose painstaking work reminds us of the sizable contribution all documentary editors make to the historical profession. Thanks as well to Julie Miller and Jeffrey Flannery at the Manuscript Division of the Library of Congress. And not to be remiss, a companionable nod to James P. McClure of the Jefferson Papers (Princeton); Andrew Jackson O'Shaughnessy and Jack Robertson at the International Center for Jefferson Studies; and Special Collections at the University of Virginia Library.

At the institution where we have taught for over a decade now, we extend our particular thanks to Bill Cooper, who took temporary leave of the old

South to become an Adams scholar. We are in debt as well to our LSU colleagues Chuck Shindo, Aaron Sheehan-Dean, Christine Kooi, Sue Marchand, Steven Ross, Ali Wolfe, and the department chair, Victor Stater, all of whom have provided valuable information and encouragement.

Sincere thanks to George Gibson, now at Grove Atlantic, who first saw merit in our project; and to our agent, Geri Thoma, for her persistence in finding a stable home for the book. For their care and dependability throughout the production process, our thanks to Terezia Cicel and Bruce Giffords. We are most of all grateful for Wendy Wolf, our editor at Viking, who communicates the art of the book like no one else we've met and who eagerly supported an atypical approach to the time-worn, platitudinous genre of "founders studies."

As readers can easily detect, the Adamses obliged us to rediscover the life and works of Marcus Tullius Cicero. In *De re publica,* more than twenty centuries ago, the wise Roman wrote that even under constitutional government, equality can never be realized where people *appear* to be free but are free in words only. Democracy (in the mature republic the Adamses wished for) demands nothing less than taking the measure of words and matching them to what functionally exists. This has been our guiding principle as authors, and we can only hope that readers feel we have chosen our words carefully and reached conclusions impartially.

Notes

ABBREVIATIONS

AA	Abigail Adams.
AFC	*Adams Family Correspondence*. Edited by L. H. Butterfield et al. 12 vols. Cambridge, Mass.: Belknap/Harvard University Press, 1963–.
AP/FOL	Adams Papers, Founders Online (National Archives).
AP/microfilm	Adams Papers, on microfilm (Massachusetts Historical Society).
BPL	John Adams Library at the Boston Public Library.
DAJA	*Diary and Autobiography of John Adams*. Edited by L. H. Butterfield et al. 4 vols. Cambridge, Mass.: Belknap/Harvard University Press, 1961.
DALCA	*Diary and Autobiography of Louisa Catherine Adams*. Edited by Judith S. Graham et al. 2 vols. Cambridge, Mass.: Belknap/Harvard University Press, 2013.
DHFFC	*Documentary History of the First Federal Congress, 1789–1791*. Edited by Linda Grant De Pauw et al. 22 vols. Baltimore: Johns Hopkins University Press, 1972–.
DHRC	*Documentary History of the Ratification of the Constitution*. Edited by John P. Kaminski et al. 22 vols. Madison: State Historical Society of Wisconsin, 1976–.
DJQA	*The Diaries of John Quincy Adams, a Digital Collection*. Massachusetts Historical Society.
JA	John Adams.
JQA	John Quincy Adams.
LCA	Louisa Catherine Adams.
LPJA	*Legal Papers of John Adams*. Edited by L. Kinvin Wroth and Hiller B. Zobel. 3 vols. Cambridge, Mass.: Belknap Press, 1965.
MHS	Massachusetts Historical Society.
PGW-P	*The Papers of George Washington: Presidential Series*. Edited by W. W. Abbot et al. 4 vols. Charlottesville: University of Virginia Press, 1987–.
PGW-R	*The Papers of George Washington: Retirement Series*. Edited by W. W. Abbot et al. 4 vols. Charlottesville: University of Virginia Press, 1998.
PJA	*Papers of John Adams: General Correspondence*. Edited by Robert J. Taylor et al. 17 vols. Cambridge, Mass.: Belknap/Harvard University Press, 1977–.
PTJ	*Papers of Thomas Jefferson*. Edited by Julian P. Boyd et al. 43 vols. Princeton, N.J.: Princeton University Press, 1950–.

EXORDIUM

1. To long-trusted friend Dr. Benjamin Rush, John Adams wrote on March 23, 1809, "Monuments will never be erected to me. I wish them not" (AP/FOL). In 2001, Congress first entertained the prospect of an Adams Memorial to be erected at an unspecified location in the area of the National Mall, but funding and related issues kept the plan from advancing. The idea was to honor John Adams and his legacy, with further honor accorded to both his wife and his eldest son. On July 23, 2018, after this book went to press, H.R. 1220 resuscitated the near-defunct plan by establishing the Adams Memorial Commission. H.R. 1220 is set to expire in December 2020.
2. Serviceable myths persist for humane reasons as much as they do for less noble political reasons, in either case seeking to strengthen belief in the flow of history toward general uplift, toward public happiness or tranquility on a large scale. We presume there is no need to document the fact that social consciousness is influenced by forces that misrepresent the constant flux of events so as to remove uncertainty and create closure.
3. Emblematic of the ecstatic Jeffersonian script previewing American exceptionalism is his statement to Joseph Priestley just after inauguration as president: "We can no longer say there is nothing new under the sun. For this whole chapter in the history of man is new. The great extent of our republic is new. Its sparse habitation is new." March 21, 1801, *PTJ*, 33:393–94.

4. The Adamses used the phrase "party spirit" or "spirit of party" with regularity; in general, see Hofstadter, *Idea of a Party System;* www.presidency.ucsb.edu/ws/index.php?pid=25809.
5. JQA to JA, Nov. 25, 1800, AP/FOL.
6. There are two intersecting definitions of "cult of personality." One is the psychotherapeutic ethos that arose in the early twentieth century alongside consumerism: an individual's "pursuit of happiness" was no longer about assiduous work habits within a community but now a matter of personal expression and a lifestyle. A second, politically drawn definition has flourished since the 1950s. *The Oxford English Dictionary* refers to mass psychology: "a collective obsession with . . . or uncritical admiration for, a particular public figure or leader." The term was most widely used, mid-century, to describe the manufactured support for communist rulers. See Heinze, "Schizophrenia Americana."

   As given currency in the 1950s, "cult of personality" fused discussions about conformity in American public life with the phenomenon of the strongman in communist countries. In 1956, in an essay so titled, a seasoned observer of media and culture examined these two definitions side by side, writing in the *American Scholar* that the U.S. tradition of encouraging the young to develop "outgoing and gregarious" personalities was "alien to" Asian and European societies, and especially repugnant to the British. While the cult surrounding the late Soviet leader Joseph Stalin was being overturned by his successors, it was equally the case that American culture had long been distinguished for a certain lack of restraint relative to the self-suppression favored elsewhere in the world. Outgoing behavior continues to be seen as "democratic" in origin. Strunsky, "Cult of Personality," 266. Strunsky was a print journalist who spent a good portion of his career at CBS.
7. JA to James Warren, Dec. 2, 1778, in *PJA,* 7:244.
8. Frances Trollope, *Domestic Manners of the Americans* (London: Richard Bentley, 1839); Alexis de Tocqueville, *Democracy in America* (New York: Penguin, 2003). In the aftermath of his victory in the Battle of New Orleans, in 1815, and throughout his political rise in the 1820s, Jackson was popularly referred to as "the Hero." Fredrika J. Teute and David S. Shields trace a consciousness of the phenomenon to questions surrounding George Washington's pre-presidential image, writing, "Washington understood that a cult of personality was no enduring foundation for nationhood or focus for civil society. A government of persons rather than laws subjected a state to the whims of the rulers' personalities. The state had to be governed by laws, civil society by manners, and public life by virtues. . . . The success of the American Revolution had unleashed unrestrained ambitions and personal expectations. These ambitions, if they were directed toward Old World images of rank, fashion, and social privilege, would make the republic a caricature of decadent Europe." See Teute and Shields, "Confederation Court," 225.
9. The obvious exception is David McCullough's "love letter" to John Adams, his mega-selling biography of 2001, *John Adams.* McCullough successfully converted a "loser" into a "winner." The book's tremendous popularity was owing not to any research discoveries or originality in interpretation but to its storytelling author's outward pretense to authority. It is biography as ventriloquism, the biographer as his subject's amanuensis. Let us at least give McCullough his due as an active ambassador for the cause of history; his avuncular enthusiasm endeared him to millions. But as seductive as feel-good history is, no historian of merit would regard his Adams book as objective or particularly well informed on the conduct of politics in early America.

   In the past, American historical biography has generally featured idea builders (Thomas Jefferson and others) and men of action (Andrew Jackson, Daniel Boone, wartime leaders on and off the field of battle). For generations, nothing was so American as tales of frontier heroism and an associated folk charm that glossed over frontier mud, speculative failures, and folk poverty. America's first professional author, Washington Irving, was the nineteenth century's McCullough, in rhapsodizing an anointed George Washington and a nearly omniscient "Washingtonesque" Christopher Columbus in massively popular multivolume biographies. Somewhat more objective popular treatments did emerge, such as that of the New York journalist James Parton, who wrote somewhat conventionally about the glorified founders, but also studied with greater equanimity than most that unfortunate victim of bad publicity, Aaron Burr. On this subject, see Burstein, *Original Knickerbocker;* and Casper, *Constructing American Lives.*
10. In her developmental approach to the study of American republicanism, Jennifer R. Mercieca identifies and explores two aspects of post-Revolutionary political conditions that relate to our larger thesis. She finds in "Romantic citizenship" the triumphalist conceit of Americans as a "chosen people" who became "ironic partisans" around the time of John Quincy Adams's presidency, when popular belief was expressed through party belonging. A countervailing strain, "tragic citizenship," held that the people were always falling short of their moral promise. "Romantic citizenship served as an ideal," she writes, "while tragic citizenship offered a safer view of republicanism for those who found romantic citizenship too democratic, chaotic, and idealistic." See Mercieca, *Founding Fictions,* esp. 34–38, 198–201.
11. A majority of historians, for purposes of convention in distinguishing between the party of Jefferson and party of Jackson, date the origin of a formal "Democratic-Republican" party to the period 1791–1792. No such party

actually existed. Before the end of George Washington's first term as president, Congressman James Madison, Secretary of State Thomas Jefferson, and their allies recoiled at the seemingly unchecked influence of Alexander Hamilton in the administration and saw a need to consolidate opposition. Ardent supporters of the administration, acquiring the name of "Federalists," often identified the critics with the pejorative name of "Democrats."

In 1794, during Washington's second term, political associations arose in various locales that designated themselves as "Democratic-Republican Societies" (also abbreviated, at this time, as "Democratic Societies"). The administration roundly criticized their activities. Their members tended to support the positions taken by the Madison-Jefferson coalition. However, the societies did not survive long, and they did not presume to give a name to any national party. When a surprise election result occurred in Federalist-dominated Massachusetts in 1795, and a critic of the administration won a seat in Congress, a prominent anti-administration newspaper referred to the victor as "an independent Democratic Republican, and of consequence a true Federalist (according to the real sense of the word)." This was as close to an embrace of the "Democratic-Republican" label as the era ever offered, more importantly demonstrating the amorphous character of party altogether. (*Aurora General Advertiser,* April 30, 1795.)

When John Adams and Thomas Jefferson stood for the presidency in 1796, neither made mention of a "Democratic-Republican" party. By 1800, when the same two vied a second time, more newspapers were referring to candidates in elections for state legislatures as "Democratic Republicans," but it was still a convenient label, not a formal one. Typically, writers made reference to "the Republican portion of our fellow citizens." Therefore, in this book, we do not use the term "Democratic-Republican," instead referring to the cause of Madison and Jefferson not as it is sometimes retrospectively known but as it was colloquially referred to across the United States from the mid-1790s through the conclusion of the Jeffersonian era, namely, "Republican." (Party designations are discussed in *History of U.S. Political Parties,* vol. 1 [New York: Chelsea House, 1973]; and Phil Lampi, "A New Nation Votes," https://elections.lib.tufts.edu.)

12. *Political Works of Marcus Tullius Cicero,* xi.
13. Broadly speaking, "loser"-directed early American histories of today studiously engage with the sordid lives of smugglers, filibusters, counterfeiters, con men, slave stealers, experimental religious sects, prostitutes, and the like. It sometimes appears that a majority of scholars of the present generation, with their immense devotion to the cause of historical justice, are recasting tradition by rendering obsolete histories that celebrate all-white, principally male achievements and by revivifying the millions of women, slaves, free blacks, and others whose trials and triumphs have found their way into a new national narrative that charts the inexorable march to race awareness.

    However framed, academic scholarship recognizes history's complexity, its elusiveness. It is to be pondered as a jigsaw puzzle. Historians analyze information and disinformation contained in hundreds of years of books, newspapers, magazines, diaries, letters, published pamphlets, account books, political cartoons, social satires, and so on, so as to blur the boundaries (as much as is possible) that separate specializations into such subgenres as political, intellectual, cultural, social, economic, emotional, literary, gender, diplomatic, and military history. It is within this often-unwieldy framework, with its array of choices, that we operate here.
14. During these years, the slogan "principles, not men" was frequently heard, yet it was the personalities of Monroe's chief cabinet members (J. Q. Adams, William H. Crawford, and John C. Calhoun) that dominated the national conversation. Their competition was relatively muted in the period before the outsider Jackson entered the race, and "one-upmanship" depended on perceptions in the gossipy public realm, fed by speculation in the pages of newspapers.
15. For a good example of such language in the context of state politics, see JQA to JA, Feb. 4, 1792, AP/FOL.
16. Burstein and Isenberg, *Madison and Jefferson,* chaps. 6 and 7.
17. At times, factions within the two parties resisted, with varying degrees of invective, the mainstream wing of the party: the Republicans of the early nineteenth century had their "Quids," and the Federalists a disunionist element, but opposition criticism served mostly to alienate and never truly threatened to derail either party as a congressional majority or in presidential contests.
18. Historians acknowledge lingering uncertainty over Adams's defense of those accused of murder in the Boston Massacre. How much coordination existed between the defense team and the patriot leadership remains a matter of speculation. See Hiller B. Zobel, *The Boston Massacre* (New York: W. W. Norton, 1970).

    The nickname "Old Man Eloquent" is something of a misnomer, according to the historian of public speaking Horace G. Rahskopf, who devoted considerable time to a deconstruction of John Quincy Adams's career as a student and practitioner of political oratory. Acknowledging the power of JQA's emotional appeals, forcefulness, and animation, Rahskopf regarded his voice itself as "not strong," less eloquent, and less effective than that of other well-known congressional orators of the age, such as Henry Clay, John C. Calhoun, and Daniel Webster. He writes, "Discrepancies between Adams' theory and practice were numerous. Some precepts in the *Lectures on Rhetoric and Oratory* were not exemplified in Adams' speeches." See Rahskopf, "John Quincy Adams' Theory and Practice of Public Speaking," esp. 86, 90, 92.
19. Oct. 27, 1827, *DJQA.*

1: EXEMPLARS

1. Jan. 30, 1768, Paper Book 15, journal fragments, *DAJA,* 1:337–38; AA to JA, Sept. 14, 1767, in *AFC,* 1:62. In his *Autobiography,* John Adams wrote of this period, "In the Years 1766 and 1767 my Business increased, as my Reputation spread, I got Money and bought Books and Land. I had heard my father say that he never knew a Piece of Land run away or break, and I was too much enamoured with Books, to spend many thoughts upon Speculation on Money." *DAJA,* 3:286.
2. *DAJA,* 3:287.
3. The best character study remains Shaw, *Character of John Adams,* esp. 19–40.
4. Krapp, *English Language in America,* 1:214–17.
5. JA to AA, June 30, 1774, in *AFC,* 1:117.
6. See, among other titles, Gelles, *Abigail and John;* Gelles, *Portia;* Ellis, *First Family;* Nagel, *Descent from Glory;* Parsons, *John Quincy Adams.* For a particularly well-focused treatment of the world of manners that absorbed the Adamses' minds, see Barker-Benfield, *Abigail and John Adams.*
7. Pattee, *History of Old Braintree and Quincy,* 1–12, 54–57.
8. Naming the town Quincy was concluded at a public meeting after a vote on the recommendation of Richard Cranch (1726–1811), who was married to Abigail Adams's sister Mary. See ibid., 63; Cranch, *Memoir of John Adams,* 16.
9. Newell, *From Dependency to Independence,* introduction, chaps. 10 and 12; Carr, *After the Siege,* chap. 4.
10. Oct. 24, 1762, *DAJA,* 1:229–30; Cranch, *Memoir of John Adams,* 11–12.
11. March 14 and 18, 1759, *DAJA,* 1:78–81; Crocker, *Reminiscences and Traditions of Boston.*
12. *DAJA,* 3:272.
13. JA to Lovell, Dec. 24, 1777, in *PJA,* 5:369.
14. Pattee, *History of Old Braintree and Quincy,* 59–63; Newell, *From Dependency to Independence;* Winifred B. Rothenberg, "The Emergence of a Capital Market in Rural Massachusetts, 1730–1838," in Hoffman et al., *Economy of Early America,* 126–65; Taylor, *American Colonies,* 304–8.
15. JA to AA, June 30, 1774, in *AFC,* 1:117.
16. Holton, *Abigail Adams,* 125–26, 133, 141–46; Woody Holton, "The Battle Against Patriarchy That Abigail Adams Won," in Young, Nash, and Raphael, *Revolutionary Founders,* 273–83.
17. JA to Tufts, Aug. 27, 1787, in *AFC,* 8:149.
18. Gabriel Bonnot de Mably (1709–1785) had already published widely on ancient and modern history and political morality. Around the end of the Revolution, Adams, too, considered writing a history of American independence but dropped the idea; Editorial Note, "John Adams and the Writing of the History of the American Revolution," and JA to Mably, Jan. 15, 1783, in *PJA,* 14:165–68, 172–81. On the importance of pseudonyms, see Shalev, "Ancient Masks, American Fathers," esp. 154–56, 159, 163.
19. "King v. Stewart, 1773–1774," "Deposition of Silas Burbank," June 28, 1773, "Adams's Minutes of the Review, Cumberland Superior Court, Falmouth, July 1774," in *LPJA,* 1:106–8, 121–41. "Scurlogging" does not appear in newspapers, nor does it seem to have been used in British legal sources; it is not in the *OED.* It could be a combination of "scurrile" (vulgar taunt and invective) and "logger," meaning "of rank growth." "Scurrile" was similar to "scurrility," which, in English law, meant subjecting religion, states, families, or persons to contempt and ridicule. Note that coarse jesting without defamatory insult was labeled "rusticity." See Cumberland and Maxwell, *Treatise of the Laws of Nature,* 335.
20. JA to Richard Cranch, Sept. 2, 1755, in *PJA,* 1:3–4; *DAJA,* 3:264–66. Adams wrote in his diary (Feb. 4, 1772) of "rustic imaginations" more strongly tempted by militia commissions than by "Learning, Eloquence, and Genius, of which common Persons have no idea." *DAJA,* 2:52.
21. JA to AA, Oct. 29, 1775, and Aug. 3, 1776, in *AFC,* 1:318, 2:75–76. He wrote something similar to James Warren: "our New England Educations, are quite unequal to the Production of Such Great Characters" as British or Roman generals and senators. See JA to Warren, July 17, 1774, in *PJA,* 2:109.
22. According to the *OED,* "ploughjogger" was first used in England in 1600 and was at once a humorous and a derogatory label. See "The Author's Apology," in Richard Ploughjogger, *A Brief Inquiry into the Dissenting Institution* (Boston, 1758), 2; an advertisement that identifies the author as "Richard Plough-jogger," *Boston Weekly Advertiser,* Aug. 7, 1758. John Adams intentionally misspelled "Humphrey" as "Humphry," though the editors of the Adams Papers have corrected the spelling in titling the essays: see esp. "Humphrey Ploughjogger to the *Boston Evening-Post* [June 20, 1763]," in *PJA,* 1:63–66. When, in print, Adams pretended to be an educated gentleman responding to "Ploughjogger's" letter, he added the *e* to "Humphrey"; see letter signed "U," *Boston Gazette,* July 18, 1763; see also Saltman, "John Adams's Earliest Essays."
23. JA to Edmund Jenings, April 3, 1782, in *PJA,* 12:382–83. For supporters of the new Constitution using the Ploughjogger style, see Massachusetts state ratifying convention speech in *Freeman's Oracle* (Exeter, N.H.), Feb.

1, 1788; Ebenezer Hazard to Jeremy Belknap, Feb. 3, 1788; *Newburyport Herald,* April 17, 1788; for Anti-Federalists, see Hugh Ledlie to John Lamb, Jan. 15, 1788, Ledlie to William Samuel Johnson, Dec. 1–3, 1788; "Honestus," in *New York Journal,* April 26, 1788; "John Humble," "Address of the Lowborn," *Independent Gazetteer,* Oct. 29, 1788, all in *DHRC,* 5:848, 6:1348–50, 24:253–55, 3:485–86, 575–84, 17:219–21, 2:205–6. Plowmen were important as symbols in ceremonies surrounding the adoption of the federal Constitution. The Grand Federal Procession in Manhattan featured ten divisions representing various occupations: the first division led by a plow drawn by six oxen, at their head a man in "farmer's dress." See "Description of the New York City Federal Procession," *New York Daily Advertiser,* Aug. 2, 1788; attack on Jefferson in *Concord (N.H.) Republican Gazette,* Dec. 23, 1801.

24. Longmore, "'Good English Without Idiom or Tone,'" 517; Jayne Crane Harder, "James Russell Lowell: Linguistic Patriot," *American Speech* 29 (Oct. 1954): 183. Claiming more distinctive, more permanent connections from parts of Great Britain to the American colonies, David Hackett Fischer offers a popular interpretation in *Albion's Seed: Four British Folkways in America* (New York: Oxford University Press, 1989).
25. For these distinctions, see esp. Kenneth Cmiel, *Democratic Eloquence: The Fight over Popular Speech in Nineteenth-Century America* (Berkeley: University of California Press, 1990).
26. Krapp, *English Language in America,* 2:22–35, 180–83, 196–200; Lederer, *Colonial American English; The New Encyclopedia of Southern Culture,* vol. 5, *Language* (Chapel Hill: University of North Carolina Press, 2007), 42–43; Benjamin Bangs Diary, April 1744 and Oct. 1759; Isaac Bangs Diary, April–July 1776, both at MHS; Bangs, *Journal of Lieutenant Isaac Bangs, 1776,* 3–6; Dec. 18, 1765, *DAJA,* 1:263.
27. Howe, *Language and Political Meaning in Revolutionary America,* 23–34; Kramer, *Imagining Language in America,* 30–31 and chap. 1.
28. "Notes and Queries," *Journal of American Folklore* 11 (April–June 1898): 162–64; David Simpson, *The Politics of American English, 1776–1850* (New York: Oxford University Press, 1986), esp. 26–33; Tanner and Collings, "How Adams and Jefferson Read Milton and Milton Read Them."
29. June 20, 1779, *DAJA,* 2:385; JA to Abigail "Nabby" Adams, Aug. 13, 1783, in *Journal and Correspondence of Miss Adams, Daughter of John Adams,* 202–3.
30. AA to JA, Dec. 15, 1783, in *AFC,* 5:280.
31. Ferling, *John Adams,* 45–49; Alexander, *Samuel Adams;* William M. Fowler Jr., *Samuel Adams, Radical Puritan* (New York: Longman, 1997); Samuel Forman, *Dr. Joseph Warren: The Boston Tea Party, Bunker Hill, and the Birth of American Liberty* (Gretna, La.: Pelican, 2011); Burstein, *Sentimental Democracy,* chap. 3.
32. On Warren's role in the Revere story, and the events of April 1775 more generally, see David Hackett Fischer, *Paul Revere's Ride* (New York: Oxford University Press, 1994); and Forman, *Dr. Joseph Warren;* Samuel Swett, *History of Bunker Hill Battle* (Boston: Munroe and Francis, 1827).
33. AA to JA, June 18, 1775, in *AFC,* 1:222–23.
34. Quincy, *Memoir of the Life of John Quincy Adams,* 2–3; *AFC,* 1:223–24n; *DAJA,* 2:290–91.
35. JA to AA, June 23 and July 7, 1775, in *AFC,* 1:226, 241.
36. Ryerson, *John Adams's Republic,* 182–85.
37. Ibid., 185.
38. JA to AA, June 2, 1776, in *AFC,* 2:3; Ferling, *John Adams,* 142–48.
39. JA to AA, April 15, 1776; AA to JQA, Jan. 19, 1780, in *AFC,* 1:384, 3:268.
40. JA to AA, June 30, 1774, and Feb. 18, 1776; AA to JA, Aug. 14, 1776, in *AFC,* 1:117, 349, 2:93–94. John forbade Nabby to learn Latin or Greek; see Holton, *Abigail Adams,* 104; Nagel, *John Quincy Adams,* 11. While giving credit to his wife in 1776 ("I wish I understood French as well as you"), John took special pride, in his diary in 1779, when a French military engineer assured him that his French was very impressive, indeed fluent. May 20, 1779, *DAJA,* 2:377.
41. AA to JA, May 7, 1776, in *AFC,* 1:401–3.
42. JA to Nabby Adams, April 18, 1776; JA to AA, June 29, 1777, in *AFC,* 1:388, 2:270–71.
43. JA to JQA, July 27, 1777, in *AFC,* 2:289–91.
44. AA to JQA [ca. March 15, 1784], in *AFC,* 5:309–10.
45. Dec. 3–5[?], 1758, *DAJA,* 1:61; "A Dissertation on Canon and Feudal Law," Nos. 4 & 6, *Boston Gazette,* Oct. 21, 1765, in *PJA,* 1:123–27; Shaw, *Character of John Adams,* 49–50.
46. AA to JA, June 25, 1775, and March 2 [1776], in *AFC,* 1:230, 354–55.
47. AA to Edward Dilly, May 22, 1775; AA to JA, Aug. 14, 1776, in *AFC,* 1:200–203, 2:93–94; Nov. 2–3, 1818, *DJQA.*
48. The most famous letter-writing manual, *The Complete Letter Writer; or, New and Polite English Secretary,* was first published in London in 1755; it described letters as "performance." The manual was sold in the American colonies by 1760; see *New-York Gazette,* May 26, 1760. There were advice books written for ladies, and Daniel Defoe published one for ambitious tradesmen. The author of *The Ladies Complete Letter-Writer* (1763; Newcastle upon

Tyne: Cambridge Scholars, 2010) had traveled to North America in the 1740s. On reading letters aloud, see *The Complete Letter-Writer, Containing Familiar Letters on the Most Common Occasions in Life* (Edinburgh, 1778), 5; also L. Hannon, "The Imperfect Letter-Writer: Escaping the Advice Manuals," in Corfield and Hannon, *Hats Off, Gentlemen!*, 53–72; Myers, "Model Letters, Moral Living"; Mercy Otis Warren to AA, March 15, 1779, AP/FOL.

49. JA to Unknown, April 27, 1777, in *PJA*, 5:162–63.
50. AA to Edward Dilly, May 22, 1775, in *AFC*, 1:201; Philip Hicks, "Portia and Marcia: Female Political Identity and the Historical Imagination, 1770–1800," *William and Mary Quarterly* 62 (April 2005): 265–94. It is significant that a shorter sketch of *The Group* first appeared in the same newspaper edition as John Adams's "Novanglus" essay; Warren mentioned "Novanglus" in her pamphlet version of *The Group;* see Sarkela, "Freedom's Call"; *Boston Gazette*, Jan. 23, 1775; and [Mercy Otis Warren], *The Group, as Lately Acted* (Boston, 1775), 20, 22. In a variety of writings, John Adams donned classical masks as well: Cicero, Solon, Lycurgus, and Lysander—the last was a mighty Spartan admiral and a name John used while courting his future wife. Abigail would also have known the Portia who was Shakespeare's cross-dressing noblewoman in *The Merchant of Venice*, who masquerades as a trial attorney in order to rescue her husband. Crane, "Political Dialogue and the Spring of Abigail's Discontent."
51. Joseph Addison, the influential British editor best known as an author of the celebrated *Spectator* essays (1710–1711), called the classical Portia an eminent philosopher and a "stoick in petticoats"; see "No.155, Utility of Learning to the Female Sex," *Guardian*, in *The Works of Joseph Addison*, 6 vols. (London, 1903), 4:284. Addison's phrase appeared in the colonies; see, for example, *New-York Weekly Journal*, May 19, 1735; "every manly virtue," in *New Universal Magazine*, Nov. 1753, cited in *Pennsylvania Gazette*, June 20, 1754. A popular novel sold in the colonies was titled *A History of Portia. Written by a Lady*, 2 vols. (London, 1759); see also *New-Hampshire Gazette*, June 7 and 21, 1771; "Visions of the Paradise of Female Patriotism," *United States Magazine*, May 1779, 121–23. For a discussion of the dream story, see Burstein, *Sentimental Democracy*, 99; and Hicks, "Portia and Marcia," 273.
52. See esp. Nicole Pohl and Betty A. Schellenberg, "Introduction: A Bluestocking Historiography," *Huntington Library Quarterly* 65 (2002): 1–19.
53. Abigail wrote to her cousin in London that she had a "great desire to be made acquainted with Mrs. Maccaulays history. One of my own Sex so eminent in a tract so uncommon naturally raises my curiosity and all I could ever learn relative to her." See AA to Isaac Smith Jr., April 20, 1771, in *AFC*, 1:76–77; draft of John's letter to Catharine Macaulay, Aug. 9, 1770, *DAJA*, 1:360; Macaulay to JA, Sept. 11, 1774, in *PJA*, 2:164–65; Aug. 9, 1770, *DAJA*, 1:360; *Boston Gazette*, Oct. 21, 1765, in *PJA*, 1:123–27; also see Macaulay's published letter in *Pennsylvania Journal*, Sept. 21, 1774; Hicks, "Roman Matron in Britain."
54. AA to Warren, Aug. 14, 1777, AP/FOL.
55. AA to JA, March 31, 1776, in *AFC*, 1:270. Englishwomen had already issued public critiques of sexual tyranny in government, exposing the harshness of the law of coverture. Some of these writings were reprinted in the colonies; see "Of English *Wives Hardships*," *New-York Evening Post*, Aug. 24, 1775.

    We learn a great deal about Abigail by studying her choice of quotations. It was Daniel Defoe, in the 1706 *Jure Divino*, who introduced his irony-laced epic poem with the lines "Nature has left *this Tincture in the Blood* / That all Men *would be Tyrants* if they cou'd." Defoe was satirizing the divine right of kings in *Jure Divino* while acknowledging the overthrow of tyrants as a natural act of self-defense. Abigail was not in the least satirical when she wrote that "Men of Sense" believed in liberty as a God-given right and should detest those customs that treat women as "vassals" and give up the "harsh title of master." Defoe dedicated his poem to "Lady Reason: First Monarch of the World." When Abigail reached out to the "Men of Sense" in Congress, urging that it should "Remember the Ladies," she was embracing Defoe's model of "Lady Reason." Women, she insisted, must have the right of "representation" and a clear "voice." In Defoe's satire, the phrase "All men would be tyrants if they could" appears three times. See *Jure Divino*, 1:1, 4:72, 5:15. A shorter version of the quotation appeared in John Trenchard and Thomas Gordon's popular newspaper series, *Cato's Letters* (1723), and in *Providence Gazette and Country Journal*, Nov. 7, 1772; *PJA*, 1:81.
56. JA to AA, April 14, 1776, in *AFC*, 1:382–83.
57. JA to James Sullivan, May 26, 1776, in *PJA*, 4:208–12; also see Brown, *Self-Evident Truths*, 174–75.

    As uncomfortable as his response was to his wife's letter, a mere two days later he wrote a very different letter to Mercy Otis Warren. "The Ladies I think are the greatest Politicians," he declared; they acted on the "Sublimest of all the Principles of Policy" and considered political questions "more coolly than those who are heated with Party Zeal." Somehow, at this moment, he was convinced that women were better than men at keeping their prejudices in check when it came to suppressing selfish desires. "Every Man must seriously set himself to root out his Passions, Prejudices and Attachments," he said, "to get the better of his private Interest." He thanked God that he knew "two Ladies" who comprehended political reality and adhered to the republican principles he did. JA to Warren, April 16, 1776, in *PJA*, 4:123–26.

58. AA to JA, Aug. 14, 1776; JA to AA, Aug. 25, 1776, in *AFC,* 1:93–94, 109–10; AA to Warren, April 27, 1776, AP/FOL.
59. JA to AA, July 8, 10, 18, and 28, 1777; AA to JA, July 9, 10, and 16, 1777; Thaxter to JA, July 13, 1777, in *AFC,* 2:276–80, 282–85, 292. On the depth of emotion in the Adamses' correspondence and their expectations from each other at this time, see also Gelles, *Portia,* chap. 2.
60. JA to Hezekiah Niles, Feb. 13, 1818, AP/FOL; March 1, 1776, *DAJA,* 2:235; John D. Spillane, *The Doctrine of the Nerves* (Oxford: Oxford University Press, 1981); Knott, *Sensibility and the American Revolution;* and esp. Barker-Benfield, *Abigail and John Adams.* As for our metaphor of the clock in John Adams's celebration of Revolutionary communion, Barker-Benfield offers the following explanation: "*Sensibility* denoted a 'mechanical' operation anyway, and its rise was accompanied by various efforts to give it moral and spiritual meaning" (137).
61. Part of the problem is the confusion that exists over the words "democracy" and "republic" in the eighteenth century. Both democracies and republics get their authority from "the people," but simple democracies, as James Madison argued, "meet and exercise the government in person; in a republic," they rely on representatives and agents. And yet, as Adams realized, the House of Commons was the "democratical branch" in England, which allowed freemen to elect representatives and have a voice. Annual elections gave the system legitimacy. On confusion over the two concepts, see Shoemaker, "'Democracy' and 'Republic' as Understood in Late Eighteenth-Century America," esp. 89–91.
62. "To the Inhabitants of the Colony of Massachusetts," March 6, 1775, in *PJA,* 2:309–14. Most colonial legislatures adopted the characteristics of Parliament, which reinforced the sense of autonomy, and were far more representative. Parliament had one member to every 14,300 persons, the colonies approximately 1 to every 1,200. See Pole, "Historians and the Problem of Early Democracy." Adams made a similar case in his "Reply of the House to Hutchinson's First Message," Jan. 26, 1773. He strenuously argued that the colonial dominions were never annexed to England, which was the only way Parliament could extend its authority over the colonies. See *PJA,* 1:315–31, esp. 321–23.
63. JA, *Thoughts on Government,* 6, 10. The May 1776 resolution in the Continental Congress, which Adams helped draft, ended all governments exercising authority under the crown. Along with the Declaration of Independence, it set the stage for the elimination of all established forms of British political power, that is, appointments of governors, members of the upper houses, judges, and other officials. During his time in office, 1758–1774, the royal governor Thomas Hutchinson created an oligarchy in Massachusetts, appointing relatives and allies to virtually all major political offices. See Jensen, "Democracy and the American Revolution."
64. JA to John Winthrop, June 23, 1776, in *PJA,* 4:331. Professor Winthrop was a direct descendant of the famed Puritan who arrived in Massachusetts Bay in 1630.

2: WANDERERS

1. Parsons, *John Quincy Adams,* 13–16.
2. Feb. 14 and 21–26, 1778, *DAJA,* 2:271–78.
3. Staves, "Don Quixote in Eighteenth-Century England"; Frohock, "'Picaresque' in France Before *Gil Blas*"; Wood, *Quixotic Fictions of the USA,* 59–60.
4. JA to Arthur Lee, March 24, 1779, in *PJA,* 8:171; May 7, 15, 18, and 22, 1779, *DAJA,* 2:364–66, 373, 375–77.
5. Captain Landais had gotten himself into hot water by contesting the American naval hero John Paul Jones for command of the vessel *Alliance.* A Frenchman in service to America, he would come to be court-martialed. When appealed to by Landais, Adams chose not to involve himself in the controversy and at a later time heaped praise on the talents of Paul Jones. See Benjamin Pierce to JA, June 1, 1780; Landais to JA, June 14, 1780; Arthur Lee to JA, June 14, 1780, in *PJA,* 9:412–14; Peter Landais, *Memorial to Justify Peter Landai's Conduct in the Late War* (Boston: Peter Edes, 1784), BPL.
6. *DAJA,* 1:92–93.
7. Holton, *Abigail Adams,* 86; *DAJA,* 1:74. Adams indicated an interest in the parson's perspective on human nature at an earlier time, when Wibird willfully undertook, in a professional manner, to observe the single and the married, young and old. His mind was, Adams wrote, "stuffed with Remarks and stories of human Virtues, and Vices, Wisdom and folly." It was only when it came to personal engagement that the poor bachelor proved incompetent. "His Soul is lost, in a dronish effeminacy," Adams concluded. "He says he has not Resolution enough to court a Woman." For his own amusement, Adams pictured the minister as a turkey, flitting about nervously while looking for a place to roost.
8. Aug. 9, 1780, *DJQA;* Henry Adams, *Catalogue of the Books of John Quincy Adams,* 106–7; Jefferson to Robert Skipwith, Aug. 3, 1771; to Marbois, Dec. 5, 1783, in *PTJ,* 1:76–81, 6:373–74.
9. Lesage, *Adventures of Gil Blas,* bk. 1, chap. 2; bk. 3, chap. 5.

10. Forbes, *New England Diaries;* J. L. Bell, "The Revolutionary-Era Boy and 'His Joyrnal': Diary Keeping as a Step Toward Manhood," in Benes, *In Our Own Words,* 113–25; Woodward, "Journal at Nassau Hall." JQA's namesake, John Quincy (1689–1767), kept a diary for many years, but it was primarily a record book of court cases he presided over as judge. The most famous early diary in the English language, that of Samuel Pepys, was composed in the 1660s but was not published until the 1820s. James Boswell's, dating to the 1760s, was not published until the mid-twentieth century; the same is true of the colonial Virginian William Byrd II, who kept a revealing diary for a few years a decade or so before John Adams began his.
11. Perhaps the best single piece of evidence of an Adams commitment to openness in this mode of writing is a quotation from Francis Bacon's *De augmentis scientiarum* that John Quincy recorded at the start of a volume of his diaries in the second decade of the nineteenth century: "And the journals of Alexander the Great contained even trivial matters. Yet journals are not destined for trivial things alone, as annals are for serious ones; but contain all things promiscuously, whether greater or less concern." (Original diary viewed at MHS.)
12. JQA to AA, Sept. 27, 1778, in *AFC,* 3:92.
13. April 26 and May 10 and 12, 1779, *DAJA,* 2:362–63, 366–69.
14. *OED,* s.v. "Commonwealth"; JA to Edmund Jenings, June 7, 1780, in *PJA,* 9:338; "The Report of a Constitution or Form of Government for the Commonwealth of Massachusetts," [Oct. 28–31, 1779], in *PJA,* 8:236–62, esp. 237, 239, 242, 260. Harrington believed that the people had to be regularly instructed on the meaning of their constitution. A politician with no knowledge of history, he wrote, "cannot tell what has been; and if he has not been a Traveler, he cannot tell what is: but he that neither know what has been, nor what is, can never tell what must be, or what may be." Again, Harrington: "The formation of a Citizen in the Womb of the Commonwealth is his Education." See John Toland, comp., *Oceana* (London: n.p., 1700), 37–39, 56, 173, 179–83; Joe Horrell, "Education in Oceana," *Peabody Journal of Education* 13 (Jan. 1936): 195–202. Harrington was the inspiration for the notion that a government be of laws and not of men. And he defined an ideal republic as one that comprises mixed branches of government. John Adams owned at least two editions, one published in 1747, another in 1771. He had earlier called for the "liberal education of youth, especially those of the lower classes," in *Thoughts on Government,* in *PJA,* 4:91. Abigail's quotation from *Oceana* related to Britain as a ship: "She had sprung her planks and split her Ballast" (AA to John Thaxter, May 21, 1778, in *AFC,* 3:25). On JA's role in drafting the constitution and its undemocratic suffrage rules, see also Ryerson, *John Adams's Republic,* 212–13, 215–16, 218–19, 223, 225–26.
15. July 11, 1788, *DJQA.*
16. The sort of hero we are thinking of here is one whose virtue and suffering combined, who braved dangers willingly, who faced temptation and resisted. One possible way to look at Adams's brand is his choice of Hercules for the Great Seal of the United States in July 1776. As he wrote to Abigail at the time, he would have the seal show "Virtue pointing to her rugged Mountain, on one Hand, and perswading him to ascend. Sloth, glancing at her flowery Paths of Pleasure, wantonly reclining on the Ground, displaying the Charms both of her Eloquence and Person, to seduce him into Vice." JA to AA, Aug. 14, 1776, in *AFC,* 2:95–98. Adams's subsequent disparagement of Benjamin Franklin also plays upon this model, in that he identifies Franklin's vice as that of sloth.
17. Nov. 12–Dec. 8, 1779, *DJQA;* Dec. 10, 1779, *DAJA,* 2:405. For a recent study of the trials, deprivations, tedium, occasional camaraderie, and common anxieties of ocean travel in the eighteenth century, see Berry, *Path in the Mighty Waters,* esp. chaps. 6–8.
18. Dec. 14, 1779, *DJQA.* It is worth pointing out that John Adams made it a habit to expose his two sons to the pomp and circumstance of a diplomat's routine; in El Ferrol, they joined him at dinner in the company of a couple dozen Spanish and French military officers.
19. Dec. 17, 1779, *DAJA,* 2:410–11; 4:194–95.
20. Dec. 5, 1779, *DAJA,* 2:403–4.
21. Dec. 15, 24–26, 1779, *DJQA.*
22. One can generally detect when the son wrote from his own head and when he read his father's notes and felt obliged to change his tune. Reaching camp at the end of a day, junior reproduced senior's commentary. "The roads in General are very bad," he synthesized, after his father detailed, with greater implications, "a fertile Country, not half cultivated, People ragged and dirty, and the Houses universally nothing but Mire, Smoke, Fleas and Lice. Nothing appears rich but the Churches, nobody fat but the Clergy." Too young to have developed a real critique of the religious order, Johnny deferred: "I must not say any thing against their religion while I am in their country." Imitation was the principal form of education in this era, especially when a father (or a tutor) hovered over a child. Dec. 28–30, 1779, *DAJA,* 2:415–17; JA, *Autobiography, DAJA,* 4:216; Dec. 25, 1779, and Jan. 3, 1780, *DJQA.* Note that by the time of his post-presidency, when the first president Adams incorporated their Spanish odyssey into his *Autobiography,* it became "an hundred years ago" in comparing Boston's more primitive conveyances to the calash.

23. July 30, 1780, *DAJA;* AA to JQA, March 20, 1780, in *AFC,* 3:312. For a close examination of the exhortative letter to John Quincy and its larger implications, see Barker-Benfield, *Abigail and John Adams,* 308–10.
24. Sept. 14, 1782, *DAJA.*
25. On JQA's fondness for Dana, see Levin, *Remarkable Education of John Quincy Adams,* 69.
26. JQA to JA, Sept. 1, 1781; JA to JQA, Dec. 14, 1781, in *AFC,* 4:206–7, 263.
27. Ekirch, *At Day's Close;* McCrossen, *Marking Modern Times,* 33–38. McCrossen states that household clocks were more a mark of gentility than they were of functional value and would become common only in the 1820s. The elder Adams was one of many among his political cohort who liked to employ "timely" metaphors when writing of the human body or the body politic. "A Clock also has a Constitution," he scrawled in his diary in 1766, "Weights, Springs, Wheels and Levers, calculated for certain Uses and Ends. This Use and End is the Mensuration of Time. Now the same Reasoning may be employed with equal Propriety, concerning a Clock as concerning the human Body."
28. Paul Ricoeur, *Memory, History, Forgetting* (Chicago: University of Chicago Press, 2004), esp. 28–33; Edward S. Carey, "Edges of Time, Edges of Memory," in *Time, Memory, Institution: Merleau-Ponty's New Ontology of Self,* ed. David Morris and Kym Maclaren (Athens: Ohio University Press, 2015), 254–74; and Maurice Merleau-Ponty, *The Visible and the Invisible* (Evanston, Ill.: Northwestern University Press, 1968). John Dewey writes of the past, with an almost Adamsian sensibility in mind, "The conception that contemplative thought is *the* end in itself was at once a compensation for inability to make reason effective in practice, and a means for perpetuating a division of social classes." See Dewey, *Experience and Nature* (New York: Dover, 1958), chap. 3, quotation at 119; Hutton, *History as an Art of Memory,* chap. 3. Note, too, that Jean-Jacques Rousseau's *Confessions,* an emotional self-portrait, was published in 1782.
29. Feb.–March 1782, *DJQA.*
30. Kaplan, *John Quincy Adams,* 48–50; Nagel, *John Quincy Adams,* 27–29; various entries of Nov. 1782, *DJQA.*
31. AA to JA, Oct. 8 and 25, 1782; JA to AA, Dec. 4 and 28, 1782, in *AFC,* 5:4–5, 21–22, 46, 60; JQA to JA, Feb. 1, 1783, AP/FOL.
32. Jan. 21, 1783, *DJQA.*
33. AA to JQA, ca. March 15, 1784, in *AFC,* 5:309–11.
34. JA to Dana, April 18, 1783, in *PJA,* 14:420; *DAJA,* vol. 3, appended to entry of Oct. 27, 1783, and extracted from JA's autobiographical submission to the *Boston Patriot,* Feb. 17, 1812.
35. JA to AA, Jan. 23, 1795, in *AFC,* 10:357. We are grateful to Sara Martin of the Adams Papers for calling this letter to our attention.

3: ENVOYS

1. JA to Gerry, Jan. 31, 1785, in *PJA,* 16:505–7.
2. Ferling, *John Adams,* 285–86; more generally, Shaw, *Character of John Adams,* chaps. 5 and 6; quotation in Grant, *John Adams,* 337.
3. Fawcett, "Creating Character in '*Chiaro Oscuro,*'" 141–42.
4. On Franklin's image and popularity, see Hale and Hale, *Franklin in France,* 69–70, 90, 150; Aldridge, *Franklin and His French Contemporaries,* 61, 65, 75. On his relationship with prominent women, see Claude-Anne Lopez, *Mon Cher Papa: Franklin and the Ladies of Paris* (New Haven, Conn.: Yale University Press, 1966); "Bon Mot," *Dunlap's Maryland Gazette or the Baltimore Advertiser,* Sept. 2, 1777; Frank Moore, *Diary of the American Revolution,* 2 vols. (New York, 1860), 1:389–90. On rumors of Franklin's assassination, see AA to James Lowell, March 1, 1778, Samuel Cooper to AA, March 2, 1778, in *AFC,* 2:396, 398; *Boston Gazette,* Feb. 23, 1778.
5. Hale and Hale, *Franklin in France,* 82; J. Bennett Nolan, "Monsieur Franklin," *Pennsylvania History* 23 (July 1956): 346–75, esp. 356–60; JA to Mercy Otis Warren, Aug. 3, 1807, as quoted in Evans, "John Adams' Opinion of Benjamin Franklin," 221.
6. April 29, 1778, *DAJA,* 4:80–81. It was noted at the time that Franklin was making public appearances at both low- and highbrow events; see Aldridge, *Franklin and His French Contemporaries,* 11, 16, 65, 75.
7. Dull, *Diplomatic History of the American Revolution,* chap. 9, quotation at 77.
8. Ferling, *John Adams,* 224–27; Richard Alan Ryerson, "A John Adams Paradox: Provincial Lawyer, Cosmopolitan Reader, Ardent Nationalist," and Gregg L. Lint, "John Adams, Thomas Pownall, and Peace in 1780," in Baron and Wright, *Libraries, Leadership, and Legacy of John Adams and Thomas Jefferson,* 197–99, 207–23. For perhaps the most extensive, most damning characterizations Adams made of Vergennes, along with Franklin, see JA to James Warren, March 21 and April 13, 1783, in *PJA,* 14:350–53, 402–3.
9. JA to Jenings, The Hague, July 20, 1782; to James Warren, April 13, 1783, in *PJA,* 13:189, 14:403.
10. Sept. 9, 1776, *DAJA.*
11. May 12, 1779, *DAJA;* Landais, *Memorial to Justify Peter Landai's Conduct in the Late War,* 14.

12. Adams allowed that he would continue to act in concert with Franklin in "publick affairs," but "further than that I can feel for him no other sentiments than Contempt or Abhorrence." It is revealing of his unqualified loathing of the man that Adams used the very same phrase at the start of his involvement in Revolutionary politics to "hold in Utter Contempt and Abhorrence every Stamp Officer, and every Favourer of the Stamp Act," which was thought a design to tax colonists into submission to Parliament. JA to Jenings, July 20, 1782, in *PJA,* 13:189. On Jenings (1731–1819), see diary entry of March 4, 1779, *DAJA,* 2:355–56; Jan. 2, 1766, *DAJA;* Shaw, *Character of John Adams,* 114–19, 160–61; Evans, "John Adams' Opinion of Benjamin Franklin"; Ferling, "John Adams, Diplomat," nicely contextualizing the alteration of JA's feelings toward Franklin from 1775 to 1779.
13. JA to Arthur Lee, Oct. 10, 1782, in *PJA,* 13:525; Arthur Lee to JA, Sept. 10, 1780, in *PJA,* 10:140; JA to William Lee, April 10, 1783, in *PJA,* 14:390; JA to James Warren, April 13, 1783, in *PJA,* 14:402–5; also: "Dr. F. is disgusted with nothing but Integrity & cares for nothing but his place" (JA to William Gordon, April 15, 1783, in *PJA,* 14:411); *DAJA,* 4:69–70. John Adams's uncensored letters to James Warren during this period recall a statement he made as the Revolution heated up: "I write every Thing to you, who know how to take me. You dont Expect Correctness nor Ceremony from me." JA to Warren, Oct. 25, 1775, AP/FOL.
14. With his usual need to vindicate his own actions, Adams began one letter to Livingston, "You do me the honor, Sir, in applauding the Judgement I have formed, from time to time, of the Court of Britain, and future Ages will give me Credit for the Judgement I have formed of some other Courts." And then, indirectly addressing his problem with Franklin's credulity and lack of penetration: "The true designs of a Minister of State are not difficult to be penetrated, by an honest man of common Sense." Adams added the obvious: "My opinions, as you observe, sometimes run Counter to those generally received, but . . . Truth and Justice have sometimes obliged me." JA to Livingston, Jan. 22–23, 1783, and May 25, 1783, in *PJA,* 14:201–5, 495.
15. JA to Trumbull, April 25, 1790, AP/FOL. In a diary entry of 1796, Adams delighted in having figured out the meaning of the great English satirist Dean Swift's takedown of the poet John Dryden, when the former compared the latter to "the lady in a lobster." The meaning eluded Adams for decades, until served lobster meat at dinner one night; it was the shriveled meat in the "cradle" from which it had emerged. Dryden had demeaned Swift's poetry, and Swift never forgave the slight. The equally unforgiving Adams looked at the shelled lobster and saw "an old Lady—she looks like Dr. Franklin, i.e. like an Egyptian Mummy." Adams associated the "lady" lobster tail meat with the aged Franklin's physical appearance in Paris, and a reminder of a reputation so much greater than the man's genius as to be comical. In the same diary entry, Adams extended his diminution of greatness to encompass George Washington: "A little old Woman in a spacious Habitation as the Cradle would be a proper Emblem of a President in the new House at Philadelphia." July 28, 1796, *DAJA.* On the Swift-Dryden matter, see John Timbs, *Anecdote Lives of Wits and Humourists* (London: Richard Bentley and Son, 1872), 8–9.
16. *Boston Patriot,* July 24, 1811; Feb. 26, 1785, *DJQA;* "Almanack des Rendez-Vous," diary of William Temple Franklin for 1785, American Philosophical Society, Philadelphia. Temple's diary shows, for instance, dinner at the Lafayettes' with "All the Americans in Paris" on Feb. 14 and dinner at the Adamses' on April 7.
17. *DAJA,* 4:118, 120.
18. Franklin to Livingston, July 22–26, 1783; to Morris, Dec. 25, 1783, in *Papers of Benjamin Franklin,* 40:358, 41:345–46; Jefferson to Madison, July 29, 1789, in *PTJ,* 15:315–16; Ferling, *John Adams,* 257. For a richly detailed, unsympathetic view of Adams's Franklin fixation, see Hutson, *John Adams and the Diplomacy of the American Revolution,* 44–47, 138–41, in which the author sees evidence pointing to an affliction that is akin to "paranoid disorder, the principal symptom of which is durable, inflexible delusions of persecution" (141). The French finance counselor Turgot, who once said, "America is the hope of the human race," noted in 1778 that Adams was "cankered with excessive envy" of Franklin (45); Barnard, *Sketch of Anne Robert Jacques Turgot,* 6, 27.
19. Nordholt, *Dutch Republic and American Independence,* chap. 10.
20. JA to AA, Sept. 15, 1780, in *AFC,* 3:413–14; JA to the president of Congress, Sept. 5, 1780, in *PJA,* 10:176–78.
21. Nordholt, *Dutch Republic and American Independence,* chap. 7; JA to Franklin, May 2, 1782, in *PJA,* 13:2–3.
22. Nordholt, *Dutch Republic and American Independence,* chap. 3; Nagel, *John Quincy Adams,* 29; Ferling, *John Adams,* 241. Dumas's daughter Nancy, slightly older than John Quincy, was as taken with both Adamses and composed in French a rhyming song about the elder's Revolutionary glory. The first stanza (rendered here into English) construed a relationship between the biblical Adam and his more judicious namesake:

    The first of the Adams
    Enslaved his children
    By eating too much,
    But a wiser Adams
    Preserved their destiny,
    Giving them independence
    In our own time.

In French, "Le premier des Adams / asservit ses Enfans / En trop mangeant / Mais un plus sage Adams / Leur destin menageant / Les rend de notre temps / Independans." C. W. F. Dumas to JA, March 28, 1783, in *PJA,* 14:378, 380.

23. JA to Franklin, June 13, 1782; to Jay, Aug. 13, 1782, in *PJA,* 13:116, 236–38.
24. Kloek and Mijnhardt, *1800,* 88–92; *Le politique hollandais,* 1:18, 22–23, 86, in BPL; JA to Robert Livingston, May 16, 1782; JA to Cerisier, Jan. 14, 1783; Cerisier to JA, Feb. 26, 1783, in *PJA,* 13:50, 14:169–71, 296–300; Cranch, *Memoir of John Adams,* 27–31. Among Adams's purchases was a Dutch-to-French dictionary. The Plymouth visitor was Elkanah Watson, who not only characterizes Europeans' esteem for Adams's "deep sagacity and extensive political acquirements" but also relates an incident in his memoir of seeing Adams attempt to rescue a drowning child in a Dutch canal. Curiously, Watson says of the John Adams he knew, "He talked but little." See Watson, *Men and Times of the Revolution,* 204–7.
25. "Memorial to the States General," in *PJA,* 11:272–81.
26. Kossmann, *Low Countries,* 34–45; Kloek and Mijnhardt, *1800,* 208–9. The house of Orange had ceased to be popular, or even representative of Dutch identity. Meanwhile, as was true of American shipping interests, Dutch merchants were resentful of British actions against neutral vessels on the high seas. Hundreds of Dutch ships had been seized, including a sizable number returning from the East Indies. But William V was not sufficiently moved to resist British actions.
27. Shaw, *Character of John Adams,* 146–47; Ferling, *John Adams,* 244; *PJA,* 13:379–81.
28. Francis Dana's Russia notebook, Dana Family Papers, box 34, MHS; Parsons, *John Quincy Adams,* 22–24; Nagel, *John Quincy Adams,* 25–30.
29. JA to Dana, Sept. 17 and 29, 1782; Dana to JA, Sept. 17 and Oct. 7–18, 1782, in *PJA,* 13:469–72, 498–99, 533; Dumas to JA, March 28, 1783, in *PJA,* 14:378–79; June–Oct. 1782, *DJQA.*
30. JA to Dumas, May 1, 1783, in *PJA,* 14:465–66.
31. JA to Livingston, May 16, 1782, in *PJA,* 13:51.
32. A good example is found in the Oct. 2, 1782, entry, *DAJA.*
33. Nov. 5, 1782, *DAJA.* Of Jay's general agreement with Adams's critique of Franklin and Vergennes, see Pencak, "From 'Salt of the Earth' to 'Poison and Curse'"; to Elbridge Gerry, Adams reiterated his critique, with particular emphasis on the fisheries issue, wherein Adams alone stood firm in demanding U.S. access to Newfoundland's prodigious Grand Banks as a precondition to the conclusion of any treaty: "*British* Finesse did not Use to impose upon any Americans much less Yankees.—French Finesse has been more successful." JA to Gerry, Dec. 4, 1782, in *PJA,* 14:124–25; see also notes on Draft Peace Treaty, in ibid., 88–89n.
34. Lafayette's outsize personality was widely felt. Even Jefferson, a pronounced Francophile, found him to possess a "canine appetite for fame." Adams went one step further in psychoanalyzing his titled subject. Addressing Warren, and using the second-person plural to mean "all of America," he warned, "You have given him a great deal too much of Popularity." JA to James Warren, Dec. 15, 1782, in *PJA,* 14:132–33.
35. JA to James Warren, April 16, 1783, in *PJA,* 14:417–19.
36. To Edmund Jenings, a few days after this, he wondered who of his acquaintances might next be seduced into believing lies about him: "In all Events don't let you and me be caught in any Snare.—I have never had many intimate Friends, and I am not disposed to part with one easily." JA to Jenings, April 21, 1783, in *PJA,* 14:423.
37. Nov. 5 and 11, 1782, *DAJA;* Stahr, *John Jay,* 139–40, 153–54, 227. John Quincy Adams, in later years, continued to adhere to his father's interpretation, but his son Charles Francis Adams considered the real possibility that Franklin behaved as he did toward the French government because his primary role was as minister to the country, and only secondarily as a peace negotiator; lacking responsibility for managing the bilateral relationship, John Adams and John Jay could adopt bolder positions than Franklin; see Pellew, *John Jay,* 186.
38. Ferling, *John Adams,* 247–56.
39. The record may not provide the detail we are accustomed to seeing in the trove of Adams correspondence, but it is hard to imagine that at this juncture JQA was not privy to his father's complete reports.
40. JA to AA, Feb. 27, 1783, in *AFC,* 5:101–2.
41. JA to AA, Dec. 4, 1782, in *AFC,* 5:46.
42. Nagel, *John Quincy Adams,* 33; JA to JQA, May 28, 1784, in *AFC,* 5:333–34.
43. Jonathan R. Dull, "Franklin the Diplomat: The French Mission," *Transactions of the American Philosophical Society* 72 (1982): 1–76, esp. 11, 15, 17, 49–50; JA to president of Congress, Aug. 4, 1779, in *PJA,* 8:112. The approximate value of the eighteenth-century livre in modern currency is $10, thus the equivalent of a $210 million loan.
44. JA to Dumas, Jan. 31, 1781, in *PJA,* 11:86.
45. Even in his first year in France, Adams felt that Franklin indulged his female fans and their children with silly daily audiences. His fans, Adams wrote, wanted to concoct "Stories about his Simplicity, his bald head and scattered stray hairs." Afternoons and evenings, the ladies made him tea, and he listened to them "play their

piano fortes and other instruments of Musick," while he frittered away his day playing chess or checkers. In this way, Adams reduced Franklin to a womanish cipher, in a dotage resembling a second childhood. See May 27, 1778, *DAJA,* 4:118–19. On the common diplomatic strategy always to prepare for war in order to gain peace, see Hutson, "Intellectual Foundations of Early Diplomacy." *On* Adams's legal training in shaping his approach to statecraft, see Kurtz, "Political Science of John Adams"; Shaw, *Character of John Adams,* 178–79.

4: EXILES

1. JA to Mercy Otis Warren, Jan. 29, 1783, in *PJA,* 14:219–20.
2. JA to C. W. F. Dumas, May 19, 1783, in *PJA,* 14:483; AA to JA, Oct. 25, 1782, in *AFC,* 5:21–23.
3. AA to JA, Nov. 11, 1783, in *AFC,* 5:266–69.
4. May 13, 1779, *DAJA,* 2:370.
5. On Sterne, see esp. Valerie Grosvenor Myer, ed., *Laurence Sterne: Riddles and Mysteries* (London: Vision Press, 1984); Wilbur L. Cross, *The Life and Times of Laurence Sterne* (New York: Russell & Russell, 1967); Kraft, "Laurence Sterne and the Ethics of Sexual Difference"; Porter, *Flesh in the Age of Reason,* chap. 17; on the earthiness of the society the Adamses adapted to, see Gattrell, *City of Laughter.*
6. June 12, 1779, *DAJA,* 2:380. As Jefferson also put it, "The writings of Sterne form the best course of morality that ever was written"; on Jefferson and Sterne, see Burstein, *Inner Jefferson,* chap. 2.
7. Oct. 22, 1783, *DAJA,* 3:147n1, with reference to JQA to Peter Jay Munro, Nov. 19, 1783, and Nabby Adams's *Journal and Correspondence;* Charles Adams to JQA, April 24, 1796, in *AFC,* 11:268. Writing to Jefferson from London in 1786, Abigail Adams described her situation as that of "Sterne's starling," whose pathetic, childlike cry—"I can't get out!"—caused Yorick's heart to bleed. Desirous of escaping her luxurious quarters and returning to a quiet domesticity, "the rural cottage" and "purer and honester manners" of her "native land," she tapped into Sterne's symbolism. He was the lingua franca that connected people of feeling. The younger brother Charles would commit a saucy Sternean allusion to the page of a letter to John Quincy. And at the age of seventy, John Adams still defended Sterne against charges of dissipation, holding that "the Benevolence, Sympathy and Humanity that fill the Eyes and bosoms of the readers of his Works, will plead forever for their immortality." AA to Jefferson, Feb. 11, 1786, in *Adams-Jefferson Letters,* 119; JA to Benjamin Waterhouse, Oct. 29, 1805, AP/FOL; regarding Abigail Adams and Sterne, see Barker-Benfield, *Abigail and John Adams,* 185–87, 385.
8. March 30, 1785, *DJQA.* For an example of a Sterne (*Tristram Shandy*) allusion in a letter from JQA to AA in 1790, see *AFC,* 9:89–90.
9. JQA to JA, June 6, 1784, in *AFC,* 5:339–40.
10. JA to Richard Cranch, April 3, 1784; to JQA, June 6, 1784, in *AFC,* 5:284, 315.
11. AA to JA, July 23 and 30, 1784; JA to AA, July 26, 1784, in *AFC,* 5:397–99, 408–9; Gelles, *Abigail and John,* 157–61; Aug. 7, 1784, *DAJA.*
12. Gelles, *Abigail and John,* 162–66.
13. JA to William Gordon, April 27, 1785, in *PJA,* 17:58.
14. JA to Jefferson, Jan. 22, 1825, in *Adams-Jefferson Letters,* 606–7; Nov. 7, 1830, *DJQA;* Howard C. Rice Jr., *Thomas Jefferson's Paris* (Princeton, N.J.: Princeton University Press, 1976), 48–49.
15. Much has been written on the comparative temperaments of Adams and Jefferson. See esp. Ferling, *John Adams,* 174–75; Ferling, *Adams vs. Jefferson;* Valsania, *Nature's Man;* Burstein, *Inner Jefferson,* 172–76; Merrill D. Peterson, *Adams and Jefferson: A Revolutionary Dialogue* (Athens: University of Georgia Press, 1976); Koch, *Power, Morals, and the Founding Fathers.*
16. JA to Jefferson, Feb. 17, June 6, and July 3 and 31, 1786; Jefferson to JA, May 30 and July 11, 1786, in *Adams-Jefferson Letters,* 121–23, 132–34, 138–39, 142–47.
17. William Howard Adams, *Paris Years of Thomas Jefferson,* 172, 217–19; Cahill, *Liberty of the Imagination.*
18. May 11–16, 1785, *DJQA;* JA to Jefferson, May 23, 1785, in *Adams-Jefferson Letters.*
19. JA to Willard, April 22, 1785; to Waterhouse, April 23, 1785, in *PJA,* 17:33–37.
20. July 4, 1785, *DJQA.* After a sudden, harrowing storm, he wrote of the veritable Bermuda Triangle, "Very few Vessels pass near the Bermudas, without meeting with more or less of this kind of weather."
21. JA to Jay, June 2, 1785, AP/FOL.
22. Nabby Adams to Mary Smith Cranch, June 22, 1785; AA to Mary Smith Cranch, June 24, 1785, in *AFC,* 6:181–88; Samuel Adams to JA, April 13, 1786, in *PJA,* 18:247–48. For a comparison between John and Abigail Adams's feelings with respect to London and Paris, see also Ellis, *First Family,* 107–14, 121–25.
23. Back in Paris, when news of his father's assignment was still fresh, he had penned in his diary, "Mr. Adams is appointed Minister to the Court in London. I believe he will promote the Interests of the United States, as much as any man: but I fear his Duty will induce him to make exertions which may be detrimental to his Health.

I wish however it may be otherwise. Were I now to go with him, probably my immediate Satisfaction might be greater than it will be in returning to America." April 26, 1785, *DJQA.*

24. July 27–Aug. 8, 1785, *DJQA.* Delivering letters from Europe to a range of American gentlemen, he bore one as well for Susan Livingston, of a prominent political family: "Miss L. appears to me to be a great talker but says very little. Somewhat superficial if I am not mistaken, which must always be pardoned in a Lady." The more he saw of her, the more she pleased him, and he acknowledged having misjudged her. The diaries reveal the social costs of his time away.
25. Oct. 1–6 and Nov. 2, 1785, and March 3, 1786, *DJQA.*
26. Haraszti, *John Adams and the Prophets of Progress,* 139–40; Thompson, *John Adams and the Spirit of Liberty,* 242–44. John Adams was the "principal Engineer" of his state's constitution, responsible for its "Essence and substance," as he informed his European-based American friend Edmund Jenings. JA to Jenings, June 7, 1780, in *PJA,* 9:388–89.
27. Price, *Observations on the Importance of the American Revolution,* 64–65, 84.
28. Ibid., 92–93, 99, 113–17, 123; Haraszti, *John Adams and the Prophets of Progress,* chap. 8. "Hope of the world" is the original translator's rendering of "Il est l'espérance du genre humain."
29. Slauter, "Constructive Misreadings," 37n16. John Adams's name was also prominently associated with another French commentator on the American state constitutions, Abbé de Mably, whose work was suspect on numerous levels and similarly distorted facts, yet Adams remained friendlier toward Mably, who credited him with inspiring his 1784 work, *Observations sur le gouvernement et les lois des États-Unis de l'Amérique.* Mably had had no separate connection to Franklin; see Aldridge, "John Adams Meets the Abbé Mably."
30. JA to AA, Dec. 25, 1786; AA to Cotton Tufts, March 12, 1787; AA to JQA, March 20, 1787, in *AFC,* 7:411–12, 8:8–9, 12.
31. JA, *Defence,* vol. 1, preface. For the best overall analysis of the *Defence,* see Thompson, *John Adams and the Spirit of Liberty,* chaps. 5–7.
32. JA, *Defence,* letter 20.
33. Ibid.
34. Ibid., letter 25. Puckishly insincere, Adams recounts in his *Defence* a "common anecdote" told about the constitutional assembly in Philadelphia over which Franklin presided. The debate was whether one or two legislative branches would be set up. As Franklin rose to speak, "two assemblies appeared to him, like a practice he had somewhere seen, of certain waggoners who, when about to descend a steep hill, with a heavy load, if they had four cattle, took off one pair from before, and chaining them to the hinder part of the waggon drove them up hill; while the pair before, and the weight of the load, overbalancing the strength of those behind, drew them slowly and moderately down the hill." Mocking the popular philosopher's legendary recurrence to fables when a critical measure was brought before a political assembly, Adams projected real science onto the matter at hand, suggesting, in mock response, the superiority of Sir Isaac Newton's laws of motion.

    By using Franklin to undermine Franklin, Adams went on to provide his own analogy of the heavens over Philadelphia being out of balance amid a lightning storm. All one needed to do to resolve the problem was, as the famous inventor ought to have known, to attach "a pointed rod" to terrestrial structures, a machine so simple that "a waggoner, or a monarch, or a governor" could "disarm" the storm with it. If "a single assembly thus constituted, without any counterpoise, balance, or equilibrium, is to have all authority, legislative, executive, and judicial, concentered in it," Adams offered a better way: he would withdraw from his political quiver a lightning rod in the form of well-balanced government to prevent tyranny that could be legislated and executed by a unicameral government.
35. *Notes of Debates in the Federal Convention of 1787 Reported by James Madison,* 659; James McHenry diary, Sept. 18, 1787, Manuscripts Division, Library of Congress.
36. JA, *Defence,* preface, iii, ix–xi, xiii, 96.
37. JA, *Thoughts on Government,* 6; JA, *Defence,* iii, xvii, 96. In praising America, he wrote that "our people are undoubtedly sovereign—all the landed and other property is in the hands of citizens—not only their representatives, but their senators and governors, are annually chosen—there are no hereditary titles, honours, offices, or distinctions." He also wrote in the preface that the duration of terms "should not be so long that the deputy should have time to forget the opinions of his constituents."
38. JA, *Defence,* postscript, 390–91. In the Boston edition of the first volume of the *Defence,* his answer to Mably was rendered into English; the London edition printed the letter in French.
39. JA, *Defence,* letter 50, 329.
40. Ibid., letter 33, 188–89. Abigail Adams acknowledged that her husband had taken up the same cause as Plato "when he wrote his Laws and Republick"; AA to Cotton Tufts, Oct. 10, 1786, in *AFC,* 7:359–63.
41. JA, *Defence,* letter 33, 192–95.

42. Ibid., letter 29, 158; Bruce Miroff, "John Adams: Merit, Fame, and Political Leadership," *Journal of Politics* 48 (Feb. 1986): 116–32, quotation at 121.
43. JA, *Defence,* letter 29, 163, 165.
44. Ibid., letter 7, 28–29. On the importance of the Swiss confederation to the founding generation, and the sources used by Adams, see Halbrook, "Swiss Confederation in the Eyes of America's Founders," esp. 47–48. Adams took his idea of the wood houses from William Coxe, *Sketches of the Natural, Civil, and Political State of Swisserland* (Dublin, 1779), 61.
45. JA, *Defence,* letter 22, 194–99.
46. Ibid., letter 29, 154.
47. Ibid., letter 31, 82.
48. JA to Warren, Dec. 2, 1778, in *PJA,* 7:244; Miroff, "John Adams," 125–28. Professor Miroff is a notable exception to our comment on the majority of historians and biographers who perceive John Adams as insecure and predictably perverse.
49. JA, *Defence,* letter 25, 110–15.
50. Nelson, *Royalist Revolution,* 336n125; Franklin to JA, May 18, 1787; Madison to Jefferson, June 6, 1787, AP/FOL.
51. Nelson, *Royalist Revolution,* 216–17; JA to Jefferson, Dec. 6, 1787; Robert F. Williams, "The Influences of Pennsylvania's 1776 Constitution on American Constitutionalism During the Founding Decade," *Pennsylvania Magazine of History and Biography* 112 (Jan. 1988): 25–48, esp. 39–41.
52. JA, *Defence,* letter 3, 299; Ryerson, *John Adams's Republic,* 269. Adams's emphasis on class relations was featured in excerpts published in magazines. See "The Right Constitution of the Commonwealth Examined—Extracts from Dr. Adams's (Vice President of the United States) Defense of the Constitutions of Government of the United States," *New York Magazine; or, Literary Repository,* Oct. 1790, 589–90. As Ryerson has written elsewhere, Adams's *Defence* and "virtually all his political writings" were informed by the conviction "that social class was not a social construct but an inherent, immutable, eternal property of human nature." See Ryerson, "John Adams in Europe: A Provincial Cosmopolitan Confronts the Metropolitan World, 1778–1788," in Sadosky et al., *Old World, New World,* 142.
53. JQA to Cranch, Oct. 14, 1787, in *DHRC,* 4:74–76.
54. JQA to Cranch, Dec. 8, 1787, in *DHRC,* 4:227–29.
55. JQA thought it strange that no one "dares attack this institution openly"; if allowed to gain strength, it would prove to be "fatal to the Constitution." The elder Adams was even more vicious in his rebuke, labeling this "new order of Knights" the "deepest project of evil which has yet been laid." Jefferson urged Washington to steer clear of the society. Oct. 12, 1787, *DJQA;* JA to Samuel Osgood, April 9, 1784, in *PJA,* 16:123.
56. JA, "Letter I: Preliminary Observations," in *Defence,* 4; JQA to JA, June 30, 1787, in *AFC,* 8:97–99; William Pencak, "Samuel Adams and Shays's Rebellion," *New England Quarterly* 62 (March 1989): 63–74; Nov. 30, 1786, *DJQA;* Burstein and Isenberg, *Madison and Jefferson,* 146–47; Holton, "Did Democracy Cause the Recession That Led to the Constitution?," 444–46; Leonard L. Richards, *Shays's Rebellion: The American Revolution's Final Battle* (Philadelphia: University of Pennsylvania Press, 2002), 23, 26–27, 63, 83–88; *Vermont Gazette,* July 16, 1787. Newspapers lining up on the same side as the Adamses damned the rebels for "licentiousness" and a wanton disregard for laws. James Warren, like his friend Adams, equated licentiousness with the decadence of youth and described the people as a "child" in their rash calls for eliminating the Massachusetts Senate in response to Shays's action. See Warren to JA, May 18, 1787, Adams Papers, MHS.
57. See Paul D. Ellenbogen, "Another Explanation for the Senate: The Anti-Federalists, John Adams, and the Natural Aristocracy," *Polity* 29 (Winter 1996): 247–71.
58. July 11, 1787, *DJQA.*
59. Nagel, *John Quincy Adams,* 37–61; Cooper, *Lost Founding Father,* 36–40; Parsons, *John Quincy Adams,* 32–35; Burstein, *Sentimental Democracy,* 134–40; March 15, 1786, and July 18, 1787, *DJQA.*
60. Lucy Cranch to AA, Aug. 18, 1787, in *AFC,* 8:142.
61. Nov. 3, 1787, *DJQA.*
62. Gelles, *Abigail and John,* 172.

5: INSTIGATORS

1. Haraszti, *John Adams and the Prophets of Progress,* 15.
2. JA to Abigail "Nabby" Adams Smith, July 16, 1788, in *AFC,* 8:278–80.
3. AA to JQA, July 11, 1790, in *AFC,* 9:78. When she finally got wind of her son's attachment to the teenage Mary, a disquieted Abigail urged extreme caution: "Common Fame reports [that is, word has it] that you are attachd to a young Lady. I am sorry such a report should prevail, because whether there is or is not cause for such a

Roumour, the report may do an injury to the future prospects of the Lady as your own are not such as can warrent you in entering into any engagements, and an entanglement of this kind will only tend to depress your spirits should you be any time before you get into Buisness [*sic*] and believe me my dear son a too early marriage will involve you in troubles that may render you & yours unhappy the remainder of Your Life." AA to JQA, Nov. 7, 1790, in *AFC,* 9:142; JQA to Nathaniel Freeman, Aug. 8, 1789, Gilder Lehrman Collection, New York, ref. #GLC00881.

4. Nagel, *John Quincy Adams,* 63–70; Nov. 18, 1838, *DJQA.*
5. AA to JQA, May 30, 1789, and Aug. 20, 1790, in *AFC,* 8:363, 9:93; Barker-Benfield, *Abigail and John Adams,* 390; Ellis, *First Family,* 158–59, 198.
6. AA to JQA, July 11, 1790, in *AFC,* 9:78.
7. JQA to Cranch, July 12, 1790, in *AFC,* 9:80.
8. JA to JQA, July 9, 1789; JQA to JA, March 19, 1790, in *AFC,* 8:386–87, 9:29–31. Another father-son letter in this period is as earnest and protective, and its brisk cadence feels like a direct translation of mind to page: "Preserve my Son, at every Risque;—at every Loss;—even to extreme Poverty and obscurity; Your Honour and Integrity Your Generosity and Benevolence, your enlarged Views and liberal Philanthropy. Candour and Honour, are of more importance in your Profession even than Eloquence Learning or Genius. You will be miserable without them whatever might be your Success. The Family is well—Yours affectionatly." JA to JQA, Feb. 9, 1790, in *AFC,* 9:16.
9. AA to Mary Cranch, March 12, 1791, in *New Letters of Abigail Adams,* 70.
10. JA to JQA, prior to Sept. 8 and Oct. 24, 1790, in *AFC,* 9:105–6, 128–30. John Adams did not have access to his old diaries and letters in New York, or he could have extracted more examples of his own emotionalism mirrored in his son's experience. "My Conscience reproaches me with a long series of such Self Perfidy!" he admitted to a friend at twenty-three. "I start sometimes, and shudder at myself, when the Thought comes into my mind how many million Hours I have squandered in a stupid Inactivity neither furnishing my mind nor exercising my Body. . . . My Resolutions are like bubbles. . . . Yet new ones rise and die in perpetual succession." Draft letter to Samuel Quincy, *DAJA,* Oct.–Nov. 1758.
11. AA to Mary Cranch, March 12, 1791, in *New Letters of Abigail Adams,* 70; April 13, 1792, *DJQA.*
12. Porter, *Flesh in the Age of Reason,* chap. 13, quotation at 232. Nervous sensibility described heightened awareness but was a two-sided coin. A sensible imagination could inspire generous behavior, or it could sentence one to melancholy, even madness. The science behind the concept was tenacious: words impregnated with "sensible" meaning were transmitted as signals or impressions and engaged the soul from the pain-and-pleasure centers of the brain. The acknowledged authority on the eighteenth-century culture of sensibility in its various Anglo-American incarnations is G. J. Barker-Benfield. See his *Culture of Sensibility* and in particular his *Abigail and John Adams;* also see Benes, *In Our Own Words.*
13. Ryerson, *John Adams's Republic,* 315–16. Ryerson gives particular credit to two of General Washington's most trusted former officers, Generals Benjamin Lincoln and Henry Knox, both of Massachusetts, in smoothing the way for Adams.
14. Comte de Moustier to Comte de Montmorin, May 17, 1789, in *DHFFC,* 15:577–81.
15. JA to Lovell, July 16, 1789, in *DHFFC,* 16:1037–39; JA to JQA, July 9, 1789, in *DHFFC,* 16:982–83.
16. At the time of ratification, those favoring the Constitution saw the vice president's role in relatively democratic terms. One commentator drew comparisons to the British system, where the president of the upper house (or chancellor) was "appointed by the king, while our vice president, who is chosen *by the people* through electors and the senate, *is not dependent on the president,* but may exercise equal powers on some occasions." The meaning of "some occasions" ostensibly referred to his succession if the president died or was unable to serve out his term. Adams, then, was democratically elected but, being deprived of a regular vote, seen as holding an ex officio role. See "An American Citizen I: On Federal Government," *Independent Gazetteer,* Sept. 26, 1788, in *DHRC,* 13:250. On the vice president's unimportance, see also "Federal Farmer: Letter to the Republic," Nov. 8, 1787, in *DHRC,* 19:221. Adams early recognized the problem; see JA to Benjamin Rush, May 17, 1789, in *DHFFC,* 15:573–74.
17. Burstein and Isenberg, *Madison and Jefferson,* 189–91; Hutson, "John Adams's Title Campaign."
18. Adams did not like "His Excellency." Yet his wife, after learning of his election, addressed her letter to "His Excellency John Adams/vice president of the united states." AA to JA, April 22, 1789, in *AFC,* 8:333–35; May 9, 1789, Diary of William Maclay, in *DHFFC,* 9:29–32; Bartoloni-Tuazon, *For Fear of an Elective King,* 100–101.
19. JA to William Tudor, May 3, 1789, in *DHFFC,* 15:435–36; May 8–9, 1789, Diary of William Maclay, in *DHFFC,* 9:27–32.
20. "Biography of William Maclay," in *DHFFC,* 9:431–41; April 28 and May 19, 1789, Diary of William Maclay, in *DHFFC,* 9:8–9, 35–40; Thomas Fitzsimons to Benjamin Rush, May 15, 1789, in *DHFFC,* 15:558–59.

21. David Stuart to George Washington, July 14, 1789, *PGW-P,* 3:198; Page to St. George Tucker, Feb. 25, 1790, in *DHFFC,* 18:632; on crambo, see Isenberg, *Fallen Founder,* 65; May 11, 1789, Diary of William Maclay, in *DHFFC,* 9:33–34; "Ralph Izard, Senator from South Carolina," in *DHFFC,* 14:830–36.
22. May 14, 1789, Diary of William Maclay, in *DHFFC,* 9:35–40. Fisher Ames described his sense of "awe" over Washington's "modesty" in his delivery of the inaugural address. See Ames to George R. Minot, May 3, 1789, in *DHFFC,* 15:436–38.
23. Madison to Jefferson, Oct. 17, 1788, in *PTJ,* 14:17–18. Adams learned that during the 1788 election rumor of a "maneuver" had been used to invite a general distrust of New Englanders; it said that certain states would not vote for Washington so as to catapult Adams to the presidency. See JA to William Tudor Sr., May 27, 1789; Tudor to JA, Sept. 30, 1789, in *DHFFC,* 15:635–36, 17:1644–45.
24. *Annals of Congress,* May 11, 1789, in *DHFFC,* 10:595–607. For an example of the contrast between Washington and Adams, satirically drawn, see [Edward Church], *The Dangerous Vice* (Boston: n.p., 1789), 14, 16.
25. The attack on Abigail is in [Church], *Dangerous Vice,* 9. One Boston paper included a longer version of it that appended other women associated with the federal government; see *Independent Chronicle,* Nov. 27, 1789. Maclay compared Adams's love of titles to "fopperies fineries and pomp of Royal etiquette," in opposition to the stern manliness of republican virtue; see May 8, 1789, Diary of William Maclay, and [Maclay], "Letter to the Printer," Feb. 20, 1790, in *DHFFC,* 9:27–29, 18:586–88. The Virginian St. George Tucker wrote a vicious farce, "Up and Ride," casting Adams as "Jonathan Goosequill" and Washington as "George Wheatsheaf." He mocked Adams's physique with an analogy to gold leaf, which "can hide crassest materials and give luster to the clumsiest image." On Washington's tours, see Moats, *Celebrating the Republic,* 49–55; Bartoloni-Tuazon, *For Fear of an Elective King,* 4–5, 30–31, 50–52, 80–81, 117, 142, 156.
26. JA to Sherman, July 18, 1789, in *DHFFC,* 16:1061–64; JA to John Jebb, Sept. 10, 1785, in *PJA,* 17:424.
27. JA to Rush, June 9 and July 5 and 28, 1789, and April 4, 1790, in *DHFFC,* 16:727–28, 943–45, 1154–55, 19:1122–25. On the "language of signs," see JA, *Discourses on Davila,* 40–41; Miroff, "John Adams," 122. Representative James Jackson of Georgia said that to call Washington his "Serene Highness, His Grace, or Mightiness" would fail to "add one title to the solid properties he possessed." *Annals of Congress,* May 11, 1789, in *DHFFC,* 10:595–607.
28. JA to John Trumbull, March 12, 1790, AP/FOL and *DHFFC,* 18:833–38. As to the newspaper reports on Adams's lack of a meaningful English pedigree, the offended vice president wrote to Trumbull with an irrepressible air:

> My Father was an honest Man, a Lover of his Country and an independent Spirit. . . . My Father, Grand Father, Great Grand father and Great Great Grand father, were all Inhabitants of Braintree and all independent Country Gentlemen—I mean officers in the Militia and Deacons in the Church. I am the first who has degenerated from the Virtues of the House so far, as not to have been an officer in the Militia nor a Deacon. . . . Although I am proud of my Family, I should Be very much mortified, if I thought that I enjoyed any share of public or private Esteem, Admiration or Consideration, for the Virtues of my Ancestors. By my own Actions I wish to be tried.

29. On *M'Fingal,* see Burstein, *Sentimental Democracy,* 115, 153–54.
30. Trumbull to JA, Feb. 6, 1790; JA to Trumbull, March 9, 1790, AP/FOL.
31. Trumbull to JA, March 14, 1790, AP/FOL.
32. JA to Trumbull, March 12 and April 2, 1790, AP/FOL and *DHFFC,* 19:1101–5; see also Ryerson, "'Like a Hare Before the Hunters.'"
33. Pattee, *History of Old Braintree and Quincy,* 61–63. In general, see Fowler, *Baron of Beacon Hill;* and Unger, *John Hancock.*
34. JA to Trumbull, March 9, 1790, AP/FOL.
35. See discussion in Thompson, *John Adams and the Spirit of Liberty,* 42–43, 113–16; and C. Bradley Thompson, "John Adams's Machiavellian Moment," in Rahe, *Machiavelli's Liberal Republican Legacy,* chap. 8. JQA did not at any time accord such importance to Machiavelli.
36. Machiavelli, *Works of Nicholas Machiavel,* bk. 7, 2:3, 8–12, in BPL.
37. The famed *Spectator* essays of Addison and Steele, published in 1710/1711, presented the spectator as a curious, well-educated, neutral observer of people and places. Adams's elaboration claimed that spectatorship had a passive underside as well. In twelve of his thirty-two *Davila* essays (nos. 4–15), he departed from his discussion of sixteenth-century French political intrigue to explain the human desire for fame, worship of the rich, and the political consequences of celebrity in democratic elections. See *Discourses on Davila,* 25–93, esp. 39; on spectatorship, see Darren Staloff, "John Adams and the Enlightenment," in Waldstreicher, *Companion to John Adams and John Quincy Adams,* 50–51; and on the importance of spectatorship to Adam Smith's *Theory of Moral Sentiments,* see Marshall, "Adam Smith and the Theatricality of Moral Sentiments"; also Ryerson, *John Adams's Republic,* 325–27. However, none of these studies engage with the meaning and importance of celebrity.

38. JA, *Discourses on Davila,* 25, 27, 44. Adams built on eighteenth-century utilitarian philosophy. Simply put, it stated that human beings sought out pleasure and contrived to avoid pain. He upped the discussion from these fundamentals to the more psychological subject of public approval: men who loved praise exhibited an equal passion to escape neglect.
39. Ibid., 51, 64.
40. Ibid., 29–31.
41. Ibid., 35, 61, 70.
42. JA to Trumbull, March 9, 1790, AP/FOL. A long postscript restates the ways in which Adams believes that he exceeded all other public men in honest emotion. He was, he declared, immune to all envy. Part of this goes: "John Adams has done services for North America of which no Man is ignorant, and which cannot be forgotten. They appear to be least of all known and felt in New England. The Southern Gentlemen I must confess have shewn a better disposition to do me Justice than New Englandmen have." Adams ends with "This is confidential, you see wholly, I mean the whole Letter."
43. JQA to JA, March 19, 1790, in *AFC,* 9:29–32.
44. JA to JQA, April 1, 1790; JQA to JA, April 5, 1790, in *AFC,* 9:36–37.
45. JA to JQA, Oct. 19, 1790, in *AFC,* 9:138–40.
46. Ibid.
47. JA to JQA, April 16, 1790, AP/FOL.
48. JA to John Trumbull, April 2, 1790, AP/FOL and *DHFFC,* 19:1101–5.
49. Whereas John Trumbull might have goaded the vice president into spilling his worst thoughts, John Quincy maintained an even temperament and generally positive outlook in communicating with his father on political subjects. "The real fact is that the new [national] Government is very rapidly acquiring a broad and solid foundation of popularity," he wrote in Oct. 1790, after observing election season in and around Boston. JQA to JA, Oct. 19, 1790, in *AFC,* 9:133–35.
50. Paolo Andreani to the Venezuelan general Francisco de Miranda, July 8, 1790, in *Along the Hudson and Mohawk: The 1790 Journey of Count Paolo Andreani,* ed. Cesare Marino and Karim M. Tiro (Philadelphia: University of Pennsylvania Press, 2006), 99–104, as cited in *DHFFC,* vol. 20.
51. Jefferson to JA, July 17 and Aug. 30, 1791; JA to Jefferson, July 29, 1791, and July 13, 1813, in *Adams-Jefferson Letters,* 245–51, 356. Jefferson's most prolific twentieth-century biographer, Dumas Malone, states that there is no evidence of Jefferson's having read *Discourses on Davila* in more than a cursory manner; see Malone, *Jefferson and the Rights of Man* (Boston: Little, Brown, 1951), 354–59.
52. Rush to JA, June 4, 1789, in *Letters of Benjamin Rush,* ed. L. H. Butterfield (Princeton, N.J.: Princeton University Press, 1951), 514; JA to Rush, June 9, 1789, AP/FOL. To John Trumbull, Adams wrote as firmly that pageantry did not "imply abuse," because government used it as patriotic display: "Was there not as much Pomp in escorting Delegates to Congress in 1774 and 1775 . . . ? What was all the Parade of the Presidents late Tour through New England?" Pomp and circumstance was everywhere, and it served no one to pretend otherwise. JA to Trumbull, April 25, 1790, AP/FOL.
53. Rush to JA, July 21, 1789, in *Letters of Benjamin Rush,* 522–25; Ferling, *John Adams,* 302–4.
54. *Rights of Man,* in *Selected Writings of Thomas Paine,* 208–10. The English radical and political philosopher William Godwin, an admirer of Paine, wrote: "The case of mere titles is so absurd that it would deserve to be treated only with ridicule, were it not for the serious mischiefs it imposes on mankind." Godwin, *An Enquiry Concerning Political Justice* (London: G. G. J. and J. Robinson, 1793), bk. 5, chap. 12.
55. JA to Jefferson, July 29, 1791, in *Adams-Jefferson Letters,* 248; Seward, *Life and Public Services of John Quincy Adams,* 51–52.
56. Jefferson to JA, Aug. 30, 1791, in *Adams-Jefferson Letters,* 250–51. Jefferson wrote of his disgust with Adams's critics to Madison, while expressing his belief that the senior Adams was indeed "Publicola": "Nobody doubts here [Philadelphia] who is the author of Publicola, any more than of Davila. He is very indecently attacked in Brown's and Bache's papers" (*Federal Gazette* and *General Advertiser,* respectively); see Jefferson to Madison, June 28, 1791, in *PTJ,* 20:582–83; see also Jefferson to Thomas Mann Randolph (his son-in-law), July 3, 1791, in ibid., 295–96. Subsequent to this letter, Madison threw his weight behind John Quincy's likelier authorship: "If young Adams be capable of giving the dress in which publicola presents himself, it is very probable he may have been made the Editor of his Father's doctrines. I hardly think the Printer would so directly disavow the fact if Mr. Adams was himself the writer"; see Madison to Jefferson, July 13, 1791, in ibid., 298–99. A thorough examination of the Publicola controversy can be found in Ryerson, *John Adams's Republic,* 339–44, 505–6n; Ryerson is of the opinion that Jefferson had no doubt at all that "Publicola" was in fact the vice president's son.
57. The *Advertiser* had to assure its readers on Aug. 22 that Vice President Adams was not the author, and here it said nothing to back up the strong suggestion it had earlier printed as to Publicola's actual identity. Five years later, when the elder Adams stood for president, the same newspaper printed a veiled reference to the "real and

genuinely reputed writings of Mr. Adams, and or his eldest son." Jefferson noted to his protégé James Monroe, as rumors swirled, that "the stile and sentiments raise so strong a presumption" pointing to John Adams's sole authorship. But the latter's explicit denial a short while later rendered the question moot. At that point, Jefferson might have put two and two together, but his familiarity with JQA dated to their time in France, before the boy had sailed home to attend Harvard. *General Advertiser,* July 27 and Aug. 22, 1791, and Dec. 9, 1796; Jefferson to Monroe, July 10, 1791, in *PTJ,* 20:296–98.

58. *Columbian Centinel,* June 4 and 11, 1791. Though Paine's *Rights of Man* has been widely discussed as a reaction to Edmund Burke's *Reflections on the Revolution in France,* in which Burke extolled the virtues of institutional order and social stability, JQA as "Publicola" aimed his barbed pen at Paine far more than he exhibited an interest in defending Burke's thesis; nor did JQA's father ever describe himself as a follower of the conservative Burke. See Maciag, *Edmund Burke in America,* chap. 3.
59. *Columbian Centinel,* June 22 and July 5, 1791.
60. *Columbian Centinel,* July 23, 1791. Brown reused Jefferson's phrasing when he said he found the work of "Publicola" to consist of "abominable *heresies.*"
61. *Independent Chronicle,* July 7, 1791. In the same issue, see also the incisive "Agricola to Publicola, No. III," a critique of "Publicola" for being soft on tyranny and skeptical of a people's ability to discern, let alone take action against, their own loss of liberty.
62. Abigail "Nabby" Adams Smith to JQA, July 3, 1792, in *AFC,* 9:292–93. Her husband, William S. Smith, was in England seeking to attract investors in New York state lands.
63. Eric Stockdale, "John Stockdale, London Bookseller and Publisher of Adams and Jefferson," in Baron and Wright, *Libraries, Leadership, and Legacy of John Adams and Thomas Jefferson,* 41–58.
64. JA to AA, Feb. 27, 1793, in *AFC,* 9:413.

6: EXTORTERS

1. JQA to JA, Dec. 16, 1792, in *AFC,* 9:348–50.
2. July 26, 1796, *DAJA;* JA to Charles Adams, Sept. 11, 1794, in *AFC,* 10:229–30; JA to Waterhouse, Oct. 29, 1805, AP/FOL. While reading Cicero's *De officiis,* which he described as "a Treatise on moral obligation," JA gave a more spirited defense of Christianity in a diary entry of Aug. 13–14, 1796: "One great Advantage of the Christian Religion is that it brings the great Principle of the Law of Nature and Nations, Love your Neighbour as yourself, and do to others as you would that others should do to you, to the Knowledge, Belief and Veneration of the whole People. . . . No other Institution for Education, no kind of political Discipline, could diffuse this kind of necessary Information, so universally among all Ranks and Descriptions of Citizens. . . . Prudence, Justice, Temperance and Fortitude, are thus taught to be the means and Conditions of future as well as present Happiness."

   There was nothing new in Adams's charged use of the word "mischief." Political society had never been at a loss for it; it could be deliberate or an unintended result. Shakespeare, with alliteration, makes "mischief" a synonym for deception—"to apply a moral medicine to a mortifying mischief. . . ." (*Much Ado About Nothing,* act I, scene 3). Benjamin Franklin's *Poor Richard's Almanack* for 1744 cites with calculated irony: "Blunt Truths more Mischief than Nice Falshoods do." He quotes Alexander Pope's *An Essay on Criticism,* part 3, which Abigail Adams in turn quotes in a letter to her sister, Elizabeth Smith Shaw, July 19, 1786. As he sat in the Continental Congress in 1776, John Adams wrote fearfully to his friend James Warren of imperfect politicians: "Common sense . . . will do more Mischief, in dividing the Friends of Liberty, than all the Tory Writings together"; JA to James Warren, May 12, 1776, in *PJA,* 4:181–83. "Mischief" was widely used in legal documents to indicate harm done to a party, whether intended or unintended.
3. JA to JQA, Dec. 9, 1792, in *AFC,* 9:342–43.
4. Ross, "Legal Career of John Quincy Adams," 424–25, detailing JQA's income year by year.
5. *American Apollo* (Boston), July 5, 1793; *Massachusetts Mercury,* July 5, 1793; Cato the Younger, great-grandson (alas, not son) of the first Cato, was known as well for eloquence and personal integrity.
6. Aside from that rare historical moment when "enthusiasm" (the watchword for potentially dangerous passions) became appropriate, patriotism meant cherishing stable relations within society and sustaining the original, harmonious feeling that enabled Americans to seize upon their ennobling concepts of freedom and fairness. For an analysis, see Engels, *Enemyship,* 157–61. Engels, a scholar who specializes in the rhetoric of the post-Revolutionary era, observes that the younger Adams personalized the experience of being American. In his *Lectures on Rhetoric and Oratory,* a decade and a half later, JQA would give definition to the genre of Fourth of July addresses as a holiday when it was appropriate "to point the finger of admiration or scorn." In order to acquire the positive character demanded of the patriot, the hearer needed to understand what manner of behavior was to be shunned as well as followed.
7. Along these lines, see Reddy, *Navigation of Feeling,* chaps. 5 and 6; Cleves, *Reign of Terror in America,* chap. 1.

8. On Genet's welcome in Charleston and Philadelphia, and Morris's Jan. 6, 1793, letter to Washington, see Dumas Malone, *Jefferson and the Ordeal of Liberty* (Boston: Little, Brown, 1962), chap. 6. The most authoritative work on Morris's years as America's minister to France is Miller, *Envoy to the Terror.*
9. *Columbian Centinel,* Nov. 30, 1793.
10. JA to JQA, Dec. 14, 1793, in *AFC,* 9:469–70. The mother of "Columbus" wrote to her son supportively two weeks later, doubling down on her husband's critique of Genet, whom she labeled "contemptable." AA to JA, Dec. 20, 1793; AA to JQA, Dec. 30, 1793, in *AFC,* 9:478, 489.
11. JA to Jefferson, June 30, 1813, in *Adams-Jefferson Letters,* 346–47. If Adams felt this way in 1793, he did not say so at the time.
12. JA to AA, Dec. 20, 1793, in *AFC,* 9:490.
13. JQA to JA, April 12, 1794, in *AFC,* 10:141–43.
14. JQA to JA, Jan. 5, 1794, in *AFC,* 10:11–13.
15. JA to JQA, April 3, 1794, in *AFC,* 10:134–35.
16. JA to JQA, May 7, 1794, in *AFC,* 10:166–67.
17. JA to AA, April 5 and May 19, 1794, in *AFC,* 10:135, 183–84.
18. JQA to JA, April 12, 1794, in *AFC,* 10:141–43.
19. JA to JQA, April 23, 1794, in *AFC,* 10:150–51.
20. June 8, 1794, *DJQA.*
21. JQA to JA, July 27, 1794; JA to JQA, Aug. 24, 1794, in *AFC,* 10:218–22, 227–28.
22. Oct. 14, 1794, *DJQA.*
23. Oct. 20, 1794, *DJQA.*
24. Oct. 22, 1794, *DJQA;* Ferling, *John Adams,* 338–39. On Republicans' dismissal of Federalist war fears, see Irving Brant, *James Madison: Father of the Constitution, 1787–1800* (Indianapolis: Bobbs-Merrill, 1950), 437–38.
25. Jefferson to James Monroe, May 5, 1793, in *PTJ,* 25:660–62; Oct. 22 and 25, 1794, *DJQA.*
26. JA to JQA, Aug. 25, 1795, AP/FOL. For an overview of the preceding, see Harper, *American Machiavelli,* chaps. 10–13; and Malone, *Jefferson and the Rights of Man,* chap. 16.
27. JA to AA, Nov. 23 and 26, 1794, in *AFC,* 10:270, 275–76.
28. Kloppenberg, *Toward Democracy,* 498–99; see also Cleves, *Reign of Terror in America,* 75–90.
29. JA to AA, Dec. 1, 1794, in *AFC,* 10:281–82.
30. JA to JQA, March 26, 1795; JQA to JA, June 27 and Dec. 29, 1795, AP/FOL.
31. JQA to JA, April 1, 1795, AP/FOL.
32. Ibid.; JQA to JA, May 5, 1795, AP/FOL. "I was not sent here to make myself a partisan of Dutch factions," he underscored in his next letter to the vice president. "I must reconcile myself philosophically to the certainty of being no favourite with either side." JQA to JA, June 27, 1795, AP/FOL.
33. JQA to JA, June 27, 1795, AP/FOL. JQA's most definitive account of British bullying is given in another letter to his father, that of Sept. 19, 1795: "The force of Great Britain is so far from being exhausted, that her maritime power was never at any period so great as it is at present. Her naval superiority is every where so indisputably established, that in the mediterranean, on the ocean, in the channel or in the north sea, a french or a Dutch armed vessel can scarce venture out of an harbour without being intercepted."
34. Ibid.
35. JQA to JA, Aug. 31, 1795, AP/FOL.
36. JA to JQA, Aug. 25, 1795, in *AFC,* 11:20–22. JQA patiently set his father straight as to his reluctance to return to the bar: "I think it necessary candidly to acknowledge, that my feelings on this subject, become daily more strongly confirmed." While he assured his father that his advice would always have "great weight in my mind," life in Holland did satisfy him. The marriage calculation he did not reply to. JQA to JA, Oct. 31, 1795, in *AFC,* 11:46–50.
37. JQA to JA, Dec. 29, 1795, AP/FOL.
38. JA to JQA, Sept. 19, 1795, in *AFC,* 11:31–33.
39. July 31, 1796, *DAJA.*
40. JA to Rush, Jan. 4, 1813, AP/FOL.

7: INTELLECTS

1. See especially Winterer, *Culture of Classicism;* Shalev, *Rome Reborn on Western Shores;* Richard, *Founders and the Classics.*
2. Rush to JA, July 21, 1789, in *Letters of Benjamin Rush,* 522–25.
3. Oct. 17, 1829, Adams Papers, microfilm, reel 39, cited in Morris, "John Quincy Adams's German Library, with a Catalog of His German Books," 321; Haraszti, *John Adams and the Prophets of Progress,* 106. John Adams owned the forty-volume 1775 edition of Voltaire's complete works.

4. See list of Adams books in BPL, available online.
5. JA to AA, May 24, 1789, in *AFC,* 8:357–58. Among the eighteenth-century titles he specifically asked Abigail to carry were the works of David Hume, plus any books of "amusement" she chose. He required legal treatises and here named "Blackstone and De Sohne on the English Constitution and the Collection of American Constitutions."
6. JQA to JA, March 19, 1790, in *AFC,* 9:31.
7. April 11 and 25 and May 2, 17, and 19, 1797, *DJQA.*
8. Haraszti, *John Adams and the Prophets of Progress,* 253; Coleman, *Virtues of Abandon,* 229–35; Peter Gay, *The Enlightenment: An Interpretation: The Science of Freedom* (New York: Norton, 1969), 440–45. Rousseau did not abandon the concept of God, but he did speak the language of neurophysiological sensations. He placed few limits on reason, and he could not ignore the dogmatic tendencies and the exploitative effects of prevailing Christian doctrine. As Robert Darnton writes, "Rousseau spoke with his own voice and addressed the reader directly, as if the printed word could carry unmediated effusions from heart to heart." He created an extraordinary "sense of contact . . . sustaining the illusion of exposure to an overflowing soul." Darnton, *The Forbidden Bestsellers of Pre-revolutionary France* (New York: Norton, 1996), 117. The impact of *Émile* was immediate and extensive, forcing the fugitive author to escape to Switzerland.
9. *DAJA,* 3:271–72. Within his extant library, it is thought that the first book purchase John Adams made was Cicero's orations; see Beth Prindle, "Boston Public Library, John Adams Unbound," *History News* 63 (Spring 2008): 27.
10. April 14, 1792, *DJQA;* AA to JQA, Jan. 19, 1780, in *AFC,* 3:268–69. The editors of the Adams Papers point out that Abigail's engagement of Roman history did not compare to her husband's, and that Milo was Cicero's supporter, not adversary, one whom Cicero had defended in court.
11. JA to JQA, Jan. 23, 1788, in *AFC,* 8:219.
12. JA to JQA, Oct. 4, 1790, in *AFC,* 9:128–29. The oft-thumbed standard reference work both father and son turned to was *Robert Ainsworth's Dictionary, English and Latin* (London: Charles Rivington and William Woodfall, 1773), in BPL. The Adams bookplate featured the Latin "Libertatem amicitiam retinebis et fidem," or "Freedom, friendship, and fidelity." In general, on the two Adamses' common appreciation for Cicero, see Rathbun, "Ciceronian Rhetoric of John Quincy Adams."
13. April 14, 1792, and Aug. 7, 1796, *DAJA.* Cicero was often paired with Quintilian and Tacitus in the Adamses' self-schooling. Writing a century after Cicero, Quintilian defined rhetoric for JQA as "the science of speaking well." JQA very much approved Quintilian's statement that "incorruptible integrity is the most powerful of all the engines of persuasion." JQA, *Lectures on Rhetoric and Oratory,* lecture 6.
14. April 9 and 15, 1801, Aug. 25, 1804, and Oct. 24, 1830, *DJQA;* JQA, *Lectures on Rhetoric and Oratory,* lectures 1, 2, and 5; Rathbun, "Ciceronian Rhetoric of John Quincy Adams."
15. JQA, *Lectures on Rhetoric and Oratory,* lecture 1, 20–44; lecture 2, 66; lecture 6, 157.
16. Ibid., adapted primarily from lecture 4 (quotations at 109, 115), lecture 7, and lecture 8.
17. From Harvard in 1787, JQA wrote to his constitution-pondering father, long absent from the scenes of nation building, and enclosed an oration he'd delivered. "Demosthenes, in Greece," he noted, "to avoid being given up by his ungrateful countrymen to the tyrant of Macedon," put an end to his own life; Cicero, in Rome, "was banished from the very city, which by his vigorous exertions, and indefatigable vigilance, had been saved from impending destruction."

    JQA knew what his father was up to, and knew, too, the sense of victimization to which John Adams was prone. In lamenting the cruel treatment inflicted upon Cicero, the son analogized: hope of popularity was in both cases sacrificed to higher truths. Cicero undertook his dangerous dance with ambitious tribunes and would-be emperors, and eventually paid with his life; John Adams dared to stand toe to toe with the legendary Franklin, and to question that gentleman's diplomatic skills—and fame. Refusing to be a team player, an Adams could expect to suffer in reputation. According to the college orator, one who exhibited Adamsian/Ciceronian qualities was "actuated by some nobler motive than the desire of obtaining [society's] gratitude and applause." JQA to JA, June 30, 1787, in *AFC,* 8:96–99; "A Conference upon the Comparative Utility of *Law, Physic,* and *Divinity,*" April 10, 1787, in *DJQA.* John Adams read his son's oration and heartily approved it: "It seems to me . . . to be full of manly Sense and Spirit." A resolute mind, focused attitude, meant more to him than "Style Elegance and Mellifluence." To diversify one's base of knowledge was the Ciceronian key to success. JA to JQA, Jan. 23, 1788, in *AFC,* 8:219.
18. JQA, *Lectures on Rhetoric and Oratory,* lecture 2, 57–58, 68–69, 72; lecture 4, 99; lecture 5, 123–24; lecture 8, 187–88, 197; lecture 11, 253–56.
19. Anthony Everitt, *Cicero* (New York: Random House, 2001), quotation on jealousy at 147, also 124. We are in debt to the author of this scholarly portrait for so effectively explaining the personal psychology of the Roman, and much more.
20. Plutarch quoted in Shaw, *Character of John Adams,* 271.

21. JA to JQA, Dec. 23, 1805, AP/FOL; Weeks, *John Quincy Adams and American Global Empire,* 190; Portolano, *Passionate Empiricist,* 24–25. JQA acquired vastly more books in Europe than his father before him. An astounding fifty-three titles in their library—in several languages, of course—were of or by Cicero. When JQA died in 1848, New York's senator-to-be William Henry Seward eulogized him knowledgeably: "The model by which he formed his life was Cicero. Not the living Cicero, . . . always covetous of applause. But Cicero as he aimed to be, and as he appears revealed in those immortal emanations of his genius which have been the delight and the guide of intellect and virtue in every succeeding age." See Seward, *Life and Public Services of John Quincy Adams,* 397–98.
22. JA to JQA, Feb. 19, 1790, in *AFC,* 9:16.
23. Henry Home, Lord Kames, *Elements of Criticism* (1762; Indianapolis: Liberty Fund, 2005), chap. 2, parts 6 and 7.
24. April 14, 16, and 20 and May 3, 1792, *DJQA;* Kames, *Elements of Criticism,* chap. 2, part 1.
25. Phillipson, *Adam Smith,* 147–58, 299n12; Coleman, *Virtues of Abandon,* chap. 6.
26. Aug. 20, 1770, *DAJA;* Adam Smith, *The Theory of Moral Sentiments,* part 7, chap. 3. So ingrained in his thinking was *Theory of Moral Sentiments* that in his *Discourses on Davila,* the elder Adams copied enough of its essence that it would today be considered plagiarism; in so doing, he referred to the author not by name but only as "a great writer." See Haraszti, *John Adams and the Prophets of Progress,* 169–70.
27. Becker, *Structure of Evil,* 34.
28. JQA to AA, Sept. 17, 1810, AP/FOL.
29. The power of sympathy began with intimates and extended (as practicable) into society. This was what Thomas Jefferson meant in his heralded first inaugural address when he said, "Let us restore to social intercourse that harmony and affection without which liberty and even life itself are but dreary things." Honest introspection led to self-reformation. In the section of his work titled "Of Duty," Smith took note of problems created by constant rationalization: "This self-deceit, this fatal weakness of mankind, is the source of half the disorders of human life. If we saw ourselves in the light in which others see us, or in which they would see us if they knew all, a reformation would generally be unavoidable." Smith, *The Theory of Moral Sentiments,* part 3, chaps. 3 and 4; part 6, chap. 2.
30. JA to president of Congress, Sept. 5, 1780; Howe, *Language and Political Meaning in Revolutionary America,* 29–30; Adams, *Lectures on Rhetoric and Oratory,* 25, 431.
31. JQA, *Lectures on Rhetoric and Oratory,* inaugural lecture (1806). George Washington and James Madison also favored the concept of a national university; see Brown, *Strength of a People,* 95–97.
32. JA to JQA, Jan. 23, 1788, in *AFC,* 8:219. As JQA came into his own as a thinker, he saw Blair's *Lectures* in a somewhat critical light. They were "very good to answer their purpose as a school book," he wrote with a lordly edge, and as a whole "a work of taste and information, but not of genius." (He did not say precisely how he reached this conclusion, adding more charitably, "The opinions in general are judicious.") The Scottish classicist echoed republican strains in the writings of both Adamses, observing that the emotional power of language was fed by political liberty and suffered in its absence. When liberty was lost, oratory "languished." Blair, *Lectures on Rhetoric and Belles Lettres,* esp. lectures 25–28; March 5, 1797, *DJQA;* Potkay, "Theorizing Civic Eloquence in the Early Republic."
33. JA to JQA, March 19, 1786, in *AFC,* 7:96; Aug. 27 and Dec. 16, 1797, *DJQA;* Wasser, "John Quincy Adams and the Opening Lines of Milton's *Paradise Lost.*"
34. Paul Goring, *The Rhetoric of Sensibility in Eighteenth-Century Culture* (New York: Cambridge University Press, 2005). Thomas Sheridan (spelled by Adams with two *r*'s) was the father of the celebrated dramatist Richard Brinsley Sheridan.

8: SECOND PRESIDENT

1. JA to AA, Jan. 5, 1796, in *AFC,* 11:122–23.
2. Levin, *Remarkable Education of John Quincy Adams,* 253–57; Charles N. Edel, *Nation Builder: John Quincy Adams and the Grand Strategy of the Republic* (Cambridge, Mass.: Harvard University Press, 2014), 72–73.
3. This formulation was first (or at least most concretely) examined in Koch, *Power, Morals, and the Founding Fathers,* chap 5.
4. JA to AA, Jan. 5, 1796, in *AFC,* 11:122–23.
5. Sept. 5, 1774, and Sept. 5, 1796, *DAJA; Baltimore Federal Gazette,* Oct. 4, 1796. The prominent Virginian was Charles Simms, a lawyer and member of the Virginia House of Delegates. On Henry's lack of desire to enter the presidential race, see "Extract of a Letter from a Gentleman in Williamsburg," in *Poughkeepsie* (N.Y.) *Journal,* Oct. 12, 1796; *Charleston* (S.C.) *City Gazette,* Oct. 13, 1796. Virginia's electoral power was owing to the infamous three-fifths clause in the Constitution, which awarded slave states additional representation on the basis of the unfree black population.
6. DeConde, "Washington's Farewell, the French Alliance, and the Election of 1796"; JA to AA, Dec. 4, 1796, AP/FOL.

7. Kurtz, *Presidency of John Adams,* 109–13, 166–76, 204–6; Heidenreich, "Conspiracy Politics in the Election of 1796."
8. Jefferson to Madison, Jan. 1, 1797, in *PTJ,* 29:247–49.
9. Inaugural Address, March 4, 1797, avalon.law.yale.edu/18th_century/adams.asp.
10. Mary Smith Cranch to AA, June 13, 1797, in *AFC,* 16:157–58; Dauer, *Adams Federalists,* 114–17; Burstein and Isenberg, *Madison and Jefferson,* 315–20.
11. March 4, 1797, *DJQA.*
12. JQA to AA, Nov. 7, 1795, and May 5 and July 25, 1796; AA to JQA, July 11, 1796, in *AFC,* 11:60–61, 286, 332–33, 338–39.
13. AA to JQA, Aug. 10, 1796; JQA to AA, Aug. 16 and Nov. 14, 1796, in *AFC,* 11:356–57, 362, 404–5.
14. JA to JQA, Nov. 11, 1796, in *AFC,* 11:401. "Your appointment To Berlin was carried in Senate 17 to 12[.] The cause of opposition I imagine was an objection to renew our Treaty with Prussia. but of this I am not certain." Charles Adams to JQA, June 8, 1797, in *AFC,* 12:150–51n.
15. JQA to Charles Adams, June 9, 1796, in *AFC,* 11:312–13.
16. *DALCA,* 1:11, 16, 44–45, 64–65.
17. March 25 and May 14, 1797, May–July 1797, Jan. 13 and 20, 1798, *DJQA;* Levin, *Remarkable Education of John Quincy Adams,* chaps. 21 and 22; Nagel, *John Quincy Adams,* 92–110.
18. JA to JQA, Oct. 25, 1797, AP/FOL.
19. JA to JQA, Nov. 3, 1797, AP/FOL.
20. AA to Elizabeth Smith Show Peabody, Sept. 25, 1797, in *AFC,* 16:246; Heffron, *Louisa Catherine,* 106–7.
21. Nov. 7–11, 1797, *DJQA.*
22. Christopher Clark, *Iron Kingdom: The Rise and Downfall of Prussia, 1600–1947* (Cambridge, Mass.: Harvard University Press, 2006), 251–57, 280–82, 292–96.
23. JQA to JA, Dec. 16, 1797, AP/FOL; Clark, *Iron Kingdom,* 276.
24. Burstein and Isenberg, *Madison and Jefferson,* 316–27.
25. Mercy Warren to James Warren Jr., May 14, 1796; to Winslow Warren, June 4, 1797, Mercy Otis Warren Letterbook, Mercy Otis Warren Papers, MHS. For background, see Zagarri, *Woman's Dilemma.*
26. Message of May 16, 1797, www.presidency.ucsb.edu/ws/index.php?pid=65636.
27. Billias, *Elbridge Gerry,* chap. 17; Elizabeth Ellery Dana statement to AA on her husband's health, in *AFC,* 12:146n7; family biographical statement (in unknown hand), Dana Family Papers, MHS. John Adams was never surprised by anything Pickering said, and his disgust with Pickering's meanness and hypocrisy only grew as the years passed; in 1812, he recounted for Benjamin Rush the several occasions on which he heard Pickering loudly disparage Washington as semiliterate, "even on military affairs," yet affiliate himself proudly with organizations celebrating Washington's genius. JA to Rush, April 22, 1812, AP/FOL.
28. JQA to JA, Sept. 21, 1797, AP/FOL.
29. June 4, 1797, *DJQA.*
30. AA to Mary Smith Cranch, June 3, 1797, in *AFC,* 12:139; *Authentic Copies of the Correspondence of Charles Cotesworth Pinckney, John Marshall, and Elbridge Gerry,* esp. 65–69; Newmyer, *John Marshall and the Heroic Age of the Supreme Court,* 111–17; "A History of Lloyd House, Part I," *Historic Alexandria Quarterly* (Fall 2003/Winter 2004): 4–5; Kurtz, *Presidency of John Adams,* 230, 235; Stinchcombe, *XYZ Affair;* Austin, *Life of Elbridge Gerry,* chaps. 5 and 6.
31. AA to JQA, April 21 and May 26, 1798, AP/FOL.
32. Thomas Ray has shown that some of the strongest endorsements of President Adams's leadership came from the South. See Ray, "'Not One Cent for Tribute': The Public Addresses and American Popular Reaction to the XYZ Affair, 1798–1799," *Journal of the Early Republic* 3 (Winter 1983): 389–412; also *Providence Gazette,* April 28, 1798. A Baltimore dinner in honor of the "beloved President" appears in *Greenfield Gazette,* May 7, 1798. Critics accused wealthy Federalists of rounding up poor men at grogshops to sign their addresses, arguing along the same lines as Federalists who earlier dismissed the Democratic-Republican clubs that protested Washington's policies. In both cases, voters and their representatives were identified as the legitimate voice of the people, and unelected bodies collecting signatures were left suspect. See "Mr. Adams," *Independent Chronicle and Universal Advertiser,* May 28, 1798.
33. JA to Inhabitants of Hartford, May 10, 1798; to Isaac Lebaron, June 8, 1798; to John M. Gill, June 12, 1798; to Nathaniel Mitchell, June 18, 1798, AP/FOL; Ray, "'Not One Cent for Tribute,'" 400n. Adams received at least 296 addresses and answered at least 71; see Ferling, *John Adams,* 357.
34. William J. Murphy, "John Adams"; JA to Washington, June 22, 1798, in *PGW-R,* 2:351; caricature in "The Times: A Political Portrait" (1798), reprinted in Nancy Isenberg, "Death and Satire: Dismembering the Body Politic," in Isenberg and Burstein, *Mortal Remains,* 82–84; on Adams's critics, see "Letter IV: To the President

of the United States," *Time-Piece,* May 23, 1798; Jefferson to James Madison, May 3, 1798, in *PTJ,* 30:323; also see Ray, "'Not One Cent for Tribute,'" 395; Ferling, *John Adams,* 356.

35. July 3, 1798, *DJQA;* Stinchcombe, *XYZ Affair,* 125–26.
36. JQA to Joseph Pitcairn, Aug. 14, 1797, cited in Stinchcombe, *XYZ Affair,* 35. On Talleyrand's understanding of President Adams's position and prospects for an improvement in relations, see ibid., 43–45.
37. JQA to JA, May 18 and Sept. 25, 1798, AP/FOL; Beveridge, *Life of John Marshall,* 1:343–45.
38. Destler, *Joshua Coit;* Burstein and Isenberg, *Madison and Jefferson,* 331.
39. Washington to James Markham Marshall, July 16, 1798, in *PGW-R,* 2:426–27.
40. DeConde, *Quasi-war,* 140–47.
41. "If we did not know them . . . ," Murray preceded his cautious remarks to the younger Adams about the French government. On Pichon's entreaties, he observed slyly, "all complaining tenderness, conciliatory, full of wishes, and fears sometimes too—for us." And less critically: "All conciliation and assurances of amity, and with an urgency that confirms me in my opinion that he is ordered to do so." See William Vans Murray to JQA, July 20 and Aug. 2, 1798, reiterated Sept. 25, 1798; Murray to Timothy Pickering, Sept. 1, 1798, in *Letters of William Vans Murray to John Quincy Adams,* 436–37, 442–46, 463–67, 473–74; JQA to JA, Sept. 25, 1798, AP/FOL; DeConde, *Quasi-war,* 147–54, 159, 162.
42. DeConde, *Quasi-war,* 160, 163–64; Kurtz, *Presidency of John Adams,* 332.
43. Morison, *Harrison Gray Otis,* 158–61.
44. AA to JA, March 3, 1799, AP/FOL.
45. AA to JQA, July 30, 1799; JQA to AA, July 25, 1798, AP/FOL.
46. DeConde, "Role of William Vans Murray in the Peace Negotiations Between France and the United States, 1800," 192.
47. May, *Jefferson's Treasure,* chap. 4; AA to JQA, Feb. 10, 1799, AP/FOL; Smith, *Freedom's Fetters;* JQA to King, Aug. 27, 1798, King Papers, cited in ibid., 25. Throughout the fractious 1790s, John Adams fretted about possible sedition arising from those quarters where, in his words, "dangerous ambition," "irregular rivalries," and "destructive factions" drained a republic of life.
48. Notes on Sedition, Francis Dana Papers, box 34, MHS; Blumberg, *Repressive Jurisprudence in the Early American Republic,* 110–11. Somehow, Dana knew that "the pole was erected in the day time by a Company of about thirty persons."

    Federalists focused on fighting French influence, but antagonistic opinion writing did not come from radical émigrés alone. Prejudice spewed from presses in Philadelphia, Boston, New York, and places big and small. See Pasley, *"Tyranny of Printers";* and for a good synthesis, Ferling, *Leap in the Dark,* chap. 12.
49. JQA to AA, May 7, 1799, AP/FOL; Burstein and Isenberg, *Madison and Jefferson,* 328–29. Knowing his letter would be shared with his father, John Quincy continued to relate the problems of perception: "Here in Germany, a man by the name of Bulow, after travelling twice in the United States, has published two volumes intituled 'The Republic of North America, in its present condition.'" What sounded like an informational travelogue was anything but. "It is one continued libel upon the character and manners of the American People, written with considerable ingenuity. It contains beyond all doubt a vast deal of falsehood; but every American who feels for the honour of his Country, must confess with shame that it also contains too much of truth." All the author had to do was to follow the American press to uncover the "private malignity" that prevailed there.
50. JQA to AA, July 3, 1799, AP/FOL.
51. Morris to Washington, Dec. 9, 1799, in *PGW-R,* 4:452.
52. Before he finished his tirade, the president berated McHenry for affecting knowledge of international diplomacy, in juvenile efforts, combined with Hamilton and others, to "suspend" the mission of Ellsworth and Davie to France. McHenry to JA, May 31, 1800, in *Papers of Alexander Hamilton,* ed. Harold C. Syrett (New York: Columbia University Press, 1976), 24:552–65; also, McHenry to Hamilton, May 20, 1800, in ibid., 506–11, with the enclosure of a copy of a letter detailing McHenry's logic, which was sent to his nephew.
53. AA to JQA, May 15, 1800, AP/FOL; *Aurora General Advertiser,* May 15, 1800. The *Aurora,* rich in insults, had grated on Abigail Adams's mind since the start of the administration, when it was edited by Benjamin Bache, grandson of Benjamin Franklin, who died in 1798. She was especially perturbed when corruption was imputed to her husband in authorizing JQA to renew a treaty with Sweden. See AA to Mary Cranch, March 20, 1798, in *New Letters of Abigail Adams,* 324.
54. Clarfield, *Timothy Pickering and the American Republic,* chaps. 13–15; Billias, *Elbridge Gerry,* 296–98.
55. "Conversation with Arthur Fenner," in *Papers of Alexander Hamilton,* 24:595–75.
56. Hamilton, *Letter from Alexander Hamilton Concerning the Public Conduct and Character of John Adams.* On Hamilton's dispute with Adams after 1796, see generally Harper, *American Machiavelli,* chaps. 16–19.
57. Stahr, *John Jay,* 360–61.

58. [Cheetham], *Answer to Alexander Hamilton's Letter, Concerning the Public Conduct and Character of John Adams,* 5.
59. [Webster], *Letter to General Hamilton, Occasioned by His Letter to President Adams.*
60. *Albany Register,* Nov. 11, 1800; Smith, "President John Adams, Thomas Cooper, and Sedition." Cooper (1759–1839) turned from the law to chemistry, served as a science adviser to President James Madison, and went on to become president of South Carolina College in Columbia.
61. Isenberg, *Fallen Founder.*
62. AA to JQA, May 15 and Sept. 1, 1800, AP/FOL; entries of May 2–13, 1800, Gouverneur Morris diary (microfilm), Library of Congress. Meeting JQA in London five years before, Morris had thought ill of the son as well, writing that he found his countenance "insipid" and believed the young diplomat to be "deeply tinctured with suspicion" and incapable of making a good impression on others in the diplomatic service. Dec. 5, 1795, and Jan. 18, 1796, Morris diary; on Morris's mixed legacy, see Miller, *Envoy to the Terror.* The rumor of a Jefferson-Adams coalition was not without foundation: Samuel Smith, a Maryland congressman, tried to broker a deal between the erstwhile president and vice president that would have kept Adams in office for another term, with Jefferson as his agreed-upon successor. See Isenberg, *Fallen Founder,* 203.
63. JQA to AA, May 25 and July 11, 1800, AP/FOL.
64. JA to Stoddert, May 20, 1798; William Lewis (Fries's attorney) to JA, May 19, 1800; JA to Charles Lee, May 21, 1800, all in AP/FOL; Newman, *Fries's Rebellion,* 175, 182–83; Elsmere, "Trials of John Fries." Fries was tried twice: the first was declared a mistrial. Abigail Adams informed her husband that the Republicans were surprised by his pardon of Fries. AA to JA, May 23, 1800, AP/FOL.
65. AA to JQA, Sept. 1, 1800, AP/FOL.
66. Ferling, *Adams vs. Jefferson,* chap. 12; Isenberg, *Fallen Founder,* chap. 6.

9: PARTY IRREGULARS

1. JA to *Boston Patriot,* May 26, 1809, AP/FOL.
2. Seale, *President's House,* 1:77–81; Ferling, *John Adams,* 409–13; JA to Jefferson, March 24, 1801, in *Adams-Jefferson Letters,* 264.
3. March 1–25, 1801, *DJQA.*
4. JQA to JA, March 24 and 28, 1801, AP/FOL.
5. AA to JQA, Jan. 29, 1801, AP/FOL; Burstein, *Lincoln Dreamt He Died,* 14–15.
6. Sept. 4, 1801, *DJQA; DALCA,* 1:157; JQA to Thomas Boylston Adams, May 5, 1801, AP/FOL; Nagel, *John Quincy Adams,* 124–25; Heffron, *Louisa Catherine,* 134–37.
7. Sept. 10–11, 1801, *DJQA;* Burstein and Isenberg, *Madison and Jefferson,* 419–21, 446; Dumas Malone, *Jefferson the President: First Term, 1801–1805* (Boston: Little, Brown, 1970), 228–29; Kerber and Morris, "Politics and Literature." For JQA's advice to Dennie on the means of making his periodical popular, see JQA to Thomas Boylston Adams, April 4, 1801, AP/FOL.
8. Sept. 12–Oct. 14, 1801, *DJQA.*
9. Oct. 22–Nov. 3 and Nov. 16–17, 1801, *DJQA; DALCA,* 1:159–60, 190.
10. *DALCA,* 1:165–70; Heffron, *Louisa Catherine,* chap. 6.
11. Kerber and Morris, "Politics and Literature," 461.
12. JA to Citizens of Quincy, Oct. 28, 1802, AP/FOL.
13. *DALCA,* 1:171–78, 185.
14. Malone, *Jefferson the President, First Term,* chap. 12; Burstein and Isenberg, *Madison and Jefferson,* 354–55, 369–70; Ferling, *Adams vs. Jefferson,* 134–37. In light of Callender's vitriolic stories, one newspaper writer insisted that Jefferson was "unworthy to stoop down and unloose" John Adams's shoes; see *Hampshire Gazette,* Aug. 4, 1802.
15. Gordon-Reed, *Hemingses of Monticello,* 584–85; Parsons, *John Quincy Adams,* 80. JQA was more inclined toward salacious humor than his father had ever been. In mid-1803, while sprinting through the comedies of Shakespeare, he took a stab at the Roman comedic playwright Titus Maccius Plautus, enjoying the sexually explicit *Pseudolus* (a favorite, he says, of Cicero's) and *Captivi* and *Curculio,* with their focus on the humor of slaves who resort to trickery in persuading a gentleman to part with his money. "The wit is sometimes excellent, often vulgar," JQA noted. He had been introduced to Plautus at sixteen, in Holland, by Monsieur Dumas. That was when he read *Poenulus,* about a man who falls in love with a prostitute. It has often been said that Shakespeare borrowed from the style of wit employed by Plautus, many of whose characters were credulous men whose lust was worn on their sleeve. JQA was mildly amused, though not titillated, by such situation comedy, but he evidently got pleasure from the opportunity to jeer at President Jefferson. June 24–July 1 and July 9 and 19–23, 1803, *DJQA.*
16. JA to Francis Adrian Van der Kemp, Sept. 28, 1802, AP/FOL.
17. Parsons, *John Quincy Adams,* 76; Nagel, *John Quincy Adams,* 141–42; *DALCA,* 1:185–86; April 1–3, 1803, *DJQA.*
18. Various entries in April 1803, *DJQA.*

19. Ames to Dwight Foster, Feb. 6, 1803; to Christopher Gore, Feb. 24, 1803, in *Works of Fisher Ames* (Indianapolis: Liberty Fund, 1983), 2:1454–59; Fischer, *Revolution of American Conservatism,* 17–19; *DALCA,* 1:210.
20. There is something occasionally comic in the meandering movement of his pen in his daily journal, so it seems relevant to mention that the Shakespeare he took in these days were the comedies. He ranged between *All's Well That Ends Well* and *Taming of the Shrew,* with a dip into the ancient comedies of Plautus with their sex-starved slaves and boastful soldiers. In July, JQA revisited the voyages of Columbus and Michel de Montaigne's essay "On Vanity," wherein he found "excellent observations on Party Spirit." This was how the ravenous reader and senator in training applied himself. April 5–9 and 21–22, May 15, June 11, June 24–July 1, July 9 and 19–23, Aug. 3, and Sept. 14, 1803, *DJQA;* Verhoeven, *Americomania and the French Revolution Debate in Britain,* 207–14.
21. JQA Literary Commonplace Book, July 28, 1803, AP/microfilm, reel 230; William Peden, ed., *Notes on the State of Virginia* (Chapel Hill: University of North Carolina Press, 1954), query 6.
22. Aug. 14–22 and Sept. 18 and 26, 1803, *DJQA; DALCA,* 1:188–89; JA to JQA, sometime after June 23, 1803, AP/FOL.
23. JA to JQA, Dec. 2, 1804, AP/FOL.
24. *Edes' Kennebec Gazette,* March 3, 1803.
25. "Democracy," *Gazette of the United States,* Oct. 19, 1802; *Edes' Kennebec Gazette,* March 3, 1803. Years before, John Adams called Jefferson and New York's governor George Clinton "idols of Jacobinism and democracy"; see JA to Charles Adams, Dec. 13, 1795, in *AFC,* 11:86.
26. "What Is Democracy," *Political Magazine and Miscellaneous Repository,* Oct. 1, 1800. A similar argument was made in the pro-Jefferson *National Intelligencer,* in explaining that Adams's proud Massachusetts state constitution and all other state governments were "*modified, regulated, limited and elective democracies*" ("On Democracy," *National Intelligencer,* via *Boston Chronicle,* Aug. 1, 1803). The Virginia Federalist John Marshall was quoted as saying, "The principles of the federal constitution are strictly democratical." See "Democracy," in *Newport* (R.I.) *Guardian of Liberty,* March 7, 1801. Another story told of a youth who looked up the definition of "democracy" and found that it meant "Government in the people." *Constitutional Telegraph,* May 9, 1801.
27. "Republicanism & Democracy," *New-England Palladium,* Nov. 10, 1801; *Carlisle Weekly Gazette,* Jan. 1, 1801. On demagogues and elections as brothels, see "Where There Are Men There Will Be Passions . . . ," *Gazette of the United States,* April 27, 1804; *True American,* Jan. 24, 1803. A new Baltimore newspaper was created to combat "dangerous doctrines" and defend the distinction between republicanism and democracy. See the newspaper's opening statement, *Republican; or, Anti-Democrat,* Jan. 1, 1802; also "Democrats Are Not Republicans," *Weekly Inspector,* Sept. 20, 1806.
28. JA to Thomas Adams, July 11, 1801, and Jan. 28, 1803, AP/FOL.
29. JQA to Thomas Adams, Dec. 3, 1800, AP/FOL. JQA was hardly the first person to make the point about slave-owning democrats. Another writer argued that it was "preposterous to the last degree for southerners to claim to themselves the principles of democracy, so long as they support slavery" ("To the Printers of the Connecticut Courant," via *Eagle, or, Dartmouth Centinel,* Sept. 18, 1797). If genuine democracy existed, it existed in New England; slavery, and the rigid class order that supported it, made southerners more partial to the "aristocratical state of society."
30. JQA to JA, Nov. 25, 1800, AP/FOL.
31. JA to William Cunningham, March 15, 1804; JA to JQA, Nov. 4, 1804, AP/FOL. Unbeknownst to Adams, Aaron Burr had used a similar strategy when he engineered the Democratic-Republican win of a majority of seats in the legislature of New York state in 1800 and helped defeat him in the national election. It was not, as charged, bribery.
32. JA to Benjamin Rush, Sept. 19, 1806, AP/FOL.
33. Parsons, *John Quincy Adams,* 79.
34. Morison, *Harrison Gray Otis,* 4–6, 53.
35. Jan. 7, 1804, *DJQA.*
36. Oct. 31, 1803, *DJQA.*
37. *DALCA,* 1:204, 223–24. On Louisa's evolution in official Washington, see esp. Allgor, *Parlor Politics,* chap. 4.
38. Nov. 15 and 23, 1804, and Jan. 11 and Nov. 25, 1805, *DJQA.*
39. AA to Jefferson, May 20, July 1, Aug. 18, and Oct. 15, 1804; Jefferson to AA, June 13, July 22, and Sept. 11, 1804, in *Adams-Jefferson Letters,* 268–82; see also the rich interpretation of the 1804 exchange in Gelles, *Portia,* chap. 6.
40. Sept. 30 and Oct. 3, 1804, *DJQA.* The decision to stay with their respective kin over these months caused bad feelings between husband and wife. As a matter of financial exigency, their Boston home had been sold, and Louisa was doubtless wary of getting in Abigail's way. Immediately upon his return to Washington in late October, JQA purchased for Louisa Lady Mary Wortley Montagu's works. Because Lady Montagu was an independent, outspoken woman of early-eighteenth-century Britain who traveled widely with her ambassador

husband, wrote graphically on subjects that were generally considered a male preserve, and openly contested male literary authority, the book purchase might have been a form of apology. JQA, too, read and appreciated Lady Mary Wortley's letters. Oct. 27, 1804, *DJQA*.

41. *Repertory* (Boston), Oct. 27–Nov. 2, 1804; *Notes on Virginia,* query 19.
42. Oct. 31, 1804, *DJQA*.
43. Dec. 31, 1804, *DJQA*.
44. Jan. 15, 1805, *DJQA*.
45. JQA to JA, Jan. 24, 1805, AP/FOL.
46. JA to JQA, Feb. 7, 1805, AP/FOL.
47. JA to JQA, Jan. 27, 1805, AP/FOL.
48. JA to JQA, Jan. 27 and Feb. 7, 1805, AP/FOL.

10: SHAPE-SHIFTERS

1. Isenberg, *Fallen Founder,* 272–79; Blair and Coblentz, "Trials of Mr. Justice Samuel D. Chase."
2. JQA to JA, March 14, 1805, AP/FOL.
3. JQA to JA, March 8, 1805, AP/FOL.
4. Nagel, *John Quincy Adams,* 148–49; various entries during the summers of 1804 and 1805, *DJQA*.
5. JA to JQA, Feb. 26, 1806, AP/FOL.
6. JA to JQA, Dec. 23, 1805, AP/FOL.
7. Recall that President Jefferson dismissed JQA from the position of bankruptcy commissioner, after having already spoken highly of him on his return from Berlin. JQA might or might not have known at this point that Jefferson vehemently denied to Abigail Adams having taken away that federal emolument. Jefferson also consulted with JQA, a bit cagily, asking for a recommendation of a French-speaking someone to assume a trusted position in the new territory of Louisiana. Nov. 23, 1804, and Nov. 25, 1805, *DJQA*.
8. Dec. 8, 1805, *DJQA;* JQA to JA, Dec. 6, 1805, AP/FOL; *Annals of Congress,* 10th Cong. 1st sess., H. of R., Dec. 28, 1807, 1229–31.
9. JQA to LCA, June 30, 1806, AP/FOL.
10. July 25–26, Aug. 1 and 16–18, and Sept. 13, 1807, *DJQA; DALCA,* 1:251–52, 255.
11. JA to JQA, Dec. 23, 1805; JQA to JA, Jan. 14, 1806, AP/FOL.
12. JA to JQA, Feb. 26, 1806, AP/FOL.
13. JA to JQA, Jan. 29, 1806, AP/FOL.
14. JA to JQA, Jan. 29 and Feb. 5, 1806, AP/FOL. "Our Commerce may all fall into their hands: and we have no resource but reprisals," he wrote. "I Should rather begin with this. If I once voted for an Embargo on Merchant Ships, I would let loose all the Privateers and Vessells of force at the same time to prey upon the British Commerce."
15. JQA to JA, Feb. 11, 1806, AP/FOL.
16. Dumas Malone, *Jefferson the President, Second Term, 1805–1809* (Boston: Little, Brown, 1974), chap. 23; *Public Advertiser,* June 30, 1807; *Repertory* (Boston), July 3, 1807; June 30, 1807, *DJQA*.
17. Nagel, *John Quincy Adams,* 172; Broussard, *Southern Federalists,* 76–77; July 4 and 10, 1807, *DJQA*.
18. Isenberg, *Fallen Founder,* chaps. 8 and 9; *United States Senate Election, Expulsion, and Censure Cases,* 18–21.
19. Feb. 1, 1808, *DJQA;* JQA to JA, Dec. 27, 1807, AP/FOL.
20. JA to JQA, Jan. 8, 1808, AP/FOL.
21. JA to JQA, Feb. 19, 1808, AP/FOL.
22. JA to JQA, Jan. 8, 1808, AP/FOL. The Federalists named in the letter were John Jay of New York, who retired from politics in 1801; Rufus King, also of New York, who resigned from the U.S. Senate in 1796 and served President Adams as U.S. minister to Great Britain; Oliver Ellsworth of Connecticut, U.S. senator (1789–1796) and Supreme Court chief justice until 1800; Fisher Ames, a Harvard-trained attorney and outspoken Massachusetts congressman from 1789 to 1797; and Samuel Dexter of Massachusetts, an Adams man who served briefly in the Senate in 1799–1800 and in his cabinet after that.
23. Warren, *History of the Rise, Progress, and Termination of the American Revolution,* 1:131–32, 135, 188, 211.
24. Ibid., 1:307; 2:140, 301.
25. Ibid., 3:161–77.
26. Ibid., 3:392–95.
27. JA to Warren, July 11, July 30, and Aug. 19, 1807; Warren to JA, July 16, 1807, in "Correspondence Between John Adams and Mercy Warren," 317ff.
28. Warren to JA, Aug. 27, 1807, in "Correspondence Between John Adams and Mercy Warren." By way of comparison, the first published history of the Revolution (1789), authored by a South Carolinian, Dr. David Ramsay, emphasized John Adams's leading role in debating independence in Congress in 1776 and lionized his diplomacy in Holland; Ramsay did not discuss his political philosophy or address Adams's personal quirks at all.

29. Aug. 30, 1807, *DJQA*.
30. JA to Warren, July 20 and Aug. 8 and 19, 1807; Warren to JA, Aug. 1, 1807, AP/FOL.
31. Warren wrote that Adams's 1800 defeat occurred because "the people suspected your aristocratic and monarchic biases, though they were not generally and fully convinced of this solemn truth, until after your elevation to the Presidential Chair." She accused him of being tempted by "diadem and scepter," as one "who thinks himself the 'greatest man'" in the country; Jefferson's election was a "revolution of opinion . . . by the general voice and consent of the people." See Mercy Otis Warren to JA, Aug. 15, 1807, in "Correspondence Between John Adams and Mercy Warren"; *Independent Chronicle*, June 25, 1804; *Aurora General Advertiser*, March 5, 1805. Note that Warren's book was prominently advertised in the *Aurora*. For Paine's claim, see "Thomas Paine, to the Citizens of the U. States," *Aurora General Advertiser*, June 7, 1805.
32. Jan. 20–23, 1808, *DJQA*. After attending the gathering, JQA sized up the attendees and concluded that the Senate leader from Vermont who presided did so merely to score points and gain a federal appointment for his son—that the real "instigation" of the meeting came from "Virginian Madisonians."
33. Fischer, *Revolution of American Conservatism*, 41–43; Jan. 30 and Feb. 2, 1808, *DJQA*; *Annals of Congress*, 10th Cong., 1st sess., Senate, Jan. 8, 1808, 69–77.
34. Giles to Jefferson, Dec. 14, 1825; Jefferson to Giles, Dec. 25, 1825, Thomas Jefferson Papers, Library of Congress.
35. AA to JQA, Feb. 15, 1808, AP/FOL.
36. JA to JQA, Feb. 19, 1808, AP/FOL.
37. JA to JQA, April 12, 1808, AP/FOL.
38. Pickering, *Letter from the Honorable Timothy Pickering, a Senator of the United States from the State of Massachusetts, Exhibiting to His Constituents a View of the Imminent Danger of an Unnecessary and Ruinous War*, esp. 7–9.
39. March 18 and 31, 1808, *DJQA*.
40. JQA, *Letter to Mr. Harrison Gray Otis, a Member of the Senate of Massachusetts, on the Present State of Our National Affairs*, 1; Thomas Boylston Adams to JQA, April 10, 1808, AP/FOL.
41. [Coleman], *Remarks and Criticisms of the Hon. John Quincy Adams's Letter to the Hon. Harrison Gray Otis*, preface, 1, 6–7, 26–29.
42. Nagel, *John Quincy Adams*, 179–80; June 1, 1808, *DJQA*.
43. LCA to JQA, March 1, 1809, AP/FOL; May, *Jefferson's Treasure*, chap. 8.

11: DISTANT COMPANIONS

1. JQA to JA, July 21, 1811, AP/FOL; Heffron, *Louisa Catherine*, 193–94.
2. *Boston Patriot*, May 6, 1809. Everett graduated from Dartmouth College in 1795 and in addition to his career in journalism studied law and wrote poetry. See Goddard, *Newspapers and Newspaper Writers in New England*, 27–28.
3. March 4–6, 1809, *DJQA*.
4. *Boston Gazette*, March 27 and April 20 and 24, 1809; *Anti-monarchist*, April 5, 1809, originally published in the *Worcester* (Mass.) *National Aegis*; *Massachusetts Spy*, April 5, 1809; *Boston Patriot*, April 22, 1809.
5. Morris to unknown recipient, late March 1809, in Morris's unpublished letterbook, Gouverneur Morris Papers, Library of Congress. We are grateful to Melanie Miller, editor of the Gouverneur Morris Papers, for communicating this revealing letter.
6. *Boston Patriot*, April 15, 1809.
7. JA, *Correspondence of the Late President Adams, Originally Published in the "Boston Patriot."*
8. David Everett personally called on JQA on April 17, and again the next day, seeking "a promise of assistance for the conduct of his paper" (*DJQA*). At a Fourth of July celebration in Boston in 1809, Everett expounded the Adams critique of "that malignant fiend—party spirit." See White, *Oration, in Commemoration of the Anniversary of American Independence, Delivered in Boston, July 4, 1809, at the Request of the Bunker-Hill Association*, 16. JQA was not convinced that enough people were reading his Ames pieces. "Very little notice is taken of them any where," he recorded at the end of April, adding one month later that the commitment to writing was "a sort of dissipation, and I know not whether it will do any good." April 30 and May 27 and 31, 1809, *DJQA*.
9. JQA, *American Principles*, preface and letter no. 1. The Ames series ran through June 1809. Notably, the entire first page of the July 19 issue of the *Patriot* was divided between a continuation of John Adams's personal history and the preface to the son's compilation of his uninhibited opinion pieces.
10. "I do not wish to See you under existing circumstances any other than the private citizen you now are," she wrote to him in Feb. 1809, AP/FOL, no precise date.
11. July 4–5, 11, 20, and 24, 1809, *DJQA*; Nagel, *John Quincy Adams*, 185.
12. In 1807, when JQA first learned of Plumer's plan to compose a history, and was made aware that Plumer had already broached the subject with Jefferson, JQA was amazed: "The President cannot be a lover of

history—there are prominent traits in his character, & important actions in his life, that he would not wish should be delineated, & transmitted to posterity." JQA to Plumer, Aug. 16, 1809, AP/microfilm, reel 228; *William Plumer's Memorandum of Proceedings in the United States Senate, 1803–1807,* ed. Everett Somerville Brown (New York: Macmillan, 1923), esp. 604–6. In Plumer's diary, JQA is portrayed quite favorably as one who shared confidences.

13. To all appearances a man with a hard shell, JQA faced demons plenty. He lost his composure in Russia on a night when Louisa suddenly began a "violent bleeding" from her nose and mouth. The symptoms were "nothing to excite uneasiness," said the doctor who made a house call. But when he next took to his diary, John Quincy wrote, "I was too much affected by the Scene. . . . I pray God that not even my affection for my wife and children may deprive me of my self-possession most necessary upon the severest trials. . . . I often think that an excessive attachment to my children may be an offense in the eye of Heaven, and dread that they may be taken from me for my punishment." Having left his two eldest in the care of his aging parents, having forced his family to accept his choices, he was left with a moralist's challenge to treat his heretical impulses. Holton, *Abigail Adams,* 358; April 7, 1812, *DJQA.*
14. JA to JQA, March 16, 1810, and Jan. 15, 1811, AP/FOL. When the first copy of John Quincy's *Lectures on Rhetoric and Oratory* appeared at his door, the author's father "renounced all other Things and read them through in three days." Of the lectures, he crowed, "They have laid a Foundation for Improvement in polite Litterature in this Country." It took the son two years to find an opportunity to give credit to his father as a published author. Upon meeting the world-famous Madame Germaine de Staël, an accomplished *salonnière* and scholar, and daughter of Jacques Necker, financial adviser attached to King Louis XIV, JQA told his father, "She soon asked me if I was related to that celebrated Mr Adams who wrote the book upon Government. I said I had the happiness of being his son. She said she had read it and admired it very much that her Father Mr Necker had always expressd a very high opinion of it." JQA to JA, March 22, 1813, AP/FOL.
15. Richard Rush received effusive thanks for his "beautiful letter" from the author's father—with unsolicited added commentary: "Mr. Adams's Speeches in the Senate of this Commonwealth and in the Senate of The United States as well as at the Bar, have always been in a Strain of cool Reasoning without any affectation. . . . From his ardent Love of Poetry I have often wondered that more of it has not appeared in his Speeches. His head is full of the Poets. I never knew a Man more universally read and Studied in the English Poets." JA to Richard Rush, Jan. 15, 1811, AP/FOL.
16. JA to JQA, March 16, 1810, and Jan. 15, 1811, AP/FOL.
17. McFadden, "John Quincy Adams, American Commercial Diplomacy, and Russia."
18. Jan. 18–21 and March 11–April 3, 1810, *DJQA; DALCA,* 1:297–300. The leg inflammation was due to erysipelas, a bacteriological skin infection, which he had suffered some years prior, at Quincy.
19. JQA to JA, April 30, 1810, AP/FOL; Aug. 5 and 11, 1810, *DJQA.* Before finally receiving the letter from his father that lavishly praised the *Lectures,* John Quincy wrote home that all he had of his father's wisdom came from "the satisfaction of reading your writings in the Patriot."
20. Variously through spring and summer 1810, quotation at March 27, 1810, *DJQA.*
21. Jan. 2–3 and 19, 1811, *DJQA;* S. B. Okun, *The Russian-American Company* (Cambridge, Mass.: Harvard University Press, 1951); Paul Gary Sterling, "The Voyage of the *Rurik:* An Historic 1816 Russian Voyage to San Francisco Bay," *Argonaut: Journal of the San Francisco Museum and Historical Society* 22 (Winter 2011): 6–35.
22. Jan. 8, 1810, *DJQA.*
23. *DALCA,* 1:318, 321, 325–26, 335–36, 349–50; JA to JQA, March 11, 1813, AP/FOL. Louisa's younger sister Catherine (Kitty), who had become intimate with JQA's nephew and private secretary William S. Smith, also danced with the tsar and was invited with Louisa to the theater.
24. JQA to JA, Sept. 2, 1810, AP/FOL.
25. Even as Russia allied with England in their common fight against Napoleon, JQA continued to trust the tsar's instincts. See Palmer, *Alexander I;* Janet M. Hartley, *Alexander I* (New York: Longman, 1994), 3–5; Paléologue, *Enigmatic Czar,* 62–63; Russell, *John Quincy Adams and the Public Virtues of Diplomacy,* 42.
26. Sept. 10–17, 1812, *DJQA;* JQA to JA, Oct. 4, 1812, AP/FOL; *DALCA,* 1:354–57. As Louisa was describing the pain in her heart, John Quincy wrote to his father, "My child I fondly hope and believe is a purified Spirit, in bliss" (Oct. 4, 1812). In one letter, John Adams referred to the granddaughter he would never meet as "Louisa junior." The lost child was, to him, "a lovely Rose" (March 11, 1813).
27. JQA to JA, June 29, 1812, AP/FOL.
28. JA to JQA, Nov. 30, 1812, AP/FOL.
29. Sept. 9, 21, and 29, 1812, *DJQA; DALCA,* 1:359–60.
30. JQA to JA, June 29, 1812; JA to Elkanah Watson, Aug. 11, 1812, AP/FOL. Prior to this, JQA complained to his father that the last letter from him was dated nine months earlier; JQA to JA, Jan. 13, 1812, AP/FOL.
31. JA to JQA, Feb. 19, 1812, AP/FOL; Gelles, *Abigail and John,* 270–71; Heffron, *Louisa Catherine,* 213–14.
32. JA to JQA, Feb. 19, 1812, AP/FOL.

33. Jan. 12 and 31 and Feb. 28, 1813, *DJQA*.
34. JQA to JA, Nov. 5, 1812, AP/FOL.
35. JQA to JA, Jan. 12, 1813, AP/FOL.
36. JA to JQA, April 22, 1813, AP/FOL.
37. JQA to JA, May 8 and July 7, 1814; JA to JQA, June 12, 1814, AP/FOL.
38. JQA to JA, Aug. 20, 1814, AP/FOL.
39. Hickey, *War of 1812,* chap. 5; Dungan, *Gallatin,* chaps. 4–6, quotation at 111; May, *Jefferson's Treasure;* Peterson, *Great Triumvirate,* 44–45.
40. Sept. 1 and Oct. 1, 1814, *DJQA;* Bradford Perkins, *Castlereagh and Adams: England and the United States, 1812–1823* (Berkeley: University of California Press, 1964), chap. 4; Parsons, *John Quincy Adams,* 113–16.
41. Sept. 5 and 20 and Oct. 8 and 12, 1814, *DJQA;* Heidler and Heidler, *Henry Clay,* 110–11.
42. Perkins, *Castlereagh and Adams,* chaps. 5–6.
43. Oct. 25, 1814, *DJQA;* JQA to AA, Oct. 25, 1814, AP/FOL.
44. JQA to JA, Oct. 27, 1814, AP/FOL.
45. Perkins, *Castlereagh and Adams,* 116–27; JQA to JA, Dec. 26, 1814, and April 24 and Aug. 31, 1815; JA to JQA, June 7, 1815, AP/FOL. The British raised as comparable to Adams's bid for fishing rights their own desire for navigation rights along the Mississippi River, which they knew the U.S. government would never grant (though the principled Gallatin alone expressed some flexibility on legal interpretation of the issue).
46. JQA to JA, Dec. 26, 1814, AP/FOL. "The consolation of having rendered an acceptable service to our Country," JQA wrote, "has been ample Satisfaction and compensation for all the disquietudes with which it was attended." JQA to JA, April 24, 1815, AP/FOL.
47. Heffron, *Louisa Catherine,* chap. 11; *DALCA,* 1:375–406, quotation at 406; March 23, 1815, *DJQA*.
48. May, *Jefferson's Treasure,* chap. 10.
49. JQA to JA, April 24, 1815, AP/FOL.
50. Washington Irving, "John Bull," in *Sketch Book.*
51. Heffron, *Louisa Catherine,* 272–74.
52. JA to JQA, May 1, 14, and 16, June 8, and Oct. 13, 1815, AP/FOL.
53. JA to JQA, May 16 and June 4 and 30, 1815, AP/FOL.
54. JQA to JA, June 19, 1815, AP/FOL; Samuel Flagg Bemis, *John Quincy Adams and the Foundations of American Foreign Policy* (New York: Knopf, 1949), 227–36; Weeks, *John Quincy Adams and American Global Empire,* 44–46; Lewis, *John Quincy Adams,* 30–33.
55. JA to JQA, Aug. 30, 1815, AP/FOL.
56. JA to JQA, Sept. 2, 1815, AP/FOL.
57. JQA to JA, Aug. 31 and Oct. 9, 1815, AP/FOL; Clay quotation in Perkins, *Castlereagh and Adams,* 158.
58. JA to Jefferson, May 6 and Sept. 3 and 30, 1816, in *Adams-Jefferson Letters,* 472–74, 487–90; JA to JQA, Sept. 23, 1816; JQA to JA, Jan. 3, 1817, AP/FOL; Quincy, *Memoir of the Life of John Quincy Adams,* 410–11, 428.
59. Jefferson to JA, July 5, 1814; JA to Jefferson, July 9, 1813, and July 16, 1814, in *Adams-Jefferson Letters,* 351, 431, 435–36.
60. JA to Jefferson, Nov. 15, 1813, in *Adams-Jefferson Letters,* 400–401.
61. JA to JQA, May 3, 1816, AP/FOL. The elder Adams quoted, "As Voltaire always whined, 'Octogenaire et malade.'"
62. Explaining why he did not fear a Catholic menace to the extent his father did, JQA told a story at once unnerving and calming to him. "I had a diplomatic Colleague, in Russia," it began, "A man of excellent heart, of amiable temper, of amusing and sportive wit"—a true scholar in every sense who nonetheless held, "from the deepest conviction of his soul," that all things are ever under the immediate control of God. The same man considered John Locke a "pestilence" and the "founder of the French Revolution and all its horrors." Another man of their times, a professor in Madrid, refused to teach his students "the higher branches" of mathematics, because it had been "proved" that such an education only advanced atheism. JQA to JA, Jan. 5 and Aug. 1, 1816; JA to JQA, March 28, 1816, AP/FOL.
63. Georgini, "John Quincy Adams at Prayer"; Cooper, *Lost Founding Father,* 102–5, 384–86; Jan. 3, 1788, *DJQA;* JQA to JA, Oct. 29, 1816; JA to JQA, Nov. 13, 1816, AP/FOL.
64. JQA to JA, Aug. 1, 1816; JA to JQA, Sept. 23, 1816, AP/FOL.
65. JA to JQA, Sept. 23, 1816; JQA to JA, Oct. 29, 1816, AP/FOL.
66. JA to JQA, Nov. 26, 1816, AP/FOL.
67. Aug. 6 and 18–19, 1817, *DJQA;* JA to JQA, Aug. 10, 1817, AP/FOL. George would matriculate in 1818 and graduate in 1821, the year Charles entered; the middle brother, John, would find his Harvard education cut short upon expulsion for taking part in protests.
68. Aug. 26–27, 1817, *DJQA.*

69. July 11, 1817, *DJQA.* When John Adams urged his son to seize upon Monroe's offer of the most coveted cabinet post, he made note of the approaching milestone, as a rationale for JQA to "share the fortunes of your Country. . . . You must risque all." JA to JQA, March 13, 1817, AP/FOL.
70. On the Monroe style, see variously, Ammon, *James Monroe;* Peterson, *Great Triumvirate;* Forbes, *Missouri Compromise and Its Aftermath,* chap. 1.
71. JA to JQA, Oct. 28, 1817, AP/FOL.
72. JQA to JA, Nov. 24, 1817; JA to JQA, Dec. 8 and 31, 1817, AP/FOL. JQA quoted an old French saying: "Tant va la cruche à l'eau qu'à la fin elle se casse." Literally: If one dips an old jug into the well enough times, it is going to crack. This meant that the repeated occurrence of an action is eventually bound to produce a decisive and often catastrophic result. He knew what impended, but he went ahead because this was his time: "Whether the pitcher is filled or whether it is broken, it was made to go to the water, and go to the water it must. Break it also must, a little sooner or a little later." As their correspondence continued, the father acknowledged his own history of overreaction: "I often Suspect myself, and that my Imagination deceives me; that I mistake posibilities for probabilities and Non Entities for probabilities; that I See '*Au dessous des cartes*' [shady and fallible] many things which in reality may not be there."
73. JQA to JA, Dec. 21, 1817; JA to JQA, Dec. 31, 1817, AP/FOL; JA to Jefferson, Dec. 30, 1818, in *Adams-Jefferson Letters,* 531.
74. JA to JQA, Jan. 8, 1818, AP/FOL.
75. JQA to JA, Dec. 17, 1817, AP/FOL; Bemis, *John Quincy Adams and the Foundations of American Foreign Policy,* chap. 17; Lewis, *American Union and the Problem of Neighborhood,* chap. 4; on the full dimension of the privateering problem, see Head, *Privateers of the Americas.*
76. Gelles, *Abigail and John,* 272–74, 282–83; Kaplan, *John Quincy Adams,* 98, 219–20; Oct. 31–Nov. 2, 1818, *DJQA.*
77. JQA to JA, Nov. 2, 1818; JA to JQA, Nov. 10, 1818, AP/FOL.
78. Nagel, *John Quincy Adams,* 257–58; Ferling, *John Adams,* 438.
79. Pellew, *John Jay,* 312–13; JA to Jefferson, Oct. 17, 1817, in *Adams-Jefferson Letters,* 521.
80. Burstein, *Passions of Andrew Jackson,* chap. 5; Ammon, *James Monroe,* chaps. 23 and 24.
81. Edel, *Nation Builder,* 138–59; Bemis, *John Quincy Adams and the Foundations of American Foreign Policy,* chap. 16; Parsons, *John Quincy Adams,* 139–44.
82. Jan. 5 and March 3, 1820, *DJQA.*
83. Howe, *What Hath God Wrought,* 147–60; Peterson, *Great Triumvirate,* 57–65; Parsons, *John Quincy Adams,* 159–62; Forbes, *Missouri Compromise and Its Aftermath;* Nov. 22, 1823, *DJQA.*
84. June 2 and 20, Aug. 27–29, and Nov. 26–30, 1822, *DJQA.*
85. JQA, *Address, Delivered at the Request of the Committee of Arrangements for Celebrating the Anniversary of Independence, at the City of Washington on the Fourth of July 1821,* esp. 11–12, 34.
86. JQA to LCA, Aug. 2 and 12, 1822; LCA to JQA, Aug. 9, 1822, all in AP/microfilm, reel 456; JQA to JA, Sept. 24, 1822; JA to JQA, Oct. 7, 1822, AP/FOL; April 22–30, 1822, *DJQA; Essex Register* (Salem, Mass.), May 15 and 29, 1822; Nagel, *John Quincy Adams,* 283–85; Parsons, *John Quincy Adams,* 167–68.

12: SIXTH PRESIDENT

1. B. F. Watson, "A New Story of John Adams," *Independent,* Nov. 12, 1896, 48.
2. Burstein, *Passions of Andrew Jackson,* 146–54. For a valuable reinterpretation of the role of party and conduct of politics in the 1820s, see Peart, *Era of Experimentation.*
3. JQA to LCA, Oct. 7, 1822, AP/microfilm, reel 456. On Monroe's neutrality, see Nov. 24, 1826, *DJQA;* JQA to LCA, Aug. 11, 1821, AP/FOL. In the context of his belief of having earned the presidency, JQA cited the "literary and scientific distinctions" conferred on him in addition to the "honorable and important trusts" of appointed and elective office.
4. JQA to LCA, Aug. 11, 1821, AP/FOL. These remarks were in direct response to a letter he had just received from his wife, in which she'd said, "To me who understand perfectly what the real motives are by which you are actuated, and who can fully appreciate them, it would be perfectly unnecessary to assign reasons; but the world seldom examine farther than the surface of things and our very virtues are frequently tortured into vices by [missing word] misconception—You in consequence of the natural coldness and reserve of your manners are more calculated to produce a harsh judgment than most men; more particularly as the publick opinion inclines to believe this coldness to proceed from pride; instead of being as I know from modesty, and a desire to avoid display." LCA to JQA, Aug. 3, 1821, AP/FOL.
5. Aug. 25 and Sept. 3, 1823, *DJQA;* Brooks, *Flowering of New England,* 1; Oliver, *Portraits of John and Abigail Adams,* 188–89.

6. Sept. 9 and 14, 1823, *DJQA;* Jefferson to JA, Oct. 12, 1823; JA to Jefferson, Nov. 10, 1823, in *Adams-Jefferson Letters,* 600–601; Burstein, *America's Jubilee,* 255–57. At least one newspaper referred to the Cunningham pamphlet as "industriously but rather clandestinely circulated"; see *Cooperstown* (N.Y.) *Watch Tower,* Jan. 12, 1824. To the best of his knowledge, JQA had never set eyes on the twenty-year-old correspondence before its release as a pamphlet.
7. Jefferson to Johnson, March 4, 1823, Jefferson Papers.
8. "To the Republicans of Georgia," *Georgia Journal* (Milledgeville), Sept. 2, 1823.
9. Sept. 19, 1823, *DJQA.*
10. March 20, 1824, *DJQA.*
11. *Essex Register* (Salem, Mass.), Jan. 1, 1823; "To the Editor of the Connecticut Gazette," *Norwich* (Conn.) *Courier,* Dec. 17, 1823; *Middlesex Gazette* (Middletown, Conn.), Feb. 11, 1824; *Essex Register,* March 25, 1824; see also, "Short Sketch of John Quincy Adams," *Farmer's Cabinet* (Amherst, N.H.), July 17, 1824, reprinted elsewhere; Bethel Saler, "John Quincy Adams, Cosmopolitan," in Waldstreicher, *Companion to John Adams and John Quincy Adams,* chap. 19; Lipsky, *John Quincy Adams,* 195–97. Regarding the range of efforts employed in parrying JQA's critics, see also Edel, *Nation Builder,* 196–99.
12. *Independent Chronicle,* Jan. 10, 1824. The same issue suggested that Adams would pick up votes among Crawford supporters in view of that gentleman's having suffered a stroke.
13. Firsthand accounts in the *New York Commercial Advertiser* and *New York Statesman,* reprinted in the *Rhode Island American,* Jan. 20, 1824; additional quotation from *Richmond Enquirer,* Jan. 13, 1824; also *Trenton* (N.J.) *Federalist,* Jan. 19, 1824; *DALCA,* 2:680, 687–88; see also Allgor, *Parlor Politics,* chap. 4; Cooper, *Lost Founding Father,* 272–75.
14. On Jackson's self-presentation, see Wise, *Seven Decades of the Union,* 98–99; *DALCA,* 2:678; *New Hampshire Patriot and Statesman,* Jan. 12, 1824; *Independent Chronicle and Boston Patriot,* May 15, 1824, adapted from *New Haven Pilot; Augusta* (Ga.) *Chronicle,* May 15, 1824; Burstein, *Passions of Andrew Jackson,* 152.
15. JQA to JA, June 24, 1824; JQA to Jefferson, June 24, 1824, AP/FOL; Burstein, *America's Jubilee,* 144. There is a certain irony in all of this, because John Adams frequently disparaged the likes of Jefferson and Thomas Paine for having been given too much credit for their writings in 1776, when Massachusetts had done so much to prepare the country for independence; see Renker, "'Declaration-Men' and the Rhetoric of Self-Presentation."
16. July 31 and Aug. 6, 27, and 31, 1824, *DJQA;* Nagel, *John Quincy Adams,* 288–89. At the end of the month, JQA diarized that "eight or ten newspapers of extensive circulation" had teamed up for the purpose of sinking his chances; in a cruel coordination, they were "pouring forth continual streams of slander upon my character and reputation, public and private." He breathed, "No falsehood is too broad, and no insinuation too base for them." One ridiculous rumor claimed that father and son had had a serious falling-out.
17. Sept. 7–20, 1824, *DJQA.*
18. Oct. 3–7, 1824, *DJQA;* Levasseur, *Lafayette in America,* 1:160–62; Burstein, *America's Jubilee,* 14.
19. Oct. 8–15, 1824, *DJQA;* Levasseur, *Lafayette in America,* 1:164–75.
20. Dec. 15, 1824, *DJQA;* Burstein, *America's Jubilee,* 20–21.
21. *Columbian Centinel,* Jan. 10, 1824. Of the many who have weighed in on the "corrupt bargain" question, see esp. Nagel, *John Quincy Adams,* 292–98; Peterson, *Great Triumvirate,* 129–33; Howe, *What Hath God Wrought,* 246–50; Heidler and Heidler, *Henry Clay,* 174–92, 203–4. The Heidlers point out that the Jackson stalwart Thomas Hart Benton, Missouri senator, admitted to Clay years later that the Democrats' inner circle never really believed that a corrupt deal was made, but saying so earned them considerable political capital, which was the point (ibid., 490).
22. Seale, *President's House,* 159–61, 166–67.
23. LCA to Charles Francis Adams, April 20, 1825, AP/microfilm, reel 469.
24. Inaugural Address, www.presidency.ucsb.edu/ws/index.php?pid=25809.
25. Storrs, *Address, Delivered in Braintree, on the Occasion of the Inauguration of John Quincy Adams, Esq., to the Presidency of the United States,* 8, 28–30.
26. Foote to JQA, April 9, 1825, AP/microfilm, reel 469.
27. Adams's message effectively adopted the blueprint for American prosperity first articulated by Clay and popularly referred to as the "American System." See Peterson, *Great Triumvirate,* 133–34; for political ramifications, see Edel, *Nation Builder,* 210–15.
28. JQA, First Annual Message, Dec. 6, 1825, millercenter.org/president/jqadams/speeches/speech-3514.
29. "Diary of Life," George Washington Adams, Miscellany, AP/microfilm, reel 287.
30. LCA to JQA, June 24–25, 1824, AP/FOL; George W. Adams, *Oration Delivered at Quincy, on the Fifth of July 1824.*

31. *Columbian Centinel,* July 14, 1824. This particular Fourth of July witnessed more than the usual coverage for local heroes. In Boston proper, the official Independence Day oration had praise for John Adams as "one of the few patriots of the Revolution that Providence has yet left among us." Those assembled at Faneuil Hall heard sung an original ode called "Adams and Liberty." In nearby Dorchester, the *Boston Patriot* reported on another oration, which "paid a deserving eulogium to the talents and services of our distinguished fellow citizen JOHN Q. ADAMS." It, too, "was received with great applause." "National Jubilee," *Haverhill Gazette,* July 10, 1824; *Independent Chronicle and Boston Patriot,* July 10, 1824.
32. "Diary of Life," George Washington Adams, Miscellany, AP/microfilm, reel 287.
33. *Daniel Webster's First Oration at Bunker Hill,* June 17, 1825.
34. JQA to G. W. Adams, Aug. 18 and 25, 1825, AP/FOL.
35. JA to G. W. Adams, March 12, 1826, AP/FOL.
36. Charles Francis Adams diary, AP/microfilm, reel 56; Pattee, *History of Old Braintree and Quincy,* 62.
37. Burstein, *America's Jubilee,* 266–68.
38. JQA Letterbook entries of July 15–17, 1826, AP/microfilm, reel 149. Because Louisa had stayed behind in Washington, he shared via the mails his fear that the choices he now faced would sink him into debt. Which led to, "Should I live through my term of service, my purpose is to come and close my days here, to be deposited with my father and mother." JQA to LCA, July 14, 1826, JQA Letterbook, AP/microfilm, reel 149.
39. Oliver, *Portraits of John and Abigail Adams,* 190–91; *Selection of Eulogies,* 193–234. JQA said he received "high though melancholy gratification" from the solemn service. Well-wishers greeted him wherever he went now; long-lost relatives appeared, and decades-old anecdotes of John and Abigail circulated. Four Penobscot Indians from Maine showed up at his door, curious to meet "their father the President," but mainly, he said, to ask for a handout. Aug. 1–4, 1826, *DJQA.*
40. Aug. 6–20 and Sept. 6, 18–19, and 24–25, 1826, *DJQA.*
41. Aug. 25, Sept. 8, 12, and 16, and Oct. 1–2 and 5, 1826, *DJQA;* Pattee, *History of Old Braintree and Quincy,* 105–7; Charles Francis Adams, *Life of John Adams,* 2:408; Nagel, *Descent from Glory,* 145–46. Before the jubilee year ended, JQA had purchased so much of his father's estate that he ended up owing a considerable amount to various others who had been named as John Adams's heirs. He paid $22,000 for his father's house and the surrounding ninety-five acres.
42. Oct. 6–7, 1826, *DJQA;* Nagel, *John Quincy Adams,* 313–14. Reaching New York, JQA wrote to his eldest that he was "anxious more than perhaps I ought to be for you and hoping that you will not forget or disregard the faithful paternal advice that I have given you." JQA to George W. Adams, Oct. 16, 1826, AP/FOL.
43. Oct. 19, 1826, *DJQA.*
44. *Niles' Weekly Register,* June 20, 1818. The popular editor, Hezekiah Niles, prefaced the publication of Adams's letters to Wirt with a statement of his regard for the octogenarian's still-vigorous mind.
45. LCA to JQA, July 15, 17, and 20, 1826, AP/microfilm, reel 476; Oct. 21, 1826, *DJQA;* Burstein, *America's Jubilee,* 282–83.
46. *Selection of Eulogies,* 378–426. An audience member writing for the *Baltimore Patriot* (Oct. 25, 1826) commended Wirt's "peculiar felicity" of expression and said that the oration went far toward dissolving the "asperity and violence of party feeling generally in this country." The president, the same man reported, was "evidently absorbed" in the emotions that were to be expected upon such an occasion. Louisa Adams, so often waylaid by one indisposition or another, along with her son John, arrived by carriage two days later, having tarried in Philadelphia. She was not at the Capitol to hear Wirt speak.
47. Edel, *Nation Builder,* chap. 4; Parsons, *John Quincy Adams,* 183. In a typical, but especially maudlin, diary entry, JQA described sitting at his ill wife's bedside, eventually moving with her to the sofa, and pursuing a conversation about the future in which he hoped to have her understanding presence, "for aid and encouragement, which the world will not give." Sept. 27, 1826, *DJQA.*
48. Nov. 17, 25, and 30, 1826, *DJQA.* On the thirtieth, Trumbull presented Adams with a folio containing engravings of his works, including *Declaration of Independence.*
49. Nov. 30 and Dec. 7, 1826, *DJQA.*
50. Frothingham, *Edward Everett.*
51. Dec. 1, 1826, *DJQA;* Jefferson to Van Buren, June 29, 1824, Jefferson Papers; Cole, *Vindicating Andrew Jackson,* 71–73; Burstein, *Passions of Andrew Jackson,* chap. 5.
52. Lewis, *American Union and the Problem of Neighborhood,* chap. 7; Lewis, *John Quincy Adams,* chap. 5.
53. Dec. 23, 1826, *DJQA.*
54. Nov. 30 and Dec. 16, 1826, *DJQA;* "John Quincy Adams' Would-Be Assassin: George P. Todsen," www.masshist.org/blog/1558; Nagel, *John Quincy Adams,* 306.
55. Charles Francis Adams diary, AP/microfilm, reel 56; Oct. 30, 1826, *DJQA;* Charles Francis Adams, *Life of John Adams,* 2:409–11.

13: SURVIVING SON

1. March 16, 1827, *DJQA;* Cranch, *Memoir of John Adams,* 40.
2. Richards, *The Life and Times of Congressman John Quincy Adams,* 18–20.
3. March 15–18, 1827, *DJQA.* Before Todson left the president's office, he presented a letter of "remonstrance" at the behest of yet another man cashiered from the army.
4. May 11, 1827, *DJQA; National Daily Journal* (Washington, D.C.), April 17, 1827; *New-London* (Conn.) *Gazette,* May 2, 1827.
5. Burstein, *America's Jubilee,* chap. 8; Johnson, *John Randolph of Roanoke,* chap. 16, quotation at 207. In later years, Henry Adams wrote a less than flattering biography of the Virginian.
6. *Political Character of John Quincy Adams Delineated.*
7. See esp. Hofstadter, *Idea of a Party System,* chap. 6; Cole, *Vindicating Andrew Jackson,* 88–98, 129–32; Howe, *What Hath God Wrought,* 279–80. The pro-Adams "Administration Convention," held in Harrisburg, Pennsylvania, on Jan. 4, 1828, acknowledged the opposition as both the "democratic party" and "Jackson Democrats." It observed in the same paragraph, "Every political party is presumed to be founded on, and governed by, certain principles, on the security of which they ask public confidence.—*Parties* are governed by principles; *Factions* by *Men*" (*Baltimore Patriot,* Jan. 10, 1828). Leading up to the election of 1824, Crawford of Georgia was sometimes referred to by supporters as the "Democratic candidate" (for example, *Richmond Enquirer,* Jan. 1, 1824). In New England, Adams was at the same time associated with the "democratic party" (for example, *New-Hampshire Patriot,* via *New Hampshire Sentinel,* Jan. 2, 1824). Yet the two-party system was effectively suppressed in 1824. By 1829, "Democratic Party" was widely used in newspapers to describe adherents of the Jackson administration.
8. Parsons, "Continuing Crusade"; Burstein, *Passions of Andrew Jackson,* 161–62, 170–72, 234. Hamilton would do a stint as acting secretary of state in 1829, until Van Buren could make his way to Washington to assume the post. He eventually found himself defending Jackson's war against the national bank his father had created in the 1790s. Meanwhile, JQA acquired a grudging respect for some of the elder Hamilton's economic theories—touches of irony that make politics artful as well as confounding.
9. Van Buren, *Inquiry into the Origin and Course of Political Parties in the United States,* 8–9, 229, 251–56, 262. Van Buren remarked of Madison that "he was neither as great a man nor as thorough a Republican, certainly not as thorough a Democrat, as Mr. Jefferson" (ibid., 201–2).
10. The "aristocratic" label worked on New Yorkers, because their state was only just emerging from a system in which preponderant power was lodged in the hands of a few giant families—mainly Clintons and Livingstons. The unexpected death of DeWitt Clinton in 1828 catapulted Van Buren to a preeminent position. See Niven, *Martin Van Buren,* 205–12.
11. Parsons, *John Quincy Adams,* 189–92; Parsons, *Birth of Modern Politics,* 136–69; Pasley, *"Tyranny of Printers,"* 355–56, 391–95; Heidler and Heidler, *Henry Clay,* 205–6; Howe, *What Hath God Wrought,* 277–79. Van Buren had gotten behind the tariff bill, speaking up for northern and western protectionists (for its high duties on imported wool) while assuring opposing southerners the bill would likely not pass; it contained provisions unpalatable to New Englanders. See Peterson, *Great Triumvirate,* 159–61.
12. Mercieca, *Founding Fictions,* 170–82; Burstein, *America's Jubilee,* chap. 9.
13. Barbara McEwan, *White House Landscapes: Horticultural Achievements of American Presidents* (New York: Walker, 1992).
14. Edel, *Nation Builder,* 239–45; Cole, *Vindicating Andrew Jackson,* chap. 8; Howe, *What Hath God Wrought,* 280–83; Parsons, *Birth of Modern Politics,* 184–87.
15. Nagel, *Descent from Glory,* 147–51, 157–59.
16. June 13–14, 1829, *DJQA.*
17. June 8, 1829, *DJQA.*
18. June 7, 1829, *DJQA;* Irving, *Life and Voyages of Christopher Columbus,* bk. 4, chap. 5, bk. 5, chaps. 1 and 5; Burstein, *Original Knickerbocker.*
19. Nagel, *Descent from Glory,* 164–71.
20. April 15–16, 1831, *DJQA.*
21. Nagel, *John Quincy Adams,* 346.
22. JQA, *Dermot Mac Morrogh.* It should be said that Adams himself did not write anything that could be used as direct evidence of a desire to further embarrass Jackson over bigamy committed forty years earlier, softened by Rachel Jackson's years of pious behavior as a conventional wife. See esp. April 18–19, 1831, *DJQA,* with regard to the analogous Eaton Affair that set Jackson against those in his immediate circle who refused to associate with the discredited lower-class wife of his first-term secretary of war, the Tennessean John Eaton. Still, the moral component of the tabloid-like Eaton Affair did contribute to Adams's overall opinion of Jackson's conduct in office.

23. Kaplan, *John Quincy Adams,* 445–46.
24. Nov. 6–8, 1830, *DJQA.* Comparing private scholarship with public service, he mused, "Had I forty years ago . . . devoted the leisure of one year without interruption to the study of Cicero in his own language, my time would have been better occupied than it was and perhaps my life would have been more useful to my Country and my fellow creatures."
25. Dec. 24 and 27, 1830, and Jan. 10–12, 1831, *DJQA.* Curiously, JQA was at the same time reading for pleasure the famously debauched poet Lord Byron's classic *Childe Harold's Pilgrimage.*
26. Dec. 22, 1830, Jan. 13, 1831, and March 2, 1832, *DJQA;* Larson, *Internal Improvement;* Richards, *Life and Times of Congressman John Quincy Adams,* 65–75; Heidler and Heidler, *Henry Clay,* 226–50.
27. March 17, 1832, *DJQA.* Trained in the law, Tom made a brief appearance in the Massachusetts legislature but stood interminably in the eldest brother's shadow. He seemed to be okay with that from the time he served John Quincy as a personal secretary in the Netherlands and Prussia in the late 1790s. By the time he left Europe, he was conversant in French, German, and Dutch. Given control of John Quincy's financial affairs back home, however, Tom squandered thousands of dollars that weren't his and gave his brother no explanation for his failure. Each time Tom struck out on his own, he proved incapable of prospering.
28. Oct. 20–25, 1834, *DJQA.*

14: STANDARD-BEARER

1. McLoughlin, "Georgia's Role in Instigating Compulsory Indian Removal"; Parsons, "'Perpetual Harrow upon My Feelings'"; Richards, *Life and Times of Congressman John Quincy Adams,* 146–51; Burstein, *America's Jubilee,* 218–19; Howe, *What Hath God Wrought,* 255–56, 346–48; Kaplan, *John Quincy Adams,* 379–80, 398–400, 545–47; Teed, *John Quincy Adams, Yankee Nationalist,* 102–5.
2. Jan. 10, 1831, *DJQA;* Parsons, *John Quincy Adams,* 222–23; "Origin of the Late War," *Southern Historical Society Papers* 1 (Jan. 1876): 6–7; "The Vindication of the South," *Richmond Times,* Oct. 22, 1899; Sinha, *Slave's Cause,* 28, 209, 213, 225–27, 503.
3. In his diary, he wrote that "from the South, almost daily, [I receive] letters of insult, profane obscenity, and filth." May 21, 1842, *DJQA.* One of the assassination letters was read in Congress; he was called the "prince of devils" as the writer vowed, upon arrival in Washington, "I will shoot you." The would-be assassin signed his name and even announced the date he would be in Washington, Jan. 2, 1839. A man attacked Adams in 1844, and Adams restrained him until he could be taken into custody. When Adams asked the House to act in response to the death threat, a colleague dismissed it as a hoax, and the body in which Adams sat voted against doing anything. *New-Bedford Mercury,* Jan. 11, 1839; also *New York Daily Advertiser,* whose Capitol Hill correspondent observed that Adams was "almost daily receiving anonymous communications from the South and elsewhere threatening him with assassination, mobbing, and especially *Lynching*"; see "John Quincy Adams," reprinted in Goodell, *Legion of Liberty!,* 291; "Attack on Mr. Adams," *Emancipator and Weekly Chronicle,* Dec. 25, 1844.
4. Isenberg, *White Trash,* 152.
5. JQA acquired a reputation in Congress for his "tenacious" memory and was often asked to recount the details of earlier transactions. He outclassed his opponents and with "no time for preparation" could enter into "an extempore history of the political affairs of that period." See Maury, "John Quincy Adams," in *Statesmen of America in 1846,* 245–47.
6. July 5, 1819, Feb. 18, 1820, Jan. 11, 1826, Jan. 1, 1830, and April 19, 1837, *DJQA.*
7. Feb. 28, 1820, *DJQA.*
8. JQA, *Parties in the United States,* 37–38. Jefferson conceived of Louisiana's ethnicities as quasi-children, in need of a probationary period of training and colonial subjection before they could be fully incorporated into the United States. See Burstein and Isenberg, *Madison and Jefferson,* 395–96.
9. JQA, *An Address Delivered at the Request of a Committee of Citizens of Washington: On the Occasion of Reading the Declaration of Independence, on the Fourth of July, 1821* (Washington, D.C.: Davis and Force, 1821), 21, 27, 31; Oct. 30, 1826, *DJQA;* Waldstreicher and Mason, *John Quincy Adams and the Politics of Slavery,* 134–35.
10. JQA, *Parties in the United States,* 4, 39–40, 119.
11. Feb. 20, 1820, and Jan. 27, 1831, *DJQA.* On southern elites' hatred for poor whites, see Isenberg, *White Trash;* for an analysis of Calhoun's early defense of slavery, see Ford, "Reconfiguring the Old South," esp. 118–21. On JQA's emerging reputation as a powerful advocate in the House, see *Ohio State Journal and Columbus Gazette,* May 18, 1836; he was already considered "one of the best speakers in the House" in 1831, according to the *New-York Gazette* (via *New-London Gazette*), Dec. 21, 1831; when he spoke, "there reigned in the hall the most profound silence," in *Portsmouth Journal,* Dec. 24, 1831.
12. Ford, "Inventing the Concurrent Majority"; Don Higgenbotham, "Fomenters of Revolution: Massachusetts and South Carolina," *Journal of the Early Republic* 14 (Spring 1994): 1–33, esp. 14–15; Ellis, *Union at Risk,* 8–11, 193;

Childers, *Webster-Hayne Debate,* 26–31; "Mr. Madison and Gov. Troup," *Macon* (Ga.) *Telegraph,* Nov. 13, 1830; "Mr. Calhoun," *Newport Mercury,* Aug. 27, 1831. Calhoun's backers were initially undecided whether he should conciliate northerners and run for president in 1832 or embrace nullification full-on, which would make a presidential run impossible; see Peterson, *Great Triumvirate,* 189–91.

13. JQA, *Oration Addressed to the Citizens of the Town of Quincy, on the Fourth of July, 1831,* 11–18, 22–23, 34–36. Adams was comparing nullification to the Declaratory Act (1766), which stated that "all resolutions" in the colonies were "utterly null and void" if they denied "the power and authority of the Parliament of *Great Britain* to make laws and statutes." Calhoun's treatise used the same language, asserting state sovereignty by declaring any law "null and void" that challenged South Carolina's supremacy. See 6 George III, c. 12, *The Statutes at Large,* ed. Danby Pickering (London, 1767), XXVII, 1920. The Declaratory Act echoed the Irish Declaratory Act (1719), which put Ireland into a position of servitude to Parliament—and that was JQA's point: nullification was based on a master and slave relationship, the primal authority dictating to a subordinate entity. His rejection of sovereign power piggybacked on the constitutional precedent set by James Wilson, who argued in *Chisholm v. Georgia* (1793) that in the new American science of jurisprudence, "the term SOVEREIGN, is totally unknown." Thus, for the British, "sovereign" was traced to the king, Parliament, and the state, while in the United States sovereignty was found in man. See Dyer, "After the Revolution."
14. "Speech by Mr. Clayton, of Geo.," *Register of Debates in Congress, 22nd Congress, Second Session* (Washington, D.C., 1833), 9:1583. Clayton founded a cotton factory in protest against the tariff laws; see *Macon* (Ga.) *Telegraph,* April 11, 1829; *Milledgeville* (Ga.) *Federal Union,* Jan. 3, 1833; these and related sources available in *The Early Republic thru Local History,* earlyushistory.net/clayton-nullification-documents.
15. See "Debate on the Tariff, Speech of Mr. Adams, of Mass.," *Salem Gazette,* Feb. 26, 1833. In 1831, federal troops were employed against slave revolts in Louisiana, North Carolina, and Virginia. Nat Turner's rebellion in Virginia involved eleven federal companies, more than three thousand Virginia militia, and the state militias of North Carolina and Maryland. Federal troops were used to repress slave revolts in Florida in 1816 and 1820, even though Florida was under Spanish control. See David Adams, "Internal Military Intervention in the United States," esp. 199.
16. JQA and Condit, *Report of the Minority of the Committee on Manufactures, Submitted to the House of Representatives of the United States, February 28, 1833,* 3–4, 29, 33, 35, 37, 40–42; Aug. 11, 1835, *DJQA.*
17. "Debate on the Tariff, Speech of Mr. Adams," *Salem Gazette,* Feb. 26, 1833; "Ex-president Adams—the Tariff—Slavery," *New Hampshire Sentinel,* March 7, 1833.
18. Jan. 20 and June 6 and 22, 1830, Dec. 5, 1832, and Aug. 18 and 22, 1835, *DJQA.*
19. Dec. 5, 1837, *DJQA;* Shade, "'Most Delicate and Exciting Topics.'" Supporters of the Whig presidential candidate Hugh Lawson White of Tennessee, a onetime Jackson ally, attacked Van Buren both as an abolitionist who supported black male suffrage rights in New York and as one with close connections to those who had supported JQA in 1824. See "Great White Meeting in Fayette," *National Banner and Nashville Whig,* May 30, 1836.
20. "A Confederate Republic," *Richmond Enquirer,* Sept. 19, 1833; Campbell, *Empire for Slavery;* Lack, "Slavery and the Texas Revolution"; Schroeder, "Annexation or Independence."
21. JQA, *Speech of the Hon. John Quincy Adams, in the House of Representatives, on the State of the Nation,* 5–15.
22. Mr. Adams, May 7 and May 25, 1836, *Register of Debates,* 24th Cong., 1st sess., 3519, 4046.
23. June 6, 10, and 13, 1836, *DJQA.* Also see Waldstreicher and Mason, *John Quincy Adams and the Politics of Slavery,* 192–93; "Slavery," *Portsmouth Journal of Literature and Politics,* June 25, 1836; *Connecticut Courant,* June 20, 1836.
24. Aug. 11, 1836, *DJQA.*
25. JQA, *Eulogy on the Life and Character of James Madison, Fourth President of the United States,* 12, 54, 57–61, 82–84; *Proceedings and Debates of the Virginia State Convention of 1828–30,* 538. JQA saw nullification as one of Jefferson's "great and portentous Errors," and while aware that Madison admitted that "erroneous constructions are often not sufficiently guarded against," he still felt that Madison's principal reason for supporting the 1799 Virginia Resolution (a weaker version of nullification than Jefferson's Kentucky draft) was an "electioneering" tactic to increase Jefferson's presidential chances. See JQA to Alexander Everett, May 24, 1830, and Sept. 18, 1831, in "Letters of John Quincy Adams to Alexander Hamilton Everett, 1811–1837," esp. 340, 342; for the differences in Jefferson's and Madison's theories (Madison did not use the word "nullification"), and Madison's *Report of 1800,* more strongly disavowing nullification, see Burstein and Isenberg, *Madison and Jefferson,* 338–40, 350; also Ketcham, "Jefferson and Madison and the Doctrines of Interposition and Nullification."
26. Mr. Adams, May 25, 1836, *Register of Debates,* 24th Cong., 1st sess., 4030; Hammond's speech in the House, Feb. 1, 1836, ibid., 2449, 2455–56, 2458, 2461–62; Michael Kent Curtis, *Free Speech, "the People's Darling Privilege": Struggles for Freedom of Expression in American History* (Durham, N.C.: Duke University Press, 2000), 156–59, 177–78; *The Addresses and Messages of the Presidents of the United States, Inaugural, Annual, and Special, from 1789 to 1849* (New York: Edward Walker, 1849), 2:911–12; on the Senate's approach, see Peter Charles

Hoffer, *John Quincy Adams and the Gag Rule, 1835–1850* (Baltimore: Johns Hopkins University Press, 2017), 25. For contextualization of the gag rule within the broader abolition movement, see Sinha, *Slave's Cause.*

27. On the Federalists' theory of sedition, see Martin, "When Repression Is Democratic and Constitutional"; also Higginson, "Short History."
28. In England, sedition laws were nicknamed gagging bills, and the 1798 Sedition Law was also called a gag bill. On Adams and Lovejoy, see "Mr. Adams, Texas, and Slavery," *New-Bedford Mercury,* Dec. 22, 1837. Adams wrote the introduction to a book titled *Memoir of the Rev. E. P. Lovejoy* (1838); *Emancipator,* May 17, 1838; on critics of the 1798 Sedition Act, see *Aurora General Advertiser,* July 11, 1798; *Boston Constitution Telegraph,* Dec. 21, 1799; *Newark* (N.J.) *Centinel of Freedom,* March 19, 1799; *Alexandria Advertiser,* Sept. 5, 1798; *New-York Gazette,* July 14, 1798; "gag bill" even appeared in a poem, "The New Federal Song," *Trenton* (N.J.) *True American,* April 21, 1801; Higginson, "Short History," 160–61.
29. Mr. Hammond, Feb. 1, 1836, *Register of Debates,* 24th Cong., 1st sess., 2451, 2459; for coverage of Adams's defiant stand, see "Scene in Congress, May 25–Pinckney's Resolutions," *Haverhill* (Mass.) *Gazette,* June 4, 1836. During his speech, Hammond displayed lurid illustrations of slaves' bodies after whippings. His purpose was to expose abolitionists who would sensationalize, even sexualize, slave society. For him, it wasn't that slavery dehumanized: the issue was that the abolitionist enemy combined libelous with licentious purposes.
30. "Abolition Frowned Down," 1839 lithograph by Henry R. Robinson, Library of Congress; Wood, *Black Milk,* 98–99. The Clay-Jackson caricature is David Claypoole Johnston's "Symptoms of Lock Jaw. Plain Sewing Done Here," which concerns the censure of President Jackson for refusing to hand over documents pertaining to his controversial bank veto, also at Library of Congress; "Votes, Votes, and Violence," *Richmond Enquirer,* Sept. 19, 1832; "gagged and collared" in a party meeting, in *Ohio State Journal and Columbus Gazette,* May 22, 1835; gagging the press compared to highway robbery, in "Noble Sentiments," *Essex Gazette* (Salem, Mass.), Aug. 20, 1836; "Letter from Mr. Adams," *Emancipator,* Sept. 6, 1838.
31. LCA to Charles F. Adams, Feb. 24, 1837, AP/microfilm, MHS. A counter-resolution charged that by giving slaves the same right of petition as free men, Adams was inviting the slave population to revolt. As Adams read the scene, he was up against the grotesque spectacle he called "slaveholding freedom," which wasn't freedom at all; suppression was no kind of freedom and should be called unconstitutional. Later, as he ruminated on the drama he caused, JQA laughed off those who would have him "burnt with his petition at the stake" (Feb. 6, 1837, *Register of Debates,* 24th Cong., 2nd sess., 1587–88, 1594–95); *New-Bedford Mercury,* Feb. 10, 1837; JQA, *Letters from John Quincy Adams to His Constituents,* 11–13.
32. See Mr. Adams, Feb. 6, 9, and 11, 1837, *Register of Debates,* 24th Cong., 2nd sess., 1587, 1596, 1675–78, 1595–96, 1723; on black female petitioners, see Susan Zaeske, "'The South Arose as One Man': Gender and Sectionalism in Antislavery Petition Debates, 1835–1845," *Rhetoric and Public Affairs* 12 (Fall 2009): 341–68; one newspaper reported that in the petition from purported slaves the slaves "petitioned his expulsion from the House before he made their condition harder"; *Portsmouth and Great Falls* (N.H.) *Journal of Literature and Politics,* Feb. 11, 1837; also *Telegraph and Texas Register,* March 7, 1837. Adams admitted that he thought the petition was a forgery written by a slaveholder. On Adams's awareness of the hoax, see David C. Frederick, "John Quincy Adams, Slavery, and the Disappearance of the Right of Petition," *Law and History Review* 9 (Spring 1991): 113–55, esp. 135. Adams loved the theater, so it is not surprising that he would use this kind of dramatic device.
33. Mr. Adams, Feb. 7, 8, and 9, 1837, *Register of Debates,* 24th Cong., 2nd sess., 1610–12, 1632, 1658; *Letters from John Quincy Adams to His Constituents,* 19–21, 24–26.
34. *Letters from John Quincy Adams to His Constituents,* 25–26, 40–43; *Register of Debates* recorded Adams as saying, "If you once admit the principle that the right of petition is limited, and will not apply to slaves, the next thing will be to limit it still further, by extending the limitation to free colored people; and, after this, the next limitation will be to the question of the character of the petitioners; then the limitation will be to inquire on what side of political parties are the petitioners." Feb. 9, 1837, *Register of Debates,* 24th Cong., 2nd sess., 1674–76.
35. On "outgeneraling," see *Portsmouth Journal of Literature and Politics,* July 14, 1838. Adams would begin a speech in the morning hour, before the call to order, as a way to get around the gag rule; see "The Right of Petition," *Farmer's Cabinet,* July 20, 1838; and "Mr. Adams' Texas Speech," *New Bedford Mercury,* July 20, 1838. On outsmarting his opponents, see "Right of Petition in New Form," *Salem Gazette,* Dec. 25, 1838. Adams read a petition from the ladies of his district for abolishing slavery in the District of Columbia, which was received because they were from his district. He defended another petition from women and asked Congress why anyone would be afraid of females: "Blood, insurrection, murders?" See *New-Bedford Mercury,* Jan. 13, 1837. For criticisms of his improper behavior, which was "querulous, boisterous, passionate, silly," see "Abolition, Petitions, &c.," *Richmond Enquirer,* Dec. 27, 1837; he was called a "worn-out statesman and broken down politician" in *Macon* (Ga.) *Telegraph,* March 3, 1837.
36. *Register of Debates* notes that "Mr. A then addressed the House at length," which meant that most of his speech was omitted. See Feb. 10, 1837, and Mr. Adams, Feb. 11, 1837, *Register of Debates,* 24th Cong., 2nd sess., 1683–85, 1723; Frederick, "John Quincy Adams, Slavery, and the Disappearance of the Right of Petition," 137.

37. Holton, *Abigail Adams,* 242, 304–6. By 1810, John Adams saw Jefferson's relationship with Sally Hemings as "Blotts" on his character, part of the "foul contagion in the human Character Negro Slavery"; see JA to Joseph Ward, Jan. 8, 1810, AP/FOL. On Missouri and the "bleaching process," see Feb. 24, 1820, *DJQA.* On Texas as a nursery for slaves, see "Address at Braintree," June 7, 1842, 8. On "internal piracy," see "Letter from Mr. Adams, October 27, 1838," *Niles' National Register,* Nov. 17, 1838; and "Mr. Adams to His Constituents," *Farmer's Cabinet,* Nov. 9, 1838; also MacLean, "Othello Scorned."
38. Mason, "Battle of the Slaveholding Liberators," 675–76. On Haiti, see Douglas R. Egerton, "The Empire of Liberty Reconsidered," in Horn, Lewis, and Onuf, *Revolution of 1800,* 309–30; Johnson, *Diplomacy in Black and White,* esp. 17–18, 54–56, 60–61, 97. For a good synthesis of Washington's hands-off policy and assumption that slavery would eventually expire of its own accord, see Dorothy Twohig, "'That Species of Property': Washington's Role in the Controversy over Slavery," in Higgenbotham, *George Washington Reconsidered,* 114–38.
39. Nov. 24, 1824, *DJQA;* "From the Quincy Patriot: Letter from Mr. Adams," in *Emancipator,* Sept. 6, 1838, referring to JQA's August 13, 1837, letter to his constituents; "Address at Braintree," 17; June 8–27, 1840, *DJQA;* Waldstreicher and Mason, *John Quincy Adams and Slavery,* 239–40.
40. JQA to E. Wright Jr., April 16, 1837, AP/microfilm, reel 153; MacLean, "Othello Scorned," 152. The degeneration charge is from the August 1837 letter to his constituents, in which he also praised Washington for having liberated his slaves. See "From the Quincy Patriot: Letter from Mr. Adams."
41. *Letters from John Quincy Adams to His Constituents,* 41; "Visit of Hon. J. Q. Adams to Hingham. His Reception by the Ladies," *Portsmouth Journal of Literature and Politics,* Aug. 18, 1838; in 1801, with his father, he attended "The Sons of the Pilgrims" anniversary ceremony; see *Columbian Courier,* Dec. 25, 1801; JQA mentioned the 1790 census in a May 21, 1836, letter to a constituent, S. Sampson, Collector of Customs, Plymouth, Mass.; in "John Quincy Adams and Martial Law," 447–48; and he repeated and expanded the same argument in the published "Letter from J. Q. Adams, to the Elders of the Old Colony Memorial, the Hingham Patriot, and the Quincy Patriot, in the Twelfth Congressional District of Massachusetts, July 23, 1841," *Emancipator,* Sept. 2, 1841; and "Trial of Mr. Adams," Jan. 26, 1842, *Emancipator and Free Republican,* Feb. 2, 1842; Mr. Adams, Jan. 26, 1842, *Cong. Globe,* 27th Cong., 2nd sess., 176–77. The Massachusetts abolitionist and poet John Greenleaf Whittier praised JQA as finally free from the constraints of being a public functionary, saying that he had recovered the "free spirit of the puritan" and was "standing on his own patrimonial acres, the representative of men not unworthy of their ancestors who from the Mayflower stepped upon the Rock of Plymouth." See "Letter of John Adams," *Emancipator,* Sept. 6, 1838.
42. On Webster's John Adams, see "American Eloquence," *New Hampshire Patriot and State Gazette,* July 31, 1837. Among others quoting the words as if they came directly from John Adams's mouth are "Hear a Patriot of '76," *Baltimore Patriot,* July 11, 1831; "John Adams," *Rhode Island American and Gazette,* July 15, 1831; "John Adams," *Newburyport Herald,* July 22, 1831; "Speech of John Adams," *Madison* (Wis.) *Enquirer,* Aug. 4, 1839. Some newspapers altered some of the language of the apocryphal Adams speech in Webster's eulogy, for reasons unknown, though the gist of it was the same.
43. "A Great Outrage!," *Richmond Enquirer,* Feb. 20, 1838; see also "Northern Insolence," *Daily Atlas,* Feb. 15, 1842, reprinted by *Petersburg* (Va.) *Intelligencer.*
44. Craig M. Simpson, *A Good Southerner: The Life of Henry A. Wise of Virginia* (Chapel Hill: University of North Carolina Press, 1985), 38–43; Saltonstall's defense, in *Daily Atlas,* Jan. 31, 1842; his speech was only briefly mentioned in the official record of congressional proceedings, *Cong. Globe,* Jan. 27, 1842, 27th Cong., 2nd sess., 184; Erastus Brooks, "Sketches of Our Public Men, Number Three: John Quincy Adams of Massachusetts," *Literary Examiner and Western Monthly Review,* July 1, 1839. A precious account of JQA's self-defense when the House debated his censure in January–February 1842, is in Quincy, *Memoir of the Life of John Quincy Adams,* 343–52.
45. When he presented a petition for abolishing slavery in the District of Columbia, JQA stated outright that he did not support it himself; see *Pittsfield Sun,* Dec. 22, 1831; JQA attacked for not supporting the Quakers, in *Salem Gazette,* May 18, 1832; as a "flaming abolitionist" in "A Portrait of Consistency," *Richmond Enquirer,* Nov. 4, 1836; also see *New Hampshire Sentinel,* Feb. 23, 1837; "Mr. Adams's Opinion on Slavery," *Barre* (Mass.) *Gazette,* Feb. 24, 1837; "Abolition and John Quincy Adams," *New-Bedford Mercury,* May 3, 1839; "Second Letter on Slavery," *New-Bedford Mercury,* May 6, 1839; *Emancipator,* June 13, 1839; "Adams' Letter," *Essex Gazette* (Salem, Mass.), May 14, 1839; anti-association views in "The Counsels of Wisdom," *New-London Gazette,* March 3, 1840; "A Letter from John Quincy Adams," *New Bedford Mercury,* March 3, 1840.
46. Jan. 1, 1840, *DJQA;* JQA, *Letters to His Constituents,* 3; *Address of John Quincy Adams, to His Constituents of the Twelfth Congressional District, at Braintree, September 17, 1842* (Boston: J. H. Eastburn, 1842), 16–18, an address originally published in *Daily Atlas,* Nov. 17, 1842.
47. JQA, *Parties in the United States,* 64, 72; Jeffrey Glover, "Witnessing African War: Slavery, the Laws of War, and Anglo-American Abolitionism," *William and Mary Quarterly* 74 (July 2017): 503–32. It was common to

compare slaves and impressed sailors; see "Another List of Slaves, Not Africans, but Americans," *Independent Chronicle,* Aug. 5, 1811; also Mason, "Battle of the Slaveholding Liberators."

48. "Letter from John Quincy Adams, Respecting the Captured Africans of the Amistad, Nov. 19, 1839," *Connecticut Courant,* Jan. 1, 1840. For background on the case, see Jones, *Mutiny on the* Amistad; and Rediker, Amistad *Rebellion.*
49. JQA, *Argument of John Quincy Adams,* 6, 12, 86; Roberts-Miller, "John Quincy Adams's Amistad Argument."
50. JQA, *Argument of John Quincy Adams,* 25, 16–17.
51. Ibid., 39–40, 43, 134–45; Feb. 23, 1841, *DJQA;* Waldstreicher and Mason, *John Quincy Adams and the Politics of Slavery,* 248–49; after the trial, JQA highlighted the key issues in "Another Letter from Mr. Adams," *Emancipator,* April 1, 1841. One scholar has argued that the executive branch "did its best to re-enslave the captives and ship them back to Cuba"; see Wiecek, "Slavery and Abolition Before the United States Supreme Court," esp. 41. The issue of habeas corpus was a crucial right denied to sailors when impressed into the British navy. It was an issue in the Amistad case as well. In the earlier circuit court proceedings, the presiding judge, Associate Justice Smith Thompson, denied the writ of habeas corpus because it would have released the prisoners without determining whether they were slaves and thus given them legal standing as free persons. See *The African Captives: Trial of the Prisoners of the* Amistad *on the Writ of Habeas Corpus . . . September Term 1839* (New York: n.p., 1839); and Howard Jones, "The Impact of the Amistad Case on Race and Law in America," in Gordon-Reed, *Race on Trial,* 14–25.
52. April 4, 1841, and June 3, 1843, *DJQA.*
53. *U.S. v. The Amistad,* 15 Pet. 518 (1841); Simpson, *Good Southerner,* 42–43; Spaulding, "Dueling in the District of Columbia"; Pasley, "Minnows, Spies, and Aristocrats," esp. 616, 627–29; on prostitutes, see Nancy Isenberg, "The Infamous Anne Royall: Jacksonian Gossip, Scribbler, and Scold," in Feeley and Frost, *When Private Talk Goes Public,* 78–100. For his part, Adams described Wise's speaking style as "a motley compound of eloquence and folly, of braggart impudence and childish vanity, of self-laudation and Virginian narrow-mindedness." See JQA, *Memoirs,* 10:409.
54. JQA, *Social Compact,* 10–11, 18, 30–31.
55. July 11, 30, and 31, 1847, *DALCA,* 2:766–67.
56. March 14, 1847, *DJQA.*
57. Dec. 18, 1847, *DALCA,* 2:768.
58. Richards, *Life and Times of Congressman John Quincy Adams,* 170–90; Greenberg, *Wicked War,* 104–6; Parsons, *John Quincy Adams,* 263–67.
59. Benton, *Thirty Years' View,* 2:707–9; "Illness and Death of Mr. Adams," *Farmer's Cabinet,* March 2, 1848.
60. "Men and Things at the Capital," *Wachusett Star* (Barre, Mass.), March 14, 1848; "Death of John Quincy Adams," *Wisconsin Democrat,* March 4, 1848; *Emancipator,* March 15, 1848; "Habits of Mr. Adams," *Charleston* (S.C.) *Southern Patriot,* March 1, 1848.
61. Burstein, *America's Jubilee,* 303–4; "On the Life and Character of the Late Ex-president Adams," *New York Herald,* March 9, 1848.
62. Lord, *Eulogy on the Honorable John Quincy Adams.*
63. Quincy, *Municipal History of the Town and City of Boston,* 11–13, 28.
64. Everett, *Eulogy on the Life and Character of John Quincy Adams.*
65. Reynolds, *Walt Whitman's America,* 107–22; Walt Whitman, *The People and John Quincy Adams,* ed. William White (Berkeley Heights, N.J.: Oriole Press, 1961).

AD CONSUMMANDUM

1. JQA to Nabby Adams, April 15, 1795, in *AFC,* 10:410.
2. JA to JQA, May 3, 1816, AP/FOL.
3. July 1826, Charles Francis Adams Diary, AP/microfilm, reel 56.
4. "Mr. Adams' Coachman," *Emancipator,* Feb. 25, 1841.
5. JQA as a "worn-out," "broken-down" statesman is in the *Macon* (Ga.) *Telegraph,* March 2, 1837. Jefferson conceived neurophysiological categories, which he first elaborated on in correspondence of 1795 and which were repeated in newspapers of 1830: the "sickly, weakly, timid man [that is, the aristocrat or Federalist] fears the people, and is a tory by nature. The healthy, strong and bold man [that is, the democrat] cherishes them [the people] and is a Whig by nature." See *Portland* (Maine) *Weekly Argus,* June 19, 1830; Burstein, *Jefferson's Secrets,* 199–205. The "British Party" attack was used by Representative Henry Wise of Virginia when he called for JQA's censure; see *Boston Daily Atlas,* Jan. 31, 1842.
6. Set apart even from the usual hyperbole, Bancroft repeatedly celebrates Jackson's rashness, his "defiance of others' authority," terming him "the passionate, the impetuous." See Dusenberry, *Monument to the Memory of General*

Andrew Jackson, 34–35, 40, 46–48, 75–76, 85, 101, 103. On Jefferson's posthumous reputation as a herald of democracy, see Merrill D. Peterson, *The Jefferson Image in the American Mind* (New York: Oxford University Press, 1960); Francis D. Cogliano, *Thomas Jefferson: Reputation and Legacy* (Charlottesville: University of Virginia Press, 2008); and Andrew Burstein, *Democracy's Muse: How Thomas Jefferson Became an FDR Liberal, a Reagan Republican, and a Tea Party Fanatic, All the While Being Dead* (Charlottesville: University of Virginia Press, 2015).

7. Burstein, *Passions of Andrew Jackson,* 233–35.
8. John Henry Sherburne, editor's introduction to Wood, *Suppressed History of the Administration of John Adams,* 15. Twenty years earlier, Sherburne authored a biography of John Paul Jones, soliciting material from Jefferson at the time and reminding Jefferson that he had named Sherburne's father to a judgeship in New Hampshire. See Sherburne to Jefferson, Feb. 23, 1825, Founders Online.
9. Shaw, *Character of John Adams,* 309.
10. We have each, independently, written at length about the rhetorical versus the real political personalities of the historical actors in question. See variously, *Passions of Andrew Jackson, Fallen Founder, White Trash,* and *Democracy's Muse.*
11. On the character and development of nineteenth-century American biographical studies, see Casper, *Constructing American Lives,* esp. chap. 4; on middle-class reading habits, see Zboray, *Fictive People;* on the press, see Pasley, *"Tyranny of Printers."*
12. Wiltse, "John Quincy Adams and the Party System."
13. JA to Rush, Nov. 11, 1807, AP/FOL.
14. These characterizations come from JQA, *Parties in the United States,* esp. 21–33, 97–105. Jefferson himself wavered on the viability and reliability of party organs. As president, he adhered to the sunny optimism for which he was known, feeling he could count on the wisdom of the American people to rally round his party. He refused to see himself as even the titular head of a party yet realized (at least in the short run) that it was necessary to organize, though good-hearted citizens would not require the institution of the party as an engine to galvanize voters and turn back a permanent opposition party. He went so far as to project a kind of snowball effect, by which moderate Federalists would be brought into the fold; he meant those who disagreed on foreign policy matters but whose republican impulses otherwise directed them toward his party. (From the first inaugural: "We are all Republicans; we are all Federalists.") Toward the end of his second term as president, however, Jefferson grew, and remained thereafter, fearful of a resurgence of the Federalists. And toward the end of his life, he even considered JQA as a possible catalyst.
15. Ketcham, *Individualism and Public Life,* 169–70. To make matters worse, the tactics parties used at the state and local levels (to gain advantage in the Electoral College) increasingly bore the marks of a religious revival. This element became especially striking in the election of 1840, when the Whig Party discovered that it could beat the Democrats at their own game; see Major Wilson, *The Presidency of Martin Van Buren* (Lawrence: University Press of Kansas, 1984), 191–93.
16. Various diary entries of 1840, in Waldstreicher and Mason, *John Quincy Adams and the Politics of Slavery,* 239–40.
17. Along with JQA's *Parties in the United States* and Van Buren's *Inquiry into the Origin and Course of Political Parties in the United States,* Jefferson's obsession with the "history of parties" is treated in Burstein, *Jefferson's Secrets,* chap. 8.
18. Nagel, *Descent from Glory;* Smith, "Claiming the Centennial."
19. Joseph Epstein, *Snobbery: The American Version* (Boston: Houghton Mifflin, 2002), chaps. 2–4. "Snobbery thrives where society is most open," the author curiously observes (29).
20. Rush to JA, June 13, 1808, in *Letters of Benjamin Rush,* 965–67; JA to Rush, June 20, 1808, AP/FOL. "Sacred and undeniable" were Jefferson's original choice of words to modify "truths," edited to read "self-evident."
21. See the good critical essay by David Waldstreicher, "John Quincy Adams: The Life, the Diary, and the Biographers," in Waldstreicher, *Companion to John Adams and John Quincy Adams,* chap. 12.
22. "Liberty" can be paradoxical, meant to be cautiously self-activated and actively self-moderated. It is magnanimous. It celebrates existence under politically clear skies with a lack of restriction in everyday life. But it also implies the granting of rights; whereas "freedom," even as it incorporates a lack of restrictions, associates more with protections *against* untoward effects, that is, *freedom from* tyranny, oppression, fear, want. In their most banal, indeed perverse, formulations, both "liberty" and "freedom" have been attached to gun ownership.
23. See esp. Winterer, *American Enlightenments,* 240–51; Paul Giles, *Transatlantic Insurrections: British Culture and the Formation of American Literature* (Philadelphia: University of Pennsylvania Press, 2001); Andrew Burstein and Nancy Isenberg, "What They Really Mean by American Exceptionalism," Salon.com, April 8, 2011.
24. JA, *Defence,* letter 22, 194–99.
25. JA, *Discourses on Davila,* nos. 2 and 9.

26. JQA, *Lectures on Rhetoric and Oratory,* lecture 5, 127–28.
27. Distinction spelled out in *Baltimore Patriot,* Jan. 10, 1828, and elsewhere.
28. Cicero, *De re publica,* book 3, 28.
29. Shakespeare, *Richard II,* act 1, scene 1; *Othello,* act 2, scene 3.
30. July 7, 1794, *DJQA;* Cicero, *De re publica,* book 3, 33.
31. Glick, "Best Possible World of John Quincy Adams."
32. JQA, *Social Compact;* Rahskopf, "John Quincy Adams' Theory and Practice of Public Speaking," esp. 33–35.
33. Gustafson, "Histories of Democracy and Empire," 116.

Bibliography

UNPUBLISHED PAPERS (NON-ADAMS)

AMERICAN PHILOSOPHICAL SOCIETY
William Temple Franklin Diary

LIBRARY OF CONGRESS
Thomas Jefferson Papers
James McHenry Papers
Gouverneur Morris Papers

MASSACHUSETTS HISTORICAL SOCIETY
Benjamin Bangs Diary
Isaac Bangs Diary
Francis Dana Papers
Mercy Otis Warren Papers

ORIGINAL ADAMS TEXTS

Adams, Charles Francis. *The Life of John Adams*. 2 vols. Philadelphia: J. B. Lippincott, 1871.

Adams, George W. *An Oration Delivered at Quincy, on the Fifth of July 1824*. Boston: Ezra Lincoln, 1824.

Adams, Henry. *A Catalogue of the Books of John Quincy Adams at the Boston Athenæum*. Boston: Athenæum, 1938.

Adams, John. *Correspondence of the Late President Adams, Originally Published in the "Boston Patriot."* Boston: Everett and Munroe, 1809.

———. *A Defence of the Constitutions of Government of the United States of America*. London: C. Dilly, 1787.

———. *Discourses on Davila: A Series of Papers, on Political History*. Boston: Russell and Cutler, 1805.

———. *Thoughts on Government*. Philadelphia: John Gill, 1776.

Adams, John Quincy. *An Address, Delivered at the Request of the Committee of Arrangements for Celebrating the Anniversary of Independence, at the City of Washington on the Fourth of July 1821*. Cambridge, Mass.: Hilliard and Metcalf, 1821.

———. *American Principles: A Review of the Works of Fisher Ames*. Boston: Everett and Munroe, 1809.

———. *Argument of John Quincy Adams, Before the Supreme Court of the United States, in the Case of the United States, Appellants, vs. Cinque, and Others, Africans, Captured in the Schooner* Amistad. . . . New York: S. W. Benedict, 1841.

———. *Dermot Mac Morrogh; or, The Conquest of Ireland: An Historical Tale of the Twelfth Century in Four Cantos*. Boston: Carter, Hendee, 1832.

———. *An Eulogy on the Life and Character of James Madison, Fourth President of the United States*. Boston: American Stationers' Co., 1836.

———. *Lectures on Rhetoric and Oratory*. Cambridge, Mass.: Hilliard and Metcalf, 1810.

———. *Letter to Mr. Harrison Gray Otis, a Member of the Senate of Massachusetts, on the Present State of Our National Affairs*. 1808. Baltimore: Office of the *Baltimore Patriot*, 1824.

———. *Letters from John Quincy Adams to His Constituents of the Twelfth Congressional District in Massachusetts: To Which Is Added His Speech in Congress, Delivered February 9, 1837*. Boston: Isaac Knapp, 1837.

———. *An Oration Addressed to the Citizens of the Town of Quincy, on the Fourth of July, 1831*. Boston: Richardson, Lord, and Holbrook, 1831.

———. *Parties in the United States*. New York: Greenberg, 1941.

———. *Poems of Religion and Society*. New York: William H. Graham, 1848.

———. *The Social Compact: Exemplified in the Constitution of the Commonwealth of Massachusetts*. . . . Providence, R.I.: Knowles and Vose, 1842.

———. *Speech of the Hon. John Quincy Adams, in the House of Representatives, on the State of the Nation: Delivered May 25, 1836*. New York: H. R. Piercy, 1836.

Adams, John Quincy, and Lewis Condit. *Report of the Minority of the Committee on Manufactures, Submitted to the House of Representatives of the United States, February 28, 1833*. Boston: Beals, Homer, 1833.

The Adams-Jefferson Letters: The Complete Correspondence Between Thomas Jefferson and Abigail and John Adams. Edited by Lester J. Cappon. Chapel Hill: University of North Carolina Press, 1959.

"Correspondence Between John Adams and Mercy Warren." *Collections of the Massachusetts Historical Society*. Vol. 4. Boston: Massachusetts Historical Society, 1878.

Journal and Correspondence of Miss Adams, Daughter of John Adams. Edited by Caroline Amelia Smith deWindt. New York: Wiley and Putnam, 1841.

"Letters of John Quincy Adams to Alexander Hamilton Everett, 1811–1837." *American Historical Review* 11 (Jan. 1906): 332–54.

Memoirs of John Quincy Adams. Edited by Charles Francis Adams. Philadelphia: J. B. Lippincott, 1874.

New Letters of Abigail Adams. Edited by Stewart Mitchell. Boston: Houghton Mifflin, 1947.

OTHER EIGHTEENTH- AND NINETEENTH-CENTURY WORKS

The Adams Memorial, Containing a Sketch of John Adams, the Elder, Together with the Life, Character, Public Services, Last Sickness, Death, and Funeral Obsequies of the Late Venerable John Quincy Adams. Boston: J. B. Hall, 1848.

Austin, James T. *The Life of Elbridge Gerry*. Boston: Wells and Lilly, 1829.

Authentic Copies of the Correspondence of Charles Cotesworth Pinckney, John Marshall, and Elbridge Gerry, Esqrs., Envoys Extraordinary and Ministers Plenipotentiary to the Republic of France. London: J. Debrett, 1798.

Bangs, Edward, ed. *Journal of Lieutenant Isaac Bangs, 1776*. Cambridge, Mass.: John Wilson and Son, 1890.

Benton, Thomas Hart. *Thirty Years' View; or, A History of the Working of the American Government for Thirty Years, from 1820 to 1850*. 2 vols. New York: D. Appleton, 1856.

Blair, Hugh. *Lectures on Rhetoric and Belles Lettres*. 1783. Philadelphia: Troutman & Hayes, 1852.

[Cheetham, James]. *An Answer to Alexander Hamilton's Letter, Concerning the Public Conduct and Character of John Adams*. New York: Johnson and Stryker, 1800.

[Cicero, Marcus Tullius]. *The Political Works of Marcus Tullius Cicero*. Translated by Francis Barham. London: Edmund Spettigue, 1841.

[Coleman, William]. *Remarks and Criticisms of the Hon. John Quincy Adams's Letter to the Hon. Harrison Gray Otis*. Boston: Joshua Cushing, 1808.

Cranch, William. *Memoir of the Life, Character, and Writings of John Adams*. Washington, D.C.: S. A. Elliot, 1827.

Crocker, Hannah Mather. *Reminiscences and Traditions of Boston*. Edited by Eileen Hunt Botting and Sarah L. Houser. Boston: New England Historic Genealogical Society, 2011. Prepared by 1827, hitherto unpublished.

Cumberland, Richard, and John Maxwell. *A Treatise of the Laws of Nature*. London: n.p., 1727.

Defoe, Daniel. *Jure Divino: A Satyr: In Twelve Books*. London: n.p., 1706.

The Diaries of Gouverneur Morris. Edited by Melanie Randolph Miller. 2 vols. Charlottesville: University of Virginia Press, 2011–2018.

Dusenberry, B. M. *Monument to the Memory of General Andrew Jackson*. Philadelphia: Walker and Gillis, 1846.

Everett, Edward. *A Eulogy on the Life and Character of John Quincy Adams*. Boston: Dutton and Wentworth, 1848.

Goddard, Delano A. *Newspapers and Newspaper Writers in New England, 1787–1815*. Boston: A. Williams, 1880.

Goodell, William. *The Legion of Liberty! And Force of Truth*. New York: American A.S. [Anti-Slavery] Society, 1842.

Hale, Edward Everett, and Edward Everett Hale Jr. *Franklin in France*. Boston: Roberts Brothers, 1887.

Hamilton, Alexander. *Letter from Alexander Hamilton Concerning the Public Conduct and Character of John Adams*. New York: John Furman, 1800.

Irving, Washington. *The Life and Voyages of Christopher Columbus*. Edited by John Harmon McElroy. Boston: Twayne, 1981 [1828].

———. *Sketch Book*. Edited by Haskell Springer. Boston: Twayne, 1978 [1819–1820].

Jefferson, Thomas. *Notes on the State of Virginia*. Edited by William Peden. Chapel Hill: University of North Carolina Press, 1954 [1787].

Lesage, Alain-René. *The Adventures of Gil Blas of Santillane*. London: J. Rivington, 1761.

Letters of William Vans Murray to John Quincy Adams, 1797–1803. Edited by Worthington Chauncey Ford. Washington, D.C.: American Historical Association, 1914.

Levasseur, Auguste. *Lafayette in America in 1824 and 1825; or, Journal of a Voyage to the United States*. 2 vols. Philadelphia: Carey & Lea, 1829. Facsimile reprint by Research Reprints. New York, 1970.

Lord, Nathan. *A Eulogy on the Honorable John Quincy Adams, Delivered March 24, 1848*. Hanover, N.H.: Dartmouth Press, 1848.

Machiavelli, Niccolò. *The Works of Nicholas Machiavel*. 4 vols. London: T. Davies, 1775. Adams-owned volume containing John Adams's marginalia.

Maury, Sarah Mytton. *The Statesmen of America in 1846*. London: Longman, Brown, Green, and Longmans, 1847.

Notes of Debates in the Federal Convention of 1787 Reported by James Madison. Athens: Ohio University Press, 1966.

Papers of Benjamin Franklin. Edited by Leonard W. Labaree et al. 42 vols. New Haven: Yale University Press, 1959–.

Pattee, William S. *A History of Old Braintree and Quincy*. Quincy, Mass.: Green & Prescott, 1878.

Pickering, Timothy. *A Letter from the Honorable Timothy Pickering, a Senator of the United States from the State of Massachusetts, Exhibiting to His Constituents a View of the Imminent Danger of an Unnecessary and Ruinous War*. Boston: Greenough and Stebbins, 1808.

The Political Character of John Quincy Adams Delineated. Albany, N.Y.: Albany Argus, 1828.

Le politique hollandais. Amsterdam: J. A. Crajenschot, 1781.

Porter, Edward G. *Rambles in Old Boston New England*. Boston: Cupples and Hurd, 1887.

Price, Richard. *Observations on the Importance of the American Revolution, and the Means of Making It a Benefit to the World, to Which Is Added, a Letter from M. Turgot*. London: T. Cadell, 1785.

Proceedings and Debates of the Virginia State Convention of 1828–30. Richmond: Samuel Shepherd, 1830.

"Quandary, Christopher." *Some Serious Considerations on the Present State of Parties*. Richmond: Thomas W. White, 1827.

Quincy, Josiah. *Memoir of the Life of John Quincy Adams*. Boston: Phillips, Sampson, 1859.

———. *A Municipal History of the Town and City of Boston, During the Two Centuries from September 17, 1630, to September 17, 1830*. Boston: Charles C. Little and James Brown, 1852.

Selected Writings of Thomas Paine. Edited by Ian Shapiro and Jane E. Calvert. New Haven, Conn.: Yale University Press, 2014.

A Selection of Eulogies, Pronounced in the Several States, in Honor of Those Illustrious Patriots and Statesmen, John Adams and Thomas Jefferson. Hartford, Conn.: D. F. Robinson, 1826.

Seward, William H. *Life and Public Services of John Quincy Adams*. Auburn, N.Y.: Derby, Miller, 1849.

Smith, Adam. *The Theory of Moral Sentiments*. Amherst, N.Y.: Prometheus Books, 2000 [1759].

[Smith, William Loughton]. *The Pretensions of Thomas Jefferson to the Presidency Examined; and the Charges Against John Adams Refuted*. Philadelphia: n.p., 1796.

Storrs, Richard S. *An Address, Delivered in Braintree, on the Occasion of the Inauguration of John Quincy Adams, Esq., to the Presidency of the United States*. Boston: Munroe and Francis, 1825.

Van Buren, Martin. *Inquiry into the Origin and Course of Political Parties in the United States*. New York: Hurd and Houghton, 1867.

Warren, Mercy Otis. *History of the Rise, Progress, and Termination of the American Revolution*. 3 vols. Boston: Manning and Loring, 1805.

Watson, Winslow C., ed. *Men and Times of the Revolution; or, Memoirs of Elkanah Watson*. New York: Dana, 1856.

[Webster, Daniel]. *Daniel Webster's First Oration at Bunker Hill, June 17, 1825*. New York: Silver, Burdett, 1897.

[Webster, Noah]. *A Letter to General Hamilton, Occasioned by His Letter to President Adams*. Philadelphia, 1800.

White, William Charles. *An Oration, in Commemoration of the Anniversary of American Independence, Delivered in Boston, July 4, 1809, at the Request of the Bunker-Hill Association*. Boston: J. Belcher, 1809.

Wise, Henry A. *Seven Decades of the Union*. Philadelphia: J. B. Lippincott, 1872.

Wood, John. *Suppressed History of the Administration of John Adams*. Philadelphia: Walker and Gillis, 1846.

MODERN SECONDARY SOURCES

Adams, David. "Internal Military Intervention in the United States." *Journal of Peace Research* 32 (May 1995): 197–211.

Adams, William Howard. *The Paris Years of Thomas Jefferson*. New Haven, Conn.: Yale University Press, 1997.

Aldridge, Alfred Owen. *Franklin and His French Contemporaries*. New York: New York University Press, 1957.

———. "John Adams Meets the Abbé Mably." *Dalhousie French Studies* 52 (Fall 2000): 88–99.

Alexander, John. *Samuel Adams: The Life of an American Revolutionary*. Lanham, Md.: Rowman & Littlefield, 2002.

Allgor, Catherine. *Parlor Politics: In Which the Ladies of Washington Help Build a City and a Government*. Charlottesville: University Press of Virginia, 2000.

Ammon, Harry. *James Monroe: The Quest for National Identity*. 1971. Charlottesville: University Press of Virginia, 1990.

Barker-Benfield, G. J. *Abigail and John Adams: The Americanization of Sensibility*. Chicago: University of Chicago Press, 2010.

———. *The Culture of Sensibility: Sex and Society in Eighteenth-Century Britain*. Chicago: University of Chicago Press, 1992.

Barnard, James Munson. *A Sketch of Anne Robert Jacques Turgot*. Boston: Geo. H. Ellis, 1899.

Baron, Robert C., and Conrad Edick Wright, eds. *The Libraries, Leadership, and Legacy of John Adams and Thomas Jefferson*. Golden, Colo.: Fulcrum, 2010.

Bartoloni-Tuazon, Kathleen. *For Fear of an Elective King: George Washington and the Presidential Title Controversy of 1789*. Ithaca, N.Y.: Cornell University Press, 2014.

Becker, Ernest. *The Structure of Evil: An Essay on the Unification of the Science of Man*. New York: Free Press, 1968.

Bemis, Samuel Flagg. *John Quincy Adams and the Union*. New York: Knopf, 1956.

Ben-Atar, Doron, and Barbara B. Oberg, eds. *Federalists Reconsidered*. Charlottesville: University Press of Virginia, 1998.

Benes, Peter, ed. *In Our Own Words: New England Diaries, 1600 to the Present*. Boston: Dublin Seminar for New England Folklife, Boston University, 2006/2007.

Berry, Stephen R. *A Path in the Mighty Waters: Shipboard Life and Atlantic Crossings to the New World*. New Haven, Conn.: Yale University Press, 2015.

Beveridge, Albert J. *The Life of John Marshall*. 4 vols. Boston: Houghton Mifflin, 1916–1919.

Billias, George Athan. *Elbridge Gerry: Founding Father and Republican Statesman*. New York: McGraw-Hill, 1976.

Blair, Robert R., and Robin D. Coblentz. "The Trials of Mr. Justice Samuel D. Chase." *Maryland Law Review* 27 (1967): 365–86.

Blumberg, Philip I. *Repressive Jurisprudence in the Early American Republic: The First Amendment and the Legacy of English Law*. New York: Cambridge University Press, 2010.

Brooks, Van Wyck. *The Flowering of New England, 1815–1865*. New York: E. P. Dutton, 1936.

Broussard, James H. *The Southern Federalists, 1800–1816*. Baton Rouge: Louisiana State University Press, 1978.

Brown, Richard D. *Self-Evident Truths: Contesting Equal Rights from the Revolution to the Civil War*. New Haven, Conn.: Yale University Press, 2017.

———. *The Strength of a People: The Idea of an Informed Citizenry in America, 1650–1870*. Chapel Hill: University of North Carolina Press, 1996.

Burstein, Andrew. *America's Jubilee*. New York: Knopf, 2001.

———. *The Inner Jefferson: Portrait of a Grieving Optimist*. Charlottesville: University Press of Virginia, 1995.

———. *Jefferson's Secrets: Death and Desire at Monticello*. New York: Basic Books, 2005.

———. *Lincoln Dreamt He Died: The Midnight Visions of Remarkable Americans from Colonial Times to Freud*. New York: Palgrave, 2013.

———. *The Original Knickerbocker: The Life of Washington Irving*. New York: Basic Books, 2007.

———. *The Passions of Andrew Jackson*. New York: Knopf, 2003.

———. "The Political Character of Sympathy." *Journal of the Early Republic* 21 (Winter 2001): 601–32.

———. *Sentimental Democracy: The Evolution of America's Romantic Self-Image*. New York: Hill and Wang, 1999.

Burstein, Andrew, and Nancy Isenberg. *Madison and Jefferson*. New York: Random House, 2010.

Cahill, Edward. *Liberty of the Imagination: Aesthetic Theory, Literary Form, and Politics in the Early United States*. Philadelphia: University of Pennsylvania Press, 2012.

Campbell, Randolph B. *An Empire for Slavery: The Peculiar Institution of Slavery in Texas, 1821–1865*. Baton Rouge: Louisiana State University Press, 1989.

Carr, Jacqueline Barbara. *After the Siege: A Social History of Boston, 1775–1800*. Boston: Northeastern University Press, 2005.

Casper, Scott E. *Constructing American Lives: Biography and Culture in Nineteenth-Century America*. Chapel Hill: University of North Carolina Press, 1999.

Childers, Christopher. *The Webster-Hayne Debate: Defining Nationhood in the Early American Republic*. Baltimore: Johns Hopkins University Press, 2018.

[Cicero, Marcus Tullius]. *De re publica; De legibus*. Translated by Clinton W. Keyes. Cambridge, Mass.: Harvard University Press, 1928.

Clarfield, Gerard H. *Timothy Pickering and the American Republic*. Pittsburgh: University of Pittsburgh Press, 1980.

Cleves, Rachel Hope. *The Reign of Terror in America: Visions of Violence from Anti-Jacobinism to Antislavery*. New York: Cambridge University Press, 2009.

Cole, Donald B. *Vindicating Andrew Jackson: The 1828 Election and the Rise of the Two-Party System*. Lawrence: University Press of Kansas, 2009.

Coleman, Charly. *The Virtues of Abandon: An Anti-individualist History of the French Revolution*. Stanford, Calif.: Stanford University Press, 2014.

Cooper, William J. *The Lost Founding Father: John Quincy Adams and the Transformation of American Politics*. New York: Liveright, 2017.

Corfield, P. J., and L. Hannon, eds. *Hats Off, Gentlemen! Changing Arts of Communication in the Eighteenth Century*. Paris: Honoré Champion, 2017.

Crane, Elaine Forman. "Abigail Adams, Gender Politics, and *The History of Emily Montague*: A Postscript." *William and Mary Quarterly* 64 (Oct. 2007): 839–44.

———. "Political Dialogue and the Spring of Abigail's Discontent." *William and Mary Quarterly* 56 (Oct. 1999): 745–74.

Cunningham, Noble E., Jr. *The Jeffersonian Republicans in Power*. Chapel Hill: University of North Carolina Press, 1963.

Dauer, Manning J. *The Adams Federalists*. Baltimore: Johns Hopkins University Press, 1953.

DeConde, Alexander. *The Quasi-war: The Politics and Diplomacy of the Undeclared War with France, 1797–1801*. New York: Scribner, 1966.

———. "The Role of William Vans Murray in the Peace Negotiations Between France and the United States, 1800." *Huntington Library Quarterly* 15 (Feb. 1952): 185–94.

———. "Washington's Farewell, the French Alliance, and the Election of 1796." *Mississippi Valley Historical Review* 43 (March 1957): 641–58.

Den Hartog, Jonathan J. *Patriotism and Piety: Federalist Politics and Religious Struggle in the New American Nation*. Charlottesville: University of Virginia Press, 2015.

Destler, Chester McArthur. *Joshua Coit: American Federalist, 1758–1798*. Middletown, Conn.: Wesleyan University Press, 1962.

Dull, Jonathan R. *A Diplomatic History of the American Revolution*. New Haven, Conn.: Yale University Press, 1985.

Dungan, Nicholas. *Gallatin: America's Swiss Founding Father*. New York: New York University Press, 2010.

Dyer, Justin Buckley. "After the Revolution: *Somerset* and the Antislavery Tradition in Anglo-American Constitutional Development." *Journal of Politics* 71 (Oct. 2009): 1422–34.

Ekirch, A. Roger. *At Day's Close: Night in Times Past*. New York: Norton, 2005.

Ellis, Joseph J. *First Family: Abigail and John Adams*. New York: Knopf, 2010.

———. *Passionate Sage: The Character and Legacy of John Adams*. New York: W. W. Norton, 1993.

Ellis, Richard E. *The Union at Risk: Jacksonian Democracy, States' Rights, and the Nullification Crisis*. New York: Oxford University Press, 1987.

Elsmere, Jane Shaffer. "Trials of John Fries." *Pennsylvania Magazine of History and Biography* 103 (Oct. 1979): 432–45.

Engels, Jeremy. *Enemyship: Democracy and Counter-revolution in the Early Republic*. East Lansing: Michigan State University Press, 2010.

Evans, William B. "John Adams' Opinion of Benjamin Franklin." *Pennsylvania Magazine of History and Biography* 92 (April 1968): 220–38.

Farrell, James M. "The Writs of Assistance and Public Memory: John Adams and the Legacy of James Otis." *New England Quarterly* 79 (Dec. 2006): 533–56.

Fawcett, Julia H. "Creating Character in '*Chiaro Oscuro*': Sterne's Celebrity, Cibber's *Apology*, and the Life of *Tristram Shandy*." *Eighteenth Century* 53 (Summer 2012): 141–61.

Feeley, Kathleen, and Jennifer Frost, eds. *When Private Talk Goes Public: Gossip in the United States*. New York: Palgrave Macmillan, 2014.

Ferling, John. *Adams vs. Jefferson: The Tumultuous Election of 1800*. New York: Oxford University Press, 2004.

———. *John Adams: A Life*. Knoxville: University of Tennessee Press, 1992.

———. "John Adams, Diplomat." *William and Mary Quarterly* 51 (April 1994): 227–52.

———. *A Leap in the Dark: The Struggle to Create the American Republic*. New York: Oxford University Press, 2003.

———. *Setting the World Ablaze: Washington, Adams, and Jefferson and the American Revolution*. New York: Oxford University Press, 2000.

Ferling, John, and Lewis E. Braverman. "John Adams's Health Reconsidered." *William and Mary Quarterly* 55 (Jan. 1998): 83–104.

Fischer, David Hackett. *The Revolution of American Conservatism: The Federalist Party in the Era of Jeffersonian Democracy*. New York: Harper & Row, 1965.

Forbes, Harriette Merrifield. *New England Diaries, 1602–1800*. New York: Russell & Russell, 1923.

Forbes, Robert Pierce. *The Missouri Compromise and Its Aftermath: Slavery and the Meaning of America*. Chapel Hill: University of North Carolina Press, 2007.

Ford, Lacy K., Jr. "Inventing the Concurrent Majority: Madison, Calhoun, and the Problem of Majoritarianism in American Political Thought." *Journal of Southern History* 60 (Feb. 1994): 19–58.

———. "Reconfiguring the Old South: 'Solving' the Problem of Slavery, 1787–1838." *Journal of American History* 95 (June 2008): 95–122.

Fowler, William M., Jr. *Baron of Beacon Hill: A Biography of John Hancock*. Boston: Houghton Mifflin, 1980.

Frey, Linda S., and Marsha L. Frey. *"Proven Patriots": The French Diplomatic Corps, 1789–1799*. St. Andrews, U.K.: St. Andrews Studies in French History and Culture, 2011.

Fritzsche, Peter. *Stranded in the Present: Modern Time and the Melancholy of History*. Cambridge, Mass.: Harvard University Press, 2004.

Frohock, W. M. "The 'Picaresque' in France Before *Gil Blas*." *Yale French Studies* 38 (1976): 222–29.

Frothingham, Paul Revere. *Edward Everett: Orator and Statesman*. Boston: Houghton Mifflin, 1925.

Gattrell, Vic. *City of Laughter: Sex and Satire in Eighteenth-Century London*. New York: Walker, 2006.

Gelles, Edith. *Abigail and John: Portrait of a Marriage*. New York: William Morrow, 2009.

———. *Portia: The World of Abigail Adams*. Bloomington: Indiana University Press, 1992.

Georgini, Sara. "John Quincy Adams at Prayer." *Church History* 82 (Sept. 2013): 649–58.

Glick, Wendell. "The Best Possible World of John Quincy Adams." *New England Quarterly* 37 (March 1964): 3–17.

Gordon-Reed, Annette. *The Hemingses of Monticello*. New York: W. W. Norton, 2008.

———, ed. *Race on Trial: Law and Justice in American History*. New York: Oxford University Press, 2002.

Grant, James. *John Adams: Party of One*. New York: Farrar, Straus and Giroux, 2005.

Green, Nathaniel C. "'The Focus of the Wills of Converging Millions': Public Opposition to the Jay Treaty and the Origins of the People's Presidency." *Journal of the Early Republic* 37 (Fall 2017): 429–69.

Greenberg, Amy S. *A Wicked War: Polk, Clay, Lincoln, and the 1846 U.S. Invasion of Mexico*. New York: Knopf, 2012.

Gustafson, Sandra M. "Histories of Democracy and Empire." *American Quarterly* 59 (March 2007): 107–33.

Halbrook, Stephen P. "The Swiss Confederation in the Eyes of America's Founders." *Swiss American Historical Society Review* (Nov. 2012): 32–69.

Hammill, Faye, ed. *Literary Culture and Female Authorship in Canada, 1760–2000*. New York: Rodopi, 2003.

Haraszti, Zoltán. *John Adams and the Prophets of Progress*. New York: Grosset and Dunlap, 1952.

Harper, John Lamberton. *American Machiavelli: Alexander Hamilton and the Origins of U.S. Foreign Policy*. New York: Cambridge University Press, 2004.

Head, David. *Privateers of the Americas: Spanish American Privateering from the United States in the Early Republic*. Athens: University of Georgia Press, 2015.

Heffron, Margery M. *Louisa Catherine: The Other Mrs. Adams*. New Haven, Conn.: Yale University Press, 2014.

Heidenreich, Donald E., Jr. "Conspiracy Politics in the Election of 1796." *New York History* 92 (Summer 2011): 151–65.

Heidler, David S., and Jeanne T. Heidler. *Henry Clay: The Essential American*. New York: Random House, 2010.

Heinze, Andrew R. "Schizophrenia Americana: Aliens, Alienists, and the 'Personality Shift' of Twentieth-Century Culture." *American Quarterly* 55 (June 2003): 227–56.

Hickey, Donald R. *The War of 1812*. Urbana: University of Illinois Press, 1989.

Hicks, Philip. "The Roman Matron in Britain: Female Political Influence and Republican Response, ca. 1750–1800." *Journal of Modern History* 77 (March 2005): 35–69.

Higgenbotham, Don, ed. *George Washington Reconsidered*. Charlottesville: University of Virginia Press, 2001.

Higginson, Stephen A. "A Short History of the Right to Petition Government for the Redress of Grievances." *Yale Law Journal* 96 (Nov. 1996): 142–66.

Hoffman, Ronald, et al., eds. *The Economy of Early America: The Revolutionary Period, 1763–1790*. Charlottesville: University Press of Virginia, 1988.

Hofstadter, Richard. *The Idea of a Party System*. Berkeley: University of California Press, 1969.

Holton, Woody. *Abigail Adams*. New York: Free Press, 2009.

———. "Did Democracy Cause the Recession That Led to the Constitution?" *Journal of American History* 92 (Sept. 2005): 442–69.

Horn, James, Jan Ellen Lewis, and Peter S. Onuf, eds. *The Revolution of 1800: Democracy, Race, and the New Republic*. Charlottesville: University of Virginia Press, 2002.

Howe, Daniel Walker. *What Hath God Wrought: The Transformation of America, 1815–1848*. New York: Oxford University Press, 2007.

Howe, John. *Language and Political Meaning in Revolutionary America*. Amherst: University of Massachusetts Press, 2004.

Hutson, James H. "Intellectual Foundations of Early Diplomacy." *Diplomatic History* 1 (Winter 1977): 1–19.

———. *John Adams and the Diplomacy of the American Revolution*. Lexington: University Press of Kentucky, 1980.

———. "John Adams's Title Campaign." *New England Quarterly* 41 (March 1968): 30–39.

Hutton, Patrick H. *History as an Art of Memory*. Hanover, N.H.: University Press of New England, 1993.

Isenberg, Nancy. *Fallen Founder: The Life of Aaron Burr*. New York: Viking, 2007.

———. *White Trash: The 400-Year Untold History of Class in America*. New York: Viking, 2016.

Isenberg, Nancy, and Andrew Burstein, eds. *Mortal Remains: Death in Early America*. Philadelphia: University of Pennsylvania Press, 2003.

Jensen, Merrill. "Democracy and the American Revolution." *Huntington Library Quarterly* 20 (Aug. 1957): 321–41.

Johnson, David. *John Randolph of Roanoke*. Baton Rouge: Louisiana State University Press, 2012.

Johnson, Paul. *The Birth of the Modern: World Society, 1815–1850*. New York: HarperCollins, 1991.

Johnson, Ronald Angelo. *Diplomacy in Black and White: John Adams, Toussaint Louverture, and Their Atlantic World Alliance*. Athens: University of Georgia Press, 2014.

Jones, Howard. *Mutiny on the* Amistad: *The Saga of a Slave Revolt and Its Impact on American Abolition, Law, and Diplomacy*. New York: Oxford University Press, 1987.

Kaplan, Fred. *John Quincy Adams: American Visionary*. New York: HarperCollins, 2014.

Kerber, Linda K., and Walter John Morris. "Politics and Literature: The Adams Family and the Port Folio." *William and Mary Quarterly* 23 (July 1966): 450–76.

Ketcham, Ralph. *Individualism and Public Life: A Modern Dilemma*. New York: Basil Blackwell, 1987.

———. "Jefferson and Madison and the Doctrines of Interposition and Nullification: A Letter of John Quincy Adams." *Virginia Magazine of History and Biography* 66 (April 1958): 178–82.

Kirker, Harold, and James Kirker. *Bulfinch's Boston, 1787–1817*. New York: Oxford University Press, 1964.

Kloek, Joost, and Wijnand Mijnhardt. *1800: Blueprints for a National Community*. Vol. 2 of *Dutch Culture in a European Perspective*. London: Palgrave, 2004.

Kloppenberg, James T. *Toward Democracy: The Struggle for Self-Rule in European and American Thought*. New York: Oxford University Press, 2016.

Knott, Sarah. *Sensibility and the American Revolution*. Chapel Hill: University of North Carolina Press, 2009.

Koch, Adrienne. *Power, Morals, and the Founding Fathers: Essays in the Interpretation of the American Enlightenment*. Ithaca, N.Y.: Cornell University Press, 1961.

Kossmann, E. H. *The Low Countries, 1780–1940*. Oxford: Clarendon Press, 1978.

Kraft, Elizabeth. "Laurence Sterne and the Ethics of Sexual Difference: Chiasmic Narration and Double Desire." *Christianity and Literature* 51 (Spring 2002): 363–85.

Kramer, Michael P. *Imagining Language in America: From the Revolution to the Civil War*. Princeton, N.J.: Princeton University Press, 1992.

Krapp, George Philip. *The English Language in America*. 2 vols. New York: Century, 1925.

Kurtz, Stephen G. "The Political Science of John Adams: A Guide to His Statecraft." *William and Mary Quarterly* 25 (Oct. 1968): 605–13.

———. *The Presidency of John Adams: The Collapse of Federalism, 1795–1800*. Philadelphia: University of Pennsylvania Press, 1957.

Lack, Paul D. "Slavery and the Texas Revolution." *Southwestern Historical Quarterly* 89 (Oct. 1985): 181–202.

Larson, John Lauritz. *Internal Improvement: National Public Works and the Promise of Popular Government in the Early United States*. Chapel Hill: University of North Carolina Press, 2001.

Lederer, Richard M., Jr. *Colonial American English*. Essex, Conn.: Verbatim, 1985.

Levin, Phyllis Lee. *The Remarkable Education of John Quincy Adams*. New York: Palgrave Macmillan, 2015.

Lewis, James E., Jr. *The American Union and the Problem of Neighborhood: The United States and the Collapse of the Spanish Empire, 1783–1829*. Chapel Hill: University of North Carolina Press, 1998.

———. *John Quincy Adams: Policymaker for the Union*. Wilmington, Del.: Scholarly Resources, 2001.

Lipsky, George A. *John Quincy Adams: His Theory and Ideas*. New York: Crowell, 1950.

Lombard, Anne S. *Making Manhood: Growing Up Male in Colonial New England*. Cambridge, Mass.: Harvard University Press, 2003.

Longmore, Paul K. "'Good English Without Idiom or Tone': The Colonial Origins of American Speech." *Journal of Interdisciplinary History* 37 (Spring 2007): 513–42.

Maciag, Drew. *Edmund Burke in America: The Contested Career of the Father of Modern Conservatism*. Ithaca, N.Y.: Cornell University Press, 2013.

MacLean, William Jerry. "Othello Scorned: The Racial Thought of John Quincy Adams." *Journal of the Early Republic* 4 (Summer 1984): 143–60.

Malone, Dumas. *Jefferson and His Time*. 6 vols. Boston: Little, Brown, 1948–1980.

Marshall, David. "Adam Smith and the Theatricality of Moral Sentiments." *Critical Inquiry* 10 (June 1984): 592–613.

Martin, James P. "When Repression Is Democratic and Constitutional: The Federalist Theory of Representation and the Sedition Act of 1798." *University of Chicago Law Review* 66 (Winter 1999): 117–82.

Mason, Matthew. *Apostle of Union: A Political Biography of Edward Everett*. Chapel Hill: University of North Carolina Press, 2016.

———. "The Battle of the Slaveholding Liberators: Great Britain, the United States, and Slavery in the Early Nineteenth Century." *William and Mary Quarterly* 59 (July 2002): 665–96.

Matt, Susan J. *Homesickness: An American History*. New York: Oxford University Press, 2011.

May, Gregory. *Jefferson's Treasure: How Albert Gallatin Saved the New Nation from Debt*. New York: Regnery, 2018.

Mayville, Luke. *John Adams and the Fear of American Oligarchy*. Princeton, N.J.: Princeton University Press, 2016.

McCrossen, Alexis. *Marking Modern Times: A History of Clocks, Watches, and Other Timekeepers in American Life*. Chicago: University of Chicago Press, 2013.

McFadden, David W. "John Quincy Adams, American Commercial Diplomacy, and Russia, 1809–1825." *New England Quarterly* 66 (Dec. 1993): 613–29.

McGlone, Robert E. "Deciphering Memory: John Adams and the Authorship of the Declaration of Independence." *Journal of American History* 85 (Sept. 1998): 411–38.

McLoughlin, William G. "Georgia's Role in Instigating Compulsory Indian Removal." *Georgia Historical Quarterly* 70 (Winter 1986): 605–32.

Mercieca, Jennifer R. *Founding Fictions*. Tuscaloosa: University of Alabama Press, 2010.

Milford, T. A. "Boston's Theatre Controversy and Liberal Notions of Advantage." *New England Quarterly* 72 (March 1999): 61–88.

Miller, Melanie Randolph. *Envoy to the Terror: Gouverneur Morris and the French Revolution*. Dulles, Va.: Potomac Books, 2005.

Moats, Sandra. *Celebrating the Republic: Presidential Ceremony and Popular Sovereignty from Washington to Monroe*. DeKalb: Northern Illinois University Press, 2010.

Morison, Samuel Eliot. *Harrison Gray Otis, 1756–1848: The Urbane Federalist*. Boston: Houghton Mifflin, 1969.

Morris, Walter J. "John Quincy Adams's German Library, with a Catalog of His German Books." *Proceedings of the American Philosophical Society* 118 (Aug. 1974): 321–33.

Murphy, Orville T. "The Comte de Vergennes, the Newfoundland Fisheries, and the Peace Negotiations of 1783: A Reconsideration." *Canadian Historical Review* 46 (March 1965): 32–46.

Murphy, William J., Jr. "John Adams: The Politics of the Additional Army, 1798–1800." *New England Quarterly* 52 (June 1979): 234–49.

Myers, Victoria. "Model Letters, Moral Living: Letter-Writing Manuals by Daniel Defoe and Samuel Richardson." *Huntington Library Quarterly* 66 (2003): 373–91.

Nagel, Paul C. *Descent from Glory: Four Generations of the John Adams Family*. New York: Oxford University Press, 1983.

———. *John Quincy Adams: A Public Life, a Private Life*. New York: Knopf, 1997.

Nelson, Eric. *The Royalist Revolution: Monarchy and the American Founding*. Cambridge, Mass.: Harvard University Press, 2014.

Newell, Margaret Ellen. *From Dependency to Independence: Economic Revolution in Colonial New England*. Ithaca, N.Y.: Cornell University Press, 1998.

Newman, Paul Douglas. *Fries's Rebellion: The Enduring Struggle for the American Revolution*. Philadelphia: University of Pennsylvania Press, 2004.

Newmyer, R. Kent. *John Marshall and the Heroic Age of the Supreme Court*. Baton Rouge: Louisiana State University Press, 2001.

Niven, John. *Martin Van Buren: The Romantic Age of American Politics*. New York: Oxford University Press, 1983.

Nordholt, Jan Willem Schulte. *The Dutch Republic and American Independence*. Chapel Hill: University of North Carolina Press, 1982.

Oliver, Andrew. *Portraits of John and Abigail Adams*. Cambridge, Mass.: Belknap Press, 1967.

O'Neill, Daniel I. "John Adams Versus Mary Wollstonecraft on the French Revolution and Democracy." *Journal of the History of Ideas* 68 (July 2007): 451–76.

Onuf, Peter S. *Jefferson's Empire: The Language of American Nationhood*. Charlottesville: University of Virginia Press, 2000.

———. *The Mind of Thomas Jefferson*. Charlottesville: University of Virginia Press, 2007.

Ostrander, Gilman M. *Republic of Letters: The American Intellectual Community, 1775–1865*. Madison, Wis.: Madison House, 1999.

Paléologue, Maurice. *The Enigmatic Czar: The Life of Alexander I of Russia*. London: H. Hamilton, 1938.

Palmer, Alan. *Alexander I: Tsar of War and Peace*. New York: Harper & Row, 1974.

Park, Benjamin E. *American Nationalisms: Imagining Union in the Age of Revolutions, 1783–1833*. New York: Cambridge University Press, 2018.

Parsons, Lynn Hudson. *The Birth of Modern Politics: Andrew Jackson, John Quincy Adams, and the Election of 1828*. New York: Oxford University Press, 2009.

———. "Continuing Crusade: Four Generations of the Adams Family View Alexander Hamilton." *New England Quarterly* 37 (March 1964): 43–63.

———. *John Quincy Adams*. Madison, Wis.: Madison House, 1998.

———. "'A Perpetual Harrow upon My Feelings': John Quincy Adams and the American Indian." *New England Quarterly* 46 (Sept. 1973): 339–79.

Pasley, Jeffrey L. *The First Presidential Contest: 1796 and the Founding of American Democracy*. Lawrence: University Press of Kansas, 2013.

———. "Minnows, Spies, and Aristocrats: The Social Crisis of Congress in the Age of Martin Van Buren." *Journal of the Early Republic* 27 (Winter 2007): 599–653.

———. *"The Tyranny of Printers": Newspaper Politics in the Early American Republic*. Charlottesville: University Press of Virginia, 2001.

Peart, Daniel. *Era of Experimentation: American Political Practices in the Early Republic*. Charlottesville: University of Virginia Press, 2014.

Pellew, George. *John Jay*. New York: Chelsea House, 1980.

Pencak, William. "From 'Salt of the Earth' to 'Poison and Curse': The Jay and Adams Families and Construction of American Historical Memory." *Early American Studies* 2 (2004): 228–65.

Perl-Rosenthal, Nathan. "Private Letters and Public Diplomacy: The Adams Network and the Quasi-war, 1797–1798." *Journal of the Early Republic* 31 (Summer 2011): 283–311.

Peterson, Merrill D. *The Great Triumvirate: Webster, Clay, and Calhoun*. New York: Oxford University Press, 1987.

Phillipson, Nicholas. *Adam Smith: An Enlightened Life*. New Haven, Conn.: Yale University Press, 2009.

Pole, J. R. "Historians and the Problem of Early Democracy." *American Historical Review* 67 (April 1962): 629–46.

Porter, Roy. *Flesh in the Age of Reason*. New York: W. W. Norton, 2003.

Portolano, Marlana. *The Passionate Empiricist: The Eloquence of John Quincy Adams in the Service of Science*. Albany: State University of New York Press, 2009.

Potkay, Adam S. "Theorizing Civic Eloquence in the Early Republic: The Road from David Hume to John Quincy Adams." *Early American Literature* 34 (1999): 147–70.

Rahe, Paul, ed. *Machiavelli's Liberal Republican Legacy*. New York: Cambridge University Press, 2006.

Rahskopf, Horace G. "John Quincy Adams' Theory and Practice of Public Speaking." *Archives of Speech* 1 (Sept. 1936): 7–98.

Ratcliffe, Donald. *The One-Party Presidential Contest: Adams, Jackson, and 1824's Five-Horse Race*. Lawrence: University Press of Kansas, 2015.

———. "Popular Preferences in the Presidential Election of 1824." *Journal of the Early Republic* 34 (Spring 2014): 45–77.

Rathbun, Lyon. "The Ciceronian Rhetoric of John Quincy Adams." *Rhetorica* 18 (Spring 2000): 175–215.

Reddy, William. *The Navigation of Feeling: A Framework for the History of Emotions*. New York: Cambridge University Press, 2001.

Rediker, Marcus. *The* Amistad *Rebellion: An Atlantic Odyssey of Slavery and Rebellion*. New York: Penguin Press, 2013.

Renker, Elizabeth M. "'Declaration-Men' and the Rhetoric of Self-Presentation." *Early American Literature* 24 (1989): 120–34.

Reynolds, David S. *Walt Whitman's America: A Cultural Biography*. New York: Knopf, 1996.

Richard, Carl J. *The Founders and the Classics: Greece, Rome, and the American Enlightenment*. Cambridge, Mass.: Harvard University Press, 1994.

Richards, Leonard L. *The Life and Times of Congressman John Quincy Adams*. New York: Oxford University Press, 1986.

Roberts-Miller, Patricia. "John Quincy Adams's Amistad Argument: The Problem of Outrage; or, The Constraints of Decorum." *Rhetoric Society Quarterly* 32 (Spring 2002): 3–25.

Rosen, George E. "Political Order and Human Health in Jeffersonian Thought." *Bulletin of the History of Medicine* 26 (1952): 32–44.

Ross, William G. "The Legal Career of John Quincy Adams." *University of Akron Law Review* 23 (Spring 1990): 415–53.

Rothman, Irving N. "Two Juvenalian Satires by John Quincy Adams." *Early American Literature* 6 (Winter 1971/1972): 234–51.

Russell, Greg. *John Quincy Adams and the Public Virtues of Diplomacy*. Columbia: University of Missouri Press, 1995.

Ryerson, Richard Alan. *John Adams's Republic: The One, the Few, and the Many*. Baltimore: Johns Hopkins University Press, 2016.

———. "'Like a Hare Before the Hunters': John Adams and the Idea of Republican Monarchy." *Proceedings of the Massachusetts Historical Society* 107 (1995): 16–29.

———, ed. *John Adams and the Founding of the Republic*. Boston: Northeastern University Press, 2001.

Sadosky, Leonard J., Peter Nicolaisen, Peter S. Onuf, and Andrew J. O'Shaughnessy, eds. *Old World, New World: America and Europe in the Age of Jefferson*. Charlottesville: University of Virginia Press, 2010.

Saltman, Helen Saltzberg. "John Adams's Earliest Essays: The Humphrey Ploughjogger Letters." *William and Mary Quarterly* 37 (Jan. 1980): 125–35.

Sarkela, Sandra J. "Freedom's Call: The Persuasive Power of Mercy Otis Warren's Dramatic Sketches, 1772–1775." *Early American Literature* 44 (2009): 541–68.

Schroeder, John H. "Annexation or Independence: The Texas Issue in American Politics, 1836–1845." *Southwestern Historical Quarterly* 89 (Oct. 1985): 137–64.

Seale, William. *The President's House: A History*. 2 vols. Washington, D.C.: White House Historical Association, 1986.

Shade, William G. "'The Most Delicate and Exciting Topics': Martin Van Buren, Slavery, and the Election of 1836." *Journal of the Early Republic* 18 (Autumn 1998): 456–84.

Shalev, Eran. "Ancient Masks, American Fathers: Classical Pseudonyms During the American Revolution and Early Republic." *Journal of the Early Republic* 23 (Summer 2003): 151–72.

———. *Rome Reborn on Western Shores: Historical Imagination and the Creation of the American Republic*. Charlottesville: University of Virginia Press, 2009.

Shaw, Peter. *The Character of John Adams*. Chapel Hill: University of North Carolina Press, 1976.

Shoemaker, Robert W. "'Democracy' and 'Republic' as Understood in Late Eighteenth-Century America." *American Speech* 41 (May 1966): 83–95.

Sinha, Manisha. *The Slave's Cause: A History of Abolition*. New Haven, Conn.: Yale University Press, 2016.

Slauter, Will. "Constructive Misreadings: Adams, Turgot, and the American State Constitutions." *Papers of the Bibliographical Society of America* 105 (2011): 33–67.

Smith, Craig Bruce. "Claiming the Centennial: The American Revolution's Blood and Spirit in Boston, 1870–1876." *Massachusetts Historical Review* 15 (2013): 7–53.

Smith, James Morton. *Freedom's Fetters: The Alien and Sedition Laws and American Civil Liberties*. Ithaca, N.Y.: Cornell University Press, 1956.

———. "President John Adams, Thomas Cooper, and Sedition: A Case Study in Suppression." *Mississippi Valley Historical Review* 42 (Dec. 1955): 438–65.

Spaulding, Myra L. "Dueling in the District of Columbia." *Records of the Columbia Historical Society* 25 (1928): 117–210.

Stahr, Walter. *John Jay: Founding Father*. New York: Palgrave Macmillan, 2005.

Staloff, Darren. *Hamilton, Adams, Jefferson: The Politics of Enlightenment and the American Founding*. New York: Hill and Wang, 2005.

Staves, Susan. "Don Quixote in Eighteenth-Century England." *Comparative Literature* 24 (Summer 1972): 193–215.

Stinchcombe, William. *The XYZ Affair*. Westport, Conn.: Greenwood Press, 1980.

Strunsky, Robert. "The Cult of Personality." *American Scholar* 25 (Summer 1956): 165–72.

Tanner, John S., and Justin Collings. "How Adams and Jefferson Read Milton and Milton Read Them." *Milton Quarterly* 40 (Oct. 2006): 207–19.

Taylor, Alan S. *American Colonies*. New York: Viking, 2001.

Teed, Paul E. *John Quincy Adams, Yankee Nationalist*. New York: Nova Science, 2006.

Teute, Fredrika J., and David S. Shields. "The Confederation Court." *Journal of the Early Republic* 35 (Summer 2015): 215–26.

Thompson, C. Bradley. *John Adams and the Spirit of Liberty*. Lawrence: University Press of Kansas, 1998.

Thompson, Robert R. "John Quincy Adams, Apostate: From 'Outrageous Federalist' to 'Republican Exile,' 1801–1809." *Journal of the Early Republic* 11 (Summer 1991): 161–83.

Unger, Harlow Giles. *John Hancock: Merchant King and American Patriot*. New York: John Wiley & Sons, 2000.

United States Senate Election, Expulsion, and Censure Cases, 1793–1990. Washington, D.C.: Government Printing Office, 1995.

Valsania, Maurizio. *Jefferson's Body: A Corporeal Biography*. Charlottesville: University of Virginia Press, 2017.

———. *Nature's Man: Thomas Jefferson's Philosophical Anthropology*. Charlottesville: University of Virginia Press, 2013.

Verhoeven, Wil. *Americomania and the French Revolution Debate in Britain, 1789–1802*. New York: Cambridge University Press, 2013.

Waldstreicher, David, ed. *A Companion to John Adams and John Quincy Adams*. Chichester, West Sussex, U.K.: Wiley-Blackwell, 2013.

Waldstreicher, David, and Matthew Mason. *John Quincy Adams and the Politics of Slavery: Selections from the Diary*. New York: Oxford University Press, 2017.

Wasser, Henry. "John Quincy Adams and the Opening Lines of Milton's *Paradise Lost*." *American Literature* 42 (Nov. 1970): 373–75.

Weeks, William Earl. *John Quincy Adams and American Global Empire*. Lexington: University Press of Kentucky, 1992.

Wheeler, William Bruce. "Pennsylvania and the Presidential Election of 1800: Republican Acceptance of the 8–7 Compromise." *Pennsylvania History* 36 (Oct. 1969): 424–29.

Wiecek, William M. "Slavery and Abolition Before the United States Supreme Court, 1820–1860." *Journal of American History* 65 (June 1978): 34–59.

Wiltse, Charles M. "John Quincy Adams and the Party System: A Review Article." *Journal of Politics* 4 (Aug. 1942): 407–14.

Winterer, Caroline. *American Enlightenments: Pursuing Happiness in the Age of Reason*. New Haven, Conn.: Yale University Press, 2016.

———. *The Culture of Classicism: Ancient Greece and Rome in American Intellectual Life, 1780–1910*. Baltimore: Johns Hopkins University Press, 2002.

Wood, Marcus. *Black Milk: Imagining Slavery in the Visual Cultures of Brazil and America*. Oxford: Oxford University Press, 2013.

Wood, Sarah F. *Quixotic Fictions of the USA, 1792–1815*. New York: Oxford University Press, 2005.

Woodward, Ruth L., ed. "Journal at Nassau Hall: The Diary of John Rhea Smith, 1786." *Princeton University Library Chronicle* 46 (1985): 269–91.

Young, Alfred F., Gary B. Nash, and Ray Raphael, eds. *Revolutionary Founders: Rebels, Radicals, and Reformers in the Making of the Nation*. New York: Knopf, 2011.

Zagarri, Rosemarie. *A Woman's Dilemma: Mercy Otis Warren and the American Revolution*. Wheeling, Ill.: Harlan Davidson, 1995.

Zboray, Ronald J. *A Fictive People: Antebellum Economic Development and the American Reading Public*. New York: Oxford University Press, 1993.

Index

Pages numbers in *italics* refer to illustrations and captions. Page numbers beginning with 473 refer to endnotes.